T0134893

Lecture Notes in Computer Science 14012

Founding Editors

Gerhard Goos
Juris Hartmanis

The series Lecture Notes in Computer Science (LNCS), including its subseries Lecture Notes in Artificial Intelligence (LNAI) and Lecture Notes in Bioinformatics (LNBI), has established itself as a medium for the publication of new developments in computer science and information technology research, teaching, and education.

LNCS enjoys close cooperation with the computer science R & D community, the series counts many renowned academics among its volume editors and paper authors, and collaborates with prestigious societies. Its mission is to serve this international community by providing an invaluable service, mainly focused on the publication of conference and workshop proceedings and postproceedings. LNCS commenced publication in 1973.

Masaaki Kurosu · Ayako Hashizume
Editors

Human-Computer Interaction

Thematic Area, HCI 2023
Held as Part of the 25th HCI International Conference, HCII 2023
Copenhagen, Denmark, July 23–28, 2023
Proceedings, Part II

 Springer

Editors
Masaaki Kurosu
The Open University of Japan
Chiba, Japan

Ayako Hashizume
Hosei University
Tokyo, Japan

ISSN 0302-9743   ISSN 1611-3349 (electronic)
Lecture Notes in Computer Science
ISBN 978-3-031-35598-1   ISBN 978-3-031-35599-8 (eBook)
https://doi.org/10.1007/978-3-031-35599-8

This Springer imprint is published by the registered company Springer Nature Switzerland AG
The registered company address is: Gewerbestrasse 11, 6330 Cham, Switzerland

Foreword

Human-computer interaction (HCI) is acquiring an ever-increasing scientific and industrial importance, as well as having more impact on people's everyday lives, as an ever-growing number of human activities are progressively moving from the physical to the digital world. This process, which has been ongoing for some time now, was further accelerated during the acute period of the COVID-19 pandemic. The HCI International (HCII) conference series, held annually, aims to respond to the compelling need to advance the exchange of knowledge and research and development efforts on the human aspects of design and use of computing systems.

The 25th International Conference on Human-Computer Interaction, HCI International 2023 (HCII 2023), was held in the emerging post-pandemic era as a 'hybrid' event at the AC Bella Sky Hotel and Bella Center, Copenhagen, Denmark, during July 23–28, 2023. It incorporated the 21 thematic areas and affiliated conferences listed below.

A total of 7472 individuals from academia, research institutes, industry, and government agencies from 85 countries submitted contributions, and 1578 papers and 396 posters were included in the volumes of the proceedings that were published just before the start of the conference, these are listed below. The contributions thoroughly cover the entire field of human-computer interaction, addressing major advances in knowledge and effective use of computers in a variety of application areas. These papers provide academics, researchers, engineers, scientists, practitioners and students with state-of-the-art information on the most recent advances in HCI.

The HCI International (HCII) conference also offers the option of presenting 'Late Breaking Work', and this applies both for papers and posters, with corresponding volumes of proceedings that will be published after the conference. Full papers will be included in the 'HCII 2023 - Late Breaking Work - Papers' volumes of the proceedings to be published in the Springer LNCS series, while 'Poster Extended Abstracts' will be included as short research papers in the 'HCII 2023 - Late Breaking Work - Posters' volumes to be published in the Springer CCIS series.

I would like to thank the Program Board Chairs and the members of the Program Boards of all thematic areas and affiliated conferences for their contribution towards the high scientific quality and overall success of the HCI International 2023 conference. Their manifold support in terms of paper reviewing (single-blind review process, with a minimum of two reviews per submission), session organization and their willingness to act as goodwill ambassadors for the conference is most highly appreciated.

This conference would not have been possible without the continuous and unwavering support and advice of Gavriel Salvendy, founder, General Chair Emeritus, and Scientific Advisor. For his outstanding efforts, I would like to express my sincere appreciation to Abbas Moallem, Communications Chair and Editor of HCI International News.

July 2023   Constantine Stephanidis

HCI International 2023 Thematic Areas and Affiliated Conferences

Thematic Areas

- HCI: Human-Computer Interaction
- HIMI: Human Interface and the Management of Information

Affiliated Conferences

- EPCE: 20th International Conference on Engineering Psychology and Cognitive Ergonomics
- AC: 17th International Conference on Augmented Cognition
- UAHCI: 17th International Conference on Universal Access in Human-Computer Interaction
- CCD: 15th International Conference on Cross-Cultural Design
- SCSM: 15th International Conference on Social Computing and Social Media
- VAMR: 15th International Conference on Virtual, Augmented and Mixed Reality
- DHM: 14th International Conference on Digital Human Modeling and Applications in Health, Safety, Ergonomics and Risk Management
- DUXU: 12th International Conference on Design, User Experience and Usability
- C&C: 11th International Conference on Culture and Computing
- DAPI: 11th International Conference on Distributed, Ambient and Pervasive Interactions
- HCIBGO: 10th International Conference on HCI in Business, Government and Organizations
- LCT: 10th International Conference on Learning and Collaboration Technologies
- ITAP: 9th International Conference on Human Aspects of IT for the Aged Population
- AIS: 5th International Conference on Adaptive Instructional Systems
- HCI-CPT: 5th International Conference on HCI for Cybersecurity, Privacy and Trust
- HCI-Games: 5th International Conference on HCI in Games
- MobiTAS: 5th International Conference on HCI in Mobility, Transport and Automotive Systems
- AI-HCI: 4th International Conference on Artificial Intelligence in HCI
- MOBILE: 4th International Conference on Design, Operation and Evaluation of Mobile Communications

List of Conference Proceedings Volumes Appearing Before the Conference

1. LNCS 14011, Human-Computer Interaction: Part I, edited by Masaaki Kurosu and Ayako Hashizume
2. LNCS 14012, Human-Computer Interaction: Part II, edited by Masaaki Kurosu and Ayako Hashizume
3. LNCS 14013, Human-Computer Interaction: Part III, edited by Masaaki Kurosu and Ayako Hashizume
4. LNCS 14014, Human-Computer Interaction: Part IV, edited by Masaaki Kurosu and Ayako Hashizume
5. LNCS 14015, Human Interface and the Management of Information: Part I, edited by Hirohiko Mori and Yumi Asahi
6. LNCS 14016, Human Interface and the Management of Information: Part II, edited by Hirohiko Mori and Yumi Asahi
7. LNAI 14017, Engineering Psychology and Cognitive Ergonomics: Part I, edited by Don Harris and Wen-Chin Li
8. LNAI 14018, Engineering Psychology and Cognitive Ergonomics: Part II, edited by Don Harris and Wen-Chin Li
9. LNAI 14019, Augmented Cognition, edited by Dylan D. Schmorrow and Cali M. Fidopiastis
10. LNCS 14020, Universal Access in Human-Computer Interaction: Part I, edited by Margherita Antona and Constantine Stephanidis
11. LNCS 14021, Universal Access in Human-Computer Interaction: Part II, edited by Margherita Antona and Constantine Stephanidis
12. LNCS 14022, Cross-Cultural Design: Part I, edited by Pei-Luen Patrick Rau
13. LNCS 14023, Cross-Cultural Design: Part II, edited by Pei-Luen Patrick Rau
14. LNCS 14024, Cross-Cultural Design: Part III, edited by Pei-Luen Patrick Rau
15. LNCS 14025, Social Computing and Social Media: Part I, edited by Adela Coman and Simona Vasilache
16. LNCS 14026, Social Computing and Social Media: Part II, edited by Adela Coman and Simona Vasilache
17. LNCS 14027, Virtual, Augmented and Mixed Reality, edited by Jessie Y. C. Chen and Gino Fragomeni
18. LNCS 14028, Digital Human Modeling and Applications in Health, Safety, Ergonomics and Risk Management: Part I, edited by Vincent G. Duffy
19. LNCS 14029, Digital Human Modeling and Applications in Health, Safety, Ergonomics and Risk Management: Part II, edited by Vincent G. Duffy
20. LNCS 14030, Design, User Experience, and Usability: Part I, edited by Aaron Marcus, Elizabeth Rosenzweig and Marcelo Soares
21. LNCS 14031, Design, User Experience, and Usability: Part II, edited by Aaron Marcus, Elizabeth Rosenzweig and Marcelo Soares

22. LNCS 14032, Design, User Experience, and Usability: Part III, edited by Aaron Marcus, Elizabeth Rosenzweig and Marcelo Soares
23. LNCS 14033, Design, User Experience, and Usability: Part IV, edited by Aaron Marcus, Elizabeth Rosenzweig and Marcelo Soares
24. LNCS 14034, Design, User Experience, and Usability: Part V, edited by Aaron Marcus, Elizabeth Rosenzweig and Marcelo Soares
25. LNCS 14035, Culture and Computing, edited by Matthias Rauterberg
26. LNCS 14036, Distributed, Ambient and Pervasive Interactions: Part I, edited by Norbert Streitz and Shin'ichi Konomi
27. LNCS 14037, Distributed, Ambient and Pervasive Interactions: Part II, edited by Norbert Streitz and Shin'ichi Konomi
28. LNCS 14038, HCI in Business, Government and Organizations: Part I, edited by Fiona Fui-Hoon Nah and Keng Siau
29. LNCS 14039, HCI in Business, Government and Organizations: Part II, edited by Fiona Fui-Hoon Nah and Keng Siau
30. LNCS 14040, Learning and Collaboration Technologies: Part I, edited by Panayiotis Zaphiris and Andri Ioannou
31. LNCS 14041, Learning and Collaboration Technologies: Part II, edited by Panayiotis Zaphiris and Andri Ioannou
32. LNCS 14042, Human Aspects of IT for the Aged Population: Part I, edited by Qin Gao and Jia Zhou
33. LNCS 14043, Human Aspects of IT for the Aged Population: Part II, edited by Qin Gao and Jia Zhou
34. LNCS 14044, Adaptive Instructional Systems, edited by Robert A. Sottilare and Jessica Schwarz
35. LNCS 14045, HCI for Cybersecurity, Privacy and Trust, edited by Abbas Moallem
36. LNCS 14046, HCI in Games: Part I, edited by Xiaowen Fang
37. LNCS 14047, HCI in Games: Part II, edited by Xiaowen Fang
38. LNCS 14048, HCI in Mobility, Transport and Automotive Systems: Part I, edited by Heidi Krömker
39. LNCS 14049, HCI in Mobility, Transport and Automotive Systems: Part II, edited by Heidi Krömker
40. LNAI 14050, Artificial Intelligence in HCI: Part I, edited by Helmut Degen and Stavroula Ntoa
41. LNAI 14051, Artificial Intelligence in HCI: Part II, edited by Helmut Degen and Stavroula Ntoa
42. LNCS 14052, Design, Operation and Evaluation of Mobile Communications, edited by Gavriel Salvendy and June Wei
43. CCIS 1832, HCI International 2023 Posters - Part I, edited by Constantine Stephanidis, Margherita Antona, Stavroula Ntoa and Gavriel Salvendy
44. CCIS 1833, HCI International 2023 Posters - Part II, edited by Constantine Stephanidis, Margherita Antona, Stavroula Ntoa and Gavriel Salvendy
45. CCIS 1834, HCI International 2023 Posters - Part III, edited by Constantine Stephanidis, Margherita Antona, Stavroula Ntoa and Gavriel Salvendy
46. CCIS 1835, HCI International 2023 Posters - Part IV, edited by Constantine Stephanidis, Margherita Antona, Stavroula Ntoa and Gavriel Salvendy

47. CCIS 1836, HCI International 2023 Posters - Part V, edited by Constantine Stephanidis, Margherita Antona, Stavroula Ntoa and Gavriel Salvendy

https://2023.hci.international/proceedings

Preface

Human-Computer Interaction is a Thematic Area of the International Conference on Human-Computer Interaction (HCII). The HCI field is today undergoing a wave of significant innovation and breakthroughs towards radically new future forms of interaction. The HCI Thematic Area constitutes a forum for scientific research and innovation in human-computer interaction, addressing challenging and innovative topics in human-computer interaction theory, methodology, and practice, including, for example, novel theoretical approaches to interaction, novel user interface concepts and technologies, novel interaction devices, UI development methods, environments and tools, multimodal user interfaces, human-robot interaction, emotions in HCI, aesthetic issues, HCI and children, evaluation methods and tools, and many others.

The HCI Thematic Area covers four major dimensions, namely theory and methodology, technology, human beings, and societal impact. The following four volumes of the HCII 2023 proceedings reflect these dimensions:

- Human-Computer Interaction (Part I), addressing topics related to design and evaluation methods, techniques and tools, and interaction methods and techniques
- Human-Computer Interaction (Part II), addressing topics related to children-computer interaction, emotions in HCI, and understanding the user experience
- Human-Computer Interaction (Part III), addressing topics related to human-robot interaction, chatbots and voice-based interaction, and interacting in the metaverse
- Human-Computer Interaction (Part IV), addressing topics related to supporting health, quality of life and everyday activities, as well as topics related to HCI for learning, culture, creativity, and societal impact.

Papers of these volumes are included for publication after a minimum of two single-blind reviews from the members of the HCI Program Board or, in some cases, from members of the Program Boards of other affiliated conferences. We would like to thank all of them for their invaluable contribution, support, and efforts.

July 2023

Masaaki Kurosu
Ayako Hashizume

Human-Computer Interaction Thematic Area (HCI 2023)

Program Board Chairs: **Masaaki Kurosu**, *The Open University of Japan, Japan* and **Ayako Hashizume**, *Hosei University, Japan*

Program Board:

- Salah Ahmed, *University of South-Eastern Norway, Norway*
- Valdecir Becker, *Federal University of Paraiba, Brazil*
- Nimish Biloria, *University of Technology Sydney, Australia*
- Zhigang Chen, *Shanghai University, P.R. China*
- C. M. Nadeem Faisal, *National Textile University, Pakistan*
- Yu-Hsiu Hung, *National Cheng Kung University, Taiwan*
- Jun Iio, *Chuo University, Japan*
- Yi Ji, *Guangdong University of Technology, P.R. China*
- Hiroshi Noborio, *Osaka Electro-Communication University, Japan*
- Katsuhiko Onishi, *Osaka Electro-Communication University, Japan*
- Mohammad Shidujaman, *Independent University, Bangladesh, Bangladesh*

The full list with the Program Board Chairs and the members of the Program Boards of all thematic areas and affiliated conferences of HCII2023 is available online at:

http://www.hci.international/board-members-2023.php

HCI International 2024 Conference

The 26th International Conference on Human-Computer Interaction, HCI International 2024, will be held jointly with the affiliated conferences at the Washington Hilton Hotel, Washington, DC, USA, June 29 – July 4, 2024. It will cover a broad spectrum of themes related to Human-Computer Interaction, including theoretical issues, methods, tools, processes, and case studies in HCI design, as well as novel interaction techniques, interfaces, and applications. The proceedings will be published by Springer. More information will be made available on the conference website: http://2024.hci.international/.

General Chair
Prof. Constantine Stephanidis
University of Crete and ICS-FORTH
Heraklion, Crete, Greece
Email: general_chair@hcii2024.org

https://2024.hci.international/

Contents – Part II

Emotions in HCI

Understanding the User Experience

Children Computer Interaction

Participatory Designs for Computational Play

A Study of Children's Play Across Traditional and Digital Domains

Eva Brooks[1]([✉]) [iD] and Emma Edstrand[2] [iD]

[1] Aalborg University, Kroghstræde 3, 9220 Aalborg, Denmark
eb@ikl.aau.dk
[2] Halmstad University, Kristian IV:S Väg 3, 301 18 Halmstad, Sweden
emma.edstrand@hh.se

Abstract. In this paper, we outline a perspective on *participatory designs for computational play* as a social and material activity, beyond an understanding of computational activities as an individual "thinking" endeavor. The overall aim of this study is to explore how a participatory design approach including traditional and digital resources trigger children's computational play. By this, our intention is to contribute to the contemporary debate on the increased use of computational thinking related activities in early childhood education and their potentials for play and learning. Framed by a perspective considering traditional and digital resources as access points to play and learning, the empirical study involves 50 children from 2nd grade, aged 8–9 years from two different primary schools in northern Denmark. The outcomes demonstrates that computational play has the potential to reconfigure learning activities by providing new, previously unthinkable, activities that can support children in early childhood education and their development of computational literacy. At the same time, the analyses show that computational play requires new ways to be scaffolded to not counteract children's independent experimentation, testing, and creativity.

Keywords: Participatory design · Computational play · Children in Early Childhood Education · Traditional creative resources · Digital technology · Workshops · Access points · Instruction

1 Introduction

In this paper, we outline a perspective on *participatory designs for computational play* as a social and material activity, beyond an understanding of computational activities as an individual "thinking" endeavor. The concept of computational is increasingly recognized in relation to the digitalization of society emphasizing a need for improved computational tools, information storing and distributed digital solutions. In the wake of a digitalized society, computational thinking has been highly acknowledged in the field of education as a fundamental skill for the 21st century where citizens are required to become digital literate [1, 2]. In addition, skills such as collaboration, problem-solving,

M. Kurosu and A. Hashizume (Eds.): HCII 2023, LNCS 14012, pp. 3–25, 2023.
https://doi.org/10.1007/978-3-031-35599-8_1

critical thinking, communication, innovation, and creativity have been highlighted as essential for the 21st century [3]. In response to these issues, it becomes critical to design and implement relevant activities for children to acquire this kind of computational and other kinds of transversal skills.

Computational thinking (CT) was introduced by Seymour Papert [4] but is commonly related to Jeanette Wing's [5] definition of the concept saying that CT is not only for computer scientists but a fundamental skill for everyone. Barr and Stephenson [6] identified CT strategies in a classroom setting, for example, increased use of computational vocabulary, group work with explicit use of computational processes such as decomposition, pattern recognition, negotiation and consensus building, and a mindset that can accept failed solution attempts. However, CT has primarily been recognized in relation to upper primary school and secondary school education, in particular in subject such as mathematics and computer science [7]. Studies focusing on young children's CT are currently limited and thus more knowledge is needed in regard to how the concept can be implemented in early years' education.

Researchers have attempted to reframe CT in directions such as computational making [8], computational participation [9], tangible computing [10], and computational empowerment [11]. Moreover, researchers have framed CT in terms of play activities in classrooms to support CT [12], participatory methods to teach CT skills [13], and designerly approaches as a foundation for CT [14]. When implementing frameworks for CT in early years' education it is essential to consider children's interests [14]. Research has shown that for young children to develop new knowledge, hands-on and play-based activities are central [15], allowing them to explore and co-create crossing over traditional (analogue) and digital domains [16, 17]. However, it lacks an agenda of supporting young children's computational discovery, i.e. their ways to in play-oriented ways discovery. In addition, CT seems to be an elusive phenomenon that currently does not encompass a wider concern that follows digitalization in the field of early childhood. We argue that participatory design can respond to this knowledge gap by creating social and play-oriented conditions necessary for young children to engage on their own terms; something we have termed as *children's computational play*.

The overall aim of this study is to explore how a participatory design approach including traditional and digital resources trigger children's computational play. By this, our intention is to contribute to the contemporary debate on the increased use of computational thinking related activities in schools and their potentials for play and learning. This will give insights into a renewed understanding of children's contemporary play. The study is based on workshop activities with schoolchildren (8 years of age), where computational thinking activities were applied using both traditional material (e.g. foam clay, cardboard, sharpies, LEGO) and digital educational resources (educational robots). The general research questions addressed are:

– In what ways do interactions unfold in participatory design activities including a combination of traditional and digital resources.
– What implications will the use of a combination of traditional and digital resources have for children's computational play in participatory design activities?

2   Related Work

This section presents an overview of research carried out in the field of computational thinking and how its application in early childhood moves towards computational play. Moreover, the research area of participatory design is investigated, particularly focusing on its relevance for and relationship to the research field of computational play.

2.1   From Computational Thinking to Computational Play

Currently, there is an increasing interest about Computational Thinking (CT) in primary and secondary schools. Despite this, it does not yet have an uncontested definition [6, 11–14, 18, 19]. Wing [5] states that CT concerns problem-solving, designing systems, and understanding human behavior. In one way, this definition is broad and offers a wide range of implementation possibilities, but in another way the definition is limited when it comes to the concept's concrete application. In 2010, Wing [20] extended this understanding of CT by proposing that CT is "the thought processes involved in formulating problems and their solutions so that the solutions are represented in a form that can be effectively carried out by an information-processing agent." The Computer Science Teachers Association (CSTA) [21] and the International Society for Technology in Education (ISTE) [22] expand on this by adding characteristics of CT processes, for example:

- formulating problems in a way that enable individuals to use a computer and other tools to solve them,
- logically organizing and analyzing data,
- representing data through abstractions such as models and simulations,
- automating solutions through algorithmic thinking, i.e. through a series of ordered steps,
- identifying, analyzing, and implementing possible solutions with the goal of achieving the most efficient and effective combination of steps and resources, and
- generalizing and transferring this problem-solving process to a wide variety of problems (CSTA, 2017; ISTE, 2021).

In particular, CSTA and ISTE have identified four broad thinking skills of CT, namely: *decomposition, abstraction, pattern recognition*, and *algorithm*. Decomposition includes a process of breaking down a complex problem into smaller bits [23]. Pattern recognition includes a sorting process identifying similarities and differences or, alternatively, finding patterns within problems. Abstraction concerns a filtering out of unnecessary details for solving a problem. Algorithm skills are based on a step-by-step plan for solving problems, which should be correctly ordered and include all necessary information [1, 19].

CT is globally integrated in educational programs [24]. In Europe several countries have incorporated CT in compulsory subjects, and some other countries integrate CT based on a computer science tradition [25]. CT is generally addressing learners' skills to understand, apply, and evaluate computational issues [20]. Brennan and Resnick [18] have proposed a broader understanding of CT including other perspectives. The authors introduced a framework based on *computational concepts* (the concepts designers engage with as they program), *computational practices* (the practices designers develop as they program), and *computational perspectives* (the perspectives designers form about the world around them and about themselves). This framework acknowledges CT as a social activity including consequences for society at large. This is aligned with the research carried out by Kafai and Burke [26], who describes CT as computational participation, where computational objects are key for children to share experiences with others.

Dindler et al. [11] propose a perspective on CT, which is based on the Participatory Design (PD) values of democratization and empowerment emphasizing opportunities for children to develop their capacity for engaging with digital technology. The authors describe computational empowerment as an approach and a PD response to existing challenges related to digital literacy in lower secondary education. The computational empowerment approach is envisioned to empower youth through constructive, analytical, and critical engagement with technology. Based on this, the authors conclude that PD has the potential to drive a computational empowerment agenda in education.

Research describes the making-approach to CT as playful in its nature due to the inclusion of material engagement and the role this approach has to learners' sharing of experiences when it comes to developing literacies [27]. In addition, it is emphasized that creativity, problem-solving, hands-on, do-it-yourself, and empowering strategies are vital for creating sociotechnical identity [cf. 28, 29, 27, 30].

The concept of CT is primary applied in upper primary and secondary schools, and a relatively new concept in early childhood education. Hence, little is known about how to promote children's CT when implementing such activities in early childhood classrooms [cf. 12]. Brooks and Sjöberg [14] propose a designerly approach to promote the implementation of CT in lower primary school settings. The authors illustrated how children in playful ways could develop CT capabilities while engaged with designing digital games using a combination of creative and digital resources. Children's exploration, questioning, reflection, and reasoning of the resources, problems, and solutions offered opportunities for them to develop CT capabilities, confidence, and pride in their work. Lee et al. [12] argue that when incorporating CT in early childhood education, children's needs, and development have to be considered to ensure the progression of children's thinking processes. The authors conclude their article by emphasizing the importance of a play-like classroom setting as it can enable them to become creative problem solvers. In their study, Murcia and Tang [31] investigated CT in early childhood education and acknowledged the nature of children's play with tangible coding technologies, and the role of multimodal resources in their development of CT. In their study, children learned to code a Cubetto robot, and the outcomes from this showed that the tangible robot interface facilitated children's development of multimodal digital literacies.

It is worth noting that challenges in implementing and understanding the meaning and usefulness of CT in educational settings still remain, specifically in ECE. It is evident that more research on the application of CT in ECE is needed. In their editorial, Li et al. [32] state that CT is more about thinking than computing and point to the multifaceted theoretical nature of the concept, in particular related to STEM education. Considering this in the context of CT in ECE, we claim that there is a need for moving beyond this kind of deficient models of CT. The research field of CT in ECE could be more robust by integrating overlooked needs and interests of children and thus engaging them more substantially in CT on their own premises. This is why we propose a reverse approach to CT in ECE. By this we mean that instead of emphasizing the 'thinking' part of CT, a more playful and expressive approach need to be considered to nurture children's participation and natural ways of communicating and learning. Play represents a dynamic and complex activity requiring and leading to complex symbolic constructions. Vygotsky [33] noted play as children's primary source of development. Vygotsky [34] also pointed to creativity as a process that includes play as well as imagination asking the question of "what-if". Play, then, can become a powerful source for children's way of approaching computational activities. Hence, the proposed reverse framing of CT starts with play, and with play strategies in mind we introduce children to computational matters. We consider play as an integral part of participatory design processes with children, which will be further elaborated in the next section.

2.2   Participatory Design and Computational Play

Participation is described as fundamental for children's learning and development [35] in the sense that they should be able to express their ideas, preferences, and choices, for instance in school settings [36]. This is aligned with Article 12 of the Conventions of the Right of the Child (CRC), which addresses children's right to express their own views as well as their right to heard and taken seriously [37]. Research has shown that early childhood teachers' considerations of children's participation is influenced by their own purposes and practices and thus realized in diverse ways, for example in the form of councils, negotiation, and dialogue [38–40]. In this sense, the concept of participation has a democratic annotation and implies a commitment to values and principles of democracy as well as respect to children's interests, voices, and capabilities [41].

Democracy has been a cornerstone of Participatory Design (PD) and became prominent in Scandinavia in the 1970s, reflected by political engagement and democratic awareness [42]. The Scandinavian approach to PD was about integrating users into processes of designing and prototyping new technologies and thereby attuning them to their needs [43]. PD is thus characterized by iterative, collaborative work aimed to joint learning and for users to learn about technology to pose more qualified demands [11]. Similarly, applying PD processes in classrooms can help to involve children in situations where they mutually can develop ideas, conceptualize, and reflect. Hence, PD applied in classrooms includes more than constructing and solving problems in a design process. It also concerns activities enabling children to make use of their prior knowledge to collaboratively tackle complex problems [13].

We believe that PD processes can provide children with inspiration and enable dialogue and collaboration with potential to drive children's computational play. In PD activities, children are engaged in creative hands-on processes to obtain ideas and explore interactions. Here, the selection of material to use is important. Materials such as clay, foam, and cardboard have potentials and constraints, in terms of Gibson [44] different affordances. An interesting aspect of affordances regards how children approach them, e.g. how they pick up, choose, and combine materials at hand. Research within the field of PD present different ways of organising PD sessions, including the use of various material [45] and methods [46].

Being engrossed in design activities where ideas can be expressed by means of material, has connotations with play. Play as a concept has several explications [47–50], but the traditional understanding of play has changed in recent years because of the development of play-oriented digital technology. Play processes open for different arrangements of traditional and digital resources pose new play landscapes. Such arrangements can be seen as a way of making meaning material or expressed differently, to realize meaning such as ideas or understandings. This kind of play, i.e. crossing over domains, is new and therefore the implications for children's play are still scarce [51, 52]. To approach this gap in research, we set out to explore the intersections of play across traditional and digital domains in a PD framed activity. In particular, we are interested in how the materiality of traditional-digital resources enable school children (8 years of age) to develop ideas, code, and collaborate with others. The PD set-up was intended to create a spirit of play to drive the activity.

2.3   Accessing the Analogue and Digital

In this study, traditional learning material in early childhood education (e.g. foam clay, markers, LEGO) and the digital resource (Ozobot), used by children are examples of mediating tools [53, 54] for children's computational play. Traditional and digital resources open up possibilities for children to, as mentioned earlier, develop ideas, code, and collaborate in a playful learning context. An aspect which is related to the role of mediating tools in play and learning situations is that they enable "access points" [55, 56] to knowledge. In line with the study by Brooks and Møller [57], analogue characteristics of traditional material are in the present study seen as resources that support children in their work of generating ideas through design. This is done by, for example, materializing and testing ideas and assumptions related to the fairytale in collaborative problem-solving manners. Considering the digital resource, it enables activities and reasoning related to coding without requiring any extensive prior knowledge. In this way, the complex knowledge involved in coding which is integrated into the tool (the robot) provides "short-cuts" for the children's making and reasoning. Thus, the digital resource contains knowledge that the children may have access to without fully mastering them in their original scientific form [58]. In this sense, the traditional and digital resources are examples of different mediating tools. However, both are examples of tools that offers children to perform activities with coding and design.

3   Method

The empirical field included in this paper is based on long-term study of workshops with children 4–9 years of age, where children's interaction with technologies and traditional creative material was investigated. This particular study involves 50 children from 2nd grade, aged 8–9 years from two different primary schools in northern Denmark (see Table 1).

The study is based on a qualitative workshop methodology aimed to inspire children to explore, and experiment in playful ways. This methodology has had an increased use within different research fields [59]. The concept of 'workshop' is often related to

Table 1. Overview of participants in the study.

Primary school ID	Participants	Gender
School A	29	12 girls; 17 boys
School B	21	10 girls; 11 boys

the concept of 'participation' and used in various contexts arranged so that participants can learn and be engaged in creative problem-solving in relation to domain-specific situations [60, 61]. The workshop methodology performed within this study was design to meet the participants' expectations as well as accomplish our research goal. The core of the workshop arrangement was to create conditions for the participants' active participation and influence. Aligned with this, the workshop design included a range of tools to support the children's activities and energize a sense of inspiration and ownership [62]. According to Ørngreen and Levinsen [61], workshops should be designed to fulfil predefined, but not predictable, aims.

In the following, we describe the material that was used during the workshops, and the procedure, followed by a description of the data collection, ethical considerations, and finally we present our analytical approach.

3.1 Material

The workshop activity was designed to offer children different ways of working with coding and design. Thus, the children were introduced to a combination of traditional material and digital resources. Our intention was to meet children's everyday ways of using different resources in play and learning, and thereby create an activity that could be meaningful and engaging in a multimodal way, thus responding to children's way of playing and communicating. A classic fairytale theme constituted the framework in which the mentioned combination of traditional and digital resources was used. The coding activity was carried out with the educational robot Ozobot. The children were free to elaborate on and re-design the fairytale and thus make it their own. Ozobot could represent one or more of the characters within a storyline of the fairytale. In this way, Ozobot was used by the children to reenact the storyline by conceptualizing and redesigning the fairytale using coding. In addition, creative material (e.g. foam clay, markers, LEGO, cardboard, paper, yarn, glue, and scissors) was used by the children to physically enact this storyline. As a result, Ozobots as characters in the fairytale was coded by the children to act the storyline scenes that the children had created, like actors in a play. It is this combination of the traditional and digital that constituted a predefined framework, which at the same time was not predictable as the children had the privilege to redesign this framework as they wished. This setup is inspired by a narrative inquiry method [63–66].

Ozobot is a versatile robot designed to enhance children's interest in programming. The size of an Ozobot is at par with a golf ball and it can be programmed both analogously and digitally by either using color codes on paper with sharpies or in apps on a tablet such as iPad or using block programming in web browsers on a computer or tablet.

The color codes are supposed to teach basic coding concepts, for example cause-effect, and critical thinking. In the present study, the coding was carried out analogously with different colored sharpies (black, red, blue, and green). These different colors can be combined in various ways and thereby create different codes. For example, specific speed codes can change the robot's velocity from lowest (snail dose) to fastest (nitro boost). It is also possible to change its direction, to code cool moves, and counter codes (Fig. 1).

Fig. 1. Children engaged in coding with Ozobot robots and creative material.

The fairytales were selected by the researchers beforehand and included classical fairytales, which are outlined in the below Table 2:

Table 2. Overview of the fairytales used in the workshop activity.

Fairytale	Background and Author
The boy who cried wolf	A fable addressed back to ancient Greece. One of Aesop's fables
Little red riding hood	European fairytale. Based on Charles Perrault and Brothers Grimm's fairytales
What the old man does is always right	A humorous short story by H. C. Andersen
The little match girl	A literary fairytale by H. C. Andersen
There is no doubt about it	Short story by H. C. Andersen

Each of the chosen fairytales are classical and a moral message is included in the storyline:

The boy who cried wolf concerns a shepherd boy who repeatedly fools villagers into thinking a wolf is attacking his town's flock. When an actual wolf appears and the boy calls for help, the villagers believe that it is another false alarm, and the sheep are eaten by the wolf.

Little red riding hood is a European fairy tale about a girl and a wolf. The story tells of how the girl comes across a cunning wolf on the way to her grandmother's home.

What the old man does is always right is about a farmer and his wife, who trust him because she believes that every decision that he makes is always the best possible one. The farmer's wife tells him to exchange their horse for something more useful. After a series of trades, the farmer ends up with a bag of rotten apples. However, the farmer is certain that his wife will be pleased.

The little match girl is about a girl who is sent out by her parents to sell matches on the last evening of the year. She has lost her shoes and is barefoot and freezing. She is however afraid to go home because her father would beat her for failing to sell any matches.

There is no doubt about it is about an incident in a hen-roost. When evening came, a respectable hen nibbled, and a feather fell. Because she liked to joke, the hen said that with each feather she fell, she became more beautiful. An owl that was on a branch above the hen-roost, was horrified at the idea of a hen getting without feathers in front of the rooster, especially since she could die of cold.

Each fairytale was read out aloud to the children either by the teacher or researchers. Based on the sometimes difficult content, it was also discussed with the children for them to grasp both the content and the sometimes-hidden messages (Fig. 2).

Fig. 2. Children and researcher engaged in reading and talking about the fairytale.

3.2   Procedure

The workshops were carried out in two primary school settings in northern Denmark and lasted for totally 2.5 h including breaks. The participating children were divided into groups of 3–5 children. This resulted in a total of six groups in school A and a total of five groups in school B. Each group had their own workstation, which was equipped by Ozobot robots (at least two at each workstation), sharpies, coding schemes, and calibration station.

Based on the participatory design approach to the workshops, they were divided into four phases, which is illustrated in Table 3:

Table 3. Overview of the four workshop phases.

Phase	Content	Time Allocation
Introduction	Introduction to the activity, reading of and talking about the fairytale, exploring the creative and digital resources	30 min

(continued)

Table 3. (*continued*)

Phase	Content	Time Allocation
Exploration, Discovery, and Design	Discussing the problem, idea generation of solutions, materializing and testing ideas, designing, and arranging the fairytale storyline and the coding pathways	75 min
Communication	The children present their outcomes to each other	30 min
Reflection	Reflection and evaluation of the workshop	15 min

The objective of the first phase (introduction) was to introduce the children to the activity, the task and its purpose, and the different resources. Each group of children were introduced to their specific fairytale, which was read out loud by a teacher or researcher. To clarify the content of the fairytale, this was followed by a facilitated group discussion focusing on questions related to the fairytale, for example regarding underlying moral messages of the fairytale. This ended with a shared understanding of the fairytale as a starting point for the next phase. After this, the children were introduced to the Ozobot, how it worked and could be coded, and also to the creative material.

In the second phase (exploration, discovery, and design), the children started with idea generation and division of work. In parallel, they explored different opportunities, for example how to build grandmother's house in the Little red riding hood fairytale so that it was stable enough and that grandmother's bed could fit into it. They also explored different coding opportunities, for example how tight a curve could be or how thick or thin the lines could be for Ozobot to read by means of its sensor-technology. The phase ended with an arrangement of the whole storyline, including a proper set up of the different storyline props and a proper coding pathway for Ozobot to reenact the storyline.

The objective of the third phase (communication) was for the children to present their conclusive storyline to the other children. They were encouraged to present their solutions, choices and considerations that were included relative to the specific resources as well as to the solution as a whole. Before communicating the solution, the children were occupied with questions such as: Is the coding appropriate so that Ozobot's reenacting is trustworthy represented? Is the material representation of the fairytale relevant and adequately conveying our ideas?

The final fourth phase (reflection) was dedicated to a plenary discussion, where the children were encouraged to reflect on the task as such, their experiences of the collaborative work, the interaction with each other and the different resources, and any other questions.

3.3 Data Collection

The data collection included video observations and photographs from the different workstations. Each one of the workstations was equipped with a video camera recording the children's interactions while working with the task at hand. In addition, we occasionally photographed situations at the workstations. Primary school A produced approximately 92 min video data at each of the six workstations, in total 552 min. Primary school B produced 127 min of video data at each of the five workstations, totally 635 min. All together, we collected 19.8 h of video data (1187 min). In addition, we gathered around 49 photographs.

Collecting video data in the workshops offered insights into how the children used the full range of material and digital components to express meaning. This kind of multimodal episodes characterize children's play and learning in early years settings by revealing eye contact, body movement, facial expressions, and the manipulation of resources [67]. Video cameras have thus opened for potentials to scrutinize activities in different modes.

3.4 Ethical Considerations

The study was aligned with common research-ethical principles of transparency and quality of documentation as well as to the protection of sources and individuals throughout the research process [68, 69]. Prior to the study, teachers and parents were informed about the study in writing. All parents confirmed their child's participation in the study by signing informed consent forms, which included approval for us to use videos and photographs for scientific purposes. The ethical considerations include full respect for the United Nations Convention of the Rights of the Child (UNCRC) [70]. The participating children were informed about the study, the aim of the workshop and its procedures, and how we collected data through video recordings. The video cameras were shown to the children, and they were informed that if they in any way felt uncomfortable with their participation, they could interrupt their participation without any explanation. They could in such cases just tell their teachers or the researchers. After this information, the children gave verbal consent, which was negotiated during the full workshop activity.

3.5 Analytic Framework

The analysis was carried out using a thematic approach [71]. The video data and the photographs were analyzed and selected sample episodes were identified and transcribed. This process of viewing the video recordings to study the interactions (verbal speech and non-verbal actions), was carefully carried out by the researchers. The children's conversations were in Danish, and the selected transcripts were translated to English.

Inspired by Braun & Clarke [71], the analytic process was informed by the following steps:

– **Transcribing:** Video recordings and photographs were studied several times. Episodes were chosen and transcribed. These episodes were tested for their relevance by each of the researcher.

- **Coding:** Data was arranged relevant to codes. There was an overlap with the transcribing step. During the transcription when notes were taken highlighting episodes and quotes held to be interesting for the study. Some dialogues were recurring and thus also marked as interesting. When revisiting the transcriptions, these notes were helpful.
- **Identifying themes:** Codes were organized into themes. This was an iterative process starting with loose themes based on the codes using mind maps on physical paper and step-by-step reducing the several themes into three overarching themes.
- **Reviewing themes:** The final themes were tested, quotes and episodes were selected and tested for their relevance.
- **Finalizing themes for the study:** The resulting three themes, episodes, and quotes were finalized: (i) Experimenting and organizing; (ii) Modelling and arranging; and (iii) Instruction and problem-solving. The episodes have been chosen as they show frequently occurring patterns in the empirical material of how the chosen traditional and digital resources framed by a participatory design approach generated signs of computational play.

In the following, we present these outcomes of the study.

4   Findings

The analysis of the 11 workstations within the two workshops allowed us to understand how a participatory design approach triggered children's computational play across traditional and digital domains. It was possible to identify how PD mediated by a workshop structure and a combination of analogue and digital resources mediated children's interactions in playful ways. Further, these playful ways were enacted in a participatory design process configured in experimenting and organizing, modelling and arranging, and instruction and problem-solving actions, demonstrating insights into computational play. In the following sub-sections, we unfold these themes.

4.1   Experimenting and Organizing

The process of realizing code through the pre-existing code schemes to align this coding with the storyline of the fairytale was not straightforward. Nevertheless, it included experimentation of several codes where the organizing of coding actions was done in a step-by-step way towards an adequate representation of the storyline. This theme unfolds the different representational choices made available in the process of reassembling a multitude of coding opportunities into the best fit. One of the episodes shows how the children's production of code was organized to make it convincing in relation to the storyline. In doing so, they experimented with spatial organization and directionality to realize the interconnection between a code and the storyline. Another episode demonstrates the concentration and focus that was predominant in the transformation of the code represented on the coding scheme sheet to a concrete code representation in a series of work sheets.

Episode 1 – School B, Group 2. The group of three children (two boys and a girl) is in the process of coding the pathway for Ozobot to move in accordance with their storyline of the fairytale *What the old man does is always right*. Their storyline represents how Ozobot representing the old man walk through the farmer's market and exchange his horse for a cow, the cow to a sheep, the sheep to a hen, and finally to a bag of rotten apples. The research assistant shows the coding scheme and asks them what kind of codes they would consider. One of the boys says, *it is a long way for Ozobot to move from the horse to the cow, we need to find a code so that takes him quickly around the market*. The boy points to that there need to be time for the group to code the whole storyline that they have planned for. The girl and the boy take turns coding, they carefully connect lines with specific codes so that Ozobot surely can read the code without interruption of unconnected lines (code). Together, the two boys check the codes that they have decided to use on a separate sheet of paper to check so that the codes work properly for their storyline. It works and they sketch the codes on the big sheet of paper where they are to set up the whole storyline. When this is done, the girl again tests so that the codes work properly. It works and the boy who did the coding and happily exclaims, *yeeees*!

The episode demonstrates the children's careful considerations of the interrelationship between the code and the storyline. They test and verify their coding in a recursive and modularization manner. These practices are also central to reasoning and problem solving in design. Their choice and organization of the code provided information about the meaning of the storyline was based on several experimentation with codes. They designed a circular organization of the storyline including a spatial proximity between the objects (the horse, cow, sheep, etc.) to represent the most important issue, namely for Ozobot to have the time to run through the whole storyline when they should present their task for the other children. The children's use of spatial organization enabled them to connect Ozobot's pathway and thus realize their storyline the way that was meaningful for them. The pathway was linked to objects included in the fairytale, where the linking of them express relational processes such as when Ozobot moves from having exchanged the horse to a cow, to the next object of exchanging the cow to a sheep. In this way, the children used spatial organization to indicate part-whole interrelations.

Episode 2 – School A, Group 2. The group includes five boys and three of them explore and experiment with Ozobot. They have two Ozobots and check out the sensors and how Ozobot by means of the sensors can identify colors and accordingly detect codes. They sketch different codes using sharpies on sheets of paper. They experiment with testing how sharp curves can be for Ozobot to still identify the pathway without becoming confused. They also check how close the different lines and codes need to be for Ozobot to keep moving without disconnection.

Even though the children have not been given explicit and detailed instructions of the coding procedure, they are actively experimenting with it and make their way into coding in an experimental and goal-oriented way. They explore what is possible to do with the coding of Ozobot and what is not possible.

4.2 Modelling and Arranging

Modelling and arranging refer to the children's materializing processes, articulating their interests in decorating, and arranging the props in the storyline and Ozobot in aesthetically and trustworthy manners. The children's modelling transformed the fairytale by ornaments and details of the clay figures and transformed elements of them to make them more expressive and salient but still trustworthy to the fairytale. The expansion from the affordances inherent in the fairytale, made available potentials for representing the characters and props and the relations between them. The children put lot of efforts into this way of articulating their ideas and conclusions. The following episode illustrates the children's arrangement and transformation of the props and of Ozobot.

> **Episode 3 – School A, Group 2.** This group consists of three children (two boys and a girls) dealing with the fairytale of *What the old man does is always right*. The girl has collected black foam clay and starts modelling to an animal. According to her, it looks both like a sheep and a cow. She then gets some yellow foam clay and puts yellow dots on the animal. She is satisfied as this detail transforms the black creature to a cow.

> **School A, Group 1.** The group of three girls and two boys are occupied with the fairytale of, *The boy who cried wolf*. Two of the girls are decorating the two Ozobots representing a sheep and the boy by arranging so that one of the Ozobots is covered by yellow foam clay and eyes (a sheep) and the other one with an orange cap representing the boy.

The next episode describes how the children by the end of the workshop preparing for their presentation to the other children, with engagement and concentration arranged the whole storyline, including coding and the arrangements of the props that all together represented the children's way of transforming the classic fairytale to a new representation.

> **Episode 4 – School B, Group 2.** The group of two boys and a girl is occupied with the fairytale, *What the old man does is always right*. One of the research assistants has told the children that they soon should be ready to present their storylines to each other. The girls start to place small bushes that she quickly creates with green foam clay on the sheet of paper where they have placed their coded pathway, which represents Ozobot's (the old man's) pathway around the marketplace. She continues by creating trees that she also places along the coded pathway. One of them places a wind power mill created by LEGO next to the farmhouse. The girl has placed the horse in a corner far away from the farmhouse and realizes that she needs to move the horse so that it is placed next to the farmhouse as it is there that Ozobot should start the trip around the marketplace. This causes a discussion in the group regarding the order of the placement of the different animals that are represented at the market. In doing so, they follow the order of the original fairytale. The boys point out where the animals should be placed to represent that order and the girl moves the animals around to fit the fairytale.

While modelling and arranging all groups admire each other's creations and they also demonstrate pride in their arrangements, for example *Surely, this is beautiful*, or *Look, I have done this one!*

4.3 Instruction and Problem-Solving

The workshop environment framed by a participatory design approach promoting children's play across traditional and digital domains had implications for the children's way of solving the problem at hand. In particular, this was related to the ways they were instructed to approach the task, i.e. to solve the problem at hand including interactions with traditional (analogue) and digital resources. The opportunities inherent in a participatory approach for children to play across modalities presented itself in relation to the children's emerging interests throughout the process. This interest became a source for supporting the instruction in an informal way in the sense that the task as such was structured in different phases and guided by the teachers/researchers, but within this structure there was an openness. This guided openness revealed a process where the problem-solving was grounded in a desire to explore and experiment with what was possible and what was not; investigating a 'what if' character of the process, i.e. what would happen if we do like this? However, in one of the groups (School A, Group 2) the teacher and the researcher instructed the children in a step-by-step way. The facilitators (teacher or researcher) were by the table most of the time instructing the children to, for example, discuss the fairytale, investigate the robots, create props, and decide on the storyline. In both ways of instruction, the children demonstrated a motive to actively participate in problem-solving. But when drawing attention to how these different ways of instructing the children focuses attention on the key role of the facilitator in establishing and orchestrating the workshop interactions. These problem-solving instructions are exemplified through the next two episodes.

> **Episode 5 – School A, Group 1.** The group (three girls and two boys) are engaged in the *The boy who cried wolf* fairytale. One of the girls points out that they needed to do the wolf as it was missing and that they needed to start with the coding. A researcher comes by the workstation and instruct them in coding the Ozobot. The girl hands over the coding scheme to the researcher so that the researcher can show different codes making the robot to move fast, slow, to the right, and to the left. Another girl tells the researcher by showing on a paper how they want Ozobot to move, and she points to the code that best can fit to this wish. The research quickly demonstrates how to sketch the codes and leaves the workstation. Two of the girls start to jointly code. One of them holds the coding sharpies and the other girl points on the paper how she should draw the lines. When they have finished the coding, they test the codes with Ozobot. They are all engaged in the task, three of them with coding, one of them with arranging the props to the storyline, and one of them preparing the presentation for the other groups.

In this episode the instruction was focused on the role the tools played in the children's problem-solving, i.e. the tools co-determined the way the children were facilitated by the researcher.

Episode 6 – School B, Group 1. The group of two boys and a girl is occupied with the fairytale, *What the old man does is always right.* One of the researchers is sitting by the workstation and asks the children, *do you remember what the fairytale was about?* After a talk about the fairytale, the researcher carefully instructs the children about the coding procedures and techniques. The children test the coding. Next, the researcher says, *Now, you need to create the storyline, you can use this paper and test the foam clay.* The researcher discusses with the children how they can create the storyline and the props. One of the teachers comes to the workstation and add to what the researcher said, *yes, you need to think about what you want to create.* The teacher turns to the girl, *what do you want to create?* She replies that she could create the animals and the teacher says, *it is a really good idea, so start with that.*

In this episode, the children were not so explorative or experimental, rather they followed what the researcher or teacher instructed them to do. The children picked up what the researcher or teacher said and did not make their own distinctions of the creation of the storyline, the robot, or the creative material.

5 Discussion

5.1 Access Points to Knowledge

The findings of this study demonstrate how the children in the coding task show computational thinking (CT) skills in terms of identifying and articulating problems directed to the digital tool to solve, analyzing, and implementing solutions [6, 21, 22]. For instance, through collaboration the children seek solutions to the problem of getting the Ozobot to move forward in the environment they have created within a time frame that fits the storyline or whether it can manage to take the curves without getting lost. In this sense, the Ozobot could be regarded as "an information-processing agent", as Wing [20] puts it, including children's decomposing, verifying, and iterative actions [1, 19, 23]. Furthermore, the design of the digital resource is easy for the children to make sense of, and they use it in an exploratory way characterized by interactions that are directed towards experimentation and organization. The interactions with the Ozobot give the children an entrance to programming which is pedagogically interesting. With a short introduction by the facilitators the children engage in coding without having any extensive prior knowledge about complex knowledge that are incorporated in the digital tool [58]. The Ozobot, thus, provides access points [55, 56] to CT skills. The study illustrates that the children's reasoning about codes and coding schemes constantly was related to the fairytale and to the environment that they had created. In this way, traditional and digital resources constituted mediating tools [53, 54] for children's computational play and for their development of CT skills. Thus, the study demonstrates how traditional and digital resources provide new learning activities and that they co-determine the conditions for learning in new ways.

5.2 The Role of Scaffolding

The outcomes of the study reveal that the combination of traditional/analogue and digital resources contribute to computational play but at the same time the children need to understand complex knowledge [11], for instance what a problem represents and what information one will gain by experimenting with coding aligned with conducting the storytelling [3, 14]. In the findings, the importance of the facilitators' interaction with the children was apparent when investigating how the children reasoned about coding and designing/creating while experimenting with a combination of analogue and digital resources. In five of the six groups, the children reassembled the researchers' introductory discussion about the fairytale and demonstration of the creative materials, the robot, and its coding opportunities while exploring and experimenting in the participatory design activity. Worth noting is how the multimodality of the materials and the way of scaffolding the activity, triggered children's interest as well as structured the content related to the activity. In this sense, the multimodal set-up facilitated children's digital play [31] crossover analogue and digital domains [16, 17] to become "creative problem-solvers", as Lee et al. [12] put it. Video-recorded episodes of the children's participatory design activity show how they pick up aspects of the introduction and appropriated the facilitators' reasoning and made them "their own", as Wertsch [54] puts it. In one of the groups, however, the facilitators were constantly instructing the children while they carried out the activity, which guided them to take decisions that were framed by these instructions. In this case, the facilitators anticipated the kinds of actions, choices, and decisions the children would need to make meaning of the activity, which the children followed along the way rather than exploring by themselves. Here, video-recorded episodes show how the children's work were focused on instructions as they approached the materials by doing without any reflections on what they themselves could do with the materials. These two ways of scaffolding clearly illustrates it as a delicate matter where facilitators need to find windows of opportunities in their scaffolding approach to not counteract children's independent experimentation, testing, and creativity.

5.3 Developing Computational Play

Learning about computational issues in ECE require children to adopt a collaborative, creative, experimenting, and critical approach to problem-solving in a multimodal setting. A focus in this study was on how a PD approach including traditional and digital resources trigger children's computational play. It has been argued earlier that a step-by-step approach to solving problems [1, 19] can both foster and inhibit children's computational play (c.f. Sect. 4.3). The children have to become familiar with the decisive steps of the computational problem in a creative and playful way if it is to be counted as computational play. Here, the issue is to consider the dynamic, complex, and imaginative character of play [33, 34, 45, 46, 49, 51] when designing for computational play. The findings of this study demonstrate how children by arranging traditional and digital resources in modularized, recursive, and iterative manners, showed signs of both computational and design/creative learning. For instance, the children's creativity while combining the different materials was apparent when they combined clay with LEGO to provide robust and trustworthy creations, or when they dressed Ozobot with hats of clay to make the robot alike the fairytale character that it was representing. This shows that materiality was a significant component of computational play. The ways in which the children managed to deconstruct own computational and creative arrangements and reasonings as well as realizing whether their suppositions were acceptable or not, illustrate that they understand some of the procedures of computational matters. In their reasonings, the children invoked domain-specific as well as domain-crossing capabilities by using coding terminology, that they appropriated through active and collaborative participation in the task. The findings demonstrate that when the children prepare for their final presentation by transforming the classic fairytale to a new representation. The coding become meaningful when it is framed by play and design allowing children to co-create across traditional and digital domains [16, 17]. This illustrates how the children within a play-like activity setting are enabled to become creative problem solvers [12] due to the inclusion material engagement and the role that PD entails to children's sharing of experiences [27] when developing computational play. To engage in tasks requiring children to discuss, negotiate, and assess the relevance of multimodal arrangements aligned with coding strategies is an important part of computational literacy. Activities in which children get the opportunity to solve problem and reason about computational matters within a PD framing open the door to what we have termed computational play.

5.4 Conclusion

In this study, we have investigated how a participatory design (PD) approach including traditional and digital resources trigger children's computational play. Our intention was to contribute with knowledge about the processes involved in such activities. Informed by a participatory design approach to computational play, our research analyzed children's interactions while being involved in PD activities with a combination of traditional and digital resources. Moreover, we had an interest in the implications such interactions have for computational play.

The findings show that a participatory design approach including a combination of traditional and digital resources incorporate distinctions and operations that provide "shortcuts" for the children's computational play by providing access points to complex CT capabilities. This means that the children are able to engage in sophisticated reasoning about computational issues closely linked to parallel hands-on activities with creative material and the storyline of the classic fairytale, without requiring too much specific prior knowledge about coding. It is notable that the computational and design practices have similarities, for instance the computational practice of testing, verification, and recursive modularization are also central to reasoning and problem solving in design. However, the results also point to dilemmas connected to the instruction and scaffolding of computational play activities. That is, for nurturing this kind of play, facilitators need to create conditions for children to experiment, test, and being creative. In this sense, children in early childhood education can make meaning in ways that are natural for them, namely through play and creativity. Through engaging in this kind of playful and resource-mediated design activities, children develop new ways of interacting and reasoning, which are enabled through the support of the resources. To conclude, the study demonstrates that computational play has the potential to reconfigure learning activities by providing new, previously unthinkable, activities that can support children in early childhood education and their development of computational literacy. At the same time, the analyses show that computational play requires new ways to be scaffolded to not counteract children's independent experimentation, testing, and creativity.

References

1. Piedade, J., Dorotea, N., Pedro, A., Matos, J.F.: On teaching programming fundamentals and computational thinking with educational robotics: a didactic experience with pre-service teachers. Educ. Sci. **10**, 214 (2020). https://doi.org/10.3390/educsci10090214
2. Soulé, H., Warrick, T.: Defining 21st century readiness for all students: what we know and how to get there. Psychol. Aesthet. Creat. Arts **9**, 178–186 (2015)
3. Binkley, M., et al.: Defining twenty-first century skills In: Griffin, P., McGraw, B., Care, E. (eds.) Assessment and Teaching of 21st Century Skills, pp. 17–66. Springer, Dordrecht (2012). https://doi.org/10.1007/978-94-007-2324-5_2
4. Papert, S.: The Children's Machine: Rethinking School in the Age of the Computer. Basic Books, New York (1993)
5. Wing, J.M.: Computational thinking. Commun. ACM **49**(3), 33–35 (2006)
6. Barr, V., Stephenson, C.: Bringing computational thinking to K-12: what is involved and what is the role of the computer science education community? ACM Inroads **2**(1), 48–54 (2011). https://doi.org/10.1080/21594937.2018.1496002
7. Chongo, S., Osman, K., Nayan, N.A.: Level of computational thinking skills among secondary science students. Sci. Educ. Int. **31**(2), 159–163 (2020). https://doi.org/10.33828/sei.v31.i2
8. Rode, J.A., et al.: From computational thinking to computational making. In: 2015 International Conference on Pervasive and Ubiquitous Computing (UBICOMP '15), Onaka, Japan, pp. 240–250. ACM (2015). https://doi.org/10.1145/2750858.2804261
9. Kafai, Y.B.: From computational thinking to computational participation in K-12 education. Seeking to reframe computational thinking as computational participation. Commun. ACM **59**(8), 26–27 (2016). https://doi.org/10.1145/2955114
10. Soleimani, A., Herro, D., Green, K.E.: CyberPLAYce - a tangible, interactive learning tool fostering children's computational thinking through storytelling. Int. J. Child-Comput. Interact. **20**, 9–23 (2019). https://doi.org/10.1016/j.ijcci.2019.01.002
11. Dindler, C., Smith, R., Iversen, O.S.: Computational empowerment: participatory design in education. CoDesign **16**(1), 66–80 (2020). https://doi.org/10.1109/EDUCON.2018.8363498
12. Lee, J., Joswick, C., Pole, K.: Classroom play and activities to support computational thinking development in early childhood. Early Childhood Educ. J. (2022). https://doi.org/10.1007/s10643-022-01319-0
13. Theodoropoulos, A.: Participatory design and participatory debugging: listening to students to improve computational thinking by creating games. Int. J. Child-Comput. Interact. **34**(100525), 1–11 (2022). https://doi.org/10.1016/j.ijcci.2022.100525
14. Brooks, E., Sjöberg, J.: A designerly approach as a foundation for school children's computational thinking skills while developing digital games. In: IDC '20: Proceedings of the Interaction Design and Children Conference, pp. 87–95. ACM (2020). https://doi.org/10.1145/3392063.3394402
15. Bers, M.U.: Coding, playgrounds and literacy in early childhood education: the development of KIBO robotics and ScratchJr. In: 2018 IEEE Global Engineering Education Conference (EDUCON), pp. 2094–2102. Santa Cruz de Tenerife, Spain (2018). https://doi.org/10.1109/EDUCON.2018.8363498
16. Bajovic, M.: Playing and learning across the concrete and digital realms: a new context for the new learners. Int. J. Play **7**(2), 199–209 (2018). https://doi.org/10.1080/21594937.2018.1496002

17. Brooks, E., Sjöberg, J.: Playfulness and creativity as vital features when school children develop game-based designs. Des. Learn. **14**(1), 137–150 (2022). https://doi.org/10.16993/dfl.170

18. Brennan, K., Resnick, M.: New frameworks for studying and assessing the development of computational thinking. In: Proceedings of the 2012 Annual Meeting of the American Educational Association, pp. 1–25. Vancouver, BC, Canada (2012)

19. Silva, R., Fonseca, B., Costa, C., Martins, F.: Fostering computational thinking skills: a didactic proposal for elementary school grades. Educ. Sci. **11**, 518 (2021). https://doi.org/10.3390/educsci11090518

20. Wing, J.: Computational thinking: what and why? CMU School of Computer Science (2010). https://www.cs.cmu.edu/~CompThink/resources/TheLinkWing.pdf. Accessed 10 Feb 2023

21. Computer Science Teachers Association: CSTA K-12 computer science standards, revised 2017 (2017). https://www.doe.k12.de.us/cms/lib/DE01922744/Centricity/Domain/176/CSTA%20Computer%20Science%20Standards%20Revised%202017.pdf. Accessed 16 Feb 2023

22. International Society for Technology in Education: ISTE standards (2021). https://cdn.iste.org/www-root/ISTE%20Standards-One-Sheet_Combined_11-22-2021_vF4%20(1)%20(4).pdf. Accessed 16 Feb 2023

23. Valenzuela, J.: How to develop computational thinkers (2022). https://www.iste.org/explore/computational-thinking. Accessed 25 Feb 2023

24. Modan, N.: 33 states adopted 57 computer science ed policies since 2018 (2019). https://www.k12dive.com/news/33-states-adopted-57-computer-science-ed-policies-since-2018/562530/. Accessed 15 Feb 2023

25. Bocconi, S., et al.: Developing computational thinking in compulsory education. JRC Science for Policy Report (2016). European Commission. https://publications.jrc.ec.europa.eu/repository/handle/JRC104188. Accessed 15 Feb 2023

26. Kafai, Y.B., Burke, Q.: The social turn in K-1$2 programming: moving from computational thinking to computational participation. In: Proceedings of the 44th ACM Technical Symposium on Computer Science Education (SIGCSE '13), 603–608. ACM, New York, NY (2013). https://doi.org/10.1145/2445196.2445373

27. Tanenbaum. J.G., Williams, A.M., Desjardins, A., Tanenbaum. K.: Democratizing technology: pleasure, utility and expressiveness in DIY and maker practice. In: Proceedings of the SIGCHI Conference on Human Factors in Computing Systems, pp. 2603–2612. ACM (2013). https://doi.org/10.1145/2470654.2481360

28. Kafai, Y.B., Fields, D.A., Searle, K.A.: Everyday creativity in novice e-textile. In: Proceedings of the 8th ACM Conference on Creativity and Cognition (C&C '11), pp. 353–354. ACM (2011). https://doi.org/10.1145/2069618.2069692

29. Lewis, T.: Creativity in technology education: providing children with glimpses of their inventive potential. Int. J. Technol. Des. Educ. **19**(3), 255–268 (2009). https://doi.org/10.1007/s10798-008-9051-y

30. Blikstein, P.: Travels in troy with freire: technology as an agent of emancipation. Educ. Pesqui. **42**(3), 837–856 (2016). https://doi.org/10.1590/S1517-970220164203003

31. Murcia, K.J., Tang, K.S.: Exploring the multimodality of young children's coding. Aust. Educ. Comput. **34**(1) (2019)

32. Li, Y., et al.: Computational thinking is more about thinking than computing. J. STEM Educ. Res. **3**(1), 1–18 (2020). https://doi.org/10.1007/s41979-020-00030-2

33. Vygotsky, L.S.: Play and its role in the mental development of the child. In: Bruner, J.S., Jolly, A., Sylva, K. (eds.) Play – Its Role in Development and Evolution, pp. 537–554. Penguin Books Ltd., New York (1933/1976)

34. Vygotsky, L.S.: Imagination and its development in childhood (N. Minick, Trans.). In: Rieber, R.W., Carton, A.S. (eds.) The Collected Works of L. S. Vygotsky, vol. 2, pp. 339–350. Plenum Press, New York (1987)

35. Sylva, K., Melhuish, E., Sammons, P., Siraj-Blatchford, I., Taggart, B.: Early Childhood Matters: Evidence from the Effective Preschool and Primary Education Project. Routledge, Abingdon (2010)

36. Correia, N., Camilo, C., Aguiar, C., Amaro, F.: Children's right to participate in early childhood education settings: a systematic review. Child Youth Serv. Rev. **100**, 76–88 (2019)

37. United Nations Committee on the Rights of the Child: Convention on the Rights of the Child: General comment no. 12: the right of the child to be heard (2009). https://resourcecentre.sav ethechildren.net/pdf/5040.pdf/. Accessed 10 Feb 2023

38. Correia, N., Aguiar, C.: Children's participation in early childhood education: a theoretical overview. Contemporary Issues in Early Childhood (2021). https://doi.org/10.1177/146394 9120981789

39. Kanyal, M.: Children's rights: 0–8 years. In: Kanyal. M. (ed.) Children's Rights 0–8: Promoting Participation in Education and Care, pp. xi–xiv. Routledge, New York (2014)

40. Niemi, R.: From active joining to child-led participation: a new approach to examine participation in teaching practice. South Afr. J. Childhood Educ. **9**(1), 1–7 (2019). https://doi.org/10.4102/sajce.v9i1.663

41. Lansdown, G., Jimerson, S. R., Shahroozi, R.: Children's rights and school psychology: children's right to participation. J. Sch. Psychol. **52**(1), 3–12 (2014). https://0.1016/j.jsp.2013.12.006

42. Bjerknes, G., Ehn, P., Kyng, M., Nygaard, K.: Computers and Democracy: A Scandinavian Challenge. Gower Publishing, Aldershot (1987)

43. Björgvinsson, E., Ehn, P., Hillgren, P-A.: Participatory design and "democratizing innovation". In: PDC '10: Proceedings of the 11th Biennial Participatory Design Conference, pp. 41–50. ACM, New York, NY (2010). https://doi.org/10.1145/1900441.1900448

44. Gibson, J.J.: The Senses Considered as Perceptual Systems. Cornell University, London (1966)

45. Sanders, E.B.N., Brandt, E., Binder, T.: A framework for organizing the tools and techniques of participatory design. In: PDC '10: Proceedings of the 11th Biennial Participatory Design Conference, pp. 195–198. ACM, New York, NY (2010). https://doi.org/10.1145/1900441.1900476

46. Walsh, G., Foss, E., Yip, J., Druin, A.: FACIT PD: a framework for analysis and creation of intergenerational techniques of participatory design. In: Proceedings of the SIGCHI Conference on Human Factors in Computing Systems (CHI '13), pp. 2893–2902. ACM, New York, NY (2013). https://doi.org/10.1145/2470654.2481400

47. Pellegrini, A.D.: Research and policy on children's play. Play Policy **3**(2), 131–136 (2009)

48. Schwartzman, H.B.: The anthropological study of children's play. Annu. Rev. Anthropol. **5**, 289–328 (1976)

49. Sutton-Smith, B.: The Ambiguity of Play. Harvard University Press (1997)

50. Wood, E.: Conceptualizing a pedagogy of play: international perspectives from theory, policy and practice. In: Kuschener, D.S. (ed.) From Children to Red Hatters: Diverse Images and Issues of Play, pp. 166–190. University Press of America (2009)

51. Edwards, S., Mantilla, A., Grieshaber, Nuttall, J., Wood. E.: Converged play characteristics for early childhood education: multi-modal, global-local, and traditional-digital. Oxford Rev. Educ. **46**(5), 637–660 (2020). https://doi.org/10.1080/03054985.2020.1750358

52. Torres, P.E., et al.: A systematic review of physical-digital play technology and developmentally relevant child behaviour. Int. J. Child-Comput. Interact. **30**, 100323 (2021). https://doi.org/10.1016/j.ijcci.2021.100323

53. Vygotsky, L.S.: Mind in Society: The Development of Higher Psychological Processes. Harvard University Press, Cambridge (1978)
54. Wertsch, J.V.: Mind as Action. Oxford University Press, New York (1998)
55. Edstrand, E.: Learning to reason in environmental education. Digital tools, access points to knowledge and science literacy, (Diss.) Studies in Educational Sciences, University of Gothenburg (2017)
56. Giddens, A.: Runaway World: How Globalisation is Shaping Our Lives. Profile Books, London (2002)
57. Brooks, E., Møller, A.K.: Children's generative play with a combination of analogue and digital resources. In: Brooks, A. (ed.) Creating Digitally. Springer, Cham (in press)
58. Vygotsky, L.S.: The instrumental method in psychology. In: Reiber, R., Wollock, J. (eds.) The Collected Works of L. S. Vygotsky, vol. 3: Problems of the Theory and History of Psychology, pp. 85–89. Plenum Press, London (1997)
59. Storvang, P., Mortensen, B., Clarke, A. H.: Using workshops in business research: a framework to diagnose, plan, facilitate and analyze workshops. In: Freytag, P., Young, L. (eds.) Collaborative Research Design. Working with Business for Meaningful Findings, pp. 155–174. Springer, Singapore (2018). https://doi.org/10.1007/978-981-10-5008-4_7
60. Ødegaard, E.E., Oen, M., Birkeland, J.: Success of and barriers to workshop methodology: experiences from exploration and pedagogical innovation laboratories (EX-PED-LAB). In: Wallerstedt, C., Brooks, E., Ødegaard, E.E., Pramling, N. (eds.) Methodology for Research with Early Childhood Education and Care Professionals. Example Studies and Theoretical Elaboration, vol. 38, pp. 57–82. Springer, Cham (2023). https://doi.org/10.1007/978-3-031-14583-4_5
61. Ørngreen, R., Levinsen, K.: Workshops as a research methodology. Electron. J. E-Learn. **15**(1), 70–81 (2017)
62. Schei, T.B., Ødegaard, E.E.: Stories of style – exploring teachers' self-staging with musical artefacts. In: Garvis, S., Pramling, N. (eds.) Exploring Lived Experiences: Narratives and Early Childhood, pp. 59–69. Routledge, London (2017)
63. Caine, V., Clandinin, J.D., Lessard, S.: Narrative Inquiry – Philosophical Roots. Bloombury (2021)
64. Kurtz, C.F.: Working with Stories in Your Community or Organization: Participatory Narrative Inquiry. Kurtz-Fernhout Publishing (2014)
65. Clandinin, D.J.: Engaging in Narrative Inquiry. Left Coast Press (2013)
66. Dewey, J.: How We Think; A Restatement of the Relation of Reflective Thinking to the Educative Process. D. C. Heath & Co Publishers (2010)
67. Flewitt, R.: Using Video to Investigate Preschool Classroom Interaction: Education Research Assumptions and Methodological Practices. Vis. Commun. **5**(1), 25–50 (2016). https://doi.org/10.1177/14703572060609
68. Danish code of conduct for research integrity: Ministry of Higher Education and Research, Copenhagen, Denmark (2014). Retrieved 7 Mar 2021. https://ufm.dk/en/publications/2014/files-2014-1/the-danish-code-of-conduct-for-research-integrity.pdf. Access 24 Feb 2023
69. General data protection regulations (GDPR) (2016/679). Off. J. Eur. Union. https://eur-lex.europa.eu/legal-content/EN/TXT/PDF/?uri=CELEX:32016R0679. Accessed 24 Feb 2023
70. Convention on the rights of the child (1989). Treaty no. 27531. United Nations Treaty Series, vol. 1577, pp. 3–178. https://treaties.un.org/doc/Treaties/1990/09/19900902%2003-14%20AM/Ch_IV_11p.pdf. Accessed 25 Feb 2023
71. Braun, V., Clarke, V.: Using thematic analysis in psychology. Qual. Res. Psychol. **3**(2), 77–101 (2006)

Do 3–4-Year-Old Preschoolers Know that the Fictional Characters in Television Programs Are not Real?

Yanan Chen$^{(\boxtimes)}$ (iD), Ting Zhang (iD), and Liwei Zhao (iD)

Central China Normal University, Wuhan 430070, Hubei, People's Republic of China
{chenyanan,zhangting77,zhaoliwei}@mails.ccnu.edu.cn

Abstract. It is of great significance for children's development to correctly distinguish between reality and fantasy. The purpose of this study was to investigate whether 3–4-year-old children can distinguish between reality and fantasy and whether they can distinguish between different fictional worlds as adults do, and to further analyze their understanding of fictional characters acted by real people based on previous studies. In the study, 36 pairs of combinations were created by pairing three real people, four fictional characters, and two fictional characters acted by real people. Both young children and adults were asked to rate how easily these characters could meet on a scale of 1 to 3. The results revealed that 3–4-year-olds could distinguish between different fictional worlds like adults but were less able to distinguish between reality and fantasy than adults. In addition, 3–4-year-olds and adults had different understandings of fictional characters acted by real people. Children interpreted these characters as fictional characters rather than real people, while adults interpreted these characters as real people rather than fictional characters.

Keywords: Fantasy/reality distinction · Fantasy/fantasy distinction · Non-metric multidimensional scaling

1 Introduction

The rapid advancement of technology has led to the widespread popularity of television in households, becoming a significant component of children's leisure time [1]. A recent study conducted by Common Sense Media in 2020 assessed electronic media usage among children aged 0–8 years in the United States and found that children aged 2–4 spent an average of 2.5 h per day using electronic media, while children aged 5–8 spent 3.05 h per day. Furthermore, the study revealed that children aged 0–8 years spent 73% of their total screen time viewing television and video content each day [2]. Other researchers have investigated television viewing habits among Chinese children, discovering that television was the most utilized form of media by young children aged 3–6 years, accounting for 35.1% of media use time [3]. Li et al. [4] found that a staggering 93.39% of children aged 3–6 years watched television every day, with an average viewing time of 90.88 min.

© The Author(s), under exclusive license to Springer Nature Switzerland AG 2023
M. Kurosu and A. Hashizume (Eds.): HCII 2023, LNCS 14012, pp. 26–40, 2023.
https://doi.org/10.1007/978-3-031-35599-8_2

Cartoons are deeply loved by children among various television programs. Children spend a lot of time watching cartoons every day and gain knowledge about the world from them [5]. A study conducted by Yu [6] revealed that over 50% of children watched cartoons for about 0.5–1 h per day. Cartoons are featured with their abundance of fictional content, including entities and events that are not possible in the physical world or contravene physical laws [7]. This includes talking animals and characters with superpowers. Conversely, real entities and events refer to things or occurrences that exist in everyday life and align with the laws of reality [8], such as cleaning the classroom.

The presence of fictional content in cartoons presents a duality of benefits and challenges. On the one hand, it has been demonstrated to stimulate children's imagination and creativity [9, 10]. A study by Subbotsky et al. [10] found that preschool children who watched movies with fictional content performed significantly better on creativity tests compared to those who had not seen these movies. On the other hand, researchers have shown that some cartoons can lead to a decrease in children's executive function [7, 11], as the fictional content may interfere with their ability to properly execute tasks [12]. Additionally, as children are prone to imitating what they see, failure to distinguish between reality and fantasy can result in dangerous imitation of fantastical events [13]. It is thus of utmost importance for children's development to be able to distinguish between reality and fantasy.

Over the past few years, the field of psychology has witnessed a proliferation of studies examining children's differentiation between reality and fantasy [8, 14, 15]. Despite these efforts, there remains much contention among scholars regarding the ability of young children to distinguish between these two domains. Some researchers have doubted young children's ability to distinguish between reality and fantasy. They argued that children often had a strong belief in the existence of fictional characters [16, 17]. For example, Prentice et al. [16] found that most children under the age of 6 believed in the existence of Santa Claus, the Tooth Fairy, and the Easter Bunny. In addition, young children may accept the possibility of impossible events if they are presented with them [18–20]. However, a significant body of research has demonstrated that the ability to distinguish between reality and fantasy develops in early childhood. By the age of 3, children can already distinguish between pretend and real actions [21], imagination and reality [22], and toys and the objects they represent [23]. For instance, Wellman and Estes [24] reported that 3-year-olds can distinguish between real entities and mental imagery, comprehending that real entities can be touched while mental imagery cannot. By five years of age, children are able to accurately distinguish between real and fantastical entities [25, 26], as well as real and fantastical events [27, 28].

In addition to the real world, children are frequently exposed to a variety of fictional worlds, such as storybooks, dreams, cartoons, pretend play, etc. Therefore, it is important for them to be able to distinguish not only reality from fantasy but also different fictional worlds [29]. Adults have the ability to recognize the existence of multiple fictional worlds, beyond the binary distinction between reality and fantasy [30]. For example, it is well known that Snow White, Spider-Man, and Mickey Mouse are all fictional characters, but they each occupy a different fictional world. Will young children behave like adults? Goulding and Friedman [31] conducted three experiments in which children aged 4–7 were asked to judge whether improbable and impossible events could happen in dreams, stories, and reality. The results indicated that children believed such events were most likely to occur in dreams, followed by stories, and finally in reality. This demonstrates that children hold subtle beliefs about every world [32, 33], and these different beliefs influence their judgments. For example, children may view dreams as farther away from reality than stories, leading them to believe that a greater number of events can occur in the more distant world [34]. Skolnick and Bloom [32] explored the beliefs of 4-year-old children and adults about fictional characters in media and their relationship with other characters in the same world (e.g., Batman and Robin) or different worlds (e.g., Batman and Spongebob). The results showed that 4-year-old children could distinguish different fictional worlds like adults, and pointed out that this was an unlearned default understanding. However, the binary judgment task used in the study (Experiment 1 required children to choose between "real" and "make-believe," and Experiment 2 required them to choose between "yes" and "no") makes it difficult to draw definite conclusions about the relationship between different fictional worlds [29]. Martarelli et al. [29] improved this by changing the binary judgment task into a progressive judgment task. The study selected 3 photos of real people and 12 photos of fictional characters and then asked children to rate how easily these characters could meet on a scale of 1 to 6. Non-metric multidimensional scaling (NMDS) was used to convert ratings of how easy it was for characters to meet into a spatial map representing the distance between them. The results indicated that children aged 3–4 could distinguish different fictional worlds like adults, but they couldn't distinguish the real world from the fictional world.

Besides, there is a special kind of character in real life——the fictional characters acted by real people, such as Snow White acted by actors in Disneyland. These characters are special links between fictional characters and real life. How do young children understand their existence? Do they interpret them as fictional characters or real people? This is also one of the important issues in this study. Woolley et al. [35] found that 4-year-old children who were visited by Candy Witch acted by real people were more likely to believe in the existence of this novel entity. The enlightenment of this result is that if young children interact with a fictional character acted by real people in real life, children may believe in the existence of this fictional character more.

With the growing popularity of television in families, cartoons are becoming popular among children. This raises concerns about the potential impact of the fictional content contained within cartoons on children who may not be able to distinguish between reality and fantasy. Although previous studies have investigated the ability of young children to distinguish between reality and fantasy, the results have been inconsistent, warranting further investigation. In addition, substantial research on young children's understanding of reality and fantasy was conducted in western countries, and this study adds a valuable cross-cultural perspective to the research by using Chinese children as the study population. This study refers to and extends the study by Martarelli et al. [29] to examine the ability of 3–4-year-old children to distinguish between reality and fantasy (reality/fantasy), as well as between different fictional worlds (fantasy/fantasy). Furthermore, the study also explores children's understanding of fictional characters acted by real people in real life.

2 Methods

2.1 Participants

A total of 23 children aged 3–4 and 16 adults participated in this study. The children were recruited from kindergartens in Wuhan, Hubei Province, China, while the adults were undergraduate students also from the same location. However, one child and one adult were excluded from the study due to their data not meeting the experimental requirements. The final sample consisted of 22 young children ($M = 44.13$ months, $SD = 3.63$, with 10 boys and 12 girls) and 15 adults ($M = 21.6$ years, $SD = 0.49$, with 6 boys and 9 girls).

2.2 Materials and Procedures

The materials used in the experiment included four pictures of fictional characters (Sun Wukong and Zhu Bajie from the Chinese cartoon *Journey to the West*; Snow White and the dwarf from the animated films *Snow White and the Seven Dwarfs*), three pictures of real people (the participant, the participant's father, and mother) and two pictures of fictional characters acted by real people (Snow White and Zhu Bajie) (see Appendix 1). The consistency of the characters' expressive actions and emotional attributes was taken into consideration during the selection of the pictures, as previous studies have shown that the emotions of characters can influence children's reality/fantasy judgments [27, 36–38].

Due to the COVID-19 epidemic, face-to-face contact with the participants was not possible, and the experiment was conducted online. The children were asked to evaluate the combination of characters in pairs, and 36 pairs of characters (n × (n–1)/2 pairs comparisons with n = 9 stimuli) were presented with Microsoft PowerPoint software. The experiment was recorded with the consent of the kindergarten teachers during a video call with the children, which was facilitated by the screen-sharing function of Tencent Meeting.

Initially, the knowledge of four fictional characters was assessed among the children by the experimenter asking them to identify the characters. If the children were unable to accurately recognize the character, the experimenter provided the correct answer. Subsequently, both children and adults were asked to rate how easily these 36 pairs of characters could meet on a scale of 1 to 3, where 1 signified that the two characters had never met and would not meet in the future, 2 indicated that it was somewhat easy for them to meet, and 3 meant they were easy to meet and had met at least once. To assist children in making judgments, column charts were utilized to provide a better understanding of the relationship between degrees (see Appendix 2).

The experimental procedure was based on the study by Martarelli et al. [29], with a modification in the method used for children to rate the ease of meeting between characters. The rating range was narrowed from 1–6 to 1–3, and the smiley face scale was replaced by a more intuitive and vivid column chart. This alteration was made as it was found that it was challenging for 3–4-year-olds to differentiate between six different smiley faces during the prediction.

For adults, they filled out the online questionnaire prepared in advance by the experimenter and the content was also to rate how easily these 36 pairs of characters could meet on a scale of 1 to 3.

2.3 Data Analysis

The collected data were analyzed by one-way ANOVA, non-metric multidimensional scaling analysis, and repeated measures ANOVA using SPSS25.0.

3 Results

Firstly, in examining the distinction between adults and children in different fictional worlds, the analysis excluded fictional characters acted by real people. The results showed that the distinction was based on pairing other characters, including within-real worlds (reality/reality pairs, e.g., the participant and his or her father), within-fictional worlds (fantasy/fantasy pairs of characters from the same fictional world, e.g., Sun Wukong and Zhu Bajie), between-fictional worlds (fantasy/fantasy pairs of characters from different fictional worlds, e.g., Sun Wukong and Snow White), and between real-fantasy worlds (reality/fantasy pairs, e.g., the participant and Zhu Bajie). Children and adults had to rate how easily these 36 pairs of characters could meet on a scale of 1 to 3, with higher scores indicating a higher possibility of a meeting between characters. Descriptive statistics are shown in Appendix 3.

Referring to the study of Martarelli et al. [29], the distinction between adults and young children for reality/fantasy and fantasy/fantasy was calculated at the individual level through the following formula:

For the degree of reality/fantasy distinction (RFD):

$$(M_{RR} - M_{RF}) \times sd_{tot} \tag{1}$$

M_{RR} is the mean of all reality/fantasy judgments, M_{RF} is the mean of all reality/fantasy judgments, and sd_{tot} is the standard deviation of all judgments.

For the degree of fantasy/fantasy distinction (FFD):

$$sd_{FF}/sd_{tot} \tag{2}$$

sd_{FF} is the standard deviation of all fantasy/fantasy judgments.

Two one-way ANOVAs were conducted with age as the independent variable and RFD and FFD as the dependent variables. The results revealed that there was a significant difference between adults and children in the degree of reality/fantasy distinctions, $F(1, 35) = 27.66, p < 0.001, \eta_p^2 = 0.44$, but not in the degree of fantasy/fantasy distinctions, $F(1, 35) = 0.12, p > 0.05, \eta_p^2 = 0.03$, indicating that 3–4 years old are as capable as adults of distinguishing between different fictional worlds, but not good at distinguishing between reality and fantasy as adults can do.

Secondly, the mental representation of real and fictional worlds was analyzed using non-metric multidimensional scaling (NMDS). Ratings of how easy it was for characters to meet into a spatial map that represents the distance between them. For instance, if a participant rated Snow White as 3 for ease of meeting with the dwarf, but 1 for ease of meeting with Zhu Bajie, the map would display that Snow White was relatively close to the dwarf, but relatively far from Zhu Bajie.

The NMDS was first conducted using the ALSCAL procedure in SPSS 25.0, resulting in average maps for adults and children, as shown in Appendix 4 and Appendix 5. Both average maps correctly divided the four fictional characters into two groups: the *Journey to the West* group (Sun Wukong and Zhu Bajie) and the *Snow White and the Seven Dwarfs* group (Snow White and the dwarf). This indicates that both adults and children perceive the existence of different fictional worlds and that characters within the same fictional world are judged as easier to meet. In addition, children were able to distinguish the real people group (the participant, the participant's father, and the participant's mother) from the fictional character group (the *Journey to the West* group and the *Snow White and the Seven Dwarfs*), suggesting that they could distinguish between the real and fictional worlds.

However, they have different understandings of fictional characters acted by real people. In the children's average map, these acted fictional characters were closer to the characters in their respective fictional worlds, indicating that the children interpreted the acted characters as fictional characters rather than real people. In contrast, in the adults' average map, the fictional characters acted by real people were closer to the real people. It indicates that the adults considered these characters as real people rather than fictional characters.

Subsequently, since the fit of the average maps model for young children generated by the process of ALSCAL was not satisfactory (stress $= 0.45$), we utilized the PROSXCAL procedure in SPSS 25.0 for further analysis. The PROSXCAL procedure introduces an optimal scale transformation into the multidimensional scaling analysis model, thereby enabling more precise results with sufficient sample size. Consequently, average maps with improved fits were generated for both adults and children, as shown in Appendix 6 and Appendix 7. These results reinforced the findings previously discussed.

Finally, in order to eliminate the potential impact of repeated measures on the results, the above results were validated through the use of a repeated measures analysis of variance (ANOVA). The results of Mauchly's test indicated that the data was in compliance with the assumption of sphericity ($p = 0.617 > 0.05$), further reinforcing the conclusion that there were significant differences between the understanding of fictional characters acted by real people among young children and adults ($F_{(1,35)} = 404.69$, $p < 0.01$, $\eta_p^2 = 0.92$).

4   Discussion

In the present study, we examined the ability of 3–4-year-old children and adults to distinguish reality/fantasy and fantasy/fantasy, and also explored their understanding of fictional characters acted by real people. We found that 3–4-year-olds were able to distinguish between different fictional worlds as well as adults, but were not as good as adults at distinguishing between reality and fantasy. Besides, 3–4-year-olds and adults had different understandings of fictional characters acted by real people. 3–4-year-olds interpreted these characters as fictional characters rather than real people, while adults interpreted these characters as real people rather than fictional characters.

First of all, the result is in line with previous studies by Martarelli et al. [29] and Skolnick et al. [32], which showed that children aged 3–4 can distinguish different fictional worlds. For instance, they believed that characters within the same world, such as Snow White and the dwarf, could interact with each other, but not with characters from different worlds, like Sun WuKong. This ability to distinguish between fictional worlds has been explained as a product of early childhood development and as an unlearned default option for children [29, 32]. When children encounter a fictional world, they tend to create unique attributes that distinguish it from other fictional worlds. This conclusion was supported by a subsequent study that investigated the behavior of 3- and 4-year-old children during pretend play. The results showed that, regardless of whether they presented two pretend games simultaneously or sequentially, children were unwilling to transfer objects between the two games, indicating their recognition of multiple pretend worlds and their spontaneous differentiation between different pretend worlds [33].

Secondly, the study revealed that the ability of 3–4-year-old children to distinguish between reality and fantasy was not as good as that of adults, consistent with the results of Martarelli et al. [29]. However, previous studies have shown that young children can already distinguish between reality and fantasy [28, 39]. This may be because in our experimental task, children must judge the physical possibility of events, and these skills seem to develop around the age of 4 [40]. This task was challenging for 3-year-old children.

The results of our study differ from those of Martarelli et al. [29], who found that young children perceive the real world as one of many and cannot yet distinguish it from the fictional world. However, in our study, children were found to be able to distinguish the real world from the fictional world. This discrepancy in results could be attributed to three factors. First, Martarelli et al. [29] presented children with 105 character evaluations, which could have resulted in fatigue and decreased accuracy in judging reality and fantasy for the 3–4-year-old participants. In contrast, our study required the evaluation of only 36 character pairs, which was relatively less taxing for the young children. Second, research has demonstrated that the familiarization with stimulus materials affects children's judgments of reality and fantasy [41–43]. The real people used in our study were the participant, the participant's father, and the mother, whereas the real people they used were the participant, the experimenter, and the participant's teacher. The greater familiarity of the characters in our study could have impacted the results of the experiment. Lastly, due to the limited comprehension of 3–4-year-old children, we altered the 6-point smiley face scale used in Martarelli et al. [29] to a 3-point column chart scale, which reduced the error in the results to some extent, but also precluded a more in-depth analysis of the differentiation capacity of the children.

Finally, our findings revealed that there was a difference in the understanding of fictional characters acted by real people between 3–4-year-old children and adults. Children interpreted these characters as fictional characters, whereas adults interpreted them as real people. The result is consistent with the traditional view of cognitive development that young children are gullible and tend to believe in the existence of fictional characters [44–46]. As they grow older, children become increasingly rational, similar to adults. Moreover, previous research has shown that the emotional content embedded in stimulus material influences children's distinction between reality and fantasy. Children are more likely to believe that events with neutral or positive emotions occur in reality, as opposed to events with negative emotions [27, 36–38]. The animated characters used in this study are popular among young children and elicit positive emotions, which may have led the children to perceive these fictional characters as real.

5 Limitations

The present study has several limitations that should be addressed in future research. First of all, in order to enhance the visibility and precision of differences in the average maps of children and adults, it would be beneficial to perform Procrustes transformations on the average maps obtained through the application of ALSCAL and PROSXCAL. Secondly, the method used to assess the ease with which different characters could meet may have led to confusion among the participants, as they may have interpreted "meeting" as viewing characters on television or in storybooks, rather than in reality. Future research should consider how to avoid this situation. Finally, the ongoing COVID-19 pandemic necessitated conducting the survey online, which may have introduced additional variables such as inconsistent equipment and network stability, or the presence of a teacher, which may have influenced the results of the experiment. Future studies should seek to mitigate these sources of variability.

Appendix 1

The experimental materials used in the study. (A) the real people: the participant, the participant's father, and the participant's mother; (B) the characters in *Journey to the West*: the fictional characters (Sun Wukong and Zhu Bajie) and the fictional character acted by real people (Zhu Bajie); (C) the characters in *Snow White and the Seven Dwarfs*: the fictional characters (Snow White and the dwarf) and the fictional character acted by real people (Snow White).

A		
Photograph of the participant	Photograph of the participant's father	Photograph of the participant's mother
B		

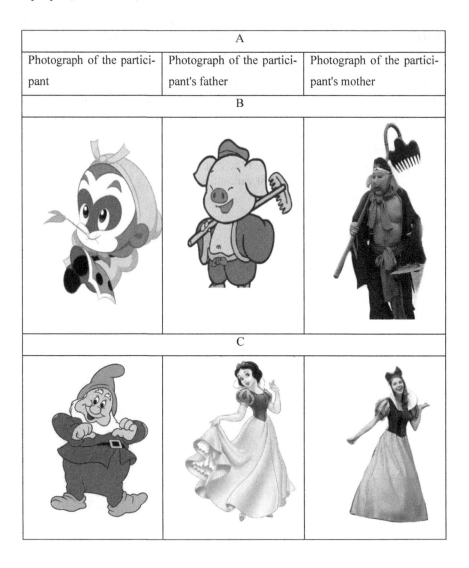

C		

Appendix 2

The easiness scale of a pair of characters to meet

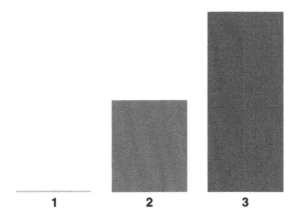

Appendix 3

Means and standard deviations of adults and Children's ratings for the easiness of different characters could meet.

	Within-real		Within-fictional		Between-fictional		Between-real-fictional	
	M	SD	M	SD	M	SD	M	SD
children	2.68	0.61	2.39	0.78	2.14	0.87	2.07	0.87
adults	2.91	0.35	2.30	0.90	1.17	0.41	1.08	0.32

Appendix 4

Adults' average map (stress = 0.08)

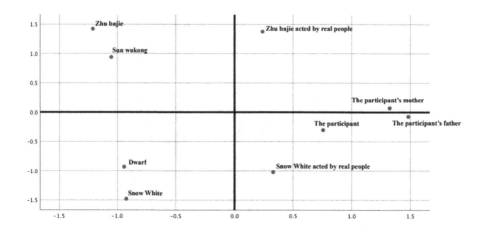

Appendix 5

3–4-year-olds' average map (stress = 0.45)

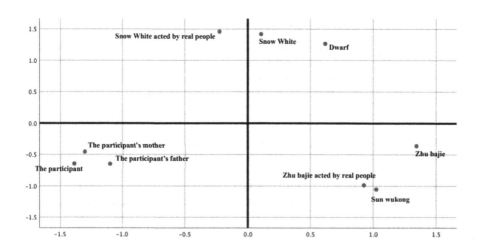

Appendix 6

Adults' average map (stress = 0.01)

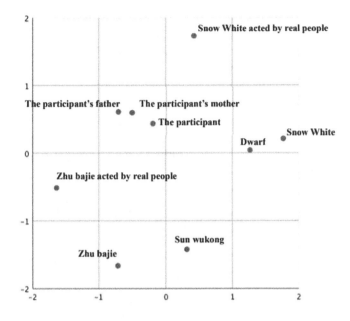

Appendix 7

3–4-year-olds' average map (stress = 0.05)

References

1. Christakis, D.A., Ebel, B.E., Rivara, F.P., Zimmerman, F.J.: Television, video, and computer game usage in children under 11 years of age. J. Pediatr. **145**(5), 652–656 (2004)
2. Rideout, V., Robb, M.B.: The common sense census: media use by kids age zero to eight, San Francisco (2020)
3. Liu, G.Y., Li, J.X., Xie, S., Liu, X.F., Ma, S.S.: The effect of electronic devices on preschool children's social ability: the mediating role of family environment. Chin. Spec. Educ. **11**, 90–96 (2020)
4. Li, H., Zhou, Z.K., Wu, X.P.: 3–6 year old children's media use. Shanghai Res. Educ. **5**, 57–59 (2014)
5. Dong, S.M., Song, Y.J., Jiang Y.R., Sun, G.Q., Wang. Y., Jiang, F.: A multicenter study on the effect of television viewing behavior on sleep quality in children under 4 years of age in China. Chin. J. Pediatr. **53**(12), 907–912 (2015)
6. Yu, J.: Education value of cartoon for preschoolers. Master's thesis, Hunan Normal University (2016)
7. Lillard, A.S., Peterson, J.: The immediate impact of different types of television on young children's executive function. Pediatrics **128**, 644–649 (2011)
8. Woolley, J.D.: Thinking about fantasy: are children fundamentally different thinkers and believers from adults? Child Dev. **68**(6), 991–1011 (1997)

9. Tower, R.B., Singer, D.G., Singer, J.L., Biggs, A.: Differential effects of television programming on preschoolers' cognition, imagination, and social play. Am. J. Orthopsychiatry **49**(2), 265–281 (1979)

10. Subbotsky, E., Hysted, C., Jones, N.: Watching films with magical content facilitates creativity in children. Percept. Mot. Skills **111**(1), 261–277 (2010)

11. Li, H., Hsueh, Y., Yu, H., Kitzmann, K.M.: Viewing fantastical events in animated television shows: immediate effects on Chinese preschoolers' executive function. Front. Psychol. **11**, 583174 (2020)

12. Lillard, A.S., Drell, M., Richey, E., Boguszewski, K., Smith, E.: Further examination of the immediate impact of television on children's executive function. Dev. Psychol. **51**, 792–805 (2015)

13. Bandura, A.: Social Learning Theory. Prentice-Hall, Oxford (1) (1977)

14. Woolley, J.D., Ghossainy, M.E.: Revisiting the fantasy–reality distinction: children as naïve skeptics. Child Dev. **84**(5), 1496–1510 (2013)

15. Chen, X.Y., Wang, Y.F., Zhao, J.Y., Meng, Q.: The developmental characteristics and mechanism of children's distinction between fantasy and reality. Adv. Psychol. Sci. **07**, 1232–1237 (2019)

16. Prentice, N.M., Manosevitz, M., Hubbs, L.: Imaginary figures of early childhood: Santa Claus, Easter Bunny, and the Tooth Fairy. Am. J. Orthopsychiatry **48**, 618–628 (1978)

17. Principe, G.F., Smith, E.: Seeing things unseen: fantasy beliefs and false reports. J. Cogn. Dev. **9**, 89–111 (2008)

18. Chandler, M.J., Lalonde, C.E.: Surprising, magical, and miraculous turns of events: children's reactions to violations of their early theories of mind and matter. Br. J. Dev. Psychol. **12**, 83–95 (1994)

19. Rosengren, K.S., Hickling, A.K.: Seeing is believing: children's explanations of commonplace, magical and extraordinary transformations. Child Dev. **65**, 1605–1626 (1994)

20. Subbotsky, E.: Magical thinking in judgments of causation: can anomalous phenomena affect ontological causal beliefs in children and adults? Br. J. Dev. Psychol. **22**, 123–152 (2004)

21. Flavell, J.H., Flavell, E.R., Green, F.L.: Young children's knowledge about the apparent-real and pretend-real distinctions. Dev. Psychol. **23**, 816–822 (1987)

22. Woolley, J.D., Wellman, H.M.: Origin and truth: young children's understanding of imaginary mental representations. Child Dev. **64**, 1–17 (1993)

23. Woolley, J.D., Wellman, H.M.: Young children's understanding of realities, nonrealities, and appearances. Child Dev. **61**, 946–961 (1990)

24. Wellman, H.M., Estes, D.: Early understanding of mental entities: a reexamination of childhood realism. Child Dev. **57**, 910–923 (1986)

25. Sharon, T., Woolley, J.D.: Do monsters dream? Young children's understanding of the fantasy/reality distinction. Br. J. Dev. Psychol. **22**, 293–310 (2004)

26. Taylor, B.J., Howell, R.J.: The ability of three-, four-, and five-year-old children to distinguish fantasy from reality. J. Genet. Psychol. **121**, 315–318 (1973)

27. Samuels, A., Taylor, M.: Children's ability to distinguish fantasy events from real life events. Br. J. Dev. Psychol. **12**, 417–427 (1994)

28. Golomb, C., Galasso, L.: Make believe and reality: explorations of the imaginary realm. Dev. Psychol. **31**, 800–810 (1995)

29. Martarelli, C.S., Mast, F.W., Läge, D., Roebers, C.M.: The distinction between real and fictional worlds: investigating individual differences in fantasy understanding. Cogn. Dev. **36**, 111–126 (2015)

30. Lewis, D.: Truth in fiction. Am. Philos. Q. **15**, 37–46 (1978)

31. Goulding, B.W., Friedman, O.: Children's beliefs about possibility differ across dreams, stories, and reality. Child Dev. **91**(6), 1843–1853 (2020)

32. Skolnick, D., Bloom, P.: What does Batman think about SpongeBob? Children's understanding of the fantasy/fantasy distinction. Cognition **101**(1), B9-18 (2006)
33. Skolnick Weisberg, D., Bloom, P.: Young children separate multiple pretend worlds. Dev. Sci. **12**(5), 699–705 (2009)
34. Weisberg, D.S., Goodstein, J.: What belongs in a fictional world? J. Cogn. Cult. **9**, 69–78 (2009)
35. Woolley, J.D., Boerger, E.A., Markman, A.B.: A visit from the Candy Witch: factors influencing young children's belief in a novel fantastical being. Dev. Sci. **7**, 456–468 (2004)
36. Carrick, N., Quas, J.A.: Effects of discrete emotions on young children's ability to discern fantasy and reality. Dev. Psychol. **42**(6), 1278–1288 (2006)
37. Li, Y.H., Wang, Y.F., Chen, X.Y., Li, S., Zhang, L.M.: Do children know that fantastic events in television programs are not real? Cogn. Dev. **58**, 101020 (2021)
38. Metlicar, S.: Happy dragon is real, frightening dragon is not: children's fantasy-reality distinction of emotional stimuli. Stud. Psychol. **56**(2), 155–167 (2014)
39. DiLalla, L.F., Watson, M.W.: Differentiation of fantasy and reality: preschoolers' reactions to interruptions in their play. Dev. Psychol. **24**(2), 286–291 (1988)
40. Skolnick Weisberg, D., Sobel, D.M.: Young children discriminate improbable from impossible events in fiction. Cogn. Dev. **27**(1), 90–98 (2012)
41. Vaden, V.C., Woolley, J.D.: Does god make it real? Children's belief in religious stories from the Judeo-Christian tradition. Child Dev. **82**, 1120–1135 (2011)
42. Woolley, J.D., van Reet, J.: Effects of context on judgments concerning the reality status of novel entities. Child Dev. **77**(6), 1778–1793 (2006)
43. Cook, C., Sobel, D.M.: Children's beliefs about the fantasy/reality status of hypothesized machines, **14**(1), 1–8 (2011)
44. Dawkins, R.: Putting away childish things. Skeptical Inquirer, January/February, pp. 31–36 (1995)
45. Gilbert, D.T.: How mental systems believe. Am. Psychol. **46**, 107–119 (1991)
46. Subbotsky, E.V.: Foundations of the Mind: Children's Understanding of Reality. Harvard University Press, Cambridge (1993)

Story-Time Machine-Low-Tech Attachment Design for Pre-school Children

Wen-Huei Chou[1], Shi-Liang Chang[2(✉)], and Chung-Wen Hung[3]

[1] Department and Graduate School of Digital Media Design, College of Design, National Yunlin University of Science and Technology, Douliu, Taiwan
cris@yuntech.edu.tw
[2] Graduate School of Design, National Yunlin University of Science and Technology, Douliu, Yunlin, Taiwan
shiliang@yuntech.edu.tw
[3] Department of Electrical Engineering, National Yunlin University of Science and Technology, Douliu, Taiwan
wenhung@yuntech.edu.tw

Abstract. Parents' behavior has a great influence on pre-school children, and children's living habits are closely related to family lifestyle. This study combined design research and technology to develop a teaching aid for parent–child reading. The goal was to reduce the excessive use of computers, communication devices, and consumer electronics (3C), as such devices have been found to negatively affect the parent–child relationship and may result in the child feeling disinterested and anxious. The Double Diamond design process model was adopted for the design research. A literature review and product comparison were used to identify the weaknesses of existing products and five design and development principles were proposed accordingly. Next, a focus group of experts was organized to review and modify the viewpoints and insights proposed based on their observations. Then, the value propositions were drafted to meet customer needs and to ensure product value; the product perspectives were defined. Porter's five forces analysis was applied to improve competitiveness. Innovative business models that integrated profits for business, English learning, and parent–child learning were suggested to enhance the sustainability and increase the product value of teaching aids for children. As actual product design research, a prototype of the designed product was produced. Following repeated testing, the product was completed to the first stage. In the near future, an iterative approach will be adopted to raise some funding; therefore, the future remains promising.

Keywords: Parent–Child Learning · English Learning · Innovative Business Model · Non-technology-oriented · Teaching Aids for Children

1 Introduction

Parents have great influence on preschool children's behaviors through their own attitudes and behaviors, which, in turn, affects children's habits and lifestyles [1, 2]. In recent years, digital products have gained increasing popularity and have gradually dominated physical books, toys, and dolls. This trend has led to changes in children's learning environments and lifestyles and caused behavioral and emotional problems related to the excessive use of cellphones, impaired parent–child relationships, and increased boredom and anxiety [3, 4]. Therefore, it is a significant goal in product design to transform parent–child reading and learning into intimate and valued parent–child time in a society with an increasingly fast pace and limited time together. Children learn optimally between birth and three years old, when they start learning two languages and have high-quality interactions with other people [5]. In the company of their parents, children may learn English more easily than if they were separated from their parents. Methods such as bedtime reading and storytelling allow children to naturally integrate into an English-learning environment, while storytelling facilitated by projectors and sound-and-lighting performances is conducive to engaging children and helping them to relax, so that they are able to absorb knowledge in a stress-free environment. Such non-technology-oriented methods combine virtual and physical materials to minimize addiction to high-tech products, promote emotional communication between parents and children, and enhance intimate parent–child relationships. This study was conducted in cooperation with BigByte Education, an English education institution. Based on the teaching materials that BigByte Education is skilled at developing, and on the basis of advocating children's English learning and education, a Story Time Machine for bedtime reading was designed. The Story Time Machine is a technology-based application that is oriented toward human interaction, to support the distancing of parents and children from computers, communication devices, and consumer electronics (the 3Cs), and to increase engagement in parent–child interactions.

The purpose of this study was to combine design research and technology to develop a design for a teaching aid for parent–child reading. Through a corporate needs analysis, market analysis, and a literature review, the product was designed to provide parent–child learning and reading opportunities, reduce excessive use of personal technology products, minimize dependence on technology through a combination of virtual and physical approaches, promote parent–child relationships, and establish a daily learning environment for children. It was also expected that this study would help enterprises to establish innovative business models that integrate business profits, English learning, and parent–child learning to improve the sustainability and product value of teaching aids for children.

2   Literature Review

2.1   Importance of Parent–Child Interaction and Parent–Child Reading and the Impact of 3C Devices on Parent–Child Relationships

Parents have a great influence on pre-school children's behavior. Parents' attitudes and behaviors, including how they position themselves as a parent, are associated with children's habits and lifestyles [1, 2]. Studies have shown that parent–child interaction has a positive and healthy effect on children's thinking and psychological development, promotes perceived happiness and their ability to quickly adapt to and learn social interaction, and has a critical influence on children's growth [6–8]. Parent–child interaction may take many forms, such as nature-based activities, parent–child reading, leisure sports, and board games [9, 10]. Parent–child reading usually starts with reading picture books together and serves as a direct family connection [11]. Family reading is also helpful for the development of children's language and vocabulary, as well as learning to read. Parent–child reading is thus an essential component of children's learning and serves as an opportunity for families to spend quality time together [12]. Therefore, establishing a strong parent–child relationship is of great significance to strengthening a family [13].

With the decrease in birth rates and increase in dual-career families in Taiwan, parents are spending more time at work and less time with their children [7]. Taiwan has also witnessed a decline in the average age of Internet users, as many parents use the 3Cs as a means to appease and reward their children. Although such an approach is effective over the short term, it reduces parent–child interaction, leads to children's addiction to 3C devices, and may even escalate to mental conditions and self-harm behaviors [14–16]. In addition, children learn from parents' behaviors. When parents use 3C devices frequently, children are likely to emulate them. Excessive use of 3C devices has been found to cause learning disabilities, apathy, and social alienation [17, 30]. Bedtime stories are a way to enhance parent–child interaction and reduce dependence on 3C devices.

2.2 Bedtime Stories and Smart Toys

Bedtime stories are an important activity in early childhood development, as they promote perceived well-being and improve sleep, language development, literacy, emotional control, and behavior. Studies have pointed out that reading with parents enhances parent–child relationships and has a positive effect on children's development [18, 19, 31]. In recent years, bedtime stories have evolved from simple reading to the use of smart toys [21, 23], leading to an increase in market demand for smart toys that facilitate learning. It has also been found that games are an important factor in developing social skills and intelligence [32]. In 2004 Kehoe et al. developed a virtual peer system that allowed children to interact with a virtual character to create interesting stories [33]. Language style has also been found to impact the effectiveness of smart toys. Hence, it has been suggested that both the narrator's voice and the way the stories are narrated should feel warm and familiar to children to enhance their learning [34, 35]. Cassell and Ryokai [36] designed a smart toy called StoryMat and found that cooperating with adults in playing games can effectively promote children's intellectual development. Similarly, Digital English learning can help make learning English more attractive to new learners, generating a positive attitude and willingness to engage with the learning process [24, 26]. Since many studies have pointed out that both bedtime stories and smart toys affect children's development, while learning English is a modern trend for parents, with many children exposed to American English from a very young age, the authors intended to design a smart toy that focused on combining bedtime reading and English learning.

2.3 Comparison of Teaching Aids for Children

This study selected competing teaching aids (such as pop-up books for games, audio-books, and mobile-shaped audio books) sold on the market; compared their function, content, price, and advantages and disadvantages; and summarized the key competitive features required for the product to be designed and developed in this study. The detailed comparison is presented in Table 1.

Table 1. Analysis of competing teaching aids for children.

No.	Name and Image	Function and Content	Differences
1	Pop-up book with game Extracted on Jun 17, 2021, from https://reurl.cc/9r1d2a	(1) A pop-up book for playing house (2) Fun (3) Cultivates imagination (4) Encourages interaction with the toy (5) Comes with a stuffed doll (6) The 3D book can be extended (7) The stickers can stick to the cardboard Selling price: NT $750	(1) Limited content (2) Vulnerable to wear and tear (3) Difficult to store (4) No audio (5) Content cannot be expanded (6) Short product lifespan
2	Physical audio book Extracted on Jun 17, 2021, from https://reurl.cc/O0E2lA	(1) Teaches daily conversation and corresponding vocabulary (2) Comes with a barcode scanner (3) Contains conversations in various scenarios, such as when shopping and at supermarkets, and about product categories. (4) Introduces payment tools Selling price: NT $880	(1) Content is limited and cannot be expanded (2) Content is fixed (3) Limited parent–child interaction (4) Large in size (5) Components need to be replaced as a whole when broken (6) Difficult to store
3	Mobile-shaped audio book Extracted on Jun 17, 2021, from https://reurl.cc/lRZ3Dd	(1) Includes six English nursery rhymes (2) A mobile-shaped toy that sings and tells stories (3) Comes with storybooks (4) Illustrated buttons that facilitate selection (5) Has a simple flashing light Selling price: NT $680	(1) Allows reading and listen to nursery rhymes at the same time (2) Bilingual (English and Chinese) (3) Facilitates language development (4) Content cannot be expanded

(*continued*)

Table 1. (*continued*)

			(5) Heavy (6) Difficult to store
4	Story projection torch Extracted on Jun 17, 2021, from https://reurl.cc/9r1dev	(1) Torch-shaped projector that projects story images (2) Comes with three slides of films (stories) (3) Comes with three story books (4) Can be used in the evening Selling price: NT $380	(1) Limited stories (2) Difficult to add other story films due to manufacturing specifications (3) Difficult to keep the projected image stable as it is handheld (4) May cause eye tiredness (5) Limited projection range (6) Low image quality (7) Cheap
5	Interactive puzzle game Extracted on Jun 17, 2021, from https://reurl.cc/Yd211o	(1) Requires a tablet and other physical tools (2) Allows multiple accounts to correspond to different difficulty levels (3) Includes games for learning English, math, reasoning, physics, and music (4) Includes various modules to facilitate the learning of different subjects Selling price: NT $6,440	(1) May cause eye discomfort when used for long periods (2) Needs storage space for the various accessories (3) Limited parent–child interaction (4) Expensive (5) May cause addiction to high-tech devices (6) Limited parent–child interaction

(Data source: Compiled by the authors)

It can be seen from the comparison that the biggest weakness of traditional pop-up books lies in the lack of audio feedback and inability to expand the content. As a result, children may get bored easily, which allows for easy elimination from the market. Physical audio books are usually large in size, have limited content, and do not allow expansion nor facilitate parent–child interaction. Therefore, children tend to lose interest in them after a short period of time. The problem with story projection torches lies in the low quality of the projected image, which reduces children's and parents' interest in interacting with the device. In recent years, smart interactive puzzle games have become more popular. However, such games require the support of high-end software and hardware; hence, they tend to be expensive and require frequent maintenance by the producers. Devices that lack sufficient maintenance tend to stop functioning, interrupting the learning process. In addition, long-term use of these products may cause fatigue and eye discomfort, reduce parent–child interaction, and affect children's development. The weaknesses of the teaching aids on the market are summarized in Table 2.

Table 2. Summary of weaknesses of existing products.

Type	Traditional pop-up books	Physical audio books	Story projection torches	Interactive puzzle games
Weaknesses	No audio Limited learning content Limited pages in the physical books Vulnerable to wear and tear Short product lifespan	Limited categories Large in size Content cannot be expanded Limited parent–child interaction	Limited projection lightness Limited projection range Low projection image quality Manufacturer specific specs	Requires the use of a tablet Fast elimination of software Insufficient maintenance of the system May cause eye discomfort when used for long periods Limited parent–child interaction

(Data source: Compiled by the authors)

The literature review and product comparison showed that, in order to provide a sound English environment in daily life and develop a habit of reading with parents, a game-based teaching aid should integrate technologies, contain structures and functions that meet learning needs, and incorporate the advantages of existing products while avoiding the disadvantages. Only products with flexible learning content, swift updates and supporting technology, and expandable and extensible learning content can satisfy consumers' changing demands and need for diversification, cope with changes in the market, secure long-term profits, and ensure sustainability. As such, this study proposed five design and development principles for the product to be designed, including (1) expandable learning content, (2) high audio and image quality, (3) reasonable weight, (4) suitable for parent–child interactions, and (5) long product life cycle.

3 Methodology

3.1 Design Research Plan

This study adopted the Double Diamond design model, which is a design process proposed by the British Design Council in 2005. The model includes four phases of design: discover, define, develop, and deliver. Every two phases involve a "divergence-convergence" process, which allows in-depth understanding of the problem, uncovers core issues, seeks various solutions outside of inertial thinking, and aims to develop a product that solves problems (Fig. 1). Studies have found that sliding tactile feedback wristbands developed using the Double Diamond model were able to assist the visually impaired in learning in virtual and real-world scenarios and effectively help them to engage with society [28, 29]. Therefore, this study applied the model to designing and developing a human-centered, non-technology-oriented interactive teaching aid. The four phases of the design process are illustrated in Fig. 1.

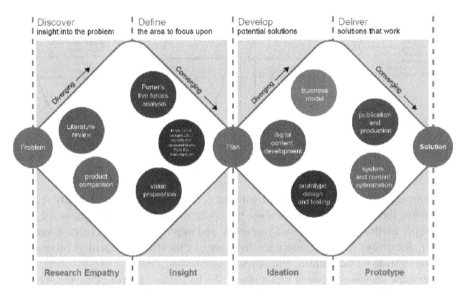

Fig. 1. Double Diamond design model (design process of this study).

3.2 Design Research

(1) Discover: In this phase, past studies on English teaching materials and parent–child reading were collected and reviewed, and competing English teaching aids for children in domestic and foreign markets were compared and their advantages and disadvantages analyzed.

(2) Define: In this phase, a focus group composed of experts and representatives from the partner company was organized to determine the design direction of the product. The focus group was composed of English lecturers and core textbook developers from

BigByte, and 12 to 15 experts in parenting education and child education, as well as cross-disciplinary experts in digital content design, mechanism design, and sensor module design. The goal was to review viewpoints proposed by the research team based on their observations and to propose new insights. A semi-structured questionnaire was used, and the duration of the focus group was three hours. The findings were compiled and used for the subsequent design planning and compliance guidelines. Next, the core value of the product was created using a value proposition map. A brainstorming session was organized to understand consumer needs, propose product benefits, resolve issues with existing products, and identify product characteristics, to gain customer recognition, satisfy customer needs, create core value, and define the product design principles. The initial value proposition is presented in Fig. 2.

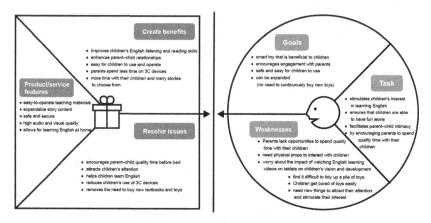

Fig. 2. Value proposition of the product.

Following the proposals developed within the value proposition, this study applied Porter's five forces framework to analyze the opportunities and challenges of the market, identify methods to resolve said problems, and improve the competitive advantage [27, 37]. According to Porter, there are five factors that affect competitive advantage: competitive rivalry (the number and strength of existing competitors), the threat of a new entry, the bargaining power of suppliers, the bargaining power of buyers, and the threat of substitutes (products/services). Porter's five forces analysis of the Story Time Machine (the product to be developed in this study) is exhibited in Fig. 3.

(3) Develop: The design principles, weaknesses of existing products, and new product value proposition identified in the previous phases were used as a reference for development. Porter's five forces provided a better understanding of the competitiveness of the product. Prior to developing a prototype, it is necessary to discuss the business model with the partner company in order to better understand its commercial value, help the company to create an innovative business model, identify target customers, and determine the market positioning of the product. Business models include nine interrelated elements, which can be categorized into four dimensions: supply, demand, value, and finance. The business model of the Story Time Machine is illustrated in Fig. 4. Once the business model was determined, the authors began to design the digital content of the

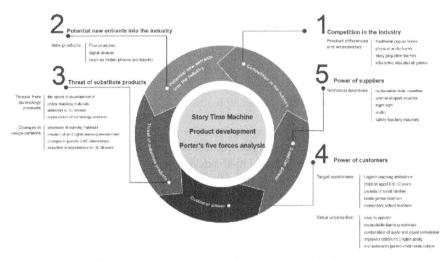

Fig. 3. Porter's five forces analysis of the Story Time Machine.

product and test the prototype. Specifically, English stories were converted into interactive digital content that facilitates parent–child reading. Next, the outlook of the product was designed, the color scheme was determined, and the user experience was planned. A prototype was then produced, and experts and representatives of the partner company were invited to test the projection technology and operating system and to identify their limitations. A revision of the design was conducted accordingly.

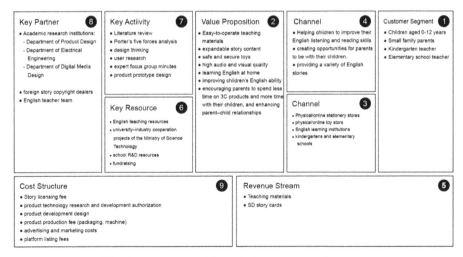

Fig. 4. Business model (preliminary concept diagram).

(4) Deliver: In this phase, the system and content of the product were optimized based on the test results of the prototype. The design was intended to be published and commercialized in preparation for market launch.

4   Results and Discussion

This study applied a cross-disciplinary design. The goal was to develop a children's English teaching aid that combines digital content and physical supports. The product design, computer machinery, and digital media design were conducted jointly by a professional design team and BigByte. Porter's five forces analysis showed that, although there were many types of product related to children's learning, the majority of them did not facilitate parent–child reading and the content was not expandable. Past studies have shown that children's learning effectiveness is correlated with parents' involvement. Therefore, this study aimed to develop a product surrounding the core concept of parent–child reading. With an emphasis on user experience, the design was expected to be customer centered. Moritz [38] asserted that service design should be holistic, multidisciplinary, and integrative, with comprehensive consideration of customer experience. The aspects designed and developed by the team are shown in Fig. 5.

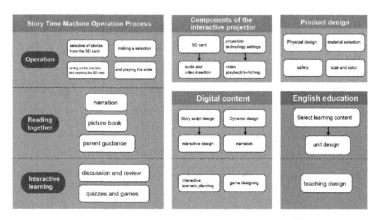

Fig. 5. Aspects designed and developed.

(1) Product Mechanism and Outlook

Based on the market research and analysis of existing products, the design team proposed the first conceptual mechanism and outlook of the product. The proposal was sent to the manufacturer for advice and the following suggestions were received: 1) The heat dissipation and sound emission holes were insufficient. They should be located on the same side as the projection to prevent hot air from blowing on to the user. 2) The heat dissipation holes, charging hole, and USB slot should also be moved to the front of the product to avoid disturbing users. 3) The USB access port is a feature of the main body; hence, different design options should be provided to the users. 4) The height of the projector should be 20 cm. 5) The buttons should be larger. 6) The visual aspects of the product should be either cute, lively, or exotic to attract children's interest. 7) The shape could be changed to a bear or dinosaur. The first version (in the shape of a penguin) is presented in Fig. 6.

Fig. 6. The penguin-shaped projector.

Five more rounds of discussions with the manufacturer were conducted and the following suggestions were proposed: 1) Use a dinosaur as the shape of the product and ensure that the product is comfortable to hold. A milder color should be used to suit children's preferences. 2) There should be one or two more outlet holes for sound emission and heat dissipation, and the shape should be changed from long to round. 3) Push buttons with a beveled surface should be used so that they are comfortable to push. One button should be used for one function only. The buttons should be designed as spikes on the back of the device, the size for the "on," "off," pause," and "start" buttons should be made smaller, while that of the middle four buttons should be enlarged, so that they are easier to identify. 4) The material proposed in the original design was soft silicone. However, since the product contains a projector and sophisticated electronic devices, soft silicone may not provide sufficient protection and may lead to damage of the delicate components due to frequent holding and physical contact. It was suggested that hard silicone or plastic material should be used to protect the internal components, covered with an outer layer made of softer material. 5) Only one battery should be used, positioned upright with clear markings for positive and negative. A light should be installed as a battery indicator (no light when there is no battery). 6) The internal circuits and component settings were confirmed (Figs. 7, 8, 9, 10, 11 and 12).

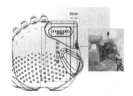

Fig. 7. Design of dinosaur-shaped projector

Fig. 8. Distance between projector and shell

Fig. 9. Prototype of dinosaur-shaped projector

(2) Interface Design and Usability
The design concept of the product focused on portability, ease of operation, replaceable

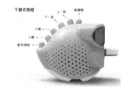

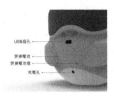

Fig. 10. Button style   **Fig. 11.** Button function   **Fig. 12.** Hole function

slide cassettes, cuddling, and the shape of an animal character. ABS plastic, food-grade silicone (pacifier silicone), and other composite materials with high temperature resistance and high safety were used so that the internal components were well protected, the product was durable, and the appearance was appealing. The product specifications were determined based on the product comparison and literature review. Specifically, a micro SD card slot was used as the game cartridge, the size of the product was 15 × 25 cm (diameter × height), the weight was 800 to 1000 g, the material was ABS plastic and food-grade silicone, the battery used was 5 V–2 A, the music file format was mp3, and stereo speakers were used.

5 Contributions and Future Research

(1) This Study Developed a Game-Based Teaching Aid That Promotes Parent–Child Reading

The parent–child reading projector was a real product design that incorporated digital and physical materials to create a parent–child interactive experience. The projector was designed to be portable, easy to operate, cuddlable, and with a replaceable slide cassette. The outside was designed to look like an animal character, and the materials were made of a safe composite and were durable, strong, and collision resistant. This study applied the Double Diamond design process and used comparisons with existing products to identify potential weaknesses that needed improving in the product design. In addition, product value proposition, Porter's five forces analysis, and innovative business model development techniques were applied to identify market trends and to determine product value. After developing the prototype and conducting repeated testing, the first phase of product development was completed. The product was designed to combine commercial profits, English learning, and parent–child learning to expand the sustainability and product value of teaching aids for children.

(2) This Study Explored a New Approach to Parent–Child English Learning and Cultivated Cross-disciplinary Talent

When the prototype is completed, the intellectual property rights of the technology will be transferred to the manufacturer to improve the English learning ability of young children in Taiwan, help parents make good use of the product, enhance parent–child relationships, and facilitate children's learning and physical and mental development. The ability to communicate in English is a soft skill that parents value. Physical audiobooks provide parents with high-quality materials, which is in line with the orientation of literacy education in the 2019 curriculum guidelines. With the product, children were expected to read/listen to at least 30 books suitable for their level in a year. The product provides children who are interested in English reading with more options and also stimulates the interest of children with no English foundation.

The Story Time Machine was the result of cross-disciplinary practical research. Its research scope covered parent–child reading and interaction, children's English teaching material design, sensory projection technology, product design, and English teaching toy design. The study also involved training the development team in the application of qualitative analysis, such as user engagement, service design, and design thinking skills. Participation in the design process was conducive to cultivating integral talent for cross-domain research and design practice needed in the future market.

(3) Future Versions and Market Evaluations

The Story Time Machine was the first generation of parent–child interactive teaching aids developed by the present research team. At present, prototype development has been completed, but the actual product testing has yet to be conducted. The subsequent focus will be on product concept reviews and product testing to resolve problems that arise during concept development, such as issues with the software and hardware and actual production of initial prototypes. A team of testers will be recruited to assist in testing the functions to ensure the quality of the product. Next, a front-end function test will be conducted to check for errors in the code to ensure sufficient stability for the product launch. A trial market will be planned, and marketing campaigns will be put in place and made ready for the launch prior to mass production. The final product concept will be determined following initial tests and released to the target customers. The product will be designed to suit future upgrades in response to the changing needs of consumers. The newest designs are expected to stimulate demand and lead the market.

The market for high-quality game-based teaching aids based on storytelling is stable. Since the stories are in English, it is not limited to markets that use traditional Chinese. Therefore, the research team is expecting to promote the product in the international market with the cooperation of BigByte. Based on the company's current customer needs and market planning, the demand for the product during the first stage is expected to reach 45,000 units. During the second stage, market demand is expected to reach 225,000 units. In addition to the projector, there will be additional stories and content available on the market, which will allow consumers to choose their learning materials in a way that corresponds to the language level and interests of their children. The product design will also be further refined. The initial selling price of the product is NT $1,850 per piece, and the price for each additional story will be NT $100 per piece, to maintain a moderate price on the market. The estimated turnover during the first stage is expected to be approximately NT $83.25 million and that of the second stage should be approximately $416.25 million. It is expected that the product will contribute to an increase in industry income and can be promoted in foreign markets.

References

1. Laible, D.J., Carlo, G., Raffaelli, M.: The Differential relations of parent and peer attachment to adolescent adjustment. J. Youth Adolesc. **29**, 45–59 (2000)

2. Arredondo, E.M., Elder, J.P., Ayala, G.X., Campbell, N., Baquero, B., Duerksen, S.: Is parenting style related to children's healthy eating and physical activity in Latino families? Health Educ. Res. **21**(6), 862–871 (2006)

3. Sahu, M., Gandhi, S., Sharma, M.K.: Mobile phone addiction among children and adolescents: a systematic review. J. Addict. Nurs. **30**(4), 261–268 (2019)

4. Nasution, M.: Factors affecting smartphone addiction in children. In: Proceeding International Seminar of Islamic Studies, vol. 2, no. 1, pp. 108–115. Medan, January 2021

5. Ramirez, N.F., Kuhl, P.K.: Bilingual language learning in children. Institute for Learning and Brain Sciences 10, Washington (2016)

6. 洪梅葵: 幼兒氣質與親子互動之探討幼兒氣質與親子互動的關係。(未出版碩士論文)。中國文化大學, 臺北市 (2018)。

7. 陳孟媛:親子互動關係對兒童成長學習影響之研究對兒童發展及親子互動關係的影響研究。(未出版碩士論文)。中國文化大學, 臺北市(2020)。

8. 林佩蓉:台北市國小高年級學童親子互動、手足關係與同儕關係之研究台北市高年級小學生親子互動、兄弟姐妹關係及同伴關係研究。(未出版碩士論文)。中國文化大學, 臺北市 (2014)。

9. Fallon, T.J., Roth, I.M., Bondoc, J.: Modeling EFL classes after parent-child reading interactions. J. Nagoya Gakuin Univ. **26**(1), 95–101, Japan (2014)

10. 蔡政霖:參與親子桌遊團體對國小孩童與家長之影響經驗研究。(未出版碩士論文)。台灣師範大學, 臺北市 (2020)。

11. Thompson, R.A.: On what is read, shared, and felt: parent-child conversation about stories. Empir. Work Commentaries, 85–89 (2019)

12. Vezzoli, Y., Kalantari, S., Kucirkova, N., Vasalou, A.: Exploring the design space for parent-child reading. In: Proceedings of the 2020 CHI Conference on Human Factors in Computing Systems, pp. 1–12, Honolulu, HI, USA (2020)

13. Zivan, M., Horowitz-Kraus, T.: Parent–child joint reading is related to an increased fixation time on print during storytelling among preschool children. Brain Cogn. **143** (2020)

14. 陳芯瀅:幼兒3C產品使用情況與親子互動相關性之探討。(未出版碩士論文)。屏東大學。屏東縣 (2020)。

15. Kildare, C.A., Middlemiss, W.: Impact of parents mobile device use on parent-child interaction: a literature review. Comput. Hum. Behav. **75**, 579–593 (2017)

16. 丁美惠: 3C 時代親子關係的營造之道。台灣教育評論月刊, 8(10), 150–154。2019。2021/6/18 取自 http://www.ater.org.tw/journal/article/8-10/free/05.pdf

17. Hughes, C., Devine, R.T.: For better or for worse? Positive and negative parental influences on young children's executive function. Child Dev. **90**(2), 593–609, U.K (2017)

18. Mindell, J.A., Williamson, A.A.: Benefits of a bedtime routine in young children: sleep, development, and beyond. Sleep Med. Rev. **40**, 93–108 (2018)

19. Pereira, D.: Bedtime books, the bedtime story ritual, and goodnight moon. Child. Lit. Assoc. Q. **44**(2), 156–172 (2019)

20. Wismaliya, R., Supriatna, M.: Internalizing the value of patience in telling bedtime stories activity in Sundanese societies. In: International Conference on Local Wisdom (2019)

21. Heljakka, K., Ihamäki, P.: Preschoolers learning with the Internet of Toys: from toy-based edutainment to transmedia literacy. In: Seminar. net, vol. 14, no. 1, pp. 85–102 (2018)

22. Islami, X., Topuzovska Latkovikj, M., Drakulevski, L., Borota Popovska, M.: Does differentiation strategy model matter? Desig. Org. Perform. Using Differ. Strateg. Instrum. Empir. Anal. 158–177 (2020)

23. Krishnaswamy, M., Bori, L., Murthy, C., Rosenfeld, H.: An immersive storytelling tool for healthy bedtime routine. In: Proceedings of the Eleventh International Conference on Tangible, Embedded and Embodied Interaction, pp. 603–608. ACM (2017)

24. Tsymbal, S.: Gamified training sessions as means of enhancing students' motivation in learning English. Psychol. J. **4**(7) (2018)

25. Ekin, C.C., Cagiltay, K., Karasu, N.: Effectiveness of smart toy applications in teaching children with intellectual disability. J. Syst. Architect. **89**, 41–48 (2018)

26. Hashim, H., Rafiq, K.R.M., Yunus, M.M.: Improving ESL learners' grammar with gamified-learning. Arab World Engl. J. (AWEJ), **5**, 41–50 (2019)

27. Porter, M.E.: Competitive strategy. Meas. Bus. Excell. **1**(2), 12–17 (1997)

28. Zhang, X., Zhang, H., Zhang, L., Zhu, Y., Hu, F.: Double-diamond model-based orientation guidance in wearable human–machine navigation systems for blind and visually impaired people. Sensors **19**(21), 4670 (2019)

29. Zhou, Z., Han, X., Xi, T.: The design of outpatient services in children's hospitals based on the double diamond model. In: Duffy, V.G. (ed.) HCII 2021. LNCS, vol. 12778, pp. 182–193. Springer, Cham (2021). https://doi.org/10.1007/978-3-030-77820-0_14

30. 李玉惠:家長對兒童使用 3C 產品看法與態度之研究. 學校行政, (103), 118–139. (2016)

31. Supriatna, M., Wismaliya, R.: Internalizing the value of patience in telling bedtime stories activity in Sundanese societies. In: Proceedings of the 2nd International Conference on Local Wisdom, INCOLWIS 2019, Padang, West Sumatera, Indonesia (2019)

32. Ekin, C.Ç., Çağiltay, K., Karasu, N.: Usability study of a smart toy on students with intellectual disabilities. J. Syst. Architect. **89**, 95–102 (2018)

33. Kehoe, C., et al.: Out of the lab and into the world: bringing story listening systems to the classroom. In: Poster presented at the Meeting of the American Educational Research Association (2004)

34. Kara, N., Cagiltay, K.: Smart toys for preschool children: a design and development research. Electron. Commer. Res. Appl. **39**, 100909 (2020)

35. Trioktaviani, S.: Language styles on bedtime story in free kids' online books. Doctoral dissertation, Universitas Islam Negeri Maulana Malik Ibrahim (2019)

36. Cassell, J., Ryokai, K.: Making space for voice: technologies to support children's fantasy and storytelling. Pers. Ubiquit. Comput. **5**, 169–190 (2001)

37. Regina, C., Raharjo, S.T.: The Role of Research and Development on Sustainable Competitive Advantage (2022)

38. Moritz, S.: Service design: practical access to an evolving field. M.Sc. thesis, KISD (2005)

Buddie: Design Exploration for Remote Interactions to Support Kids

Soo Wan Chun and Jinsil Hwaryoung Seo[(⊠)] [iD]

Texas A&M University, College Station, TX 77843, USA
{soowanchun,hwaryoung}@tamu.edu

Abstract. We present *Buddie*, a prototype designed to support remote interaction utilizing a mobile app and a soft toy. The project was initially created to facilitate remote parent-child communication for parents who are physically separated from their children due to work commitments. Because of the widespread prevalence of Covid-19, many parents avoided business trips. We broadened our research to include not only children and their parents, but also teachers, families, and friends. In this pictorial, we present the design process of *Buddie*, final prototypes, and a case study with two children and their parents.

Keywords: Remote Interaction · Tangible Interaction · Child-Parent Relationship · Traveling Parents · Social Isolation

1 Introduction

Remote communication tools are popular in our daily lives. People work remotely using video conferencing applications; students participate in online courses using online learning platforms; children send photos and videos to their parents and grandparents. The COVID-19 pandemic forced us to adapt to remote communication systems for work, education, entertainment, community activities and many more. However, many existing remote communication technologies are not friendly to young children and older adults. Many children do not own their own phones to connect with other family members and older adults are not familiar with utilizing advanced applications on their phones.

To date, many projects have addressed the challenges in remote communications for children. In tangible interaction design, researchers and designers have explored how children's relationships with their loved ones can improve by utilizing interactive tangible systems and present unique approaches and design outcomes [26–28].

Initially our project focused on designing a mobile application with a tangible object for children and their traveling parents to make them feel connected and create shared experiences when they are apart. The original idea was started from the main designer's childhood experience. Her father often traveled around the world for his work. She always wanted to travel with him and missed him so much when he was away. The prototype was developed based on the following scenario: a parent takes photos with a digital version of the child's favorite toy while they are traveling; the parent sends the photos

© The Author(s), under exclusive license to Springer Nature Switzerland AG 2023
M. Kurosu and A. Hashizume (Eds.): HCII 2023, LNCS 14012, pp. 56–71, 2023.
https://doi.org/10.1007/978-3-031-35599-8_4

to the child's tangible toy and the toy glows when photos are received from the parent's mobile app; the child hugs the toy and prints the photos on a portable print. This project followed a typical interaction design process and developed a prototype that includes an interactive soft toy for a child and a mobile app for a parent/other. The prototype, *Buddie*, was tested with a few invited children and their parents who travel often. This pictorial presents the final prototype, the design process, and the users' feedback.

We expanded our study to explore how children adapt and utilize this project in their daily lives. Because of the COVID-19 pandemic, children couldn't travel anywhere or meet friends, teachers, and families, which limited their social and emotional development. We examined how *Buddie* can be used to connect children to their loved ones during an emotionally challenging time.

2 Background

2.1 Parent-Child Communication

Fostering quality time between parents and children is crucial in building strong relationships. It not only boosts a child's self-esteem, but also fortifies family bonds and promotes desirable behavior patterns [19, 21]. However, lack of quality time with kids may result in children feeling emotionally distressed, having difficulty handling negative emotions, and experiencing antisocial behavior [20]. Investing in quality family time can cultivate a tight family bond and provide emotional, behavioral, and academic benefits for children.

Some families may not be able to have regular family time because a family member works in a different city or travels frequently due to their work. As reported by the Travel Industry Association, business travel saw a 14% increase between 1994 and 2001 and is expected to continue its upward trend [22]. It's common for parents to feel guilty about traveling without their children. Although temporary separation from a parent can play

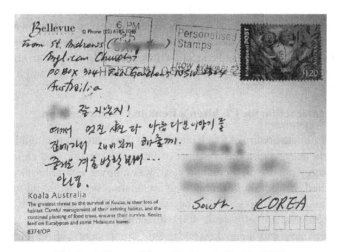

Fig. 1. A Postcard from Designer's Dad in 2007.

a crucial role in a child's social and emotional growth, it may also result in feelings of anxiety, clinginess, and anger. To mitigate the impact of separation, some parents take a special approach, such as bringing their child's favorite stuffed animal on business trips and taking pictures to stay connected. This can help ease the child's mind while the parent is away [2–4]. Some parents also send their children cute postcards. The postcard (Fig. 1) is from the designer of the project. She still keeps many postcards from her dad.

2.2 Impacts of Social Isolation on Children During the COVID Pandemic

During the COVID pandemic, many children experienced lockdowns and school closures. They had to deal with sudden changes in their social lives and daily routines, causing an inability to go out and play with other children. It is still true that some children are not socially engaging with their peers in the same way as before. In the Royal Children's Hospital's National Child Health Poll in June 2020, more than one-third of parents reported the pandemic has had negative consequences on their children's mental health [23]. Research shows that social isolation increases the risk of depression and possibly anxiety, these effects could last several years [24]. It is important to provide the right support to overcome these challenging times. During the pandemic, supporting tools and systems for remote education and communication were provided. On average, both parents and their children had increased technology and social media use since the beginning of social distancing [25].

2.3 Flat Stanley Project

Flat Stanley is a beloved children's book series written by Jeff Brown, in which the protagonist Stanley is flattened while sleeping and goes on exciting adventures. The Flat Stanley Project, created by teacher Dale Hubert in 1995, allows students to bring the story to life by creating their own Flat Stanley paper dolls, documenting their adventures and sending them to students at other schools. This project provides an opportunity for children to connect and engage with students from different locations. The project was revitalized during the COVID-19 pandemic, with teachers creating their own Flat teacher paper dolls and sending them to students, fostering a sense of connection and community. The Flat Stanley Project is a fun and educational way for children to learn about different places and cultures, while also fostering communication and collaboration skills.

2.4 Tangible Interaction for Children's Remote Communication

Because of the intimate quality of touch interactions, there are many tangible interaction research projects that explore the concepts of family interaction and children's social interactions. Huggy pajama by Fernando et al. was a novel wearable system aimed at evoking embodied interaction in remote communication between child and parent. It allows parents and children to send and receive touch and hug interactions. The project consists of two objects: a small mobile doll with a touch/pressure sensing module and a haptic wearable pajama with air pockets and heating components [1]. Seo et al. developed inTouch Wearables to support remote parent -child interaction. This project consists of a dress and a shoulder piece for each end, and it allows mother and child to share remote touches through garments with ambient color change on fabrics [16]. CloudPets is a stuffed animal that supports parent-child remote communication. Parents send over voice messages to the toy and children send voice messages back [5].

2.5 *Buddie*: Design Process

Fig. 2. Design process of *Buddies*

Buddie consists of a mobile app and a soft toy that are connected via the Internet. This project aims to ease children's separation anxiety and parent's guiltiness of traveling. The main objective of this project is to make parent-child communication more enjoyable and to make them feel connected while they are apart. We took a typical Interaction design (IxD) process to create a prototype of Buddie. IxD process is an iterative human centered design technique that aims to understand the user, define their challenges, identify insights, and come up with solutions [6]. The IxD process for our project involves five stages: discover, define, ideate, create, and evaluate (Fig. 2).

"What are the current communication practices and challenges for parents and children in families separated by work?"

This is the question we asked ourselves at the beginning of the Discover phase. From this we were able to find what the user's needs and wants were. We also identified the challenges of remote parent-child communication by reviewing literature.

In the following phase, the Define phase, we figured out the problems. We analyzed users' needs and pain points and synthesized the insights.

"How might we create an interactive communication system that supports enjoyable and accessible long-distance communication for parents and children?"

For the Ideate phase we asked ourselves this question. Based on this we generated as many possible solutions as possible by creating personas, a persona-based scenario, a user journey map, and user flows.

Persona and persona-based scenarios aid designers in understanding and focusing on a set of users. Persona is an IxD technique that uses real data, such as users' experience, to generate fictional characters [7]. Scenarios are a natural element of persona-based design and development. For our project, two personas (a parent and a child, Jane and Shelby, respectively) and a persona-based scenario were developed. Jane is a sales representative, with a 5-year-old daughter Shelby, who frequently travels for work. Shelby experiences anxiety as a result of Jane's absences. Thanks to technology, they can video call each other, but they face various obstacles, such as Shelby's low communication skills and technological understanding. Jane is looking for a new way to communicate with her child while she is away from home. The user scenario describes Jane and Shelby's situation, as well as how Jane became aware of Buddie.

From these ideations, we were able to set goals for our project, listed below:

- Asynchronous: Help parents and children feel connected even when it is not possible to interact in real-time.
- Easy to use: To interact with each other without any difficulties or other people's help.
- Playful: Create more engaging and comprehensible user experiences and interactions (Fig. 3)

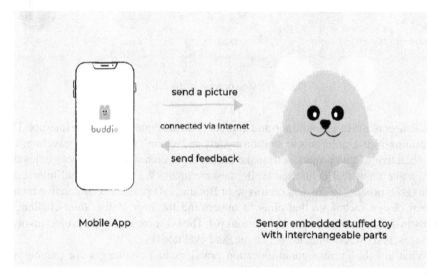

Fig. 3. System Flow Diagram.

3 Prototyping

Our project consists of two prototypes, a mobile application, and a tangible object. On the parents' side, they have a mobile application that saves their child's stuffed toy as an AR character. Instead of carrying their children's toys on the trip, they may simply take a picture of it with their mobile app. On the children's side, they have a sensor-embedded stuffed toy with interchangeable pieces. Children can mix and match whatever they choose with interchangeable ears and bodies. In the Design phase, we developed prototype sketches and low fidelity to high-fidelity prototypes.

3.1 The App

In the IxD process, sketching is a process which designers use to quickly visualize ideas and clarify design decisions before prototyping. We began the design process with quick sketches. By having multiple sketches of the design, we were able to explore multiple design directions and implement them into low-fidelity prototypes to high-fidelity prototypes. Adobe XD, a design tool used to create prototypes for web and mobile apps [12], was used to create the prototypes.

3.2   The Soft Toy

Buddie comes in a variety of colors with different ear shapes and sizes. We considered the following factors when designing the physical object: shape, size, and function. We intended the tangible object to be about the same size as a child's torso so that it could be huggable and comfortable to carry around. To be perceived as cute and friendly, the soft toys are round in shape. They have a marshmallow-like body which can be combined with bunny, bear, or cloud-shaped ears (Fig. 4).

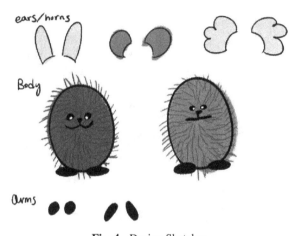

Fig. 4. Design Sketches.

Autodesk Maya, a software for creating 3D elements [13], was used to create the virtual characters based on the concept sketch (Fig. 5).

The physical stuffed toys were fabricated to match the virtual characters. Fabric was chosen based on its material. We chose felt fabric because it has a fuzzy texture that Velcro adheres to and allows for easy mixing and matching without the need for stitching or gluing. Velcro was attached to the ears so that they could be attached to the bodies.

Our prototypes required both software and hardware integrated prototyping in order to communicate between the app and the toy. Our prototypes were made with Protopie, a digital prototyping software [14], and Arduino, an open-source physical computing tool [15]. With Protopie's bridge feature, we were able to create interactive prototypes by sending signals and receiving triggers. For the communication testing, we created a simple app prototype with a round button that sends a signal to Arduino and turns the LED light on when the signal is received. When the pressure sensor detects pressure, the app receives a trigger, which shuts off the LED light and shows a square. This function was then added to our prototypes (Fig. 6).

Fig. 5. 3D Models.

Fig. 6. *Buddie* Physical Components.

4   Children's Experiences

4.1   Participants

The research team invited two children (Eric and Ava, pseudonyms) and their parents to try *Buddie* and share their experiences with us. Eric is an 8 year old boy living in Texas. He likes playing video games, origami, reading, making art and playing piano. Eric's mom is a university professor in the arts. She travels around the world to attend conferences and to work with collaborators. The research team visited Eric's home and introduced the project to him and his mother. His experience was recorded, and a semi-structured interview was conducted throughout the session. Ava is a 9-year-old, and she likes reading, swimming, ballet, and arts. She lives with her mom in New York while works in Seattle. Because of his work schedule, they meet almost every 6 months. Ava's experience was captured via Zoom and email.

4.2 Background Interviews with Participants

We conducted brief interviews with the participants. The interviews were carried out as semi-structured conversations focusing on traveling and remote communication with existing technologies. Although the two families' situations were different their experiences have common aspects.

4.3 Separation Anxiety

Eric and Ava said that they would miss their traveling parents a lot when they are away. However, they didn't express any behavioral issues or anxiety. According to their parents, Eric and Ava did not express separation anxiety when their parents were traveling or away. This could be because they had their own routine including school and they would FaceTime almost every day with their traveling parents while also maintaining their bond with their non-traveling parents. The traveling parents always brought gifts from the trips for their children. So, Eric and Ava were always waiting for their parents to come back home soon with their gifts. Even though they didn't present serious separation anxiety, they still wanted to travel with their parents all the time.

4.4 Feeling Guilty

Once parents travel for their work, they usually have tight schedules and don't think too much about their children and home. However, after work or during mealtime, they think about their children a lot. Eric and Ava moms said that they felt guilty because they were not able to stay all the time with their kids and they forgot about their kids for a short time. They also said that being in different time zones was another factor for them to make them feel guilty, for this reason they couldn't easily call their children.

4.5 Communication Technology

Both families utilized Facetime once a day to see each other and share their stories. For asynchronous communication (e.g., sending pictures and messages), they used Messenger. The kids often drew pictures and made something for traveling parents. They would take photos of their creations and send them to their traveling parents. There were no other technologies or methods utilized to enhance their remote communications.

4.6 Experiences with *Buddie*

Because of COVID, Eric's mom's business trips got cancelled. Therefore, we had to test *Buddie* while she was working in her office in the University. The research team explained to Eric to imagine that his mother is traveling, and she will send him her travel photos taken with his favorite toy. Ava's dad was still working in Seattle; therefore, we didn't need to alter anything for Ava's family. In general, Eric and Ava enjoyed interacting with *Buddie*. They liked the design and softness of the soft toy and were thrilled that they could print photos by squeezing the toy (Fig. 7).

Fig. 7. Eric experiences *Buddie*.

4.7 Feeling Connected

When Eric and Ava were introduced to the *Buddie* soft toy, Eric chose the blue one and Ava chose the pink one to be connected to their parent's application. A portable printer was placed next to the soft toy. Children liked the glowing effects with LEDs embedded in the *Buddie* soft toy. During the session, Eric and Ava talked a lot about the printed photos that their parents sent.

"Oh, mom went there. That looks nice. I think I remember that from the Internet. Now I know where she went. I want to go there with her next time. At least she is with Buddie." - Eric

"Dad told me about that place last time. Buddie looks really nice in the picture. He probably feels lonely without mom and me now. I would like to call him soon" – Ava

Wanting to use *Buddie* with grandparents and friends, Eric and Ava understood the system and how it worked fairly quickly. After they printed a couple of photos, they wanted to take a more active role in the project.

"Can I make my own picture? I want my toy in the picture. I want to send my picture to my grandmother. My grandma lives in Korea. She will be so happy about it." - Eric

"Can I send my photos to my mom? She will be curious about what my dad and I are doing now. I would like to send her some photos. Oh, can I send some pictures to my friend, Sophie. I don't see her very often these days." - Ava

4.8 Personalization of *Buddie* Project

Based on the feedback from Eric and Ava's families, the team decided to expand our session to workshops for future idea exploration and prototyping. During the experience sessions, both Eric and Ava strongly expressed that they wanted to send photos to other people including grandparents and friends. They also wanted to make their own toys and place them in their own travel photos. These workshop sessions were explorative, and the participants were loosely guided but not instructed (Fig. 8).

Fig. 8. *Buddie* with Eric and Ava's Travel Photos.

4.9   Collecting Kids' Favorite Objects

The first step of the workshop was to create a digital version of their favorite objects or toys. Eric brought four objects to consider making a digital toy for this project (Fig. 9). The first object was a pillow he created in an art workshop he attended when he was four years old. He said that the funny monster drawing was done by him, that's why he still likes it. The second object was a blue character pillow from his mom that she brought back with her from a conference in Japan. Eric likes it because it's fluffy and the surface

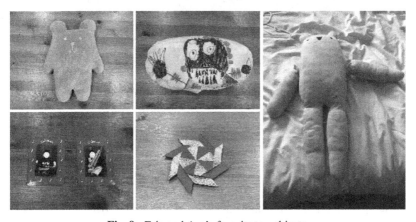

Fig. 9. Eric and Ava's favorite toy objects.

is very smooth. The third object is a set of pictures with flat frames where he is playing instruments. He said that he put these photos on the refrigerator all the time. The fourth object was a folded ninja star which he was very proud of. He has folded several dozens of ninja stars, but he thinks this is the best. Ava chose only one object, a stuffed doll. She said that the doll's name is Tori, and she always sleeps with it.

4.10   Creation of Digital Toys

Through multiple iterations, Eric chose the blue stuffed toy for the final digital toy design. Eric and the design team discussed whether he wanted to create the digital toy using computer software or not. He decided to draw it by himself using a blue colored pencil and a blue marker. He did not like the outcome too much; however, he was still willing to use it for his travel pictures. Since Ava has only one candidate for the digital toy, she used Tori. She wanted Tori as it is, so she used Photoshop and got rid of the background (Figs. 10 and 11).

Fig. 10. Ava's digital toy creation.

Fig. 11. Eric's digital toy creation.

4.11   Placing Digital Toys in the Pictures

After creating their own digital toys based on their real favorite toys, Eric and Ava successfully chose some of their travel photos and located the digital version of their favorite toy on each photo. After finishing placing the digital toys using *Buddie*, they wanted to print them and display them in their rooms.

4.12   Flat Eric and Ava Project

Once the *Buddie* project was initially presented to Eric, he immediately connected this project to his Flat Teacher project, which he experienced in first grade. He received Flat Mrs. Huggins during the pandemic. He used to place his flat paper teacher on his desk and would do homework with her (Fig. 12).

Extending the project, Eric and Ava really wanted to put themselves in the picture and send their pictures to grandparents and friends. Since both children loved drawing and making artworks, they felt comfortable drawing/painting their own digital characters. The Fig. 13 presents their digital characters (Flat Eric and Flat Ava). Flat Eric's and Ava's were placed on their favorite travel photos using *Buddie*.

Upon request by the participating children, the design team quickly prototyped a tablet version of *Buddie* for them. As their ideas grew, Eric created the Flat grandparents and Ava created the Flat version of her family. Their creations were implemented into *Buddie*. When they were able to send their final photos with their digital flat characters, Eric and Ava were very happy and proud of themselves. Ava hugged her iPad with the

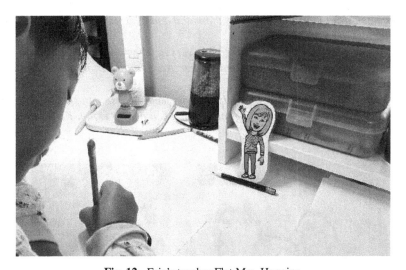

Fig. 12. Eric's teacher Flat Mrs. Huggins.

Fig. 13. Flat Eric and Flat Ava.

digital characters. Eric printed several photos with Flat Grandparents and put them on the side of his bookshelf.

4.13 Participants' Reflections

Overall, the participants enjoyed the *Buddie* project and felt as if they shared more things using *Buddie* when they are not with their loved ones. This encouraged the kids to be creative and actively engaged in the process. *Buddie* supported families being connected and created memorable moments when some of the family members travel without their kids (Figs. 14 and 15).

"This was fun. I will make more. Now I can show my Flat Grandparent everywhere. I am carrying them around. Haha. They couldn't visit us for a long time because of COVID. They are cute." - Eric

"I wish we had this kind of application before. I always felt guilty when I was traveling but now, I can do creative activities with my son using Buddie and we are apparently together" - Eric's mom

"I liked Buddie. I want to make my Tori glowing. I want to have the tiny printer at home. So, I can print many photos of my mom and dad. Next time, I can do a better job on drawing myself" - Ava

"I think this is brilliant. I don't talk to Ava very much when I am away. I think I can do more interesting works using Buddie with her. Are you going to sell the application soon?" - Ava's dad

"I love the idea. I think this will help parents feel always connected to kids when they are traveling. Just placing the digital character in photos is fun. Kids will like it." - Ava's mom

Fig. 14. Ava's customized pictures.

Fig. 15. Eric's customized pictures.

5 Conclusion

In this project, we explored how mobile and tangible interactions can support children with traveling parents. *Buddie* was developed utilizing a mobile application, a tangible soft toy and a small printer. Through *Buddie*, a traveling parent can take pictures and place a digital version of their child's favourite toy in travel photos. When the child receives pictures through the soft toy, she can print them and know where her mother is. The early prototype was expanded through participants' workshops with two families during the COVID pandemic. The children participating in the workshop developed their own versions of digital characters that could be embedded into the *Buddie* app. Through this process, we learned that kids' separations or isolations caused by a family member's traveling or the COVID lockdown could be overcome by utilizing the *Buddie* application concept. Families and friends can stay connected in these challenging times. After the pandemic, we would like to invite more family participants to test the system. For that, we are going to develop an easy method to include users' own digital characters or flat characters in the application.

References

1. Teh, J.K.S., Cheok, A.D., Peiris, R.L., Choi, Y., Thuong, V., Lai, S.: Huggy Pajama: a mobile parent and child hugging communication system. In: Proceedings of the 7th International Conference on Interaction Design and Children (IDC '08), pp. 250–257. Association for Computing Machinery, New York (2008). https://doi.org/10.1145/1463689.1463763
2. https://winnie.com/post/wanted-to-share-something-my-bd34b41b
3. https://www.ariesresidencesuites.com/8-ways-make-business-travel-bearable-parents-kids-alike/
4. AT&T Commercial "Sweet Pea". https://youtu.be/HoxpudVMLcs

5. https://en.wikipedia.org/wiki/CloudPets
6. Dam, R., Siang, T.: What is design thinking and why is it so popular. Interact. Des. Found. (2018)
7. Pruitt, J., Grudin, J.: Personas: practice and theory. In: Proceedings of the 2003 Conference on Designing for User Experiences (2003)
8. Richardson, A.: Using customer journey maps to improve customer experience. Harv. Bus. Rev. **15**(1), 2–5 (2010)
9. Howard, T.: Journey mapping: a brief overview. Commun. Des. Q. Rev. **2**(3), 10–13 (2014)
10. Modlitba, L.P.: Globetoddler: enhancing the experience of remote interaction for preschool children and their traveling parents. Diss. Massachusetts Institute of Technology, School of Architecture and Planning, Program in Media Arts and Sciences (2008)
11. Chan, M.-Y., et al.: WAKEY: assisting parent-child communication for better morning routines. In: Proceedings of the 2017 ACM Conference on Computer Supported Cooperative Work and Social Computing (CSCW '17), pp. 2287–2299. Association for Computing Machinery, New York (2017). https://doi.org/10.1145/2998181.2998233
12. https://www.adobe.com/products/xd.html
13. https://www.autodesk.com/products/maya/overview
14. https://www.protopie.io/
15. Yarosh, S., Chieh, Y., Abowd, G.D.: Supporting parent–child communication in divorced families. Int. J. Hum.-Comput. Stud. **67**(2), 192–203 (2009)
16. Seo, J.H., Sungkajun, A., Cook, M.: InTouch wearables: exploring ambient remote touch in child-parent relationships. In: Proceedings of the Eleventh International Conference on Tangible, Embedded, and Embodied Interaction (2017)
17. Yarosh, S., et al.: "Almost touching" parent-child remote communication using the sharetable system. In: Proceedings of the 2013 Conference on Computer Supported Cooperative Work (2013)
18. Tsetserukou, D.: Haptihug: a novel haptic display for communication of hug over a distance. In: Kappers, A.M.L., van Erp, J.B.F., Bergmann-Tiest, W.M., van der Helm, F.C.T. (eds.) EuroHaptics 2010. LNCS, vol. 6191, pp. 340–347. Springer, Heidelberg (2010). https://doi.org/10.1007/978-3-642-14064-8_49
19. Mowder, B.A., et al.: Parent role characteristics: parent views and their implications for school psychologists. Psychol. Sch. **32**(1), 27–37 (1995)
20. Jacobs, K.: Parent and child together time. In: Handbook of Family Literacy, pp. 213–232. Routledge, London (2004)
21. Chang, J.-H., Yeh, T.-L.: The influence of parent-child toys and time of playing together on attachment. Procedia Manuf. **3**, 4921–4926 (2015)
22. http://www.tia.org/index.html (12/01/2007)
23. https://theconversation.com/are-the-kids-alright-social-isolation-can-take-a-toll-but-play-can-help-146023
24. Loades, M.E., et al.: Rapid systematic review: the impact of social isolation and loneliness on the mental health of children and adolescents in the context of COVID-19. J. Am. Acad. Child Adolesc. Psychiatry **59**(11), 1218–1239 (2020)
25. https://www.liebertpub.com/doi/10.1089/CYBER.2020.0284
26. Hindus, D., Mainwaring, S.D., Leduc, N., Hagström, A.E., Bayley, O.: Casablanca: designing social communication devices for the home. In: Proceedings of the SIGCHI Conference on Human Factors in Computing Systems (CHI '01), pp. 325–332 (2001)

27. Keller, I., van der Hoog, W., Stappers, P.J.: Gust of me: reconnecting mother and son. IEEE Pervasive Comput. **3**(1), 22–28 (2004)
28. Romero, N., Markopoulos, P., van Baren, J., deRuyter, B., Ijsselsteijn, W., Farshchian, B.: Connecting the family with awareness systems. Pers. Ubiquit. Comput. **11**(4), 299–312 (2007)
29. Shi, H., Wang, Y., Li, M., et al.: Impact of parent-child separation on children's social-emotional development: a cross-sectional study of left-behind children in poor rural areas of China. BMC Publ. Health **21**, 823 (2021). https://doi.org/10.1186/s12889-021-10831-8

Research Design Based on Children's Participative Edutainment Products

Chang Ge, Feng jiao Wang, and Zhu Gao$^{(\boxtimes)}$

Department of Art and Design, Xi'an University of Technology, Xi'an, China
2954985006@qq.com

Abstract. Objective: To protect children's eyesight by reducing the frequency and duration of children playing electronic products through children's participation in the design of children's interesting entertainment products. Methods: 15 primary school students aged 8–12 were selected by random sampling method to improve the existing incomplete design scheme of entertainment products together with designers, so that children would become the main participants in the early stage of the design of children's entertainment products. Then GR-AES was used to calculate children's emotional responses to each design scheme, and the final design scheme was drawn up from the perspective of children. Results: The entertainment products conforming to children's emotional experience were designed. Children participated in the drawing of the design sketch, and the entertainment products with the highest user satisfaction were finally designed based on children's preferences. Conclusion: It is beneficial to cultivate children's consciousness of innovation and cooperation, make children's entertainment projects rich and diversified, help children to train the adjustment function of the eyes, improve the adjustment ability of the ciliary muscle, so as to improve the resistance ability of the eyes.

Keywords: Children's entertainment products · Participatory design · User demand

1 Introduction

With the advent of the intelligent era, intelligent electronic products have become a necessity in family life. Children's eyes will be irreversible damage if they look at electronic products for a long time. In the investigation of children's use of electronic games at home and abroad, the phenomenon of addiction to electronic games has been found. At the same time, with the increase of children's continuous staring time on the screen, the rate of visual impairment has increased significantly [1]. Children lack self-control and are difficult to distinguish right from wrong and are easily disturbed by the Internet world [2]. Driven by commerce and economy, it is rare for children's products with serious plagiarism and actual consideration for children [3]. Most children's products do not know enough about the physiological and psychological needs of children at all ages, so they ignore the experience of children themselves. As the final product users, children's participation is obviously not high [4]. Therefore, there is an urgent need for an entertainment product that conforms to the emotional experience of children, both as the final consumer and as the main design participant in the pre-design process. This study puts forward the concept of children's participatory design of entertainment products and the process of participating in the implementation. A child's favorite entertainment product can "share" children's time playing electronic products, enrich and diversify children's entertainment items, bring more pleasant use experience to children and reduce the adverse effects of electronic products on children's vision. Children's real needs can be well taken into account through children's participatory design method. This process brings children a sense of achievement, is conducive to cultivating children's sense of cooperation and spirit of innovation, and can avoid the risk of adverse effects on children in the age of intelligence.

2 Design of Participatory Entertainment Products

Participatory design, also known as co-design and collaborative design, is a design method that attempts to make all stakeholders actively participate in the design process and make users change from passive to active, so as to ensure that the results meet their needs and have practical feasibility [5]. In order to understand what users really think, participatory design is often used to engage users in order to design products with the highest user satisfaction. The participatory design method can have a deeper understanding of users, solve their problems more pertinently, and meet their needs. The participatory design method used in this paper makes children the primary participants in the early stage of children's entertainment products. Other design participants include: at least two expert designers and educational experts with children, primary school teachers, and parents or other guardians of children. In the stage of participatory design, conditions are created for children to obtain aesthetic feeling. Children draw the appearance of ideal products on paper, intuitively present their inner thoughts, improve their aesthetic ability, and learn to create beauty by various means [6].

2.1 Design for Users

Participatory design is mainly used to understand user characteristics and needs, such as cognition, habits, behaviors, etc. Because it is difficult for designers to truly feel all the experiences and ideas of users, they use participatory design to engage users in creativity, During the incubation stage of design ideas and the preliminary research stage, users are allowed to communicate with designers. From function to form, from material to color, users are free to give full play to their innovative ability [7], and users' needs are deeply explored. Children can intuitively express their design ideas [8].

The designer, as a service provider, takes children as the object of design. Starting from the perspective of children, the designer enables children to give full play to their imagination and creativity in the process of children's participatory design. The designer provides the basic functions of entertainment products and simple graphic prototypes, such as the circular or square sketch of a small night light with only switches and bulbs for several children, and gives the rest of the design to children. Children are free to add the functions they need. In addition, children's psychology and usage habits should be fully investigated. Children aged 8–12 years old have high neural excitability in the brain and respond quickly to external stimuli [9]. They like to explore and are good at observing things around with their eyes. They are inattentive and like to be hyperactive. At this stage, children's physical functions are gradually improved, their memory is gradually enhanced, their emotions are gradually enriched, and their inner world is gradually formed, which is also the best period for the development of children's imagination [10]. Children older than 7 years have the ability to sort and process numbers, ask questions about spatial concepts, distinguish between reality and fantasy, and express their thoughts simply through verbal descriptions or drawings. Children older than 10 years old can imagine the three-dimensional perspective of the human body from different perspectives, have the ability of abstract thinking, hypothetics-reasoning, solve present problems with what they have learned in the past, and make plans for the future [11]. In terms of gender: Boys have a slight advantage in math and spatial imagination, and girls have a slight advantage in language.

2.2 Design Method

The design methods used in this study include GR-AES method and GaCoCo participatory game design method [12]. This study randomly selected 15 primary school students aged 8–12 to participate in the design. GR-AES is the full name of graduation achievement emotion Set. In this paper, the focus of GR-AES is to investigate children's emotions in each activity, and take each activity stage as a page. Above the page is a question about user participation in design experience of this activity. The children were asked to make choices after completing each of the five emotionally-increasing faces displayed on the page, such as "not at all," "slightly," "moderately," "very much," and "extremely." Children's emotions and opinions can be more accurately collected through language and graphics [12]. As shown below (Fig. 1).

How much did you ENJOY yourself?

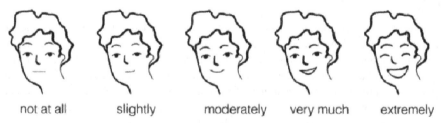

not at all   slightly   moderately   very much   extremely

Fig. 1. GR-AES (Graduation Achievement Emotion Set) page on male enjoyment ([12])

GR-AES is a verbal - image self-report tool capable of assessing the emotional intensity of achievement. At the end of each task, the researchers conducted a GR-AES examination to investigate the children's achievement emotions in participating in the design of entertainment products.

GaCoCo participatory game design method, the full name of GaCoCo is gamified Cooperative design and Cooperative Learning, which was first proposed by Dodero et al. (2014a) and gradually improved in the study of school game design (e.g.,Dodero et al., 2014b) [12]. In this article, the GaCoCo participatory game design approach is used as follows: Using GaCoCo's landmark ideas: cooperative learning and gamification. The design of edutainment products, namely (1) the knowledge that children explore when playing entertainment products; (2) Promote children's participation in design.

2.3 Design Role Participation

The participants included 15 primary school children aged 8–12, at least two expert designers with children, two educational experts, three primary school teachers and two parents or other guardians of the children. The total number of participants was 23. In user participatory design, designers play a role as an organization and manager of information communication for users [13]. Designers are responsible for proposing preliminary design schemes, guiding children to give full play to their imagination and creativity in products, and conducting GR-AES checks at each test stage to investigate children's achievement emotions in participating in the design of entertainment products.

Children at the school stage are at the stage of rapid growth of knowledge reserve, their cognition gradually opens, their vision becomes broader, their curiosity becomes strong, and they begin to explore the whole world [14]. Children are mainly responsible for cooperating with designers in the early stage of design.

Due to the particularity of their profession, primary school teachers are the ones who know the primary school children aged 8–12 best. They are responsible for choosing topics and directions that children are interested in together with designers, and expanding children's knowledge through entertainment products. During children's participatory design, primary school teachers are mainly responsible for the selection of the final scheme, and their opinions also play an important role.

Education experts are mainly involved in judging the reasonableness of edutainment products. If there is something inappropriate about the proposed program of edutainment products for children, the education experts are responsible for pointing out, and the education experts have a vote on the selection of the final program.

Parents or other guardians of children are the consumers of this design. Consumer word-of-mouth has an important impact on product innovation, and the aesthetic and symbolic significance of products have an impact on the dissemination of word-of-mouth [15]. In the early stage of design, consumers' concerns and opinions on new products should be fully considered. The child's parents or other guardians have the option to vote during the child participatory design phase.

2.4 Design Process

In this study, the design stage is divided into five parts, namely, the requirement confirmation stage, the participatory design stage, the research and analysis stage, the integrated development stage and the design evaluation stage. The participatory design process is shown in Fig. 2.

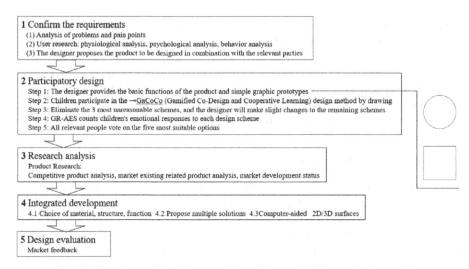

Fig. 2. Flow chart of Participatory design (Source: Self-drawn by the author)

Confirming Requirements. (1) Analysis of problems and pain points; (2) User research: physiological analysis, psychological analysis and behavioral analysis; (3) Designers propose products to be designed in combination with stakeholders.

Participative Design Phase. Materials preparation: 15 copies of product intention drawing, 15 copies of design basic shape, 15 copies of corrugated paper, 8 copies of voting cards in Fig. 6, 23 copies of voting cards in Fig. 7, 15 copies of GR-AES emotion analysis set 1, 15 copies of GR-AES emotion analysis set 2, and 1 corrugated paper model. The required experimental materials are shown in Fig. 3. Step 1: The designer provides the basic design shape drawn by the children. Step 2: Children participate through drawing → GaCoCo (Gamification Collaborative Design and Cooperative Learning) design method. Designers refer to the product intention diagram for children, as shown in Fig. 7, and circle the parts that need to be designed by children. During the period of children's participation in design, children can discuss with each other, and children can communicate with designers and primary school teachers at any time where they feel vague. Step 3: After the completion of children's design, select the three children's "works" with the lowest number of votes in the voting board, and eliminate the three most unreasonable schemes. The voting board is shown in Fig. 4. The designer slightly changes the children's works approved in the first round of voting. Step 4: GR-AES measured children's satisfaction with their own works and their emotional reactions in the process of participating in the design. Step 5: Secondary voting. All relevant personnel select the five schemes that best fit the design theme on the voting cards, among which, the voting cards used are shown in Fig. 5.

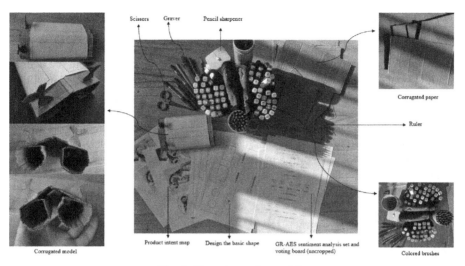

Fig. 3. Experimental materials

Research and Analysis Phase. Analyze the existing relevant products in the market, investigate the market development status, analyze competing products, design questionnaires and sort out the survey results.

Integrated Development Stage. Material, structure, function selection, put forward multiple solutions, computer aided to do 2D/3D drawings.

Design Evaluation Phase. Accept market feedback.

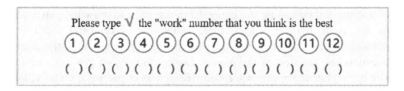

Fig. 4. Step 3 Voting card (Source: self-drawn by the author)

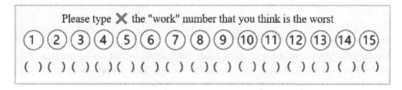

Fig. 5. Step 5 Voting card (Source: self-drawn by the author)

3 Implementation Process

The implementation of this study takes "animal telescope" as an example. According to the survey, most children love small animals and are full of curiosity about the animal world, but children need to explore the science knowledge about animals. An animal telescope that can see the world in the eyes of animals enables children to see the world in the eyes of animals and have a deeper understanding of creatures in nature. The main part is modeled in the general shape of children's telescope, as shown in Fig. 7. When changing the world in the eyes of animals, the lenses need to be replaced. Different animal lenses need to correspond to different shapes and colors, so children are encouraged to use bionic design, and the planning of the shapes and colors of these lens shells is left to children.

Implementation process—Take the "animal telescope" as an example

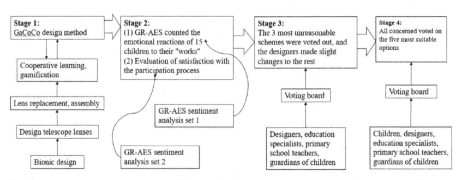

Fig. 6. Implementation process – Taking "Animal Telescope" as an example (Source: Self-drawn by the author)

In the first stage, the bionic design is used to design the lens of the corresponding animal. Children choose an animal they like, start association and imagination around the selected animal, and draw their ideas on the paper. The parts that require children to participate in the design are divided into 1 lens shell in the product intention drawing in Fig. 7, 2 stickers on the side of the telescope, and 3 ornaments matching the corresponding lens.

In the process of participation, children freely create the basic shape of the product and draw their inner thoughts on the paper. Children need to draw the pattern in front of the lens shell in the red box or make three-dimensional accessories with corrugated paper, such as cat ears and bee wings. Finally, the designer will stick the accessories in the corresponding position of the model. During the design process, children can discuss with each other and ask questions from designers or parents for advice. GaCoCo participatory game design encourages children to exchange ideas and collaborate. The basic shape of its products is shown in Fig. 8, and the general process of the first stage is shown in Fig. 9.

The second stage: The GR-AES method was used to test 15 children's satisfaction with their "works" and their emotional reactions in the process of participation. GR-AES

Fig. 7. Product intention (photo credit: https://www.taobao.com/)

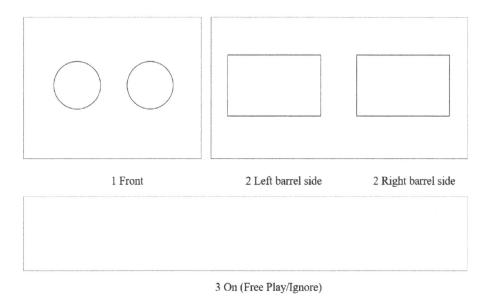

1 Front   2 Left barrel side   2 Right barrel side

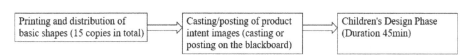

3 On (Free Play/Ignore)

Fig. 8. Basic shape design (picture source: self-drawn by the author)

| Printing and distribution of basic shapes (15 copies in total) | → | Casting/posting of product intent images (casting or posting on the blackboard) | → | Children's Design Phase (Duration 45min) |

Fig. 9. Process of the first stage (picture source: self-drawn by the author)

emotion analysis set 1 was used to measure children's satisfaction with their "works", as shown in Fig. 10. The satisfaction increased from left to right, and children marked "√" under their corresponding emotions. GR-AES emotion Analysis Set 2 was used to measure children's emotional responses in the process of participation, as shown in

Fig. 11. Pleasure degree increased from left to right, and children marked "√" under their corresponding emotions.

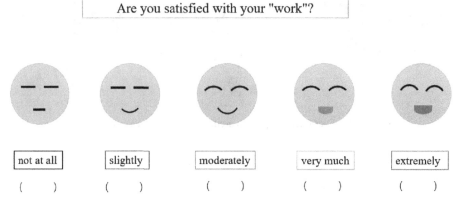

| Are you satisfied with your "work"? |

| not at all | slightly | moderately | very much | extremely |
| ( ) | ( ) | ( ) | ( ) | ( ) |

Fig. 10. GR-AES Emotion Analysis Set 1 (Source: Self-drawn by the author)

| Were you happy participating in the design process? |

| not at all | slightly | moderately | very much | extremely |
| ( ) | ( ) | ( ) | ( ) | ( ) |

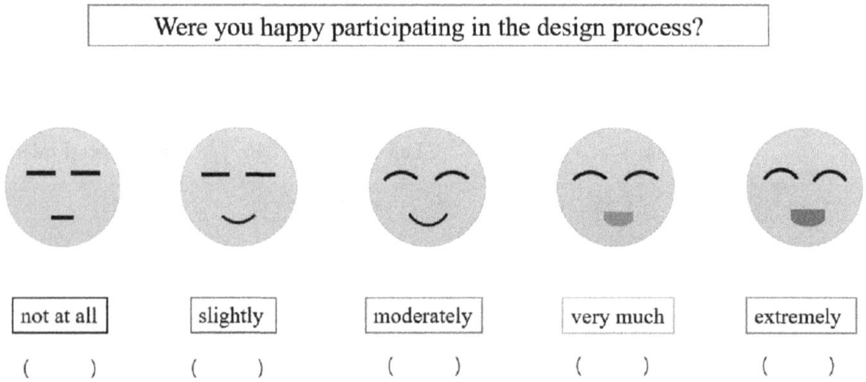

Fig. 11. GR-AES Emotion Analysis Set 2 (Source: Self-drawn by the author)

The third stage: the three most unreasonable schemes are eliminated by voting. The voting board is shown in Fig. 4. Voters included designers, education experts, primary school teachers and children's guardians. The designer made minor changes to the rest of the selected scheme.

Stage 4: All relevant personnel vote to select the five most suitable schemes. The voting cards are shown in Fig. 5. Participants include children, designers, education experts, primary school teachers and guardians of children. The participation process of children is shown in Figs. 12, 13 and 14.

Fig. 12. Child participation process diagram

Fig. 13. Children talking to each other

4   Research Results

Through the experiment, 87% of children are extremely happy in the process of participation, and 13% feel very happy. Children have a high participation in the design of participatory entertainment products. Cooperation and communication between children is conducive to the exchange of information, which can stimulate children's more

Fig. 14. Making decorations out of corrugated paper

inspiration and imagination. Most children are very happy with their "creations" and are interested in the upcoming products they have designed. There are two main reasons for the elimination of the schemes in Table 1. Reason 1: They have no correlation with the selected animals; Reason 2: The "works" are not finished. According to the statistics of the second round of voting, it is found that the most suitable five schemes are implementable and conform to the aesthetic design principle, which is easy to be slightly modified by designers and manufactured by factories. The most popular animal behaviors among children were found through experiments: cat, tortoise, dog, rabbit, giant panda, dragonfly and fish.

Take cat, the most popular small animal among children, for example. According to the scheme with the highest number of votes, the digital model of its scheme is shown in Fig. 15.

The "animal telescope" is designed by children themselves. Children choose their favourite animals and design the side, lens and decoration of the telescope by themselves, which can improve their love for this entertainment product. They can use the entertainment products they are interested in to pull children back to the outdoors from being addicted to electronic products, and improve the cooperation and communication ability between children through participatory design. Use animal telescopes to encourage children to observe nature and explore the secrets of all kinds of small animals. An animal telescope that can see the world through the eyes of animals can give children a deeper understanding of the creatures in nature, thus broadening their horizons and understanding more popular science knowledge.

Table 1. Experimental results of animal telescope based on children's participatory design

Obsolete scenarios	The five most suitable options	The proposal with the highest number of votes	Ranking of the most popular animals for children
			Cats, turtles, dogs, rabbits, pandas, dragonflies, fish

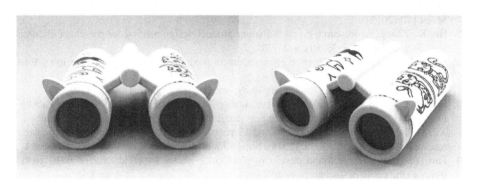

Fig. 15. Digital model of animal telescope based on children's participatory design

5   Conclusion

In the context of the rapid development of intelligence and electronic technology, children enter the adult world earlier, "childhood" gradually fades away, and the boundary between adults and children is gradually blurred [16]. A child's favorite entertainment product can "share" the time children spend on electronic devices, thereby preventing children from becoming addicted to video games. Edutainment products designed by children can not only increase children's love for the products, but also bring different experiences and knowledge to children. Disadvantages: children copy each other in the process of participation, and the sample size is relatively small, which is not suitable for the mass production of products. The advantage is that children choose and "design" the scheme according to their own preferences in the early stage of design. These ideas and the performance of children in the process of participation can provide the designer with good materials and inspire the design, so as to design entertainment products in line with the emotional experience of children. Children's participatory design can understand what children like and what children expect the product to have. Personalized products in line with children's emotional experience can help brands better understand customers' preferences and have more advantages than competitors in the market, which is conducive to cultivating children's awareness of innovation and cooperation, enriching and diversifying children's entertainment programs, and effectively reducing the myopia rate of children.

References

1. Zhang, Y., Shang, C., Chen, B., Du, K., Huang, X.: Effects of electronic sports and video games on visual health of children and adolescents. China Sports Sci. Technol. **58**(06), 10–16 (2022). https://doi.org/10.16470/j.csst.2021069
2. Qin, Y., Wang, Y.: Preventing minors from becoming a "generation delayed by mobile phones" – analysis and educational intervention on minors' addiction to mobile phones. China Audio-Vis. Educ. **421**(02), 1–7+14 (2022)
3. Liu, Z.: On the application of interaction design in children's toy products. Beauty Times (11), 104–106 (2016). https://doi.org/10.16129/j.cnki.mysds.2016.11.035
4. Ma, H.: Research on product innovation design with user participation. Res. Des. Art **2**(01), 56–61+70 (2012)
5. Hu, K., Zhang, F.: Research on participatory product design method for preschool children aged 5–6 years. J. Des. **35**(10), 8–11 (202)
6. Wang, C., Li, T., Bo, Q.: Children's entertainment products and their design principles. Fine Arts Rev. **1**, 106 (2014)
7. Zhao, N.: Construction of participatory design method. Design **07**, 183–185 (2013)
8. Hu, K., Cai, W.: Classification and visualization of participatory design methods. Packag. Eng. 1–16 (2023). http://kns.cnki.net/kcms/detail/50.1094.TB.20220823.1523.002.html
9. Xu, M.: For children aged between 6 and 12 years of auxiliary visual acuity product design research. Beijing Inst. Technol. (2018). https://doi.org/10.26948/d.cnki.gbjlu.2018.001364
10. Sun, Y.: Design research and development of color games for children aged 6–12 years. Beijing University of Technology (2016)
11. Hu, R.: Research and application of intelligent product design method for school-age children. Xiangtan University (2019). https://doi.org/10.27426/d.cnki.gxtdu.2019.000308
12. Gennari, R., et al.: Children's emotions and quality of products in participatory game design. Int. J. Hum.-Comput. Stud. **101**, 45–61 (2017). ISSN 1071-5819. https://doi.org/10.1016/j.ijhcs.2017.01.006
13. Barcellini, F., Detienne, F., Burkhardt, J.M.: Users and developer mediation in an open source software community: boundary spanning through cross participation in online discussions. Int. J. Hum. Comput. Stud **66**(7), 558–570 (2008)
14. Pan, Z., Fu, Q., Wang, Y.: Research on the design of children's educational products based on the theory of sensory integration. Beauty Times **796**(05), 106–109 (2019). https://doi.org/10.16129/j.cnki.mysds.2019.05.033
15. Zhu, Z., Liu, F., Wei, H., Wu, J.: Research on the influence mechanism of product design on consumer word-of-mouth communication: the mediating effect of emotion and perceived quality. J. Dalian Univ. Technol. (Soc. Sci. Ed.) **43**(04), 55–62 (2022). https://doi.org/10.19525/j.issn1008-407x.2022.04.006
16. Li, Q., Cheng, S., Yang, X., Chen, B.: Research on personalized product design based on extension innovation method. Packag. Eng. **43**(22), 87–94 (2022). https://doi.org/10.19554/j.cnki.1001-3563.2022.22.010

Metacognitive Processes Involved in Human Robot Interaction in the School Learning Environment

Deepti Mishra[1,2,3](✉) , Ricardo G. Lugo[2,5] , Karen Parish[4] ,
and Solveig Tilden[6]

[1] Department of Computer Science (IDI), University of Science and Technology, Trondheim,
Norway
Deepti.Mishra@ntnu.no

[2] Department of Information Security and Communication Technology (IIK), Norwegian,
University of Science and Technology, Trondheim, Norway
Ricardo.G.Lugo@ntnu.no

[3] Business Analytics Research Group, Inland School of Business and Social Sciences, Inland
Norway University of Applied Sciences, Hamar, Norway

[4] Faculty of Education, Inland Norway University of Applied Sciences, Hamar, Norway
Karen.Parish@inn.no

[5] Estonian Maritime Academy of Tallinn University of Technology, Tallinn, Estonia

[6] Faculty of Social Sciences, Department of Psychology, University of Copenhagen,
Copenhagen, Denmark

Abstract. With the ongoing digital revolution and the ever-increasing development of new technology, schools must provide students with a grounding in certain technical skills, such as computational thinking, which are likely to be required for future roles, including working with and operating robots. For such robot human interaction to be successful, introduction of robots into school learning environments is crucial. However, we also need to better understand the learning processes involved in this human robot interaction. Acknowledging the importance of metacognitive processes as an essential aspect in achieving learning outcomes in educational contexts, this article investigates the experiences of students in human-robotic interactions and related tasks (programming and math) by exploring the student's self-assessment of perceived performance (JOP), motivation (fun and difficulty) and learning. This aim has been achieved through a pilot study whereby the authors conducted a three-day workshop with grade 6 students and collected pre and post survey data. The findings contribute knowledge to our understanding of the importance of metacognition and in particular accurate self-assessment as crucial for both motivation and learning with humanoid robots.

Keywords: self-assessment · motivation · learning · humanoid robots · robot-assisted teaching

M. Kurosu and A. Hashizume (Eds.): HCII 2023, LNCS 14012, pp. 85–100, 2023.
https://doi.org/10.1007/978-3-031-35599-8_6

1 Introduction

With the ongoing digital revolution and the ever-increasing development of new technology, schools must provide students with a grounding in certain technical skills, such as computational thinking, which are likely to be required in many future roles [1]. Many such roles will also require an understanding of robotics [1]. At the same time, in order for the application of robots into school learning environments (SLEs) to be successful, we need to have a better understanding of the human robot interaction, the skills required for learning with robots, and in particular the metacognitive processes surrounding this interaction.

Metacognition is defined as 'awareness of one's own knowledge—what one does and does not know—and one's ability to understand, control, and manipulate one's cognitive processes' [2]. Specifically, metacognition includes three processes: knowledge of one's own abilities, an understanding of a situation, and how to regulate one's own behaviours [3]. Students who show higher metacognitive skills are accurate and confident in their judgments of their own performance in relation to task demands and are better able to accurately describe their strengths, weaknesses, and their potential to improve (see [4] for overview). The development of metacognitive skills is therefore essential in achieving learning outcomes in educational contexts and accurate judgement of one's own learning can be a useful measure of performance in both familiar and unfamiliar domains [5]. In addition, self-evaluative skills need to be developed through direct mastery experiences targeted at specific tasks that develop over time [6]. Metacognitive judgements require students to retrospectively evaluate the effectiveness of their learning after establishing an initial evaluation of their skills and confidence in the ability to problem-solve by effectively using their abilities [7]. Metacognition is therefore an important consideration when introducing humanoid robots into SLEs and indeed for a future with robots.

Much of the research on the application of robots in SLEs to date has focused on the technological capabilities of robots, or the social aspect of learning with robots [8–10]. In addition, humanoid robots are used largely as novices, tutors [11], classmates, peers, or entertainers [12]. Often these applications are driven by technological feasibility [9, 13]. The NAO, RoboVie and Tiro robots have been used to explore the psychological dynamics that characterize the social human-robot interactions in educational settings [14]. Multiple studies [15, 16] have acknowledged a lack of understanding regarding the efficacy of humanoid robots in SLEs [14]. In particular, further investigation is needed to explore what the self-efficacy of humanoid robots is to promote learning, and in particular in how students perceive such interactions as part of their metacognitive development.

This paper presents some of the findings from a larger study on the use of humanoid robots in SLEs. The larger study uses a multi-disciplinary framework that incorporates, pedagogical/didactical development, technical development for human robot interaction, psycho-social development, and ethical development (ref). The aim of this article is to investigate the experiences of students in human-robotic interactions and related tasks (programming and math) by exploring the student's self-assessment of perceived performance (JOP), motivation (fun and difficulty) and learning as aspects of their metacognitive processes.

This paper is organized as follows: firstly, we explore the state of the art looking at research related to metacognition, programming, mathematics, and human robot interaction. Following this we present our hypotheses, methods and results. To finish we discuss the results in light of the state of the art, followed by conclusion.

2   State of the Art

In research that is related to metacognitive judgements it is shown that performance and relative accuracy are considered a reliable and robust method for predicting learning assessment [17]. This is valid for metacognitive judgements done well after the learning, though with smaller effect sizes, indicating that immediate or delayed metacognitive judgements help in learning consolidation. In addition, accurate metacognitive judgements are calibrated with performance outcomes [18]. Research has also examined the accuracy of self-efficacy beliefs, showing that overconfident self-efficacy beliefs can have detrimental effects on later performance [19].

2.1   Self-assessment and Enjoyment in Mathematics, Programming and Tasks with Robots

It has been shown that there is a strong positive relationship between student's confident self-assessment about learning mathematics and enjoyment of mathematics [20] and that students who overestimate their mathematic competence tend to report higher engagement and higher interest in Mathematics [21]. In research that focuses on programming tasks, student self-assessment is often conceptualized as self-efficacy. Research suggests that the self-efficacy beliefs of novice programmers has been found to have a strong influence on their engagement, while effort, enjoyment, deep learning, and surface learning were predictors of programming performance [22]. Students with higher interest (including enjoyment) in programming have greater programming self-efficacy [23]. It has also been found that children's positive experiences with technology can lead to enjoyment in both programming and higher self-efficacy when working with robots [24]. Shim, Kwon [25] illustrated that when using a robot game to learn and practice computer programming, students showed enjoyment in using the programming concepts taught by the robot.

2.2   Accurate Self-assessment and Difficulty in Mathematics, Programming and Robot Tasks

There is little research that focuses on self-assessment and difficulty in programming and robots. It has been found that variations in Mathematic task difficulty is among the potential causes of inaccuracy in students' efficacy self-calibration since students reported more accurate calibration, higher self-efficacy beliefs, and more favorable self-evaluations on easier math problems than more difficult ones [26]. Chen and Zimmerman [27] also claimed that there is a decrease in student's self-efficacy beliefs and calibration accuracy as the Mathematics tasks became more difficult. However, more generally it has been found that inaccuracy in one's judgments can stem from either an underestimation or overestimation of one's abilities in relation to the task novelty and difficulty, and optimism or pessimism of the outcomes [18, 28]. Tasks that are deemed easy, even if novel, can be misjudged and an over precision estimation can negatively affect performance. While tasks that are deemed novel and too difficult in relation to one's abilities can lead to an underestimation of precision and also negatively impact performance [18, 29]. While some studies have shown that individual tendencies to overestimate competence may have a number of adjustment benefits, other studies have suggested that realistic self-estimation is more beneficial [21, 30].

2.3 Accurate Self-assessment and Learning in Mathematics, Programming and Using Robots

With regards to self-assessment specifically in mathematics and learning, the results are somewhat mixed when it comes to accurate self-assessment and actual performance. Hosein and Harle [31] found that, on average, students were underestimating their performance in mathematics while Dupeyrat, Escribe [32] in their study with 8th and 9th graders reported that students who overestimated their math competence had significantly higher performance approach goals than those who underestimated their math competence but did not significantly differ from those who were accurate. Lee [21] also revealed that students' overestimation of mathematics competence positively predicted their mathematics achievement. On the other hand, Hardy [33] found that accurate mathematical self-efficacy beliefs were better predictors of performance than overconfident self-efficacy beliefs.

Learning through computer programming provides opportunities for students to develop self-regulated learning competencies to interactively see the outcomes of their actions, and review and reflect on them [34]. This process is even more effective when students program a humanoid robot due to increased interactivity since programming statements translate to robot actions. In computer science, successful students tend to underestimate whereas unsuccessful students tend to over-estimate, their own performance [35, 36] and performance on the exam is strongly correlated with the ability to correctly predict marks [35]. Students in general seem to be quite accurate in assessing their own knowledge in programming and there is a statistically significant correlation between accurate self-assessment and performance in exams [37].

2.4 Relationship Between Perceived Ease of Task and Enjoyment in Mathematics, Programming and Robot Tasks

Perceived difficulty and lack of confidence are found to be important reasons why students do not continue with mathematics, as well as perceived dislike and boredom, and lack of relevance [38]. Similarly, programming has acquired the reputation of being difficult and there is an image of a "programmer" as a socially inadequate "nerd", spending all hours producing arcane and unintelligible code [39]. If students approach programming with an expectation that it will be difficult, and with a negative image of those who excel in the subject, it is very hard to imagine their being especially motivated to achieve success [39]. Giannakos and Jaccheri [40] found that children's positive attitudes regarding an activity's easiness and usefulness significantly affected engagement and their intention to participate in coding activities. Likewise, children who encounter fewer difficulties in coding tasks and could handle the cognitive load better have higher positive attitude and learning [41]. However, when children experience difficulties in coding, they feel less excited, as fun and enjoyment derive from successfully completing tasks [42, 43]. In addition, a study conducted at four middle schools found that pre-computer science conceptual understanding, confidence in using the computer and positive computer science attitudes significantly predict post-computer science conceptual understanding and greater confidence in using the computer post intervention [44].

On the other hand, research into robots is variable. It has been found that the perception of learning tasks as difficult and complex may be regarded as an advantage and supportive process for the students in terms of learning during robotic coding; however, some studies suggest the vice versa [45]. In a study conducted to investigate middle school students' attitudes toward and motivation for robotics activities and learning STEM, students demonstrated positive intrinsic and extrinsic motivation, self-determination and self-efficacy concerning robotics at the beginning of the activities and maintained the results after the activities [46]. In addition, students reported perceived ease of use as a determinant for perceived usefulness and actual use of robotics to learn computer programming [47]. On the contrary, Ohnishi, Honda [48] in their research on robotics classes for elementary and junior high school students, found that robotics programming is difficult for the participants but also fun and important which may make them motivated to work on difficult problems because they feel programming is fun.

2.5 Association Between Accurate Self-assessment of Perceived Performance Between Mathematics, Programming and Robot Tasks

Research has established that mathematics is a very important tool for many other subjects and there is a strong positive correlation between the student's performance in mathematics and programming [49]. Problem-solving and logical-mathematical thinking skills are also essential for programming; however, it can also be said that learning computer programming is also an effective way to develop these skills [50]. Analytical and logical thinking skills are also necessary to perform successfully in Mathematics as well as in procedural, object-oriented, and visual programming courses [51]. Multiple studies [52–54] have revealed that there is a significant correlation between the students' performance in the programming courses and their mathematics achievement. Qahmash, Joy [55] also confirmed by analyzing a large data set spanning nineteen years that there is a significant positive correlation between students' performance in mathematics and programming. In addition to mathematics, student's self-perception of their understanding as well as their comfort level with the programming task is also a strong predictor of their performance in programming [56]. Whilst studies directly related to robots are scarce, in a study conducted with middle school students for learning robotics and STEM, participants believed that STEM knowledge (in particular in Computer Science and Mathematics) were necessary for robotics [46].

3   Research Aim and Hypotheses

The above state of the art reveals much research into the different metacognitive process related to the individual subjects of programming, Mathematics, and robots. by building on this we will investigate the experiences of students in human-robotic interactions and related tasks (programming and math) by exploring the student's self-assessment of perceived performance (JOP), motivation (fun and difficulty) and learning. We propose that a better understanding of these processes will contribute to our understanding of these metacognitive processes and move forward the research into human robot interactions in SLEs.

This aim is operationalized through the investigation of the following hypotheses and as illustrated in Fig. 1.

H_1: The more accurate the self-assessment of perceived performance (JOP) the greater the level of, enjoyment, in Programming, Mathematics and robot interaction.

H_2: The more accurate the self-assessment of perceived performance (JOP) the greater the level of, difficulty in Programming, Mathematics and robot interaction.

H3: The more accurate the self-assessment of perceived performance (JOP) the greater the level of learning in general.

H_4: Perceived ease of task will result in more enjoyment in programming, Mathematics and robot interaction.

H_5: There will be an association of accurate self-assessment of perceived performance between Mathematic, robot interaction and Programming.

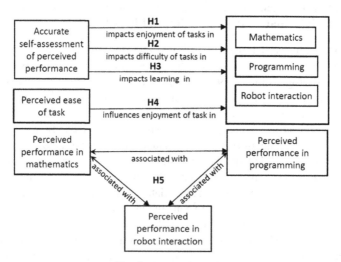

Fig. 1. Research model

4 Methods

4.1 Participants

Sample: The participants were Grade 6 students attending a primary school in a medium sized town in Norway ($N = 17$; $n_{female} = 6$).

4.2 Measurements

Independent Variable - Metacognitive assessment (JOP): Participants were asked for a metacognitive judgment concerning how they expected to perform working with the Math, Robot, and Programming. Participant answered the following question: "How well do you think you will do with the Robot/ math/ programming?". After their workshop with the robots, the participants were then asked: "How well did you do with the Robot/math/programming?". Both items were answered on a 5-point scale (badly - very well). Judgement of performance index was computed using the formula:

$$\text{JOP} = \left(\text{Post X}_{ijk} - \text{Pre X}_{ijk}\right)/\text{Post X}$$

where scores closest to zero (0) signified an accurate calibration of their performance, negative scores indicated an overestimation, and positive score indicated under confidence. Students were then grouped either in underestimation, accurate, or overconfident group for each of the categories (Robot, Math, Programming). Underestimation and Overconfidence are deemed as more negative evaluations.

Dependent Variables: The dependent variables were defined as learning, fun, and difficult in each category (Robot, math, Programming). Learning perceptions was measured on a 5-point Likert scale (not-very) with the item 'Do you feel you learned from the robot'. Perceptions of fun and difficulty were assessed by 'How much fun/ difficult was XXX' and was scored on a 5-point Likert scale (not-very). A total score for fun was also computed by summing the individual fun scores (Cronbach's $\alpha = .762$).

4.3 Procedure

The data was collected during a 3-day workshop which involved the following activities:

Activity 1 - Introduction to robot's presentation and class discussion led by the researchers.

Activity 2 - The participants completed a secure online pre-test structured questionnaire. The data collected was anonymous.

Activity 3 - The participants were separated into gendered groups of four or five by the regular class teachers. Each group participated in a one-hour session led by the researchers. The session included basic programming and math tasks using the robot. The Math tasks were designed in collaboration with the regular class teachers to ensure that they were set at an appropriate level and relevant to the curriculum.

Activity 4 - The participants completed a secure online post-test structured questionnaire. The data collected was anonymous.

Activity 5 - The researchers conducted semi-structured group interviews with each of the four groups.

More details about the procedure can be found in (ref).

Ethical Approval. The study conformed to the ethical guidelines for experimental studies set by the Norwegian Social Science Data Services (NSD). After the initial NSD online application was filled in, formal application was not required since only non-identifiable and non-health-related data were used in this research. Written informed consent was obtained from parents/guardians of the participating students. In addition, the students were informed about the aims of the project, their role in it, planned use of the data, and their right to withdraw. Participants were informed that they could withdraw from participation at any time and without any consequences throughout and after the session. However, it was made clear to them that the pre-test and post-test data was anonymous and therefore their survey data could not be withdrawn. The secure online provider used for the pre- and post-test surveys is authorized by the author's research institutions.

5 Results

The results related with means and correlations are given in Table 1.

To further test the hypothesis that accurate JOP would do better than either the under-estimation group and overconfidence group, non-parametric ANOVAs were performed on all DV in relation to the subjects (Robot, Math, Programming) and the results are shown in Table 2. Dunn's post hoc comparisons were used for pairwise comparison.

H_1: The more accurate the self-assessment of perceived performance (JOP) the greater the level of, enjoyment, in Programming, Mathematics and robot interaction.

To test for associations JOP predicts fun (H_1) in mathematics, programming and working with the robot, correlational analysis showed that higher JOP for mathematics and JOP for programming had high significant associations with enjoying mathematics ($\rho_s = 0,537*$) and programming ($\rho_s = .454$, $p < .05$) respectively. Non-significant associations ($p > .05$) were found for JOP Robotics and enjoying robotics ($\rho_s = .339$), math ($\rho_s = -.252$), JOP Math and enjoying robotics ($\rho_s = .275$), and programming ($\rho_s = .023$); and JOP programming and enjoying math ($\rho_s = -.063$). Additionally, *JOP* in programming has a positive correlation with fun working with robots ($\rho_s = .745$, $p < .05$) and fun with robot is positively correlated with fun with programming ($\rho_s = .639$, $p < .05$).

ANOVA - There were significant findings ($W = 9.05$, $p = .011$) for JOP Math on fun with large effect sizes ($\eta^2 = .504$). Post-hoc comparisons showed that the under-estimation group had more fun than the overestimation group *($z = 2.69$, $p = .004$,* Cohen's $d = 2.17$) and that the accurate perception group also reported more fun than the overestimation group *($z = 2.55$, $p = .005$, Cohen's $d = 1.94$).*

Table 1. Correlations (Spearman's ρ)

	1	2	3	4	5	6	7	8	9
1. Gender	–								
2. JOP Robot	−.301	–							
3. JOP Math	−.129	.176	–						
4. JOP Blocky	−.064	.582**	.153	–					
5. How fun was robot	−.119	.339	.275	.745**	–				
6. How fun was math	−.081	−.252	.537*	−.063	.228	–			
7. How fun was programming	.227	−.181	.023	.454*	.639**	.291	–		
8. How difficult was math	.174	−.420*	.174	−−.187	−.151	-.08	.047	–	
9. Difficult working with robot	−.327	−.109	−.117	−.298	−.461*	−.248	−.535*	.383	–
10. How much I Learned	−.094	−.426*	−.448*	−.209	.035	−.383	0.09	.211	.207

Table 2. Analysis of Variance for JOP and Fun, Difficulty & Learned($df = 2$)

	DV	W	p	η^2
JOP Math	Fun	9.05*	.011	.504
	Difficult	1.07	.587	.066
	Learned	2.72	.257	.051
JOP Robot	Fun	3.38	.185	.099
	Difficult	1.79	.409	.015
	Learned	5.81	.055	.272
JOP Programming	Fun	6.55*	.038	.325
	Difficult	not reported	-	-
	¨Learned	2.83	.243	.059

DV: Dependent variable
* Correlation is significant at the 0.05 level (1-tailed)
** Correlation is significant at the 0.01 level (1-tailed)

There was also a significant effect of JOP calibration for programming on how fun the task was ($W = 6.55$, $p = .038$) with large effect sizes ($\eta^2 = .325$) *and post hoc comparisons showed a significant difference between the* overestimation and underestimation group ($z = 2.50$, $p = .006$, Cohen's $d = 1.95$) and accurate group over the overestimation group ($z = 1.85$, $p = .032$, Cohen's $d = 1.72$). However, no significant findings for JOP robotics and fun ($W = 3.38$, $p = .185$).

H$_2$: The more accurate the self-assessment of perceived performance (JOP) the greater the level of, difficulty in Programming, Mathematics and robot interaction.

To test for associations between JOP negatively predicts difficulty (**H2**) in working with the robot. Students with better JOP Robotic calibration reported significantly less difficulty in math ($\rho_s = -.420$, $p < .05$) but not working with robots ($\rho_s = -.109$). Difficulty with math and programming was not associated ($p > .05$) with either JOP Math ($\rho_s = .174$; $\rho_s = -.187$) and JOP Programming ($\rho_s = -.117$; $\rho_s = .298$).

ANOVA - No significant associations were found for JOP Math and difficulty ($W = 1.07$, $p = .587$). No significant findings for JOP robotics and difficulty ($W = 1.79$, $p = .409$).

H3: The more accurate the self-assessment of perceived performance (JOP) the greater the level of learning in general.

To test for associations between JOP negatively predicts learning (**H3**), higher JOP scores were negatively associated with learning ($\rho_s = -.448 -- .426$, $p < .05$) in robot and Math.

ANOVA - While not significant, there were trends for JOP robotics and learning ($W = 5.81$, $p = .055$) with medium to large effect sizes ($\eta^2 = .272$). No other significant associations were found for JOP Math and learning ($W = 2.72$, $p = .257$). No significant findings for JOP programming and learning ($W = .283$, $p = .243$).

H4: Perceived ease of task will result in more enjoyment in programming, Mathematics and robot interaction.

To test the hypothesis that perceived difficulty will influence how fun the task is perceived (**H4**), a regression analysis was performed. Fun scores were entered as dependent variables while difficulty scores and the JOP calibrations were entered as independent variables. A significant relationship for JOP Robots accuracy scores ($\beta = .317$, $t = 1.41$, $p = .179$) and difficulty ($\beta = -.422$, $t = -1.88$, $p = .081$) could predict ($F = 3.04$, $R^2 = .303$, $p = .040$ (1-tailed) how much fun the students reported.

JOP math ($\beta = .689$, $t = 3.51$, $p = .003$) and difficulty ($\beta = -.277$, $t = -1.16$, $p = .266$) could predict enjoyment with math ($F = 6.34$ $R^2 = .475$, $p = .011$).

Due to the omission of the item measuring difficulty for programming, the regression analysis for fun with programming could not be computed.

H5: There will be an association of self-assessment of perceived performance between Mathematic, robot interaction and Programming.

To test the association between maths, programming and robotic interaction (**H5**), correlational analysis showed that JOP robotic interaction was only associated with JOP programming ($\rho_s = .582$, $p < .01$) partially supporting the hypothesis. No association was found between JOP Math and JOP Robotics ($\rho_s = .176$, $p > .05$) JOP robotics and JOP Programming ($\rho_s = .153$, $p > .05$), and JOP Math and JOP Programming ($\rho_s = -.187$, $p > .05$).

6 Discussion

The following discussion of the results focuses on the hypotheses as shown in Fig. 1.

H_1: The more accurate the self-assessment of perceived performance (JOP) the greater the level of, enjoyment, in Programming, Mathematics and robot interaction.

To test the accuracy of student metacognitive judgements on their learning, enjoyment and difficulties ($\mathbf{H_1}$) in a humanoid-robot interaction learning task. Results show that students who reported higher levels of estimation (JOP) in Maths and programming enjoyed the tasks more with medium to large effect sizes ($\rho_s = .454-.745$). Both accurate self-assessment and under-estimator groups had more fun in maths and programming tasks. While not significant, large effect sizes for fun ($\eta^2 = .272$) were also found in JOP Robot group. To the best of the author's knowledge, research has not been conducted to identify the association between accurate self-assessment and enjoyment in tasks related with mathematics, programming and robots therefore future studies would need to further investigate how JOP calibration for mathematics, programming and robot tasks can predict enjoyment of the task. Of the three tasks, the teacher led tasks (math and programming) were deemed more fun by all students. This may be due to access to direct feedback from the teachers, whereas in the robot condition, the students had to provide their own self-assessment. This may be for the following reasons. The students in this study were young (grade 6) and their ages ranged from 10–12. Age has been identified as a moderator for the quality of metacognitive judgements [57]. Also, the math and programming task conditions were teacher led, and the teachers may have provided feedback that helped the students assess their performance as identified by Sadler [58] or students may have lacked the self-regulatory skills to self-assess [59]. This may explain why metacognitive judgements were not significant in the novel robot interaction situation. This may be due to the disruptive nature of learning novel skills as reported by [60].

H_2: The more accurate the self-assessment of perceived performance (JOP) the greater the level of, difficulty in Programming, Mathematics and robot interaction.

Although this study did not show any differences between the underestimation and accurate estimation groups nor did any findings emerge between the groups on the difficulty of tasks in maths, robot, programming. Studies have reported more accurate calibration and higher self-efficacy beliefs with easier math problems than with more difficult ones [26] and decrease in student's self-efficacy beliefs and calibration accuracy (and increase their calibration bias) as the math items become more difficult [27]. More studies need to be conducted to identify association between student's calibration accuracy and mathematics, programming and robot related task difficulty.

H3: The more accurate the self-assessment of perceived performance (JOP) the greater the level of learning in general.

Moore and Healy [18] along with Rachmatullah and Ha [30] identified that under- and overestimation of one's skills can have detrimental effects on performance. When the students were divided into groups based on their estimation calibration (JOP) - underestimation, accurate, overestimation [6] - accuracy in their metacognitive judgements could significantly predict 50.4% of the how well they did on the math task. However, both underestimation (Cohen's d = 2.17) and accurate (Cohen's d = 1.94) metacognitive judgements outperformed the overestimation group. Higher ratings (overconfidence in JOP) in math reported less learning. These results contradict previous findings by Dupeyrat, Escribe [32] in which students who overestimated their math competence had significantly higher performance than those who underestimated their performance. In addition, their performance did not differ significantly from those who accurately predicted their math competence. Lee [21] revealed that students' overestimation of maths competence positively predicted their maths achievement. However, another study by Hardy [33] established that accurate mathematical self-efficacy beliefs were better predictors of performance than overconfident self-efficacy beliefs. Accurate self-reflection is important to students' success in maths [61].

Similar findings emerged when the students' accuracy of performance (JOP) for programming also produced large effects for the underestimation (Cohen's d = 1.95) and accurate group (Cohen's d = 1.72). Higher ratings (overconfidence in JOP) in robot skills also reported less learning. These results are in line with the findings from Klayman, Soll [29] and Moore and Healy [18] where accurate estimation led to optimal performance, underestimation may have led to mis performance, and overestimation had the worst outcomes of performance. Similarly, Alaoutinen and Smolander [37] and Harrington, Peng [35] found in their studies related with programming and computer science respectively that student's accurate self-assessment resulted in optimal performance in exams. This is also supported by Durak, Yilmaz [45] who stated that perception of learning tasks as difficult and complex may be regarded as an advantage and supportive process for the students in terms of learning during robotic coding.

H4: Perceived ease of task will result in more enjoyment in programming, Mathematics and robot interaction.

This study also investigated the difficulty of the tasks on how the students enjoyed the different conditions. Research has identified that task difficulty can influence perceptions of performance [18, 29]. JOP calibrations for math ($\beta = .689$) and lower perceived difficulty ($\beta = -.277$) predicted 47.5% of enjoyment of the math task. This is in line with Brown, Brown [38] who also reported that perceived difficulty in mathematics resulted in less enjoyment. Likewise, JOP calibrations for robot interaction ($\beta = .317$) and lower perceived difficulty ($\beta = -.422$) could predict 30.3% of the enjoyment of the robot tasks, supporting the hypothesis.

H5: There will be an association of self-assessment of perceived performance between Mathematic, robot interaction and Programming.

Previous studies have shown relationships between maths, programming and robotic interaction. This study investigated to see if the same associations arose in our sample. Contrary to previous findings [51], this study found that robotic interaction was only related to programming skills and not math. These findings may be due to more metacognitive factors [54] that are more domain general (critical thinking, self-regulation). However, not only programming skills but also STEM knowledge, in particular in mathematics and computer science, are necessary for robotics [46]. Additionally, logical-mathematical skills are essential for programming education and the reverse is also true i.e. learning programming develops logical-mathematical skills [50]. Multiple studies [52–54] demonstrated a significant correlation between the students' performance in the programming and mathematics.

7   Conclusion

The aim of this article has been to investigate the experiences of students in mathematics, programming and working with robots by exploring the student's self-assessment of perceived performance (JOP), motivation (fun and difficulty) and learning. Key findings of this pilot study reveal that the more accurate the self-assessment a student has the greater the level of enjoyment in mathematics and programming. In addition, those who accurately self-assess or under-assess their ability report more learning in both mathematics and programming. The perceived ease of task also increases the enjoyment that students have in doing the mathematics and tasks with robots. Finally, those who report high perceived performance in programming also had high perceived performance in tasks with robots.

These results therefore highlight the importance of metacognition in SLEs. As educators we need to facilitate the students in the development of their own self-assessment skills by giving them opportunities to retrospectively evaluate the effectiveness of their learning (Yeung & Summerfield, 2012). In the case of human robotic interaction, it is clear that confident self-assessment of their programming skills is beneficial and therefore helping students to develop their programming skills will be beneficial to working with robots. These findings also highlight the importance of setting tasks that are on appropriate level of difficulty for the individual student. If the tasks are perceived by the student as too difficult the enjoyment will be lower. By adopting a metacognitive approach to learning with humanoid robots, students will not only be better prepared for a future with robots, but in addition, they will become more skilled at both mathematics and programming, which are necessary for ongoing digital revolution and the ever-increasing development of new technology.

The findings of this study need to be taken with scrutiny. The low number of participants may affect the results both positively and negatively. Small samples can either inflate statistical findings (Type I errors) or not find associations due to low power (Type II errors). The dependent variables were produced and novel for this study and have not been otherwise validated. While showing acceptable reliability scores, they, as the independent variables used in this study, are self-reported and not objective learning outcomes. Students worked in groups; thus they may have experienced frustration in working with other students that can have influenced their perceptions. Future studies would need to validate outcome variables, with individual tasks with higher number of participants to achieve better statistical analysis. In addition, further investigation into the qualitative experiences of the students and teachers involved in the human robot interaction would contribute to a more wholistic understanding of these experiences.

Disclosure of Potential Conflicts of Interest.   The authors have no competing interests to declare that are relevant to the content of this article.

References

1. Crompton, H., Gregory, K., Burke, D.: Humanoid robots supporting children's learning in an early childhood setting. Br. J. Edu. Technol. **49**(5), 911–927 (2018)

2. Meichenbaum, D.: Teaching thinking: a cognitive-behavioral perspective. Thinking Learn. Skills **2**, 407–426 (1985)
3. Flavell, J.H.: Metacognition and cognitive monitoring: a new area of cognitive–developmental inquiry. Am. Psychol. **34**(10), 906 (1979)
4. Efklides, A.: Metacognition: Defining its facets and levels of functioning in relation to self-regulation and co-regulation. Eur. Psychol. **13**(4), 277–287 (2008)
5. Schripsema, N.R., et al.: Impact of vocational interests, previous academic experience, gender and age on situational judgement test performance. Adv. Health Sci. Educ. **22**(2), 521–532 (2017)
6. Boud, D., Lawson, R., Thompson, D.G.: The calibration of student judgement through self-assessment: disruptive effects of assessment patterns. High. Educ. Res. Dev. **34**(1), 45–59 (2015)
7. Yeung, N., Summerfield, C.: Metacognition in human decision-making: confidence and error monitoring. Philos. Trans. Roy. Soc. B: Biol. Sci. **367**(1594), 1310–1321 (2012)
8. Balogh, R. Educational robotic platform based on arduino. in Proceedings of the 1st international conference on Robotics in Education, RiE2010. FEI STU, Slovakia. 2010
9. Powers, K., et al. Tools for teaching introductory programming: what works? In: Proceedings of the 37th SIGCSE Technical Symposium on Computer Science Education (2006)
10. Leite, I., et al.: Modelling empathic behaviour in a robotic game companion for children: an ethnographic study in real-world settings. In: Proceedings of the Seventh Annual ACM/IEEE International Conference on Human-Robot Interaction (2012)
11. Newton, D.P., Newton, L.D.: Humanoid robots as teachers and a proposed code of practice. in Frontiers in Education. Frontiers (2019)
12. Pandey, A.K., Gelin, R.: Humanoid robots in education: a short review. In: Goswami, A. Vadakkepat, P. (eds.) Humanoid Robotics: A Reference, pp. 2617–2632. Springer, Dordrecht (2017). /https://doi.org/10.1007/978-94-007-6046-2_113
13. Belpaeme, T., et al.: Social robots for education: a review. Sci. Robot. **3**(21), eaat5954 (2018)
14. Lehmann, H., Rossi, P.G.: Social robots in educational contexts: developing an application in enactive didactics. J. e-Learning Knowl. Soc. **15**(2) (2019)
15. Kazakoff, E.R., Sullivan, A., Bers, M.U.: The effect of a classroom-based intensive robotics and programming workshop on sequencing ability in early childhood. Early Childhood Educ. J. **41**(4), 245–255 (2013)
16. Ros, R., Baroni, I., Demiris, Y.: Adaptive human–robot interaction in sensorimotor task instruction: from human to robot dance tutors. Robot. Auton. Syst. **62**(6), 707–720 (2014)
17. Rhodes, M.G., Tauber, S.K.: The influence of delaying judgments of learning on metacognitive accuracy: a meta-analytic review. Psychol. Bull. **137**(1), 131 (2011)
18. Moore, D.A., Healy, P.J.: The trouble with overconfidence. Psychol. Rev. **115**(2), 502 (2008)
19. Pajares, F., Graham, L.: Self-efficacy, motivation constructs, and mathematics performance of entering middle school students. Contemp. Educ. Psychol. **24**(2), 124–139 (1999)
20. Zhang, C.: An Inquiry into Student Math Self-Efficacy, As Told from the Perspective of Ontario Secondary Teachers (2017)
21. Lee, E.J.: Biased self-estimation of maths competence and subsequent motivation and achievement: differential effects for high-and low-achieving students. Educ. Psychol. 1–21 (2020)
22. Kanaparan, G.: Self-efficacy and engagement as predictors of student programming performance: an international perspective (2016)
23. Kong, S.-C., Chiu, M.M., Lai, M.: A study of primary school students' interest, collaboration attitude, and programming empowerment in computational thinking education. Comput. Educ. **127**, 178–189 (2018)
24. Master, A., et al.: Programming experience promotes higher STEM motivation among first-grade girls. J. Exp. Child Psychol. **160**, 92–106 (2017)

25. Shim, J., Kwon, D., Lee, W.: The effects of a robot game environment on computer programming education for elementary school students. IEEE Trans. Educ. **60**(2), 164–172 (2016)
26. Chen, P.: Exploring the accuracy and predictability of the self-efficacy beliefs of seventh-grade mathematics students. Learn. Individ. Differ. **14**(1), 77–90 (2003)
27. Chen, P., Zimmerman, B.: A cross-national comparison study on the accuracy of self-efficacy beliefs of middle-school mathematics students. J. Exp. Educ. **75**(3), 221–244 (2007)
28. Moore, D.A., Cain, D.M.: Overconfidence and underconfidence: when and why people underestimate (and overestimate) the competition. Organ. Behav. Hum. Decis. Process. **103**(2), 197–213 (2007)
29. Klayman, J., et al.: Overconfidence: it depends on how, what, and whom you ask. Organ. Behav. Hum. Decis. Process. **79**(3), 216–247 (1999)
30. Rachmatullah, A., Ha, M.: Examining high-school students' overconfidence bias in biology exam: a focus on the effects of country and gender. Int. J. Sci. Educ. **41**(5), 652–673 (2019)
31. Hosein, A., Harle, J.: The relationship between students' prior mathematical attainment, knowledge and confidence on their self-assessment accuracy. Stud. Educ. Eval. **56**, 32–41 (2018)
32. Dupeyrat, C., et al.: Positive biases in self-assessment of mathematics competence, achievement goals, and mathematics performance. Int. J. Educ. Res. **50**(4), 241–250 (2011)
33. Hardy, E.: Fostering accurate self-efficacy beliefs in middle school mathematics students. Evergreen State College (2013)
34. Rachmatullah, A., Mayhorn, C.B., Wiebe, E.N.: The effects of prior experience and gender on middle school students' computer science learning and monitoring accuracy in the Use-Modify-Create progression. Learn. Individ. Differ. **86**, 101983 (2021)
35. Harrington, B., et al.: Gender, confidence, and mark prediction in CS examinations. In: Proceedings of the 23rd Annual ACM Conference on Innovation and Technology in Computer Science Education (2018)
36. Mishra, D., Ostrovska, S., Hacaloglu, T.: Assessing team work in engineering projects. Int. J. Eng. Educ. **31**(2), 627–634 (2015)
37. Alaoutinen, S., Smolander, K.: Student self-assessment in a programming course using bloom's revised taxonomy. In: Proceedings of the fifteenth annual conference on Innovation and technology in computer science education. 2010
38. Brown, M., Brown, P., Bibby, T.: "I would rather die": reasons given by 16-year-olds for not continuing their study of mathematics. Res. Math. Educ. **10**(1), 3–18 (2008)
39. Jenkins, T.: On the difficulty of learning to program. In: Proceedings of the 3rd Annual Conference of the LTSN Centre for Information and Computer Sciences. Citeseer (2002)
40. Giannakos, M.N., Jaccheri, L.: What motivates children to become creators of digital enriched artifacts? In: Proceedings of the 9th ACM Conference on Creativity & Cognition (2013)
41. Papavlasopoulou, S., Sharma, K., Giannakos, M.N.: How do you feel about learning to code? Investigating the effect of children's attitudes towards coding using eye-tracking. Int. J. Child-Comput. Int. **17**, 50–60 (2018)
42. Qiu, K., et al.: A curriculum for teaching computer science through computational textiles. In: Proceedings of the 12th International Conference on Interaction Design and Children (2013)
43. Searle, K.A., et al.: Diversifying high school students' views about computing with electronic textiles. In: Proceedings of the Tenth Annual Conference on International Computing Education Research (2014)
44. Hinckle, M., et al.: The relationship of gender, experiential, and psychological factors to achievement in computer science. In: Proceedings of the 2020 ACM Conference on Innovation and Technology in Computer Science Education (2020)

45. Durak, H.Y., Yilmaz, F.G.K., Yilmaz, R.: Computational thinking, programming self-efficacy, problem solving and experiences in the programming process conducted with robotic activities. Contemp. Educ. Technol. **10**(2), 173–197 (2019)
46. Kaloti-Hallak, F., Armoni, M., Ben-Ari, M.: Students' attitudes and motivation during robotics activities. In: Proceedings of the Workshop in Primary and Secondary Computing Education (2015)
47. Aparicio, J.T., et al.: Learning programming using educational robotics. In: 2019 14th Iberian Conference on Information Systems and Technologies (CISTI). IEEE (2019)
48. Ohnishi, Y., et al.: Robotics programming learning for elementary and junior high school students. J. Robot. Mechatron. **29**(6), 992–998 (2017)
49. Fabros-Tyler, G.: English, Mathematics, and Programming grades in the secondary level as predictors of academic performance in the college level. In: IISA 2014, The 5th International Conference on Information, Intelligence, Systems and Applications. IEEE (2014)
50. Korkmaz, Ö.: The effect of scratch-and lego mindstorms Ev3-based programming activities on academic achievement, problem-solving skills and logical-mathematical thinking skills of students. MOJES: Malaysian Online J. Educ. Sci. **4**(3), 73–88 (2018)
51. White, G., Sivitanides, M.: An empirical investigation of the relationship between success in mathematics and visual programming courses. J. Inf. Syst. Educ. **14**(4), 409 (2003)
52. Balmes, I.L.: Correlation of mathematical ability and programming ability of the computer science students. Asia Pacific J. Educ. Arts Sci. **4**(3), 85–88 (2017)
53. de Souza, L.M., et al.: Mathematics and programming: marriage or divorce? In: 2019 IEEE World Conference on Engineering Education (EDUNINE). IEEE (2019)
54. Erdogan, Y., Aydin, E., Kabaca, T.: Exploring the psychological predictors of programming achievement. J. Inst. Psychol. **35**(3) (2008)
55. Qahmash, A., Joy, M., Boddison, A.: To what extent mathematics correlates with programming: statistical analysis. In: International Conference on Computer Science Education Innovation & Technology (CSEIT). Proceedings. 2015. Global Science and Technology Forum (2015)
56. Bergin, S., Reilly, R.: Programming: factors that influence success. In: Proceedings of the 36th SIGCSE Technical Symposium on Computer Science Education (2005)
57. Bellon, E., Fias, W., De Smedt, B.: Metacognition across domains: Is the association between arithmetic and metacognitive monitoring domain-specific? PLoS ONE **15**(3), e0229932 (2020)
58. Sadler, D.R.: Formative assessment and the design of instructional systems. Instr. Sci. **18**(2), 119–144 (1989)
59. Zimmerman, B.J., Schunk, D.H.: Handbook of self-regulation of learning and performance. Routledge/Taylor & Francis Group. (2011)
60. Boud, D., Molloy, E.: Rethinking models of feedback for learning: the challenge of design. Assess. Eval. High. Educ. **38**(6), 698–712 (2013)
61. Ramdass, D., Zimmerman, B.J.: Effects of self-correction strategy training on middle school students' self-efficacy, self-evaluation, and mathematics division learning. J. Adv. Acad. **20**(1), 18–41 (2008)

Children's Indiscriminate Helping Behavior Toward the Robot Dog: Can Voice Influence It?

Yi Pang[✉] [iD], Qianxi Jia[iD], and Jiaxin Lee[iD]

Central China Normal University, Wuhan 430070, Hubei, People's Republic of China
{pangyi,qianxijia,jiaxinlee}@mails.ccnu.edu.cn

Abstract. In humans and robots' vast and complex interaction mechanism, children's study of prosocial behavior toward robots is a unique and humanized perspective. Many studies have confirmed that children can extend their helping behavior from humans to social robots. Meanwhile, the robots' different characteristics and expressions are the essential factors affecting children showing their helping behavior to the robots. This study aims to investigate whether the robot dog's "grievance" voice can affect the performance of children's altruistic behavior when it can't come out from a cage itself. Forty-four 4-year-old children were randomly assigned the two conditions, and the results showed that the presence or absence of aggressive voices does have an impact on the display of helping behaviors in young children. The findings can provide meaningful advice to parents and workers in the field of preschool.

Keywords: Robot dog · Prosocial behavior · Instrumental helping · Child-robot interaction

1 Introduction

Technological devices fill our world now, such as the phone, the internet and even the social robot. Robots as a vital result of the development of modern technology are permeating our usual lives [1]. Robots can play important roles in our society, the main roles are as tutors, companions and learners [2]. For example, in the classroom, educational robots can teach students science [3], languages [4] and mathematics [5]. In a sense, robot teachers can even replace human teachers to teach students. In general, a social robot is an autonomous agent that can act in a socially appropriate manner based on its role in an interaction [6, 7]. Social robots are an important branch of robotics. There are several different definitions of social bots. One definition is that a social robot is an autonomous or semi-autonomous robot that can interact and communicate with humans based on the machine's calculations and norms that are consistent with human social expectations [8]. Social robots are an important party to human-computer interaction, and they are seen as one of the technologies of the future with the potential for development. Therefore, it is an irreversible trend in the Internet era to study the mechanisms and laws of human-robot communication and interaction, which will be of great value to our proper understanding and use of social robots for the convenience of life, the development of education, and the growth of students.

M. Kurosu and A. Hashizume (Eds.): HCII 2023, LNCS 14012, pp. 101–111, 2023.
https://doi.org/10.1007/978-3-031-35599-8_7

Robot toys are the most likely future applications of social robots in the future [9]. As the most common and everyday form of pet that children have access to, robot dogs have many characteristics that influence young children's perceptions of them. Robot dogs' welcoming appearance (soundscape, aesthetics and gentle movement) can attract children [10]. Meanwhile, sound and movement were chosen as the main interaction modalities between the robot and the children. This combination was considered one of the most efficient non-verbal multimodal communication for non-anthropomorphic robots [11]. Voice can reflect emotions through its nonverbal voice features that can either strengthen or lessen the feeling of empathy [12]. Empathy is the ability of an individual to detect and indirectly experience the emotions of others. Children will have an innate nature to help humans in need [23], Even children who are learning to walk can help adults in need by helping to remove barriers. Even though there will be no reward or requirement for this behavior. This act of helping is motivated by some concern for others, not by a desire to gain personal fame or recognition from others [13, 32]. This nature has been shown to occur with robots. Therefore, we chose the combination of the robot dog's movements and sounds to investigate whether the children's pro-social behavior towards it would be due to empathy.

In humans and robots' vast and complex interaction mechanism, children's study of prosocial behavior toward robots is a unique and humanized perspective. Pro-social behavior is defined as a valuable behavior that may not be rewarding to the person initiating the help, but helps those who are still "watching" the behavior by facilitating the development of their psychological mechanisms. Prosocial behavior includes instrumental helping behavior, sharing, comforting and cooperative behaviors. The study and development of pro-social behavior is an important topic in the field of psychology. For children, the level of development of pro-social behavior can predict their future social adjustment and even academic status [14, 15]. From a sociological point of view, pro-social behavior plays a key role in maintaining the stability of human society [16]. Pro-social behavior is related to many individual and social factors. An active understanding of these factors will help us to provide a more complete and comprehensive understanding, promote the development of pro-social behavior in children and provide a good foundation for their development throughout life [17]. Children initiate pro-social behavior in three main steps. The first step is for children to first become aware that the other person is caught in a difficult situation and that they can confront the other person's cues of need. In the second step, children can engage in appropriate behaviors to alleviate the other person's difficult situation. In the third step, the child is motivated to behave in a way that gives them an internal incentive to help others [18]. Then, a small branch of pro-social behavior was selected for this study, namely, to explore the factors that influence children's helping behavior. According to the three steps of pro-social behavior in children, when a child wants to help another individual, he or she must first understand that the other individual is in a difficult situation, must know what appropriate behavior he or she should do and must have the motivation to do so, at which point the child's altruistic helping behavior occurs. Many past studies have explored the mechanisms, developmental history, and factors influencing children's helping behaviors. Infants around 18 months of age can help with most tasks in set situations. Most infants help with at least one task. Of course, infants will not help if the adult shows no intention of reaching the task at all [19]. A 2006 study showed that infants between 12 and 18 months of age are able to help others not only by helping them accomplish something but also by providing information. For example, if an adult inadvertently drops an object and starts looking for it, the infant finds it and points to it, directing the adult's attention [20]. Further, what factors influence young children's helping behaviors? Previous experiments have shown that a number of socially motivated factors can influence young children's helping behavior, such as adult gaze; verbal or material rewards can influence young children's motivation for instrumental helping behavior; and past experiences of the helper, as well as the characteristics of person in need of help themselves can have an impact on helping behavior [21–23].

Studies have shown that children's altruistic helping behavior does extend to social robots [24]. That is, children's empathic responses to human demanders also occur with inanimate entities (e.g., robots). Children's empathic mechanisms for robots are actually very similar to those of humans. Young children are able to apply their animistic thoughts to robots [25]; children around the age of 10 develop empathy for robots that display similar negative emotions [26]; and children around the age of 11–13 interpret robots that display specific body postures as them displaying a specific emotional state [27]. These findings suggest that children can indeed respond accordingly to certain characteristics emitted by robots. Further, children are not just able to be helped by robots based on the social cues they provide. One experiment showed that children recognize that non-human agents deserve help when they need it. When the barrier blocked the drug, infants would be more likely to help the drug cross the barrier than when the barrier did not block the drug. Although the help rate in this experiment was lower than for humans overall, these results suggest that children perceive that nonhuman agents are needed and available for their help [28, 29]. Different characteristics and expressions of robots are essential factors affecting children to show their helping behavior to robots [25]. Different robotic appearance features influence children's acceptance of them. For example, a 2016 study comparing children's acceptance of three different robots with different appearances (Sphero-like spheres, Romo with an active face and ChiCaRo with a robot that transmits live images and has hand-like features) found that children's acceptance of Sphero was significantly higher and acceptance of Romo was significantly lower [30]. Normal children prefer to interact with robots with animal-like or mixed human-machine features, and robots with such features are perceived as "friendly and kind" by children. Robots with "two legs, a rectangular body and strong facial features" were perceived as "negative and bossy" by children, so their desire to interact was low [31]. Among them, whether it has a certain degree of anthropomorphic appearance and verbal and nonverbal communication is crucial. A robot needs to have some facial and physical characteristics to enable positive human interaction (this does not mean that the more human-like it is, the better; for example, a robot suitable for "security" work would look more machine-like). It is also critical that the robot has good emotional expression, such as making a "cry" like sound, which will elicit the same emotional mechanisms that humans use to raise human babies [32].

Past research has addressed children's pro-social behavior toward robots, but not many studies have focused on robotic pets. Therefore, our current study selected a robot dog as our experimental material to test the question: does its making/not making aggressive noises when the robot dog is stuck in a difficult situation affect children's unconditional helping behavior toward them? We selected 4-year-old children and showed them a robot dog that was locked in a dog cage and wanted to get out but could not get out by itself. Our experimental hypothesis was that the robot dog making a grievance voice would cause children to help it more and faster than if it did not make aggressive noises. Considering the desire for a more comprehensive understanding of children's perceptions of the robot dog, we also designed an animacy interview, a helper's reason interview, and other open-ended questions (e.g., would you like to have a dog).

2 Method

2.1 Participants

Forty-four children (14 boys) aged 4 years old ($M = 62.32$, $SD = 3.72$) were recruited from a kindergarten in Eastern China. All of the children are ethnically Chinese. They were randomly assigned to the experimental and control groups. Two children were excluded because procedural error ($n = 2$). Finally, data from 42 children (29.4% boys and 70.6% girls) were included in the analysis.

2.2 Materials

About 30 cm long "Ke wang" robot dog and a cage will be used as our primary experimental materials. Its body is composed of simple black and white colors, and it can make simple movements, make different expressions and make specified sounds. Most importantly, it can perform different behaviors and voices according to the experimenter's different orders. The robot dog has a "grievance" mode, when turning it on, the robot dog can express the voice like crying. In addition to a robot dog, we also need a cage, a laboratory room and video equipment that can record the experimental process.

2.3 Design

This study used a single-factor two-level (grievance voice: with vs. without) between-subjects design. Forty-four children were randomly assigned to the experimental and control groups. The whole experiment included three stages: the pre-test phase, the test phase and the interview phase. In the pre-test phase, our main purpose was to set up the site for the experiment, as well as to have some interaction between the main test and the children to ensure that the children were in a more normal and relaxed state when conducting this experiment. In the test phase, we randomly assigned children to the experimental and control groups and recorded the whole process to facilitate later coding and data analysis. This experiment included two conditions: grievance voice condition ($n = 22$) and without grievance voice ($n = 22$). In the interview phase, we will conduct about 5 min of interviews with each child, mainly encapsulating the vitality interview and the help cause interview.

2.4 Procedure

We adopted the research of Martin et al., whose study used a social robot to test whether children's instrumental helpfulness crosses the human-robot divide. Testing included the pre-test phase, test phase and interview phase.

Pre-test phase: in the laboratory room, E2 put the robot dog in the cage and put the cage on a table. Then, E1 brought every child into this room, in order to prevent the children cannot notice the robot dog in time, E1 reminded every children "Look, what's that on the table? Please sit down in front of this table."

Test-phase: The experimental and control condition (see Table 1 and Fig. 1) are based on the procedure used in Martin's (2020) study. In both conditions, the robot dog attempted to go out from the cage in the first 10s. In the second 10s, the experimental condition's dog expressed its grievance voice, while the control condition's keep silent and just aimed to go out. When the child touched the cage, tried to open the door, took out the robot dog, or asked E1 for help (or made an attempt to do any of the above), we judged that the child has shown helping behavior.

Table 1. The Robot dog's behaviors in a trial

Time	Experimental Condition	Control Condition
Onset	Be locked in a cage and put on the table	Be locked in a cage and put on the table
1−10 s	Try out unsuccessfully	Try out unsuccessfully
11−20 s	Enter grievance mode and make a whimpering sound	Keep quiet for 10s
20 s	Turning off the mode indicates the end of the trial	The end of the trial

Fig. 1. The robot dog's different voices in the Experimental condition (left) and Control condition (right).

Interview phase: when the test phase finished, E1 conducted a 5-min interview with each child. After an animacy interview, E1 asked every child why chose (or not) to help the robot dog. Each child was asked a total of nine questions concerning physiological, cognitive, and affective characteristics. The interview questions can be seen in Table 2.

Table 2. The interview outline

Interview category	Group	Question
Animacy interview	Every child	Do you think it is alive?
		Does it need water or food?
		Does it grow?
		Can it breathe?
		Can it think?
		Can it feel happy or unhappy?
Interviews on the reasons why children performed(or did not) helping behavior	When the children touched the cage	Why did you choose to touch the cage? How does it feel in the cage? Do you think it needs help?
	When the children didn't touch the cage	Why you didn't touch the cage? How does it feel in the cage? Do you think it needs help?

2.5 Video Coding

Helping behavior was coded as a dichotomous variable. When the child touches the cage, tries to open the door, takes out the robot dog, or asks E1 for help (or makes an attempt to do any of the above), we can judge that the child has shown helping behavior. We also recorded the latency to help, in this study, it is determined the duration from the start of the experiment to the child exhibited their helping behavior. Children's answers in the animacy interview were coded as yes or no.

3   Results

Our study aims to test if the robot dog's grievance voice can influence the children's helping behavior. The hypothesis is that the children would be more and faster willing to help the robot dog when it performs voice than it was not. We used SPSS Win 25.0 to analyze the data and evaluate the hypothesis. The methods we used were descriptive analysis and a chi-square test.

Firstly, 9 out of 21 children helped the robot dog in the experimental condition, however, only 3 of 21 children helped in the control condition. The variable "grievance voice" had a significant effect on the results ($X^2 = 4.20$, df $= 1$, p $< .05$), not the gender ($X^2 = 0.66$, df $= 1$, p $= .42$).

Further, latency to help was overall shorter in the experimental condition (M $= 13.11$s, SD $= 3.06$) than in the control condition (M $= 19.67$ s, SD $= 7.51$), it illustrated that children were faster to help the robot dog that in need in the experimental condition than in the control condition. But we didn't find a significant difference in this aspect (p $= .68$).

The range of scores of children's answers in the animacy interview is 0–6. When children answered all "no", he (or she) got 0, when answered all "yes", he (or she) got 6. Results showed relatively high average scores on the questions "Do you think it is alive?" and "Can it feel happy or unhappy?". Overall, children's average scores on physical and cognitive questions were lower compared to the psychological aspects (see Fig. 2).

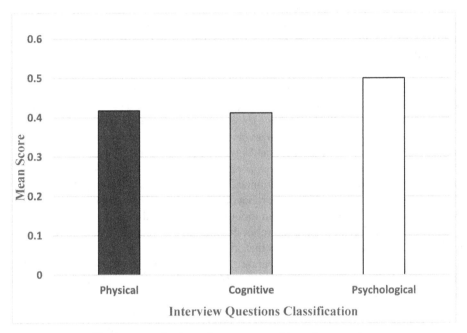

Fig. 2. Example chart of mean scores of interview questions

4 Discussion

The current study examined whether the robot dog's making or not making a grievance sound when it was stuck in a difficult situation had an effect on the children's helping behavior. The results showed that the presence or absence of grievance sounds did affect the demonstration of children's helping behavior, and the effect was significant. When the robot dog made a grievance sound, it prompted the children to be more willing and quicker to help. Conversely, when the robot dog did not make any sound, only a small percentage of children were willing to show their helping behavior. The current study is linked to a previous study [25], which explored children's undifferentiated helping behaviors towards social robots, and this study focused the scope of the inquiry on the robot dog.

Many previous studies have shown that young children reach a certain age and develop a tendency to actively help each other in difficult situations [22]. An important prerequisite for young children to be able to engage in helping behavior is their ability to understand the other person's goal of helping, and, what kind of help the other person needs from them [19]. This cognitive ability of young children can be extended to robots [33] so that when a robot dog is put in a cage and fails to try to get out, young children can understand what the needs of the robot dog are at that moment and try to free the robot dog from the cage. In spite of being able to understand the other person's needs and know what action to take, their own willingness to help is also a key component [34]. Young children have a natural tendency to help both animate and inanimate entities [24, 25], and when we conducted unstructured interviews with each subject child, many of the children who provided helping behaviors reported that they touched the cage or wanted to open the cage door because they felt that the robot dog was in the cage and "wanted to get out", "unhappy" and "wanted my help". The present study again demonstrates that young children's empathic abilities can extend to inanimate entities. In addition, this study found that four-year-old children were able to demonstrate helping behaviors more often and quicker when the robot dog exhibited grievance sounds compared to when it did not. The vocal quality of a person's voice is often an accurate representation of his or her emotional state at the moment, and aggravated, whimpering sounds can reflect an individual's emotions of sadness, anxiety, or even anger at the moment. Also, the voice is an important part of a person's interaction with social robots [12]. The empathy of young children can indeed be extended to the robot dog, so we hypothesize that the "aggrieved" voice will serve as a guideline that can mobilize empathy and motivate young children to show helpful behavior toward the robot dog. Based on the analysis of the responses to the interview questions, it is clear that in the age group of 4–5 years, there is still a tendency for some children to be pantheistic about inanimate entities such as robot dogs, believing that robot dogs can drink/eat, breathe, grow, think, and feel happy or sad emotions just like humans. In particular, the mean interview scores for questions about psychological categories were significantly higher than those for physical and cognitive categories. We speculate that it may be that children around the age of 4 are not yet able to fully perceive that robotic dogs do not have psychological properties, and that they still pay more attention to psychological properties when judging whether robotic dogs are alive [35]. However, overall, the mean scores for the overall interview questions were relatively low ($M = 2.56$, mean score not reaching the one-half level), and some of the children were very adamant during the interview that "It is a fake dog", suggesting that some children around the age of 4 can already realize that the robot dog is an inanimate entity and that it does not have physical, cognitive, or psychological capabilities.

It is worth mentioning that when we asked the children "Do you want to have a dog", "Have you ever had a puppy", and "Have you ever been chased or bitten by a puppy", more than half of the children indicated that they wanted to have a "dog". When asked if they wanted a "real dog", more than half of the children indicated that they wanted a "real dog", but almost all of them had never had a puppy (when we asked the reason, almost all of them had lost the opportunity to get a puppy because their parents refused to get a dog). Even when children indicated that they had been chased by puppies or were afraid that they would bite them, they still indicated that "puppies are cute" and "I would like to have a puppy of my own". This may give educators and parents of young children some insight into how they can gain different feelings from human interaction by allowing them to have more contact with small animals while ensuring their personal safety.

Of course, there are still many shortcomings in this study. For example, when we asked the children why they did not show helping behaviors, some of them indicated that they "did not know how to help it" or "felt that it could knock the cage off by itself", which indicates that we need to consider the details of the experimental procedure more carefully. In addition, when asked about "any experience of being chased or bitten by a dog", one child indicated that he was very scared when being chased by a dog, despite our strict attention to the style and tone of the question, which may have brought back bad memories and experiences and was an important reminder for the follow-up interview. Finally, the proportion of male and female children among the subjects was randomized, which might have had some effect on the results.

This study provides important clues and inspiration for understanding young children's perceptions and interactions with robot pets, and some of the study's interesting findings provide important educational insights for parents and teachers of young children today. Future research can be but is not limited to look at other characteristics of the robot dog, such as its expressions and movements, to explore its interesting connections with young children's prosocial behavior.

Acknowledgments. We sincerely thank the children, teachers, and parents who supported and participated in this experiment.

References

1. National Robotics Initiative 2.0: Ubiquitous Collaborative Robots (NRI-2.0) (2017). https://www.nsf.gov/pubs/2017/nsf17518/nsf17518.htm. Accessed 8 Feb 2023
2. Chen, H., Park, H.W., Breazeal, C.: Teaching and learning with children: Impact of reciprocal peer learning with a social robot on children's learning and emotive engagement. Comput. Educ. **150**, 103836 (2020). https://doi.org/10.1016/j.compedu.2020.103836
3. Hashimoto, T., Kobayashi, H., Polishuk, A., Verner, I.: Elementary science lesson delivered by robot. In: Proceedings of the 8th ACM/IEEE International Conference on Human Robot Interaction, pp. 133–134. IEEE Press, Piscataway (2013). https://doi.org/10.1109/HRI.2013.6483537
4. Movellan, J., Eckhardt, M., Virnes, M., Rodriguez, A.: Sociable robot improves toddler vocabulary skills. In: Proceedings of the 4th ACM/IEEE International Conference on Human Robot Interaction, La Jolla, CA, pp. 307–308. IEEE Press (2009). https://doi.org/10.1145/1514095.1514189
5. Wei, C.-W., Hung, I.-C., Lee, L., Chen, N.-S.: A joyful classroom learning system with robot learning companion for children to learn mathematics multiplication. Turkish Online J. Educ. Technol. **10**, 11–23 (2011). https://doi.org/10.2753/RES1060-9393530406
6. Duffy, B.: Anthropomorphism and the social robot. Robot. Auton. Syst. 42(3), 177–190 (2003). https://doi.org/10.1016/S0921-8890(02)00374-3
7. Sarrica, M., Brondi, S., Fortunati, L.: How many facets does a "social robot" have? a review of scientific and popular definitions online. Inf. Technol. People **33**(1), 1–21 (2020). https://doi.org/10.1108/ITP-04-2018-0203

8. Bartneck, C., Nomura, T., Kanda, T., Suzuki, T., Kennsuke, K.: A cross-cultural study on attitudes towards robots. In: Salvendy, G. (ed.) Proceedings of the HCI International. Lawrence Erlbaum Associates, New Jersey (2005). https://doi.org/10.13140/RG.2.2.35929.11367

9. Druin, A.: The design of children's technology. Morgan Kaufmann Publishers Inc, Burlington (1998)

10. Ihamäki, P., Heljakka, K.: Social and emotional learning with a robot dog: Technology, empathy and playful learning in kindergarten. In: Proceedings of the 9th Annual Arts, Humanities, Social Sciences and Education Conference (2020)

11. Löffler, D., Schmidt, N., Tscharn, R.: Multimodal expression of artificial emotion in social robots using color, motion and sound. In: Proceedings of the 13th ACM/IEEE International Conference on Human-Robot Interaction (HRI), pp. 334–343. ACM, New York (2018). https://doi.org/10.1145/3171221.3171261

12. Kim, J., Kim, W., Nam, J., Song, H.: "I can feel your empathic voice": Effects of nonverbal vocal cues in voice user interface. In: Extended Abstracts of the 2020 CHI Conference on Human Factors in Computing Systems, pp. 1–8. ACM, New York (2020). https://doi.org/10.1145/3334480.3383075

13. Hepach, R., Haberl, K., Lambert, S., Tomasello, M.: Toddlers help anonymously. Infancy 22(1), 130–145 (2016). https://doi.org/10.1111/infa.12143

14. Caprara, G.V., Barbaranelli, C., Pastorelli, C., Bandura, A., Zimbardo, G.: Prosocial foundations of children's academic achievement. Psychol. Sci. 11, 302–306 (2000). https://doi.org/10.1111/1467-9280.00260

15. Crick, N.R.: The role of overt aggression, relational aggression, and prosocial behavior in the prediction of children's future social adjustment. Child Dev. 67, 2317–2327 (1996). https://doi.org/10.1111/j.1467-8624.1996.tb01859.x

16. Keesing, R., Strathern, A.: Cultural anthropology: a contemporary perspective. Harcourt Brace College Publishers, Fort Worth (1998). https://doi.org/10.2307/3317238

17. Hay, D.F.: Prosocial development. J. Child Psychol. Psychiatrie 35, 29–71 (1994). https://doi.org/10.1111/j.1469-7610.1994.tb01132.x

18. Dunfield, K.A., Kuhlmeier, V.: Classifying prosocial behavior: children's responses to instrumental need, emotional distress, and material desire. Child Dev. 84, 1766–1776 (2013). https://doi.org/10.1111/cdev.12075

19. Warneken, F., Tomasello, M.: Altruistic helping in human infants and young chimpanzees. Science 311, 1301–1303 (2006). https://doi.org/10.2307/3845841

20. Liszkowski, U., Carpenter, M., Striano, T., Tomasello, M.: Twelve- and 18-month-olds point to provide information for others. J. Cogn. Dev. 7, 173–187 (2006). https://doi.org/10.1207/s15327647jcd0702_2

21. Over, H., Carpenter, M.: Eighteen-month-old infants show increased helping following priming with affiliation. Psychol. Sci. 20, 1189–1193 (2008). https://doi.org/10.1111/j.1467-9280.2009.02419.x

22. Warneken, F., Tomasello, M.: Extrinsic rewards undermine altruistic tendencies in 20-month-olds. Dev. Psychol. 44(6), 1785–1788 (2008). https://doi.org/10.1037/a0013860

23. Vaish, A., Carpenter, M., Tomasello, M.: Young children selectively avoid helping people with harmful intentions. Child Dev. 81, 1661–1669 (2010). https://doi.org/10.1111/j.1467-8624.2010.01500.x

24. Beran, T.N., Ramirez-Serrano, A., Kuzyk, R., Nugent, S., Fior, M.: Would children help a robot in need? Int. J. Soc. Robot. 3(1), 83–93 (2011). https://doi.org/10.1007/s12369-010-0074-7

25. Martin, D.U., MacIntyre, M.I., Perry, C., Clift, G., Pedell, S., Kaufman, J.: Young children's indiscriminate helping behavior toward a humanoid robot. Front. Psychol. 11, 239 (2020). https://doi.org/10.3389/fpsyg.2020.00239

26. Kim, E.H., Kwak, S.S., Kwak, Y.K.: Can robotic emotional expressions induce a human to empathize with a robot? In: 18th IEEE International Symposium on Robot and Human Interactive Communication (RO-MAN 2009), pp. 358–362. IEEE Press, Piscataway (2009). https://doi.org/10.1109/ROMAN.2009.5326282

27. Beck, A., et al.: Interpretation of emotional body language displayed by a humanoid robot: a case study with children. Int. J. Soc. Robot. 5(3), 325–334 (2013). https://doi.org/10.1007/s12369-013-0193-z

28. Kühnlenz, B., Sosnowski, S., Buß, M., Wollherr, D., Kühnlenz, K., Buss, M.: Increasing Helpfulness towards a Robot by Emotional Adaption to the User. Int. J. Soc. Robot. 5(4), 457–476 (2013). https://doi.org/10.1007/s12369-013-0182-2

29. Hamlin, J.K.: The case for social evaluation in preverbal infants: Gazing toward one's goal drives infants' preferences for helpers over hinderers in the hill paradigm. Front. Psychol. 5(1563), 1–9 (2015). https://doi.org/10.3389/fpsyg.2014.01563

30. Shiomi, M., Abe, K., Pei, Y., Ikeda, N., Nagai, T.: "I'm Scared" Little children reject robots. In: Proceedings of the 4th International Conference on Human Agent Interaction, pp. 245–247. ACM, New York (2016). https://doi.org/10.1145/2974804.2980493

31. Woods, S., Dautenhahn, K., Schulz, J.: The design space of robots: investigating children's views. In: RO-MAN 2004. Proceeding of the 13th IEEE International Workshop on Robot and Human Interactive Communication, pp. 47–52. IEEE Press, Piscataway (2004). https://doi.org/10.1109/ROMAN.2004.1374728

32. Breazeal, C.: Emotion and sociable humanoid robots. Int. J. Hum. Comput. Stud. 59, 119–155 (2003). https://doi.org/10.1016/S1071-5819(03)00018-1

33. Itakura, S., Ishida, H., Kanda, T., Shimada, Y., Ishiguro, H., Lee, K.: How to build an intentional android: Infants' imitation of a robot's goal-directed actions. Infancy 13(5), 519–532 (2008). https://doi.org/10.1080/15250000802329503

34. Hepach, R., Vaish, A., Tomasello, M.: Young children are intrinsically motivated to see others helped. Psychol. Sci. 23(9), 967–972 (2012). https://doi.org/10.1177/0956797612440571

35. Kim, M., Yi, S., Lee, D.: Between living and nonliving: young children's animacy judgments and reasoning about humanoid robots. PLoS ONE 14(6), e0216869 (2019). https://doi.org/10.1371/journal.pone.0216869

Children's Toy Design Based on Multiple Intelligence Theory–Research Case of "Spatial Intelligence Children's Toy Design"

Xiaoyang Qian[1], Yixuan Li[1], Lei Xue[1(✉)] [ORCID], and Mohammad Shidujaman[2] [ORCID]

[1] School of Art and Design, Beijing Forestry University, Beijing, China
xue10222@bjfu.edu.cn
[2] Department of Computer Science and Engineering, Independent University, Dhaka, Bangladesh
Shantothusets@iub.edu.bd

Abstract. Learning by playing is a learning goal for future talent training. It is a learning method that optimizes the learning process through game elements as the main carrier of the concept of "learning by playing", toys have a profound impact on the early stages of children's development. With the improvement of families' awareness of children's education, society has put forward higher requirements for children's educational resources, comprehensive development, and intelligent exercise. Based on the theory of multiple intelligences, combined with Piaget's theory of children's cognitive development, FBS design model and emotional design, and comprehensive user research results, this research aims to improve children's multiple intelligences, and proposes a RBFES (requirement- behavior-function-emotion-structure) children's toy design model. In terms of design practice, through in-depth analysis of field research and user research data, combined with semi-structured interviews, questionnaires, observation methods and other methods, taking the design practice of spatial intelligent children's toys as an example, to demonstrate the design process and research ideas of RBFES, and design a spatial intelligent toy Product and supporting UI interface, and conducted a usability test to get feedback and future improvement direction. The research angle and the design model proposed in this paper can provide reference and guidance for the design of children's toys with multiple intelligences in the future.

Keywords: Multiple intelligence theory · FBS model · Emotional design · Learning by playing

1 Introduction

Play has a profound impact on the early stages of a child's development. Play can promote children's mental development [1], and even bring about neurophysiological changes, increasing the plasticity of the brain. Piaget pointed out that games are the most basic way of communication that occurs before language and art. Games are also a means for children to explore and understand the world [2]. The experience learners gain from these early developmental games can be transferred to later study and work; play is conducive to learners' participation in deep learning [3]. In today's world, technology continues to develop, and future careers, economic development, and social life are full of uncertainties. Learners need to acquire the skills, develop the mindset to face these uncertain challenges in the future, and continue to learn throughout their lives. The joyful and emotional experiences of play help learners face this uncertainty and realize their potential to become cooperative, creative, competent, and responsible citizens. Under the educational concepts of all-round human development, lifelong learning, and embodied cognition, [4] the educational value of "games" has been paid more and more attention, and people expect "games" to undertake the mission of education. Learning by playing is a learning goal for future talent training. It is a learning method that optimizes the learning process through game elements, and guides learners to use imagination and a playful attitude towards learning and practice, making learning more attractive, and toys as" The main carrier of the concept of learning through play has a profound impact on the early stages of children's development.

With the improvement of families' awareness of children's education, society has put forward higher requirements for children's educational resources, comprehensive development, and intellectual exercise. Based on the theory of multiple intelligences, this study combines Piaget's children's cognitive development theory, FBS design model and emotional design, and integrates the results of user research, with the purpose of improving children's multiple intelligences, and proposes a RBFES children's toy design based on multiple intelligences theory Model.

In terms of design practice, through in-depth analysis of field research and user research data, combined with semi-structured interviews, questionnaires, observation methods and other methods, taking the design practice of spatial intelligent children's toys as an example, to demonstrate the design process and research ideas of RBFES, and design a spatial intelligent toy Product and supporting UI interface, and conducted a usability test to get feedback and future improvement direction. The research angle and the design model proposed in this paper can provide reference and guidance for the design of children's toys with multiple intelligences in the future.

2   Overview of Multiple Intelligences Theory

The theory of multiple intelligences is a new concept of international education that has been popular all over the world since the mid-1980s [5]. It was published in 1983 by Howard Gardner: The Structure of Intelligence: The Theory of Multiple Intelligences (1983) was the first to systematically put forward the theory of human intelligence structure that was continuously developed and improved in subsequent research [6].

The definition and understanding of intelligence in multiple intelligence theory is different from the traditional view of intelligence. Intelligence is not a kind of ability but a group of abilities. Intelligence does not exist in an integrated way but exists in an independent way [7].

Since the connotation of this theory is closely related to the well-rounded education that our country is currently advocating and implementing, our country has introduced more about the theory of multiple intelligences since the 1990s and has increasingly recognized the important value of the theory of multiple intelligences. "The theory of multiple intelligences is the best interpretation of well-rounded education" [8] (Fig. 1).

Fig. 1. Multiple intelligence theory

Gardner believes that human beings have a total of eight kinds of intelligence. Linguistic Intelligence is manifested in thinking with words and expressing complex meanings in different ways of language and words; the prominent feature of Logical Mathematical Intelligence is to use logical methods to solve problems, and to use numbers and the ability to understand abstract patterns; the prominent features of Spatial Intelligence are the accurate perception of the visual world, the ability to think in three-dimensional space, and the ability to discern the connection between objects in the perceived space; the feature of Musical Intelligence is the ability to understand non-verbal sounds in the environment, including Sensitivity to rhythm, melody, rhythm, etc.; Bodily Kinesthetic Intelligence is reflected in the activities of object manipulation and motor skills; Interpersonal Intelligence is manifested in the individual's ability to perceive, experience, and respond to other people's emotions and emotions; the outstanding characteristics of Intrapersonal Intelligence sensitive to one's own feelings and emotions, aware of one's own strengths and weaknesses, and self-directed decision-making; Naturalist Intelligence manifests as thinking and ability to gain insight into natural or man-made systems [9].

3   Design Model Based on Multiple Intelligence Theory

3.1   FBS Model

Based on the innovation and optimization of the design process, scholars at home and abroad have proposed different product design models and methods, aiming at perfecting product structure design. Among them, the FBS (function-behavior-structure) model proposed by GERO in 1990 is a design process model. By analyzing the three main variables in the design process, namely function, behavior and structure, the conceptual design problem is transformed from abstract to abstract by using step-by-step mapping. Converting to concrete makes the innovative design process more logical and scientific, optimizes the product design process, and establishes a mapping mechanism between design concepts and product structures [10]. It has been widely used in the field of design (Fig. 2).

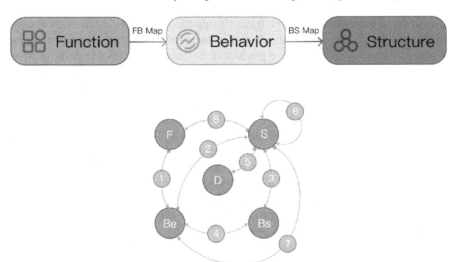

Fig. 2. FBS design model mapping relationship

GERO divides the FBS process into 8 steps. First, transform the function F into the expected behavior Be that can perform the function; second, transform the expected behavior Be into the structure S that performs the behavior; third, deduce the actual behavior Bs according to the structure S; fourth, transform the expected behavior Be is compared with actual behavior Bs to judge whether the designed structural scheme is feasible; fifth, if feasible, generate design description D; otherwise, return to the previous step to re-select. Through these steps, the designer transforms the intended function F of the artifact into a design description D [11].

As a widely used design model, FBS provides guidance for designers in terms of product structure improvement, but it lacks non-technical factors such as user needs and emotional experience. Therefore, we hope to interpret the needs of target children based on the theory of multiple intelligences and children's development stages and enrich the existing FBS model through the concept of Emotional Design.

3.2 Emotional Design

Emotional Design proposed three levels of design based on Don Norman's cognitive psychology, namely: visceral, behavioral, and reflective.

In terms of the instinctive level, by analyzing the five senses of the user when in contact with the product, guide the design of the product's appearance and form, so that the user can resonate with the product from the inner emotional point of view. For multiple intelligent children's toys, the instinctive level is reflected in the color and shape of the appearance and materials; in terms of behavior, Emotional Design focuses on operating experience to bring users efficiency and pleasure, and puts forward requirements on the usability, ease of use and continuity of toys. Multi-intelligence children's toys need to pay more attention to functionality. That is, the improvement effect of intelligence; in the aspect of reflection, it refers to the emotionalization of product characteristics, such as "self-image, personal satisfaction and memory", etc., to establish the emotional bond between users and products, requiring designers to think about the use of toys and its significance, such as the functions of "self-realization, knowledge popularization, intelligence improvement, and parent-child relationship promotion" of multiple intelligence children's toys [4].

In this paper, emotional design is used to combine Emotional Design with FBS model. While satisfying product functionality, it can deeply explore the user's spiritual satisfaction and emotional resonance, to pursue the balance between functional technology and emotion (Fig. 3).

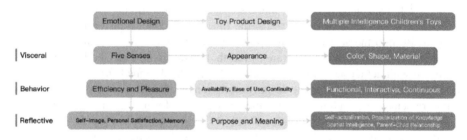

Fig. 3. Extended model of emotional design

3.3 Overview of Piaget's Theory of Child Development Stages

As is known, Piaget analyzed the mental development from the first childhood to the puberty and put forward many developmental stages [12]. The stage theory of cognitive development put forward by Jean Piaget (Jean Piaget, 1896–1980), a world-renowned contemporary child psychologist, believes that children's cognitive development can be divided into the following four basic stages [13] (Table 1).

To design children's toys, it is necessary to deeply explore children's growth needs and design toys according to children's psychological and physical changes. The theory of children's cognitive development stages proposed by Jean Piaget helps designers understand how children understand the world, how to think about problems, analyze user needs, understand children's different age stages, and the differences in cognitive development, and interpret children's different stages Ability, etc. provide effective theoretical guidance. It can help children to understand knowledge step by step until it can be fully scientifically constructed [14].

Table 1. Stage characteristics of Jean Piaget's theory of cognitive development

Stage	Age	Stage Characteristics
Sensorimotor Stage	0–2	The development of this stage is mainly the differentiation of sensation and movement. Infants and young children learn and understand the objective world through sensation and movement
Preoperational Stage	2–7	With the emergence and development of language, children internalize perceived actions into symbols, representations, and intuitive thinking
Concrete Operational Stage	7–11	Children at this stage already have abstract concepts in their cognitive structure and can carry out concrete logical reasoning
Formal Operation Stage	11–15	Children at this stage can not only logically consider realistic situations, but also consider possible situations (hypothetical situations)

3.4 RBFES Children's Toy Design Model Based on Multiple Intelligence Theory

To sum up, because the FBS design model lacks non-technical factors such as user needs and emotional experience, it cannot design multiple intelligent children's toys that meet children's cognitive development stage and can achieve a balance between emotion and functional technology. Taking this as a starting point, based on the theory of multiple intelligences, this paper combines user needs and emotional experience into the FBS design process model through the early user demand research and the combination of the three-level theory of emotion, to establish the combination of user needs, logic and emotion. The RBFES children's toy design model based on the theory of multiple intelligences that connects product functions, user behavior, and user cognition can be used in the process of cultivating children's toy designs with different intelligences and lays the foundation for the proposal of multiple intelligence children's toy design methods [15] (Fig. 4).

The keywords in the table are abbreviated as follows: User requirement(R), Emotional design(E), Emotional design reflective layer (Er), Emotional design behavior layer(Eb), Emotional design visceral layer(Ei), Behavior expectation(Be), Behavior subsistence(Bs), Structure(S), Function subsistence(Fs) Function expectation(Fe).

The RBFES children's toy design model based on multiple intelligence theory is shown in Fig. 6, and its detailed design operation instructions are shown in Table 2.

In Table 2, there are 10 operation steps in the RBFES children's toy design model based on multiple intelligence theory,

Step 1: Determine the target group of children according to the preliminary user research, clarify the needs of users, and combine the multiple intelligence theory and the characteristics of children's cognitive development stages to determine the type of intelligence to be improved.

Fig. 4. RBFES children's toy design model based on multiple intelligence theory

The second step: compare the "Multiple Intelligences Improvement Methods and Strategies Table", transform the intelligence improvement method into the interactive behavior of children and toys.

Step 3: According to the interaction behavior, determine the toy function required to trigger the corresponding behavior, to transform the interaction behavior between children and the toy into the expected toy product function.

Step 4: According to the three-level theory of emotion, start from the "Reflection level" and determine the non-structural functions and product characteristics of toys according to user needs.

Step 5: Deduce the "Behavior Layer" based on the "Reflection Layer", combine non-structural functions with expected product functions, and think about the corresponding interactive behavior from the three dimensions of "Usability", "ease of use" and "Continuity".

Step 6: Deduce the "instinctive layer" and develop design thinking on the appearance, color and material of the toy.

Step 7: Combining multiple intelligence promotion methods (expected product functions) and non-structural functions, develop toy structure design from three levels of emotion, and find the optimal solution of toy structure that satisfies functions and emotions.

Step 8: Deduce children's actual operation behavior according to the final structural design, to start the evaluation of multiple intelligence children's toy design scheme.

Step 9: Compare the Behavior Subsistence of the child with the Behavior Expectation to test whether the design is feasible, and if not, make iterative adjustments to the plan.

Step 10: Compare the Function Subsistence of the toy with the Function Expectation, check whether the design is feasible, and if it is not feasible, iteratively adjust the plan.

According to this step, the optimal design scheme is produced.

Table 2. Design operation instruction of RBFES children's toy design model based on multiple intelligence theory

Serial Number	Features	Design Operation Instructions
Operation 1	R	Determine the stage characteristics of cognitive development of the target group of children according to the user survey, and determine the target to improve the type of intelligence combined with the needs
Operation 2	R-Be	According to the Table of Multiple Intelligence Enhancement Modes, the intelligent enhancement modes are transformed into expected interaction behaviors between children and toys
Operation 3	Be-Fe	Transform children's expected interaction with toys into expected toy product functions
Operation 4	Be-Er	According to the theory of three levels of emotion, starting from the "reflection level", this paper guides the non-structural functions and product characteristics of toys according to user research
Operation 5	Er-Eb	The non-structural functions and expected product functions of "reflection layer" are transformed into "behavior layer" design to guide toy operation design
Operation 6	Eb-Ei	Based on the "reflection layer" and "behavior layer", the "visceral layer" is derived to guide the shape design of toys
Operation 7	Fe+E-S	The structure design of toy is developed in combination with multiple intelligence enhancement (expected product function) and emotional three-level
Operation 8	S-Bs	Evaluate the design scheme of multiple intelligent children's toys and deduce the behavior subsistence of the structure
Operation 9	Bs-Be	The behavior subsistence is compared with the expected behavior to test the feasibility of the design scheme
Operation 10	Fs-Fe	Compare the actual function with the function expectation to test the feasibility of the design scheme

The RBFES children's toy design model based on the theory of multiple intelligences is based on the classic FBS design model, through the steps of integrating emotional design and user research, combined with the theory of multiple intelligences, and through the layer-by-layer mapping of behavior, function, and structure, multiple intelligence children can be obtained. The optimal design plan of the toy, to test the effectiveness of the model and the scientific, systematisms and integrity of the design process, we will carry out design practice based on the RBFES children's toy design model based on the theory of multiple intelligences to test it.

4   Design Practice of Spatial Intelligence Children's Toys

4.1   Investigate and Survey

Based on the above-mentioned RBFES children's toy design model based on multiple intelligence theory and Piaget's children's developmental stages, we launched a multiple intelligence children's toy design about improving children's spatial intelligence. First, we visited and investigated two of the largest toy stores in Beijing—FAO Schwarz in Guomao and Hamleys in Wangfujing. Among them, FAO Schwarz is one of the oldest and iconic toy retail brands in the world, while Hamleys is a century-old British toy store (Fig. 5).

Fig. 5. Investigate and Survey of multiple intelligent toys

Through on-the-spot research on multiple intelligent children's toys in the market, it is found that most of the current toy products are entity interaction, focusing on subject knowledge popularization, closely integrated with course content, the boundary between "toys" and "teaching aids" is gradually blurred, and children's development theory is less guided Improve basic capabilities. For example, the combination of games and ancient poetry recitation, most products only apply the concept of "learning by playing", excessively pursuing knowledge, ignoring the playability of toys and the cultivation of non-disciplinary knowledge.

In terms of themes, there is a lack of perception of intangible objects, such as light and shadow, magnetism, and air. At the same time, most foreign products currently have a low degree of openness, and children cannot perform more free play and re-creation of the products. In the future, it is necessary to increase the playing methods of toys and the results of toy games to achieve randomness and diversity. Parents cannot record the growth and changes of children, and there is a lack of supporting APP platform to record products, and it is impossible to inspect children's intellectual development and cultivation at the functional level.

Based on this, we believe that "perception of intangible objects" can be used as a breakthrough to enhance children's spatial intelligence while incorporating non-subject knowledge, focusing on "turning intangible into tangible", allowing children to experience intangible objects (such as light and shadow, magnetism, air, etc.) learning topics) to allow parents to see tangible changes. On this basis, thinking divergence and refinement, we decided to create a game with the theme of light and shadow, with the help of the imaging properties of light and the way of playing with color fusion, to enhance children's spatial intelligence, and comprehensively cultivate children's imagination, color perception and three-dimensional perception Ability of multiple intelligence children's toys.

4.2 Analysis of Competing Products

Based on the results and findings of the field research, after layers of screening, a total of 4 light and shadow-themed toys (games) were selected, and market research and competitive product analysis were conducted from three aspects: applicable age, price, and product characteristics (Fig. 6).

Shadow FX Color Projector   Bulby For Kids   Acousto-optic Toys   Shadowmatic

Fig. 6. Four light and shadow themed toys (games)

Shadow FX Color Projector is suitable for children aged six and above. Children construct scene stories on the projection board by copying components or creating their own paintings, and then use three points of different colors of lights to project to form their own light and shadow works and stories. Its parts are small and have many components, which are easy to be swallowed by children. Its performance is average in terms of safety. Its construction steps are relatively simple, so it is not effective in cultivating children's spatial intelligence.

Bulby For Kids is suitable for children aged 4 and above. By splicing different components and using natural light projection, the product provides an open story guide, allowing children to imagine the time of possible sounds and the objects that appear in the scene. Like the Shadow FX Color Projector, its parts are small and have many components, and its safety is not good. However, Bulby For Kids is very portable after assembly. At the same time, the results are more open, and children have more space to use their imagination, and they perform better in the improvement of spatial intelligence.

Acousto-optic Toys is suitable for children aged 3 and above. Through projections, bedtime stories are interpreted in the form of slides, scene cards are shown through flashlights, and children and parents can use paper puppets to interpret shadow stories. As a toy in the form of a slide show, children can only use paper puppets to interpret stories in limited scenes. It does not perform well in terms of the openness of gameplay and results, and its playability is poor. Because the paper puppets have a fixed shape, children There is less space for DIY free play, and its spatial intelligence improvement effect is poor.

Different from the other three toy products, Shadowmatic is an electronic game suitable for children aged 4 and above. Players use parallax to rotate abstract objects in three-dimensional space to form recognizable projections, and set different themed levels to get recognizable You can clear the level with a specific shadow shape. As a video game, it has a natural advantage in communication, which is convenient for children to share and play with their peers. However, its openness is poor, and the gameplay is fixed and single. It is to operate a virtual three-dimensional object in a two-dimensional screen, which is not effective in improving spatial intelligence (Fig. 7).

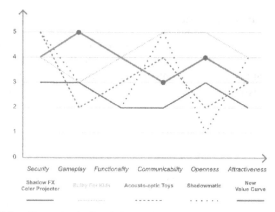

Fig. 7. Value Curve Analysis of Themed Toys (Games) Competing Products

From the six evaluation dimensions of safety, playability, functionality, dissemination, openness, and attractiveness, comprehensively analyze and evaluate the above four toys (games) to propose a value proposition for this toy design.

Based on the value curve, we put forward the design proposition of this toy: We hope that this light and shadow-themed spatial intelligent children's toy will use 3D parallax, color superimposition, and projection methods, and children will use the toy to superimpose the components in the spatial dimension to form a two-dimensional colorful shadow form. In the elementary play, children need to use spatial parallax to spell out shadow patterns of a given shape through components. In advanced play, children can use their imagination to spell out their own personalized projected images. Therefore, through the above two ways of playing, children's spatial intelligence can be improved, including the feeling of color, the perception of shape and space position, and the recognition of the connection between three-dimensional space objects.

4.3 User Needs Analysis

During the development period, young children have unique ways of cognition and thinking about things, and will show unique physical, psychological, and behavioral characteristics [16]. Therefore, for the design and development requirements of multiple intelligent toys, designers analyze according to the characteristics of children in different age groups.

According to Piaget's cognitive development stage theory, the mental operations of children in the concrete operation stage focus more on abstract concepts, and their thinking characteristics are conservative and no longer self-centered. Because of their reversible thinking, and relatively perfect motor skills, they can perform fine movements. After evaluation, we believe that it is most effective to cultivate children's spatial intelligence thinking at this stage (Fig. 8).

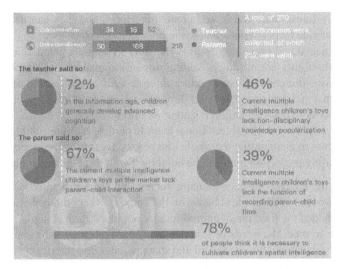

Fig. 8. Questionnaire survey analysis of user Needs

After clarifying the age range of target children, we designed a questionnaire to investigate and understand the current situation of the use of multiple intelligent children's toys in the market. We designed questionnaires for teachers and parents respectively and explored their expectations for the experience of multiple intelligent children's toys. Provide a theoretical basis for design practice. We distributed a total of 270 questionnaires online and offline, and 252 valid questionnaires. Among them, 52 questionnaires were distributed offline (34 teachers, 18 parents), and 218 questionnaires were distributed online (50 teachers, 168 parents). After analyzing the questionnaire data, as shown in the figure, under the background of the information age, children generally have early psychological development, strong thinking ability, and can carry out specific logical reasoning. We conclude that currently children generally enter the concrete operation stage early, and the age of target users of toys is suitable to be lowered from 7 to 11 years old to 3 to 7 years old. At the same time, the parent-child interaction function of toys needs to be paid more attention by designers, to maintain the "parent-child time" of parents and children." to be supported.

In terms of user interviews, to obtain more in-depth information from the target audience, we conducted semi-structured interviews with 12 parents and children to understand their needs for toys for children with multiple intelligences. After sorting out the information, we investigated the basic demographic characteristics, the use and feedback of children's existing toys, parents' expectations for children's toys with multiple intelligences, etc. By sorting out the interview results of 12 parents and children, we have the following four conclusions:

1. Children's interest in a certain single product is not high. It is necessary to increase the variability of the product to make the single product more diversified. There are multiple ways to increase playability and interest retention.

2. Children are more interested in self-created products, and they can use colors and other appearance forms to personalize the presentation effect
3. The two-dimensional projection endows the story in a timely manner, and its playability and durability are not high. Adding dimension conversion components, such as turning two-dimensional paper into a three-dimensional structure or changing a three-dimensional structure into two-dimensional light and shadow, this the class change process will attract children's attention more
4. Compared with the process of traditional module particle building, children may prefer the process of dismantling the whole into blocks. By setting the reverse gameplay, the dismantling projection map can be combined with three-dimensional fragments.

Based on the analysis of questionnaire survey and semi-structured user interview results, we proposed product ideas based on the value curve, combined with children's interests, and added the function of animal science popularization in non-subject knowledge. In order to meet the needs of "sharing and sharing", we need to build a mobile APP platform, so that parents can record and share parent-child interaction and combine it with this light and shadow theme space smart toy.

4.4 Design Process

According to the above user demand analysis, the age of the target users of the toy is 3–7 years old. According to their thinking characteristics, they are conservative and no longer self-centered. The ability to perform fine movements; and spatial intelligence refers to the correct perception and expression ability of color, shape, and spatial position, which can help children accurately perceive the visual world, deduce thinking images, have the thinking ability of three-dimensional space, and be able to distinguish and perceive space The connection between objects, in summary, it is most effective to cultivate children's spatial intelligence thinking at this stage (Table 3).

After clarifying children's spatial intelligence training goals, refer to the "Multiple Intelligence Improvement Methods and Strategies Table" to clarify the spatial intelligence improvement methods, and enhance children's spatial intelligence by cultivating children's expression and feelings of "color, shape, and spatial position". Transform the secondary training goals into the expected interactive behavior between children and toys, that is, space construction and color fusion. Combining the above analysis of competing products and the proposition of value curve design, clarify the expected function of toy products—the theme of light and shadow, with the help of the imaging properties of light and the way of playing with color fusion, to improve children's spatial intelligence and comprehensively cultivate children's imagination and color perception A multi-intelligence children's toy with three-dimensional perception.

Table 3. Ways and strategies for improving multiple intelligences

Multiple Intelligence	Promotion Methods and Strategies
Linguistic Intelligence	Enhance one's mastery of language and the ability to use it flexibly
Logical Mathematical Intelligence	Improve children's understanding, reasoning, thinking and expression ability of logical result relationship
Spatial Intelligence	Improve children's correct feeling and expression ability of color, shape, and spatial position
Musical Intelligence	Enhance children's ability to feel, distinguish, remember, and express music
Bodily Kinesthetic Intelligence	Improve children's body coordination, balance and movement of strength, speed, flexibility, and other abilities
Interpersonal Intelligence	Enhance children's ability to detect, experience and respond appropriately to the emotions and emotions of others
Intrapersonal Intelligence	Enhance children's self-awareness, insight and reflection of their own ability and understand their own emotions and strengths and weaknesses
Naturalist Intelligence	Enhance children's ability to observe various forms of nature, identify and classify objects

After determining the expected function of the toy, introduce "emotional design", start from the "reflection layer", and according to user research, clarify the non-structural function of the toy, that is, the "non-disciplinary knowledge" animal science attribute; "Science Popularization" combined with "Space Construction" and "Color Fusion" to enhance spatial intelligence, to determine how the toy is played and how it interacts.

In terms of the instinct level, comprehensive user research (semi-structured interviews and questionnaires), target user preferences and product animal science attributes, deduce the shape design of toys; and "promote parent-child relationship" and "parents record children's growth and sharing" from the needs of parents. Let's start, build a mobile APP platform, so that parents can record and share parent-child interaction, and combine it with this light and shadow theme space smart toy. To sum up, starting from the perspective of emotion and users, enrich the expected product functions, design the structure of the toy, then evaluate and iteratively adjust the design plan from the behavioral and functional levels, and finally produce a space smart children's toy, through light and shadow fusion and space jigsaw puzzle the play method, supplemented by AR animal science, comprehensively improves the spatial intelligence and subject knowledge of children aged 3–6 (Table 4).

Table 4. Application description of RBFES children's toy design model based on multiple intelligence theory in design cases

Serial Number	Features	Design Operation Instructions
Operation 1	R	Determine the target users as children aged 3–7, and determine the improvement of visual-spatial intelligence based on user needs
Operation 2	R-Be	The way to improve spatial intelligence is to cultivate children's expression and feelings of "color, shape, and spatial position", and transform them into the expected interactive behavior between children and toys - space construction, color fusion
Operation 3	Be-Fe	Transform "space construction" and "color fusion" into expected functions——light and shadow toys that enhance children's visual-spatial intelligence with the help of the imaging properties of light and the gameplay of color fusion
Operation 4	Be-Er	Starting from the "reflection level", clarify the non-structural functions of toys according to user research - "non-disciplinary knowledge" animal science attributes
Operation 5	Er-Eb	The combination of "non-subject knowledge" animal science popularization function and the "space construction" and "color fusion" that enhance spatial intelligence clarify the interaction mode of toys
Operation 6	Eb-Ei	Comprehensive user research, children's preferences, and animal science attributes, deduce the shape design of the toy and add APP design to solve the shortcomings of the research
Operation 7	Fe + E-S	Space intelligence improvement method (space construction, color fusion) and emotional three-level development of toy structure design
Operation 8	S-Bs	Evaluate design proposals for spatially intelligent children's toys on the theme of light and shadow, deduce the behavior subsistence of the structure
Operation 9	Bs-Be	Compare the behavior subsistence with the expected behavior to test the feasibility of the design solution
Operation 10	Fs-Fe	Compare the behavior subsistence with the function expectation to test the feasibility of the design scheme

4.5 Space Smart Toy Design Display

1. Toy Product Design Details

Based on the above design process, a spatially intelligent children's toy that combines physical products and APP is designed and produced. Through light and shadow fusion and spatial jigsaw puzzles, supplemented by AR animal science popularization, the spatial intelligence of children aged 3–7 is comprehensively improved. The physical toy design is inspired by the shape of dinosaurs, which is childlike and cute. Contains 1 bracket, 3 main parts, 15 acrylic components. Children can freely choose components, build toys, and adjust components to assemble.

The main parts of the toy are connected by mortise and tenon structure, which not only ensures the stability of the product structure, but also enhances children's assembly ability and hands-on ability. At the same time, the product is equipped with a universal light to meet the needs of children to build projections from different angles and can produce wonderful and brilliant light and shadow effects anytime and anywhere. The acrylic component is equipped with a magnetic latch, which cooperates with the top ring structure, which is convenient for children to adjust the spatial position of the component and enhances the flexibility of the game (Fig. 9).

Fig. 9. Product details and Effect drawing

2. Mobile Platform Design Details

Starting from the needs of parents to "promote parent-child relationship" and "parents to record and share children's growth and sharing", combined with toys, a mobile APP platform is built. Parents can use APP to interact with children, record in real time, and assist children in AR identification, recording and viewing. Intelligent growth process (Fig. 10).

The gameplay of the toy is divided into two parts: "Theme Play" and "Free Play". In the "Theme Play" mode, children can choose the corresponding level, check the animal science and the required parts, build the space under the guidance of the detailed description, and form the corresponding animal light and shadow image. After the construction is completed, enter through the AR camera function of the APP. Identify the page and judge whether it is successfully cleared. On the completed page, you can view the popular science information, hear the corresponding animal sound, and save and share the screen recording. In the "Free Play" mode, children do not have a fixed building goal, and can give full play to their imagination. After the building is completed, AR recognition will be performed, similar animal images will be automatically matched, and relevant animal science knowledge will be learned to improve the openness and playability of the toy.

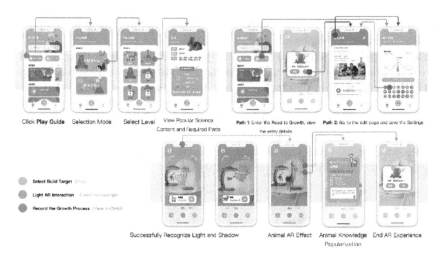

Click **Play Guide**   Selection Mode   Select Level   View Popular Science   Path 1: Enter the Road to Growth, view   Path 2: Go to the edit page and save the Settings

Content and Required Parts   the entry details

- Select Build Target (Play)
- Light AR Interaction (Learn Knowledge)
- Record the Growth Process (Parent-Child)

Successfully Recognize Light and Shadow   Animal AR Effect   Animal Knowledge   End AR Experience

Popularization

Fig. 10. App operation flow chart

The recording function is a major feature of the product. Parents can view the children's play records and details page from the "Growth Road" module on the homepage and see the improvement and change process of the corresponding intelligence through the visualization of the clearance score (Fig. 11).

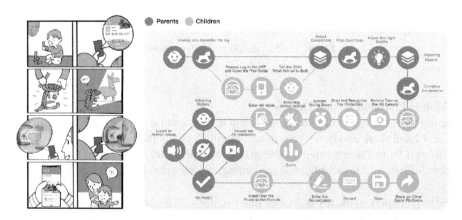

Fig. 11. Storyboard and User usage process

4.6 Usability Testing

After building a prototype, it was tested by 7 users, and based on user feedback, this toy has the following advantages: First, the three-dimensional space jigsaw puzzle is relatively novel, and compared with similar products on the market, it performs better in terms of openness and playability; At the functional level, toys can comprehensively

Fig. 12. User testing process

improve children's spatial intelligence from the dimensions of imagination, color perception, and three-dimensional perception. However, some users also reported that the appearance of the toy is not intuitive and interesting. It is hoped that through a more child-like appearance, the instinctive experience of children's "five senses" will be enhanced, and the attractiveness of the toy to children will be improved; There is a lot of room for improvement, and the difficulty of the level can be appropriately reduced to improve children's experience. To sum up, after testing, the design of this toy has practicality and high feasibility (Fig. 12).

In terms of software, we conducted a prototype test through XD, and handed it over to 4 parents for testing. Based on user feedback, APP has the following advantages: First, the page cartoon is beautiful, in line with the tonality of children's toys, and has a sense of brand. At the same time, the software AR function is highly playable, and the novel gameplay and cool AR interactive effects are very easy to attract children. It should be noted that in terms of "parent-child relationship connection", the parent feedback recording function is not enough in terms of portability, but the overall interaction logic of the APP is smooth, and the functionality is in line with expectations.

Comprehensive toy and APP user testing, 75% of the test parents believe that this toy is considered perfect in terms of safety, the toy is open and playable, and in terms of functionality, it conforms to the cognitive theory of children's psychological development and can be effective. Improve the spatial intelligence of school-age children.

5 Summary and Outlook

Based on the theory of multiple intelligences, this thesis proposes the RBFES children's toy design model, and takes the space intelligence toy as an example to verify. Focus on the guiding significance and value of multiple intelligence theory in the design of children's toys and use sufficient and detailed user research and emotional design theory to optimize the FBS design model, find the best way to improve children's multiple intelligence, and optimize and optimize the FBS model. The design of multiple intelligence children's toys provides research ideas and provides more possibilities for the design of such products.

However, due to the time limit of the project, this study still has certain limitations. The number of user samples is limited, and the multiple intelligence exercise needs and exercise methods of special children, such as mentally handicapped children and hearing-impaired children, were not paid attention to. In the future, we can focus on special groups of children and develop specialized design models. At the same time, there is still a lot of room for improvement in the user experience of the APP platform in the "parent-child interaction mode" and "recording function". Next, we will gradually realize the iterative improvement of the platform functions.

Finally, we would like to thank Wu Haoyue and Zhou Ruyi from Beijing Forestry University for their help during the toy design process. In addition, we also thank all participants for their data feedback and improvement suggestions during the usability testing process.

References

1. Pellegrini, A.D., Dupuis, D.N., Smith, P.K.: Play in evolution and development. Academic Press (2) (2007)
2. Yue, F., Tian, W., Shidujaman, M.: A design method of children playground based on bionic algorithm. In: Kurosu, M. (ed.) HCII 2021. LNCS, vol. 12764, pp. 173–183. Springer, Cham (2021). https://doi.org/10.1007/978-3-030-78468-3_12
3. Winthrop, R., McGivney, E.: Skills for a Changing World: Advancing Quality Learning for Vibrant Societies. Brookings Institution (2016)
4. Zhang, X., Sha, Y., Yu, H.: Playing middle school: returning the educational value of games. Contemporary Educ. Sci. (05), 10–15 (2021)
5. Zhang, H.: The theory of multiple intelligences and its application in college english teaching. Chinese Adult Educ. (11), 182–183 (2008)
6. Gardner, H.: Frames of Mind: The Theory of Multiple Intelligences (Basic, New York) (1983)
7. Lu, G., Chen, S.: Research on the design method of preschool educational toys based on the theory of multiple intelligences. Furniture Interior Decorat. **2**, 4 (2020)
8. Gu, M., Meng, F.: New concept of international education. Hainan Publishing House (2001)
9. Zhong, Z.: Multiple intelligence theory and educational technology. Audio-visual Educ. Res. **3**, 5 (2004)
10. Bai, Z., Zhang, Z., Li, C., et al.: A review of function-behavior-structure (FBS) modeling methods. J. Graph. **43**(5), 11 (2022)
11. Gero JS . Design Prototypes: A Knowledge Representation Schema for Design[J]. AI Magazine, 1990
12. Köylü, M.: Ölüm olayının çocuklar üzerine etkisi ve "Ölüm Eğitimi." Ondokuz Mayıs Üniversitesi İlahiyat Fakültesi Dergisi **17**(17), 95–120 (2004)
13. Kale, H.: Uso da teoria de Piaget na educação nutricional de pré-escolares. Tao Yun, Gao Fei
14. The Main Influence of Piaget's Theory on Education. J. Yunnan Normal University (Philosophy and Social Science Edition) (03), 63–67 (1993)
15. Zhang, B., Xu, Q., Yang, Y., Li, X., Gu, R.: Research on innovative design of children's playing aids based on FBS model extension. Packag. Eng. **42**(12):121–127 (2021). 10.19554/j. cnki.1001–3563.2021.12.016
16. Dan, L.: The creative design of toys for preschool children based on psychological theory. J. Changchun Univ. **20**(003), 106–108 (2010)

Impacts of Information Accessibility and Diagnosticity on Children's Visual Perception of Recommended Books

Jia-Rui Sun and Ko-Chiu Wu[✉]

National Taipei University of Technology, Taipei, Taiwan (R.O.C.)
kochiuwu@mail.ntut.edu.tw

Abstract. Searching vast library collections for books to read can be overwhelming for children. The information-seeking behavior of children differs greatly from that of adults; if the information is too complex and large in quantity, information overload may occur. Thus, book recommendation systems for children must match their information-processing abilities. This study grounded on the accessibility-diagnosticity theory proposed by Feldman and Lynch aimed to investigate the relationships among the cognitive abilities, information-seeking behavior, and eye movement behavior of children of different ages faced with different types of information. Our results indicate that age, perceptual speed, and the number of round-trip choices influence eye movement behavior for both accessible information and diagnostic information, whereas associative memory was only correlated with eye movement behavior for diagnostic information. This study employed physiological and psychological indicators to explain information identification responses to verify the cognitive effects of different types of information. These results can be applied to meet the specific needs of children regarding information-seeking while sparking their interest in self-learning, both of which will aid in the development of smart library services for digital natives.

Keywords: Visual perception · Cognitive ability · Information seeking behavior

1 Introduction

1.1 Background and Motivation

Traditionally, libraries have been evaluated based on the scope of their collections. However, as the numbers of publications and categories have increased over time, readers must spend substantial amounts of time searching for books they are interested in. Furthermore, the era of information overload has increased the cognitive burden for child readers, making it difficult for them to identify the information they need. Book recommendation systems provided on library mobile devices recommend books to readers based on their borrowing records, increase information accessibility, and, at the same time, reduce their cognitive load. Information-seeking generally begins with an individual's need for information and is influenced by the individual's cognitive abilities

© The Author(s), under exclusive license to Springer Nature Switzerland AG 2023
M. Kurosu and A. Hashizume (Eds.): HCII 2023, LNCS 14012, pp. 131–148, 2023.
https://doi.org/10.1007/978-3-031-35599-8_9

[1]. Thus, understanding the influence of differences in cognitive ability on searching behavior is crucial. As children are still in the process of developing many important cognitive skills, their relationship with information differs significantly from that of adults. Researchers [2] have used search areas to investigate the information-seeking behavior of children in smart libraries, finding that age and gender impact both searching behavior and book selection.

Past research has shown that eye movement can be used to distinguish the abilities of individuals and their performance in different tasks. For instance, gaze analysis furthers understanding on the concentration of individuals while they process different types of information [3]. For children, overly-complicated information is ignored, so their eyes focus only on the information they are interested in. Cognitive development theory suggests that the cognitive abilities and eye movement behavior of children vary with age [4]. Over 80% of the information processed by the brain is obtained via the visual system, so eye movements are the most important source of information in the cognitive search process of children [5].

This study is grounded on the accessibility-diagnosticity model proposed by Feldman and Lynch. We observed children as they operated the book recommendation system of a digital library, recording their eye movement trajectories. Our objective was to investigate the relationships among the information-seeking behavior, cognitive abilities, and eye movement behavior of elementary school children to provide reference for meeting the specific needs of children regarding information-seeking while sparking their interest in reading and self-learning. We believe these goals are key to the development of smart library services for digital natives.

2   Related Work

2.1   Accessibility-Diagnosticity Model and Message Framing

Feldman and Lynch [6] suggested that whether a certain piece of information can be extracted from an individual's memory as a basis for judgment in everyday life is determined by the accessibility and diagnosticity of the information itself. This concept was expanded into the accessibility-diagnosticity model. Accessible information is information that an individual can easily find in his or her short-term memory, and diagnostic information is information that helps an individual form judgments; that is, information that is more relevant to the judgment has greater diagnosticity. Feldman's explanation of the model was that any information serving as input for judgment is influenced by three factors: 1. The accessibility of the information in the individual's working memory after input, 2. The diagnosticity of other information in the individual's working memory after input, and 3. The perceived diagnosticity of the input information during judgment. Dick et al. [7] discovered that while individuals are forming judgments on unknown information, they will hold greater trust in credible information. In other words, individuals facing unknown information make assessments based on the context or relevant information. If an individual is judging a single piece of information, information that can help the individual analyze and evaluate the stimulus has high diagnosticity, whereas information that cannot has low diagnosticity [8].

Accessibility and diagnosticity are respectively the necessary and sufficient conditions of information utilization. Only information that can be recalled can be used to form judgment, and if a piece of information is deemed to have no connection to the judgment, then said information cannot be used [6, 9]. Broniarczyk and Alba [10] held that when an individual is choosing information, data-based information is more persuasive and diagnostic information is more easily adopted regardless of its accessibility. When an individual is browsing information and the target matches the negative information in the individual's memory, then the persuasiveness of the information declines substantially [8]. Thus, the model comprises three methods of information processing: 1. When memory-based information is diagnostic, then said information is adopted; 2. When memory-based information is less diagnostic, the individual will continue searching until the information is sufficient for judgment; 3. When memory-based information is highly diagnostic or not diagnostic, then said information is adopted.

Message framing refers to the presenting of messages based on gains or losses to message receivers and using the way the message is framed to influence their views and decisions. This concept comes from the prospect theory [11]. Gain-framing points out the gains that are obtained as the message-receivers receive the message, and loss-framing stresses the negative impacts that the message will inflict on the message-receivers if they do not choose this information [12, 13]. These gains and losses influence selection by message-receivers. For highly-involved message-receivers, loss-framed messages are more persuasive, whereas less-involved message-receivers will adopt peripheral information (e.g., the credibility of the information) as the basis for their decisions.

2.2 Information-Seeking Behavior

Access to information is a basic human need. However, the need for information in children is often overlooked because they are still in early learning stages and are not as mentally developed as adults are. Their need for information differs due to their age-varying cognitive development. Information-seeking behavior in children manifests in the activities that they engage in to fill gaps in their existing knowledge [14]. Marchionini [15] indicated that information-seeking, closely associated with learning and problem-solving, is a dynamic learning process that is affected by personality traits, interpersonal relationships, and environmental factors [16]. Moore et al. [17] stated that children must be able to locate, identify, organize, and combine information in order to become problem-solvers. Kuhlthau [18] divided information-seeking behavior into six stages: initiation, selection, exploration, formulation, collection, and presentation. She also developed an information-seeking framework comprising concepts such as the information search process, the principle of uncertainty, and the zone of intervention.

2.3 Eye Movement

In 1879, French ophthalmologist Louis Émile Javal discovered that as an individual reads, his or her eyes do not move continuously along a line of text but stop temporarily in one spot before rapidly jumping to the next spot. Thus, by observing the individual's eye movements, one can understand the areas where the individual's interests are in the reading process and the dynamic trajectories of his or her visual attention [19–21]. Just and Carpenter [22] observed that when individuals encounter a rare word, the duration of their visual attention is longer, while common words draw less visual attention. They therefore made two assumptions regarding eye movement: the immediacy assumption, in which the cognitive system in the brain of an individual facing information immediately processes visual information, and the eye-mind assumption, in which the eyes fixate on the information until the brain has finished processing it, meaning that fixation time equals the cognitive processing time.

Eye movements can be divided into two major types: relatively still fixations and short and rapid saccades. Fixations capture images on the fovea (where vision is the clearest) for more detailed visual processing. Research has shown that when individuals engage in visual information-searching, the average durations of fixations and motion picture viewing were 275 ms and 330 ms, respectively, which indicates that the duration of fixations is highly correlated with the complexity of the visual information [23]. Saccades are short stops anywhere on an image; in this case, the vision is blurry, so information cannot be processed during saccades [24].

In addition to eye movement trajectories, eye movement analysis also includes visual analysis (e.g., heatmap analysis). Heat maps use different colors to mark the amount of time a subject's gaze dwells on a spot. Red indicates long periods of time, yellow and green indicate moderate lengths of time, and blue means short periods of time. Compared to trajectory maps, heat maps cannot present detailed information on fixation points.

2.4 Kit of Factor-Referenced Cognitive Tests

Cognitive abilities are the abilities that an individual has acquired at a certain time or stage of development, and perceptual speed is a cognitive factor that has a certain influence and is indispensable among numerous internal factor analyses. To a certain extent, the eye movement behavior of children can be applied to analyze their perceptual speed, which refers to the amount of time that children need to perform a task and reflects the speed at which children process the information in visual stimuli. However, limited by their prior knowledge and experience, differences exist in the perceptual speed of children as they perform tasks [25]. So far, research has indicated that differences in perceptual speed affect information-seeking behavior [26]. Associative memory uses certain intermediaries to establish association between two things. It is defined as the phenomenon in which part of a remembered object is recalled when another part of said object appears. Thus, what is measured is the children's short-term memory of the visual stimuli. When visual stimuli appear, sensory organs receive the external stimuli, and the central processing system determines the necessity of the information and sends the identified information to the short-term memory, where it is encoded and finally stored in the long-term memory. The brain influences our judgment of the information based on the response of the short-term memory to the visual stimuli [27]. For this reason, short-term memory plays a crucial role in search behavior.

This study utilized the kit of factor-referenced cognitive tests (FRCT) developed by Ekstrom [28]. Based on the cognitive abilities analyzed in "Human Cognitive Abilities" [25], we used perceptual speed (P) and memory, associative (MA) to measure the cognitive abilities of elementary school children (see Fig. 1). P includes the Finding A's Test (P-1), the Number Comparison Test (P-2), and the Identical Pictures Test (P-3), which require children to find certain pieces of information among large quantities of distracting information. MA includes the Picture-Number Test (MA-1) and the Object-Number Test (MA-2), which require students to recall the numbers that correspond to pictures or text.

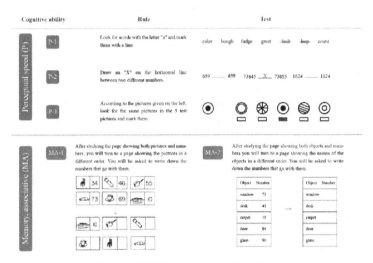

Fig. 1. FRCT Test Interpretation Chart

3   Methods

3.1   Participants

As Hourcade [29] indicated that the development of visual acuity is associated with age, we recruited children between the ages of 9 and 12 to participant in this study. We recruited a total of 30 participants, including 23 girls and 7 boys, with the consent of their parents or teachers.

To avoid interference from app information, we first had the participating students fill out a cognitive ability questionnaire before the experiment with the individual as the unit. In the second phase, the participants took part in eye movement calibration, and in the third phase, the participants viewed different types of recommendations. The entire experiment took 30–40 min in total.

3.2 Experiment Materials

The recommendation system used in this study was a function on the homepage of the interactive book-searching app, Interstellar Book Treasure Hunt. The children's book collection on the third floor of the main branch of the New Taipei City Library serves as the database of this app. The Interstellar Book Treasure Hunt is an interactive book-finding app that combines mobile technology and smartphone augmented-reality technology. Based on the concept of collective intelligence, it purpose is to strengthen interactions between libraries and children.

The homepage of the recommendation system comprises two parts: 20 recommended books and the 20 most popular books (see Fig. 2 (a) and (b)). The recommendations are based on the child's borrowing records, which means it can be considered memory-based accessible information. The most popular books are drawn from the library records of most borrowed books, so this represents non-memory information. The way that children evaluate and judge information is associated with the popularity ranking of books. That is, the popularity sequence of information holds reference value for children, so the diagnostic information in this study is defined as "the most popular". Figure 2 (c) displays the recommendation mechanisms of the recommendation system. When the user is a library reader, the system uses the user's borrowing records to recommend books. If the user has never applied for a library card before, the system will recommend books to the user based on the borrowing records of children of the same age and gender.

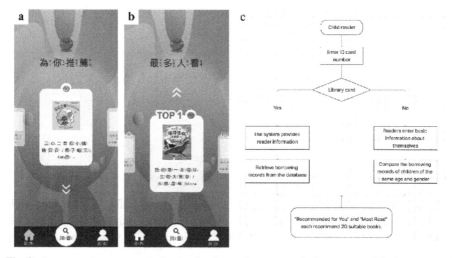

Fig. 2. Images and recommendation mechanisms of recommendation system of the homepage of Interstellar Book Treasure Hunt: (a) accessible information – interface of recommended books; (b) diagnostic information – interface of most popular books; (c) flow chart of recommendation mechanisms of recommendation system

3.3 Experiment Tool

The GP3 Eye Tracker used in the experiment of this study is a desktop eye tracker developed by Gazepoint that collects eye movement data from children in non-laboratory environments. Before the eye movement experiments, the child participants had to independently perform eye calibration. The GP3 was placed approximately 65 cm from the participants, and they had to look at five white round dots consecutively on a mobile phone. The underlying principle of the GP3 is that it uses infrared to detect eye movement. The data collected during the eye movement experiment was analyzed using Gazepoint Analysis, a software program developed by Gazepoint.

3.4 Mobile Phone Swipe Trajectory Indicator

Mobile phone swipe trajectories were collected as the children operated the app. These were quantified [30] using the number of round-trip choices and total exploration depth (see Fig. 3). The number of round-trip choices refers to the number of times that a child switches from a forward swipe to a backward swipe while browsing book information, and total exploration depth is the number of book recommendations that the children see while browsing book information (repeats are not counted).

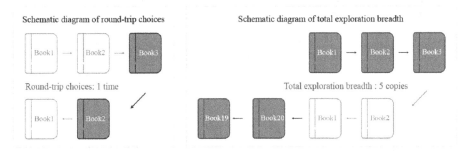

Fig. 3. Mobile phone swipe trajectory data: round-trip choices and total exploration depth

3.5 Eye Movement Indicators

The eye movement behavior analysis in this study included fixation duration, total fixation area, and fixation area per second. A fixation duration is the duration of time that a participant spent gazing at the interface when choosing a book. Total fixation area is the proportion of the overlapping heat maps collected during fixation durations in the collection of heat maps of the entire interface area. Fixation area per second is the area that the participant gazes at per second when choosing a book, equaling the total fixation area divided by the fixation duration.

4   Result

4.1   Children's Information-Seeking Behavior

Following the suggestions of Lee [30], the quantitative data for the information-seeking behavior of children in this study included the number of round-trip choices and total exploration depth. We examined the influence of the age, P, and MA of the participants on the number of round-trip choices and total exploration depth.

Round-Trip Choices. The number of round-trip choices is the number of times that a participant swiped backward. As a participant browsed from the first book to the tenth book, a swipe from the right to the left was defined as a forward swipe, whereas a swipe in the opposite direction was defined as a backward swipe. Table 1 presents the frequency analysis of the round-trip choices made by participants of different ages.

According to the results in Table 1, the most common frequency of round-trip choices made by the 30 participants with regard to accessible information was 4 times. With regard to diagnostic information, the most common frequency of round-trip choices made by the 30 participants was 2 times. On the whole, the 30 participants made fewer round-trip choices when diagnostic information was involved than when accessible information was involved. The diagnostic information consisted of the most popular books in the library, so the information had higher credibility and persuasiveness. When a piece of information has greater persuasiveness, children place more trust in it and perceive it

Table 1. Round-trip choice data analysis (N = 30)

Accessible information

Participant age	Frequency							
	0	1	2	3	4	5	6	8
9	0	2	1	1	0	0	0	0
10	0	0	2	2	3	0	1	0
11	1	3	3	0	2	0	0	0
12	0	2	0	1	3	2	0	1
Total	1	7	6	4	8	2	1	1

Diagnostic information

Participant age	Frequency						
	0	1	2	3	4	6	8
9	0	0	1	3	0	0	0
10	1	1	3	1	1	0	1
11	1	2	4	1	1	0	0
12	0	0	3	4	1	1	0
Total	2	3	11	9	3	1	1

as credible. As a result, fewer round-trip choices are made with regard to diagnostic information.

The two sets of round-trip choice data presented greater differences in various frequencies, so we redistributed the data based on the original frequencies. The children who made 2 or fewer round-trip choices were placed in Sample Set 1, and those who made 3 or more round-trip choices were placed in Sample Set 2. We used these two sample sets to determine whether the number of round-trip choices was associated with age (see Table 2). The results indicated a significant relationship between the age of the child and the number of round-trip choices he or she made with regard to accessible information.

Table 2. Chi-square test of age and number of round-trip choices

Type of information	p-value
Accessible information	0.037
Diagnostic information	0.160

To understand the relationships between the cognitive abilities P and MA in children and the number of round-trip choices they make, we performed Pearson correlation analysis. The results revealed no significant relationships ($p > 0.05$) between P and the number of round-trip choices or between MA and the number of round-trip choices, regardless of the type of information.

Total Exploration Breadth. According to the results of the Kruskal-Wallis one-way ANOVA (see Table 3), the total exploration depth of the participants with regard to accessible information or diagnostic information did not vary significantly with age ($p > 0.05$). However, the average exploration depth of the twelve-year-old participants with regard to accessible information was the greatest ($M = 18.78$), and that of the nine-year-old participants was the smallest ($M = 13.75$); with regard to diagnostic information, the average exploration depth of the nine-year-old participants was the greatest ($M = 18.75$), whereas that of the eleven-year-old participants was the smallest ($M = 13.11$).

The results of the Pearson correlation coefficient analysis of the relationship between the cognitive abilities and total exploration depth of the participants are presented in Table 4. With regard to accessible information, the correlation between P-3 and total exploration depth was significant and moderately positive ($r = 0.408, p = 0.025$), meaning that children with better P-3 abilities showed greater total exploration depth with regard to accessible information.

4.2 Eye Movement Data

While choosing books, the participants exhibited a longer average fixation duration with regard to accessible information ($M = 22.790$ s) than with regard to diagnostic information ($M = 8.046$ s), a smaller average total fixation area with regard to accessible

Table 3. Total exploration breadth data analysis

Accessible information		
Participant age	Total exploration breadth(M)	p-value
9	13.75	0.117
10	15.00	
11	14.67	
12	18.78	
Diagnostic information		
9	18.75	0.215
10	15.75	
11	13.11	
12	16.11	

Table 4. Pearson product-moment correlation analysis of cognitive abilities and total exploration depth in participants

Accessible information		
Cognitive ability	Pearson-r	p-value
P-1	0.316	0.089
P-2	0.257	0.170
P-3	0.408*	0.025
MA-1	−0.037	0.846
MA-2	0.065	0.733
Diagnostic information		
P-1	0.225	0.231
P-2	−0.021	0.914
P-3	−0.020	0.916
MA-1	−0.185	0.328
MA-2	−0.067	0.725

information ($M = 12.981\%$) than with regard to diagnostic information ($M = 21.011\%$), and a smaller average fixation area per second with regard to accessible information ($M = 3.020\%$) than with regard to diagnostic information ($M = 3.063\%$).

Analysis by Age. We performed Kruskal-Wallis tests to determine whether the eye movement behavior of the participants was significantly correlated with their age. The results showed that with regard to accessible information, the total fixation area of the participants varied significantly with their age the first ($p = 0.015$) and third times (p

= 0.035) they were choosing a book. In the remaining groups, this relationship was not significant. Pairwise post-hoc comparisons indicated that the first time the participants were choosing a book, the total fixation areas of the nine-year-old participants were significantly smaller than that of the ten-year-old participants ($p = 0.014$, $F = -2.458$), and those of the eleven-year-old participants ($p = 0.005$, $F = 2.799$) and the twelve-year-old participants ($p = 0.014$, $F = 2.468$) were significantly greater than that of the ten-year-old participants. The third time they were choosing a book, the fixation durations of the eleven-year-old participants were significantly longer than those of the ten-year-old participants ($p = 0.026$, $F = 2.234$), and those of the twelve-year-old participants were significantly longer than those of the eleven-year-old participants ($p = 0.009$, $F = 2.682$). However, with regard to diagnostic information, the eye movement behaviors of the participants did not vary significantly with age the fifth time they were choosing a book. Based on the analysis results above, we posit that this may be due to the amount of effort that children of different ages put into the task. Older children have more patience when receiving accessible information and establishing knowledge frameworks, so their fixation areas and fixation durations are larger and longer. Also, when individuals are judging diagnostic information, book rankings can help them analyze and assess whether the accessibility of the information is high or low. Thus, for children, diagnostic information is more likely to be trusted and adopted.

Analysis of Cognitive Abilities. With regard to accessible information, correlations existed between the fixation duration and P-1 ($r = 0.407$, $p = 0.028$) and between total fixation area and P-1 ($r = 0.379$, $p = 0.042$), P-2 ($r = 0.550$, $p = 0.002$), and P-3 ($r = 0.405$, $p = 0.029$) the second time the participants were choosing a book. The fourth time the participants were choosing a book, a correlation existed between total fixation area and P-1 ($r = 0.385$, $p = 0.047$). The fifth the participants were choosing a book, a correlation existed between total fixation area and P-1 ($r = 0.425$, $p = 0.043$), P-2 ($r = 0.478$, $p = 0.021$), and P-3 ($r = 0.469$, $p = 0.024$).

With regard to diagnostic information, correlations existed between total fixation area and P-2 the first time the participants were choosing a book ($r = 0.367$, $p = 0.046$), between total fixation area and P-1 the second time the participants were choosing a book ($r = 0.432$, $p = 0.022$), between fixation area per second and P-2 the third time the participants were choosing a book ($r = 0.515$, $p = 0.007$), and between total fixation area and P-2 ($r = 0.646$, $p = 0.001$), P-3 ($r = 0.438$, $p = 0.032$), and MA-2 ($r = 0.539$, $p = 0.007$) the fourth time the participants were choosing a book. The fifth time they were choosing a book, total fixation area ($r = 0.632$, $p = 0.001$) and fixation area per second ($r = 0.566$, $p = 0.005$) were both found to be correlated with P-2.

With both types of information, fixation area was correlated with P. However, with accessible information, fixation duration was only correlated with P-1, whereas with diagnostic information, fixation area was also correlated with MA-2, and fixation duration per second.

Analysis of Children's Information-Seeking Behavior. We applied Mann-Whitney tests to the round-trip choice data in Sample Set 1 and Sample Set 2, the results of which revealed that with regard to accessible information, a significant relationship existed between fixation duration and the number of round-trip choices in Sample Sets 1 and 2 the first time the participants were choosing a book ($p = 0.007$); with regard to diagnostic information, a significant relationship existed between fixation area per second and the number of round-trip choices in Sample Sets 1 and 2 the fifth time the participants were choosing a book ($p = 0.044$).

We analyzed the relationship between the eye movement behavior and total exploration depth of the participants using the Pearson correlation coefficient analysis. The results indicated no significant correlation between eye movement behavior and total exploration depth as the participants browsed the two types of information.

4.3 K-Means

To explore the individual differences in children identifying the two types of information, we used the K-means analysis (Ward's method), in which dividing the children into four groups is more suitable (see Fig. 4). This resulted in Group 1 (10 participants), Group 2 (7 participants), Group 3 (12 participants), and Group 4 (1 participant) (Table 5).

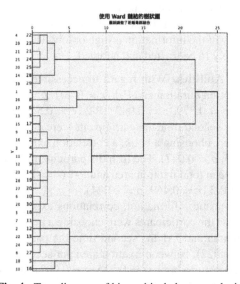

Fig. 4. Tree diagram of hierarchical cluster analysis

Table 5. Cross table of group results and age

Age/Group	1	2	3	4
9	2	1	1	0
10	2	1	5	0
11	5	3	1	0
12	1	2	5	1
Total	10	7	12	1

Group 4 presented the longest fixation durations when browsing the two types of information, and Group 2 presented the largest total fixation area. Group 4 presented the largest fixation area per second when browsing accessible information, and Group 3 presented the largest fixation area per second when browsing diagnostic information (Table 6).

Table 6. Average values of eye movement data for each group when browsing different types of information

Accessible information			
Group	Gaze duration	Total gaze area	Gaze area per second
1	7.97	10.305%	2.55%
2	9.71	39.562%	2.39%
3	12.04	29.369%	3.69%
4	29.75	23.902%	2.88%
Diagnostic information			
1	7.44	9.185%	2.44%
2	9.46	39.1%	2.25%
3	7.82	18.556%	3.73%
4	12.2	11.093%	1.71%

The chi-square test results of the four groups revealed a significant relationship between the different groups and the number of round-trip choices when browsing diagnostic information ($p = 0.006$). The results of the Kruskal-Wallis test showed that the various groups displayed significant differences in P-2 ($p = 0.009$); the number comparison abilities of Group 1 were weaker than those of Group 2 ($p = 0.001$, $F = -3.354$), but the number comparison abilities of Group 3 were stronger than those of Group 2 ($p = 0.038$, $F = 2.074$).

Half of the participants in Group 1 were 11 years old. The participants in Group 1 made the fewest round-trip choices with regard to diagnostic information ($M = 2.2$). With regard to accessible information, they also presented the shortest fixation durations ($M = 7.97$) and the smallest total fixation area ($M = 10.305\%$). With regard to diagnostic information, they presented the shortest fixation durations ($M = 7.44$) and the smallest total fixation area ($M = 9.185\%$). Thus, they displayed the lowest degree of information involvement and the poorest concentration abilities when browsing information. We infer that the amount of recommendation information inflicted a heavier burden on the short-term memory of these participants, thereby causing their need for information to be more ambiguous.

Almost half of the participants in Group 2 were 11 years old. The participants in Group 2 made the most round-trip choices with regard to diagnostic information ($M = 3.14$). With regard to accessible information, they also presented shorter fixation durations ($M = 9.71$) but the largest total fixation area ($M = 39.562\%$). With regard to diagnostic information, they presented longer fixation durations ($M = 9.46$) and the largest total fixation area ($M = 39.1\%$). Thus, gain-loss asymmetry was more likely to occur in these participants as they browsed diagnostic information. We therefore speculate that they adopt peripheral route processing.

Almost half of the participants in Group 3 were 10 years old. The participants in Group 3 made fewer round-trip choices with regard to diagnostic information ($M = 2.58$). With regard to accessible information and diagnostic information, they presented longer fixation durations, greater total fixation area, and the greatest fixation area per second ($M = 3.69\%$). With regard to diagnostic information, they presented shorter fixation durations ($M = 7.82$), greater total fixation area ($M = 18.556\%$), and the greatest fixation area per second ($M = 3.73\%$). We speculate that the participants in this group did not scrutinize the information attributes when browsing diagnostic information.

The participant in Group 4 was 12 years old and made more round-trip choices with regard to diagnostic information ($M = 3$). With regard to accessible information and diagnostic information, he/she presented the longest fixation duration and smaller total fixation area. On the whole, he/she was visually focused and willing to spend time browsing information patiently and displayed a high degree of information involvement. After encoding the presented information, he/she could more easily transfer the information from his/her short-term memory to his/her long-term memory.

5   Discussion

The objective of this study was to observe the differences in the information-seeking behavior of children with different cognitive abilities while they browsed different types of information. We measured the perceptual speed and associative memory of the children using the kit of factor-referenced cognitive tests and recorded the eye movement behavior of the children using an eye tracker to explore the relationships among cognitive abilities, information-seeking behavior, and eye movement behavior.

5.1   Effect of Cognitive Ability on Information-Seeking

The perceptual speed of children influences their judgment of different types of information. Analysis of the experiment data revealed that perceptual speed had the greatest impact on information-searching. Children with faster perceptual speed displayed more active search behavior (greater total exploration depth, total fixation area, and fixation area per second) with regard to accessible information. We speculate that this is because the accessible information comprised books recommended based on their own reading preferences. Thus, they invested more energy and effort in browsing the information than when browsing diagnostic information. Perceptual speed was gauged by assessing the speed at which the children could quickly scan information and make the correct responses, which requires a certain amount of focus and efficiency. Associative memory was not correlated with the information-seeking behavior with regard to diagnostic information; it was only correlated with total fixation area, which means that this information does not really depend on the associative memory of children. We speculate that this was due to a lack of correlation between the text and visuals in the diagnostic information.

5.2 Information-Seeking Behavior for Different Types of Information

Through our experiment, we discovered that children have a preference for accessible information and that sequence locations of the information is associated with the children's choices; that is, accessible information is more likely to be focused on by children. While the children were browsing accessible information, they made more round-trip choices than when browsing diagnostic information. We speculate that their need for information shifts depending on the context, as when they cannot grasp information clearly, they are likely to experience information anxiety. During the browsing process, their search strategies change as information appears. Wurman [31] indicated that when individuals encounter (1) information they cannot understand, (2) large quantities of information they do not know how to process, and (3) information the authenticity of which they cannot determine, they will feel information anxiety. In the judgment of information needs, there lies the difference between "what we already know" and "what we must know", and this is the fundamental cause of information anxiety. Furthermore, the mobile phone swipe trajectories of the children revealed that older children displayed greater total exploration depth with regard to accessible information, whereas younger children displayed greater total exploration depth with regard to diagnostic information. We infer that diagnostic information counts as word-of-mouth marketing, and word-of-mouth influences persuasiveness, which reduces the information burden carried by children. This further indicates that diagnostic information has credibility, thereby increasing the total exploration depth of younger children with regard to diagnostic information.

5.3 Eye Movement Behavior for Different Information Systems

Analysis of the eye movement data revealed that the first time the participants were choosing a book with accessible information, the eleven-year-old and twelve-year-old participants presented significantly greater total fixation area than the ten-year-old participants, whereas the ten-year-old participants presented significantly greater total fixation area than the nine-year-old participants. The third time the participants were choosing a book, the twelve-year-old participants presented significantly longer fixation durations than the eleven-year-old participants, and the eleven-year-old participants presented significantly longer fixation durations than the ten-year-old participants. We speculate that this was because nine-year-olds and ten-year-olds are still in the stage of static visual acuity changes. This means it takes them longer to visually process information and they may need to repeatedly gaze at the same information to identify and explain it. As a result, they presented shorter fixation durations and smaller total fixation area. The information-seeking behavior of children influences the way they gaze at information to varying degrees. Our experiment revealed that the number of round-trip choices influences fixation durations involving accessible information and fixation area per second involving diagnostic information. When children face a large amount of information, their brains will prioritize parts of the information based on their content. Information that they are interested in generally receives more attention [32].

6 Conclusion

This study contributes to the literature in its application of the accessibility-diagnosticity model. We identified and assessed the visual perception process of children based on their eye movement behavior and employed physiological and psychological indicators to speculate on and explain their information identification responses so as to verify the cognitive effectives of different types of information. Only systems matching the behavior and cognition of children can effectively interact with them. Thus, based on the results of our experiments, we put forward the following suggestions for future studies: 1. Due to the COVID-19 pandemic, we adopted random sampling for our experiment, which resulted in a biased gender ratio. We did not examine the impact of gender in our experiments, but gender differences did exist [33]. Goodway [34] also discovered more developed visual acuity among boys than among girls. We therefore suggest that future studies include gender as a variable and investigate gender differences. 2. We only analyzed perceptual speed and associative memory in this study and found that associative memory had little impact. We suggest that future studies explore the influence of other cognitive abilities (such as spatial scanning or reasoning skills) on the information-seeking behavior and eye movement behavior of children. 3. Analysis of the information-seeking behavior of the children revealed that there was too much accessible information for the younger participants, so they displayed lower degrees of information involvement than the older participants. We suggest that the number of book recommendations takes into account the degree of involvement of children of different ages so as not to exceed their capacity for information load.

References

1. Wilson, T.D.: Human information behavior. Inform. Sci. **3**, 49 (2000)
2. Reuter, K., Druin, A.: Bringing together children and books: an initial descriptive study of children's book searching and selection behavior in a digital library. Proc. Am. Soc. Inf. Sci. Technol. **41**, 339–348 (2004)
3. Knoblich, G., Ohlsson, S., Raney, G.E.: An eye movement study of insight problem solving. Mem. Cognit. **29**, 1000–1009 (2001). https://doi.org/10.3758/BF03195762
4. Fischer, K.W.: A theory of cognitive development: the control and construction of hierarchies of skills. Psychol. Rev. **87**, 477 (1980)
5. Sanders, M.S., McCormick, E.J.: Human factors in engineering and design. Ind. Robot Int. J. **25**, 153 (1998). https://doi.org/10.1108/ir.1998.25.2.153.2
6. Feldman, J.M., Lynch, J.G.: Self-generated validity and other effects of measurement on belief, attitude, intention, and behavior. J. Appl. Psychol. **73**, 421 (1988)
7. Dick, A., Chakravarti, D., Biehal, G.: Memory-based inferences during consumer choice. J. Consum. Res. **17**, 82–93 (1990). https://doi.org/10.1086/208539
8. Herr, P.M., Kardes, F.R., Kim, J.: Effects of word-of-mouth and product-attribute information on persuasion: an accessibility-diagnosticity perspective. J. Consum. Res. **17**, 454–462 (1991). https://doi.org/10.1086/208570
9. Lynch, J.G., Marmorstein, H., Weigold, M.F.: Choices from sets including remembered brands: use of recalled attributes and prior overall evaluations. J. Consum. Res. **15**, 169–184 (1988)

10. Broniarczyk, S.M., Alba, J.W.: The importance of the brand in brand extension. J. Mark. Res. **31**, 214–228 (1994)

11. Kahneman, D., Tversky, A.: Prospect theory: an analysis of decision under risk. In: Handbook of the Fundamentals of Financial Decision Making, pp. 99–127. World Scientific (2012). https://doi.org/10.1142/9789814417358_0006

12. Maheswaran, D., Meyers-Levy, J.: The influence of message framing and issue involvement. J. Mark. Res. **27**, 361–367 (1990)

13. Smith, G.E.: Framing in advertising and the moderating impact of consumer education. J. Advert. Res. **36**, 49 (1996)

14. Dervin, B.: From the Mind's Eye of the User: The Sense-Making Qualitative-Quantitative Methodology. Hampton Press (1992)

15. Marchionini, G.: Information Seeking in Electronic Environments. Cambridge University Press (1997)

16. Wilson, T.D.: On user studies and information needs. J. Doc. (1981)

17. Moore, P.: Information problem solving: a wider view of library skills. Contemp. Educ. Psychol. **20**, 1–31 (1995). https://doi.org/10.1006/ceps.1995.1001

18. Kuhlthau, C.C.: Developing a model of the library search process: cognitive and affective aspects. RQ **28**, 232–242 (1988)

19. Almourad, M.B., Bataineh, E.: Comparing the behaviour of human face capturing attention of autistic & normal developing children using eye tracking data analysis approach. In: Proceedings of the 2019 3rd International Conference on Advances in Artificial Intelligence, New York, NY, USA, pp. 221–226. Association for Computing Machinery (2019). https://doi.org/10.1145/3369114.3369122

20. Frutos-Pascual, M., García-Zapirain, B., Mehdi, Q.H.: Where do they look at? Analysis of gaze interaction in children while playing a puzzle game. In: 2015 Computer Games: AI, Animation, Mobile, Multimedia, Educational and Serious Games (CGAMES), pp. 103–106 (2015). https://doi.org/10.1109/CGames.2015.7272954

21. Syeda, U.H., et al.: Visual face scanning and emotion perception analysis between autistic and typically developing children. In: Proceedings of the 2017 ACM International Joint Conference on Pervasive and Ubiquitous Computing and Proceedings of the 2017 ACM International Symposium on Wearable Computers, New York, NY, USA, pp. 844–853. Association for Computing Machinery (2017). https://doi.org/10.1145/3123024.3125618

22. Just, M.A., Carpenter, P.A.: A theory of reading: from eye fixations to comprehension. Psychol. Rev. **87**, 329 (1980)

23. Rayner, K.: Eye movements in reading and information processing: 20 years of research. Psychol. Bull. **124**, 372 (1998)

24. Land, M.F.: Eye movements and the control of actions in everyday life. Prog. Retin. Eye Res. **25**, 296–324 (2006)

25. Carroll, J.B.: Human Cognitive Abilities: A Survey of Factor-Analytic Studies. https://doi.org/10.1017/CBO9780511571312, https://libsearch.ntut.edu.tw:3716/core/books/human-cognitive-abilities/F83D5EADF14A453F6350FF3DD39631C8. Accessed 27 May 2022

26. Allen, B.: Cognitive differences in end user searching of a CD-ROM index. In: Proceedings of the 15th annual international ACM SIGIR conference on Research and development in information retrieval, New York, NY, USA, pp. 298–309. Association for Computing Machinery (1992). https://doi.org/10.1145/133160.133212

27. Ashcraft, M.H.: Human memory and cognition. Scott, Foresman & Co (1989)

28. Ekstrom, R., French, J., Dermen, D.: Kit of factor-referenced cognitive tests. Educational Testing Service (1976)

29. Hourcade, J.P.: Interaction design and children. Now Publishers Inc. (2008)

30. LEE, Y.-W.: The Effect of Augmented Reality Navigation on Children's Learning Motivation and Information Seeking Behavior – A Case Study of the Augmented Reality Navigation Application (2019). https://ndltd.ncl.edu.tw/cgi-bin/gs32/gsweb.cgi/ccd=NDG6Kt/record?r1=2&h1=0
31. Wurman, R.S.: Information Anxiety. New York (1989)
32. Plebanek, D.J., Sloutsky, V.M.: Selective attention, filtering, and the development of working memory. Dev. Sci. **22**, e12727 (2019). https://doi.org/10.1111/desc.12727
33. Hsieh, T., Wu, K.: The Influence of Gender Difference on the Information-seeking Behaviors for the Graphical Interface of Children's Digital Library. Universal Journal of Education
34. Goodway, J.D., Ozmun, J.C., Gallahue, D.L.: Understanding Motor Development: Infants, Children, Adolescents, Adults. Jones & Bartlett Learning (2019)

Emotions in HCI

Emotion Recognition via Facial Expressions to Improve Virtual Communication in Videoconferences

Bärbel Bissinger[1]([⊠]), Anja Beer[1], Christian Märtin[1], and Michael Fellmann[2]

[1] Computer Science, Augsburg University of Applied Sciences, Augsburg, Germany
{baerbel.bissinger,anja.beer1,christian.maertin}@hs-augsburg.de
[2] Business Information Systems, University of Rostock, Rostock, Germany
michael.fellmann@uni-rostock.de

Abstract. One of the most important things for successful projects is communication. Especially in agile software development face-to-face communication plays a central role. Face-to-face conversations are also one of the most direct and most emotional forms of human interaction. Facial expressions communicate emotions to others and can have a strong impact on conversations, perception, and decision-making.

Due to the Covid-19 pandemic and digitalization more and more meetings and workshops take place virtually or hybrid. Many social cues and non-verbal signals are more difficult to share in a virtual set-up or are getting lost completely. Since face-to-face communication and facial expressions are so important for the success of a project and the perception of emotions, we are trying to find ways to bridge the gap of emotion recognition between on-site meetings and videoconferences. We are investigating, how software could support participants of videoconferences to improve virtual communications efficiently with empirical and qualitative research.

In this paper, we present the results of two experimental user studies of facial expression recognition (FER) during videoconferences. In one study we did an analysis of emotion recognition after the meeting with a FER-tool, a human observer, and self-assessments of the participants. In another study, we visualized emotional states in real-time during a business meeting with the help of human observers and a simulation. We realized that both, humans, and the FER-tool, had difficulties to recognize emotions in specific situations and that there is room for improvement. In general, positive emotions were easier to identify than negative ones. Most participants were open to visualizing emotions and considered the information during a meeting as helpful, but also mentioned that it can be distracting. Therefore, a suitable form of emotion recognition and visualization which takes the productivity and wellbeing of the participants into account needs to be developed and evaluated.

Keywords: Facial expression recognition · facial expressions · human emotions · professional environment · virtual human interaction · videoconferences

M. Kurosu and A. Hashizume (Eds.): HCII 2023, LNCS 14012, pp. 151–163, 2023.
https://doi.org/10.1007/978-3-031-35599-8_10

1   Introduction and Motivation

1.1   Success Rate of Software Projects

According to the Standish Group's CHAOS report, which looks at the success and failures of software projects through long-term studies, only 29% of software projects were successful from 2011 to 2015. Successful here means the project was *on time, on budget and within a satisfactory result*. In total, over 25,000 software projects worldwide were included in this analysis [1].

Fig. 1. Success rate of software projects according to the report of Standish Group 2015

As shown in Fig. 1, more than half of the software projects did not end on time, on budget, or with a satisfactory result. 19% of the projects could not achieve a usable result and are therefore considered to have failed. The economic damage is therefore very high.

1.2   Communication and Collaboration as Success Factor for Projects

As numerous studies and research papers show, communication and collaboration are important success factors for IT projects [2–5]. According to a project management study conducted by *GPM Deutsche Gesellschaft für Projektmanagement e.V.* and *PA Consulting Group* in 2008, e.g., the quality of communication is the second most frequently cited cause for either successful, or failed projects. A total of 79 companies were surveyed, with a high proportion from the automotive, consulting and IT sectors [4].

1.3   Virtual Collaboration

Due to the Covid-19 pandemic, many meetings are currently held virtually and this trend is likely to continue in the future [6]. This changes how humans communicate and collaborate. In virtual environments, many social cues and nonverbal communications get lost or are more difficult to exchange [7, 8]. This, e.g., makes it difficult to express or recognize emotions. Since emotions play a significant role in all human actions and are essential for our perception, communication and decision-making [9], we are trying to find ways to bridge the gap of emotion recognition between on-site meetings and videoconferences.

1.4 Previous Research

In a previous paper [10] we summarized the importance of emotions and presented possible use cases for automated, artificial intelligence (AI) based facial expression recognition (FER)-Tools, which we divided into two areas: *group level* and *individual level*. The use cases on group level aim at improving the communication in videoconferences, the use cases on individual level focus on training and self-reflection. After a literature review [11] and first tests focusing on the accuracy of emotion recognition, we verified that neither humans nor FER-tools can always definitely detect emotions based on facial expressions. In most cases, however, humans outperform the FER-tools according to a performance comparison of Dupré et al. with eight FER-tools and human observers [12]. This comparison was done with two dynamic facial expression data bases, which contain posed and spontaneous expressions.

As part of previous research, we developed a prototype, the Visualizer, which is able to analyze facial expressions with the help of a FER-tool as well as speaking times and chat activities in videoconferences [10].

2 User Studies

To investigate further, we tested one of the FER-tools, FaceReader from Noldus[1], in real-life scenarios in videoconferences. Furthermore, we performed another user study where we did not use an AI-based FER-tool. Instead, emotion recognition was done by human observers.

The goal is to find ways to bridge the gap of emotion recognition between on-site meetings and videoconferences.

2.1 User Study 1: Emotion Recognition After the Meeting by a FER-Tool

We conducted a small-scale user study in which we analyzed emotional states of videoconference participants. In this study, we used a FER-tool which analyzes the faces and interprets the associated emotional states automatically with the help of AI. In addition, we collected the subjective impressions of the participants with a self-report questionnaire after the videoconference. We compared the subjective impressions with the results of the computer-based measurements and a human observer to validate the results of the AI.

Goal. By comparing the tool's analysis with the personal impressions of the participants and with the interpretation of human observers we want to validate the FER-analysis results.

Setup. For this study, we have chosen an online meeting with personal topics to evoke many emotions in the participants. As video conferencing platform we selected Zoom.

---

[1] https://www.noldus.com/facereader.

We recorded the meeting and analyzed the facial expressions of the participants afterwards with a FER-Tool based on AI, with a questionnaire to collect personal impressions of the participants and with a human observer.

With Zoom's cloud recording, the gallery view is available with all attendees, but without separate video streams of the participants [13]. For the FER analysis, we had to cut out the participants' videos from the gallery view video for each participant because we can only analyze one face at a time with our FER-tool and license. This limited the number of participants. With more than nine participants per gallery view, the video resolution per participant becomes too low for the FER-tool to perform a useful analysis. Three female and three male participants between the ages of 26 and 29 volunteered to participate in the study. During the meeting, participants were asked to keep their camera on to not change the arrangement of the videos in the gallery view.

The meeting should trigger different emotions. Therefore, we recreated situations of a job interview or a feedback session with personal questions. During the meeting, different types of personal questions were asked, such as "What are your strengths and weaknesses?" and "How do you deal with conflicts between you and your colleagues?". We allotted four minutes for each participant in the meeting. In addition to a question-and-answer session, there was a guided discussion about individual questions.

After the meeting, participants were given a self-report questionnaire to assess their emotions during the meeting using Ekman's basic emotions [14, 15] and to indicate situations in which they felt certain emotions. A total of 16 situations were indicated by the participants.

The participants' video recordings were read into the FER tool and analyzed. In addition, the observer gave his interpretation of the participants' emotions. The results of the FER-tool and the observer's interpretation were compared with the information provided by the participants. Through the information provided by the participants, the results of the FER-tool could be validated to reveal strengths and weaknesses.

Table 1. Emotions recognized by human observer and reported by participants

Situation	Participant	Emotions indicated by the participant	Emotions interpreted by human observer
1	Participant 1	Happy	Neutral
2	Participant 1	Surprised	Happy
3	Participant 2	Happy	Happy
4	Participant 2	Angry	Contempt
5	Participant 2	Surprised	Surprised
6	Participant 3	Happy	Happy
7	Participant 3	Angry	Sad
8	Participant 3	Surprised	Happy
9	Participant 3	Scared	Scared
10	Participant 4	Happy	Happy
11	Participant 4	Surprised	Neutral
12	Participant 4	Scared	Scared
13	Participant 5	Happy	Happy
14	Participant 5	Surprised	Neutral
15	Participant 6	Happy	Happy
16	Participant 6	Surprised	Happy

Analysis and Results. The recognized emotions of the human observer and the felt emotions which were reported by the participants afterwards are shown in Table 1. The recognized emotions of the FER-tool are visible in Table 2.

Table 2. Emotions recognized by FER-tool

Situation	Participant	Emotions detected by the FER-tool							
		Neutral	Happy	Sad	Angry	Surprised	Scared	Disgusted	Contempt
1	Participant 1	0.70	**0.27**	0.03	0.00	0.00	0.00	0.00	0.12
2	Participant 1	0.11	0.84	0.01	0.00	**0.00**	0.00	0.00	0.02
3	Participant 2	0.12	**0.82**	0.00	0.00	0.00	0.00	0.00	0.06
4	Participant 2	0.52	0.03	0.05	**0.05**	0.00	0.00	0.06	0.02
5	Participant 2	0.57	0.30	0.00	0.01	**0.08**	0.00	0.00	0.08
6	Participant 3	0.05	**0.90**	0.00	0.00	0.00	0.00	0.00	0.00
7	Participant 3	0.14	0.72	0.00	**0.00**	0.00	0.00	0.04	0.00
8	Participant 3	0.15	0.70	0.00	0.00	**0.00**	0.00	0.00	0.01
9	Participant 3	0.52	0.00	0.01	0.37	0.00	**0.00**	0.00	0.00
10	Participant 4	0.03	**0.95**	0.03	0.00	0.00	0.00	0.00	0.01
11	Participant 4	0.49	0.00	0.36	0.00	0.00	0.00	0.04	0.00
12	Participant 4	0.64	0.01	0.01	0.08	0.04	0.01	0.01	0.16
13	Participant 5	0.22	**0.60**	0.00	0.00	0.00	0.00	0.00	0.00
14	Participant 5	0.03	0.96	0.00	0.00	**0.00**	0.00	0.00	0.00
15	Participant 6	0.04	**0.93**	0.00	0.00	0.00	0.00	0.00	0.00
16	Participant 6	0.80	0.09	0.00	0.00	**0.00**	0.00	0.00	0.05

The human observer correctly interpreted the positive emotion *Happy* in five out of six cases and the emotion *Surprised* in one out of six cases. The emotion *Scared* Was recognized by the human observer in two out of two cases and the emotion *Angry* in zero out of two cases. In comparison, the FER-tool was able to correctly interpret all positive emotions and one out of four of the other emotions. The result shows that both the human observer and the FER-tool can interpret positive emotions more easily than negative emotions.

It was difficult for the human observer to recognize emotions that were only slightly shown. The FER-tool was able to capture slightly shown emotions and mixed emotions, as it displayed gentle deflections for the respective emotion in each case (see for example situation 1).

From the user study, the AI-based tool's detection rate was lower when subjects moved their head or eyes, such as lowering their head or looking away from the camera. For example, the emotion *Sad* was detected when participants looked at the table in front of them. Similarly, for individuals with special physical signs, such as noticeably large eyes, the FER-tool had difficulties detecting that person's various emotions, even after calibration for that specific face. In these cases, human observers were better able to assess emotional states from additional information like context and voice.

In summary for this user study, the use of an FER-tool can lead to more insights, especially when emotions are easily shown or when participants focus on content other than the videos during a meeting. However, the accuracy of the FER-tool in real-time videoconferences was not as good as expected; especially when people move a lot, have noticeable facial signs, or when the quality of the videos is low.

2.2   User Study 2: Emotion Recognition in Real-Time by Human Observers

Since the FER-tool was not outperforming humans in real online meetings, and since the usage of AI-based tools is very complex in German companies due to unclear regulations regarding AI as well as important privacy policies and laws, we conducted another small-scale user study without the usage of AI. As an alternative we used a simulation where the emotion recognition was performed by human observers.

Goal. We aimed at investigating whether the visualization of emotional states during a business video meeting might be helpful or distracting and how emotional states can be visualized. As a start for further exploration of *Group Level – Use Case: Remote Meeting* [10], we did a user study in which we visualized emotional states of participants in real-time during a videoconference of a business meeting. By collecting feedback, we wanted to gather information for further developing the Visualizer-Prototype.

Setup. For this user study, we chose a business meeting with a limited number of participants (<10) and with focus on exchange, connectivity, and collaboration. The meeting is a regular exchange opportunity for experts and interested people to share their knowledge, challenges, and ideas on similar topics. We have chosen this type of meeting to have an open atmosphere and to have many people actively involved during the videoconference.

The study included a pre-survey with a self-assessment, a videoconference with real-time emotion visualization and a questionnaire afterwards which contained a report with a summary of interaction data of the meeting.

Participants were nine people who volunteered to take part in the study during this meeting and in the surveys before and after the meeting. Five participants were female, four were male, ages ranged from 27 to 54 years, and work experience ranged from three to 27 years. One person was unable to attend the meeting on short notice, so we had eight participants for the entire study and nine participants for the self-assessment.

We did a written survey with each participant before and after the meeting. The pre-survey included a self-assessment for emotion recognition via faces. For that purpose, we used static images of basic emotions according to Ekman. The dataset included the following acted basic emotions shown by different people: *Happy, Sad, Angry, Surprised, Scared, Disgusted and Contempt.* Each basic emotion was represented by four images. Two of the four images show the emotion on women and two images show the emotion on men. In total, 28 images needed to be evaluated by each participant during the self-assessment.

The pre-survey determined how well these emotions can be recognized from these facial images. In addition, the participants assessed the difficulty of the test and their personal test results. The purpose of this was to give us some insights on how good the participants are at recognizing emotions in images and how they rate themselves. Moreover, with the results of the self-assessments, we tested our hypothesis that if people, who are struggling to recognize emotions would see more need for assistance in emotion recognition during online meetings than people, who are good at identifying emotions in other people's faces.

During the meeting, participants were asked to turn on their cameras, but they had the opportunity to turn it off in between if they wanted to. The recognized emotions of all participants who had their camera activated were visualized as bar charts and available for everyone during the meeting.

In the Visualizer-Prototype, other interaction data like speaking time and individual emotions for example are available. To not distract people during the meeting and focus on emotions, we provided other interaction data afterwards in a report. During the meeting, we focused on emotional states only. Since the Visualizer-Prototype is based on AI, we used a simulation of it. Therefore, we created a simulation prototype with Figma[2], a collaborative software to create porotypes focusing on User Experience (UX) which feel like the real experience. The recognized emotions in the **Figma-Prototype** were adapted in real-time during the meeting which was done by human observers. A screenshot of the Figma-Prototype is shown in Fig. 2.

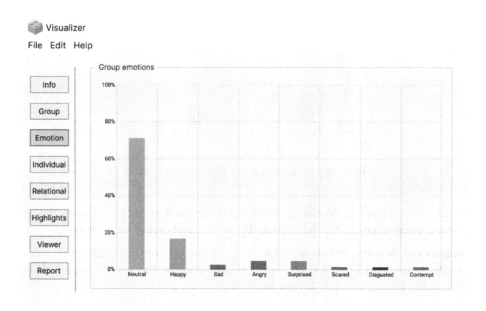

Fig. 2. Figma-Prototype – Group emotions

After the videocall, we provided participants with a session report that included information about the meeting and interaction data such as voice activity, chat messages, and a summary of emotion recognition. A screenshot of the report is shown in Fig. 3.

At the end of the study, participants were asked to complete a questionnaire. This questionnaire focused on collecting subjective impressions of the participants to verify whether the shown information during the meeting is considered as helpful and if the participants see a need for visualizing emotional states and other interaction data during

---

[2] https://www.figma.com/prototyping/.

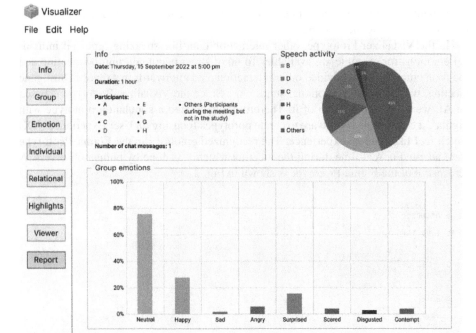

Fig. 3. Report which was provided after the meeting

or after a virtual meeting. Moreover, we asked for feedback on our prototype including structure, comprehensibility, and applicability to iteratively refine our prototype.

Analysis and Results. Pre-survey with self-assessment: In total, the nine participants collectively assessed 252 emotions via faces of the images. The answers are visible in Table 3. The correct emotions are marked in grey.

The results of the self-assessments show that the basic emotions *Happy* and *Surprised* were recognized most frequently, while the emotion *Scared* was identified least frequently. *Happy* was recognized by all participants in all four images and is the only emotion which has a 100% recognition rate. *Surprised* was recognized with a rate of 97.22%. *Scared* was registered with a rate of 16, 67%. Moreover, Table 3 shows that images indicating *anger* have a tendency to be perceived as *Contempt*.

None of the participants stated that they could easily recognize the emotions shown on the faces and none rated their own answers as very good. People who were best at recognizing emotions were people with many years of work or people with children.

Questionnaire After the Meeting with Report: In general, all respondents felt that the information was presented in an understandable way. 87.5% of the respondents (7/8) answered that the information helped them to draw conclusions about the emotional situation in the team, and 62.5% (5/8) reported, it increased their awareness of the emotional situation of individual team members. For 75% of respondents (6/8), the report is helpful to better assess their own linguistic involvement in the meeting. 75%

Table 3. Results of emotion recognition

Image	Emotion shown in image	Emotions recognized by participants						
		Happy	Sad	Angry	Surprised	Scared	Disgusted	Contempt
1	Happy	9	0	0	0	0	0	0
2	Scared	0	0	2	0	1	5	1
3	Contempt	0	2	0	0	0	0	7
4	Scared	0	2	2	2	2	0	1
5	Disgusted	0	0	1	0	0	7	1
6	Sad	0	7	0	0	1	0	1
7	Disgusted	0	0	4	0	0	2	3
8	Scared	0	0	0	9	0	0	0
9	Sad	0	5	1	0	2	0	1
10	Contempt	4	0	0	0	0	0	5
11	Surprised	0	0	0	9	0	0	0
12	Angry	1	0	6	0	0	0	2
13	Happy	9	0	0	0	0	0	0
14	Surprised	0	0	0	9	0	0	0
15	Sad	0	3	2	0	4	0	0
16	Scared	0	0	1	2	3	0	3
17	Angry	0	0	6	0	0	0	3
18	Disgusted	0	0	3	0	0	6	0
19	Contempt	0	0	0	0	0	0	9
20	Happy	9	0	0	0	0	0	0
21	Sad	0	2	2	0	2	0	3
22	Surprised	1	0	0	8	0	0	0
23	Angry	0	0	4	0	0	0	5
24	Contempt	3	0	4	1	0	0	1
25	Happy	9	0	0	0	0	0	0
26	Angry	0	0	3	1	0	2	3
27	Disgusted	0	0	0	0	0	7	2
28	Surprised	0	0	0	9	0	0	0

of the participants (6/8) had a positive attitude towards the visualization of emotions and considered having the information during a meeting as helpful. Even considering the information as helpful, 50% (4/8) mentioned that it can be distracting as well. Other individual participants felt stressed, because of the additional input or mentioned they would fear an impact on their careers, if such an approach would be used regularly.

37.5% of respondents (3/8) reported that they do not behave normally when they know that their facial expressions are analyzed.

For 25% (2/8), the information displayed in the report (computer-aided facial expression analysis and the display of chat and voice activities during a meeting) would provide added value.

Participants, who had difficulties in recognizing emotions during the survey, did not see the need for the visualization of emotions during meetings. This refutes our hypothesis that people who are struggling would see more need for this assistance. It could be explained with the well-known *Dunning-Kruger-Effect*, which describes "*how difficulties in recognizing one's own incompetence lead to inflated self-assessments*" [16].

2.3 Discussion

The small-scale studies underline that emotion recognition via facial expressions is a complex topic and that there are not always explicit or unambiguous assessments.

Even though there are certain physical signals such as facial expressions that indicate a specific emotion, one signal alone was often not enough. Both humans and the FER-tool had difficulties to always identify the emotion unequivocally. This was shown in

Study 1 as well as in the self-assessment of Study 2. In Study 1, the FER-tool detected other emotions than humans in specific situations, who had the context of the discussion and other verbal and non-verbal information as indicators for emotions in addition to facial expressions. In the self-assessment of Study 2, where people did not have any context or additional information, participants had difficulties to recognize emotions by only seeing the faces in the images.

Happy was the emotion which was recognized best. This is the only clearly positive one of the basic emotions. The other basic emotions are more difficult to distinguish from each other. In general, people did recognize fewer "negative" emotions than the FER-tool in Study 1. A possible explanation for that could be that people tend to not show or report negative emotions in a business environment or in our culture in general even though all emotions are important. The FER-tool might be a more neutral observer than colleagues in this case.

In the questionnaire of Study 2, people reported on the one hand that the prototype helps them to better understand the emotional situation in the team, on the other hand participants gave the feedback they have the expression that their emotional reactions might change knowing it will be analyzed. This means that the results could be distorted. It could also happen that people focus more on their own facial expressions and less on the reactions of others or on the content of the meeting. There might be positive and negative effects of FER, just as self-view during videoconferences can have positive and negative consequences. According to a study with 179 participants [17] which is focusing on the impact of self-view in online meetings, seeing oneself can have a positive effect on self-awareness, but a negative one on enjoyment and perceived productivity for example. The negative effects are higher in an information consuming role.

Another feedback was that the real-time display of emotional states could be an additional stressor as it is another input to watch out for. This means the approach could also increase the fatigue caused by videoconferences, which is known as a phenomenon called *Zoom-Fatigue* [18–20].

Therefore, the perceived wellbeing and fatigue should be considered as well. Another person mentioned possible negative effects on the career, if such an approach would be used regularly. This underlines that the visualization of emotions should be voluntary, there should always be the possibility to turn the emotion recognition off and that the data protection rules must be considered. Therefore, ethical standards or value-based design must be taken into account [21]. Moreover, guidelines for systematic assessment and mitigation of risks posed by emotion recognition systems need to be considered [22].

2.4 Limitations

Limitations of our studies are the small number of participants and the heterogeneity of the test groups, what limits the meaningfulness of the results. Another limitation might be that we just tested one FER-tool. The second user study was done without an AI based tool, but with a simulation of it, by using human observers as emotional interpreters. There were occasional slight delays in the display during the real-time emotional visualization. The correctness of the simulation and the slight delays could have an impact on the experience of the participants.

In Study 1 we compared the results of the FER-tool with the personal impressions of the participants. The questionnaire to collect the felt emotions was done after the meeting to not distract during the videoconference. The delayed reporting of emotions may have affected the results, as participants could not remember all the emotions they felt.

For the self-assessment in Study 2 we used static images. The static images limit the transferability of the results to videoconferences.

3   Conclusion and Future Work

The results of our studies indicate that there is a need for improvement for the recognition of emotional states during videoconferences and that there is a need for improvement of emotion recognition via faces, both for humans and AI-based FER-tools. It also emphasizes that emotions are difficult to capture and that there are many challenges. In general, the positive emotion *Happy* was the easiest to recognize. In some situations, the FER-tool could lead to more insights, especially when emotions are slightly shown, or it could assist when people are focusing on content other than the videos. In other situations, the self-reports of the participants or the human observer interpretations were more accurate because they could use information other than facial expressions alone.

Through the user studies, we have received valuable feedback that will help us in the iterative development of the prototypes. Other interaction data like chat activities and speaking times, which were presented to the participants afterwards in the report, did not add value to the majority of participants in Study 2.

Most participants were open to visualizing emotions and considered the information during a meeting as helpful, but also mentioned that it can be distracting.

Future work could validate the findings of those small-scale user studies, evaluate combined approaches that also use EEG- and voice-based recognition methods or test different alternatives to AI-based emotion recognition like real-time self-reporting's.

Our future research focuses on the question how the information should be presented or visualized to not distract people during the meetings. It should also take the perceived wellbeing and fatigue into account, to verify whether visualizations of emotions are reducing or increasing the fatigue. This could be validated in future studies with the measure for Zoom-Fatigue, for example with the *Zoom Exhaustion & Fatigue Scale* by Fauville et al. [23].

Another option to reduce the effects of self-view and fatigue from activated cameras during videoconferences could be to measure and visualize not the recognized emotions but the real facial expressions and show them in a virtual version as an animated smiley or avatar, as is for example possible with the headset Quest Pro from Meta.[3] This could help to reduce the time with activated cameras, but still be able to show emotions through facial expressions.

Another important research area are ethical design guidelines, as mentioned in Sect. 2.3 Discussion.

---

[3] https://www.meta.com/de/quest/quest-pro/.

References

1. CHAOS REPORT 2015. The Standish Group International, Inc. (2015). https://www.standi shgroup.com/sample_research_files/CHAOSReport2015-Final.pdf
2. Qian, W., Zhen-hua, S.: Research on multi-perspective communication management of software development project based on theory of project management. In: 2010 2nd International Conference on Signal Processing Systems, Dalian, China, pp. V3-192–V3-195, July 2010. https://doi.org/10.1109/ICSPS.2010.5555844
3. Fan, D.: Analysis of critical success factors in IT project management, in 2010 2nd International Conference on Industrial and Information Systems, Dalian, China, Jul. 2010, pp. 487–490. https://doi.org/10.1109/INDUSIS.2010.5565760
4. Engel, C., Tamdjidi, A., Quadejacob, N.: Projektmanagement Studie 2008 'Erfolg und Scheitern im Projektmanagement' (2008). https://www.gpm-ipma.de/fileadmin/user_upload/GPM/ Know-How/Ergebnisse_Erfolg_und_Scheitern-Studie_2008.pdf
5. Gheni, A., Jusoh, Y., Jabar, M.A., Mohd Ali, N.: The Critical Success Factors (CSFs) for IT projects. J. Telecommun. Electron. Comput. Eng. (JTEC) 9(3–3) (2017)
6. McKinsey Global Institute. The future of work after COVID-19. McKinsey (2021)
7. Acai, A., Sonnadara, R.R., O'Neill, T.A.: Getting with the times: a narrative review of the literature on group decision making in virtual environments and implications for promotions committees. Perspect. Med. Educ. 7(3), 147–155 (2018). https://doi.org/10.1007/s40037-018-0434-9
8. Oeppen, R.S., Shaw, G., Brennan, P.A.: Human factors recognition at virtual meetings and video conferencing: how to get the best performance from yourself and others. Br. J. Oral Maxillofac. Surg. 58(6), 643–646 (2020). https://doi.org/10.1016/j.bjoms.2020.04.046
9. Picard, R.W.: Affective Computing, July 2000. https://doi.org/10.7551/mitpress/1140.001. 0001
10. Bissinger, B., Märtin, C., Fellmann, M.: Support of virtual human interactions based on facial emotion recognition software. In: Kurosu, M. (ed.) Human-Computer Interaction. Technological Innovation, vol. 13303, pp. 329–339. Springer, Cham (2022). https://doi.org/10.1007/ 978-3-031-05409-9_25
11. Bissinger, B., Fellmann, M., Märtin, C., Hohmann, D.: Emotionserkennungssoftware auf Basis von Gesichtsausdrücken als Möglichkeit zur Unterstützung der virtuellen Zusammenarbeit. Gesellschaft für Informatik e.V. (2022). http://dl.gi.de/handle/20.500.12116/39674. Accessed 13 Dec 2022
12. Dupré, D., Krumhuber, E.G., Küster, D., McKeown, G.J.: A performance comparison of eight commercially available automatic classifiers for facial affect recognition. PLoS ONE 15(4), e0231968 (2020). https://doi.org/10.1371/journal.pone.0231968
13. Zoom Video Communications, Inc.: Ändern der grundlegenden und erweiterten Einstellungen für Cloud-Aufzeichnungen, Zoom Support. https://support.zoom.us/hc/de/articles/ 360060316092-%C3%84ndern-der-grundlegenden-und-erweiterten-Einstellungen-f%C3% BCr-Cloud-Aufzeichnungen. Accessed 06 Feb 2023
14. Ekman, P., Sorenson, E.R., Friesen, W.V.: Pan-cultural elements in facial displays of emotion. Science 164(3875), 86–88 (1969). https://doi.org/10.1126/science.164.3875.86
15. Ekman, P., Cordaro, D.: What is meant by calling emotions basic. Emot. Rev. 3(4), 364–370 (2011). https://doi.org/10.1177/1754073911410740
16. Kruger, J., Dunning, D.: Unskilled and unaware of it: How difficulties in recognizing one's own incompetence lead to inflated self-assessments. J. Pers. Soc. Psychol. 77(6), 1121–1134 (1999). https://doi.org/10.1037/0022-3514.77.6.1121
17. Abramova, O., Gladkaya, M., Krasnova, H.: An unusual encounter with oneself: exploring the impact of self-view on online meeting outcomes completed research paper, December 2021

18. Riedl, R.: On the stress potential of videoconferencing: definition and root causes of Zoom fatigue. Electron. Mark. (2021). https://doi.org/10.1007/s12525-021-00501-3
19. Nesher Shoshan, H., Wehrt, W.: Understanding 'Zoom fatigue': a mixed-method approach. Appl. Psychol., p. apps.12360 (2021). https://doi.org/10.1111/apps.12360
20. Wang, B., Prester, J.: The Performative and Interpretive Labour of Videoconferencing: Findings from a Literature Review on 'Zoom' Fatigue (2022)
21. Friedman, B., Hendry, D.: Value Sensitive Design: Shaping Technology with Moral Imagination. The MIT Press, Cambridge (2019)
22. Hernandez, J., et al.: Guidelines for assessing and minimizing risks of emotion recognition applications. In: 2021 9th International Conference on Affective Computing and Intelligent Interaction (ACII), Nara, Japan, pp. 1–8, September 2021. https://doi.org/10.1109/ACII52 823.2021.9597452
23. Fauville, G., Luo, M., Queiroz, A.C.M., Bailenson, J.N., Hancock, J.: Zoom Exhaustion & Fatigue Scale. SSRN J. (2021). https://doi.org/10.2139/ssrn.3786329

Combining Computer-Based Activity Tracking with Human Energy and Sentiment Self-assessment for Continuous Work-Life Reflection

Michael Fellmann⬡, Fabienne Lambusch(✉)⬡, and Angelina Clara Schmidt(✉)⬡

University of Rostock, Business Information Systems, Rostock, Germany
{michael.fellmann,fabienne.lambusch,
angelina.schmidt}@uni-rostock.de

Abstract. The modern working world offers much flexibility and freedom, but also suffers from work intensification, constant time pressure and an increase of mental illnesses and burnout. Moreover, "healthy" working habits that ensure long-term productivity and well-being increasingly can no longer be prescribed by managers in a top-down fashion, since they highly depend on the individual. Therefore, there is a need for continuous work-related self-reflection on an individual basis in order to retain a high level of human energy, productivity and well-being during work. Current tools that support this predominantly focus on either time and task management, fitness-tracking, or mental health. An integrated approach is largely missing so far. Therefore, we design and implement a prototypical application that addresses this intersection of automatic computer activity tracking and daily IT-supported self-assessment of important well-being related variables. Among the variables tracked are sleep quality (morning assessment), human energy and sentiment (fluctuations throughout the day) as well as five user-configurable variables (evening assessment) with a preset on progress, autonomy, strength use, social contacts, and stress. In the work at hand, we first derive requirements for such a tool and then present its implementation resulting in our *Desktop Work-Life Tracker* (DWLT) system. We moreover describe which questions can be answered by such a tool and present a preliminary evaluation.

Keywords: Self-Tracking · Desktop Logging · Human Energy · Pictorial Scale · Productivity Management · Energy Management · Individual Feedback

1 Introduction

These days, many employees are confronted with very high work demands [1]. High workloads, knowledge-intense products and services as well as permanent time pressure can make it hard to keep pace with all requirements. In addition to that, modern communication means can also unintentionally lead to more multitasking and interruptions. All these circumstances can make it hard to retain one's energy and drive, to stay motivated, healthy, productive and be resilient. Moreover, they can induce long-term stress, which

M. Kurosu and A. Hashizume (Eds.): HCII 2023, LNCS 14012, pp. 164–181, 2023.
https://doi.org/10.1007/978-3-031-35599-8_11

can result in serious mental health problems such as burnout. Mental health problems are a major contributor to the overall burden of disease and are particularly concentrated in the working population, leading to a loss of human capital [2]. In addition, modern information and communication technology enables a higher degree of flexibility in daily work [3, 4]. On the one hand, this enables a more seamless integration of work and life, while on the other hand it challenges employees to balance their work and private life, as those boundaries increasingly tend to vanish [4, 5]. Thus, managing balance in life has become more challenging for individuals [5, 6].

This is a potential risk to health, as research found that people fail to make best choices in their own interest [7]. It is desirable that individuals critically reflect on their own behavior to discover strengths as well as necessary changes. Critical reflection has already be defined by Dewey in 1933 as "the active, persistent and careful consideration of any belief or supposed form of knowledge in the light of the grounds that support it and the further conclusions to which it tends" [8, p. 9] (for a comprehensive review on the notion of reflection, see [9]).

In the first place, it is information that is needed to compare different states and to target a healthier behaviour through so-called self-regulation [10]. The information can be collected, for example, via *self-observation* [11], which is a strategy to systematically gather data about the own behavior. However, gathering data manually might be time-consuming and impractical, especially in the work context. Indeed, designing and implementing IT-based tools that ease the burden of data collection and analysis for self-reflection is a promising avenue of research [12–14]. In this way, advanced systems have been developed that raise people's awareness for potential productivity or health issues. In more detail, IT can be supportive by collecting personally relevant information e.g. through desktop-based time tracking tools, mobile apps [13], or via wearable devices like smartwatches and fitness trackers. They can furthermore lead to surprising insights [15], as most humans tend to underestimate time passed. So, it is difficult to reconstruct details of a workday or to find out individual patterns or correlations. There can be complex interrelations as for example shown by Abdel Hadi et al. [16] for recovery activities, work-related rumination, and motivation. Hence, to profit from IT-supported self-observation, many variables have to be recorded and their effects and interrelations must be considered e.g., via visualizations or analytical instruments.

Summarizing, IT-based tools can assist in advanced self-observation. However, existing tools predominantly focus on specific topics such as tracking of time and tasks executed, physiological variables (e.g., fitness trackers) or track various variables of mental states to improve mental health. *An integrated approach that combines tracking of work-related variables such as time and productivity with more wellbeing and health-oriented variables is largely missing so far. Therefore, we propose a novel integrated approach which we denote as Desktop Work-Life Tracking.* In this paper, we mainly report on the prototypical implementation of the corresponding tool, the *Desktop Work-Life Tracker* (DWLT).

The remainder of the paper is structured as follows. In the next section, we provide an overview on related work. In Sect. 3, we elicit requirements while in Sect. 4, we report on the implementation of the combined tracking tool for computer-based activities and human energy and sentiment. In Sect. 5, we provide a preliminary evaluation and in Sect. 6 we summarize our results and provide an outlook.

2 Related Work

2.1 From Time Tracking to the Quantified Self

To support self-observation, time tracking tools are in widespread use that automatically record what is done on a computer. They serve to record the working time of a user e.g., for project management. More advanced tools such as *RescueTime* (rescuetime.com) also provide additional analytics such as an estimation of productive time or tracking of work-related goals. Using these tools, it is possible to explore what are the most productive hours or how many time was lost e.g., on distraction websites. Research has confirmed that these insights are valuable since in an empirical study, employees were surprised about various behaviors of themselves such as their work fragmentation [15]. In other words, employees estimated various variables of their working behaviors incorrectly. Recent time tracking tools such as *Timely* (timelyapp.com) moreover try to not only track time spent working on a computer with various applications, files and websites, but also to automatically assign time allocation to projects. *However, despite these advanced features, time tracking tools predominantly have a narrow focus on work- and productivity-related measurements. They do not embrace a more holistic understanding of work-life tracking that would also require to track a person's state in terms of wellbeing- or health-related variables. Embracing such an understanding would also require to track physiological variables.*

Tracking one's physiological variables is at the heart of the *quantified self*-movement. According to a team of authors around Gary Wolf [17], its core idea is all about "self-knowledge through numbers". That is, gaining more comprehension and understanding about oneself by measuring and interpreting some values in numbers (e.g., steps per day, heartbeats, etc.). Swan [18] provides a more precise definition to extend this approach. It states that *quantified self* is an umbrella term for the practice of tracking any kind of biological, physical, behavioral, or environmental data about oneself. Moreover, individuals may be highly intrinsically motivated in gathering such data and changing their behavior accordingly. The most common tools to gather physiological data are smartwatches and other wearable devices. According to a recent study, 7 out of 10 Americans track physiological variables on a regular basis, with 20% of them using smartwatches [21]. *However, while smartwatches and other wearable devices track various parameters such as steps, heart rate, calories burnt or sleep quality, they usually do not have a possibility to track one of the most fundamental variables for motivation and work productivity, that is: human energy.*

Although some tracking devices such as the Oura Ring compute measures indicating a sort of "readiness" to take action, this does not determine if an employee will have energy in the sense of feeling vitality or enthusiasm that is important for the decision to engage or not engage in a task. *Hence also tools from the quantified self fall short in supporting a more holistic work-life tracking that combines work tracking with health-related and wellbeing variables such as human energy.*

2.2   Human Energy and Sentiment as a Source of Vitality

The concept of *human energy* has been described in [25]. In the following, we briefly summarize it. Human energy is closely linked to well-being in terms of individual resource status [19]. Strain and recovery from work lead to an increase or decrease of the individual resource status over time [20] which can be characterized in terms of fatigue, (emotional) exhaustion, need for recovery, self-control capacity or vitality [21]. These states refer to different aspects of human energy [22] which can be understood as high levels of subjective vitality and low levels of fatigue [23, 24]. Fritz et al. state: "Human energy is a 'fuel' that helps organizations run successfully" [23].

Quinn et al. reviewed several energy-related literature and developed an integrated model of human energy [22]. The model differentiates between two types of human energy: physical energy and *energetic activation*. The physical energy is furthermore classified into potential energy (ATP and glucose) and kinetic energy. Energetic activation is "the degree to which people feel energized" [22]. It is "experienced as feelings of vitality, vigor or enthusiasm" [22]. It also plays a prominent role in regard to mental wellbeing [31], burnout and depression [32] being associated with a lack of energy [33].

Summarizing, energetic activation leads to intrinsic motivation, which makes people seek new challenges. *Quinn et al. state that the energetic activation is the limiting factor whether we invest our energy into an activity or not. Moreover, empirical studies suggest that long-term survival of companies is strongly associated with the employees' energy* [30]. *Taken together, human energy seems to be of vital importance for more holistic work-life tracking.*

Energetic activation furthermore can be understood as the level of arousal of an individual. Arousal in turn can be classified according to the emotional valence associated with it being positive or negative [27]. The basic idea is to classify energy according to its intensity (high or low) and sentiment (negative or positive). This distinction is also known as the *circumplex model* and can be traced back to Russel in the 1980s [28]. *All in all, energy and sentiment are highly relevant variables but in spite of this, support for human energy and sentiment tracking e.g. via digital solutions and their integration in self-management approaches has not yet received much attention* [34].

2.3   Human Energy Tracking

In the direction of human energy assessment, Spreitzer and Grant propose an energy audit, a self-observation and intervention class to improve energy management [35]. In their article, they describe how students recorded their energy trajectories and identified behaviors that benefit or impair personal energy. The authors report positive learning experiences by students, i.e., a clearer understanding of their energy trajectories, energy depleting or promoting factors, and even strategies to improve their energy. Actually, the class led to surprising insights for students like their low energy in the afternoon. They could also identify behaviors to be improved for better recovery, e.g., sleep practices and break activities, behaviors that are not sustainable, e.g., using energy drinks, and even behavioral strategies that could help them use their energy peaks, e.g., planning important work according to their typical energy curve. Spreitzer and Grant furthermore describe how already the increased awareness for the individual energy levels caused some students to change their behavior for improved energy management. They explicitly suggest using experience sampling methods in the future to automatically request energy assessments from the students at different points in time in comparison to their manual method.

Based on these insights, we have developed a first IT-supported energy audit tool based on formR [36]. Using the tool, users are prompted to fill in a questionnaire sent via email four times a day over a course of ten days. After this, users receive personal feedback about their most influential factors that drive or drain their energetic activation during a workday. Initial results from testing the study with samples of more than 100 test persons, which have not yet been published, show that there seem to be significant beneficial effects that are caused by the reflection on human. Hence in line with the results of Spreitzer, we can confirm empirical evidence that tracking and observing one's energy seems to be beneficial for energetic wellbeing, i.e., feeling higher levels of vitality instead of fatigue. Also, this study shows how different factors like micro-breaks [37] influence an individual's energy level. However, the biggest drawback of this study is a rather lengthy survey and its limited duration of usually ten days. Consequently, determining trends spanning several weeks is not possible. *Hence including continuous human energy tracking throughout the own working day would be highly valuable in order to gain insights and proactively increase the own energy level or prevent a decrease.*

Summarizing the motivation and related work introduced so far, we come to the following propositions:

(i) Self-observation is an important prerequisite for self-reflection which in turn is a precondition for self-management which nowadays is more important than ever, due to changes in the working world.
(ii) Current time tracking tools predominantly have a narrow focus on productivity and in this direction allow to accurately record how the time is spent. But they do not integrate wellbeing or health-related variables.
(iii) Complementary to time tracking, wearables in conjunction with quantified self-practices allow to track and analyze physiological or mental variables, but they lack tracking work-related variables such as working time or productivity and moreover lack an assessment of human energy.

Therefore, we derive requirements for an integrated self-tracking approach that integrates computer-based activity tracking with a (semi-)automated assessment of wellbeing and health-related variables and denote this approach as Desktop Work-Life Tracking.

3   Requirements for Integrated Desktop Work-Life Tracking

In the following, we present requirements for our *Desktop Work-Life Tracking* (DWLT) tool. First, we derive requirements for *data tracking and self-assessment*. Next, we derive requirements for data *visualization and analysis* and finally, we devise *personalization* requirements.

3.1 Data Tracking and Self-assessment

First of all, variables differ in regard to the point in time in which they should be recorded. Basically, variables can be tracked in the morning, throughout the whole day or in the evening. For example, sleep quality is best assed directly after getting up and starting the day. In contrast, human energy which fluctuates over the day should be recorded multiple times on the day to have an accurate picture of the energetic states. Moreover, some variables are summative in nature, e.g., the feeling of overall work progress. Hence, they can be answered best at the end of the respective day. In the following, we elaborate in more detail on variables that should be tracked.

In the morning, *sleep* is an important variable since it is a predictor for work performance [38]. Sleep is also important according to recent research suggesting that long-term disturbed sleep and/or deprivation of sleep increases the risk of being affected by dementia [39]. Also, currently it is hypothesized and implied that sleep is a sort of "cleaning" of the brain via the glymphatic system and hence of vital importance for its optimal functioning [40, 41]. In the light of this research, sleep is an important variable for self-management and hence should be included in the morning assessment, leading to our first requirement:

RQ1: Morning assessment of sleep quality.

Once the individual starts her or his day, the performed *computer activities* are an indicator of what the person is doing, so they should be recorded. This is particularly important since human memory does not work accurate in time estimations [15]. This leads to our second requirement:

RQ2: Continuous capturing of computer activities.

Tracking work activities and productivity allows interesting insights regarding time [15] or other work and life patterns [16]. What is missing, however, is an assessment of the *energy* and *sentiment* that is accompanied with this work. This information is important for self-management since highly productive work in combination with long working durations may deplete the individual's resources and lead to exhaustion. If no adequate replenishment of resources e.g., via recovery activities takes place, it can lead to burnout. This has also been acknowledge by scientific studies summarized in an article "manage your energy, not your time" [42]. Also, sentiment play a significant role. For example, if negative sentiment dominates the work or has to be suppressed, it could have serious health-related consequences as it is implied by studies e.g., [43]. Hence tracking one's energy and sentiment is important for long-term health and productivity. Since energy and sentiment *fluctuate over the day*, they need to be tracked *multiple times per day*, leading to our third requirement:

RQ3: Human energy and sentiment assessment multiple times per day.

Since some variables are only meaningful at the *end of the day*, i.e., they provide a summative assessment of the whole day, we need to assess them with an evening survey. For example, a student fighting his procrastination might be interested in tracking his progress e.g., on his bachelor thesis, each evening. A manager in contrast might be interested in observing her overall perceived level of stress throughout the day. This leads to our fourth requirement:

RQ4: Evening assessment of variables that recap the day via a survey.

Recent empirical research [44] suggests that qualitative data in the form of, e.g., *personal notes* are of utmost importance for the later interpretation and sensemaking of the quantitative data, leading to our fifth requirement:

RQ5: Allow personal notes for each self-assessment.

3.2 Data Visualization and Analysis

At the heart of activity tracking is recording what is done on a computer, and hence it can lead to interesting insights to just look at the "raw" tracked data. Seeing working times and most used applications are among the most interesting facts people want to know about their work according to an empirical study [26]. In order to ease the inspection of this data, basic features for filtering (e.g., by date or unique activity) should be possible. This is also what can be seen as a basic feature in many activity tracking tools, leading to our sixth requirement:

RQ6: Activity list with basic filtering methods.

In regard to tracked activities, *productivity* is important since spending more time on the computer is not per se a success (e.g., if only social media or shopping websites are browsed). Productivity estimation is a core feature and *the* most prominent visualization in established time tracking tools with large user bases such as *RescueTime*, thus, emphasizing the vital importance of productive work over just long work. This leads to our seventh requirement:

RQ7: Visualization of the productivity score of computer activities.

One fundamental empirically proven rule of thumb for designing visual data exploration tools is to provide overview first and details upon request [12]. Hence displaying the data that has been recorded for a workday in full detail should be done in a separate component such as a daily dashboard that can be invoked only when the user is interested in this specific day and all details, leading to our eighth requirement:

RQ8: Daily dashboard for insights related to the current day.

Users of self-tracking tools in general are interested in a wide variety of questions and insights that can be obtained by *analyzing the data for relations*. Among the questions are the current status, history, goals, discrepancies, context and factors [45]. To meet these empirically observed needs, a component for the display of selected *longitudinal* tracking data and analysis of relations in the data is needed, leading to our nineth requirement:

RQ9: Relation analysis component for longitudinal data analysis.

3.3 Personalization

Life can have different episodes both short-term (e.g. completing a University degree) as well as long-term (e.g., establishing a business, become a parent). Hence the tool must provide *customization features* to be useful both for different users as well as to accommodate to users' changing needs in the long run. The emphasis on personalization is also reflected in many works in the self-tracking and persuasive systems field (e.g. [46, 47]). Hence since personalization is required because persons differ in their goals and ambitions, we define our tenth requirement accordingly:

RQ10: Variables should be user-defined.

Due to different chronotypes that result in different daily wake and sleep patterns [48] and also increasing flextime work models, time points for the surveys to automatically show up in the tool should be customizable. Moreover, the frequency for variables tracked over the course of the day should be adjustable since working conditions differ e.g., in regard to the number of different work topics or processing speed. Hence for some people, recording energy and sentiment in a time interval of an hour or even longer would be reasonable, whereas others could prefer a 30 min. Interval, hence leading to the eleventh requirement:

RQ11: Adjustable timing and frequencies for surveys.

Since *colors are beneficial* to remember things [49] and moreover people have different culturally-bounded associations with colors [50], colors should be user-defined thus leading to the twelfth requirement:

RQ12: User-defined color scheme for variables.

4 Design and Implementation of the Desktop Work-Life Tracker

In the following, we describe and illustrate how we implemented the requirements derived previously in our *Desktop Work-Life Tracker* (DWLT) in the form of *data capturing and self-assessment features* (4.1), an *activity viewer* (4.2), *daily dashboard* (4.3), *relation analysis* (4.4) as well as *user settings* (4.4).

4.1 Data Capturing and Self-assessment Features

To implement RQ2, automated data capturing is continuously performed in the background for computer-based activities. In more detail, the used applications, window title and use time of the currently active window is recorded. The tool stores all data locally in.csv files, nothing is transferred and all data can be deleted easily. Regarding the self-assessments, the dialogues (a)-(c) that implement RQ1, RQ3 and RQ4 are shown in Fig. 1.

For the morning (a) as well as the evening survey (c), we use sliders for user input. In order to easily see the current position of the slider, we use a black/white color-scheme. The evening survey moreover shows the user-defined colors of the variables (RQ12) as well as a user-defined textual prompt that appears upon mouse hovering. In the more frequently appearing energy and sentiment dialogue (b) we decided to implement visually more attractive input elements. For human energy, we use our 7-point scale in the form of a battery symbol which has been validated in an interdisciplinary research endeavor [51]. For sentiment, we use a shorter 5-point scale which is in line with empirical research on mood tracking suggesting such a scale to be appropriate [46]. Both user input

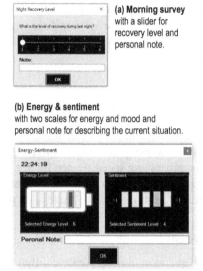

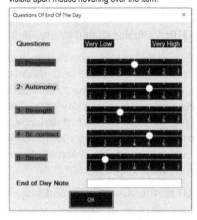

(a) **Morning survey**
with a slider for recovery level and personal note.

(b) **Energy & sentiment**
with two scales for energy and mood and personal note for describing the current situation.

(c) **End of day survey**
with sliders for five **user-defined variables** and a personal note on the day. The question of the item is visible upon mouse hovering over the item.

Fig. 1. Forms for Data Capturing via Self-Assessment

elements operate with a single click. The evening assessment enables rating five user-adjustable variables. Our default for these variables is perceived progress – one of the most motivating factors in work – as well as autonomy, strength-use, and social contacts (borrowed from the Self-Determination Theory where they are denoted as autonomy, competence and relatedness) as well as stress.

Finally, all the self-assessment dialogues have a text input field for personal notes at the bottom (RQ5).

4.2 Activity Viewer

To implement RQ6, DWLT has a component Activity Viewer (cf. Fig. 2). In the upper part, it displays all recorded activities on the computer along with the further attributes Date, Start Time, End Time, Duration, the Process Name (i.e., application name) and the Window Title. Furthermore, the user can display a filtered list in the lower part of the window. Filtering can be done according to the date and also the option to show unique process names (applications) can be selected. In the latter case, the tool will automatically sum up the duration of all separate activities with the same application. All columns can be sorted and rows can be deleted easily and then the data could be saved again as.csv file. Using the Activity Viewer, questions such as "What did I do two days ago?" or "How much time did I spent with activity x on day y" can be answered.

4.3 Daily Dashboard

To meet RQ8, we implemented the Daily Dashboard (cf. Fig. 3). With the date picker element on the top, the user can select the day for which all data should be shown. In the

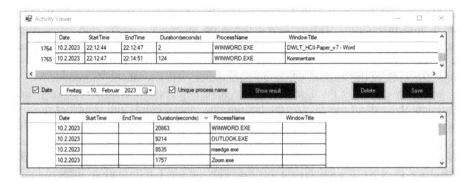

Fig. 2. Activity Viewer

upper part, a bar chart indicates working time and productivity (RQ7). For each recorded hour, a bar appears. The length of the bar represents the share of computer-based work in that hour, ranging from 0% to 100%. Switching off tracking or idle time does not count as computer-based work (idle time is recorded when the user does not press a button or moves her mouse for more than 5 min, e.g., during a coffee break).

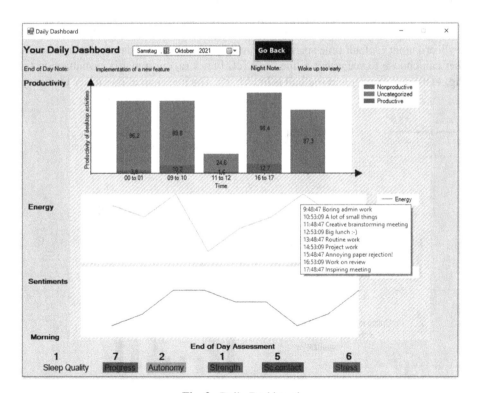

Fig. 3. Daily Dashboard

Moreover, productivity is estimated an indicated via colored segments of the bars which implements RQ7. This is accomplished via an easy to modify static application list with productivity ratings. For example, while office applications in general are rated as "productive", a web-browser is rated as "uncategorized" (since you can browse e.g., pages for work or distraction) while most computer games would be "unproductive".

In the lower part of the dashboard, line charts depict the fluctuation of energy and sentiment throughout the day. At the bottom, the labels, colors and values of the five user-defined variables of the evening-survey are displayed. Personal notes are shown for sleep (top right) as well as the whole day (top left) and also for the energy and sentiment curves. Regarding the latter, personal notes appear only upon mouse hovering over the line charts in order to not overload the user with too much information. Inspecting the visualizations in the Daily Dashboard, the user can answer self-reflective questions such as "At which hours I was most productive?" or "Overall, how did I perceive my day?".

4.4 Relation Analysis

To meet RQ9, the component Relation Analysis has been implemented (cf. Fig. 4). While in general, rich visualizations are suggested to help people in self-reflection [12], we however tried to make the visualization simple and easy to grasp. We therefore opted for rather established visualizations known from business environments such as bar charts or line charts as well as a matrix. At the top of the dialogue, the user can first specify the time range for the analysis using two date picker elements that allow mouse and keyboard input (default time span is the current day and the two days before). Next, the user can choose to see either a line chart (cf. Fig. 4 (a)) or a matrix visualization (cf. Fig. 4 (b)) in the upper part (default is line chart). The line chart allows to see the energy

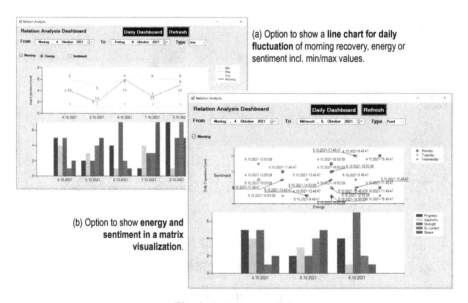

(a) Option to show a **line chart for daily fluctuation** of morning recovery, energy or sentiment incl. min/max values.

(b) Option to show **energy and sentiment in a matrix visualization**.

Fig. 4. Relation Analysis

and sentiment fluctuations in the given time frame and is optionally also enriched by the value of the morning assessment. The matrix presents energy and sentiment states in a two-dimensional system. Each point in the matrix can represent multiple measurements for which the date(s) and weekday(s) are indicated. In the bottom part, bar charts for the values of the evening survey are displayed.

Since in the Daily Dashboard, fluctuations of energy and sentiment throughout the day are plotted as a curve using a line chart, we decided to stick to this visualization also in the Relation Analysis for reasons of consistency. We moreover decided to include the morning assessment value in this line chart because the level of morning recovery relates to a "deeper" physiological, more bodily-oriented variable and as such fits well together with energy and sentiment. For energy and sentiment, we also include min/max values since a day with extreme high energy that is fully leveraged for productive work may result in exhaustion at the end of day. Thus, the average energy would be medium. Such days should be distinguishable from a rather unproductive day with constant medium energetic activation that would also result in medium average energy.

For the five user-defined variables, we decided to use vertical bars since these values represent retrospective, summative assessments of the day (e.g., in regard to perceived progress, social contacts or other events throughout the day) rather than a continuous variable going up and down (e.g., energy). Finally, the user can at any time jump into the Daily Dashboard via the respective button, and both dialogues can be used at the same time, e.g., arranged side by side on a large screen. In this way, we support the pattern of "overview first, details on demand" which is quite common in the design of dashboards and data analytics software.

Overall, by inspecting the provided visualizations, the user can answer self-reflective questions such as "Is there a relation between my energy and sleep?", "At which times/weekdays I often feel energized and happy?", or "Are progress and strength-use correlated?". Even complex relations may be discovered in the data like a pattern "High autonomy co-occurs with lower stress and higher energy on next day".

4.5 User Settings

To meet RQ10, RQ11, and RQ12, we implemented a user settings dialogue (cf. Fig. 5). In this dialogue, the user can specify the timepoint for the morning and evening survey to automatically appear on the screen as well as the time interval for the more frequently appearing small energy and sentiment dialogue (RQ11). Furthermore, custom variable names and a prompt for each variable (RQ10) can be set and a custom color can be selected (RQ12). Using these personalization options, the user can customize the tracker at his/her own disposal, e.g., include a variable "headache" with red color and see how this is influenced e.g., by working duration, sleep quality, or perceived progress.

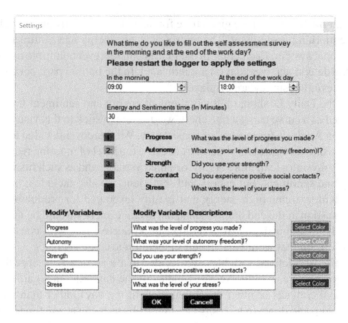

Fig. 5. User Settings

5   Preliminary Evaluation

According to the influential *Memorandum on Design-Oriented Business Informatics*, research is "differentiated by generality, originality, justification and publication from the mere development of concrete solutions for concrete problems in practice, as developed by application companies, software houses and consulting firms" [52]. The memorandum has been signed by major renown researchers from the discipline and paved the way for the further methodological advancement of the discipline. It also establishes a common ground in terms of research methodology, evaluation strategies and goals as well as epistemological questions. Regarding the principles that should be followed when conducting research, the authors state that *abstraction, originality, justification* and *utility* are fundamental. These principles can serve as a criterion to judge whether the research has been conducted properly and if the results create value. We therefore step through each of the principles in our preliminary descriptive evaluation.

Abstraction. An artifact must be applicable to a class of problems. The class of problem is clearly described in the introduction. It is the increased need for self-management due to changes of the working world that demands improved tools that not only track work-related variables such as time allocation. Instead, tools that support effective self-management should offer tracking of a wider range of work-, wellbeing- and health-related variables. *Since our tool is not tailored to specific professional activities or industries and is applicable for all types of computer-based work, hence our approach provides a good level of abstraction.*

Originality. An artifact must make an innovative contribution to the state of the art. The innovative aspect of the proposed DWLT tool design lies in the *novel combination of features known from time tracking, quantified self and electronic diaries in a single tool.* Furthermore, despite this integration of different variables, our *DWLT provides simple assessment dialogues* since users want to devote only a few minutes per day for filling in questionnaires according to our investigations [55]. Furthermore, the tool provides *personalization options* that comprise timing, variable names, prompts and colors that allow to build a "personal tracker". Also, *personal notes* can be recorded, which addresses one of the most significant deficiencies of current tracking tools according to a review study [44]. Taken together, *we provide an original approach to IT-based self-observation that can improve self-management practices.*

Justification. This principle is essential for all scientific works since they should comprehensibly be justified and validatable. *Since we justified major design requirements in Sect. 3 either with literature or own logical thinking and deductions, the artefact has been created based on justified design requirements. It is furthermore validatable since a running application exists that demonstrates the feasibility of the concept and allows to validate the theoretical design requirements.* The prototypical implementation also paves the way to explore the effects of tool usage e.g., in terms of the established model from Kirkpatrick 1976 [29] distinguishing between reaction, learning, behavior and outcome, which is planned as our future work.

Utility. An artifact must be able to generate a benefit for stakeholders today or in the future. The question about utility can be answered by a deductive and inductive line of argumentation. *Deductive arguments* are that, first, the tool has been built according to justified requirements that state favorable or necessary features, hence it can be deduced that an actual implementation of these features leads to the desired results. Second, according to internal analyses of a larger sample, which has not yet been published, there seem to be significant beneficial effects that are caused by the reflection on human energy. These results seem to underpin earlier preliminary positive statements that have been given in qualitative form by participants of our previous smaller-scale studies reported in [36]. Implementing features for continuous energy tracking and reflection as an implementation of an empirically validated concept again let us deduce that our artefact provides utility. Third, using our tool, insights can be gained that have been considered important in an empirical study [26]. Among the top-rated insights of tracking applications that also lead to behavior change are e.g., working duration, frequent applications in stat of low perceived productivity or favorable timeframe for focused work.

Inductive arguments depend on own empirical observations. In this direction, the tool was already tested in an early formative user study in which several test persons used it over a course of two weeks during their ordinary work. After using the tool, semi-structured interviews were made about how participants perceived the usefulness and ease of use of the tool and potentially points for further development. We are still in the process of analyzing the results, but preliminary insights are that people in general liked the application, but differ a lot in how they make use of the application speaking in favor of even more comprehensive personalization options.

6 Summary and Outlook

Today's working world is characterized by increased complexity, flexibility and speed thus demanding more self-management skills than ever before in order to keep pace with all requirements and stay healthy, productive and preserve one's wellbeing. For many people it is challenging to determine the activities and the impact they create on themselves, e.g. on their energy level [33]. Thus, an improved self-reflection is necessary. It can be promoted through the procedure of self-observation [11].

With our tool, the *Desktop Work-Life Tracker* (DWLT), it is possible to track eight variables in a semi-automated way. Among the variables are (i) *sleep* assessed in the morning, (ii) *computer-based activity and productivity* automatically recorded over the day, (iii) *energy and sentiment* via recurring small assessments over the day, (iv) *evening assessment* with five user-adjustable variables that can be used to keep track of important variables. Our default for these variables is perceived progress, autonomy, strength-use, social contacts, and stress.

Furthermore, the tool provides an *Activity Viewer* for inspecting computer-based work activities and their time consumption, a *Daily Dashboard* that mirrors all data recorded for a single day, and moreover a *Relation Analysis* to see developments over time, correlations of the data, and also trends. In this way, the tool supports answering simple questions such as "Is there a relation between my energy and sleep?" by just looking at the plotted data. Even more complex patterns might be spotted by conducting "visual inference" when looking on the visualizations. Examples for this could be the answer to question such as "How does working late in the evening influence my next day energy level?", or even more complex "Does high autonomy co-occur with lower stress and higher energy on next day?". Resulting knowledge could then, for example, be used to increase the proportion of energizing activities, to utilize energy peaks for important tasks, or to establish recovery phases for energy troughs.

In our future work, we plan to address two areas of improvement. First, we plan to integrate sensor data from wearable devices in order to automatically track physiological data during the course of the day and not rely on self-assessments. This will enable advanced analyses on how fitness-related activities correlate with to productive work or other desirable outcomes. The second area of improvement is the automatic detection of signals on e.g., extreme values, or trends. This could be the basis for, e.g., alerts or recommendations based on the detected signals. Such recommendations could be used for e.g. promoting relaxation [14]. IT-supported triggers might help people in implementing their targeted improvements and ultimately promote more effective self-management.

References

1. Parent-Thirion, A., et al.: 6th European Working Conditions Survey: Overview report, 2017th edn. Publications Office of the European Union, Luxembourg (2017)
2. James, S.L., et al.: Global, regional, and national incidence, prevalence, and years lived with disability for 354 diseases and injuries for 195 countries and territories, 1990–2017: a systematic analysis for the Global Burden of Disease Study 2017. Lancet **392**(10159), 1789–1858 (2018). https://doi.org/10.1016/S0140-6736(18)32279-7

3. Eurofound, W.: Conditions and Sustainable Work: An Analysis Using the Job Quality Framework. Publications Office of the European Union, Dublin (2021)

4. Green, F.: It's Been a hard day's night: the concentration and intensification of work in late twentieth-century Britain. British J. Industr. Relations **39**(1), 53–80 (2001). https://doi.org/10.1111/1467-8543.00189

5. Barber, L.K., Jenkins, J.S.: Creating technological boundaries to protect bedtime: examining work-home boundary management, psychological de-tachment and sleep. Stress. Health **30**(3), 259–264 (2014). https://doi.org/10.1002/smi.2536

6. Green, F., McIntosh, S.: The intensification of work in Europe. Labour Econ. **8**(2), 291–308 (2001). https://doi.org/10.1016/S0927-5371(01)00027-6

7. Hsee, C.K., Hastie, R.: Decision and experience: why don't we choose what makes us happy? Trends Cogn. Sci. **10**(1), 31–37 (2006). https://doi.org/10.1016/j.tics.2005.11.007

8. Dewey, J.: How we think: a restatement of the relation of reflective thinking to the educative process. Lexington, MA: D.C. Heath (1933)

9. Baumer, E.P., Khovanskaya, V., Matthews, M., Reynolds, L., Schwanda Sosik, V., Gay, G.: Reviewing reflection: on the use of reflection in interactive system design. In: Proceedings of the 2014 conference on Designing Interactive Systems, Vancouver BC Canada, pp. 93–102 (2014)

10. Burkert, S., Sniehotta, F.: Selbstregulation des Gesundheitsverhaltens. In: Handbuch der Gesundheitspsychologie und Medizinischen Psychologie, pp. 98–106

11. Manz, C.C., Sims, H.P.: Self-management as a substitute for leadership: a social learning theory perspective. AMR **5**(3), 361–367 (1980). https://doi.org/10.5465/amr.1980.4288845

12. Choe, E.K., Lee, B., Zhu, H., Riche, N.H., Baur, D.: Understanding self-reflection: how people reflect on personal data through visual data exploration. In: Proceedings of the 11th EAI International Conference on Pervasive Computing Technologies for Healthcare: PervasiveHealth 2017 : 23–26 May 2017, Barcelona, Spain, Barcelona, Spain, pp. 173–182 (2017)

13. Rapp, A., Cena, F.: Self-monitoring and Technology: Challenges and Open Issues in Personal Informatics. In: Stephanidis, C., Antona, M. (eds.) Universal Access in Human-Computer Interaction. Design for All and Accessibility Practice. UAHCI 2014. Lecture Notes in Computer Science, vol. 8516, pp. 613–622 (2014). https://doi.org/10.1007/978-3-319-07509-9_58

14. Fallon, M., Spohrer, K., Heinzl, A.: Wearable devices: a physiological and self-regulatory intervention for increasing attention in the workplace. In: Davis, F., Riedl, R., vom Brocke, J., Léger, P.M., Randolph, A. (eds.) Information Systems and Neuroscience. Lecture Notes in Information Systems and Organisation, vol. 29, pp. 229–238. Springer, Cham (2019). https://doi.org/10.1007/978-3-030-01087-4_28

15. Pammer, V., Bratic, M.: Surprise, surprise: activity log based time analytics for time management. In: CHI 2013 Extended Abstracts on Human Factors in Computing Systems, pp. 211–216. France, Paris (2013)

16. Abdel Hadi, S., Mojzisch, A., Krumm, S., Häusser, J.A.: Day-level relation-ships between work, physical activity, and well-being: Testing the physical activity-mediated demand-control (pamDC) model. Work Stress, pp. 1–22, 2021. https://doi.org/10.1080/02678373.2021.2002971

17. Quantified Self, Homepage - Quantified Self. https://quantifiedself.com/. Accessed 30 Dec 2021

18. Swan, M.: The quantified self: fundamental disruption in big data science and biological discovery. Big data **1**(2), 85–99 (2013). https://doi.org/10.1089/big.2012.0002

19. Ragsdale, J.M., Beehr, T.A.: A rigorous test of a model of employees' re-source recovery mechanisms during a weekend. J. Organ Behav. **37**(6), 911–932 (2016). https://doi.org/10.1002/job.2086

20. Zijlstra, F.R.H., Cropley, M., Rydstedt, L.W.: From recovery to regulation: an attempt to reconceptualize 'recovery from work.' Stress Health J. Int. Soc. Investig. Stress **30**(3), 244–252 (2014). https://doi.org/10.1002/smi.2604

21. Sonnentag, S., Venz, L., Casper, A.: Advances in recovery research: What have we learned? What should be done next? J. Occup. Health Psychol. **22**(3), 365–380 (2017). https://doi.org/10.1037/ocp0000079

22. Quinn, R.W., Spreitzer, G.M., Lam, C.F.: Building a sustainable model of human energy in organizations: exploring the critical role of resources. Acad. Manag. Ann. **6**(1), 337–396 (2012). https://doi.org/10.1080/19416520.2012.676762

23. Fritz, C., Lam, C.F., Spreitzer, G.M.: It's the little things that matter: an examination of knowledge workers' energy management. AMP **25**(3), 28–39 (2011). https://doi.org/10.5465/amp.25.3.zol28

24. Zacher, H., Brailsford, H.A., Parker, S.L.: Micro-breaks matter: a diary study on the effects of energy management strategies on occupational well-being. J. Vocat. Behav. **85**(3), 287–297 (2014). https://doi.org/10.1016/j.jvb.2014.08.005

25. Lambusch, F., Weigelt, O., Fellmann, M., Siestrup, K.: Application of a pictorial scale of human energy in ecological momentary assessment research. In: Harris, D., Li, WC. (eds.) Engineering Psychology and Cognitive Ergonomics. Mental Workload, Human Physiology, and Human Energy. HCII 2020. Lecture Notes in Computer Science, vol. 12186, Springer, Cham (2020). https://doi.org/10.1007/978-3-030-49044-7_16

26. Meyer, A.N., Murphy, G.C., Zimmermann, T., Fritz, T.: Design recommen-dations for self-monitoring in the workplace. Proc. ACM Hum. Comput. Interact. **1**(CSCW), 1–24 (2017). https://doi.org/10.1145/3134714

27. Bruch, H., Vogel, B.: Strategies for creating and sustaining organizational energy. Employ. Relat. Today **38**(2), 51–61 (2011)

28. Russell, J.A.: A circumplex model of affect. J. Personality Soc. Psychol. **39**(6), 1161–1178 (1980). https://doi.org/10.1037/h0077714

29. Kirkpatrick, D. L., Craig, R.L.: Evaluation of training: Evaluation of short-term training in rehabilitation. In: Training and Development Handbook, 2nd ed. (1967)

30. Welbourne, T.M.: Two numbers for growth, innovation and high performance: working and optimal employee energy. Organ. Dyn. **43**(3), 180–188 (2014). https://doi.org/10.1016/j.orgdyn.2014.08.004

31. Ryan, R.M., Frederick, C.: On energy, personality, and health: subjective vitality as a dynamic reflection of well-being. J. Pers. **65**(3), 529–565 (1997). https://doi.org/10.1111/j.1467-6494.1997.tb00326.x

32. Grobe, T.G., Frerk, T.: BARMER Gesundheitsreport 2020. Barmer, Berlin (2020)

33. Schippers, M.C., Hogenes, R.: Energy management of people in organizations: a review and research agenda. J. Bus. Psychol. **26**(2), 193–203 (2011). https://doi.org/10.1007/s10869-011-9217-6

34. Li, J., Vogel, D.: Digital health education for self-management: a systematic literature review. PACIS 2021 Proceedings, 2021. https://aisel.aisnet.org/pacis2021/164

35. Spreitzer, G.M., Grant, T.: Helping Students Manage Their Energy. J. Manag. Educ. **36**(2), 239–263 (2012). https://doi.org/10.1177/1052562911429431

36. Lambusch, F., Richter, H., Fellmann, M., Weigelt, O., Kiechle, A.-K.: Human energy diary studies with personalized feedback: a proof of concept with formr. In: Proceedings of the 15th International Joint Conference on Biomedical Engineering Systems and Technologies (BIOSTEC 2022), Vienna, Austria, pp. 789–800 (2022)

37. Kim, S., Park, Y., Headrick, L.: Daily micro-breaks and job performance: general work engagement as a cross-level moderator. J. Appl. Psychol. **103**(7), 772–786 (2018). https://doi.org/10.1037/apl0000308

38. Litwiller, B., Snyder, L.A., Taylor, W.D., Steele, L.M.: The relationship between sleep and work: a meta-analysis. J. Appl. Psychol. **102**(4), 682–699 (2017). https://doi.org/10.1037/apl 0000169

39. Sabia, S., et al.: Association of sleep duration in middle and old age with inci-dence of dementia. Nat. Commun. **12**(1), 2289 (2021). https://doi.org/10.1038/s41467-021-22354-2

40. Komaroff, A.L.: Are toxins flushed out of the brain during sleep?

41. Reddy, O.C., van der Werf, Y.D.: The Sleeping Brain: Harnessing the Power of the Glymphatic System through Lifestyle Choices. https://doi.org/10.3390/brainsci. Accessed 7 Feb 2023

42. Schwartz, T., McCarthy, C.: Manage your energy, not your time. Harvard Business Review, vol. 85, no. 10, p. 63 (2007). https://hbr.org/2007/10/manage-your-energy-not-your-time

43. Spector, P.E., Goh, A.: The role of emotions in the occupational stress process. In: Perrewé, P.L., Ganster, D.C. (eds.) Research in Occupational Stress and Well Being, vol. 1, Exploring theoretical mechanisms and perspectives. Oxford, Amsterdam: Elsevier Science; JAI, pp. 195–232 (2002)

44. Cho, J., Xu, T., Zimmermann-Niefield, A., Voida, S.: Reflection in theory and reflection in practice: an exploration of the gaps in reflection support among personal informatics apps. In: CHI2022: Proceedings of the 2022 CHI Conference on Human Factors in Computing Systems : April 30-May 5, 2022, New Orleans, LA, USA, New Orleans LA USA, pp. 1–23 (2022)

45. Li, I., Dey, A.K., Forlizzi, J.: Understanding my data, myself. In: Proceedings of the 13th International Conference on Ubiquitous Computing, Beijing, China, p. 405 (2011)

46. Yfantidou, S., Sermpezis, P., Vakali, A.: 12 Years of self-tracking for promoting physical activity from a user diversity perspective: taking stock & thinking ahead. In: Adjunct Proceedings of the 30th ACM Conference on User Modeling, Adaptation and Personalization, Barcelona Spain, pp. 211–221 (2022)

47. Busch, M., Schrammel, J., Tscheligi, M.: Personalized persuasive technology – development and validation of scales for measuring persuadability. In: Berkovsky, S., Freyne, J. (eds) Persuasive Technology. PERSUASIVE 2013. Lecture Notes in Computer Science, vol. 7822, pp. 33–38. Springer, Berlin, Heidelberg (2013). https://doi.org/10.1007/978-3-642-37157-8_6

48. Volk, S., Lowe, K.B., Barnes, C.M.: Circadian leadership: a review and integration of chronobiology and leadership. J. Organ Behav. (2022). https://doi.org/10.1002/job.2659

49. Hanna, A., Remington, R.: The representation of color and form in long-term memory. Mem. Cognit. **24**(3), 322–330 (1996). https://doi.org/10.3758/BF03213296

50. Madden, T.J., Hewett, K., Roth, M.S.: Managing images in different cultures: a cross-national study of color meanings and preferences. J. Int. Marketing **8**(4), 90–107 (2000). http://www.jstor.org/stable/25048831

51. Weigelt, O., et al.: Time to recharge batteries – development and validation of a pictorial scale of human energy. Eur. J. Work Organiz. Psychol. **31**(5), 1–18 (2022). https://doi.org/10.1080/1359432X.2022.2050218

52. Österle, H., et al.: Memorandum zur gestaltungsorientierten Wirtschaftsinformatik. Schmalenbachs Z betriebswirtsch Forsch **62**(6), 664–672 (2010). https://doi.org/10.1007/BF03372838

53. Fellmann, M., Lambusch, F., Pieper, L.: Towards combining automatic measurements with self-assessments for personal stress. In: 2019 IEEE 21st Conference on Business Informatics (CBI), July 15- 17, p. 8(00076). Moscow, Russia. IEEE (2019). https://doi.org/10.1109/CBI.2019.00076

Features Focusing on the Direction of Body Movement in Emotion Estimation Based on Laban Movement Analysis

Sota Fujiwara[1]([✉]), Fumiya Kobayashi[1], Saizo Aoyagi[2] [ID], and Michiya Yamamoto[3] [ID]

[1] School of Science and Technology, Kwansei Gakuin University, Sanda, Hyogo, Japan
hct56892@kwansei.ac.jp
[2] Faculty of Global Media Studies, Komazawa University, Kita-Ku, Tokyo, Japan
[3] School of Engineering, Kwansei Gakuin University, Sanda, Hyogo, Japan
michiya.yamamoto@kwansei.ac.jp

Abstract. Technology for sensing and understanding human behavior is being developed. We focused on the universality of Laban Movement Analysis, a body representation theory, in estimating internal states, such as emotions, and defined original feature values based on that theory. The feature values have shown their effectiveness in estimating emotions in a paired electronic instrument-making task and in a design-making task on a PC. In this study, to generalize further these features, we analyzed whether forward/backward or left/right movements contributed to emotion estimation. For this purpose, we defined new features and evaluated them by machine learning emotion estimation. For the body movement measurement experiment, we designed a video-watching task with few contrasting movements and a bespoke task with various movements. The results showed that the left-right direction feature was effective in the bias (Space) feature of the motion, and that the examination of the front-back and left-right directions improved the estimation's accuracy.

Keywords: emotion estimation · Laban Movement Analysis · feature engineering · video-watching task · bespoke task

1 Introduction

Much research on the estimation of internal states and emotions has been performed using information technology, and most of this research has been based on facial expressions by Ekman's six basic emotions (anger, disgust, fear, happiness, sadness, and surprise) for many years [1]. However, Sato et al. found that Japanese people do not follow Ekman's theory and that the actual relationship between emotions and facial expressions has not been clarified [2]. There are also issues that few studies have focused on, including scenes of naturally evoked emotions.

We have focused on how it is difficult to express emotions intentionally via body movements, which concludes to natural emotional expression by body movements. For this, we have designed a task in which two people work in pairs to create an electronic

© The Author(s), under exclusive license to Springer Nature Switzerland AG 2023
M. Kurosu and A. Hashizume (Eds.): HCII 2023, LNCS 14012, pp. 182–195, 2023.
https://doi.org/10.1007/978-3-031-35599-8_12

musical instrument in cooperation [3] and a task in which one person designs and creates a display watch [4] as scenes where both natural emotions are evoked and have made clear expressions by body movement under these conditions. In these studies, we designed our original body movement features based on Laban Movement Analysis (LMA) originally designed as a dance theory [5]. We also performed emotion estimation by machine learning, which showed a high relationship between intrinsic emotion expression and body expression theory. However, in these studies, we used the same LMA values and did not consider optimization according to movement.

In this study, we focused on the axis of the human body in expressing emotion through body movements. We did this because the body axis should be considered an essential element for quantifying body movements to estimate emotions. In detail, by considering the nature of human joints, degrees of freedom, and ease of movement, we expected to contribute to the estimation as well as to studies in rehabilitation medicine and sports medicine. LMA also discusses the relationship between Kinesphere and the direction of body movement. Therefore, in this study, we analyze the feature values of LMA that can be applied to various tasks by designing two contrasting tasks through modifying the feature values according to the direction of body movements, and through comparing the results of the emotion estimation along with these changes. The first task is to watch a video with little motion, in contrast to the task in the previous study [6]. The second task is one that assumes a bespoke scene, which is a type of custom-made interactive ordering task with various body movements including standing and sitting [7]. By evaluating the results of the emotion estimation using support vector machine (SVM) in these tasks, we discuss how the LMA values should be defined by focusing on the direction of body movements.

2 Related Works

2.1 The Importance of Body Movement in Emotion Estimation

Human body movements contain as much information as facial expressions; there-fore, we considered them an important factor in recognizing and estimating emotions. For example, research has reported that when emotions are estimated by presenting facial expressions and body movements simultaneously, body movements have a greater influence on emotion recognition, depending on the situation [8, 9]. However, two major issues remain in emotion research focusing on body movements. The first is that the target emotion, situation, sensing method, and quantification of body movement differ among studies, making it difficult to compare results among studies [10]. This is due to how the expressed body movements are highly context dependent, and the variables for interpreting body movements are often defined subjectively and qualitatively. In other words, it is difficult to establish a method that can respond to various situations to a certain degree, such as Ekman's research on facial expressions. Second, there are few studies on situations that can occur in daily life [11]. Although there are many situations where estimating emotions is required for spontaneous human behavior (e.g., in education, entertainment, medical care), there has not been much research on such situations because of the difficulty of sensing in the natural environment and controlling during experiments.

2.2 Laban Movement Analysis

Laban theory, a theory of body expression, abstracts human actions in terms of multiple elements in the representation of internal states [12]. For example, one study shows that Laban theory can be utilized not only for movements during dancing [13] but also for playing sports and games [14], and walking [15]. In contrast, our previous research focused on the versatility of LMA [5], where we applied Laban theory, which can describe the relationships between people's psychological states and body movements, to behavior analysis and emotion estimation, and we made it possible to estimate emotions from body movements. Here, we defined our original feature values and we have conducted emotion estimation during the production of an electronic block instrument in which two people work together [1] as well as emotion estimation in a task in which a single person creates a design using a PC [16]. These estimations were performed using SVM as the learning model, with the LMA values, which will be described in next section of Space, Weight, Time) because explanatory variables and emotions (e.g., joy, sleepiness, discomfort, satisfaction) are based on Russell's core affect model as the objective variables [17]. In this study, we discuss the LMA values as a challenge to expand these applications' scope.

2.3 LMA Values and Their Issues

Laban proposed a description method called "Effort-shape description'" for body move-ments [12]. In the previous study, we focused on "Effort," which represents the inner impulses that cause movement, such as attitude and motivation, and is considered to be closely related to emotion. Among these factors, we selected three and defined our original feature values as shown in Fig. 1. Space refers to biases of the directions (Direct/Indirect) of body parts in LMA and it was defined as the area of the triangle formed by the head position and the positions of the wrists. Weight refers to strength of motions (Strong/Light) in LMA and it was defined as the head's vertical position. Time refers to the haste of change (Sudden/Sustained) in body movements in LMA and it was defined as the maximum value of moving averages of the speed of the head and the wrists across 60 s.

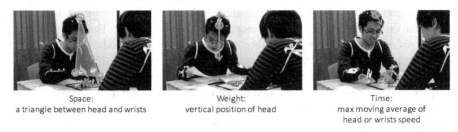

Space: Weight: Time:
a triangle between head and wrists   vertical position of head   max moving average of
                                                                     head or wrists speed

Fig. 1. Feature values for emotion estimation based on Laban Movement Analysis.

Thus, in previous studies, we demonstrated that the LMA values were effective for emotion estimation in situations of natural emotional arousal. However, we have not explored whether the LMA values definition is optimal for other tasks, and we have not examined the relationship between the likelihood and the nature of body movement features and the accuracy of emotion estimation. Therefore, in this study, we attempted to extend the range of application by setting two contrasting tasks. The first task was a video-watching task in which we focused on scenes with little motion, in contrast to the above task. This task was characterized by how it requires very few movements because a person simply watches videos in front of displays. In contrast, the task can evoke the target emotion precisely, and the timing of the emotion evocation is clear. The second task, which includes standing and sitting, was a bespoke scene, which is a type of tailor-made purchasing task. This task is characterized as a scene that includes interaction with a salesperson, and there might be various types and sizes of movements, including standing and sitting. We examine the applicability of the LMA-based emotion estimation method by optimizing LMA values in applying them for different tasks by evaluating the results of the emotion estimation using machine learning.

3   LMA Values Focusing on Various Motions and Their Directions

3.1 Space

In the case of Space, we assumed it was necessary to capture the front-back body movements that may cause postural changes rather than the left-right body bias because the hand positions and face direction/position do not change much when watching a movie. In addition, by considering the accuracy of obtaining hand coordinates due to the measurement environment, we used the area of the triangle obtained from the coordinates of the three points of the head, neck, and waist (Fig. 2 right) instead of the area of both hands and the head as in previous studies (Fig. 2 left).

Equation (1) and Eq. (2) show a vector from neck to head and a vector from neck to waist, where $p_h[t]$, $p_n[t]$, and $p_w[t]$ are positions at time t of the head, the neck, and the waist.

$$v_h[t] = p_h[t] - p_n[t] \tag{1}$$

$$v_w[t] = p_w[t] - p_n[t] \tag{2}$$

Equation (3) shows *Space[t]*, the area of the triangle consisting of the three coordinates of the head and both hands.

$$Space[t] = \frac{1}{2}\sqrt{\left| v_h[t]^2 | v_w[t] | \right|^2 - (v_h[t] \cdot v_w[t])^2} \tag{3}$$

We refer to the space obtained above as Space-FB, and to the features defined in the previous study as Space-LR.

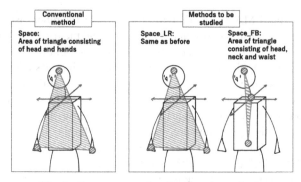

Fig. 2. Space: conventional and study methods.

3.2 Weight

For Weight, we used the head's vertical position as in previous studies (Fig. 3 left). However, postural changes greatly affect this. Therefore, in this study, we defined it as the angle between the vector consisting of the head and waist and the vector excluding the vertical component of that vector (horizontal to the ground) in front-back direction (Fig. 3 right). We also defined the angle consisting of the head, neck, and shoulders as the Weight, focusing on the left-right direction (Fig. 3 center).

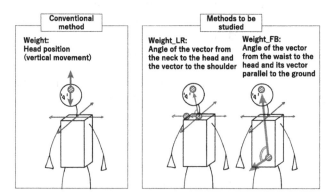

Fig. 3. Weight: conventional and study methods.

Equation (4) shows a vector from waist to head at time t, where $p_h[t]$ and $p_w[t]$ are the same as those obtained in the previous section.

$$v_s[t] = p_h[t] - p_w[t] \tag{4}$$

Equation (5) shows Weight focused on front/back direction at time t, which is the angle between the above vector and vector without the z component of the above vector. We refer to this as Weight-FB.

$$Weight\,[t] \;=\; \arccos \frac{v_s[t] \cdot u[t]}{|v_s[t]\|u[t]|} \tag{5}$$

Equation (6) shows a vector from left shoulder to neck, where $p_l[t]$ is a position of the left shoulder and $p_h[t]$ is the same as obtained in the previous section.

$$v_l[t] \;=\; p_l[t] - p_n[t] \tag{6}$$

Equation (7) shows Weight by focusing on left/right direction at time t, which is the angle between the $v_h[t]$ and $v_l[t]$.

$$Weight[t] = \arccos \frac{v_h[t] \cdot v_l[t]}{|v_h[t]\||v_l[t]|} \tag{7}$$

3.3 Time

For Time, in the previous study, we obtained the speeds of both hands and the head (Fig. 4 left). However, in this study, we obtained the speed of the head only (Fig. 4 right) by considering that the desk in the video-watching task hide the hands and that the accuracy of the measurement is low. In the previous study, we used the moving average of the speed over a one-minute period as Time, but this caused problems that the number of data was not enough for the tasks in the short experimental time, and there is a possibility that the values in characteristic movements might be rounded off. Therefore, in this study, we defined Time as the maximum speed at a specific time that was appropriately modified (Fig. 4 right).

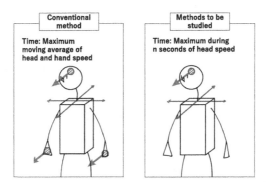

Fig. 4. Time: conventional and study methods.

Equation (8) shows speed of the head, where $p_h[t]$ and $p_h[t-1]$ are the positions of the head at time t and time $t-1$, respectively

$$v[t] \;=\; p_h[t] - p_h[t-1] \tag{8}$$

Equation (9) shows Time at time t, which is the greatest velocity during the specified n seconds from time t − (n − 1) seconds to t seconds.

$$Time[t] = \max_{t-(n-1) \leq x \leq t} |v[x]|, \; where\{t \mid t \geq n - 1\} \tag{9}$$

We used these LMA values that were calculated from each individual's body movement data obtained in each of the experiments.

For Time, we set n = 60 for the bespoke task, as in the previous study, because the length of the experiment was sufficiently long. For the video watching task, we set n = 10 because the duration of each video watching was as short as 4 min.

4 Measurement Experiment

4.1 Video-Watching Task

We designed a task where participants watched videos in which the number of physical actions was small and the magnitude of the actions was considered small. In the task, we targeted four emotions in Russel's core affect model: "pleasant (arousal, pleasant)," "fearful (arousal, unpleasant)," "boredom (calm, unpleasant)," and "healing (calm, pleasant)." First, we performed a preliminary experiment and we selected videos that could precisely evoke the target emotion by using a questionnaire and then using them as stimulus videos (Fig. 5) for measurement experiment. Next, we had the participants watch the stimulus videos and measure their body movements (Fig. 6). We did this using Azure Kinect and iPi Studio. We then showed the participants a 4-min stimulus video for each emotion, and asked them to answer a questionnaire totally 20 points for each video to indicate what emotion was aroused (Fig. 7).

Fig. 5. Selected videos.

Fig. 6. Experimental scenery.

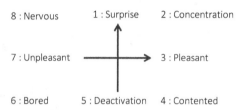

Fig. 7. Emotions used in the emotion interview.

4.2 Bespoke Task

We designed a task for bespoke, where participants purchased products by communicating with a salesperson, which is considered to incite significant changes in body movements and emotions. Here, we asked what kind of the emotions could be extracted during the purchasing of a suit in our preliminary experiment and modeled the evoked emotions. For the actual experiment, we designed a bespoke task using origami by assuming it could evoke the same emotions as the suit bespoke task. Specifically, we designed a process in which the user could select a use a sitting position (use selection process), select origami as a material in the standing position (origami selection process), and select a design from a catalog in a sitting position, and the participant input the design into a PC (design selection process) (Fig. 8). We had the participants perform a bespoke task with these three processes and we measured their body movements. Here, we used a robot (RoBoHoN: SHARP, shown in the figure) as a salesperson operated by the experimenter using the WOZ method to reproduce the interaction of a real bespoke scene in all processes (Fig. 9) [18]. Furthermore, we used a core affect model in Fig. 10, which was extracted as the emotions aroused during the actual suit bespoke process. Using this model, we had the participants answer which of the eight emotions was aroused and with what degree of intensity (on a 5-point scale from "1: not at all" to "5: very much").

Fabrication Selection Process

Origami Selection Process

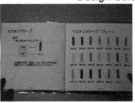

Design Selection Process

Fig. 8. Bespoke task processes.

Fig. 9. RoBoHoN as a salesclerk.

4.3 Measurement Methods and Results

In the video-watching task, we performed our measurement experiment on 36 under-graduate and graduate students (18 males and 18 females) attending Kwansei Gakuin University. In this experiment, we used motion capture software (iPi Mocap Studio 4, Fig. 11). Because 17 participants failed to track the wrists' motion, we used the body movement data of the remaining 19 participants (6 males and 13 females) for our analysis. We also obtained emotional data for each individual (stimulus image) × (questionnaire location) (= 80).

In the bespoke task, we performed measurement experiments on 22 undergraduate and graduate students (11 males and 11 females) attending Kwansei Gakuin University.

Fig. 10. Core affect model for the bespoke task.

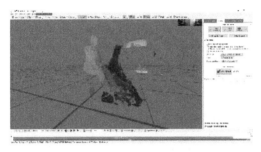

Fig. 11. Screenshot of the motion capture software "iPi Mocap Studio 4."

Here, we used a motion capture camera (Vicon Bonita 10: Crescent Inc.) to take our measurements. We used the data of all of participant for our analysis because we could compensate for the missing data. We also obtained an average of 28 emotional data points from each individual's questionnaire. We show an example of the questionnaire results in Fig. 12.

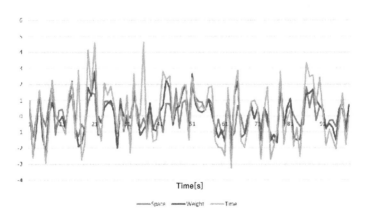

Fig. 12. An example of data transition of the LMA values.

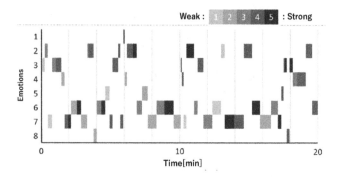

Fig. 13. An example of the questionnaire results.

We used the data obtained in this way for the estimation of emotions, both from the measurement of the body movements of the experimental participants in each task and from the results of the emotional questionnaire elicited during the performance of the task (Fig. 13).

5   Emotion Estimation and Analysis

5.1   Emotion Estimation by SVM

We calculated each LMA value from the body movement data measured in each task described in the previous section, and we created a data set together with the emotion data. We used the data set to perform emotion estimation by machine learning and compared the results to analyze the features. For emotion estimation, we constructed a learning model using SVM, which is supervised learning, and validated it using the Holdout method. We constructed the learning model using MATLAB, a numerical analysis software that MathWorks developed. The RBF kernel was used as the SVM kernel function, and the hyperparameters were optimized using grid search and 10-fold cross-validation.

5.2   Comparison of Estimation Accuracy

We evaluated the effectiveness of features focused on direction via machine learning using the learning model described in the previous section. The ratio of the training data to the test data was randomly selected so that training: test = 8: 2, and training and evaluation were conducted for each individual. In the training, the objective variables were the eight classes of emotions (seven emotions and neutrality), excluding the free-response results, and the predictor variables were three LMA values. We estimated using a combination of front-back and left-right features for Space and Weight as the features used as predictor variables, and we compared the results.

We show the results for each task in the Table 1. In the bespoke task, the combination with the highest percentage of accuracy was the case used Space-LR and Weight-LR at 80.41%, and the combination with the lowest percentage of accuracy was the case used Space-FB and Weight-FB at 62.86%. The highest percentage of accuracy in the video-watching task was the case used Space-LR and Weight-LR at 78.98%, and the lowest was the case used Space-FB and Weigh-FB at 65.84%.

Table 1. The results for each task.

Task	Space	Weight	Accuracy (SD) [%]	F-value (SD) [%]
Bespoke	FB	FB	62.86(.09)	47.73(.09)
	FB	LR	63.56(.12)	63.56(.12)
	LR	FB	78.52.(.07)	71.66(.10)
	LR	LR	80.41(.06)	74.70(.09)
Video-watching	FB	FB	65.84(.10)	52.87(.10)
	FB	LR	75.44(.09)	64.28(.09)
	LR	FB	71.27(.10)	59.33(.13)
	LR	LR	78.98(.09)	69.25(.12)

Moreover, we took the average of the percentage of accuracy in Table 1 for each task, focusing on each feature. The results showed a trend in both tasks, with higher estimation accuracy on using Space-LR and better estimation accuracy on using Weight-LR as well (Table 2).

Therefore, for the LMA values focusing on the direction of body movements in this study, results showed that features capturing the left and right directions contributed more to the improvement of accuracy than those capturing the front and back directions for both Space and Weight did.

Table 2. Comparison of accuracy using new and old feature values.

Task	Feature	Accuracy (SD) [%]	F-value (SD) [%]
Bespoke	Space	79.46(.01)	73.18(.02)
	Space	63.21(.00)	49.41(.01)
	Weight	71.98(.08)	62.90(.12)
	Weight	70.69(.08)	59.70(.12)
Video-watching	Space	75.12(.04)	64.29(.05)
	Space	70.64(.05)	58.58(.06)
	Weight	77.21(.02)	66.76(.02)
	Weight	68.55(.03)	56.10(.04)

6 Discussion

The results of the Wilcoxon signed-rank sum test for the combination with the largest percentage of accuracy (Space-LR and Weight-LR) and the combination with the smallest percentage of accuracy (Space-FB and Weight-FB) presented in the previous section, focusing on the percentage of accuracy for each individual, showed significant differences. The estimation accuracy of Space and Weight was significantly higher when the left-right direction features were used than when the front-back direction features were used. The results indicate that the left-right-focused features are effective in improving accuracy.

The results indicate that Space is better suited for features that capture the left-right spread than the front-back spread in cases where people make few physical movements, such as when watching a movie, or when there are many types of movements due to interaction, such as when bespoke. Similarly, we conclude that Weight, which represents the force of movement, is better suited for emotion estimation if it captures lateral changes in posture, such as tilting the head sideways, rather than forward and backward changes in posture.

7 Conclusion

In this study, we conducted experiments to measure body movements and emotions in two contrasting tasks, a video-watching task and a bespoke task, to expand the range of application of LMA values and to optimize their use in various tasks. We analyzed the estimation accuracy using a combination of the proposed LMA values focusing on the direction of body movements, and we examined the application of the features. The results showed that the combination of the largest (Space-LR and Weight-LR) and smallest (Space-FB and Weight-FB) accuracy were similar in both tasks, and that the estimation accuracy improved by about 18% for the bespoke task and about 13% for the video-watching task. From these results, we showed the effectiveness of emotion estimation with LMA values for tasks with few physical movements, such as the video-watching task, as well as for tasks with many types of movements, such as the bespoke task, and we obtained insight into how to define features that were more appropriate for each task.

In both tasks, the results showed that features that focused on the left-right orientation change and spread for Space and Weight contributed more to accuracy than those that focused on the front-back orientation.

In the future, we intend to improve these features, incorporate other features and estimation methods, and develop more generalized LMA values for use in purchasing procedures, watching videos explaining products, online shopping, and other situations.

References

1. Boucher, J.D., Ekman, P.: Facial areas and emotional information. J. Commun. **25**, 32–49 (1975)

2. Sato, W., Hyniewska, K., Minemoto, K., Yoshikawa, S.: Facial expressions of basic emotions in Japanese Laypeople. Frontiers Psychol., pp. 10–259, (2019)
3. Tanaka, K., Yamamoto, M., Aoyagi, S., Nagata, N.: Affect extraction in personal fabrication based on laban movement analysis: The Transactions of the Human Interface Society, Vol. 18(4), pp.363–372 (2016). (in Japanese)
4. Aoyagi, S., Yamazaki, Y., Ono, Y., Yamamoto, M., Nagata, N.: Extraction of Emotional Body Expression Types in Fabrication Based on Laban Movement Analysis and Sensitivity Analysis. Trans. Hum. Interface Soc., Vol. 22(1), pp.1–12, (2020). (in Japanese)
5. Bartenieff, I., Lewis, D.: Body Movement: coping with the environment, gordon & Breach Science (1980)
6. Kobayashi, F., Ogi, K., Aoyagi, S., Yamamoto, M.: Construction of the eye-emotion dataset and its evaluation by machine learning focusing on individual differences in emotional arousal, correspondences on Human Interface, 24(3), pp.289–296(2022). (In Japanese)
7. Fujiwara, S., Kobayashi, F., Aoyagi, S., Sugimotoi, M., Yamamoto, M., Nagata, N.: A Study on Application of Emotion Estimation based on Laban Feature Values to Bespoke Scenes. Proceedings of the Human Interface Symposium **2021**, 570–573 (2021)
8. Meeren, H.K., van Heijnsbergen, C.C., de Gelder, B.: Rapid perceptual integration of facial expression and emotional body language. Proceedings of the National Academy of Sciences of the United States of America (PNAS) **102**(45), 16518–16523 (2005)
9. Van den Stock, J., Righart, R., de Gelder, B.: Body expressions influence recognition of emotions in the face and voice. Emotion **7**(3), 487–499 (2007)
10. Kleinsmith, A., Bianchi-Berthouze, N.: Affective Body Expression Perception and Recognition: A Survey. IEEE Trans. Affect. Comput. **4**(1), 15–33 (2013)
11. Witkower, Z., Tracy, J.L.: Bodily Communication of Emotion: Evidence for Extrafacial Behavioral Expressions and Available Coding Systems. Emot. Rev. **11**(2), 184–193 (2018)
12. Laban, R.: The mastery of movement, 2nd edn. McDonald and Evans, London (1960)
13. Aristidou, A., Chrysanthou, Y.: Feature extraction for human motion indexing of acted dance performances In: 2014 International Conference on Computer Graphics Theory and Applications (GRAPP) (2014)
14. Dewan, S., Agarwal, S., Singh, N.: Laban movement analysis to classify emotions from motion. 10th International Conference on Machine Vision (ICMV 2017), 106962Q, (2017)
15. Crane, E.A., Gross, M.M.: Effort-Shape characteristics of emotion-related body movement 10th International Conference on Machine Vision (ICMV 2017), 106962Q, (2017)
16. Ono, Y., Aoyagi, S., Sugimoto, M., Yamamoto, M., Nagata, N.: Application of the emotion estimation method based on classification of expression type in laban feature values to design creation. Trans. Hum. Interface Soc. 23(3), pp.359–372, (2021). (in Japanese)
17. Russell, J.A.: A Circumplex Model of Affect. J. Pers. Soc. Psychol. **39**, 1161–1178 (1980)
18. Kobayashi, F., Sugimoto, M., Aoyagi, S., Yamamoto, M., Nagata, N.: Modeling Salesclerks' Utterances in Bespoke Scenes and Experimental Evaluation of It Using a Communication Robot. Trans. Hum. Interface Soc. 24(4), pp.263–272 (2022). (in Japanese)

User-Friendly Automated Evaluation Tool for Assessment of Emotional Intelligence

Lana Hiasat[1]([✉]) [ID], Faouzi Bouslama[2] [ID], and Sokrates Ioannou[3] [ID]

[1] General Studies Department, HCT, Dubai Men's Campus, Dubai, UAE
`lhiasat@hct.ac.ae`
[2] Computer Information Science Department, HCT, Dubai Men's Campus, Dubai, UAE
[3] Civil Engineering Department, HCT, Abu Dhabi Men's Campus, Abu Dhabi, UAE

Abstract. Educational institutions have a considerable interest in identifying links between personality traits and academic success. It has long been known that intelligence quotient (I.Q.) alone is not the sole, or a particularly good, predictor of success. Learning rarely occurs in isolation, and so our ability to accurately perceive how others feel or react may also be an indicator, or at least a contributor, to educational success. The capacity to receive emotions, simulate emotion-related feelings, understand the information of those emotions, and manage them is one definition of what has been termed Emotional Intelligence (E.I.). The innovative E.I. evaluation method developed in this study is based on an interdisciplinary approach between the computer science, engineering and humanities departments. An interdisciplinary approach is needed because the authors' goal in developing the evaluation tool is to address the problem of designing an effective yet simple and user-friendly method that educators of any background could find easy and beneficial to use. The literature on E.I. provides very few examples of effective systematic interventions where it was pointed out that, after many years of research, there are still very few examples of successful interventions that specifically increase E.I and that while self-contained seminars may raise the awareness of E.I, they are unlikely to affect permanent change.

Keywords: Emotional Intelligence · Evaluation Methods and Techniques · HCI and Humanities · Interdisciplinary · Interventions

1 Introduction

In an HCT-funded research project (Coombe, Bouslama, & Hiasat 2019), the researchers have developed a series of localized bilingual surveys to assess the students' and Faculty's E.I. skills. The skills in E.I. are crucially necessary to know how to interpret our emotions to effectively communicate with all stakeholders (other educators and students). Possessing E.I. skills is especially important for educators as it helps them face certain stressful situations in which their actions can impact their students' learning and wellbeing. In addition, it continues to be a problem as researchers have noted to measure employability of potential graduates (Dacre Pool & Qualter 2013). Another important

M. Kurosu and A. Hashizume (Eds.): HCII 2023, LNCS 14012, pp. 196–214, 2023.
https://doi.org/10.1007/978-3-031-35599-8_13

aspect to consider is the importance of passion as described in Duckworth's book on the power of grit (2016). Duckworth argues that passion combined with perseverance, is a crucial factor in determining an individual's level of success, regardless of their natural talents or abilities. The E.I. skills can assist educators with dealing with such challenges and employability demanding situations. Moreover, with the established relationship of E.I. skills and new research evidence linking E.I. to enhanced instructional performance and as a factor in teacher retention (Zeidner, Matthews & Roberts 2009), teachers at all levels could benefit from learning and using E.I. skills for both personal and professional development (Bouslama et al. 2019; Coombe 2020; Coombe et al. 2020; Chen, Jacobs & Spencer 1998). The classic text that Tinto (1993) described regarding student retention persists today and the emphasis on quality education still stands true.

One tool for the assessment of emotional intelligence is the Emotional Intelligence Quotient (EQ-i 2.0) test (Bar-On 2012). It's a self-report assessment that measures an individual's emotional and social skills, including self-awareness, self-regulation, motivation, empathy, and social skills. It's user-friendly and automated, allowing individuals to complete the assessment online and receive their results instantly. Another innovative user-friendly tool to self-assess emotional intelligence is the Emotional Intelligence Appraisal by Talent Smart (Huang 2020). This online assessment measures an individual's emotional intelligence, providing a comprehensive report with personalized feedback and suggestions for improvement. The tool is user-friendly, accessible from anywhere with an internet connection, and results are delivered instantly. A third user-friendly tool for self-assessment of emotional intelligence is the Mayer-Salovey-Caruso Emotional Intelligence Test (MSCEIT) (Mayer 2002; Mayer & Salovey 1997). It's a performance-based test that measures an individual's emotional intelligence by evaluating their ability to perceive, understand, and manage emotions.

The purpose of this paper is to present an innovative user-friendly tool to self-assess one's emotional intelligence. The proposed tool also includes an action plan for a set of interventions for improvement. The assessment consists of and validates the six developed assessments created by Bouslama et al. (2019) while offering a list of effective strategies. The choice of interface proposed in this paper is purposefully selected to be simple, and user-friendly. The tool is used in executive leadership training as a follow-up to a face-to-face training workshop to encourage participants to further develop their emotional intelligence skills. The authors of this paper provide a framework for how user friendly-based design is used to develop an interface of a simple tool for data tabulation and how results can be presented by going back to basic functions. The proposed assessment E.I. tool has been developed using Microsoft Excel (Microsoft Corporation. (2018)). Even though in recent years organizations are adopting artificial intelligence technologies and automation that can be coupled with emotional intelligence, going back to basics and creating a crisp mapping system has many benefits and also limitations that the authors explore in this paper. We present in this paper how E.I. user friendly evaluation tool can form a valuable resource for educators in their work to navigate a changing environment.

2 Defining the Six Dimensions of Emotional Intelligence

In his often-cited book, Daniel Goleman (1995) defines Emotional Intelligence as the ability to realize your own emotions and those of others, the ability to get self-motivated, and the ability to manage one's own emotions and relationships with others. Goleman (1995) uses the following four quadrants to define the skills and behaviors for emotional intelligence (Table 1):

Table 1. Daniel Goleman's (1995) Four Dimensions of Emotional Intelligence

Self-awareness:	**Social Awareness:**
• Self-awareness	• Empathy
• Accurate self-awareness	• Organizational awareness
• Self-confidence	• Service
Self-management:	**Relationship Management:**
• Self-control	• Inspiration
• Transparency	• Influence
• Adaptability	• Developing others
• Achievement	• Change catalyst
• Initiative	• Conflict management
• Optimism	• Teamwork and collaboration

In 2009, Cartwright and Solloway refined Goleman's 1995 definition and suggested that emotional intelligence "is the ability to understand, accept and recognize our own emotions and feelings, including their impact on ourselves and other people and to use this knowledge to improve our own behaviors as well as to manage and improve our relationship with others". Like Goleman, they recognized four core competencies of emotional intelligence: Self-awareness, Self-management, Social-awareness, and Relationship Management (see Fig. 1). Their model, however, places Self-awareness at the core of emotional intelligence. They believe that unless individuals have a deep and clear understanding of self, they cannot effectively develop and manage the remaining three quadrants or triangles.

After a comprehensive review of the literature and consideration of both the Goleman (1995) and Cartwright and Solloway (2017) models, Bouslama et al. (2019) expanded the scope and developed a localized six-quadrant model of Emotional Intelligence which features self-awareness at the center of the model. Two additional dimensions of adaptability and general mood were added to the previous models. Then localization was included to consider the local needs and cultural aspects particular to the Gulf region (see Fig. 1).

2.1 Self-awareness

Individuals who are self-aware know themselves through having a clear awareness of their behavior and/or disposition including strengths, weaknesses, thoughts, beliefs, incentives, and emotions. In simpler words, self-awareness means having a thoughtful

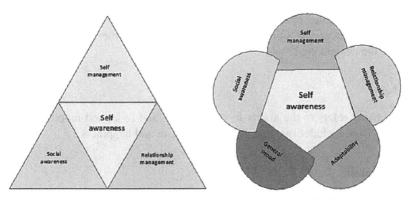

Fig. 1. Cartwright & Solloway E.I. Model (Cartwright & Solloway 2017); Bouslama et al. 6 Quadrant Model (2015); Bouslama, Housley & Steele (2015)

understanding of one's values, strengths and weaknesses, habits, and more importantly purpose in life. In fact, people who can understand their purpose in life are more capable of pursuing things that give them contentment and serenity. In education, self-awareness plays a major role as it helps teachers and thereby students understand their strengths and weaknesses and helps them develop effective strategies to become better focused on what they need to teach and learn.

2.2 Self-management

This refers to someone who uses self-coaching techniques that help them handle stress to manage their emotions and personal change in their life. Someone with high self-management has high self-esteem and can confidently show motivation to achieve personal and professional goals. They practice positive thinking and exhibit positive self-talk to help them create the life they want and believe in their abilities. A teacher with good self-management trusts their intuition to effectively problem-solve a variety of situations and manage themselves and their perception of others. Educators with good self-management can create a calm and supportive environment within the classroom. One popular stress management strategy is meditation which helps teachers decrease perceived stress and other negative emotional states that could cause health issues. Karimi et al. (2019) discovered that those with mindfulness meditation training showed significant improvements in E.I. skills compared to a control group.

2.3 Relationship Management

We define relationship management as acknowledging the emotions of others and one's own to conduct constructive interactions with a desired aim or result. If in the former dimensions, educators have been learning about themselves and others, the focus of relationship management lies in interaction. We manage relationships successfully when we use feelings and information to engage effectively with others. An educator who manages relationships effectively will need to notice and manage the effect his/her students and colleagues have on them and more importantly, why they feel that way. Only after that analysis will they be able to discern how to interact with them in order to achieve the desired goal.

2.4 Mood

This dimension refers to the ability to stay positive and in a good mood. The general mood dimension includes two main scales: optimism and happiness.

2.5 Adaptability

Adaptability refers to the ability to be flexible, and realistic and solve a range of problems as they arise. Adaptability is generally measured using three scales: reality testing, flexibility, and problem-solving. Understanding what adaptability skills are and where they come from can help you develop your skill set. The authors at the Center for Creative Leadership (Leading Effectively Staff, 2021) break down the adaptability skills into three categories: cognitive, emotional, and personality adaptability skills. Further details about each category are below:

- *Cognitive adaptability* is the ability to think through different potential scenarios and plan for various outcomes. Developing cognitive adaptability would not guarantee that the choice made is correct, but it helps in thought structuring during the decision-making process.
- *Emotional adaptability*. The idea that each colleague has unique work habits, thought processes, and individual differences may seem cliché, but it is a reality. Emotional adaptability skills allow you to recognize and appreciate these differences, enabling you to establish connections with individuals from diverse backgrounds and personalities, even those that may be distinct from your own.
- *Personality adaptability*. An adaptable personality enables one to perceive a situation objectively and envision its potential. When faced with obstacles, an adaptable person would possess a comprehensive understanding, balancing a realistic assessment of limitations with an optimistic outlook toward opportunities. This harmonious blend of realism and optimism equips the adaptable person to effectively respond to any scenario.

3 Interventions

Findings from research in a range of areas have consistently shown that people can improve their emotional competencies through systematic training (Brackett & Kutulak, 2006; Nelis et al. 2009). This has led us to conclude that E.I. can be developed through focused intervention strategies which would typically involve developing specific skills and competencies related to emotional intelligence. These interventions can be done individually, through coaching or therapy, or in a group setting through workshops or classes. The key is to find an approach that works best for the individual and to be consistent and committed to practicing and developing emotional intelligence skills over time. We consider the activities we share as E.I. packages that are divided into three parts (see Fig. 2):

- **Part I** is about knowing yourself and includes self-awareness and self-management dimensions.
- **Part II** is about knowing others and includes social awareness and relationship management.
- **Part III** is on positivity and well-being and includes the dimensions of adaptability and general mood

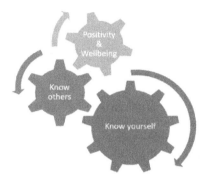

Fig. 2. Three categories of E.I. interventions

In order to implement effective interventions, the authors of this paper have developed E.I. measurement instrument in three stages that are described in this section:

- Stage 1- Paper-based and online
- Stage 2- Initial automation using Excel
- Stage 3- Adding complexity to the tool

The process of mapping the E.I. skills to interventions can be seen in Fig. 3.

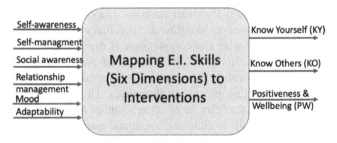

Fig. 3. E.I. skills mapping into interventions

Further to mapping the dimensions to interventions, we have developed four levels of categories: novice (low), intermediate (medium), and advanced (high) which can be seen in Table 2.

Table 2. E.I. dimensions 1 and 2 mapping to interventions.

Rule #	Self-awareness	Self-management	Know Yourself Training
1	LOW	LOW	6
2	MEDIUM	LOW	5
3	HIGH	LOW	4
4	LOW	MEDIUM	5
5	MEDIUM	MEDIUM	4
6	HIGH	MEDIUM	5
7	LOW	HIGH	4
8	MEDIUM	HIGH	3
9	HIGH	HIGH	2

4 Emotional Intelligence Innovative Measurement

We describe in this section the three stages of developing the innovative measurement and how we added complexity to the tool.

4.1 Stage 1- Paper-Based and Online Measurement

The initial stages of developing the measurement were on a traditional paper-based assessment format. The online version was developed using the institutional software Office 365 One Drive forms. The online surveys helped the researchers in the first stage of research to map participants and have some initial scores that were interpreted using the Fuzzy Logic tool (Bouslama et. al. 2015).

This initial stage was conducted at the researchers' tertiary institution and data was collected from a sample of students taking General Education and English Communication courses in 2019 (Bouslama et. al. 2019). A sample of the initial paper-based version is shown in Fig. 4.

Initially, we tried to use fuzzy logic and automatic mapping. In fact, instead of using crisp sets to model the outcomes of the online surveys, fuzzy sets were used to represent uncertainties and better deal with any complexities of the problem at hand. The four dimensions in our initial E.I. model which included self-awareness, self-management, social awareness, and relationship management, were modeled using linguistic variables defined on their respective universe of discourses. The interventions and training constituted the output which was also fuzzified in a similar manner as shown in Fig. 5.

A fuzzy rule base was built to allow the automatic mapping between the four E.I. inputs and the E.I. interventions. The system was developed and implemented using the MATLAB Fuzzy Logic toolbox. Figure 6 shows an excerpt of the mapping rules and a screenshot of the results of the simulation.

There were several limitations that researchers faced in this stage. One of the major limitations was that participants had to meet with the researchers to go over their scores and attend follow-up workshops for intervention and application of results. Participation

Fig. 4. Paper-based E.I. tools.

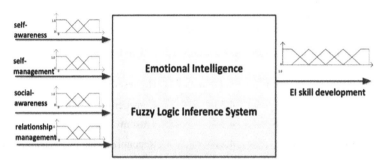

Fig. 5. E.I. Fuzzy system (Bouslama et. al. 2015)

Input 1- self-awareness	Input 2- self-management	Input 3- social awareness	Input 4- relationship management	Output- EI skill development
LOW	ANYTHING	ANYTHING		know yourself
AVERAGE			ANYTHING	know yourself
HIGH				accept your emotions
AVERAGE	LOW	LOW		know yourself
	AVERAGE		LOW	accept your emotions
	HIGH			accept your emotions
AVERAGE	LOW	AVERAGE		know yourself
	AVERAGE		LOW	accept your emotions
	HIGH			use your EI to improve
AVERAGE	AVERAGE	AVERAGE	LOW	use your EI to improve
			AVERAGE	use your EI to improve
			HIGH	recognize emotions of others
HIGH	AVERAGE	AVERAGE	LOW	recognize emotions of others
			AVERAGE	recognize emotions of others
			HIGH	improve relationships
HIGH	HIGH	HIGH	LOW	recognize emotions of others
			AVERAGE	improve relationships
			HIGH	improve relationships

Fig. 6. Fuzzy rules and simulation on MATLAB (Bouslama et. al. 2015)

in these follow-up workshops was very low. An additional limitation was that we have observed that participants were not honest in their responses. Their initial responses showed a perception of scores that we interpreted as the participants' perceived self-image and perhaps reflect their cultural influence on how to present themselves.

According to the initial results collected in 2019, the participants scored the highest in relationship management with a total score average of 4.81 out of 5 and specifically in the area of recognizing what drives one and what motivates others. The second highest score was in the dimension of social awareness where the total score average was 4.57 out of 5. Participants appeared to believe that they value differences and similarities between cultures and value differences and similarities between people as their highest scores on the E.I. measurement. This could be explained by the context we live in where many nationalities reside in Dubai, UAE and our students have opportunities to interact with many different cultures. Table 3 is a summary of the highest scores and specific areas that participants in this initial stage reported on in 2019:

Table 3. Summary of highest scores reported on E.I. surveys, 2019.

E.I. Survey Results 2019 Dimension	Score out of 5	Highest dimension
Self-Awareness	4.53	Consider myself an honest person
Self-Management	4.1	Trust my intuition
Relationship Management	4.81	Recognize what drives and motivates others
Social Awareness	4.57	I value differences and similarities between cultures I value differences and similarities between people
Adaptability	4.08	I can deal very effectively with people from different cultures
General Mood	4.09	I have good relationships with my classmates

In summary, the self-reported social-emotional intelligence profile of students in tertiary education in our study means that they have good skills for getting along with people and understanding what motivates them. They are honest and trust their intuition. They also value differences between people and cultures. This profile helps educators in understanding their students and knowing the best way to communicate and motivate them. However, as explained earlier, the limitations of this initial measurement observed was in the accuracy of self-reported results and the follow-up development of skills that were required. The need for an automated version, therefore, was identified.

4.2 Stage 2- Initial Automation Using Excel

The initial automation of the assessment tool was developed using Microsoft Excel. This was done as researchers observed discrepancies within what was initially reported in the online versions of assessments where participants disclosed their details and results were viewed by the researchers. Despite the promise of anonymity, it was observed that participants were reluctant to disclose their true strengths and weaknesses. Therefore, it became crucial not to push the participants beyond a level of disclosure that they were comfortable with and a move towards a solution that places control into the participants' hands rather than a data collection tool that saves details in the cloud.

The first automation of the tool was an Excel file where participants complete the E.I. questions by choosing a Likert score from a drop-down menu of a score between 1–5 (1 being a low score and 5 is the highest) as seen in Fig. 7. The authors used conventional VLOOKUP functions to generate the results for the participants to view following completing the assessment. The results were classified into four categories:

1. A novice score indicated that the participant's performance in this area is vulnerable: This area may be an obstacle for this person as a leader. It may be creating personal and professional challenges.
2. An intermediate score indicated that the participant's performance in this area is emerging: This is an area where the person is developing skills and awareness; it is essential to continue to practice.
3. An upper-Intermediate score indicated that the participant's performance in this area is functional: This competence is adequate and a potential strength to leverage. It will be valuable to continue further development to meet the demands of leadership.
4. An advanced score means the participant's performance in this area is skilled and may even reach expert level: This is a potential strength to leverage. Having a unique ability in this area distinguishes a person as a leader.

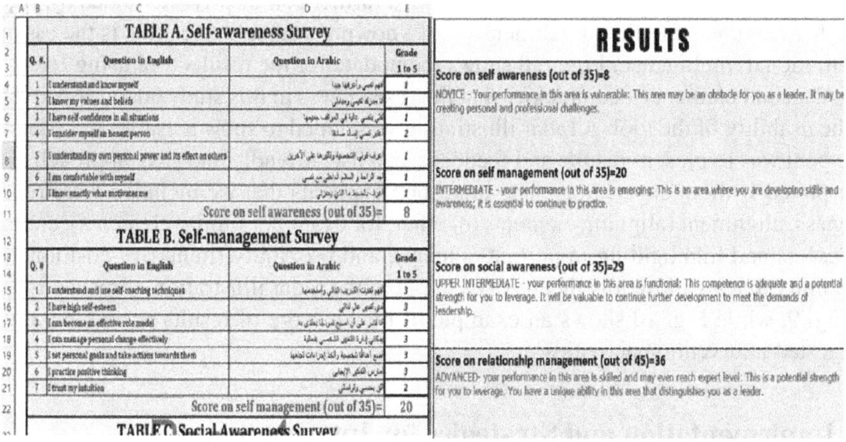

Fig. 7. Sample Excel E.I. assessment and results

In summary, the process of automating emotional intelligence assessments using an Excel sheet required creating a series of formulas and functions that can score answers to questions related to emotional intelligence. Researchers in this study have found that while automating emotional intelligence assessments using Excel can be a useful tool for self-reflection and growth; however, self-reported assessments had limitations and might not provide a comprehensive picture of an individual's emotional intelligence. Therefore, adding interventions and more complexity to this tool was needed which we describe in the next section.

4.3   Stage 3- Adding Complexity to the Tool

The initial automation using the Excel sheet was producing the results in a one-to-one crisp mapping. Crisp mapping is a method of categorizing assessment scores into clear, distinct categories or groups, often called "score bands" or "performance levels." The purpose of crisp mapping is to provide a clear interpretation of assessment scores, making it easier to understand the results and to make meaningful comparisons between individuals or groups. The alternative to crisp mapping that scientists suggest is the application of fuzzy logic (Feilhauer et al. 2021).

In the context of emotional intelligence assessments, crisp mapping involves grouping scores into categories such as high emotional intelligence which we defined as upper intermediate and advanced levels; average emotional intelligence, which we defined as intermediate level; and low emotional intelligence which we defined as novice.

Crisp mapping is often used in standardized assessments, such as aptitude tests or personality assessments, to provide a clear and concise interpretation of results. Categorical representation and mapping may not be similar to the human nature of fuzziness. Therefore, the researchers in this study believed complexity should be added to map the results into the three main dimensions of knowing yourself, giving yourself, and positivity and well-being. In doing so, a fuzzy element was added in the linguistic interpretation of the crisp score results. In addition, a further complexity was added by giving a higher percentage to the first dimension of knowing yourself since this is the essence of emotional intelligence. Figure 8 shows the update for the results tool using Excel.

A second element of complexity that the researchers in this study added was related to the usability of the tool. A radar illustration was added to show a usable and friendly. The goal was to present results and feedback in a user-friendly and easy approach to be interpreted without expert help. The important elements that we included were repetitiveness, alignment (aligning elements together, for example, similar elements), contrast (of colors and highlighting important content), and proximity (items are positioned in proximity that are close together). An example of the radar illustration of results is seen in Fig. 9, while Fig. 10 shows an example of how a score of results is presented with suggested intervention activities.

5   Implementation and Strategies for Intervention

The decision to move from a traditional one-to-one mapping to a holistic more human-like approach was to provide a holistic approach to measurement that captures human behavior and abilities. A holistic approach to mapping the results of emotional intelligence to interventions involved considering a range of factors related to an individual's overall well-being and development. This approach considered the individual as a whole,

TABLE A. Self-awareness Survey

Q. #.	Question in English	Grade 1 to 5	Question in Arabic
1	I understand and know myself	1	[illegible]
2	I know my values and beliefs	1	[illegible]
3	I have self confidence in all situations	1	[illegible]
4	I consider myself an honest person	2	[illegible]
5	I understand my own personal power and its affect on others	2	[illegible]
6	I am comfortable with myself	2	[illegible]
7	I know exactly what motivates me	2	[illegible]
Score on self awareness (out of 35)=		11	

TABLE B. Self-management Survey

Q. #	Question in English	Grade 1 to 5	Question in Arabic
1	I understand and use self coaching techniques	4	[illegible]
2	I have high self-esteem	4	[illegible]
3	I can become an effective role model	4	[illegible]
4	I can manage personal change effectively	4	[illegible]
5	I set personal goals and take actions towards them	5	[illegible]
6	I practice positive thinking	5	[illegible]
7	I trust my intuition	2	[illegible]
Score on self management (out of 35)=		28	

TABLE C. Social Awareness Survey

Q. #	Question in English	Grade 1 to 5	Question in Arabic
1	I value differences and similarities between people	3	[illegible]
2	I value differences and similarities between cultures	3	[illegible]
3	I value differences and similarities in different points of view	3	[illegible]
4	I believe I am a caring person	4	[illegible]
5	I can imagine myself in someone else's place	4	[illegible]
6	I can establish and maintain rapport with others	4	[illegible]
7	I understand the importance of values, behaviours and beliefs in the workplace	4	[illegible]
Score on social awareness (out of 35)=		25	

TABLE D. Relationship Management Survey

Q. #	Question in English	Grade 1 to 5	Question in Arabic
1	I always try to negotiate and mediate acceptable solutions to conflict	2	[illegible]
2	I know when to discuss a conflict or issue and when to walk away when solving a problem	2	[illegible]
3	I help others increase their confidence	2	[illegible]
4	I find it easy to have long-term relationships	2	[illegible]
5	I recognize what drives and motivates others	1	[illegible]
6	I consider myself an open minded person	1	[illegible]
7	I am comfortable with change	1	[illegible]
8	I can collaborate and work in a team	1	[illegible]
9	I can set and achieve goals	2	[illegible]
Score on relationship management (out of 45)=		14	

TABLE E. Adaptability Survey

Q. #	Question in English	Grade 1 to 5	Question in Arabic
1	I try to see a situation from as many perspectives as possible	5	[illegible]
2	I use my logic rather than my emotions when making decisions in life	5	[illegible]
3	When a situation happens that I don't understand I consult someone I trust to get their opinion	5	[illegible]
4	I brainstorm all the possible meanings before I make a decision	5	[illegible]
5	I have control over my thoughts and reactions	4	[illegible]
6	I am aware of what meaning I am attributing to the situations that arise in my life	4	[illegible]
7	I can deal very effectively with people from different cultures	4	[illegible]
8	I do well with non-routine tasks.	4	[illegible]
9	I can deal with stressful situations in my life	4	[illegible]
10	I try very hard to solve problems on time	4	[illegible]
Score on adaptability (out of 50)=		44	

TABLE F. General Mood Survey

Q. #	Question in English	Grade 1 to 5	Question in Arabic
1	I sleep well at night and wake up feeling ready for the day	1	[illegible]
2	I really enjoy my work	1	[illegible]
3	I take good care of my health	2	[illegible]
4	I feel positive about academic developments	1	[illegible]
5	I have good relationships with my colleagues	2	[illegible]
6	I feel that my life is going very well now	1	[illegible]
7	I feel positive about my future	1	[illegible]
Score on general mood (out of 35)=		9	

Fig. 8. Sample of an updated Excel E.I. assessment and results

rather than focusing solely on their emotional intelligence scores, and seeks to identify areas of strength and areas that may benefit from intervention. The initial strategy was to map the intervention strategies to the three categories of know yourself, know others and positivity and well-being. However, after reflection and initial trials, we noticed that the number of interventions would be high and could be overwhelming for participants to implement without expert guidance. Therefore, keeping our main objective in mind which was to create a user-friendly and easy tool to interpret without expert help, we decided to stay with the one-to-one mapping and limited the number of interventions to simply target the levels reported. We believe that the ongoing cycle approach to applying this tool would yield the most benefit. Therefore, we propose the following process:

Step 1: Take the E. I. assessment.
Step 2: Get the results and intervention plan then reflect on your E.I. profile.
Step 3: 30-day intervention plan application and reflective activities.
Step 4: Re-assess using the E.I. tool.
Step 5: Reflect on your E.I. Weighted profile with an E.I. expert consultation.

6 Implication and Recommendations: E.I. Innovative Profiling

Researchers in this study created a comprehensive and individualized tool for profiling based on the consideration that the person as a whole and taking into consideration their unique needs and circumstances. The innovative profiling tools that we recommend to further enhance our approach are described in the next section.

OVERALL TOTAL SCORE=	55.7%
SUGGESTED IMPROVEMENT=	70.0%

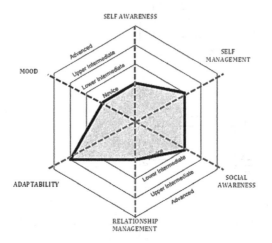

Fig. 9. Graphic illustration of results

Sample: One set of results: **R E S U L T S**

Score on self-awareness (out of 35)=11

NOVICE - Your performance in this area is vulnerable: This area may be an obstacle for you as a leader. It may be creating personal and professional challenges.

ABCs of emotions-increase your vocabulary:
Learning to name emotions accurately is one of the basic skills individuals need to work on. Useful wheels of emotions are:

Plutchik's Wheel of Emotion
(https://www.6seconds.org/2020/08/11/plutchik-wheel-emotions/)

The Emotoscope feeling Chart- can be downloaded from:
https://eq.org/library/emotoscope-feeling-chart/

Fig. 10. Sample of updated result and intervention

6.1 Part I: E.I. Johari and Nohari Windows Model

Based on our initial assessment tool, the researchers in this study observed that blind spots can be difficult to identify in addition to the participant's manipulation of the test results through the selection of responses that are desirable but not necessarily accurate or even true. Therefore, our future plans are to add another step of complexity and develop a tool for quality assurance of the reported results through a tool similar to the Johari window (available at https://kevan.org/johari) and Nohari window (available at: https://kevan.org/nohari). The Johari Window and Nohari Window are models used in psychology to understand self-awareness and self-disclosure in interpersonal relationships. They can also be applied to emotional intelligence profiling, as emotional intelligence is centered around self-awareness and the ability to understand and manage one's own emotions, as well as the emotions of others. The model was developed in 1955 by American psychologists Joseph Luft and Harry Ingham. In the Johari window model, there are four windows; an open area that is known to self and known to others, a hidden area that is not known to others but known to self, blind spots that are not known to self but known to others, and unknown areas that are both unknown to self and unknown to others (Business Balls, 2022). We suggest applying the Johari and Nohari Window to emotional intelligence profiling in the following ways:

- *Johari Window:* The Johari Window can be used to help individuals increase their self-awareness and understand how others perceive them. This can be applied to emotional intelligence by asking individuals to reflect on their own emotions and how they express them and then inviting feedback from others to gain a more complete picture of their emotional intelligence.
- *Nohari Window:* The Nohari Window can be used to explore the emotions that individuals hide or keep private, and the reasons for doing so. This can be applied to emotional intelligence by encouraging individuals to consider the emotions they tend to keep hidden and exploring the reasons behind their behavior.
- *Combining the two windows:* The Johari and Nohari Windows can be combined to create a more comprehensive picture of an individual's emotional intelligence. This might involve first using the Johari Window to increase self-awareness and understand how others perceive them, and then using the Nohari Window to explore the emotions that are kept private.

By applying the Johari and Nohari Window to emotional intelligence profiling, individuals can gain a better understanding of their own emotions, as well as how their emotions are perceived by others, and take steps to improve their emotional intelligence and overall well-being. The model diagram is seen in Fig. 11.

Further ongoing work is on developing an updated E.I. profiler considering the post-pandemic challenges and lived experiences. The suggested profilers of E.I. are presented in this section. It is crucial to emphasize that the self-leader profile is the essence of the required E.I. necessary and sufficient leadership skills. Researchers of this study believe that the E.I. profile of network leaders and happy leaders are considered sufficient but lack the necessary profile characteristics highlighted in the self-leader which could as a result pose challenges to their leadership effectiveness.

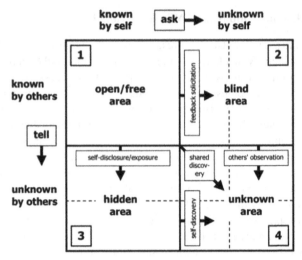

Fig. 11. The Johari window diagram is based on the Ingham and Luft Johari Window, developed and adapted by Alan Chapman. Copyright allowed from: https://www.businessballs.com/johari windowmodeldiagram.pdf

The E.I. weighted leadership profile is based on the idea that the knowing yourself category is the most important and carries the highest weight and as such the researchers assigned 50% weighted points for self-awareness and self-management. The knowing others category comes at 30% and includes social awareness and relationship management while positivity and well-being account for 20% of the profile. Emotional intelligence is a complex construct that involves several components that were discussed in this paper including self-awareness, emotional regulation, empathy, and social skills. A high level of emotional intelligence requires developing these components and applying them in daily life. Researchers of this paper have compiled the necessary and sufficient components for E.I. The necessary components that we consider are knowing yourself including the factors of self-awareness and self-management while sufficient components would be in knowing others in social awareness and relationship management. Based on the above-weighted profile calculations, we present the below three E.I. Weighted Leadership profiles which need further validation:

a) The Self Leader

We base our definition of the self-leadership models, theories and examples that are found from: https://positivepsychology.com/self-leadership/

Asset: Knowing yourself.

- Pursuing things in life that connect to your values and give you purpose in life
- Handling stress and managing your emotions effectively in life

Low score Challenges:

- Lack of focus on what really matters to you and what brings you purpose in life
- Inability to manage stressful situations and your personal reactions.

b) The Network Leader

The idea of a network leadership profile is based on network science and the invisible networks that link us (Ogden 2018). This can be found: in Network Leadership Blog - Visible Network Labs and an important classification of this profile is also based on the definition found in Ogden's article (2018):

Asset: Know Others

- Interacting effectively with others
- Achieving positive interactions and engagement with a desired aim or result with others

Low score Challenges:

- Lack of ability in connecting effectively with others and seeing how negative interactions impact successful outcomes
- Inability to establish real connections with others that motivate them to excel

c) The Happy Leader

This profile is based on positive psychology and model that Seligman has defined as PERMA (Madeson 2017; Seligman, Steen, Park & Peterson 2005):

Asset: Positivity and wellbeing

- Being resilient during a changed and uncertain environment
- Energizing yourself through seeing hidden opportunities

Low score Challenges:

- Lack of ability in finding ways to change through accepting new perspectives
- Remaining focused on the obstacles instead of hidden opportunities

Tables 4 and 5 are summaries of the potential Strengths and Vulnerabilities, respectively.

Table 4. Potential Strengths-Summary

Your Highest Scores are in…	These probably help you in…
Self-awareness	pursuing things in life that connect to your values and give you purpose in life
Self-management	handling stress and managing your emotions effectively in life
Social Awareness	interacting effectively with others
Relationship management	achieving positive interactions and engagement with a desired aim or result with others
Adaptability	being resilient during a changed and uncertain environment
General Mood	Energizing yourself through seeing hidden opportunities

Table 5. Potential Vulnerabilities- Summary

our lowest Scores are in…	These may present challenges for you around…
Self-awareness	focusing on what really matters to you and what brings you purpose in life
Self-management	managing stressful situations and your personal reactions
Social Awareness	connecting effectively with others and seeing how negative interactions impact successful outcomes
Relationship management	establishing real connections with others that motivate them to excel
Adaptability	finding ways to change through accepting new perspectives
General Mood	Remaining focused on the obstacles instead of hidden opportunities

7 Conclusion

In conclusion, the link between personality traits and academic success has been of great interest to educational institutions. While intelligence quotient (I.Q.) may not be the best predictor of success, studies have shown that other factors, such as conscientiousness and emotional intelligence (E.I.), can play a significant role in determining academic success. This is why it is important to measure the levels of E.I. in educators and educational leaders, as their influence on the academic success of their institutions is undeniable. In this paper, researchers have adapted an interdisciplinary approach to develop an effective and user-friendly evaluation tool for measuring E.I. The literature on E.I. provides examples of successful interventions, but recent studies have shown that workshops and interventions based on the Salovey and Mayer Four Branch Model of ability E.I. can effectively raise elements of E.I. in a study group. We have introduced an innovative tool to measure emotional intelligence using automation and keeping in mind the user-friendliness of the tool. The user-friendly and automated measurement tool we shared in this paper is designed for evaluating emotional intelligence. The authors aimed to provide a simple and accessible way of measuring emotional intelligence, with a focus on ease of use. The evaluation tool was based on the latest research and technological advancements in assessments, making it a reliable and effective way to assess emotional intelligence.

References

Bar-On, R.: The Impact of Emotional Intelligence on Health and Wellbeing. Emot. Intell. - NEW Perspect. Appl. (2012). https://doi.org/10.5772/32468

Business Balls website: Johari Window Model and Free Diagrams (2022). https://www.businessb alls.com/self-awareness/johari-window-model-and-free-diagrams/

Bouslama, F., Housley, M., Steele, A.: Using a fuzzy logic-based emotional intelligence framework for testing emotional literacy of students in an outcomes-based educational system. J. Netw. Innov. Comput. ISSN 2160–2174 **3**, 105–114 (2015) © MIR Labs. www.mirlabs.net/jnic/ index.html

Bouslama, F., Hiasat, L., Medina, C., Coombe, C., Manser, R.: Designing localized bilingual surveys for emotional literacy and intelligence assessment. In: Proceedings of the International Academic Conference on Education and Teaching (WEI-ET-Montreal 2019), Canada, Oct 28–30, pp. 11–27 (2019)

Brackett, M.A., Kululak, N.A.: Emotional intelligence in the classroom: skill-based training for teachers and students. In: Ciarrochi, J., Mayer, J.D. (eds.) Applying Emotional Intelligence: A practitioner's Guide, pp. 1–27. Psychology Press/Taylor and Francis, New York (2006)

Cartwright, A., Solloway, A.: Emotional intelligence: activities for developing you and your business. Routledge (2017). https://doi.org/10.4324/9781315256580

Chen, W., Jacobs, R., Spencer, L.M.: Calculating the competencies of stars. In: Goleman, D. (ed.) Working with Emotional Intelligence, pp. 377–380. Bantam Books, New York (1998)

Coombe, C.: Developing a personal and professional strategic plan. In: Coombe, C., Anderson, N.J., Stephenson, L. (eds.) Professionalizing Your English Language Teaching. Second Language Learning and Teaching. Springer, Cham (2020). https://doi.org/10.1007/978-3-030-347 62-8_9

Coombe, C., Bouslama, F., Hiasat, L.: Integrating an artificial intelligence-based emotional intelligence assessment framework with student success center interventions in UAE universities and beyond. HCT Interdisciplinary Research Grant, Grant Type and No. 1383, Fund No. 113115 (2019)

Dacre Pool, L., Qualter, P.: Emotional self-efficacy, graduate employability, and career satisfaction: testing the associations. Aust. J. Psychol. **65**(4), 214–223 (2013). https://doi.org/10.1111/ajpy. 12023

Duckworth, A.: Grit: the power of passion and perseverance. New York, NY: Scribner/Simon & Schuster (2016)

Feilhauer, H., et al.: Let your maps be fuzzy!—Class probabilities and floristic gradients as alternatives to crisp mapping for remote sensing of vegetation. Remote Sens.Ecol. Conserv. **7**(2), 292–305 (2021)

Goleman, D.: Emotional Intelligence. Bantam Books, Inc. (1995)

Huang, T.: A review of "Emotional Intelligence 2.0": travis bradberry and jean greaves, San Diego, CA: Talent Smart (2009). J. Character Leadership Develop. **7**(3)(2020)

Karimi, L., Kent, S.P., Leggat, S.G., Rada, J., Angleton, A.: Positive effects of workplace meditation training and practice. Int. J. Psychol. Stud. **11**(1), 15 (2019). https://doi.org/10.5539/ijps. v11n1p15

Leading effectively staff: adapting to change requires flexible leadership (2021). https://www.ccl. org/articles/leading-effectively-articles/adaptability-1-idea-3-facts-5-tips/

Madeson, M.: Seligman's PERMA+ Model Explained: A Theory of Wellbeing. https://positivep sychology.com/perma-model/ (2017)

Mayer, J.D.: MSCEIT: Mayer-Salovey-Caruso emotional intelligence test. Toronto, Canada: Multi-Health Systems (2002)

Mayer, J.D., Salovey, P.: What is emotional intelligence? In: Salovey, P., Sluyter, D. (eds.) Emotional development and emotional intelligence: Educational implications, pp. 3–34. Basic Books, New York (1997)

Microsoft Corporation: Microsoft Excel (2018). https://office.microsoft.com/excel

Nelis, D., Quoidbach, J., Mikolajczak, M., Hansenne, M.: Increasing emotional intelligence: (How) is it possible? Personality Individ. Differ. **47**(1), 36–41 (2009). https://doi.org/10.1016/ j.paid.2009.01.046

Ogden, C.: What is network leadership? (2018). https://www.nextgenlearning.org/articles/what-is-network-leadership

Seligman, M.E.P., Steen, T.A., Park, N., Peterson, C.: Positive psychology progress: empirical validation of interventions. Am. Psychol. **60**(5), 410–421 (2005). https://doi.org/10.1037/0003-066X.60.5.410

Tinto, V.: Leaving college: Rethinking the causes and cures of student attrition, 2nd edn. University of Chicago Press, Chicago (1993)

Zeidner, M., Matthews, G., Roberts, R.D.: What We Know about Emotional Intelligence: How It Affects Learning, Work, relationships, and Our Mental Health. MIT Press, Cambridge, MA (2009)

Visualizing Emotions Perceived in Daily Activities for Self-Awareness Development

Jungyun Kim, Toshiki Takeuchi$^{(\boxtimes)}$, and Takuji Narumi$^{(\boxtimes)}$

The University of Tokyo, Hongo 7-3-1, Bunkyo-ku, Tokyo, Japan
{jungyun,take,narumi}@cyber.t.u-tokyo.ac.jp

Abstract. The importance of developing self-awareness is increasing in the society because self-awareness helps individuals introspect to understand their own emotions and behaviors, and uncover aspects of their own personality that they had not recognized in the past. However, motivating individuals to work on developing self-awareness can be challenging because an increase in self-awareness cannot be visually tracked. Although many data visualization techniques for self-awareness development have been proposed in prior studies, they do not effectively maintain long-term engagement, and thus fail in their purpose of developing self-awareness. This study aims to: (1) improve self-awareness through data visualization of perceived happiness and stress from daily activities in the form of a house, which is treated as a metaphor for personal identity to facilitate higher engagement; and (2) investigate whether improved self-awareness through engagement with the house visualization affects individual's perception of their own lifestyle. The results from two long-term experiments demonstrate that a house as a visualization subject is effective in building individuals' self-awareness and positively influencing their intention to change their behavior.

Keywords: Visualization · Lifelog · Emotions · Self-Awareness

1 Introduction

Developing self-awareness is the process of obtaining knowledge of individuals' characteristics such as emotions, values, and behaviors [6]. It allows individuals to observe physical and emotional changes in themselves and discern how to cope with different situations [5]. Being aware of emotions, especially happiness and stress, is crucial in self-awareness, as these are universal emotions that humans experience on a day-to-day basis [19].

Although the importance of developing self-awareness is increasing in the society, it is difficult to concretely identify the benefits of developing self-awareness because its progress cannot be visibly tracked. Prior studies [9,16] attempted to support individuals in developing self-awareness, but the participants of such studies experienced difficulties in recognizing their own lifestyle

M. Kurosu and A. Hashizume (Eds.): HCII 2023, LNCS 14012, pp. 215–230, 2023.
https://doi.org/10.1007/978-3-031-35599-8_14

patterns [20], which decreased their motivation to interact with the data visualization. Additionally, they gradually lost motivation to reflect on themselves and improve their behavior. Motivation is key in self-awareness development as the process is driven by pro-active effort.

To support long-term engagement and self-awareness development, this study proposed a new way of visualizing emotions experienced in daily activities. We visualized the users' life-logging data as a house. The visualization of a house was selected because a house is often considered to be a metaphor for an individual's identity [2]. We aimed to visualize changes in the house to explicitly illustrate the daily growth and changes accomplished by the participants, that is, the users. The house design changed based on users' self-reports and symbolized the happiness and stress levels of their daily activities. We asked the following research questions using our mobile application called *How Are You*:

RQ1: How does the proposed house visualization affect the development of self-awareness in an individual?

RQ2: How does improved self-awareness due to the proposed visualization affect an individual's perception of lifestyle?

This study could contribute to providing guidelines for creating visualizations for self-awareness development in terms of data utilization and design. Additionally, it could support obtaining insights on why developing self-awareness is important and how it affects individuals' perceptions of lifestyle.

2   Related Work

Prior studies, including Emotical [9] and MoopMap [16], attempted to develop self-awareness and demonstrated that illustrating individuals' emotions through data visualization was more effective in developing self-awareness compared to referring to raw data such as numbers and texts. Emotical analyzed participants' daily activities and emotions from the past and provided an emotional forecast using a line graph along with advice to improve emotions. Their three-week experiment showed that self-awareness developed better when individuals could reflect on themselves through visualization compared with only logging data.

MoodMap aimed to enhance self-awareness and work performance by tracking and visualizing emotions using a scatter plot. It promoted self-reflection in employees and prevented mental health problems caused by work-related factors. Employees could compare their emotional trends with others and identify whether their current state required attention. The four-week experiment showed that reflecting on their visualization and comparing it with others allowed participants to feel connected with the team and open up to new perspectives.

However, individuals faced difficulties reflecting on their lifestyle patterns, which made it difficult for them to develop self-awareness successfully. For example, MoodMap focuses on understanding emotions triggered by work-related factors, while the emotions experienced in other daily activities were not taken into account. Consequently, users could not gain a clear perception of their own emotional health. Although Emotical encouraged individuals to add notes describing their daily activities in detail, such a habit was not sustainable as it was perceived as tedious and time-consuming task that added to the workload. Linking lifestyle patterns with visualization is important in supporting individuals to identify emotionally significant moments and increase their motivation to discover their inner selves [7].

Such studies also showed challenges in engaging individuals with the visualization. This was because the visualizations aimed for either providing accurate and personalized visualization or understanding the work environment thus focusing less on building connections between the visualization and individuals. This was critical as being engaged with the visualization allows individuals to evoke their experiences related to the data. They could go beyond understanding the data by feeling the message that the visualization and giving an emotional response, which forms a communication between individuals and the visualization [10]. Thus this study proposed a new visualization reflecting multiple daily activities and showing higher engagement as a solution to overcome the limitations.

Such studies also faced challenges in engaging individuals because the visualizations aimed to either provide accurate and personalized visualization or understanding the work environment, thus focusing less on building connections between the visualization and individuals. However, such a connection is critical because being engaged with the visualization allows individuals to relate what they see with their experiences and accordingly pursue changes. When a visualization is engaging it can evoke an emotional response, which can lead to introspection and self-directed change [10]. Thus, this study proposed a new visualization reflecting multiple daily activities and showing higher engagement as a solution to overcome these limitations.

3   Proposed Visualization

This study proposed a new visualization design for emotions perceived in daily activities to overcome the above-mentioned limitations and support individuals' self-awareness development. The objectives of this study are to (1) examine the effect of the proposed visualization on the development of self-awareness and (2) investigate if the improved self-awareness from the proposed visualization affects individuals' perception of lifestyle. This study could provide guidelines for creating data visualizations for self-awareness development, particularly in terms of data utilization and design. Additionally, it could provide insights into why developing self-awareness is important and how it affects individuals' perceptions about their own lifestyle.

We explored various metaphors to use in our visualization because metaphor-based visualizations allow individuals to understand the information conveyed in the visualization by connecting it to their prior knowledge [4]. As we wanted individuals to reflect on their knowledge when viewing the visualization, we chose house, which is known as a metaphor of an individual's identity [3]. A house is also used as a channel of self-expression [13], especially from a psychological perspective; thus, we wanted individuals to create an emotional representation of the self while interacting with the visualization.

The data used to generate the house design included daily activity information and the corresponding happiness and stress levels. The happiness and stress levels determine the size of the house, and the variation in daily activities determines the number of house components. In the first experiment that we conducted, data from beginning to end were gathered and reflected in the visualization. However, this confused participants when viewing the visualization because there was too much data for interpretation. Hence, in the second experiment, a house was created using only past one week's data. We organized daily activity categories based on a survey conducted in 2020 [11], as shown in Table 1. Individuals could reflect on two types of houses, where one represented happiness and the other represented stress, enabling them to focus on one emotion at a time. Eight design strategies for encouraging lifestyle behavior change [1] and five golden rules for color selection were used as design references [12].

Table 1. Daily activities categorized based on the survey [11].

Main Category	Subcategory
Socialization	None
Leisure	Sports
	Shopping
	Internet/Games
	TV/Movie
	Art/Music
	Rest
	Other
Eating	None
Sleeping	None
Studying	None
Working	None
Other	None

Figure 1 displays examples of house design. The bottom left figure shows low levels of happiness and stress, and a narrow range of daily activities. The top-left figure is similar to the bottom-left figure, but with high happiness and stress levels. Both visualizations were generated when individuals had a relatively simple lifestyle pattern. Individuals could attempt to add more decorations to the house by challenging themselves with new daily activities. If they were not satisfied with the size of the house (e.g., the size of happiness house is as shown in the bottom left figure), they could attempt to seek causes by reflecting on their lifestyle patterns.

The bottom-right figure represents low levels of happiness and stress, and a wide variety of daily activities. The top-right figure is similar to the bottom-

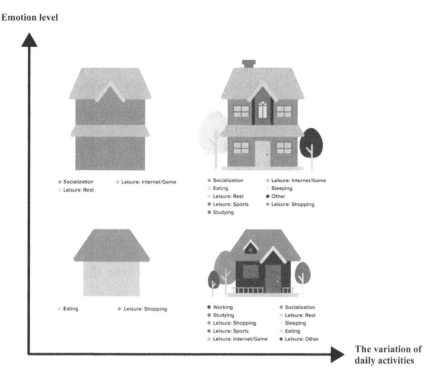

Fig. 1. Examples of house designs created from the data on daily activities and happiness and stress levels. Individuals will be provided with two houses, where one represents happiness and the other represents stress.

right, but with high levels of happiness and stress. In contrast to figures on the left side, both visualizations on the right were generated when individuals engaged in various daily activities, indicating a busy lifestyle pattern. Individuals can attempt to simplify the house design if they want to focus on a few daily activities that are important to them.

We did not set an ideal house design reflecting an optimal lifestyle pattern. Rather, the idea was to let users freely explore and engage with the visualization without a set target so as to allow awareness of emotions to emerge. Thus, they could utilize the house visualization for recording and reflecting their intentions or interact to create an ideal design.

4 Mobile Application: How Are You

We developed an iOS mobile application *How Are You* to implement the visualization (Fig. 2). It allows users to (a) add data on daily activities and corresponding happiness and stress levels on a scale of one to six where one is the lowest and six is the highest [8], and (b) perform self-reflection from visualizations. Below we list how *How Are You* provides the visualization to users.

We developed an iOS mobile application *How Are You* to implement the visualization (Fig. 2). It allows users to (a) add data on daily activities and record happiness and stress levels on a scale of one to six where one is lowest and six is highest [8], and (b) perform self-reflection based on visualization. Below we list *How Are You* provides the visualization to users.

1. Collect data: *How Are You* sends notifications approximately every two to three hours for users to carry out (a).
2. Transfer data: The data from (a) are transferred to a Realtime Database.
3. Analyze data: The happiness and stress levels for each daily activity are averaged and arranged in descending order as an array (e.g., [5, 3, 1.3]).
4. Create visualization: The array from Realtime Database is imported to *How Are You* and two house visualizations; one representing happiness status and one representing stress status, are created based on the index. Each value of the index determines the size of the house and the house components (e.g., windows, roof). A higher value generates a larger house. The total number of indices determines the number of house components; thus, a higher index number creates a more decorative house.

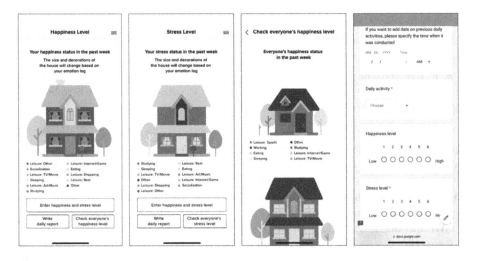

Fig. 2. The main screens of *How Are You*.

5   Experiment to Examine the Effect of the Proposed Visualization

5.1   Self-Awareness and Quality of Life

Purpose and Hypotheses. Through a long-term experiment in which the participants used *How Are You*, we investigated the effect of the proposed visualization on self-awareness and quality of life compared with commonly used visualizations, as it has been discovered that development of self-awareness allows individuals to assess quality of life [8]. Based on prior studies on data visualization [17], bar and pie charts were chosen to represent the commonly used visualization for this experiment. The hypotheses for this experiment are as follows:

H1: Visualizing individuals' perceived happiness and stress from daily activities in the form of a house motivates them to engage with it, which supports the development of self-awareness.
H2: Visualizing individuals' perceived happiness and stress from their daily activities as a house improves the quality of their lives.

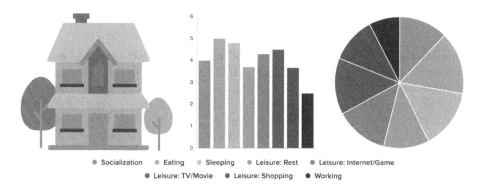

Daily activities	Average happiness level
Socialization	4
Eating	5
Sleeping	4.8
Leisure: Rest	3.7
Leisure: Internet/Game	4.3
Leisure: TV/Movie	4.5
Leisure: Shopping	3.67
Working	2.5

Fig. 3. Types of visualizations provided to the participants: house, bar chart, pie chart

Participants and Procedure. Thirty participants participated in the experiment (18 males and 12 females), with ages ranging from 21 to 50 years. They were recruited via snowball sampling through a social media platform managed by the university and friend referrals from the country where the study was conducted. Each participant was paid 10,000 JPY (approximately 87 USD) for participation.

The participants were randomly divided into three groups based on the three types of visualization-house, bar chart, and pie chart (Fig. 3). Ten participants were assigned per visualization type. All participants were required to conduct the following tasks daily using *How Are You* for four weeks: adding data of their daily activities and reporting corresponding happiness and stress levels, reflecting on themselves by viewing the visualization, and completing a report to share their feedback about using *How Are You*. To monitor their interaction with *How Are You*, there was no instruction set to specify the number of data inputs required in a day, but participants were notified that a lack of data input (e.g., once in a few days) may impact the reliability of the visualization, decreasing the development of self-awareness. Participants completed a survey on quality of life [14] every week and at the end of the experiment. They also completed a survey to review their overall experience with the visualization in terms of self-awareness development [15] and participated in a 10-min semi-structured interview.

Results and Discussion. The results of the survey on self-awareness development are shown in Fig. 4. The Kruskal-Wallis test revealed that the dimension of connectedness ($H(2)=15.11$, $p<0.01$), purpose ($H(2)=6.21$, $p<0.05$), coherence ($H(2)=6.15$, $p<0.05$), and significance ($H(2)=12.34$, $p<0.01$) were statistically significant between the visualization groups. However, there were no statistically significant differences among the three types of visualizations in the resonance dimension, a dimension representing emotional engagement, suggesting that an improvement in building emotional engagement may be required. Post-hoc analysis was conducted using the Steel-Dwass test, and the results showed that the house (Mdn=4) was rated higher in the dimension of significance compared to the bar (Mdn=3) and pie charts (Mdn=3) ($p<0.05$). Moreover, the house (Mdn=4) was better supported in building a connection (Connectedness: Mdn=3) and providing directions (Purpose: Mdn=2.5) to set goals than the pie chart ($p<0.05$).

We analyzed the interview data using thematic analysis, because it allowed us to understand how participants interacted with *How Are You*. The results indicated that the visualizations influenced participants' thoughts and behavior; they became more conscious about their happiness and stress status, which helped them discover why they experienced such emotions. For example, P29 said, *"My visualization showed that work is the biggest cause of stress, which made me realize that I was tired of working from home. However, as it is impossible to change the work schedule set by the company, I tried to reduce the amount of stress by discovering positive aspects and believing that it would support me to grow."* Opinions on viewing other participants' visualizations were divided into two groups: positive and negative. A positive opinion among the participants was that they learned about different perspectives on happiness and stress, and felt a sense of connection with individuals whose visualization was similar to their own. P27 said, *"At first, I could not understand why there were people who felt happy from studying because studying was what I hated the most. But on*

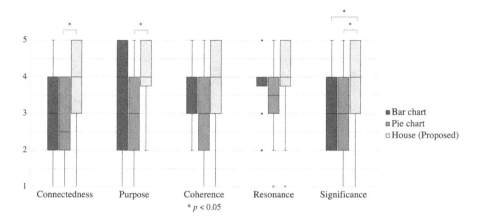

Fig. 4. The distribution of responses to the survey on self-awareness development (n=30). The x-axis represents five dimensions of grouped responses, the y-axis represents its score and the horizontal black line represents the median value.

the halfway through the experiment, I realized that maybe I should not feel too stressed about studying and find happiness inside studying by thinking outside the box. Still, I was glad that there were people who also hated studying." A negative view was that monitoring others' visualizations led participants to judge their life unfavorably, which interfered with building self-awareness. P27 added, "I felt that I was the only one with boring lifestyle pattern."

We compared participants' self-reported quality of life before and after the experiment. The Mann-Whitney U test showed that the overall quality of life improved (before: Mdn=62.5, after: Mdn=75) for participants who interacted with the house ($U=24$, $z=-1.97$, $p<0.05$) (Fig. 5). There was no significant improvement in the subdimensions of quality of life before and after the experiment and in all dimensions of the bar and pie charts.

However, participants reported that their quality of life may be more dependent on health conditions, events, and personal factors, indicating that considering the visualization as a major influence on quality of life based on daily activities was not appropriate. For example, one participant experienced a continuous decrease in their quality of life regardless of the type of daily activity because they were suffering from side effects after COVID-19 vaccination. Another participant with a similar opinion mentioned that although it was interesting to deepen self-knowledge through interaction with the visualization, the visualization did not necessarily affect the quality of life.

Participants often forgot about the daily activities they had engaged in at the beginning of the experiment, as the visualization reflected four weeks of accumulated data. This confused them while reflecting on themselves through visualization, especially when such activities showed a high level of happiness and stress. We assumed that this may be one of the reasons why the resonance dimension did not show statistical significance. Moreover, participants gradu-

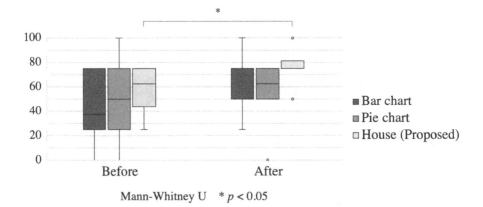

Fig. 5. The distribution of responses to the questions on overall quality of life for participants with house visualization (n=10). The x-axis represents the stage of the experiment and the y-axis represents participants' overall quality of life converted to a score of between 0 to 100, where 0 is the lowest and 100 is the highest. The horizontal black line in the box plot is the median value.

ally lost motivation to interact with the visualization towards the end of the experiment because they were uncertain how to conduct self-reflection when the visualization did not show noticeable changes in design, making it difficult to compare with past data. To create higher engagement between the visualization and individuals, it would be necessary to make changes in the visualization more obvious and reduce the workload for self-reflection so that users can easily relate their current situation with the visualization.

5.2   Self-awareness and Behavioral Change

Purpose and Hypotheses. Through another long-term experiment, we investigated the effects of the proposed visualization on self-awareness and positive behavioral change. As some participants reported that visualization may affect their thoughts and behavior, we conducted this experiment to investigate this possibility in detail. Furthermore, metaphor-based visualizations have been found to support changes in behavior [18]. In this experiment, we updated *How Are You* by visualizing users' life-logging in the past one week instead of the entire experiment. This allowed participants to easily link the visualization with their past and current lifestyle patterns when they introspected based on the visualization. The duration of the experiment was reduced from four weeks to three weeks to reduce the workload for reflecting and comparing their past and current visualizations. The hypotheses for this experiment are as follows:

H1: Visualizing individuals' perceived happiness and stress from daily activities as a house motivates them to engage with the visualization, which supports the development of self-awareness.

H3: Visualizing individuals' perceived happiness and stress from daily activities as a house encourages positive behavioral change.

Participants and Procedure. Thirty participants participated in the experiment, consisting of 15 males and 15 females aged between 21 and 58, who were divided into three groups, with 10 participants assigned per visualization type (house, bar chart, pie chart). The recruitment method was the same as that used in the first experiment. Each participant was paid 7,500 JPY (approximately 65 USD) for participation. Half of the 30 participants participated in both the first and current study. Participants who participated for a second time were assigned to the visualization that they did not experience in the first experiment, as being overfamiliar with the visualization could have impacted the result. Moreover, five repeat participants were assigned to each group to maintain an equal proportion of new and repeat participants.

During the three-week experiment, participants conducted the following tasks daily using *How Are You*, which were the same as in the first experiment: logging data, viewing the visualization, and writing the daily report. At the end of the experiment, participants completed a survey [15], followed by a 10-min semi-structured interview on their overall experience with visualization and self-awareness development.

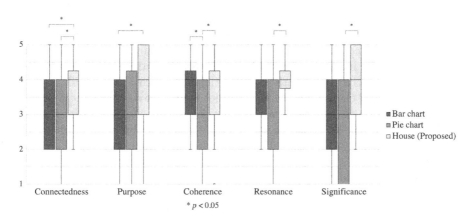

Fig. 6. The distribution of responses to the survey on self-awareness development (n=30). The x-axis represents five dimensions of grouped responses, the y-axis represents its score and the horizontal black line represents the median value.

Results. The results of the survey on self-awareness development are shown in Fig. 6. The Kruskal-Wallis test revealed significant differences in the dimensions of: connectedness($H(2)=11.4$, $p<0.01$), purpose($H(2)=4.15$, $p<0.05$), coherence($H(2)=8.49$, $p<0.05$), resonance($H(2)=6.58$, $p<0.05$), and significance($H(2)=7.29$, $p<0.05$). A post-hoc analysis was conducted using the

Steel-Dwass test, and the results showed that participants built a significantly stronger connection with the house (Mdn=4) compared to the bar (Mdn=3) and pie charts (Mdn=3) in terms of the connectedness dimension. Moreover, when interacting with house visualization (Mdn=4), participants better understood the data (Coherence: Mdn=3), showed higher engagement (Resonance: Mdn=4), and had meaningful experience (Significance: Mdn=3) compared to the pie chart ($p<0.05$). There was also a significant difference between the bar (Mdn=4) and pie charts (Mdn=3) in Coherence dimension ($p<0.05$). Regarding the purpose dimension, the house (Mdn=4) was more effective for setting goals based on understanding oneself than the bar char ($p<0.05$).

In comparison with the previous experiment, the difference within the visualization groups for the resonance dimension showed statistical significance. As the resonance dimension represents emotional engagement, participants in this experiment were more engaged with visualization. The improvement in participants' engagement may be due to adjusting the data amount for generating the visualization because reflecting the data in the past week instead of the whole duration of the experiment allowed participants to easily understand the changes in visualization.

The interview data were analyzed using thematic analysis. The results showed that 16 out of 30 interviewees reported that they were inspired to change their behavior due to the interaction with the visualization; among these, six, three, and seven participants were assigned to the bar chart, pie chart, and house, respectively. They were inspired to seek different daily activities that could help them cope with stress. Behavioral changes reported by the participants are divided into three categories: broadening variation in daily activities, increasing or maintaining the happiness level of specific daily activities, and decreasing the stress level of specific daily activities. Participants with a busy daily routine mostly focused on one or two daily activities that showed the highest or lowest level or portion in the visualization. One participant identified that sleeping was important for their happiness status because it contributed to reducing the stress experienced in other daily activities. Therefore, they aimed to maintain a consistent and healthy sleep schedule by changing their sleeping time from three in the morning to midnight.

Because some participants from the first experiment reported that it was difficult to identify changes in the visualization, the scope of data entry was adjusted. Seven participants who interacted with the house reported that monitoring changes in the visualization, such as size, proportion, colors, and decorations, gave them a sense of achievement that motivated them to reflect on their lifestyle and interact further with the visualization after changing their behavior. They said *"Viewing the changes in the house enabled me to learn more about myself. Even if I did not receive a notification from the app, I attempted to try new daily activities and see how my house changed in response"* (P25).

Participants who did not intend to change their behavior reported that they were satisfied with the design of the visualization and wanted to maintain their current lifestyle patterns instead of making changes. One participant realized that their stress level in studying was lower than expected, and that they should not worry so much about their tasks as they were doing fine with handling the stress. P27 said *"I was very stressed about the workload for my thesis especially after the peer review, and when I saw the visualization with low level of stress on studying, I realized that maybe I was coping well with the current workload. Thus, I should try not to think in a negative way."* Although such participants did not actively seek out new daily activities, delivering a feeling of comfort and understanding of the current lifestyle pattern indicated positive progress in self-awareness development, which could be one of the strengths of all visualizations.

6   Discussion

The first experiment aimed to compare the effects of the proposed visualization with commonly used visualizations on self-awareness and quality of life. The results suggest that house visualization was the most effective in developing self-awareness and improving overall quality of life. However, many participants reported that their quality of life depended on health conditions, events, or personal factors instead of daily activities. Thus, at present, it may be difficult to conclusively state that the house certainly influenced their overall quality of life.

The second experiment aimed to compare the effects of the proposed visualization with those of commonly used visualizations on self-awareness and behavior change. The results demonstrated that house visualization was the most effective method for improving self-awareness. In terms of behavioral change, 16 out of 30 participants showed a change in their behavior in different ways, such as trying new daily activities or adjusting happiness or stress levels of specific daily activities.

The house was chosen as the design for the proposed visualization because it is a metaphor for an individual's identity. In the experiment, the participants commented that growing the house by adding various components and adjusting the size delivered a sense of satisfaction, which motivated them to deepen their self-awareness and build a stronger connection with the house. Some may have concerns regarding conveying the idea of self-awareness and quality of life through a house because participants may associate large and decorative houses with happiness and small and dull houses with stress. Since there are no rules for designing houses, providing implicit goals may mislead participants when developing self-awareness. However, our study showed that the participants had different opinions regarding their ideal house design. For example, one participant was satisfied with the medium-sized house, as it seemed suitable for the current situation. Another participant wanted to make the house decorative but was not concerned about its size. This shows that participants set their own standards with regard to an ideal visualization based on their personal views, interpretations, and preferences.

In the present study, *How Are You* did you not provide any instructions to participants on how they should interact with the visualization. This is because we wanted to prevent creating stereotypes of an ideal design and allow them to think proactively for themselves. However, some participants reported that it was challenging to interact with the visualization, and they wanted *How Are You* to provide specific goals. Thus, the interaction method could be investigated to clarify whether goal-directed visualization contributes to self-awareness development and positive behavior change.

7   Future Work

Future work building on this study will involve enabling self-agency, such as customizing daily activity categories and colors. As *How Are You* predetermined the categories of daily activities and corresponding colors, some participants reported that they chose the category based on a rough assumption and were often confused about which category their daily activity belonged to. Additionally, their understanding of colors was different from what was presented in the visualization, which negatively affected forming a connection with the visualization. Personalizing visualization through self-agency could overcome such issues and further enhance engagement with visualization.

Another possible improvement for *How Are You* involves the frequency of daily activities in the visualization. The proportion of each daily activity in the visualization was decided based on the happiness and stress levels and its frequency was not reflected. Thus, participants were confused when reflecting on the visualization, as some daily activities were shown to be the most significant factor of happiness and stress even if they only occurred once or twice. Displaying the frequency can reduce confusion, clearly indicate lifestyle patterns, and better support self-awareness improvement.

One of the insights gained from the visualization was the balance of emotions experienced in daily activities. Such insights allowed participants to reflect on their current lifestyle patterns and explore possible improvements. Thus, visualization could be utilized to support discovering an ideal balance of emotions and identifying whether such discovery affects the development of self-awareness.

8   Conclusion

This study aimed to develop self-awareness using a house visualization. The house visualization was expected to build high engagement with participants so as to encourage introspection and self-directed changes. It was found that the improvement in self-awareness resulting from the house visualization positively affected individuals' intention to change their behavior. Examples of behavioral change reported by the participants include trying new daily activities, engaging in daily activities with the highest happiness level more frequently, and improving the happiness and stress level of specific daily activities.

Although understanding emotions and personal characteristics based on the development of self-awareness may not provide visible or measurable benefits to individuals, it allows them to learn how to increase their own well-being by changing their behavior. We hope that this study will encourage busy working individuals to gain insights about their own emotional health and motivate them to nurture it. In addition, we hope that this study will guide researchers in utilizing data visualization to help individuals develop self-awareness.

Acknowledgement. This work was partially supported by JST PRESTO (JPMJPR 22S9) and the Mitsubishi Electric Corporation.

References

1. Consolvo, S., McDonald, D.W., Landay, J.A.: Theory-driven design strategies for technologies that support behavior change in everyday life. In: Proceedings of the SIGCHI Conference on Human Factors in Computing Systems, pp. 405–414 (2009)
2. Coolen, H., Meesters, J.: Editorial special issue: house, home and dwelling (2012)
3. Crowhurst, S.H.: A house is a metaphor. J. Archit. Educ. **27**(2–3), 35–42 (1974)
4. Frey, T.: Telling the story in a compelling way: improving data visualization by using metaphors. Tech. rep., Working paper (2021)
5. Gharadaghi, A., Masoumi Ala, S.: Investigating the role of emotional self-awareness, cognitive emotion regulation and social adequacy in predicting marital satisfaction. Hum. Relat. Stud. **2**(4), 32–39 (2022)
6. Goleman, D.: Working with emotional intelligence (1998)
7. Hernandez, J., McDuff, D., Fletcher, R., Picard, R.W.: Inside-out: reflecting on your inner state. In: 2013 IEEE International Conference on Pervasive Computing and Communications Workshops (PERCOM Workshops), pp. 324–327. IEEE (2013)
8. Hills, P., Argyle, M.: The oxford happiness questionnaire: a compact scale for the measurement of psychological well-being. Pers. Individ. Differ. **33**(7), 1073–1082 (2002)
9. Hollis, V., et al.: What does all this data mean for my future mood? actionable analytics and targeted reflection for emotional well-being. Hum.-Comput. Interact. **32**(5–6), 208–267 (2017)
10. Kennedy, H., Hill, R.L.: The feeling of numbers: emotions in everyday engagements with data and their visualisation. Sociology **52**(4), 830–848 (2018)
11. Kim, J., Takeuchi, T., Tanikawa, T., Narumi, T., Kuzuoka, H., Hirose, M.: A study on self-awareness development by logging and gamification of daily emotions. In: Stephanidis, C., Antona, M. (eds.) HCII 2020. CCIS, vol. 1226, pp. 194–201. Springer, Cham (2020). https://doi.org/10.1007/978-3-030-50732-9_26
12. MacDonald, L.W.: Using color effectively in computer graphics. IEEE Comput. Graph. Appl. **19**(4), 20–35 (1999)
13. Marcus, C.C.: House as a mirror of self: exploring the deeper meaning of home. Nicolas-Hays, Inc. (2006)
14. Organization, W.H., et al.: The world health organization quality of life (whoqol)-bref. World Health Organization, Tech. Rep. (2004)
15. Rajcic, N., McCormack, J.: Mirror ritual: an affective interface for emotional self-reflection. In: Proceedings of the 2020 CHI Conference on Human Factors in Computing Systems, pp. 1–13 (2020)
16. Rivera-Pelayo, V., Fessl, A., Müller, L., Pammer, V.: Introducing mood self-tracking at work: empirical insights from call centers. ACM Trans. Comput.-Hum. Interact. (TOCHI) **24**(1), 1–28 (2017)

17. Sadiku, M., Shadare, A.E., Musa, S.M., Akujuobi, C.M., Perry, R.: Data visualization. Int. J. Eng. Res. Adv. Technol. (IJERAT) **2**(12), 11–16 (2016)
18. Saffer, D.: The role of metaphor in interaction design. Inf. Archit. Summit **6** (2005)
19. Seligman, M.E.P., Csikszentmihalyi, M.: Positive psychology: an introduction. In: Flow and the Foundations of Positive Psychology, pp. 279–298. Springer, Dordrecht (2014). https://doi.org/10.1007/978-94-017-9088-8_18
20. Strober, L.B., Becker, A., Randolph, J.J.: Role of positive lifestyle activities on mood, cognition, well-being, and disease characteristics in multiple sclerosis. Appl. Neuropsychol. Adult **25**(4), 304–311 (2018)

A Novel EEG-Based Real-Time Emotion Recognition Approach Using Deep Neural Networks on Raspberry Pi

Lukas A. Kleybolte[(✉)] [iD] and Christian Märtin [iD]

Faculty of Computer Science, Augsburg University of Applied Sciences, An Der Hochschule 1, 86161 Augsburg, Germany
{lukas.kleybolte,christian.maertin}@hs-augsburg.de

Abstract. Automated emotion classification becomes more and more important, as intelligent software systems can better serve users, when they can reliably assess their emotional state and adapt interactive applications accordingly and in real-time. EEG-based brain-computer interfaces (BCI) provide the individual data that can be exploited for emotion classification. However, AI-based emotion classification on EEG-data typically requires computationally intensive training and powerful hardware when the results are needed in real-time. A survey of the related work has shown that not many real-time solutions exist for energy-efficient hardware.

In this paper we present an approach for finding a global best channel set universally suitable for all subjects with high classification accuracy. In our research we used Russel's emotion model and the DEAP data set. By applying a total of six nature-based swarm channel selection algorithms and one classical selection algorithm, the different algorithms could be compared with each other. The resulting reduced channel set consists of only 7 channels.

With the set it is possible to classify emotions in real-time using low-level energy-efficient hardware. Emotion classification on the Raspberry Pi only takes between 82 and 93ms.

Keywords: Real-time classification · EEG · Emotion classification · Raspberry Pi · CNN-LSTM

1 Introduction

Interaction between humans and computers and cooperation of humans with robots is becoming increasingly important these days. Not only in research, but also in everyday life, many of us already use smart assistance systems which support us with our daily activities. Many psychologists, e.g., Ekman [1], Gilbert [2], Keltner and Lerner [3], and Oatley [4] are convinced that emotions are the driving force behind most of our significant decisions in life. Typically, during decision-making, people try to avoid negative emotions and reinforce positive emotions, which is usually done unconsciously. When people make decisions based on emotions, machines and interactive software systems

© The Author(s), under exclusive license to Springer Nature Switzerland AG 2023
M. Kurosu and A. Hashizume (Eds.): HCII 2023, LNCS 14012, pp. 231–244, 2023.
https://doi.org/10.1007/978-3-031-35599-8_15

need to understand, or more precisely, be able to read and interpret our emotions to interact with humans correctly. However, it is not enough to detect and interpret emotions; an important step is to be able to classify emotions quickly enough for machines to act in real-time. One way to detect emotions is to use brain waves, which can be recorded using an electroencephalogram (EEG). Brain waves are often measured using many electrodes placed on the head, causing a large data stream. To make EEG measurements real-time capable, among other things, the data size must be reduced. One way to solve this task is to reduce the number of electrodes and to extract meaningful features.

Therefore, the following questions arise: Is it possible to compute a reduced global channel set that is suitable for all tasks and individuals and reduces the computational complexity of emotion classification? And is it possible to design a classification procedure that runs in real-time on a Raspberry Pi?

In our paper, we succeeded in answering these questions and present a new method for detecting emotions quickly and at the same time reducing energy consumption and resource requirements, so that emotion detection can even run on a Raspberry Pi.

2 Related Work

There exist several approaches to recognize emotions in real-time. In general, the emotion recognition process is structured in a data declaration or, rather data collection activity, the classification process that uses an EEG-based emotion recognition architecture and a result interpretation activity. The first task of the emotion recognition architecture consists of removing disturbance variables, such as noise reduction, for upscaling EEG data quality. In the next step, a feature extraction process begins to identify optimal features for the following classification process. Whereby between the feature extraction and the classification process, usually a feature selection takes place to remove redundant features.

In our search for similar work for real-time emotion recognition using microcomputers, embedded devices, or single-board computers, we discovered that most of the papers used devices that were optimized for, e.g., CNNs or used GPU/TPU units to be able to classify emotions efficiently.

- In 2022 Kim et al. [5] developed a novel framework for real-time emotion recognition using a Long Short-Term Memory (LSTM) classifier. They reached 91.3% accuracy by utilizing self-recorded EEG data.
- In the same year, Pothula et al. [6] built a seizure classification architecture on an NVIDIA Jetson Nano B01 board and achieved a mean accuracy of 98.9% with the Random Forest algorithm and the FER dataset. Noteworthy classifiers with their achieved accuracies are Decision Tree algorithm (96.4%), a Neural Network with seven layers (96.3%), Support Vector Machine (SVM) with a Radial Basis Function kernel (RBF) (92.7%), k-Nearest Neighbors algorithm (k-NN) (88.1%), and logistic regression (79.6%) respectively.
- In 2021 Li et al. [7] published a review of an emotion recognition approach with a Long-Term Recurrent Convolution Network (LRCN) on hardware by considering the KMU dataset and achieved a mean accuracy of 77.41%.

- Leite et al. [8] tried to identify the emotional states of computer gamers using the Evolving Gaussian Fuzzy classifier and achieved an accuracy of 72.2%.
- Huang et al. [9] suggest a linear SVM classifier for detecting patients' emotions with a disorder of consciousness and achieved 91.5% accuracy.
- In the context of multiple emotional states identification Kim et al. [10] reach an accuracy of 82.25% by implementing a Multi-SVM with RBF and utilizing SEED and DEAP dataset.
- In the same year Bandara et al. [11] applied a Random Forest algorithm for emotion adaptive advertising and achieved 91.97% accuracy with self-recorded EEG data.
- Khateeb et al. [12] attempt to classify 9 emotions on 4 channels and achieve 65.92% accuracy with an SVM classifier considering the DEAP dataset.
- Wang et al. [13] suggested a three-class SVM classifier for enhancing emotion recognition and reaching 87.23% accuracy.
- Yang et al. [14] reported an accuracy of 88.34% by implementing a LRCN with LSTM on a hardware and considering the KMU-dataset.
- In 2020 Li et al. [15] achieved an accuracy of 72.66% by implementing an advanced CNN on CMOS hardware and considering ECG and PPG as extra features.
- Val-Calvo et al. [16] achieved an accuracy of 72.47% using various physiological signals such as EEG, Galvanic Skin Response (GSR) and heart rate variations by measuring Blood Volume Pressure (BVP) using the k-NN algorithm. They used the FER-dataset and RAVDESS-dataset for Validation. Other classifiers they used were SVM (linear & RBF), Decision Tree algorithm, Random Forest, Gaussian Naïve Bayes, Ada Boost and Quadratic Discriminant Analysis.
- Alakus et al. [17] tried to detect emotions of gamers with a new approach, the Convolutional Smooth Feedback Fuzzy Network (CSFFN) and achieved 73.20% by utilizing the DEAP dataset.
- Gonzalez et al. [18] attended to detect emotions related with neurological disorders by implementing a BioCNN in hardware and achieved 77.57% valence and 71.25% arousal accuracy. The BioCNN is a special type of the classical Convolutional Neural Network, as it is a hardware inference engine specialized for EEG-based emotion recognition. They considered the FEXD and DEAP datasets.
- Another research approach for real-time computational emotion recognition on hardware is the research of Aslam et al. [19]. They achieved 72.96% valence and 73.14% arousal accuracy with the DEAP dataset and 70.71% valence accuracy with the SEED dataset. In both approaches, the linear SVM is declared as classifier.

Most features were pre-processed with Power Spectral Density (PSD), Principal Component Analysis (PCA), (Higuchi-) Fractal Dimension and statistical methods such as mean and standard deviation and F-Score. In the context of real-time analysis commercially available headsets can be used, e.g., from the company EMOTIV Inc. The differing number of channels used in the survey above are 14 channels, 32 channels, 4 channels and 8 channels. One researcher only used 2 channels or a single channel for detecting emotions.

If we take a closer look on our literature review, we observe a research gap in detecting users' emotional state in real-time with inexpensive hardware and without an integrated GPU or TPU. If we can achieve high accuracy in real-time emotion recognition with such low-level hardware, we can open many practical Human Computer Interaction (HCI) research fields. Therefore, we investigate the possibility of implementing real-time emotion recognition on the widely used Raspberry Pi platform.

3 Methods

Before the data can be classified, several processes are required to render emotions from the data recorded with an EEG headset. The procedure and the necessary processes are quite similar in most applications. First, the recorded EEG data need to be cleaned and pre-processed. Features are then extracted since the large amount of data generated per second by an EEG headset makes it very difficult to classify emotions, as this would be computationally intensive and can lead to overfitting, which is a well-known problem in classification tasks. Feature extraction is usually followed by feature selection, because often redundant features are extracted, which would affect the classification process badly. Finally, after these steps, the data can be classified using a classification algorithm. The entire pipeline from raw data to classified emotions is usually very computationally intensive, so small micro-computers like the Raspberry Pi, with their very limited power, quickly reach their limits when it comes to classifying emotions in real-time. For this reason, the entire pipeline must be optimized.

3.1 Emotion Model

To make emotions more comprehensible and to be able to use them, for example, in computer science, there are the so-called dimensional models. Wundt [20] was one of the first who defined dimensions for his emotions: *pleasure–displeasure, arousal–calmness,* and *tension–relaxation.* With the assignment of emotions to dimensions, he created the foundations of the dimensional models.

Further research showed that human emotions can be represented in the dimensions of activation and valence. Russel [21] used this concept and introduced the probably most well-known bipolar dimensional model. In this model, he defined two axes, arousal (y-axis) and valence (x-axis), with each axis ranging from −24 to +24. The arousal axis describes the range of calmness or excitement of the emotions, and the valence axis is the "goodness" of the emotions; in other words, it describes if the emotions are more positive or negative. In this paper, we also use Russel's emotion model with the axes arousal and valence, but we have abstracted the model into the 4 quadrants. Russel's emotion model was divided into the quadrants high arousal/low valence (HALV), which contains the emotions angry and nervous, high arousal/high valence (HAHV), which represents happy and excited as emotions, low arousal/and low valence (LALV) for the emotions sad and bored, and low arousal/high valence (LAHV) with the emotions relaxed and bored. A schematic representation of the emotion quadrants in Russell's emotion model is shown in Fig. 1.

3.2 Dataset

For our research we use the very common DEAP data set by Koelstra et al. [22]. This dataset is constructed from the data of 32 subjects, each of them watching 40 music

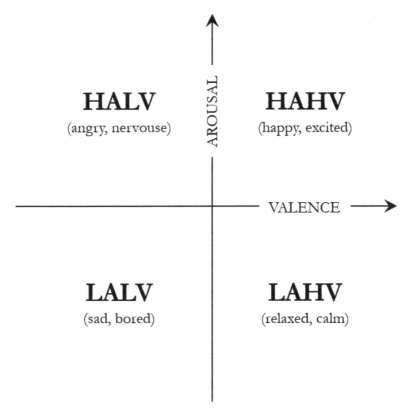

Fig. 1. Schematic representation of the Russel model reduced to the four quadrants.

videos, while their brain activity was recorded with a 32-channel EEG headset. Each recording lasts 63 s, with the first 3 s being the baseline and the music video starting after that. The baseline is an important element to identify and remove noise efficiently by using baseline correction.

The EEG headset recorded the data at a sampling rate of 512Hz, resulting in 16384 data points in just one second of recording. This results in a dataset shape (32 × 40 × 32 × 32256), which is defined by (subject × video/trail × channel × data).

There are also 8 additional channels in the data set, which measure, for example, body heat, eye movements, or muscle contractions. However, these channels are not relevant for our work.

3.3 Preprocessing

In the preprocessing step, the dataset was down sampled to a sample rate of 128Hz, which drastically reduced the number of data points per second from 16384 to 4096 data points. In addition, a bandpass filter was used to limit the frequency range of the data from 4.0 to 45.0 Hz. Furthermore, artifacts were removed from the dataset as described by Koelstra et al. in [22]. All these pre-processing steps have already been done by Koelstra et al., so they provide a pre-processed dataset for download. Another preprocessing step is to remove the 3-s baseline of the data, because the first 3 s of the data are only used for the baseline correction and not for the emotion classification since the tasks only started after these seconds. The preprocessed dataset has a shape of ($32 \times 40 \times 32 \times 7680$).

3.4 Feature Extraction

After preprocessing the EEG data, features are usually extracted to classify the emotions. These features can be divided into three different feature domains: Time, Frequency and Time-Frequency domains. The features are applied to the pre-processed EEG data and their respective time or frequency interval. For example, statistical features such as arithmetic mean and standard deviation or Shannon entropy are applied as time domain features, or the different types of power spectral density are applied as frequency domain features. The time and frequency domain features combine the above features and include, for example, the discrete wavelet transform.

One type of feature of the EEG data is the extraction of the frequency bands, as the frequency bands play an important role in brainwave analysis. The different frequency bands and during which task they occur are presented in Table 1.

Table 1. Representation of the individual frequency bands and when they occur.

Names	Frequency bands	Mental state
θ Theta	4Hz – 8Hz	meditative, sleepy, hypnotic
α Alpha	8Hz – 12Hz	mild relaxation, relaxed alertness, and closed eyes
$l\beta$ Low Beta	12Hz – 16Hz	analytical problem solving, judgment, decision making, and environmental processing, and open eyes
$h\beta$ High Beta	16Hz – 25Hz	
γ Gamma	25Hz – 45Hz	strenuous and focused work

The individual frequencies were extracted from the pre-processed EEG data using Fast Fourier Transformation (FFT). The FFT transforms the data from the Time domain to the frequency domain. In this case, the FFT was applied to small data "windows" with a fixed size of 2 s, also defined as 256 data points. The spectral power in each frequency domain was then calculated from this window. The window was then shifted by 0.125 s, equivalent to 16 data points. After extracting the features, the shape of the dataset is ($32 \times 40 \times 32 \times 480 \times 5$), where 5 represents the 5 extracted frequency bands.

3.5 Channel Selection

Usually, feature extraction is followed by feature optimization or selection, as mentioned at the beginning of the Methods chapter. However, in this paper, a specific type of feature selection is used. This is because we use channel selection instead of a feature selection to reduce the dataset, since we only have the extracted frequency bands as a feature. In this way, we remove redundant channels to achieve a more powerful classification.

First, we reduced the 32 channels of the EEG headset to the 14 channels of the EPOC X headset (EMOTIV Inc.)[1], as this is a widely used EEG headset.

We use several nature-based swarm optimization algorithms and the classical Maximum Relevance - Minimum Redundancy (mRMR) algorithm to select the channels. This procedure has already been described in Balic et al. [23] and has shown good results. The following algorithms were used as nature-based swarm optimization algorithms:

- Particle Swarm Optimizer (PSO)
- Bat Optimizer (BAT)
- Grey Wolf Optimizer (GWO)
- Two-phase Mutation Grey Wolf Optimizer (TMGWO)
- Cuckoo Search Optimizer (CSO)
- Salp Swarm Algorithm (SSA)
- Improved Salp Swarm Algorithm (ISSA)

The functionality of nature-based swarm optimization algorithms is relatively simple and always the same. The algorithm starts by randomly initializing a population, where each population instance represents a possible solution. Each solution is then evaluated with a fitness function that determines the quality of the solution. Then, based on the evaluation results, the solutions are updated by exploiting the cooperation and competition between the solutions. This can be done by adjusting the solutions' position, velocity, or other parameters. For example, in the BAT algorithm, the position of each bat is adjusted based on its current velocity. Then, the fitness function is used again to determine the quality and store the current best solution, and then the parameters, such as how the bat moves through space, are also adjusted. In the case of the bat, the velocity and direction are adjusted, among other things, by the echolocation of the "prey" which can be defined as the best solution. The algorithm is repeated until a stop criterion is reached, after which the best solution is returned. The K-nearest neighbor (K-NN) was used as a fitness function to determine the error rate and to fit the parameters of a solution candidate.

To answer one of the research questions, whether it is possible to compute a global channel set, the seven nature-based swarm optimization algorithms and the mRMR were applied to all 32 participants. The channel selection also distinguished between arousal and valence, so each participant received an optimized channel set for all algorithms and arousal and valence. This resulted in a total of 32×16 channel sets, which were tested for accuracy in emotion classification.

To calculate the accuracy of the selected channels, a bidirectional LSTM network was used, which we have already used in our previous paper [23]. To obtain a general channel set, the accuracy of each channel in the 32 x 16 channel sets was calculated using a clustering method, which was done for each classification algorithm. This resulted in a list of 16 unique channel sets. These were then checked again for accuracy using the bidirectional LSTM, which resulted in a global channel set.

---

[1] https://www.emotiv.com/epoc-X.

3.6 Classification

A convolutional neural network was combined with a long-short-term memory recurrent neural network (CNN-LSTM) to classify emotions finally. Table 2 shows the structure of the network.

CNN networks are especially popular in image classification because they are specialized in pattern recognition through convolutional layers. In our example, the CNN layers are used as a further feature extraction layer to recognize patterns from the one-dimensional input data, which are subsequently passed to the LSTM layers.

LSTMs are a special type of recurrent neural network (RNN), a type of neural network with an explicit looping mechanism in their architecture that allows them to process sequential data. This makes RNNs unique compared to other types of neural networks, such as feedforward networks, which can only process fixed-length inputs. One of the main advantages of RNNs is their ability to capture and retain information from previous time steps, making them ideal for modeling data sequences such as time series. For this reason, RNNs are well suited to solve problems where the order of the data plays a certain role, and the context and memory must be preserved over time. A special feature of the LSTMs compared to the RNNs is to forget redundant information which increases the accuracy of the network. For this reason, we use two LSTM layers in our CNN-LSTM network which receive as input the features that the CNN layers have identified. Dropout layers are used between the individual layers, which provide a more robust network and prevent overfitting. The dropout layer's function is to randomly deactivate a certain percentage of neurons during training. In this way, the network is forced to rely on other neurons for each iteration of training, which reduces the likelihood that the network will rely on a single group of neurons that may provide overfitting to the training data. The deactivated neurons are reactivated during testing, allowing the model to make predictions based on the entire network.

The Adam Optimizer was used during the training to optimize the weights in the CNN-LSTM. The special feature of the ADAM optimizer is its ability to adjust the learning rate per parameter, which allows it to reach the optimal solution quickly and efficiently. In addition, the ADAM optimizer incorporates both momentum and RMSprop techniques, resulting in faster convergence and less oscillation than other optimization algorithms.

3.7 Model Transformation

To be able to run the trained model on a Raspberry Pi to classify emotions, the model has to be transformed. The TensorFlow Framework [24] offers TensorFlow Lite for this purpose. TensorFlow Lite is a specially optimized library for embedded devices.

Since embedded devices have limited resources, and deep learning algorithms are generally considered to be resource-hungry, the built models for embedded devices need to be as light as possible. TensorFlow Lite achieves this through several model optimizations. For example, weights in the model are usually stored as Float32, these can usually be converted to Float16, Float8 or even to an 8-bit Integer, which makes the model smaller. Also, both weights and activations can be quantized by converting them to an integer, which minimizes latency, model size and computational requirements.

Table 2. Structure of the CNN-LSTM used for the classification.

Layer	Parameter	Activation
Conv1D	Input: 128, Kernel: 3x3	Relu
MaxPooling1D	Pool size: 2	--
Dropout	Rate: 20%	--
Conv1D	Input: 128, Kernel: 3x3	Relu
MaxPooling1D	Pool size: 2	--
Dropout	Rate: 20%	--
LSTM	Input: 256, Return sequence: True	Tanh
Dropout	Rate: 20%	--
LSTM	Input: 64, Return sequence: False	Tanh
Dropout	Rate: 20%	--
Flatten	--	--
Dense	Units: 128	Relu
Dense	Unit: 4	Softmax

TensorFlow Lite also uses kernel fusion to combine multiple operations into a single operation to reduce the number of computations required to run the model. This results in faster performance and lower latency.

4 Results and Discussion

In this section, the techniques discussed previously in Sect. 3 are applied, and the results are described. Furthermore, the research questions as set out in Sect. 1 are discussed.

4.1 Channel Selection

One of the most important parts of this paper is to find an optimized channel set to reduce the amount of data without affecting the classification accuracy. Therefore, as already described, we reduced the 32 electrodes used in the DEAP dataset to the 14 electrodes of the EPOC X headset. As shown in Fig. 2b, the electrodes placed in the skull's center were mainly removed. However, the electrodes placed on the outside of the skull, especially the electrodes at the frontal lobe and temporal lobe of the brain, were adopted.

The channel selection technique was then used to reduce the 14 EPOC X channels to seven, as described in the Methods section. The first step was to select the best channels for each subject and then validate the channel sets using the bidirectional LSTM. For most subjects, the validation accuracy was between 70% and 80%. To find the perfect channel set for all subjects, the individual channel sets were compared, whereby the similar accuracy of the individual subjects made the process more difficult so that the frequency of the individual channels occurring in the subjects played a major role in

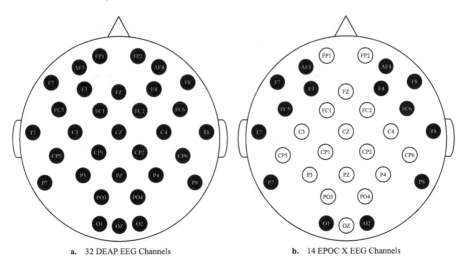

a. 32 DEAP EEG Channels   b. 14 EPOC X EEG Channels

Fig. 2. The channel reduction from the (**a**) original 32 DEAP electrodes to the (**b**) 14 (EPOC X) as the first step in the channel selection process.

finally calculating a channel set for each individual channel selection algorithm. Table 3 shows the results of the individual channel selection algorithms:

As shown in Table 3, a classification accuracy between 74% and 81% can also be observed in this case. This is more or less the same as for the individual participants. It is also noticeable that electrodes T7 and T8 appear in almost every channel set. As a generally usable channel set, we determined that the channel set from the ISSA channel selection algorithm with the classification type Arousal was the most accurate after also testing this channel set for valence, where an accuracy of 82.07% was achieved.

The optimal 7 channels which are valid for all participants in the DEAP dataset, can be seen in Fig. 3, where it is noticeable that most of the electrodes are located on the left side of the brain. Consequently, the first research question could be answered.

4.2 Training and Evaluation

After finding the general optimal channel set (['P7', 'FC5', 'T7', 'T8', 'F4', 'O1', 'AF3']), we developed the CNN-LSTM, which was designed to be an accurate but not very computationally intensive classifier for emotion classification. The CNN-LSTM network was trained in a total of 150 epochs with a batch size of 256 samples. It achieved an accuracy of 79.82%. Remarkable for this is that each training epoch only took 36 s on a GeForce GTX TITAN X. The bidirectional LSTM classifier, used for the channel selection, needed 197 s for each epoch even though the network was trained on two GeForce GTX TITAN X simultaneously. This is caused, among other things, by the fact that the bidirectional LSTM with 786,610 trainable parameters has significantly more trainable parameters than the CNN-LSTM network with 535,044.

Table 3. Overview of the selected channels during the selection algorithms and their accuracy in classifying emotions.

Channel Selection Algorithm	Russel's emotion model axes	Channels	Accuracy
mRMR	Arousal	['T7', 'T8', 'FC5', 'F7', 'P8', 'FC6', 'P7']	73.97%
mRMR	Valence	['FC5', 'T8', 'T7', 'F7', 'FC6', 'F3', 'P8']	74.9%
BAT	Arousal	['O1', 'P7', 'F8', 'FC6', 'T8', 'AF4', 'O2']	79.92%
BAT	Valence	['T7', 'P7', 'F8', 'O1', 'T8', 'O2', 'AF4']	79.42%
CS	Arousal	['T7', 'AF4', 'F7', 'F8', 'FC6', 'P8', 'T8']	76.63%
CS	Valence	['FC5', 'T8', 'AF4', 'T7', 'P7', 'AF3', 'F3']	79.55%
GWO	Arousal	['T7', 'AF4', 'F8', 'P7', 'F3', 'T8', 'AF3']	79.58%
GWO	Valence	['T8', 'FC6', 'T7', 'P7', 'AF4', 'O1', 'P8']	79.76%
TMGWO	Arousal	['FC6', 'F8', 'T8', 'P8', 'O2', 'F4', 'AF4']	78.31%
TMGWO	Valence	['T8', 'FC6', 'F8', 'P8', 'O2', 'F4', 'AF4']	79.21%
SSA	Arousal	['T7', 'F8', 'P7', 'T8', 'O1', 'F7', 'F3']	80.33%
SSA	Valence	['O2', 'P7', 'T8', 'O1', 'F7', 'FC6', 'P8']	78.84%
ISSA	Arousal	['P7', 'FC5', 'T7', 'T8', 'F4', 'O1', 'AF3']	81.38%
ISSA	Valence	['F7', 'T7', 'P7', 'FC6', 'FC5', 'O1', 'F8']	77.97%
PSO	Arousal	['P7', 'O2', 'T8', 'T7', 'O1', 'F7', 'FC6']	76.37%
PSO	Valence	['T8', 'T7', 'P8', 'O1', 'AF4', 'P7', 'F4']	79.92%

4.3 Prediction on the Raspberry Pi

To show that our proposed CNN-LSTM network is real-time capable and runs on a Raspberry Pi, the pre-trained network was converted to the TensorFlow Lite format using

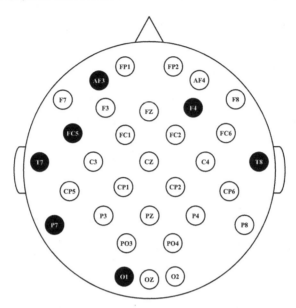

Fig. 3. Topographic representation of the optimal channel set for all subjects: ['P7', 'FC5', 'T7', 'T8', 'F4', 'O1', 'AF3'].

the TensorFlow framework. Furthermore, a server was built, which splits the DEAP data set into 2 s batches and sends it to the Raspberry Pi via Ethernet.

We used a 4th generation Raspberry Pi with 2 gigabytes of RAM and a *Quad Core ARM v8 Cortex-A72* with a clock frequency of 1.5GHz. The operating system on the Raspberry Pi was Ubuntu Server version 22.10.

To demonstrate the real-time capability, a Python script was written that received the raw 2-s EEG data batches and subsequently performed the feature extraction, which was optimized with the Python library NumPy [25] as much as possible. After the features were extracted, the data could be passed to the TensorFlow Lite model for emotion classification.

The feature extraction and classification processes only took between 82 and 93 ms on the Raspberry Pi so that the classification could be demonstrated in real-time on the Raspberry Pi 4.

5   Conclusion

In our present work, the problems according to the two research questions as set out in Sect. 1 could be solved. A global best channel set universally suitable for all subjects was found and emotions could be classified in real-time on a Raspberry Pi.

In this work, the channel selection was divided into several steps to obtain a more robust channel selection. By applying a total of six nature-based swarm channel selection algorithms and one classical selection algorithm, the different algorithms could be compared with each other, whereby it was discovered that the differences between the individual channel selection algorithms were relatively small. It has been found that the optimal channel set contains mainly electrodes positioned on the left side of the skull, which could lead to potential conclusions about particularly important regions in the brain that are especially active when watching music videos.

Furthermore, this work demonstrated that it is possible to classify emotions in real-time using low-level energy-efficient hardware. Since emotion classification on the Raspberry Pi only takes between 82 and 93ms. In the future, our findings can be used as a basis for converting more complex models to TensorFlow Lite models in order to possibly achieve more accurate classification results. The code used in our project is made available in a GitHub repository.[2]

References

1. Ekman, P.: Emotions revealed. BMJ **328**, 0405184 (2004). https://doi.org/10.1136/SBMJ.040 5184
2. Gilbert, D.T.: Stumbling on happiness. Vintage Books, New York (2007)
3. Keltner, D., Lerner, J.S.: Emotion. Handbook of. Social Psychology. (2010). https://doi.org/ 10.1002/9780470561119.SOCPSY001009
4. Oatley, K.: Best Laid Schemes: The Psychology of the Emotions (1992)
5. Kim, S.-H., Yang, H.-J., Nguyen, N.A.T., Prabhakar, S.K., Lee, S.-W.: WeDea: a new EEG-based framework for emotion recognition. IEEE J. Biomed. Health Inform. **26**, 264–275 (2022). https://doi.org/10.1109/JBHI.2021.3091187
6. Pothula, P.K., Marisetty, S., Rao, M.: A real-time seizure classification system using computer vision techniques. SysCon 2022 - 16th Annual IEEE International Systems Conference, Proceedings (2022). https://doi.org/10.1109/SYSCON53536.2022.9773923
7. Li, W.-C., Yang, C.-J., Liu, B.-T., Fang, W.-C.: A real-time affective computing platform integrated with ai system-on-chip design and multimodal signal processing system. In: 2021 43rd Annual International Conference of the IEEE Engineering in Medicine & Biology Society (EMBC), pp. 522–526. IEEE (2021). https://doi.org/10.1109/EMBC46164.2021.9630979
8. Leite, D., Frigeri, V., Medeiros, R.: Adaptive gaussian fuzzy classifier for real-time emotion recognition in computer games. In: 2021 IEEE Latin American Conference on Com-putational Intelligence, LA-CCI 2021 (2021). https://doi.org/10.48550/arxiv.2103.03488
9. Huang, H., et al.: An EEG-based brain computer interface for emotion recognition and its application in patients with disorder of consciousness. IEEE Trans. Affect Comput. **12**, 832–842 (2021). https://doi.org/10.1109/TAFFC.2019.2901456
10. Kim, S.-H., Yang, H.-J., Nguyen, N.A.T., Lee, S.-W.: AsEmo: automatic approach for EEG-based multiple emotional state identification. IEEE J Biomed. Health Inform. **25**, 1508–1518 (2021). https://doi.org/10.1109/JBHI.2020.3032678
11. Bandara, S.K., Jayalath, B.P., Wijesinghe, U.C., Bandara, S.K., Haddela, P.S., Wick-ramasinghe, L.M.: EEG based real-time system for video advertisement recommendation. In: 21st International Conference on Advances in ICT for Emerging Regions, ICter 2021 - Proceedings, pp. 201–206 (2021). https://doi.org/10.1109/ICTER53630.2021.9774791
12. Khateeb, M., Anwar, S.M., Alnowami, M.: Multi-domain feature fusion for emotion classification using DEAP dataset. IEEE Access. **9**, 12134–12142 (2021). https://doi.org/10.1109/ ACCESS.2021.3051281

---

[2] https://github.com/Mozartuss/Real-Time-Emotion-Recognition-CNN-LSTM.

13. Wang, K.Y., Huang, Y. de, Ho, Y.L., Fang, W.C.: A customized convolutional neural network design using improved softmax layer for real-time human emotion recognition. In: Proceedings 2019 IEEE International Conference on Artificial Intelligence Circuits and Systems, AICAS 2019, pp. 102–106 (2019). https://doi.org/10.1109/AICAS.2019.8771616

14. Yang, C.J., Li, W.C., Wan, M.T., Fang, W.C.: Real-time EEG-based affective computing using on-chip learning long-term recurrent convolutional network. In: Proceedings - IEEE In-ternational Symposium on Circuits and Systems. 2021-May (2021). https://doi.org/10.1109/ISCAS51556.2021.9401588

15. Li, W.-C., Yang, C.-J., Fang, W.-C.: A real-time emotion recognition system based on an AI system-on-chip design. In: 2020 International SoC Design Conference (ISOCC), pp. 29–30. IEEE (2020). https://doi.org/10.1109/ISOCC50952.2020.9333072

16. Val-Calvo, M., Alvarez-Sanchez, J.R., Ferrandez-Vicente, J.M., Fernandez, E.: Affective robot story-telling human-robot interaction: exploratory real-time emotion estimation analysis using facial expressions and physiological signals. IEEE Access. **8**, 134051–134066 (2020). https://doi.org/10.1109/ACCESS.2020.3007109

17. Alakus, T.B., Gonen, M., Turkoglu, I.: Database for an emotion recognition system based on EEG signals and various computer games – GAMEEMO. Biomed. Signal Process Control. **60**,(2020)

18. Gonzalez, H.A., Muzaffar, S., Yoo, J., Elfadel, I.M.: An inference hardware accelerator for EEG-based emotion detection. In: Proceedings - IEEE International Symposium on Circuits and Systems. 2020-October (2020). https://doi.org/10.1109/ISCAS45731.2020.9180728/VIDEO

19. Aslam, A.R., Altaf, M.A.: bin: an on-chip processor for chronic neurological disorders assistance using negative affectivity classification. IEEE Trans. Biomed. Circuits Syst. **14**, 838–851 (2020). https://doi.org/10.1109/TBCAS.2020.3008766

20. Wundt, W.: Grundzuge der Physiologischen Psychologie. Am. J. Psychol. **6**, 298 (1894). https://doi.org/10.2307/1410982

21. Russell, J.A.: A circumplex model of affect. J. Pers. Soc. Psychol. **39**, 1161–1178 (1980). https://doi.org/10.1037/h0077714

22. Koelstra, S., et al.: DEAP: a database for emotion analysis; using physiological signals. IEEE Trans. Affect Comput. **3**, 18–31 (2012). https://doi.org/10.1109/T-AFFC.2011.15

23. Balic, S., Kleybolte, L., Märtin, C.: A Swarm Intelligence Approach: Combination of Different EEG-channel optimization techniques to enhance emotion recognition. In: Kurosu, M. (eds.) Human-Computer Interaction. Technological Innovation. HCII 2022. Lecture Notes in Computer Science, vol. 13303, pp. 303–317. Springer, Cham (2022). https://doi.org/10.1007/978-3-031-05409-9_23

24. Developers, T.: TensorFlow (2022). https://doi.org/10.5281/ZENODO.7604251

25. Harris, C.R., et al.: Array programming with NumPy. Nature **585**, 357–362 (2020). https://doi.org/10.1038/s41586-020-2649-2

Evaluating the Outcome of Collaborative VR Mind Mapping Sessions with Sentiment Analysis and Emotional Intelligence

Diana Kozachek[1]([envelope]) [ORCID], Muhammad Ainul Yaqin[2] [ORCID], Kunal Prasad[3] [ORCID], and Sheng-Ming Wang[3] [ORCID]

[1] Institute Futur, Freie University of Berlin, Berlin, Germany
`kozachekdiana@gmail.com`
[2] Doctoral Program in Design, National Taipei University of Technology, Taipei, Taiwan
[3] Department of Interaction Design, National Taipei University of Technology, Taipei, Taiwan
`ryan5885@mail.ntut.edu.tw`

Abstract. Collaborative brainstorming harbours various positive effects: Enhancement of creativity and social skills, broader discussions and contributions, and instant feedback [28,46], while the technique of mind mapping simultaneously visualises the results of this process. Using a Virtual Reality (VR) application, a technology increasingly adopted for ideation [23,44], this study creates a setting that allows collaborators to produce meaningful results in an immersive digital environment. By nature, group settings remain complex and dynamic, with emotions playing a significant role in the outcome [2]. So far, emotional responses have mainly been researched through biophysical responses on a single-user basis [13].

To assess the complex relationship between emotional intelligence (EI) and the language-based results of collaborations, a mind-mapping task was analysed through performance and sentiment analysis, a natural language processing (NLP) technique that identifies the polarity of a given text. We examine the outcome of 13 sessions (N=39) in VR by distinguishing the results into problem-orientation and solution-orientation before applying a fine-tuned language model to get detailed information on the emotional polarity of the results. This mixed-level data analysis shall bridge the gap between self-assessment questionnaires and support the automated group work evaluation by analysing results on an objective scale. Although enhanced problem orientation could not be connected to specific emotions in the sentiment analysis, our results have shown significant relationships between the number of solutions created and the emotions of joy and surprise and a significant negative relationship with the emotion of sadness.

M. Kurosu and A. Hashizume (Eds.): HCII 2023, LNCS 14012, pp. 245–263, 2023.
https://doi.org/10.1007/978-3-031-35599-8_16

Keywords: Collaborative Brainstorming · Sentiment Analysis · Emotional Intelligence · Mind-Mapping · Virtual Reality (VR) · Natural Language Processing · Group Dynamics

1 Introduction

Brainstorming combines known and new information to generate original ideas [3,34]. Typically performed in groups, it is an essential technique to solve a problem in workspaces collaboratively. Our research environment embedded within an immersive VR tool allows multiple means of data collection while shielding participants from outside distractions and not interrupting their group experience through data gathering. The enhanced focus, promised by the technology itself [7], creates engaging experiences in VR that shall enable participants to work together on a mind-mapping task as efficiently as in real life. However, collaborations are also a matter of complex social dynamics, with emotional intelligence (EI) being considered a critical factor in ensuring good teamwork [16,25], implying a relationship between the performance of a team and their EI. A sole questionnaire-based evaluation of emotional intelligence may be distorted through response bias [6], a phenomenon that occurs when a participant responds inaccurately or falsely to a given question. Recent research indicates that collaborative settings enhance dishonesty even further, positively [22] and negatively [15].

Emotional intelligence is the ability to contribute to the appropriate appraisal and expression of self and others, effectively controlling emotion [31]. The effectiveness of EI adoption in many aspects finds a moderate connection between EI and perseverance as the improvement of performance and subjective well-being [1]. Therefore, in group EI application, research performed by Zarifsanaiey et al. comprised digital storytelling with the group discussion that enhanced social intelligence and EI among the control group of students [45]. Besides, the intervention of the EI in the VR application and strategic decision create a more realistic immersive assessment to evaluate user performance through intangible interaction and positive comprehension and cooperation on the strategic decision [2,37].

Until now, the evaluation of collaboration in VR has been mostly focused on performance in terms of efficiency or centred on demonstrating effectiveness on a system level [4,30,42]. Other studies have rated results in terms of creativity [20], using methods such as inter-rater reliability or counting unique ideas [17] without further analysing the content of the results. One study showed the difference between solution-oriented and problem-oriented results in collaborative problem-solving in virtual environments [27] by coding results manually. While the information on emotional factors could be gathered through sentiment analysis applied to the results, AI-supported content analysis in collaborative VR settings has been mostly used to evaluate the content of post hoc interviews [19]. On the other hand, sentiment analysis on VR applications and devices also gathered insights into customers' opinions through social media data [18,29,35].

With the manifold possibilities in multi-user environments, we still lack methods to bridge the gap between performance-based evaluations while considering the emotional factors of groups. Pre-trained language models have been shown to improve sentiment analysis [41], and thus, open the possibility of becoming a relevant method to analyse the outcome of language-based tasks beyond the measure of efficiency. In this study, we utilise a combined approach of sentiment analysis based on a pre-trained language model, performance measurements, and questionnaires to evaluate the results of thirteen VR collaborations in triads on the same mind-mapping task.

Our research question aims to investigate the possibility of a connection between the emotional intelligence of a group and the sentiment regarding the results of their problem and solution-oriented task in virtual reality collaboration. After identifying a research gap in the introduction, we developed two hypotheses to assess this research question. Our hypotheses aim to explore the complex relationship between the outcome of collaborations in Virtual Reality on a performance and sentiment level per group while considering the EI of the participants. Therefore, we conclude with two assumptions:

1. We assume that emotional intelligence (EI) influences the results of group work in virtual reality collaboration.

2. We assume that sentiment analysis offers an explanation model for solution-oriented and problem-oriented results of language-based tasks in virtual reality collaborations.

2   Research Design and Methodology

In the following section, we identify the research design and the means of hardware and software integration for data collection and evaluation to conduct this study. We begin with the setup of the hardware and software environment. Then, we provide the details of the emotional intelligence test and sentiment analysis methods.

2.1   Hardware and Software Integration Solution

For the VR study, Oculus Quest headsets with controllers were employed. We supplied the participants with the right-hand controller during the VR experiment. The headsets had the functionality of recording and transferring verbal communication into the VE, enabling the participants to talk with each other at any time. At the same time, self-recording transcribes spoken content onto the created nodes. On the other hand, the controllers opened a keyboard to write text on the nodes. Both approaches led to the same result and were quick and user-friendly.

Virtual environments (VE) refer to computer-generated spaces that offer users a sense of presence and the possibility to interact within their 3D environment [40]. When choosing the VE that facilitated the experiment, we focused on applications representing the participants using neutral avatars. On the output level, we needed an application that enables interaction on an oral level, which has been proven to enhance creative output [17], and on a written level, to enable NLP-based analysis of the results. All those functionalities should be given while not distracting them from the task of mind mapping. The virtual environment that facilitates our studies is NODA.io (Fig. 1). The application enables its users to be present in a shared virtual-reality space and thus build and share 3-dimensional mental models such as mind maps, flowchart diagrams, storyboards and networks [12]. The participants can create edges (referred to locally within the application as 'nodes') and connect them using vertices (referred to as 'connections') anywhere within the virtual space. Users can also edit the shape, colour, opacity, size and title of the edges, and each user is assigned to a specific design. Regarding interactivity, researchers agree that being able to influence an environment is an essential driver of feeling present in this environment [43], thus, making NODA.io a research environment that supports our goal.

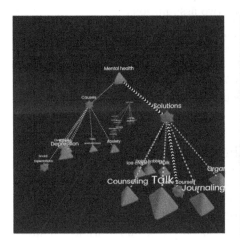 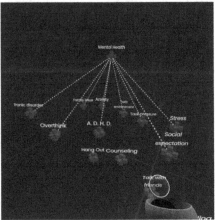

Fig. 1. Noda.IO Mind Map Screenshots

2.2 Research Design and Tasks Implementation

The study participants would go through six steps (Fig. 2), ranging from the welcoming phase to the onboarding, to the first demographic questionnaire, before entering the VR environment. Here, our participants would start with the individual exploration phase to get used to the experimental environment as a single user before starting the experiment and entering the collaborative space. Consisting of two different steps within the experiment, the participants would exit the immersive experience after filling out the questionnaire on the EI embedded within the VR application.

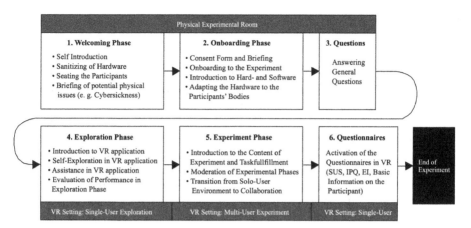

Fig. 2. The Process Design of Research Implementation

The two phases of the mind-mapping session guide the triads from problem-oriented to solution-oriented thinking. The difference in both approaches has been centred in prior research inspecting collaboration in VR [27] and offers a basis for the later analysis of the sentiment of the written output. In the first phase, participants produce unlimited sub-issues related to the main issue. Within this phase, they connect their nodes with each other or with those of the other participants. After 7 min, we would continue with the second phase. Now, we would ask the participants to collectively decide upon one sub-issue on which they collaboratively work on solutions. Within the next 7 min, they may verbally discuss their decisions or vote for one issue by adding a sign to the node before finding solutions for the chosen issue. The framework to explain this approach is posed by the Search for Ideas in Associative Memory (SIAM) model by Nijstad and Stroebe [33]. Under the SIAM model, idea generation is a two-step process. First, an individual activates knowledge concepts in long-term memory, loading them into working memory. Second, working memory is examined as the individual tries to generate a new idea by combining concepts, making new connections or applying the knowledge to a new domain.

2.3 Data Collection and Evaluation Methods

A combination of implicit and explicit data collection shall bridge the gap between technically supported content analysis and questionnaires to evaluate collaborative VR sessions on multiple levels while maintaining the users' immersive experience. The implicit data contains the gathering of performance data and, subsequently, the sentiment analysis of the results of each group distinctively. Here, we apply the efficiency measurement through the task-based distinction between problem-oriented and solution-oriented output. After this distinction, we analyse the content through sentiment analysis, utilising a pre-trained language model [41], and compare the results group-wise. The explicit data collection features demographic data and self-assessment questionnaires on the emotional intelligence questionnaire.

Emotional Intelligence Questionnaire-Based Data Collection and Evaluation. The emotional intelligence in this research conveys the implication study of EI from the Mayer-Salovey-Caruso Emotional Intelligence Test [8], which deployed four factors in analysing EI performance in perceiving emotions, facilitating thoughts, and understanding managing emotions. However, to conform the EI to the mind-mapping task, this research employed two factors of understanding and managing the emotions to be converted into the emotional intelligence questionnaire. The area scored based on these questions reveals the understanding of the emotional interpretations for the emotion-combination, progress to the relationship's transitions, and the methods to manage them to be open-feeling and modulate to oneself and others concluded as the strategic emotional intelligence area [9,32]. The questionnaire is divided into two sections with questions on emotions about the experience before and after the experiment. In contrast, the other two independent questions denote observing the emotional-based decision on regulating the feeling and evaluating the interaction towards the task assigned to manage the emotion. The ordinal score scale provides the respondents with questions from 1 to 5 (Likert Scale).

Sentiment Analysis. The sentiment analysis has been conducted on a pre-trained language model based on DistilBERT [38]. DistilBERT is a lightweight version of BERT [14], which stands for Bidirectional Encoder Representations from Transformers. BERT has been trained on English Wikipedia Articles, consisting of 2,500 million words, and the BooksCorpus, containing 800 million words. Due to the self-attention mechanism in Berts' transformer, the model can be fine-tuned and perform various tasks based on singular texts or text pairs [14]. "Distilbert-base-uncased-emotion" [39] is fine-tuned to predict emotion regarding joy, love, surprise, sadness, anger, and fear. The model card specifies a learning rate at 2e-5, meaning that the learning rate linearly increased from 0 to 2e-5 within the first 10,000 steps. With a batch size of 64 and 8 training epochs, the model achieved a high accuracy of 93.8% and an F1-Score of 93.79, making it an excellent fit to evaluate specific emotions on a language-based data set.

3   Experiment Deployment and Data Analysis

In the following section, we provide details on the experiment setup, the mind-mapping task, the process description, the participants, and the hard- and software utilised during the study.

3.1   Participants and Mind Mapping Task

This research recruited 39 participants that formed groups of 3 each. Ages ranged from 19 to 55 years (M = 27.13, SD = 7.27) and consisted of 51.3% male and

48.7% female. The participants' educational backgrounds indicated Bachelor's (33.3%), Master's degrees (59%) and PhDs (7.7%). All the participants brainstormed in teams before, and most of our participants met for the first time. Seventeen participants wore glasses (43.6%), as mentioned as their visual impairment.

In the briefing, our participants were informed about the mind map topic: mental health. As our participants are diverse regarding their nationalities, ages and gender, we chose mental health after a trend topic research, concluding that this issue is broad and activating enough to be worked on, unlike topics like climate change or politics, which are geographically specific or may trigger ideologies. It was essential for the later sentiment analysis to choose a topic that produces output that triggers ideas around issues first, thus, forming the problem-oriented phase before continuing to the solution-oriented phase, where ideas around resolutions are captured and discussed. Overall, the topic was very well-received by the participants. The open-ended output was emphasised during an initial introduction and invited them to type their ideas into the VR environment.

3.2 Data Collection

The study utilised two methods of data collection: qualitative questionnaires and quantitative measurements through performance data and the sentiment analysis of the results. The questionnaire was composed of the Emotional Intelligence Questionnaire (EI). Whereas the primary goal of this experiment was to identify differences in emotional intelligence and their relationship to performance measures in the VE, participants were free to express their notions into nodes and decide on the results through brainstorming with time limitations only. The post-questionnaires were implemented within the VR environment to acknowledge the immersive characteristics of the VR environment. The NODA.io application contains multiple data points for each group, describing the results in documentation of each user's individual and collaborative actions. The following items were used to gather information on the collaborative activity: Before the

Table 1. NODA.io Export Data Description

Datapoint	Description
Uuid	A unique Id that refers to the user's identification hash
Title	The title of the node that the participant designated
Colour	The colour of the node; each user was assigned a unique colour
Shape	The node's shape; each user was assigned a unique shape
Size	The size of the node. The main issue was set apart through the size
PositionX	The X-coordinate position of the node was used for the location measure
PositionY	The Y-coordinate position of the node was used for the location measure
PositionZ	The Z-coordinate position of the node was used for the location measure

experiment, each user specified the nodes in colour and shape: the data points Uuid, colour and shape conclude the individual user output. The connections between those nodes were evaluated based on Uuid and positional measures. By dividing the nodes based on the optical factors, it was possible to distinguish a user's interaction with their nodes solely vs the interaction between the user's nodes. The nodes in phase one, where issues surrounding the mind-mapping topic were created, formed the results regarding problem orientation. The nodes from phase two centred around the collectively chosen issue, resulting in the solution-oriented nodes. Duplicates, single characters and empty nodes were removed prior to the evaluation.

In the following part, we will discuss the results of the multi-modal data analysis. We will first discuss every means of data collection separately before drawing connections between the results.

3.3   Problems-Oriented Vs Solutions-Oriented Data Analysis

The results of the task were divided respecting the two phases of the VR session: While the first, individual mind mapping was dedicated to thinking about mental health on a problem-oriented level (P), the second phase was meant to be solution-oriented (S) and interactive in terms of collaboration within the triad. The ratio (R) between Problems and Solutions is indicated by dividing the number of problems by the number of solutions. The results on the group level (G) are as follows:

Table 2. Ratio of Problems to Solutions

G	1	2	3	4	5	6	7	8	9	10	11	12	13
P	20	12	16	21	20	24	17	20	13	17	18	7	19
S	22	6	4	19	14	16	14	27	12	12	12	17	13
R	0.9	2.0	4.0	1.1	1.4	1.5	1.2	0.7	1.1	1.4	1.5	0.4	1.5

Groups 1, 8 and 12 came up with more solutions than problems, while groups 2, 3, 6, 11 and 13 had at least 1.5 times more problems than solutions, with group 3 showing the highest ratio of 4 times more problems than solutions. The other groups, 4, 5, 7, 9 and 10, found nearly equal solutions as problems. It is important to note again that the second phase of the collaboration was the interactive group phase. Interaction during problem representation has led to higher performances during problem-solving tasks [24], potentially accounting for the high number of solutions per group. Joint attention is another fundamental aspect of the results of collaborative work during problem-solving. As the participants collectively decide on one problem to work on, the solution-critical moment can be established in the virtual workspace [5].

3.4 Sentiment Analysis

The data set consisted of 455 single words and word combinations after cleaning. The removal of the central node in each group, "mental health", empty nodes, and accidental duplicates of the same nodes were the steps of the initial cleaning process. The pre-processing of the data consists of removing punctuation, stop words, single characters (except "I"), and uneven spacing before converting them into lowercase characters. Following the cleaning process, we calculated the mean sentiment of all 455 words. For this step, we used the Natural Language Toolkit (NLTK) package VADER (Valence Aware Dictionary for Sentiment Reasoning) [21], a model used for text sentiment analysis. With this in mind, groups 4, 8 and 11 display positive values ranging from 0.060 to 0.045 above the benchmark. Groups 1, 2, 7, 9, 10, and 11 are negative but still above the benchmark, with the lower bound set at -0.017. Four groups displayed a strong negative sentiment, ranging from -0.144 to -0.028 below the benchmark and needing further evaluation.

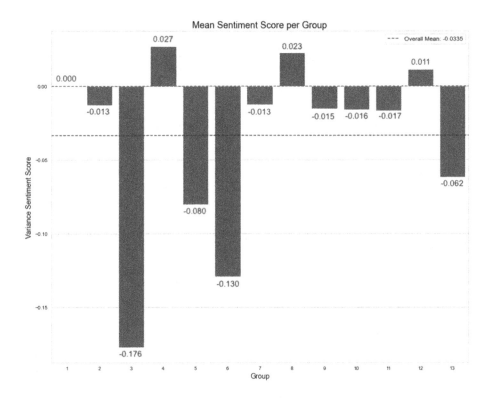

Fig. 3. Overall Mean Sentiment Values Per Group

After this general analysis of polarity per group, we are looking at the detailed emotional evaluation in terms of love, joy, surprise, anger, fear and sadness through the application "Distilbert-base-uncased-emotion" [39]. We aggregated the mean values of each node's sentiments to make them comparable across the groups.

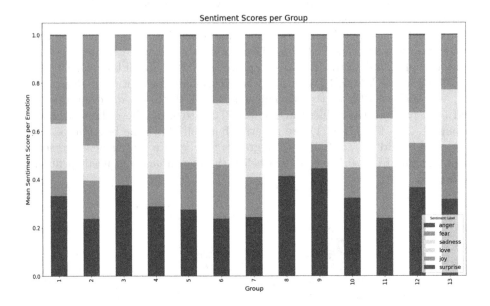

Fig. 4. Detailed Mean Emotional Values Per Group

To assess the relationship between the three positive sentiments (joy, love, surprise) and the solutions, as well as the three negative sentiments (fear, anger, sadness) and problems, we used Multiple Linear Regression analysis, as in the formula below. To test the relationships in terms of negative correlation, we evaluated the three positive sentiments (joy, love, surprise) and the problems, as well as the three negative sentiments (fear, anger, sadness) and solutions 2.

$$yi = \beta0 + \beta1xi, 1 + \beta2xi, 2 + \beta kxi, k + \epsilon i; \qquad (1)$$

As displayed below, we found significant p-values (< 0.05) for the positive and negative emotions on both the results on a group level (N=13) and individual result level (N=455) when it comes to assessing the solutions of the mind map.

The individual values of the solution-oriented nodes showed a significant positive relationship with joy with a p-value of 0.011 but a low R2 for the model of 0.020. The emotion sadness showed a strong negative relationship with the number of solutions produced, with a p-value of 0.009 and an R2 for the model of 0.636. The mean values of the dominantly represented positive emotion of joy as an independent variable with the number of solutions per group showed a significant positive relationship with a p-value of 0.027 and an R2 for the multiple linear regression model of 0.663.

Table 3. Results of the Multiple Linear Regression Model with Highlighted Significant p-values.

emotion /dependent variable	joy /solutions	love /solutions	surprise /solutions	anger /solutions	fear /solutions	sadness /solutions
p-value & coefficient Individual level	0.134 1.194	0.872 0.502	**0.011** 158.170	0.783 0.266	0.196 -1.611	**0.009** -2.817
p-value & coefficient Group level	**0.027** 41.235	0.714 -21.985	0.157 1615.109	0.326 -23.466	0.568 -22.450	**0.020** -61.745
emotion /dependent variable	joy /problems	love /problems	surprise /problems	anger /problems	fear /problems	sadness /problems
p-value & coefficient Individual level	0.999 -0.001	0.403 -1.801	0.874 -6.793	0.410 -0.5483	0.556 0.505	0.404 0.614
p-value & coefficient Group level	0.589 10.459	0.689 -30.032	0.776 -376.570	0.802 -4.527	0.401 29.262	0.740 -6.075

On the other hand, the same analysis was conducted for the first phase of the group work, investigating the number of problems the participants came up with as a dependent variable. The mean sentiment values of the emotions were the independent variables. Neither the results on a group level nor the distinct sentiment values for the individual words displayed a significant relationship.

3.5   Emotional Intelligence Questionnaire

The emotional intelligence questionnaire was distributed with two aspects leveraged to the (1) Emotional intelligence flow measurement before and after experimenting. (2.1) The Interruption of the emotional intelligence-based decision to regulate the feeling to accomplish the task in individual groups. (2.2) The Interruption of the emotional intelligence-based decision to evaluate the interaction to accomplish the task in individual groups. In measuring the EI flow, this research utilised the Wilcoxon Signed Rank Test because the participants' results were not normally distributed, and the ordinal results were adopted from a 5-point Likert Scale. We calculated this stage to two methods: the overall and group-based participants. The general measurement showed the Z value to -0.866 based on the negative ranks of the emotional measurement before and after the experiment (Before < After), the significance value was revealed to the 0.387 ($p >$ 0.05), which indicates the acceptance of the null hypothesis with no significant difference from the paired questionnaire. However, the descriptive analysis performed slightly better results on the emotions obtained after the experiment (M = 3.72, SD = 0.887) compared to before the experiment (M = 3.56, SD = 0.754) 4. In addition, the group-based analysis was also measured in the same method, and the outcome unveiled the same indicator of insignificant value greater than

0.05 in each group. Towards the descriptive analysis, the result acknowledges the emotional improvement performed by Group 2,4,5,6,9,10,13; the decreasing emotion is found in group 1,7,8; Nevertheless, the same emotion on before-after the experiment is shown to the group 3, 11, and 12, which also can refer to the Wilcoxon signed rank test that resulted to a value of 1.

Table 4. General EI Measurement Before And After The Experiments

	Descriptive			Wilcoxon Signed Rank Test	
	N	Mean	SD	Z	Asymp. Sig. (2-tailed)
Before	39	3.56	0.754	-0.866	0.387
After		3.72	0.887		

The second and third questions examine the involvement of the emotional decision to regulate the feeling and interaction in individual and group tasks in the mind-mapping experiment. With the same pattern, this research used the 5-point Likert scale to measure the attitudinal perspectives of the participants, with reflects the calculation measurement as very positive (4.20–5.00), positive (3.40–4.19), neutral (2.60–3.39), negative (1.80–2.59), and very negative (1.00–1.79) [36]. The general indicator of the questionnaire showed the neutral/moderately emotion-based decision used for both regulating the feeling and evaluating the interaction towards the task assigned in the experiment session. The descriptive statistical analysis in 6 shows it. The EI - 2 shows a mean value of 2.92 with an SD of 1.148. The variance result acknowledges 1.318, which exerted a lower value than the EI - 3 result (M = 2.79, SD 1.260). The group analysis in 7 revealed the lowest performance of group 4 (M = 1.000, SD = 0) and the highest score of group 9 (M = 4.333, SD = 0.557) for the EI - 2 question, which acknowledges how far the participants involved in the emotion in managing the feeling. Moreover, the EI - 3 questions that apprehend the emotion based on evaluating the interactions show group 2 (M = 1.333, SD = 0.577) as the lowest group compared to others, yet, the highest result can point to groups 9 and 10 (M = 4.330, SD = 0.557) which have the same outcome.

4   Results and Discussion

Lastly, we will discuss our findings regarding the hypotheses, data analysis, research design limitations, and future perspectives.

Table 5. Group-based EI Measurement Before And After The Experiment

Group	Before - After	Descriptive Mean	SD	Wilcoxon Signed Rank Test Z	Asymp. Sig. (2-tailed)
1	Before	3.333	0.577	-0.577	0.564
	After	3.000	1.000		
2	Before	4.000	1.000	-0.816	0.414
	After	4.667	0.577		
3	Before	4.000	0.816	0	1
	After	4.000	0.816		
4	Before	3.000	0.000	-0.447	0.655
	After	3.333	1.528		
5	Before	3.000	1.000	-0.447	0.655
	After	3.333	0.577		
6	Before	3.333	0.577	-1	0.317
	After	3.667	0.577		
7	Before	3.667	0.577	-0.816	0.414
	After	3.000	1.000		
8	Before	4.333	0.577	-1	0.157
	After	4.000	0.000		
9	Before	3.333	0.577	-1414	1
	After	4.000	0.000		
10	Before	3.667	1.155	-1	0.317
	After	4.000	1.000		
11	Before	4.000	1.000	0	1
	After	4.000	1.000		
12	Before	3.000	0.000	0	1
	After	3.000	1.000		
13	Before	3.500	0.707	-1	0.317
	After	4.500	0.707		

Table 6. Emotion-based Decisions To Regulate and Evaluate Feelings And Interactions - General Performance.

	Minimum	Maximum	Mean	SD
Involving emotional-based decisions to regulate personal and group members' feelings during the tasks (EI - 2)	1	5	2.92	1.148
Involving emotional-based decisions to evaluate personal and group members' interactions during the tasks (EI - 3)	1	5	2.79	1.260

Table 7. Emotion-based Decisions to Regulate and Evaluate Feelings and Interactions - Group Performance.

	EI (2)		EI (3)	
Group	Mean	SD	Mean	SD
1	2.667	0.577	2.333	1.528
2	1.333	0.577	1.333	0.577
3	2.750	0.957	2.500	0.577
4	1.000	0.000	1.667	0.577
5	3.000	1.000	3.333	1.155
6	2.667	0.577	1.667	0.577
7	2.667	1.155	3.000	1.000
8	4.000	0.000	4.000	0.000
9	4.333	0.577	4.333	0.577
10	4.000	0.000	4.333	0.577
11	3.333	1.528	3.667	1.528
12	2.667	1.155	1.667	0.577
13	3.000	1.414	2.500	0.707

4.1 Response to the Hypotheses

Regarding our two hypotheses, we concluded that partly significant tendencies for one were uncovered. The first hypothesis was "Emotional intelligence (EI) influences the results of group work in VR." Our questionnaire result provides insight into involving emotional intelligence in the decision-making to cope with the issues assigned in the task. Nevertheless, the emotional changes were observed to ensure the shifting emotion before and after the experiment. The findings distinguished into two outcomes which showed no high difference in emotional flow found both before and after the mind-mapping session for the first section of the question. A slight improvement is shown in the after emotional-question with the 0.16 value difference; still, the slight difference cannot alter the overall result observed for this section. The result was contrary to the value of the scope of education [26] that evidence the connection between the EI and the success of the academic field. The second finding exhibited the neutral emotion-decision-making to accomplish the discussion assigned. This result also reflects the moderate use of emotion in regulating feeling and evaluating the interaction in individual and group tasks. As part of the response, this research argues on the topic set to the mind-mapping discussion and questionnaire that emphasises the emotional intelligence and the related emotion developed biased responses [6]; people may not fully admit the truth when asked about their emotions.

We concluded with significant results regarding the second hypothesis, "sentiment analysis offers an explanation model for solution-oriented and problem-oriented results of language-based tasks in VR collaborations". Regarding the positive emotions, we found significant values for the relationship between higher numbers of solutions and the emotion of joy on a group level. The data on the individual results showed significance for the positive emotion of surprise. In terms of negative emotions, higher sadness values indicated decreasing solutions on individual and group levels. On the other hand, negative emotions could not be connected to an increasing number of problems created in mind mapping, neither on a group level nor an individual level. In order to fully accept the second hypothesis, further tests have to be conducted on the negative emotions and problem orientation.

While most groups created more problems than solutions, it is essential to note that the strength of the sentiment values of fewer positive words with a strong tonality may outweigh the number of problems, resulting in an overall positive sentiment on a group level and vice versa. The language model we utilised is fine-tuned on six different emotions, three of them being negative: fear, anger and sadness, and two of them being positive: joy and love. The emotional indicator for surprise can be perceived on both levels. The imbalance between positive and negative emotions might potentially distort the results.

4.2   Research Limitations

The study performed a sentiment analysis on the results of a mind mapping phase, centring on finding problems and solutions to mental health. While our 39 participants had 11.67 ideas on average each, the distinction between positive and negative content or problem-orientation and solution-orientation might have more complex origins. Chi, Glaser and Rees argue that focusing on either problem or solution might be a matter of expertise, as novices will stick to the problem representation even while working on solutions, while experts will focus on the problem-solving [11]. Further investigating a potential distinction between mental healthcare professionals' output might offer valuable insights on this topic. However, researchers analysed those processes based on physic, mathematics, or coding tasks [27]. At the same time, mental health is a more relatable, day-to-day topic, especially amongst our participants and can be discussed with little prior knowledge. On the other hand, the quality of the provided solutions was not evaluated by the triads, as the results were meant to be analysed in quantity and sentiment after the necessary data cleaning. An extended process in the VE with an additional discussion phase could lead to further quality assurances.

4.3   Future Perspectives

Virtual collaborations are a rising field of interest in research and practice. Whether those collaborations occur in virtual environments or non-immersive applications, evaluating the outcome poses challenges as soon as the results exceed an amount that a single moderator can overlook manually. With our 13 triads at separate times and only 14 min of group work, the results reached more than 500 ideas before cleaning. The need for automated evaluation arises in more dynamic settings, such as multiple break-out sessions simultaneously, as instant feedback may enhance productivity and create more efficient work. To thoroughly assist virtual group work in the future, language models that specifically understand the difference between problem orientation and solution orientation within a domain may offer meaningful assistance. The fine-tuning of such a language model would provide us with further insights and, thus, will be tested in the future. A service gap can be closed on a process level by combining a fine-tuned model with real-time evaluations, enabling more efficient collaborative experiences.

5   Conclusion

This study provides researchers with insight into using a combined approach of questionnaires on emotional intelligence, performance analysis distinguishing between problem- and solution orientation, and sentiment analysis to evaluate the results of collaborations in a virtual reality environment. While the questionnaire did not fully explain the group's output, we found significant results correlating the performance with the sentiment analysis. Groups with higher positive sentiments of joy and surprise also produced more solution-oriented results, while increased sadness caused groups to come up with fewer solutions. However, the negative emotions drawn from the sentiment analysis could not be connected statistically to the equally important results of the problem-orientated working phase. The tendencies uncovered by the study shall contribute to the exploration of automated content analysis in dynamic virtual environments, as categorising the sentiment of the results can become an important means of assistance in the evaluation of collaborations on a process level and, thus, raise efficiency as well as providing researchers and practitioners with objective insights on emotions. A domain fine-tuned language model would provide us with further insights and, thus, will be tested in the future.

Acknowledgement. We would like to show our gratitude to Shao-Ying Lin, Yu-Xuan Dai, Vu-Hong Lan, and all of the participants who have contributed to this research.

References

1. Ain, N.U., Munir, M., Suneel, I.: Role of emotional intelligence and grit in life satisfaction. Heliyon **7**(4), e06829 (2021). https://doi.org/10.1016/j.heliyon.2021.e06829
2. Alharbi, R., Alnoor, A.: The influence of emotional intelligence and personal styles of dealing with conflict on strategic decisions. PSU Research Review(ahead-of-print) (2022)
3. Amabile, T.M.: The social psychology of creativity: a componential conceptualization. J. Pers. Soc. Psychol. **45**(2), 357–376 (1983). https://doi.org/10.1037/0022-3514.45.2.357
4. Balint, B.N.: [DC] Designing VR for teamwork: the influence of HMD VR communication capabilities on teamwork competencies. In: 2019 IEEE Conference on Virtual Reality and 3D User Interfaces (VR), 2019, pp. 1365–1366 (2019). https://doi.org/10.1109/VR.2019.8798147
5. Barron, B.: When smart groups fail. J. Learn. Sci. **12**(3), 307–359 (2003). https://doi.org/10.1207/S15327809JLS1203_1

6. Bernardi, R.A., Guptill, S.T.: Social desirability response bias, gender, and factors influencing organizational commitment: an international study. J. Bus. Ethics **81**, 797–809 (2008). https://doi.org/10.1007/s10551-007-9548-4

7. Bhagwatwar, A., Massey, A., Dennis, A.: Contextual priming and the design of 3D virtual environments to improve group ideation. Inf. Syst. Res. **29**(1), 169–85 (2018)

8. Brackett, M.A., Salovey, P.: Measuring emotional intelligence with the Mayer-Salovey-Caruso emotional intelligence test (MSCEIT). Psicothema, 18 Suppl, 34–41 (2006). https://www.ncbi.nlm.nih.gov/pubmed/17295955

9. Caruso, D.R. (n.d.). Msceit resource sample report - talentlens. Mayer-Salovey-Caruso emotional intelligence test. Retrieved February 9, (2023). www.talentlens. com.au/userfiles/MSCEIT%20Resource%20Sample%20Report.pdf

10. Chen, C., Yang, C., Huang, K., Yao, K.: Augmented reality and competition in robotics education: effects on 21st century competencies, group collaboration and learning motivation. J. Comput. Assist. Learn. 36 (2020). https://doi.org/10.1111/jcal.12469

11. Chi, M.T.H., Glaser, R., Rees, E.: Expertise in problem solving. In: Sternberg, R. (ed.) Advances in the Psychology of Human Intelligence, pp. 1–75. Erlbaum, Hillsdale, NJ (1982)

12. Coding Leap. (2021). NODA.io (version 1.41). [VR app] Accessed 15 Sept 2022

13. Collins, J., Regenbrecht, H., Langlotz, T., Said Can, Y., Ersoy C., Butson. R.: Measuring cognitive load and insight: a methodology exemplified in a virtual reality learning context. In: 2019 IEEE International Symposium on Mixed and Augmented Reality (ISMAR), Beijing, China, pp. 351–362 https://doi.org/10.1109/ISMAR.2019.00033

14. Devlin, J., Chang, M., Lee, K., Toutanova, K.: BERT: pre-training of deep bidirectional transformers for language understanding. arXiv https://doi.org/10.48550/arXiv.1810.04805

15. Du, Y., Ma, W., Sun, Q., Sai, L.: Collaborative settings increase dishonesty. Front. Psychol. **12**, 650032 (2021). https://doi.org/10.3389/fpsyg.2021.650032

16. Druskat, V.U., Wolff, S.B.: Building the emotional intelligence of groups. Harvard Bus. Rev. **79**, 80–90 (2001)

17. Forens, M., Bonnardel, N., Barbier, M.-L.: How communication modalities can impact group creativity in multi-user virtual environments. In: Proceedings of the European Conference on Cognitive Ergonomics 2015, ECCE'15. Association for Computing Machinery, New York, NY, USA (2015). https://doi.org/10.1145/2788412.2788439

18. Gao, Y., Chen, A., Chi, S., Zhang, G., Hao, A.: Analysis of emotional tendency and syntactic properties of VR game reviews. In: 2022 IEEE Conference on Virtual Reality and 3D User Interfaces Abstracts and Workshops (VRW), Christchurch, New Zealand, 2022, pp. 648–649 (2022). https://doi.org/10.1109/VRW55335.2022.00175

19. Geszten, D., Komlódi, A., Hercegfi, K., Hámornik, B., Young, A., Köles, M.: A content-analysis approach for exploring usability problems in a collaborative virtual environment. Acta Polytechnica Hungarica 2018 Nov 06;**15**(5), 67 (2018)

20. Gong, Z., Nanjappan, V., Soomro, S. A., Georgiev, G.V.: Virtual brainstorming and creativity: an analysis of measures, avatars, environments, interfaces, and applications. In: Proceedings of the International Conference on Engineering Design (ICED21), Gothenburg, Sweden, 16–20 August 2021 (2021). https://doi.org/10.1017/pds.2021.601

21. Hutto, C.J., Gilbert, E.E.: VADER: a parsimonious rule-based model for sentiment analysis of social media text. In: Eighth International Conference on Weblogs and Social Media (ICWSM-14). Ann Arbor, MI, June 2014 (2014)

22. Jenkins, S., Delbridge, R.: Exploring Organizational Deception: Organizational Contexts. Organization Theory, Social Relations and Types of Lying (2020). https://doi.org/10.1177/2631787720919436

23. Jin, Y., Lee, S.: Designing in virtual reality: a comparison of problem-solving styles between desktop and VR environments. Digital Creativity **30**(2), 107–126 (2019)

24. Jonassen, D.H., Kwon, H.I.: Communication patterns in computer mediated versus face-to-face group problem solving. Education Tech. Research Dev. **49**(1), 35–51 (2001). https://doi.org/10.2307/30220298

25. Jordan, P.J., Lawrence, S.A.: Emotional intelligence in teams: development and initial validation of the short version of the workgroup emotional intelligence profile (WEIP-S). J. Manage. Organ. **15**, 452–69 (2009)

26. Khassawneh, O., Mohammad, T., Ben-Abdallah, R., Alabidi, S.: The Relationship between Emotional Intelligence and Educators' Performance in Higher Education Sector. Behav. Sci. **12**(12) (2022)

27. Kwon, K., Song, D., Sari, A.R., Khikmatillaeva, U.: Different types of collaborative problem-solving processes in an online environment: solution-oriented versus problem-oriented. J. Educ. Comput. Res. **56**(8), 1277–1295 (2019). https://doi.org/10.1177/0735633117740395

28. Lailiyah, L., Setiyaningsih, L.A., Wediyantoro, P.L., Yustisia, K.K.: Assessing an effective collaboration in higher education: a study of students' experiences and challenges on group collaboration. EnJourMe (English Journal of Merdeka): Culture, Language, and Teaching of English, 6(2) 152–162 (2021). https://doi.org/10.26905/enjourme.v6i2.691

29. Lampropoulos, G., Keramopoulos, E.: Virtual reality in education: a comparative social media data and sentiment analysis study. Int. J. Recent Contrib. Eng. Sci. IT (iJES). **10**, 19–32 (2022). https://doi.org/10.3991/ijes.v10i03.34057

30. Marsic, I., Dorohonceanu, B.: Flexible user interfaces for group collaboration. Int. J. Hum.-Comput. Interact. **15**, 337–360 (2004). https://doi.org/10.1207/S15327590IJHC1503_02

31. Mayer J.D., DiPaolo M., Salovey P. Perceiving affective content in ambiguous visual stimuli: a component of emotional intelligence. J Pers Assess. **54**(3-4), 772-781 (1990). Summer. https://doi.org/10.1080/00223891.1990.9674037. PMID: 2348356

32. Mayer, J.D.: MSCEIT: Mayer-Salovey-Caruso Emotional Intelligence Test. Multi-Health Systems, Toronto, Canada (2002)

33. Nijstad, B.A., Stroebe, W.: How the group affects the mind: a cognitive model of idea generation in groups. Personality and social psychology review: an official journal of the Society for Personality and Social Psychology Inc, 10(3), 186–213 (2006). https://doi.org/10.1207/s15327957pspr1003_1

34. Osborn, A.: Applied Imagination: Principles and Procedures of Creative Problem Solving. Charles Scribner's Sons, New York, New York (1953)

35. Palos Sánchez, P., Folgado-Fernández, J., Rojas Sánchez, M.: Virtual reality technology: analysis based on text and opinion mining. Math. Biosci. Eng. **19**(8), 7856–7885 (2022). https://doi.org/10.3934/mbe.2022367

36. Pimentel, J.L., Pimentel, J.: Some biases in Likert scaling usage and its correction. Int. J. Sci.: Basic Appl. Res. (IJSBAR) **45**(1), 183–191 (2019)

37. Sanchez, D.R., Weiner, E., Van Zelderen, A.: Virtual reality assessments (VRAs): exploring the reliability and validity of evaluations in VR. Int. J. Select. Assess. **30**(1), 103–125 (2022). https://doi.org/10.1111/ijsa.12369

38. Sanh, V., Debut, L., Chaumond, J., Wolf, T.: DistilBERT, a distilled version of BERT: smaller, faster, cheaper and lighter (2019). arXiv https://doi.org/10.48550/arXiv.1910.01108

39. Savani, B.: Distilbert-base-uncased-emotion, model card (2021). https://huggingface.co/bhadresh-savani/distilbert-base-uncased-emotion

40. Schroeder, R.: Defining Virtual worlds and virtual environments. J. Virtual Worlds Res. **1**(1), 1 (2008). https://doi.org/10.4101/jvwr.v1i1.294

41. Socher, R., et al.: Recursive deep models for semantic compositionality over a sentiment treebank. In: Proceedings of the 2013 Conference on Empirical Methods in Natural Language Processing, pp. 1631–1642 (2013)

42. Stanney, K.M., Mollaghasemi, M., Reeves, L.: Development of MAUVE: the multi-criteria assessment of usability for virtual environments system. Final report, contract no.N61339-99-C-0098, Orlando, FL: Naval Air Warfare Center, Training Systems Division, 8/00 (2000)

43. Steuer, J.: Defining virtual reality: dimensions determining telepresence. J. Commun. **42**(4), 73–93 (1992). https://doi.org/10.1111/j.1460-2466.1992.tb00812.x

44. Yang, E.K., Lee, J.H.: Cognitive impact of virtual reality sketching on designers' concept generation. Digital Creativity **31**(2), 82–97 (2020)

45. Zarifsanaiey, N., Mehrabi, Z., Kashefian-Naeeini, S., Mustapha, R.: The effects of digital storytelling with group discussion on social and emotional intelligence among female elementary school students. Cogent Psychol. **9**(1), 2004872 (2022). https://doi.org/10.1080/23311908.2021.2004872

46. Zielasko, D., et al.: Remain seated: towards fully-immersive desktop VR (2017). https://doi.org/10.1109/WEVR.2017.7957707

Measurement and Evaluation of the Healing Effect of Nature-Themed Video Projection

Tomomi Misaki[1], Chen Feng[2], Azuma Kawaguchi[1], and Midori Sugaya[2(✉)]

[1] Joshibi University of Art and Design, Tokyo, Japan
202101@isis.joshibi.jp, kawaguchi01041@venus.joshibi.jp
[2] Shibaura Institute of Technology, Tokyo, Japan
{i042370,doly}@shibaura-it.ac.jp

Abstract. Natural views have a healing effect on humans. In recent years, many studies have proven the healing effect of natural views, even with different media such as images and videos. However, current media-based natural space creation mainly involves video projection of nature shotted directly. We assume that videos processed to assimilate with the room would have a greater healing effect. We compared two video projection types and evaluated the mental healing effect. To give a comparison, we prepared two videos: a non-processed video shot directly of a natural view and a processed video being a processed video of a natural view assimilated to the wall based on our proposal. For the proposal video, we adjusted the brightness and saturation of pixels to blur the projection's border, making it appear to assimilate with the wall. A comparative analysis of the two types of videos will clarify the differences in their healing effects. We conducted a questionnaire and the semi-interview as the sentimental evaluation. We applied the biological signal related to the central nervous system and autonomic nervous system as quantitative evaluation. Furthermore, we conducted a statistical analysis on both evaluations. The results showed that both videos had a healing effect. And the impression of the processed video was significantly different between those who felt calmed after viewing the non-processed video and those who felt calmed after viewing the processed video .

Keywords: Video projection · Natural · Relax · Sentimental difference scale · Impression

1 Introduction

More than 160 years ago, Florence Nightingale proposed the notion that being able to experience and appreciate natural views had a healing effect on humans [1]. Ulrich's study [2] proposed that natural views can have a positive effect on humans, even when they are inside rooms. To test this, they divided the patients into two rooms, one with a natural view and one without. Results showed that the patients in the room with a natural view had a faster recovery rate.

In the last few years, research has shown the beneficial effects of natural views, even when experienced through various mediums such as images and videos [3]. Studies have

© The Author(s), under exclusive license to Springer Nature Switzerland AG 2023
M. Kurosu and A. Hashizume (Eds.): HCII 2023, LNCS 14012, pp. 264–278, 2023.
https://doi.org/10.1007/978-3-031-35599-8_17

employed monitors and projectors to display natural views within rooms, suggesting that these views can offer a sense of healing. Usually, rooms with natural views displayed have unprocessed, directly captured images and videos. Even if these images and videos are presented as if they were windows, they can still be very conspicuous in the room and give people a strong sense of "the video is being projected there," which can be unsettling. Thus, we proposed blurring the border of the natural view projection and making the projection assimilate into the wall to reduce the emphasis on projection in the room and create a more calming effect. As a demonstration video, we adjusted the brightness and saturation of pixels to blur the projection's border and make it assimilate into the wall.

We compared the healing effects of two types of video projections: one directly shot from a natural view and one processed to assimilate to the wall. To quantify the healing effect, we used biological signals related to the central nervous system and autonomic nervous system as quantitative evaluations [4], as well as a questionnaire and semi-interview for sentimental evaluation. The statistical analysis of the evaluations revealed the differences in the healing effects of the two videos.

In this study, the "healing effect" will be examined in its entirety as a beneficial transformation from the current physical and mental state, including "relaxation," "calmness," "comforting," "soothing," "comfort," "stress reduction effect," and so on.

2 Previous Research

2.1 Research on the Creation of Natural Environments Through Images

By creating a virtual space through video projection, it is possible to create "presence," the sense of being there [5].

A previous study shows the construct of virtual environments and their influence on presence and imagery in simulated clinical environments. It was found that "The possibility exists that displaying photographic images with high levels of presence that create a sensation of "being there" in the image may distract the viewer from stress and or pain in the healthcare environment" [6].

Environmental experiments using virtual spaces created by still images projection and video projection have been widely conducted. An experiment to investigate the effects of sunlight filtering through trees on people was conducted by creating a simulated environment in a room by displaying still images on a 50-inch LCD monitor. That experiment showed that there was a stress-reducing effect even indoors [7]. In other studies, the display monitor was also a pseudo-window to project live and environmental videos. Then, there was an experiment in which impressions were evaluated in four environments: one without a window, one with a window, one with a live video displayed on a pseudo-window, and one with an environmental video projected on a pseudo-window. The pseudo-window was evaluated more similarly to a window than to no window. In particular, the pseudo-window with a live video displayed on it was stated to be an effective substitute for a window. In addition, the environmental video was rated higher than the realistic window in the following items: healing fatigue, relaxing, refreshing, rest for the eyes, and visually stimulating, indicating its refreshing effect [8]. The Semantic Differential (SD) scale is used as a method of evaluating videos. We will use this method in our study as well. As described above, various studies have been conducted on the healing effects of nature through images and videos.

However, most current experiments have been conducted either in their natural state or by processing them to make them more realistic. We could not find any examples of our proposed video projection in a room assimilated with the wall.

2.2 Research for Video Processing to Add Healing Effects

The study that evaluated the image color preference after long-term image watching and conducted the experiments, the experiments suggested that "it was possible that viewers might feel tired of high saturation and high color contrast image colors when a visual fatigue phenomenon appeared [9]. In this study, it is assumed that the video is always on the wall. Therefore, the saturation and high color contrast are set low to avoid discomfort even if the image is projected for a long period.

According to the "prospect-refuge theory," views that can be seen without being seen, such as a "refuge," where one can hide in the foreground, and "prospect" spreads out in the background, are images that provide a sense of security from an animal behavior perspective [10, 11]. Numerous experiments have been conducted based on this theory. In a room simulating a hospital room, photographs representing "prospect and refuge," "prospect," "refuge," and "hazard" were projected onto a large screen, and experiments were conducted to measure the effects on pain. This experiment suggests that a composite image of "prospect and refuge" may predominantly decrease pain sensation [3]. Based on this study, we will also include the "prospect and refuge theory" image in the processed video in our study.

"1/f fluctuation," which is said to have a healing effect, was exhibited from videos directly shot of a natural view, such as snowfall affected by a gentle breeze, and the effect was also found in videos [12]. In this study, "1/f fluctuation" is reproduced in the processed videos by using videos shot of trees swaying in the wind.

3 Proposal

As shown in previous studies, there have been various experiments with natural images using media, and their effects have been demonstrated. However, most of these studies are based on photographs or videos of directly shot of a natural view. We proposed a video method suitable for projection in a room and created a video.

The video is designed to be viewed in a room for a long period of time. We adjusted the brightness and saturation and blurred the border of the projections for the projection assimilated with the room.

We compared two video projection types in this study and evaluated the mental healing effect: the non-processed video that is a directly shot of a natural view and the processed video that is a processed natural view video based on our proposal.

4 Method

A comparative analysis of the two types of videos will clarify the differences in their healing effects.

We conducted the statistical analysis on the biological signal, questionnaire and the semi-interview evaluation.

The statistical analysis was performed using HAD: A GUI-based free software program that contains a function for basic statistical [13].

4.1 Video Processing

Explanation of the Non-processed Video a Directly Shot of Natural View. The video was shot in Yoyogi Park in Shibuya Ward, Tokyo, on a morning in April (Nikon Z7II 24–120 mm F4 4K 30p), with the composition facing upward to avoid unnecessary obstructions in the background. This video has been rotated and cropped, but the image quality still needs to be processed or adjusted. In this study, we refer to this image as the non-processed video.

Explanation of the Processed Video Processed Based on Our Proposal. In this study, we refer to this image as the processed video. Our methodology for the processed video was shown below:

- For comfortable viewing long time in a room, saturation, and high color contrast would be suppressed [9]. In addition, brightness contrast would be also suppressed.
- Based on "prospect-refuge theory" [10, 11], the silhouetted branches are placed in the foreground, assuming "refuge," and the tree in the background is in the distance, being the "prospect."
- In the distant view, blurred details give the impression that the viewer is viewing the scene through a haze.
- The vignette effect was added to make the border naturally with the wall.
- The swaying of the trees caused by the wind and the light diffused accordingly were added. The f/1 fluctuation was reproduced by putting together the live action video of the non-processed videos with a processed natural view video based on our proposal. [12]

The numerical differences from non-processed video and processed video resulted in the following results (Fig. 1.). The histogram of the RGB and luminance values shows the level values on the horizontal axis and the number of pixels on the vertical axis. The distribution is spread over the entire area for the high-contrast non-processed video, while the distribution is concentrated in a narrow range for the low-contrast processed video. The decrease in the standard deviation value in the processed video also indicates a decrease in the contrast value. In the contour detection image using the same algorithm, the detection line in the processed video is significantly reduced, indicating a decrease in the numerical value difference between adjacent pixels. These values indicate a blurred impression of the processed video.

Non-processed video

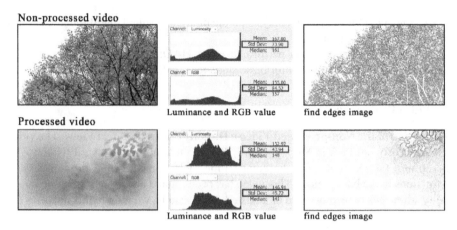

Fig. 1. Comparison of non-processed video and processed video

4.2 Sentimental Evaluation

Questionnaire
Question to Choose Which Is Closer (on a 5-Point Scale)

- Preference for nature or urban environment
- Preference for in a room or in an open air
- More calmed after viewing the non-processed video or the processed video

Questions About Impressions of Videos. Using the Semantic Differential (SD) method, we asked 12 questions about impressions of the non-processed video and the processed video. The participants were asked to answer with pairs of opposite adjectives on a 5-point scale: Nervous–Relaxed, Tired–Energetic, Irritated–Soothe, Dark–Bright, Dissonance–Harmony, Enclosed–Open, Cold–Warm, Unhealthy–Healthy, Anxious–Calm, Uncomfortable–Comfortable, Dislike–Like, Boring–Exciting.

Interview. We asked detailed questions about their impressions of each video, their mood, and feelings about it, and what they were thinking about while viewing the video.

4.3 Bio-Signals

In order to evaluate the changes in emotion caused by viewing the unprocessed and processed videos, we asked participants to wear electroencephalogram (EEG) and pulse sensors while viewing both videos. We assume that these wearable sensors evaluate the impact of pre-processing on emotional shifts by measuring the physiological changes of the body of the participants. This allowed us to collect data on their physiological reactions to their emotional changes.

EEG evaluation was conducted with the Mind Wave Mobile 2, which is a simplified one channel EEG sensor, and we used the index of low beta over low alpha to measure the attention level of the participant. The Mind Wave Mobile 2 was connected to a laptop computer, and the participant was asked to focus on a certain task while the EEG was recorded. The data was analyzed to see how the participant's attention level changed over time.

As for HRV evaluation, we applied the pulse sensor provided by the Switch Science Company. The index we applied in this study is the SDNN/RMSSD. The HRV index SDNN/RMSSD is a measure of the variability of heart rate over a period of time. It is calculated by dividing the average of the standard deviations of the normal-to-normal (NN) intervals, also known as the root mean squared successive differences (RMSSD), by the standard deviation of the normal-to-normal (SDNN) intervals. The greater the ratio of this index, the greater the heart rate variability [14]. This can be used to assess the overall health of the cardiovascular system as well as to monitor changes in cardiovascular health over time.

5 Experiment

5.1 Experimental Materials

- Non-processed video: Directly shot of the natural view (cf. 4.1 Video Processing)
- Processed video: Processed natural view video based on our proposal (cf. 4.1 Video Processing)
- Stress loading: Using the Stroop task, stress was added prior to the projection of the natural video. Characters with different word and color stimuli took longer to decode than words written in black [15]. The Stroop task has been used in various psychological studies as a stressor. In this study, red, blue, yellow, and black Chinese characters written in different color schemes from the character stimuli were displayed 2 s each for 3 min.
- Rest time image: RGB value is (155,155,155) gray with a reticle in the center.

5.2 Experimental Environment

The experiment was conducted in a windowless consultation room that had been partitioned off. The space inside the partition was about 6 m^2, and it contained a bed and a projector that was directed at the wall. The distance from the eye level to the wall was 2.450 mm, the staring height was 850 mm, the projection size was 1.600 x 900 mm, and the projection height was 1.050 mm. The video projection size and position were set in accordance with THX's standards, which are recommended for home theaters (THX being an American company that produces audio/visual reproduction standards) (Fig. 2.). The projection size of the screen was 36° of the viewer's horizontal viewing angle with a resolution of 1,920 × 1,080 high-definition pixels, while the projection height was within 15° of the elevation angles to the center of the screen based on the horizontal line at eye level.

The brightness of the room, measured at the participant's head position in the direction of the line of sight, was set within the 150–200 lx range specified by the Japanese Industrial Standards (JIS) for brightness in hospital rooms. The brightness of the gray screen projection at rest time was 177 lx, that of the non-processed video projection was 180 lx, and that of the processed video projection was 135 lx.

The room temperature during the experiment ranged from 17.6 to 23 °C, and the humidity ranged from 48% to 60%. Participants were monitored for coldness and advised to wear a jacket when the temperature was low. During the experiment, they were placed in a reclined position with their back elevated up to 60°.

The questionnaire was filled out on a Google form on the participant's smartphone. Participants responded verbally to cues and Stroop test for the progression of the experiment. And the investigator outside the room responded to audio transmitted via a microphone placed in the room. At the end of the experiment, interviews were conducted face-to-face.

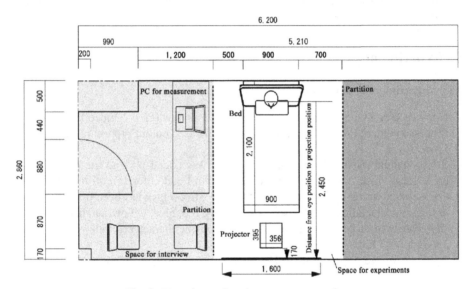

Fig. 2. Experimental environment construction

5.3 Experiment Procedure

The participants reclined on a bed and evaluated their impressions of the video projected on the wall in front of them. Each experiment took approximately 47 min, with both the non-processed video set and the processed video set comprising a 3-min rest period, a 3-min Stroop task, and a 3-min video viewing period, for a total of 9 min. The order of video projection was randomized (Fig. 3.).

5.4 Participants Attributes

A total of 49 participants (25 males and 24 females), mostly undergraduate and graduate students in their 20s or older, took part in the experiment. Of these, 49 provided valid questionnaires (male: 25, female: 24), 48 conducted valid interviews (male: 25, female: 23), and 45 had valid biometric measurements (male: 24, female: 21).

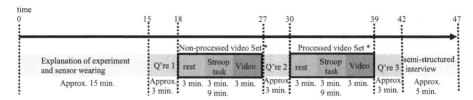

Fig. 3. Timeline of the experiment

Participants were asked to rate their preference for nature or urban environment, and for a room or an open air. The results showed that 53.06% had a prefer nature, and 28.57% prefer an urban environment, and 18.37% were neither. Also, 42.86% prefer a room, and 28.57% prefer an open air, and 28.57% were neither. Values for preference are the sum of "prefer" and "slightly prefer."

6 Result

6.1 Questionnaire

Question to Choose Which Video Made You Feel Calmer After Viewing. (Parameter: Frequency distribution (the number of people)) We asked the participants to answer on a five-point scale whether you felt calmed after viewing the non-processed video or the processed video (Fig. 4.). 51.02% (26.53% non-processed video and 24.49% slightly non-processed video) of the respondents were more calmed by the non-processed video. 44.90% (28.57% processed video and 16.33% slightly processed video) were more calmed by the processed video. 4.08% were neither.

Those who felt calmer after viewing the non-processed video are named "group A" and those who felt calmer after viewing the processed video are named "group B."

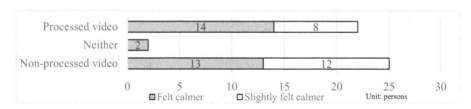

Fig. 4. Which video made feel calmer after viewing non-processed video or processed video

Impression Evaluation

Impressions of Non-processed Video and Processed Video. (Analysis method: t-test) Both videos showed high rated values indicating an average of 4.1 or higher for "Nervous–Relaxed" and 3.7 or higher for "Irritated–Soothe," "Unhealthy–Healthy," "Anxious–Calm," "Uncomfortable–Comfortable," and "Dislike–Like." In addition, a t-test showed that the non-processed video was rated significantly higher with the value of

"Dark–Bright" (t (48) = 7.203, p = .000), "Enclosed–Open" (t (48) = 4.859, p = .000), "Cold–Warm" (t (48) = 2.832, p = .007), and "Unhealthy–Healthy"(t (48) = 3.810, p = .000) (Fig. 5.).

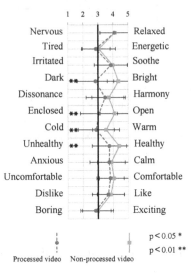

Fig. 5. Impressions of non-processed video and processed video

Impressions of Non-processed Video and Processed Video by Group A and Group B. (Analysis method: t-test) The analysis was divided into two groups: impression evaluations of the non-processed video and processed video by group A and impression evaluations of the non-processed video and processed video by group B. We excluded two who were neither.

In group A, the t-test showed that the non-processed video was rated significantly higher with the value of "Dark–Bright" (t (24) = 6.603, p = .000), "Dissonance–Harmony" (t (24) = 2.954, p = .007), "Enclosed–Open" (t (24) = 4.834, p = .000), "Cold–Warm" (t (24) = 3.645, p = .001), "Unhealthy–Healthy" (t (24) = 4.578, p = .000), "Anxious–Calm" (t (24) = 2.123, p = .044), "Uncomfortable–Comfortable" (t (24) = 3.460, p = .002), and "Dislike–Like" (t (24) = 3.302, p = .003) (Fig. 6. (A)).

In group B, the t-test showed that the non-processed video was rated significantly higher with the value of "Tired–Energetic" (t (2.160) = 21, p = .042s), "Dark–Bright" (t (4.234) = 21, p = .000), and "Enclosed–Open"(t (2.592) = 21, p = .017), and the processed video was rated significantly higher with the value of "Nervous–Relaxed" (t (3.464) = 21, p = .002), and "Dislike–Like" (t (2.485) = 21, p = .021) (Fig. 6. (B)).

Comparison: Non-processed Video and Processed Video by Group A and Group B. (Analysis method: two-way analysis of variance) Evaluation of the non-processed video by group A and B and evaluation of the processed video by group A and B were compared (Fig. 7.).

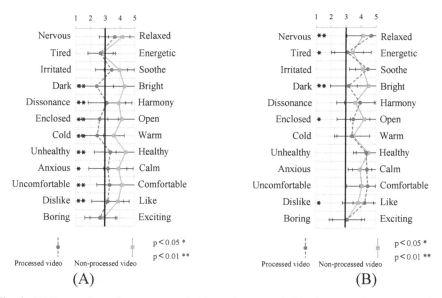

Fig. 6. (A) Impressions of non-processed video and processed video by group A; (B) Impressions of non-processed video and processed video by group B

As a result, the interaction was significantly difference for "Nervous–Relaxed" ($F(1, 45) = 11.133$, $p = .002$), "Irritated–Soothe" ($F(1, 45) = 6.269$, $p = .016$), "Dissonance–Harmony" ($F(1, 45) = 9.861$, $p = .003$), "Cold–Warm" ($F(1, 45) = 4.959$, $p = .031$), "Unhealthy–Healthy" ($F(1, 45) = 8.030$, $p = .007$), "Anxious–Calm" ($F(1, 45) = 7.229$, $p = .010$), "Uncomfortable–Comfortable" ($F(1, 45) = 12.620$, $p = .001$), and "Dislike–Like" ($F(1,45) = 16.575$, $p = .000$).

Impressions of the processed video were l significantly higher for group B for "Nervous–Relaxed" ($F(1, 90) = 14.946$, $p = .000$), "Irritated–Soothe" ($F(1, 90) = 13.035$, $p = .001$), "Dissonance–Harmony" ($F(1, 90) = 6.405$, $p = .013$), "Cold–Warm" ($F(1, 90) = 9.564$, $p = .003$), "Unhealthy–Healthy" ($F(1, 90) = 15.989$, $p = .000$), "Anxious–Calm" ($F(1, 90) = 16.019$, $p = .000$), "Uncomfortable–Comfortable" ($F(1, 90) = 21.158$, $p = .000$), and "Dislike–Like" ($F(1, 90) = 15.483$, $p = .000$).

Impressions of the non-processed video was not significantly different between group A and B.

6.2   Bio-Signal

Comparison of Average SDNN/RMSSD for Processed and Non-processed Video. The results of a t-test show a significant difference between the SDNN/RMSSD of the processed and non-processed video. The paired-sample t-test revealed that the mean SDNN/RMSSD of the non-processed video was significantly higher than that of the processed video ($t(44) = 3.822$, $p = .000 < .050$). Therefore, it can be concluded that the non-processing of the video significantly affects the SDNN/RMSSD. Since the SDNN/RMSSD represent the variance of normal-to-normal intervals of heartbeat intervals and reflect the

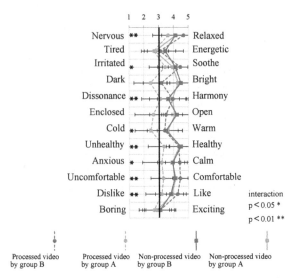

Fig. 7. Comparison of impression evaluation of non-processed video and processed video by group A and B

change of stress states and autonomic nervous activity, these results suggest that the processing of the video has a significant effect on stress levels and autonomic nervous activity (Fig. 8.).

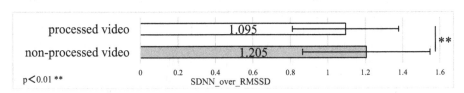

Fig. 8. Average of SDNN/RMSSD for processed and non-processed video

Comparison of Average of EEG Index for Processed and Non-processed Video. The average values of EEG index lowβ/lowα by group were compared. The average of lowβ/lowα values was not significantly different.

6.3 Discussion

Healing Effect of both Non-processed Video and Processed Video. First, the healing effects of both the non-processed video and processed video will be discussed. The rating scale questionnaire about the impression of the video for both videos show high values, indicating an average of 4.1 or higher for "Relaxed" and 3.7 or higher for "Soothe," " Healthy," "Calm," "Comfortable," and "Like" (Fig. 5.). When interviewed about whether they would prefer the video to be present or not, 40 out of 48 respondents said they would prefer the video to be present, either in the non-processed video or processed video. The reasons given were "I felt more relaxed with the videos" and "I was less bored with the videos than without them" in the interview.

From these facts, it can be suggested that both the non-processed video and processed video have a healing effect, giving a sense of relaxation, soothe, calm, like, and comfortable.

Differences in Impressions by Group A and Group B. The bio-signal results show that the non-processed video was predominantly active in sympathetic nerve and so the stress tendency was less for the processed video than for the non-processed video (Fig. 8.). However, when asked to choose the video that made them feel calmer after viewing it, participants were slightly more likely to choose the non-processed video (Fig. 4.). Based on these results, we discussed the possibility that there is a significant difference between the impressions of the non-processed video and the processed video by different people.

Therefore, the impression evaluation in Fig. 5. Was analyzed by dividing the respondents into those who felt calm after viewing the non-processed video (group A) and those who felt calm after viewing the processed video (group B) (Fig. 6. (A) (B)).

Differences in Impressions Evaluation of Each Video by Groups. There was a large difference in the evaluation of the non-processed video and the processed video by group A. In all items, the non-processed video had more positive values than the processed video. In nine of the items, the evaluation of the non-processed video was predominantly higher (Fig. 6. (A)).

However, in the impression evaluation by group B (Fig. 6. (B)), the difference in the evaluation of both videos were less than that of group A. In some items, the processed video was more positive than the non-processed video. For "Nervous-Relaxed" and "Dislike-Like," the processed video was rated significantly higher than the non-processed video.

Differences in Impression Evaluation by Groups on Individual Videos. When divided into Group A and Group B, there was a significant difference in the evaluation of each impression. Therefore, we compared the evaluation of Group A and B for the non-processed video and the evaluation of Group A and B for the processed video. As the result, there was no significant difference in the evaluation of the non-processed video for both groups. However, for the processed video, the evaluation of group A was generally low, while that of group B was high, resulting in a significant difference in impression evaluation between group A and B (Fig. 7.).

This suggests that the non-processed video has a stable healing effect, while the processed video has a different effect for each person, with a lower effect for certain people but a higher healing effect than the non-processed video for certain people.

Discussion from Interviews. To examine the details, we would like to discuss them with the interviews. The interviews have been recompiled based on the notes and audio recordings described during the interviews. Impressions that came up frequently during the interviews are summarized (Table 1.). Those that were particularly frequent are indicated in gray cells and lattice pattern cells.

We also discussed whether each impression was positive or negative. For example, opinions about brightness, such as "It is bright and makes me feel happy" were counted as positive, while those about "It is too bright and irritating" were counted as negative. Cases that were neither were excluded. Particularly salient values were indicated in striped cells.

Table 1. Semi-structured interview summary (impressions of videos)

Unit: persons	Impressions of non-processed video					Impressions of processed video				
	Positive			Negative			Positive		Negative	
	ALL	group A	group B	group A	group B	ALL	group A	group B	group A	group B
artificial	6	0	0	2	1	9	2	3	2	0
realistic	29	14	8	1	1	1	0	1	0	0
fantastic	0	0	0	0	0	11	4	3	1	0
open	7	3	3	0	0	1	0	1	0	0
enclosed	1	0	0	0	0	7	1	4	1	0
bright	16	7	5	0	4	0	0	0	0	0
dark	0	0	0	0	0	19	3	7	7	0
sharp	14	5	2	0	3	0	0	0	0	0
hazy	0	0	0	0	0	17	2	5	6	0

Details of Differences in Impressions by Groups. We discussed what impression differences between the non-processed video and processed video could be attributed to these differences. In the impression evaluation questionnaire, significant differences were found for Dark–Bright and Enclosed–Open, both for group A and B. Many of the same points were also made in the interviews (Table 1.: gray cells). And according to the interviews, it was pointed out a lot that the non-processed video gives a "realistic and clear" impression, while the processed video gives a " Fantastic and Hazy" impression (Table 1.: lattice pattern cells), which is also likely to be a major difference between the non-processed video and processed video. Therefore, we can say that the non-processed video is "Bright, Open, Realistic, Clear" and the processed video is "Dark, Closed, Fantastic, Hazy."

Differences in Impression Evaluation by Groups on Individual Videos. Next, we discussed whether these impressions were positive or negative. At first glance, we tend to think that "Bright, Open, Realistic, Clear" is a positive impression and "Dark, Closed, Fantastic, Hazy" is a negative impression, but a detailed analysis of the interviews revealed that this is not necessarily true. There was a difference between Group A and B in whether they felt negatively or positively about the non-processed video and the processed video. Some participants in group B had a positive impression of processed video's "Closed" and a negative impression of the non-processed video's "Bright" and

"Clear." Those participants were rarely found in group A. Some participants in group A had a negative impression of the processed video's "Dark" and "Hazy," but they were not in group B (Table 1.: striped cells).

These differences in feeling were revealed based on the details of the interviews. For example, in group A, some people felt positively about the "realism" of the non-processed video, saying that "it was good because it was natural." On the other hand, in group B, there are those who feel negatively about the realism of the non-processed video, saying "I do not feel particularly relaxed because it is the same as their usual scenery."

Considering these opinions, it is possible that they have contrast impressions of the video. Are these impressions personal preference?

Reasons for the Difference in Impressions. From a different perspective, some participants pointed out the different situations and moods in which they would like to see each video: "I want to see the non-processed video and the processed video at different times. I want to see the non-processed video when I need motivation and the processed video when I am tired." "I want to see the non-processed video when I want to go outside, and I want to see the processed video when I am alone." "The processed video is what I want to see before I go to sleep or when I am relaxing at home." These are only some of the opinions, but from these opinions it can be inferred that the videos that healing us vary depending on our mood and situation at the time.

Effects of the Proposed Processing of Processed Video. Concerning the results of the effects of the processed video (cf. 5.1 Experimental Materials), we consider that the blurring, vignette effect, and saturation and contrast adjustments are manifested as healing effects. Regarding light diffused by the swaying, there were 17 answers in the interview, 10 positives, 2 negative, and 5 not distinguishable. From this, we consider that the effect was generally felt. There were no specific comments on the adaptation of the "prospect-refuge theory," and it was not clear what kind of effect it had.

7   Conclusion

The results of this experiment suggested that both the non-processed video, which was a direct shot of a natural view, and the processed video, which was a processed natural view video based on the proposed method, had healing effects. Specifically, the non-processed video may have a consistent healing effect for people with a wide range of sensibilities. On the other hands, the processed video may elicit further healing effect than the non-processed video, particularly for those who had a favorable reaction to it. It was then suggested that the video projection that is healing may differ depending on the sensations of the individual, the environment, and the level of stress. Further study is needed to fully understand the causes and conditions of this difference in impressions.

8   Future Work

This study provided insight into potential directions for utilizing video to create natural healing spaces.

However, to investigate in more detail, we consider it necessary to conduct experiments with proposed videos that are feature-specific and for longer periods of time.

The study also identified issues for both the processed and the non-processed video.

By the non-processed video, some pointed out that external factors such as the weather, the color of the sky, and the insects that enter the space can be detrimental to impression. We consider it necessary to process the images to make them look more natural.

Additionally, there were indications of fear and anxiety in response to the processed video, which may be due to the dark and low-contrast processing.

These are issues that require further exploration to expand the potential of room projection.

References

1. Nightingale, F.: Notes on Nursing: What it is and What it is Not. New edition revised and enlarged. Harrison, London (1860)
2. Ulrich, R.S.: View through a window may influence recovery from surgery. Science **224**, 420–421 (1984)
3. Vincent, E., Battisto, D., Grimes, L. McCubbin, J.: The effects of nature images on pain in a simulated hospital patient room. HERD 2010 Spring **3**(3), 42–55 (2010)
4. Suzuki, K., Matsubara, R., Sugaya, M.: Construction of an emotion estimation model using EEG and heart rate variability indices as features by machine learning. JSAI2021 **3F2-GS-10j-03**, 1–4 (2021)
5. Ijsselsteijn, W.A.: Presence in depth. Eindhoven University of Technology. Doctoral dissertation. Eindhoven, pp. 1–286 (2004)
6. Vincent, E., Battisto, D. Grimes, L.: The effects of presence and influence in nature images in a simulated hospital patient room. HERD 2010 Spring, **3**(3), 56–69 (2010)
7. Takayama, N., Fujisawa, M., Aramaki, M., Morikawa, T.: Influence of subjective appraisal and personality and other traits to psychological stress reduction effect caused by "Sunshine filtering through foliage" in the forest picture. Jpn. Insts. Landscape Archit. **75**, 565–570 (2012). National Conference Research Papers Transcript, 24 (2012)
8. Kawata, N., Miki, M., Jonan, R., Terai, D., Aida, H.: The efficacy of virtual window: impression of office workers in the environment with windows and the windowless environment and examination of image projected on the virtual window. Intelligent Systems Design Laboratory, The Monthly Lecture Meeting, 164 (2015)
9. Hung, C. S.: A study on the image color preference after the long-term visual operation condition (2013)
10. Appleton, J.: The Experience of Landscape. Wiley, London (1975)
11. Appleton, J.: translator: Kanno, H.: Fukei no keiken: Keikan no bi nituite (in Japanese). Hosei University Press (2005)
12. Ishimura, K., Kato, C., Saito, Y., Rinoshika, A.: 1/f fluctuation analysis on heeling effects of video, J. Vis. Soc. Jpn. **29–1**(2), 27–30 (2009)
13. Shimizu, H.: An introduction to the statistical free software HAD: suggestions to improve teaching, learning and practice data analysis. J. Media, Inf. Commun. **1**, 59–73 (2016)
14. Tomoi, D., et al.: Estimation of stress during car race with factor analysis. In: 20th Robotics Symposia, pp.133–138 (2015)
15. Stroop, J.R.: Studies of interference in serial verbal reactions. J. Exp. Psychol. **18**(6), 643–662 (1935)

Laughter Map: Supporting System for Recalling Pleasant Memories Based on the Recording and Visualization of Laughter Experiences

Miyabi Shigi, Masayuki Ando, Kouyou Otsu, and Tomoko Izumi[✉]

Graduate School of Information Science and Engineering, Ritsumeikan University, Kusatsu, Shiga 525-8557, Japan
is0507ix@ed.ritsumei.ac.jp, {mandou,k-otsu, izumi-t}@fc.ritsumei.ac.jp

Abstract. In recent years, an increasing number of people are being diagnosed with depression. A specific tendency of recalling a memory in depressed patients is the mood-state-dependent effect, in which memories are easily recalled based on the current mood state; for example, a negative mood leads to an easier recall of negative memories. In this study, we aim to support the recall of past pleasant experiences for preventing the cycle of negative mood-state-dependent recall. To achieve this, we propose a voice-based lifelogging application "Laughter Map" that allows users to record voice of laughter and conversations before and after and to review their past laughing conversations in a map format during their daily lives. To validate the usefulness of the proposed method for conveying past laughter experience in a map format, an experiment was conducted for comparing the cases of presenting past laughter experience in a list chronologically and presenting it on a map. According to the results, presenting past laughter experience in a map format enhances detailed recall compared with when laughter experience is displayed in chronological order.

Keywords: Emotions in human–computer interactions (HCI) · Kansei engineering · lifelogging system · laughter · recall support

1 Introduction

In recent years, an increasing number of people are being diagnosed with depression globally [1]. The COVID-19 pandemic and restrictions on social activities have considerably affected people's mental health [2]. Memory and judgment skills are impaired in depression, and specific cognitive tendencies for recalling past events may be observed depending on the mood. In particular, the mood-dependent effect is well known [3], in which an experience tends to be recalled when a person is in an associated mood. In cases in which a mood-state-dependent effect is observed, past negative memories tend to be recalled when the person feels depressed. The subsequent worsening of the negative mood results in more negative memories being recalled. This repetition may result in chronic depression and cognitive distortion. To avoid this chain of negative

M. Kurosu and A. Hashizume (Eds.): HCII 2023, LNCS 14012, pp. 279–292, 2023.
https://doi.org/10.1007/978-3-031-35599-8_18

memory recall, external triggers to change the mood are necessary. In addition, previous studies have revealed that positive memories can be a promising method for improving mood [4]. In this study, we aim to help users recall pleasant past experiences to break the negative mood-dependent cycle.

In maintaining positive mental health and living a fulfilling life, it is important to recall not only conscious enjoyable experiences such as unique leisure activities but also unconsciously pleasant events in daily life. In addition to extraordinary pastimes such as traveling or dining with others, we sometimes find unconscious enjoyment in casual conversations with family and friends or in interesting events during our daily lives. Recalling these small positive experiences can effectively increase self-efficacy and help re-evaluate self-worth and life. The use of conversations to recalling these types of experiences are a technique used in clinical interviews to determine one's resources and strengths [5]. Support for recalling daily life positively might be useful for people in situations in which restrictions have been placed on social activities due to outbreaks of infectious diseases or in scenarios in which physical or mental deterioration prevent nondaily activities.

In the field of Human–Computer Interactions, studies have focused on lifelogging systems for recording daily life. Such life logging-based approach could be used for recording unconsciously pleasant memories in daily activities and supporting their recall. For example, emotional expressions such as laughter recorded in the lifelog expresses the users' feelings about the experience. Therefore, these emotional expressions recorded in the lifelog could be used for collecting and enhancing recall of past positive experiences that are outside of the user's conscious mind.

In this study, the voice-based lifelogging application "Laughter Map" is proposed to accumulate information about situations in which laughter occurs in a user's life. This application then allows recalling past positive events with visualizing past events with laughter in the form of a map on a mobile device. (Fig. 1.) In the proposed method, the voice including laughter is selectively detected from audio lifelog data recorded based on a wearable microphone using a deep learning-based audio extraction model. Such detected voices are visualized on the map with their location and timestamp data on a dedicated smartphone application. Voice data includes the conversation before and after the timing of the laugh. Therefore, a user can then review his/her past positive events with laughter by using this application. The user can also play the corresponding voice data by selecting the data on the map. By using this system, users can review the recorded voice data to recall where and why they laughed. In this study, a prototype system was developed to enable recording the voice data before and after laughter and its location. According to the proposed method, the prototype system contain functions collecting pleasant experience with laughter and visualizing them as a map on the smartphone application. By using this implementation, we evaluated the effectiveness of presenting past laughter experiences in the form of a map.

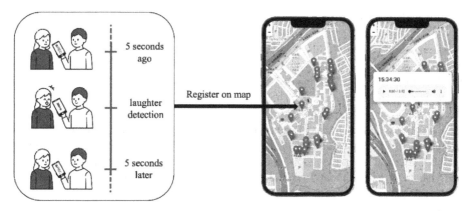

Fig. 1. Overview of the proposed system

2   Related Research

Studies on lifelogging technology have been conducted to record daily events [6]. For example, Nakashima et al. used a small camera attached to the body to record daily events [7]. A major feature of lifelogging is that information about experiences outside of the user's conscious mind can be recorded. Thus, this method can be used to obtain information of unconscious pleasant experiences in daily life. However, because existing lifelogging methods assume that all daily activities are recorded, considerable information is accumulated. Therefore, developing a method for extracting the necessary information from the log data based on the purpose of use is critical. This approach is also the same from the perspective of supporting memory recall, which is the focus of this study. In this study, we considered using the "laughing sound" information as a trigger to encourage the recall of pleasant memories in daily activities based on information from voice-related lifelogging.

Numerous studies have been conducted on information systems that aim to promote laughter by focusing on its effects. Fushimi et al. proposed a camera system that captures natural smiles by inducing laughter through the presentation of laughter sounds [8]. They found that using children's laughter as the shutter sound when capturing pictures elicited laughter from the filmed subjects. Tsujita et al. [9] revealed that the mechanism for inducing intentional smiles can improve emotional state and encourage smiling. The results of these studies revealed that such mechanisms that trigger new experiences with laughter can trigger positive emotions. In the proposed method, laughter is used as a trigger to explore pleasant memories unconsciously experienced during everyday activities. In daily life, unconscious laughter can occur when experiencing positive events. In the proposed method, the aggregation of pleasant memory information related to laughter from life records is realized by using such laughter as a clue. This study expects that whether experiences that are not clearly recognized as being pleasant in the individual's mind can be re-examined as "that time was fun" when the voice data with the laughter sound and its recorded time are presented. In this approach, the method of unconventional thinking about memories using actual event log information is yet to be studied comprehensively in the engineering domain.

3 Prototype System

In this paper, a voice-based lifelogging method, namely "Laughter Map," is proposed. The proposed method detects the user's voice reflective of pleasant experiences with laughter from recorded audio and visualizes the locations and timestamps for detected voice data on an electronic map. The voice data includes conversation before and after the timing of the laugh which is extracted from audio lifelog data recorded in daily life.

The prototype system based on the proposed method was implemented to verify the usefulness of the proposal. This prototype contains the core elements of the proposed method: voice and location recording, detection of laughter based on the recorded data, and visualization in the map format. In this section, the prototype system is introduced.

The prototype system consists of three components: a recording PC and microphone for recording audio and location data simultaneously, a smartphone for retrieving GPS location data (we used the Apple iPhone SE 2nd generation in this prototype system), and a processing PC with GPU for processing audio and generating the information view to the user. Software for this system was implemented using Python 3.11.1 and ran continuously while the system was running. This software is categorized into three main parts: the information processing part that obtains audio and location data, the audio extraction part that detects laughter from the acquired voice data, and the information presenting part that creates a display content for visualizing the audio and location data. (Fig. 2.)

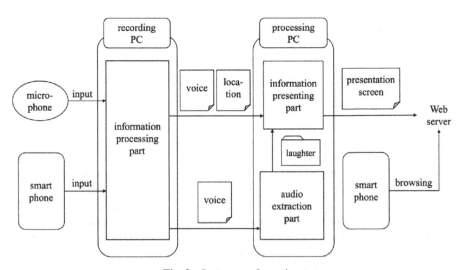

Fig. 2. System configuration

In the information processing part, the program acquires both voice and location data from user. The program consists of two functions; a voice recording function from a microphone connected to a PC, and a location acquisition function from a smartphone. The voice recording function always records audio and writes the acquired audio data as a WAV file through a recording process. For implementing the recording and saving process, PyAudio library is used. The location acquisition function is used for retrieving GPS location from the smartphone and records it to the recording PC. The PyiCloud library is used to acquire the GPS location from the smartphone. This library can acquire information on iOS devices managed on iCloud using a Python script, and the library function can refer to the location data uploaded to the personal account on iCloud from the iOS device. Furthermore, the acquisition process of voice data and location is designed to be performed in parallel. During program execution, the latitude and longitude information and the time at which that information is acquired are recorded to a text file continuously.

In the audio extraction part, a deep learning-based voice extraction model is used to detect laughter from the source audio. This model has been created based on the implementation of the method published by Gillick et al. on GitHub [10]. When using this method, some modifications have been made to the distributed sample program to include not only the laughing part but also the preceding and following 5 s in the extracted data to grasp the context of the laughter. The extracted voice is recorded on the system along with its timestamp and used for presentation.

The part information presenting dynamically generates an HTML file based on the voice files and location obtained by the information processing and audio extraction parts. Corresponding to the comparison conditions in the experiments, we have implemented three display options on voice the system for presenting data:

- Screen displays of the past complete recorded audio file (Fig. 3 (a)).
- Screen displays a list of extracted voice data before and after laughter in chronological order (Fig. 3 (b)).
- Screen displays extracted voice data before and after laughter and their location of occurrence as a map (Fig. 3 (c)).

The first screen displays all recorded information. The screen contains the raw recorded file obtained from the information processing part, its timestamp, the button to play the audio file and a seek bar for adjusting the playback location (Fig. 3(a)). In this screen, users can play and seek through the entire audio file.

The second screen displays a list of laughter in chronological order. The screen shows audio files with laughter voice with audio from 5 s before and after the extraction unit as the list format. (Fig. 3 (b)). In this screen, users can play and seek for each audio files with laughter.

The last screen displays laughter information in the map format. This screen corresponds to the proposed method. In this screen, the laughter extracted from the audio extraction part and the location data obtained from the information processing part are linked and displayed as pins on a map. The display contains a map and pins are placed at the location of laughter. When tapping the pin, users can check the time of laughter and play and seek the corresponding audio file (Fig. 3 (c)).

The first screen provides the raw audio file before extracting, while the second and third screens selectively extract and present only the voice data containing laughter. In this respect, there are differences in the information provided on each screen.

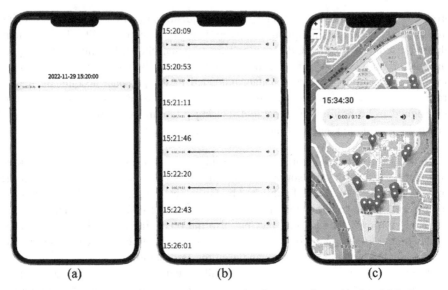

Fig. 3. Example of views corresponding to each option for presenting voice data (a) Left: screen that displays all recording information (b) Center: screen that displays a list of laughter experience chronologically (c) Right: screen that displays laughter experience on a map

4 Experiment

4.1 Experimental Purpose and Hypothesis

This study aims to examine the effectiveness of the proposed "Laughter Map" method in evoking memories and whether the presence of laughter experiences in the map format changes the content remembered when recalling experiences. Thus, an experiment was conducted in which users were asked to use the prototype system and recall their memories. In this experiment, the following hypothesis was tested:

- If past laughter experiences are presented in a map format, where voice data before and after laughter are shown at locations of laughter occurrence, the number of recalled memories increases compared with when they are presented in a list chronologically.

The motivation for setting this hypothesis is that by presenting the voice data of the laughter experience and adding location data, it is expected that the scene of the experience can be easily imagined and recalled. The image of the scene reminded from the location data is expected to become an additional element for enhancing to recall the event and more content will be recalled.

4.2 Experimental Settings

In the experiment, twenty students (10 pairs of two students, 10 men, and 10 women) from the authors' university participated. The experiment was designed as a continuous two-day experiment to realize the environment of creating and recalling laughter memories.

On the first day, participants were asked to take a walk on the campus of the university for 30 min. On the second day, participants were asked to visit the experiment room one by one to recall their experiences on the first day. The participants asked to review the contents of the experience on the first day using four review methods. Then, in each trial, participants were asked about how much content they remembered and their impression of the system through interviews and questionnaire-based surveys.

Table 1 details the four review methods used in this experiment. The first method is under the condition in which no information regarding the content of the previous day's experience is provided to participants (null condition). The second method is under the condition presenting all recorded audio through the screen of the smartphone as described in Fig. 3(a) (all condition). The trials of these two conditions are conducted sequentially in the first part of the experiment. After these two trials, participants experienced the systems under the other two conditions: the List condition and the Map condition. The method is under the list condition presents voice data clipped before and after laughter in chronological order (Fig. 3(b)). On the other hand, in the map condition, the system presents voice data clipped before and after the laughter on a map (Fig. 3(c)). The order for experiencing the list and map conditions was set differently for each participant for the evaluation to account for order bias.

Table 1. Comparison conditions

Conditions	Presented information
(0) Null condition	No information presented
(1) All condition	Present all recorded voice data (Fig. 3.(a))
(2) List condition	Present voice data extracted before and after the laughter in the chronological order (Fig. 3.(b))
(3) Map condition	Present voice data extracted before and after the laughter on a map (Fig. 3.(c))

4.3 Evaluation Item

On the second day, participants were asked to reflect on the experience and provide feedback through an interview and a questionnaire. The questionnaire (Table 2) was based on the subjective characteristic questionnaire of autobiographical memory by Sekiguchi et al. [11], excluding questions about the recall of events not experienced during the experiment (e.g., "Do you feel as if the texture and sensation of your skin are coming back?"). The participants were instructed "For each question, please answer what you recall about using this system." before answering the questionnaire. They rated each question listed in Table 2 on a five-point Likert scale, with a score of one indicating "not at all applicable" and a score of five indicating "extremely applicable." Additionally, Q8 and Q9 were included to evaluate the usefulness of the proposed interface design. Interview questions are listed in Table 3.

Table 2. Questionnaire items

No	Question content
Q1	I can recall many points and narrate them in detail
Q2	I can only recall the general details because I cannot recall fine details regarding the time and contents
Q3	The emotion is very negative
Q4	The emotion is very positive
Q5	I feel as if I am watching the event just now
Q6	I am feeling the same kind of emotions as when I experienced the event
Q7	I can recall the event one after another
Q8	I can use the system intuitively
Q9	I think the system is easy to review the past events

Table 3. Interview items

Presented information	Interview content
(1) Null condition	– Now tell me about what you remember happening yesterday when you were walking around the campus and the content of the conversation – Is there anything else you recall?
(2) All condition (3) List condition (4) Map condition	– Now, please tell me what you have recalled using the system regarding what you remember happening yesterday when you were walking around the campus and the content of the conversation – Is there anything else you recall?

4.4 Procedure

The experiment was conducted over two consecutive days. The participants were categorized into pairs and instructed to gather in the laboratory on the first day. These participant pairs are arranged to be composed by their close friends. On the first day, we carefully explained to the participants that the experiment would involve voice recording and obtained their consent to participate in the study before the experiment. The participants were then asked to walk around the campus of the university in pairs. To induce conversation between the participants, five conversation cards, were distributed. These cards were obtained from a civil product card game ("Do you know me?" Japanese edition (CONSTELLAR JAPAN Co., Ltd.)), and the participants were asked to select five cards at random. The conversation cards were freely used by the participants as they walked around the campus of the university. After choosing the conversation cards, each of the participant pair was equipped with a wearable microphone, a laptop PC, and a smartphone for recording the conversation. The pair were then asked to walk along the pre-prepared campus course, an approximately thirty-minute walk.

On the second day, the participants were to come to the laboratory one by one and asked to recall the experience of the first day without any prior information (null condition described in Sect. 4.2). Based on the interview content in Table 3, we queried them on their recollection of the conversation. First, the interview was conducted by asking the participants questions; after the interview, we requested them to answer the questionnaire items in Table 2.

We then asked them to review the recorded voice using the three different interfaces (Fig. 3.) and recall their experience. The recall task was conducted three times; all conditions were conducted as the first review, and the list and map conditions described in Sect. 4.2 were followed. The order of the list and map conditions differed for each participant. Participants were provided 5 min to review voice data using each system and were instructed to actively note their recollection. After each experience, an interview (Table 3.) was conducted. During the interview, they were allowed to reference their notes. The second to fourth interviews asked about the contents recalled during system use. After each interview, participants answered a questionnaire (Table 2.). All interviews were recorded and transcribed into text after the experiment, and the results were compared by evaluating the total number of characters and words related to the description of the scene about recalled contents, for each presentation pattern.

5   Results

5.1   Questionnaire Results

In this section, we describe the results of the questionnaires asked in each trial of the experiment. Table 4. Presents the results of the questionnaire listed in Table 2 answered during the recall of the second day of the 2-day experiment. For questions, questions Q5 and Q6 are items that ask about the degree of negative feelings, and the closer the answer is to 1, the more positive the result.

Table 4. Questionnaire results (**: $p < 0.05$, *: $p < 0.10$)

No.	All condition		List condition		Map condition		p value
	Mean	SD	Mean	SD	Mean	SD	
Q1	3.80	0.87	3.80	1.08	4.10	0.89	0.54
Q2	2.45	1.02	2.75	1.13	2.00	0.84	**0.08***
Q3	1.80	0.98	1.80	0.87	1.50	0.67	0.46
Q4	4.05	0.86	4.25	0.77	4.45	0.67	0.29
Q5	3.75	1.18	3.35	1.24	4.00	0.89	0.20
Q6	3.85	1.28	3.50	1.20	4.30	0.95	0.11
Q7	4.15	0.96	3.90	1.04	4.30	0.71	0.40
Q8	3.95	0.97	4.20	0.81	4.65	0.57	**0.03****
Q9	4.25	1.30	3.90	1.14	4.65	0.48	**0.09***

Table 5. Mean number of recalled characters and t-test results for the no recall (null condition) in the list and map conditions.

	Mean	SD	p value
List condition	1.74	2.59	6.65×10^{-4}
Map condition	2.39	3.55	

The results of questions Q1 to Q7, which asked about the impression of memories recalled, were analyzed using one-way analysis of variance. From the results, a marginally significant trend was confirmed for Q2, which asked about the detailedness of recalled situations ($p < 0.10$). In addition, multiple comparisons based on the Bonferroni method revealed a marginally significant difference in the mean values between the list-map conditions ($p < 0.10$). This result suggests that in the map condition, presenting the location data of laughter experiences could support recalling detailed memories of past enjoyable events because the location data are associated with the laughter experience.

From this point on, we describe the trend of the results from other questions based on the difference between the mean values. In Q1, the average values for all and list conditions were the same, but the highest average value was in the map condition. This is believed to be because the addition of location data made it easier to imagine the past scenario. In Q3 and Q4, participants were asked about their degree of negative and positive emotions during recall, respectively. In Q3, the average values for all and list conditions were the same, and the lowest average value was found in the map condition. In Q4, the average value was the highest in the map condition compared with the list and all conditions. Thus, although no significant trend was identified, the results suggest that participants had more positive emotions when recalling in the map condition than when recalling in other situations. For Q5, Q6, and Q7, the average values were the highest in the map condition compared with all and list conditions. From these results, it is considered to be that presenting the information in map form made the concrete scenario easier to imagine and increased its reproducibility, acting as a trigger for recalling additional events.

In terms of the interface, the results of corresponding questions Q8 and Q9 suggests the effectiveness of the map-type visualization. In Q8 about intuitively of the system, the difference in average values between all and map conditions was significant ($p < 0.05$). In addition, a significant trend ($p < 0.10$) is observed in the difference in average values between the list and map conditions in Q9 about easiness of the system. This suggests the possibility that presenting information in map form is an effective interface to recall of the past laughter experiences.

5.2   Interview Results

To verify the hypothesis of the study described in Sect. 4.1, we counted the number of characters in the interview responses of the second day's experiment and analyzing it as a recall quantity. By looking at the differences in the mention related to recall between the presentation method, it is possible to quantitatively understand the degree to which each presentation method contributes to memory recall. However, However, the number of characters in the interview responses is expected to vary depending on the personalities of the individuals (i.e., participants who talk a lot and participants who do not talk much); simply comparing the size of the number of characters cannot provide a comparison considering the difference in the number of words spoken by each participant. Therefore, the number of characters in the null condition was considered the basic number of characters when the participant spoke, and the ratio of the number of characters in the list and map conditions to the number of characters in the null condition was used as an indicator for analysis. The average value and variance of the ratios of recalled characters to the number of characters in the null condition (no information) are presented in Table 5. For the list and map conditions. The t-test was performed to examine the difference in the ratios between the list and map conditions, and a significant difference was confirmed ($p < 0.01$). This phenomenon indicates that the information provided in the map condition may be able to promote recall memory better than the information provided in the list condition.

One possible reason for the significant increase in participants' mentions during recall in the map condition is that the image of the scene complemented by the location data may have been an additional factor for recalling events and facilitate to enhance the recall. To verify this possibility, an analysis focused on the content of participants' responses regarding location in the interviews. Morphological analysis was performed on the interview responses to extract noun expressions. RMeCab was used for this extraction process. Then, focusing on the list and map conditions, only words related to the scene were extracted; these words are shown in Table 6. For 12 people (a, b, c, e, g, l, m, n, o, p, q, s), the number of words regarding the scene was greater in the map condition than in the list condition. For three people (h, j, s), the number of words was greater in the list condition than in the map condition. Based on these results, it can be concluded that the information provided in the map condition may have led to the recall of more scene-related words compared with the information provided in the list condition.

Table 6. Extracted words describing a scene from interview. In the table, "Act," "Creation-core," "Co-learning," "BKC" denote the names of university facilities located near the walking route of the experiment.

ID	List condition	Map condition
a	such a place	here, this way
b		over there, this way
c		road, shortcut
d		
e		stairs, place, here, door
f		

(*continued*)

Table 6. (*continued*)

ID	List condition	Map condition
g	Act	prefab, lower floor
h	playground, behind	building
i		
j	Building, Creation-core	
k		
l		road
m	elevator	In front of the gym, the location
n	laboratory, next laboratory	elevator, behind the Co-learning, this way
o		BKC, road
p		laboratory, tree in the back, Act
q		road, original path
r		
s		road of liberal arts
t		

5.3 Discussion

From the results of counting the number of letters when the participants were asked to recall events in the interview of the experiment, the number of letters was considerably higher when in the condition with laughter experiences presented in a map format than when they were presented in a chronological order. The results of the study supported the hypothesis that "presenting past laughter experiences information in a map format, where voice data before and after laughter are shown at locations the laughter occurred, will increase recall of the content compared to presenting them chronologically." Additionally, the results from the questionnaire, particularly Q2, revealed a significant trend toward an easy recall of events in the map condition, which implied that more detailed memories can be recalled when information is linked to location. Furthermore, the results of the other questions about recall content revealed that the mean values for the map condition were higher compared with the list condition, which consists with the main idea of the hypothesis.

The results for the interface, as seen in questions Q8 and Q9, also revealed that the map condition exhibited higher mean values compared with the list condition and a significant trend between the two conditions, which indicated that our proposed concept,

"Laughter Map" application has an effective interface compared with the chronological presentation of laughter experiences.

6 Conclusions

In this study, we proposed the voice-based lifelogging application "Laughter Map," which accumulates information of situations of laughter occurrence in the user's life and allows for recalling the past positive events with laughter in the form of a map on a mobile device. To verify the usefulness of conveying past laughter experience in a map format, an experiment was conducted to compare it to the list format. The results revealed that presenting past laughter experience in a map format increased the amount of recall compared to presenting it in a list chronologically. Furthermore, they indicated that the use of the proposed method could potentially encourage detailed recall. In the future, we will investigate whether the use of "Laughter Map" leads to the recall of pleasant experiences and positive emotions and whether long-term use can lead to a happy daily life.

Acknowledgement. This work was supported in part by the Ritsumeikan Global Innovation Research Organization (R-GIRO), Ritsumeikan University.

References

1. Institute for Health Metrics and Evaluation, https://vizhub.healthdata.org/gbd-results/?par ams=gbd-api-2019-permalink/d780dffbe8a381b25e1416884959e88b (2023). Accessed 10 Feb 2023
2. World Health Organization, https://www.who.int/publications/i/item/WHO-2019-nCoV-Sci_Brief-Mental_health-2022.1 (2023). Accessed 10 Feb 2023
3. Taniguchi, T.: Mood congruent effects and mood state dependent effects on cognition. Japanese Psychol. Rev. **34**(3), 319–344 (1991)
4. Erber, R., Erber, M.W.: Beyond mood and social judgment: mood incongruent recall and mood regulation. Eur. J. Soc. Psychol. **24**(1), 79–88 (1994)
5. De Shazer, S., Dolan, Y., Korman, H., Trepper, T., McCollum, E., Berg, I.K.: More Then Miracles: The State of the Art of Solution-Focused Brief Therapy, 2nd edn. Routledge, New York (2021)
6. Ribeiro, R., Trifan, A., Neves, A.J.: Lifelog retrieval from daily digital data: narrative review. JMIR Mhealth Uhealth **10**(5), e30517 (2022)
7. Kinoshita, E., Fujinami, K.: Impressive picture Selection from wearable camera toward pleasurable recall of group activities. In: Antona, M., Stephanidis, C. (eds.) UAHCI 2017. LNCS, vol. 10279, pp. 446–456. Springer, Cham (2017). https://doi.org/10.1007/978-3-319-58700-4_36
8. Fushimi, R., Fukushima, S., Naemura, T.: Laughin'Cam: active camera system to induce natural smiles. In: CHI'15 Extended Abstracts on Human Factors in Computing Systems, pp. 1959–1964, CHI EA'15, Assoc. Comput. Mach. New York, NY, USA (2015)
9. Tsujita, H., Rekimoto, J.: Smiling makes us happier: enhancing positive mood and communication with smile-encouraging digital appliances. In: Proceedings of the 13th International Conference on Ubiquitous Computing, pp.1–10, UbiComp'11, Assoc. Comput. Mach. New York, NY, USA (2011)

10. Gillick, J., Deng, W., Ryokai, K., Bamman, D.: Robust laughter detection in noisy environments. In: INTERSPEECH 2021, pp. 2481–2485. ISCA, Brno (2021)
11. Sekiguchi, R.: Relationship between subjective properties associated with remembering auto-biographical episodic memories, and emotion: Investigation by the subjective properties questionnaire of autobiographical memory. Kansai Univ. Psychol. Res. **3**, 15–26 (2012). (in Japanese)

In Technology We Trust! But Should We?

Arianna Sica$^{(\boxtimes)}$ ⬤ and Henrik Skaug Sætra ⬤

Østfold University College, Remmen, 1757 Halden, Norway
`Arianna.sica@hiof.no`

Abstract. Can trust be meaningfully attributed to technology? If so, under which conditions? By first presenting a conceptual analysis of trust, which differentiates between reliability and affective trust, we explore these intentionally broad questions through the analysis of the specific case of trusting social robots equipped with artificial emotional intelligence. Given their emotional capacities, which arguably strengthen the potential for deception, AEI social robots are considered the most likely candidates for experiencing trust-like attitudes towards technology. Determining whether, and what kind of, trust applies to relationships between humans and such robots will, we argue, be useful for determining what sort of trust can meaningfully be applied to human-technology interactions more broadly. This novel approach to the issue of trust in technology is underexplored in human-technology interaction, and the results presented will enable designers, citizens, and politicians to make better informed decisions regarding AEI social robots' development.

Keywords: Trust · social robots · artificial emotional intelligence

1 Introduction

In a society where we increasingly rely on algorithmic decision systems for a wide and growing range of activities, questions regarding whether we can and should trust these technologies have emerged. To what degree can we trust machines? And can we answer this question in general, or must we consider what sort of machines we encounter? The issue of trust in technology is particularly important given the direct impact this might have on the acceptance and use of the technology at stake (Freedy et al., 2007; Lankton, McKnight & Tripp, 2015; Glikson & Woolley, 2020). Furthermore, it has been argued that technology has the potential to interfere with trust, a central value in human society (Sætra, 2021a). A discussion which establishes whether human-technology interactions involve trust is therefore crucial for understanding the potential implications, such as moral value changes (Danaher & Sætra, 2022), which such relationships with technology entail.

Broadly speaking, trust in technology is defined as the willingness to depend on a given technology, in a specific context, where risk is involved, and potential negative consequences are possible (McKnight, Carter & Clay, 2009). However, we claim that a more specific definition of trust, and a clarification of how this concept is applicable

M. Kurosu and A. Hashizume (Eds.): HCII 2023, LNCS 14012, pp. 293–317, 2023.
https://doi.org/10.1007/978-3-031-35599-8_19

in the context of technology, is needed for an adequate assessment of the questions mentioned above. This article explores the concept of trust and its use in both the fields of traditional social sciences and human-technology interaction. We argue that to preserve trust as a meaningful concept, it beneficial to develop an interdisciplinary approach to the trust, enabling research on the topic to become more integrated and comparable across different fields of study. Such an assessment of trust and the related factors determining its establishment has significant consequences on the analysis of how people can and should develop trust in technologies.

We argue that if trust is a mere rational assessment of likelihood that another entity will act as we want it to, trust and *reliance* is conflated. These concepts can, however, be argued to differ significantly, and should be distinguished from each other. Furthermore, when trust is distinguished from reliance, we advance that it *does* make a difference what sort of machine are analysed. In particular, we stress the role of emotions, while highlighting how this brings us to a new dilemma as anthropomorphism and the discussion on whether machines *can* have emotions will generate disagreement regarding whether, for example, social robots with artificial emotional intelligence (AEI) could be the recipients ttrust proper.

In light of this, we choose AEI social robots as a specific case study of trust in technology. Evidence suggests that a feeling of trust towards these systems is formed more easily and spontaneously than towards other technologies. Given their characterising and specific features, these systems can express emotional, and human-like behaviours and expressions which potentially provoke emotional attachment and form attitudes of affective trust in the user. We consider whether such characteristics are relevant to justify the claim that we trust these systems. If our analysis leads to the conclusion that AEI enabled social robots' capabilities are not sufficient for a relational account of trust to be meaningfully involved in human-robot interactions, then we could argue that the same applies for technology in general.

This article is structured as follows. In Sect. 2, we present a conceptual analysis of the notion of trust and introduce two terms to emphasise the distinction between reliability and trust: namely, rationality-trust on one side, and affective trust on the other. In Sect. 3, we explore how trust is and can be used in the context of technology, questioning the possibility of affective trust in technology. Section 4 introduces AEI and social robotic technologies and considers whether the impact of their emotional and human-like capabilities on affective trust. Namely, could we claim that the AEI social robot's capabilities are enough not only to facilitate, but also to warrant trust?

Finally, Sect. 5 addresses this latter question. Despite the emotional attachment that may be formed with these systems, we argue that the synthetic nature of AEI social robots is morally relevant for the assessment of whether people should place trust in them. Namely, AEI social robots are tools designed for purposes potentially different or in conflict with the ones of their users. Although people may develop a feeling of trust towards these robots, granting trust proper in AEI social robots, and technology in general, is not morally warranted.

2   What is Trust?

Before diving into the specific issues related to trust and technology, we explore what lies in the concept of trust more broadly. How is trust used to understand the relationships between humans, what components does it consist of, and what separates it from, for example, reliability? In this section, we present different understandings of trust, before advancing our suggested use of the term.

Some authors define trust as a cognitive construct based on a rational evaluation of the trustee's ability to perform a particular job effectively, and situational features (Coleman, 1990; Kim et al., 2004; Kim, et al., 2006; Ferrin et al., 2007. Glikson & Woolley, 2020). Nickel, Franssen and Kroes (2010) presents one definition of trust derived from rational-choice theory and Coleman (1990), in which trust is conceptualised as:

> a judgement one makes when, having considered the possible costs and benefits of relying on another person's performance, as well as the salient alternatives, one comes to the conclusion that it is worth it to rely on that performance.

However, and as the authors themselves note, such an account of trust does not differ fundamentally from mere rational reliance (Nickel, Franssen & Kroes, 2010). While they include "person" in the definition, such forms of rationality-trust could arguably also apply to our evaluation of, for example, our toaster or coffee maker. The emotional aspects of the relationship with the trustee are of secondary importance or entirely omitted from trust-considerations.

Others present a different, and arguably more comprehensive, conception of trust with respect to interpersonal relationships (Lewicky & Bunker, 1995, Rousseau et al., 1998, Levine & Schweitzer, 2015, Sætra, 2021b, Aroyo et al., 2021). Rousseau et al. (1998), for example, define trust as.

> a psychological state comprising the intention to accept vulnerability based upon positive expectations of the intentions or behaviour of another.

This conceptualization of trust is based on both rational and emotional elements. As Rossi et al. (2020) argue, interpersonal trust is developed on the basis of rational factors which allow us "to access the reliability of actions and behaviours", and by affective factors which establish emotional bonds and increase "the expectation in which the involved agents invest in a common goal". Along the same line, Koyama (2016) emphasises the role of emotions in trust relationships by defining trust as an "affective attitude" which has the expectation that the other's "goodwill and competence [...] will extend to cover the domain of our interaction with" them, and that the trustee will be "directly and favorably moved by the thought that we are counting on" them. Accordingly, the emotional relationship among the trustor and the trustee "does not guarantee but provide a reason why the trustee's actions will be performed" (Koyama, 2016).

Similarly, Glikson and Woolley (2020), following McAllister's analysis (1995), address emotion-driven or affect-based trust in interpersonal relationships. They suggest that the emotional ties connecting individuals can provide a partial basis for trust based instead on an impression of the trustee's reliance and competence, and this can be seen as complementary to rational trust,

According to these discussions, researchers have individuated specific rational and emotional antecedents which help to build the foundation for the development of interpersonal trust; namely, characteristics of a trustee conducive to the generation of trust in the trustor. These are benevolence, integrity, and ability (Mayer, Davis & Schoorman, 1995; Lankton, McKnight & Tripp, 2015; Levine & Schweitzer, 2015; Glikson and Woolley, 2020). Benevolence is the degree to which an individual "is believed to want to do good to the trustor, aside from an egocentric profit motive", suggesting that the trustee has some particular attachment to the trustor (Mayer, Davis & Schoorman, 1995). Integrity corresponds to an individual's ethicality and reputation for honesty, and the belief that she adheres to a set of principles that the trustor finds adequate (Mayer, Davis & Schoorman, 1995). Finally, ability relates to an individual's technical skills, competence, and expertise in a specific context (Mayer, Davis & Schoorman, 1995), which supports the belief that the trustee *can* – in the meaning "is able to" – do what the trustor needs (McKnight, Carter & Clay., 2009).

It is key to notice that what is referred to as ability-based trust is closely linked to the rational evaluation of expected performance in a specific situation, which takes us back to reliance (see Table 1). We might, for example, ask whether a person that expresses both benevolent intents and honesty can still be generally considered trustworthy even if they lack the ability to perform what the trustor expects from them. As Mayer, Davis and Schoorman (1995) argue, the trustee's ability is relative to the required task to perform. The trustee might be "highly competent in some technical area, affording that person trust on tasks related to that area", however she might have "little aptitude, training, or experience in another area" (Mayer, Davis & Schoorman, 1995). Therefore, ability-based trust is domain specific. Benevolence and integrity, however, refer to the nature of the trustee more generally. We might expect, therefore, that in a situation where the trustee lacks the required skills and techniques for carrying out a specific task, she does not necessarily become untrustworthy in the eye of the trustor[1]. This latter might maintain the belief that she would act as expected if she had the necessary abilities, given that she possesses both the antecedents of benevolence and integrity. Rather, by lacking ability, she would be considered unreliable for that specific task. Considering this, it is essential to maintain a conceptual difference between reliability and trust based solely on benevolence and integrity, which we refer to as affective trust. As we will discuss in the following, affective trust is the most challenging in the context of in technology, as benevolence and integrity refer to qualities that many machines arguably do not, or even cannot, have. For this reason, in the remaining discussion, this article will focus specifically on affective trust.

Furthermore, we argue in favour of a universal definition of trust that is applicable across academic disciplines, and different types of human-x-relationships. By using

---

[1] Trustworthiness and trust are two interconnected however categorically distinct concepts (Nickel, Franssen & Kroes, 2010). Hardin (2006) argues that there is a casual connection between the two, as "trustworthiness begets trust". Whereas trust is usually considered an attitude, trustworthiness is a property of the trustee which satisfies and makes appropriate the attitude of trusting (Nickel, Franssen & Kroes, 2010).

trust in the same way when discussing, for example, human-human and human-robot relationships, we can avoid situations in which the same term is used to refer to a very different set of phenomena. Firstly, this allows us to distinguish between trust and reliance, and consequently allows for more conceptual clarity and helps preserve the usefulness of both terms. Secondly, such usage of the term is arguably more in line with everyday understandings of the concept, and it better promotes inter-disciplinary research, as both human-human interaction scholars and HRI scholars will to a larger degree refer to a similar phenomenon.

Table 1. Ability, benevolence, and integrity-based trust.

Trust-dimension	Refers to the trustee's…	Universality	Relies on	Relates to
Ability	…capacity or capability for performing particular actions	Domain-specific	Capabilities	Reliability
Benevolence	…desire to do good to others, including the trustor	Universal	"Goodness"	Goodness
Integrity	…honour, likelihood of abiding by their promises and proclivity to act in accordance with accepted principles	Partly universal, partly domain-specific	Intentions and principles	Principledness

3   Trust in Technology

Moving on from the general concept of trust, we explore how trust is and can be used when discussing human interaction with technology.

Lee and See's (2004) seminal article on trust in automation is often used in research on trust in various forms of technology, and they define trust as: "the attitude that an agent will help achieve an individual's goals in a situation characterized by uncertainty and vulnerability." Others working on trust in HRI often explicitly build on this definition, such as Wagner (2009), who define trust as "a belief, held by the trustor, that the trustee will act in a manner that mitigates the trustor's risk in a situation in which the trustor has put its outcomes at risk." The concept of trust is routinely used in settings in which humans interact with non-human entities, but we see from these examples that the conceptualization of trust is not necessarily integrated with the more comprehensive conceptualizations referred to in the previous section. Extant research, especially from the discipline of philosophy, expresses some reservations about "trust in technology", by defending the view that the notion of affective trust is misguided and unsuitable for ethical considerations in such a context (Friedman, Kahn & Howe, 2000; Sebastian & Feiten, 2021). The trustee's characteristics for trust to be formed include "possessing moral integrity; being capable of fulfilling one's moral obligation; actually caring about the interests of the truster; or, recognizing and responding positively to the very fact that one is being relied upon" (Nickel, Franssen & Kroes, 2010). Along the same lines, Friedman Kahn and Howe (2000) argue that entities involved in a trust relationship must possess agency and consciousness, which enable them "to express good will, extend benevolence towards others, feel vulnerable, and feel betrayed when their trust is misplaced". Such consideration could also help explain why HRI researchers seem to be referring to a somewhat different foundational concept when using the term "trust" than what is often the case in interpersonal relationships.

When discussing agency, consciousness, capability for moral agency, etc., we are talking about abilities in the form of *properties*, and these are very different from evaluations of benevolence and integrity, which arguably only make sense if the potential trustee has such required properties. We thus propose a tentative distinction in which properties-based trust is considered foundational, whereas the two latter are second-level concerns only applicable when the first level is satisfied, as shown in Fig. 1. The reason we use properties instead of abilities is that the original use of ability-based trust (Mayer, Davis & Schoorman, 1995) mainly referred to abilities relevant for reliance-based considerations of performance.

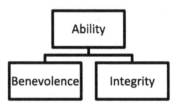

Fig. 1.   First and second-level antecedents for trust.

Some might argue that such properties are only possessed by humans and conclude that any inanimate object, including technological artifacts, can never be benevolent and honest, and therefore genuine object of trust but of mere reliability (Nickel, Franssen & Kroes, 2010; Sweeney, 2022). However, as artificial intelligence (AI) and robotics keep developing, this is increasingly being disputed. Indeed, recent development in social robotics has allowed designers to develop a kind of technology which can act like humans or living entities and establish interactions with the user on an emotional level. Research has shown that the distinguishing element of human-likeness possessed by a given technology can influence the kind of antecedents of trust developed, and consequently the conception of trust which best applies to the situation (Lankton, McKnight & Tripp, 2015). On the one hand, systems that show low human-likeness are more likely to elicit rationality-trust based on reliability, functionality, and helpfulness. On the other hand, when the technology shows high levels of human-likeness, the user might inevitably invoke constructs such as the above-mentioned integrity and benevolence to assess whether the given technology can be trusted, suggesting the possibility of experiencing human-like trust.

Designers of social robots specifically aim to build systems which elicit a feeling of trust in the user, as trust is a fundamental key factor for enabling successful cooperation and maintaining effective relationships between people and robots over time (Hancock et al., 2011; Billings et al., 2012; Broadbent, 2017; Gompei & Umemuro, 2018; Lum, 2020; Rossi et al., 2020; Prescott & Robillard, 2020). By providing not only physical help, but also emotional support, it is beneficial for social robots to be perceived as safe and trustworthy entities (Song & Luximon, 2020). Trust directly affects the willingness of people to accept information provided by robots, follow robots' suggestions, and thus benefit from the advantages inherent in robotic systems (Freedy et al., 2007; Hancock et al., 2011; Glikson & Woolley, 2020). This is because, as Song and Luximon (2020) affirm and we have previously mentioned, trust in social contexts has a significant impact on persuasion and could directly influence people's intention to follow others' suggestions.

Whereas the robot's reliability certainly plays a crucial role, developers also specifically target human emotions in the design of social robots for trust to be formed (Glikson & Woolley, 2020). As we will argue in the next sections, developing trust attitudes through emotional attachment towards the robot has the potential to allow users to access increased societal benefits from their engagement with robots (Sweeney, 2021). People's trust in robots is likely to be affected by their perception of the robot's capabilities which might depend on human-related and robot-related factors. For example, people's trust might be affected by the robot's appearance, its level of autonomy, and functionalities. It may also be influenced by user's personalities, self-confidence, and prior experience with robots. However, as we will explain below, trust-generation based on perceived benevolence and integrity, and perceived agency in machines, largely result from non-rational and non-conscious mechanisms. This helps explain why humans might self-report trust in a robot, for example, even if these could be objectively argued to be incapable of benevolence and integrity.

To sum up, authors generally agree that technology can be reliable. The possibility for the establishment of affective trust, however, is more controversial and often rejected. Nonetheless, some empirical research has proved that possessing human-like features for a specific technology marks a concrete difference in how the user perceives it and develops trust attitudes accordingly. This is shown both in self-reported trust and in human behaviour (Robinette, Howard & Wagner, 2017), but we have also seen that HRI conceptualisations of trust might not include all parts of the comprehensive concept and could be argued to mainly capture reliance. In light of this, social robots might represent an unprecedent and interesting case for the discussion about trust in technology. This brings us to the analysis of the specific case of AEI social robots, which are presented in the following section.

4   Social Robots with Artificial Emotional Intelligence

Social robots' specific physical and functional characteristics – their human-likeness – allows them to have the potential to make humans form a feeling of trust towards them. As argued in Plaks, Rodriguez and Ayad's article (2022), people are more inclined to place trust in "others who are similar to themselves on key dimensions". Social robots are consequently the most likely technology-candidates for generating trust-like experiences in humans and potentially forming trust relationships between humans and machines. Hereafter, we describe the technology of social robots and AEI. In the following sections, these systems will be investigated in more detail to identify their specific, characterising factors which distinguish them from other kinds of technologies, and which possibly contribute to develop affective trust in them.

A social robot is a "physically embodied, autonomous agent that communicates and interacts with humans on an emotional level", by following social behaviour patterns, modelling different human-like "states of mind", and adopting what they learn through their interactions (Darling, 2012). Social robots often possess humanoid or animaloid physical configurations. As we will discuss later, their appearance has implications for the effectiveness of HRI, which is based not only in visual communication but also in visual and tactile perception (Campa, 2016). The goal of social robotics is the creation of artificial agents capable of social performances and considered "above the status of instruments to that of interlocutors" in the eye of the user (Damiano & Dumouchel, 2018). In other words, humans prefer to interact with such machines in the same way they interact with other people or other social entities. Differently from inanimate computers, as well as from industrial or service robots, social robots are *designed* to elicit human feelings and mimic social cues. This implies that what we refer to as social robots are not *accidentally* but *intentionally* social, and this excludes a wide range of robots that could potentially trigger social responses in humans despite this not being intended by developers and designers (see, e.g., Scheutz, 2012, for an analysis of user's attachment to their robotic vacuum cleaners, called Roomba).

Emotions have been increasingly used in social robot design, with the aim of making AI more effective and therefore facilitate the establishment of more believable, acceptable, and effective HRI (Fong, Nourbakhsh & Dautenhahn, 2003). The capacity of social robots to cause the users to become attached to them (LaGrandeur, 2015) is expected to be intensified significantly with the implementation of AEI. Schuller and Schuller (2018) define AEI a technology that possesses the ability to "recognize emotions (both of others and oneself), generate and adapt emotions, and apply emotional information in goal accomplishment and problem solving". This new field of studies within AI research finds its greatest potential in developing computers "to be genuinely intelligent and to interact naturally with us" (Picard, 1997). As research has shown, emotional and volitional factors play a significant role in human behaviour, communication, and interaction, and are essential for the effective functioning of human intellect and thinking processes (Damasio, 1994; Lerner et al., 2015). Specifically, emotional intelligence consists in the individual's ability to understand, manage, and adjust accordingly one's own emotions, as well as to correctly interpret others' emotions and respond to their behaviours (Goleman, 1995). As a result, interactions with social robots artificially possessing emotional intelligence could be potentially, easily transformed into a much more intimate and affectionate relationship, consequently exacerbating the possibility of a user to establish an emotional bond and form trust attitudes towards the robot.

Social robots can be differentiated according to the degree of human-likeness and the level of AEI they possess, and therefore to which extent they are perceived as being sociable, warm, and personal (Lankton, McKnight & Tripp, 2015). Also, depending on the social robot's specific task, and the duration and frequency of the interaction, the user's emotional involvement might largely differ. For instance, social robots employed for teaching support necessitate to implement social cues and skills, as well as to appeal to the user's emotional state, to operate effectively. However, given that their use is limited to a few hours per week and mainly in public settings such as school, we might expect a minimum level of emotional engagement and even lower emotional attachment from the user's perspective. On the contrary, social robots intended for more personal or even intimate services, such as companionship, daily healthcare, or sex, are usually employed for a considerably prolonged, daily use, and are expected to form an affective relationship with the user. Indeed, their services work most effectively "when they are perceived as social agents, rather than tools" (Darling, 2017). This latter category is especially relevant for our analysis as it allows us to examine interpersonal trust more specifically. Indeed, the intimate, emotional relationship that this particular kind of social robots aim to establish with the user might possess the required features for human-like trust to be formed.

To summarise, as empirical studies suggest, AI social robotic systems equipped with emotional intelligence further enhance features and attitudes which resemble human ones, and the consequent possibility of trust development. As discussed above, emotions can significantly impact the perception of the antecedents of trust and consequently influence the kind of trust developed in a relationship (Schoorman, Mayer & Davis 2007). As a result, since AEI social robots are intended to interact with humans affectively, it might be assumed that their design implies for humans to develop affective trust. Hence, this case is particularly conducive for our research question, as it allows us to suggest that, if trust does or should not apply in the context of social robots, then it would be even harder to consider the possibility of establishing or experiencing trust towards other kinds of technology. The next section presents more accurately some of the AEI social robot's design characteristics which might strongly impact the user's affective trust attitudes.

4.1   How AEI Social Robots' Features Impact Affective Trust

In this section, we describe some of the specific features of AEI social robots which contribute to develop the user's affective trust. There are anthropomorphism, deception, and emotional attachment[2]. These factors are highlighted because they are tightly

---

[2] It is important to mention that the social robotics' features here presented raise ethical concerns beyond the topic of trust. Authors such as Turkle (2006, 2011) and Scheutz (2012) have expressed their concern about the anthropomorphisation of robotic technology, their deceptive potential, as well as the kind of relationship and unilateral emotional attachment that people would develop with them. However, these moral issues are not the focus of this article, and they will not therefore be addressed unless related to the issue of trust.

linked with the comprehensive concept of trust established above, and because evidence suggests that they can cause experiences of trust-like feelings in humans (Torta et al., 2014; Broadbent, 2017; Glikson & Woolley, 2020; Rossi et al., 2020; Beer, Liles, Wu & Pakala, 2017). Note also that not only social robots with AEI possess such features and can therefore appear in a personal and social way from the user's point of view. However, as it will also be argued in the following, the combination and strength of such features in AEI social robots allow these systems to be considered as different from other kinds, as a large and growing body of literature suggests (e.g., Breazeal, 2004; Sung et al., 2007; Turkle, 2010; Coeckelbergh, (2010); Darling, 2012, 2017; Gunkel, 2018; Hung et al., 2019).

Anthropomorphism. Anthropomorphism is generally defined as people's spontaneous tendency to attribute human properties and characteristics to non-human entities (Epley, Waytz & Cacioppo, 2007; Złotowski et al., 2016), but also to interpret non-human behavior as motivated by humanlike emotional and mental states (Airenti, 2015). These non-human entities include anything "that acts with apparent independence"[3], such as non-human animals, natural forces, religious deities, and mechanical or electronic devices (Epley, Waytz & Cacioppo, 2007). As research shows, artificial entities such as computers and virtual characters (Darling, 2017), or even robot vacuum cleaners (Sung et al., 2007; Scheutz, 2012) are perceived as social actors. The broader phenomenon might apply to an even broader range of artefacts, however, as similar mechanisms were described by Nass and Reeves (1996) in relation to computers and television.

Compared to other technologies, robots tend to amplify dramatically the perception of possessing human qualities such as feelings and intentions because of their specific characteristics (Darling, 2017). Specifically, anthropomorphism could be driven by interface features (e.g., human-like form of the robot), behavioural features (e.g., gaze, node), and intentional framing (e.g., giving the robot a human name) (Glikson & Woolley, 2020). Social robot design is especially intended to be anthropomorphized (Breazeal, 2003; Healy, 2022), as it can facilitate social exchange between the robot and the user, enhance familiarity, and promote interactions and integration (Damiano & Dumouchel, 2018). Furthermore, the human-likeness of a given technology potentially affect users' emotional reactions towards it (Hoff & Bashir, 2015). For these purposes, the goal for social robotic designers is to emulate humans "to the greatest extent possible" (de Visser et al., 2016). AEI plays a fundamental role here, as it enhances the tendency to anthropomorphise by depicting the robot as an entity able to *feel,* and consequently allows to perceive an attenuation of the ontological differences between humans and social robots.

As some argue (de Visser et al., 2016; Aroyo et al., 2021), the level of human-likeness of a system produces different effects on trust. Some empirical studies have shown that participants exhibited more trust, compliance, and enjoyment in the interaction with the robot than the computer (Kidd & Breazeal, 2008; Mann et al., 2015). With regard to social robotics, the more sophisticated a robots' anthropomorphic features are, the more the robot will be perceived as a subject rather than an object, and the higher the possibility for the user to form human-like trust. Furthermore, the closest the robot's appearance

---

[3] Interestingly, Tallant's thought experiment (2019) presents cases where humans are propense to anthropomorphise objects which do not appear to show any kind of agency.

to humans, the easiest is for the user to trust the robot in ways which resemble affective trust (Aroyo et al., 2021).

Deception. Deception is defined as an act or statement that intentionally misleads or promotes a belief that is not true (see, e.g., Boles, Croson & Murnighan, 2000; Gino & Shea, 2012; Levine & Schweitzer, 2015). Deceiving acts may be implemented through gestures, disguise, by means of action or inaction, or through silence (Bok, 1978).

Social robots, compared to other social technologies, show a more noticeable, stronger, and more prominent deceptive potential (Shim & Arkin, 2013; Danaher, 2020a; Sætra, 2021b). The main goal of deceiving robots is to "smoothly participate in standard human modes of communication and social interaction" (Isaac and Bridewell, 2017); i.e., to facilitate and make HRI more humanlike. This would also ease their integration into society and protect people from biases about the infallibility of such systems (Isaac & Bridewell, 2017). Deception can be achieved through different features of the robot, and on different levels. Anthropomorphic expressiveness (e.g., sad eyes, smiling), for instance, encourages the human to believe that the robot experiences emotions, hopes, and desires similar to what a human feels (Matthias, 2015; Aroyo et al., 2021). Emotional deception (Sharkey & Sharkey, 2012), which occurs when the user believes that the robot possesses real emotions, is an ability peculiarly present in AEI social robots. Such a form of deception raises unrealistic expectations regarding the robot's nature and capabilities (e.g., being benevolent or having motivations to act) and alter the possible kind of trust relationship that could be formed accordingly. Indeed, as previously mentioned, attributing certain intentions to the trusted is neglectable to form judgements of reliance, but essential for genuine affective trust (Nickel, Franssen & Kroes, 2010). With AEI social robots, the user might be more easily deceived to believe that the robot deliberately acts for her own good as she perceives the system as possessing benign intentions and feelings.

Since deceiving behaviours are generally believed to be implemented for personal gain and self-interest, some literature considers deception as particularly damaging to relationships and affective trust, sometimes in an irrevocable and enduring way (e.g., Bok, 1978; Schweitzer & Croson, 1999; Boles, Croson & Murninghan, 2000; Schweitzer, Hershey & Bradlow, 2006). In contrast, some authors argue that when deception or lying is done for the benefit of the other, such behaviours are not only considered acceptable but even perceived more ethical than telling the truth (Levine & Schweitzer, 2014, 2015; Isaac and Bridewell., 2017: Coeckelbergh, 2018; Sætra, 2021b). Isaac and Bridewell (2017) argue that ethical lies are possible because the morality of deceptive communication must be assessed in light of its underlying motive, rather than the truth or falsity of deception. The action of misleading with the purpose to do good to the deceived is a type of deception which Levine and Schweitzer (2015) call prosocial deception. Lies and deceptive behaviours, in such a case, are beneficial, prosocial, and have the effect of increasing trust (Isaac & Bridewell, 2017; Sætra, 2021b). In conclusion, deception per se does not undermine the positive interferences associated with prosocial actions (Levine & Schweitzer, 2015).

Emotional Attachment. One of the consequences of social robots' anthropomorphism and emotional deception, and the social engagement that necessarily arises from their use, is the possibility for the user to become emotionally attached to the robot (Sullins,

2012; van Maris et al., 2020; Boada, Maestre & Genís, 2021; Sharkey & Sharkey, 2020). Such characteristics are not exclusive requirements for an emotional bond to be formed. Indeed, it has been shown that people become attached to objects or other kinds of technologies even when these lack any social dimension (Sung et al., 2007; Scheutz, 2012; Carpenter, 2016). However, social robotics' anthropomorphic and deceptive features further and deeply encourage the elicitation of affection in the human. For instance, both Breazeal's studies (2004) and Riek's et al. experiment (2009) measured how anthropomorphism affects humans' empathy towards robots. Respectively, they show that when anthropomorphic robots mirror their human interlocutor's facial expressions and body movements, the user is encouraged to develop empathy towards them; and that people empathise more strongly with robots possessing human-like features than with mechanical-looking robots.

Another interesting point comes from Sweeney's analysis (2021), where she recognises that sometimes we become emotionally invested towards inanimate objects that have a sentimental value such as, for instance, a wedding ring. However, she claims that what distinguishes the emotions developed towards such objects from those towards social robots is the feeling of empathy, elicited exactly by the features described previously. In her words: "We can have emotional attachment to wedding rings, beloved bikes and plants, and we can feel sadness when they are managed, but we do not feel empathy towards them. [I]t is empathy that marks the difference in the way that we react to social robots from other objects" (Sweeney, 2021).

Also, according to their specific tasks and purposes, some robots are especially designed to elicit attachment in the user, with the aim to facilitate the use of robots as human companions and personal helpers (LaGrandeur, 2015; van Maris et al., 2020). As described above, AEI social robots particularly have the capability of communicating and engaging affectively, and being sensitive and responsive to the others' emotions. This consequently enhances the possibility to develop a form of affection towards them (Sharkey, 2016). LOVOT, for example, is a social robot specifically designed for companionship, developed to increase the user's general wellbeing. As the advertisement says: "When you touch tour LOVOT, embrace it, even just watch it, [...] It's a little like feeling love toward another person. [...] LOVOT was born for just one reason – to be loved by you" (LOVOT, 2023). LOVOT recognises its surrounding and adapts its actions in accordance with the owner's engagement with them; e.g., it looks back, laughs when tickled, and expresses joy when caressed. Similarly, another well-known commercialised companion type robot is Paro. Shaped like a cute baby harp seal, it moves and makes seal noises in response to human touch, temperature, light, noise, and orientation (Broadbent, 2017). As studies have shown, Paro reduces loneliness and increases social interactions both with Paro and other people (Heenrik et al., 2010).

AEI technology, therefore, could mark a crucial difference for determining the kind of trust that social robots elicit in humans. Indeed, since affective trust is related to affective bases, the emotional connection with the robot may have important effects on the kind of trust relationship possibly established. First, it could reinforce the belief that the involved agents act for a common goal (Rossi et al., 2020); i.e., that the robot actually cares for the user, and therefore acts for her benefit (Scheutz, 2012; Sharkey & Sharkey, 2020; Boada, Maestre & Genís, 2021). This might further promote a feeling of emotional safety and confidence in the robot, which are essential components of trust in close relationships (Levine & Schweitzer, 2015). In such cases, and mainly in the early stages of HRI, prosocial deception and lies might be particularly beneficial for strengthening such relationships. Furthermore, AEI social robots used for personal and intimate services (e.g., companionships) are intended to be regarded as fellows, companions, friends, or even lovers. When it comes to affective trust, the role of emotions and attachment make a friend to be more entrusted than a machine (Heuer, Schiering & Gerndt, 2018).

Why Social Robots are Perceived as Social Entities. To sum up, we have explored three main features which essentially characterise AEI social robots and distinguish them from technologies of other kinds for the intensity and the high degree of human-likeness they can achieve. As Coeckelbergh (2012) puts it, whether something appears as a human-like entity "is a matter of degree": by resembling humans, social robots with AEI allow to the user to perceive them not as tools, "as something in the background, or as something that has become part of ourselves (e.g., glasses), but as an other". By possessing such a significant anthropomorphic and deceptive potential, as well as the capacity to elicit emotional attachment in the user, these systems tend to reach the threshold at which, from the user's perspective, "objects become subjects" (Damiano & Dumouchel, 2018). Empirical studies show that social robots are perceived as transgressing the traditional ontological boundaries, as objects that are "sort of alive" or "alive enough" (Turkle, 2011). They fall in between the terms of old traditional dichotomies of sentient/not sentient, intelligent/not intelligent, and alive/not alive (Kahn, Friedman & Hagman, 2002; Severson & Carlson, 2010; Turkle, 2011; Gaudiello, Lefort & Zibetti, 2015; Damiano & Dumouchel, 2018).

The role of AEI in this context is crucial, as it tends to substantially intensify the user's perception – correct or not – that they are interacting with someone rather than something. This ambiguity is crucial when considering the issue of trust in technology, for two main reasons. First, it suggests that there is a possibility for humans to feel a sentiment of trust towards social robots that surpasses the way we commonly "trust" objects, i.e., rationality-trust, as empirical studies have already demonstrated. Second, given these findings, it might even support the view that users are *justified* to develop affective-trust attitudes towards AEI social robots. As Sweeney (2022) puts it, when it comes to social robots, the boundaries that make affective trust inappropriate for technology become blurred. Whether such boundaries become irrelevant when discussing trust in AEI social robots, or if it is ethically required to maintain them, will be discussed in the next section. We will present two points of view. The first, supported by Tallant's analysis (2019), conceives robots as mere tools that can be relied upon, but not necessarily *trusted*. The second follows Coeckelbergh's (2012) relational approach which suggests that so long as the user perceives robots as trustworthy social actors, such technologies *are* objects of trust. We present objections to both perspectives, and we then formulate our own view.

5 General Discussion – the Feeling of Trust vs. Trust Proper

5.1 Should We Grant Trust in AEI Social Robots?

We have established that there is a possibility humans can experience trust towards AEI social robots, as opposed to simply relying on them. However, not everyone would be convinced that, from that, it follows that we should trust them. Despite human tendency to believe the robot as good and honest and develop affective trust accordingly, such a tendency does not provide a moral permissibility to do so. Indeed, given that the do not actually possess benevolence and integrity, some might say that a mere pretence of such antecedents is not enough, and trust is inappropriate in this context.

Such a view is sustained by Tallant (2019). He argues that placing trust in objects is the result of their anthropomorphisation which make us erroneously attribute agency and intentionality to it. As we have discussed before, agency is the property which grounds the possibility for benevolence and integrity to be genuinely possessed. Hence, we must conclude that affective trust in AEI social robots is not morally justified, as "trust occurs because of the error in agency ascription" (Tallant, 2019).

Shall we then place trust in robots based on instrumentalist criteria, namely as mere tools? If this is our conclusion, then the same argument might also apply to other technological artifacts, as we have claimed that social robots equipped with AEI are the most likely candidates for establishing affective trust in this context. However, we do not believe that this would be the right track to follow. First, because it stands in contrast to what users spontaneously experience with social robots, as proved by empirical evidence. According to some, neglecting the instinctive approach of people towards such systems might hinder a correct and comprehensive analysis of trust in technology, as it has been argued that users' affective responses to a given technology are significant factors in determining ethically permissible behaviours towards these objects (Darling, 2012; Nyholm, 2020). The view that users' experiences and perceptions might provide a basis for morally justifying affective trust in social robots might be challenged. However, it is plausible to believe that by considering such experiences irrelevant and claiming that only the interactions based on reliability are permissible, it does not automatically follow that people will be prevented from developing affective trust and therefore assure that their trusting attitudes would be expressions of mere reliance.

This brings us to the second point: namely, the combination and intensity of the AEI social robots' features described above crucially affect the perception of the user. For social robots to be treated as objects that does not generative experiences of affective-like trust, the design of social robots and AEI should be significantly altered.

For instance, authors who encouraged the view of considering social robots strictly as tools, rather than social agents, have argued against the anthropomorphic features of robots (Richards & Smart, 2016). Scheutz's proposition (2012) is to legally require a robot to emit a signal continuously to remind the user that it is only a machine: it does not possess the capability to feel or have emotions, it does not act intentionally, strictly speaking, and cannot act benevolently for the user's goals. This might reduce the robot's deceptive potential, as well as the possibility and strength of emotional bonds which users might develop towards them. As a result, the likelihood to form affective trust will be decreased. However, as argued above, evidence suggests that such a strategy would not always be effective. Humans could continue to antrhopomorphise these robots, project their own mentality onto them, and form what seems like deep emotional relationships, despite their limited abilities (Breazeal, 2004; Turkle, 2011; Healy, 2022).

Furthermore, as Sharkey and Sharkey (2020) suggest, a continuous signal might impact the comfort and usefulness of having the robot around, as well as its efficacy, especially in cases where the robot is required for therapeutic reasons. Precisely this latter objection concerns any significant modification applied to the features of AEI and social robotics. As Darling (2017) sustains, and we have previously pointed out, framing social robots in anthropomorphic, deceptive, and emotional terms is functional for the robot to achieve its purposes, especially in cases when AEI social robots are employed for personal and intimate uses.

The Robot's Appearance Suffices For Granting Trust. Hereafter, by following Coeckelbergh (2009; 2012), we analyse a different approach to the question whether granting trust towards AEI social robots is permissible. This view focuses on the perspective of the user, and their perception of the social robot, rather than on the nature of the robot itself. We then present two objections.

Coeckelbergh's view (2009; 2012) is particularly interesting for our analysis as specifically focused on a concept of trust built on social relations. He claims that a genuine attribution of agency to social robots is of secondary importance. What counts is the way they appear to their users and how the users perceive some relationship with the machine. In Coeckelbergh's (2009) words:

> My suggestion is that we can permit ourselves to remain agnostic about what 'really' goes on 'in' there, and focus on the 'outer', the interaction, and in particular on how this interaction is co-shaped and co-constituted by how A[rtificial] A[gent]s appear to us, humans.

It is the appearance of agency that makes these systems eligible recipients of trust in the user's eye, because a fictional but supposed agency is enough to allow them to participate in and shape our social dimension. This is also similar to Danaher's ethical behaviourism, which suggests that the internal states of the robot are as inaccessibly to us as is the minds of other humans, and that we are consequently always left with relying on external signs and behaviour (Danaher, 2020b). In so far as robots are part of our social relations, we are inclined to trust them since trust is not produced but "already there, in the social". Contrary to Tallant's view (2019), therefore, which claims that perceiving social robots as agents is a fallacy in human reasoning, Coeckelbergh values this aspect as sufficient to justify our impression of robots as trustworthy: "Appearing-making, sometimes named 'deception', [...] is part of 'the social game' and it does not undermine trust but supports it' (Coeckelbergh, 2012). After all, it might be said that even in human-human relationships, affective trust is based on appearances. Benevolence and integrity of the other are presumed, as there is no objective certainty that this latter will behave for our own goal and benefit. As it was for the robot, also for a human trustee it is not possible to know what "really goes on in there" (Coeckelbergh, 2009), since it is perfectly plausible for the other to show nothing more than "a façade of friendliness and care" (Sweeney, 2022). Therefore, for both malevolent people or deceiving robots, the trustor will be able to appreciate the same – or significantly similar – outwardly benevolent expressions, behaviours, and language. As indicated in the second section, the vulnerability of the trustor is integrally part of an affective trust-based relationship, as our judgement for trusting someone is largely based on how the other presents themselves to us, and whether we believe them trustworthy (Sweeney, 2022). Such vulnerability does not necessarily relate to the performance of the trustee for a specific task, but rather to the possibility of being betrayed.

To this argument, two objections can be advanced. The first relates to the comparison between human-human trust, and human-robot trust, as both based on perceptions and appearances. Differently from humans, the robot's benevolence and integrity would always be pretended (Sætra, 2020). On the contrary, the human façade is intentional and situational. Pretending, it is not the standard in a human-human trust relationship, or trust would not be possible in the first place (Sweeney, 2022).

Secondly, merely focusing on the user's perspective might make us overlook various implications, potentially negative, of granting trust towards AEI social robots, specifically because of their appearance and "always-faking" nature. Differences between trust among humans and trust in robots become, therefore, relevant again when considering the risks associated. AEI social robots are not only social actors, companions, or even friends from the user's point of view. As we will argue, they also are, and should always be seen as, synthetic tools, owned and designed by others for goals and moral values which might differ from the ones of the user (Sætra, 2021b). In the next section, we present some of the consequences of placing trust in social robots – as subjects and not objects.

5.2   Too Much Trust (in Robots) is not a Good Thing

For a comprehensive assessment of the morality of trust in AEI social robots, considerations regarding the consequences of such trust are needed. As mentioned above, granting trust in robots might involve consequences possibly harmful to the user, which risk being neglected if we consider the robot's appearance as sufficient to morally justify trust. Indeed, as Aroyo et al. (2021) argue, our disposition to trust robots based on their appearance as benevolent and honest systems might lead to overtrusting these systems. Hereafter, we first describe what overtrusting technologies entails and the causes that might induce it. We then briefly explore some of the consequences of overtrust in social robots with AEI. Our analysis includes moral implications both from the perspective of the individual and in relation to human society in general.

Overtrust. Overtrust is defined as "poor calibration in which trust exceeds system capabilities" (Lee & See, 2004), leading to misuse which might expose the user to risks (Borenstein, Wagner & Howards, 2018). The possibility to overtrust occurs not only in cases of anthropomorphic and deceiving technologies – as in the case of social robots with AEI – but also for other kinds of technological artifacts when the phenomenon known as automation bias is triggered (Mosier et al., 1998; Aroyo et al., 2021). Automation bias occurs when people erroneously ascribe "higher authority, greater expected performance, and higher initial trust" to technologies (de Visser et al., 2016), with a consequent reduction of scrutiny and monitoring of the functioning of the system (Aroyo et al., 2021). With respect to automation, therefore, a key component linked to overtrust is the perception of the system as very reliable even when they might not be (Wagner & Nayyar, 2017).

In normal circumstances, the initial trust towards a given technology tends to decrease when erroneous functioning occurs (Hoff & Bashir, 2015). In cases of overtrust, instead, malfunctioning is not perceived per se and do not lead to a recalibration of the user's positive expectations of the system's potential (Aroyo et al., 2021). However, even in situations where there is no clear evidence of malfunctioning or defective behaviour, the user might be inclined to overestimate the capacities of the technology.

As for robotics, overtrust leads to a situation where "a person accepts risk because the robot appears to, or is expected to, perform a function it cannot" (Aroyo et al., 2021). More so than with other forms of automation, we have seen that in HRI the user tends to create an illusion of agency and intentionality in the robot's actions. The presence of affection in HRI, as well as anthropomorphic and deceptive features of the robot, might mislead and biased users' understanding of the robot's actual abilities, and induce the user to overtrust the system. Overtrust in autonomous systems, therefore, seems to relate more closely to affective trust than trust in automation (Wagner & Nayyar, 2017).

Privacy, Manipulation, and Surveillance. Placing trust in robots can have adverse implications. Among the most discussed, there is the concern of the protection of private information, as robots can collect personal identifying data that could be accessed by other people. Social robots with AEI raise more serious worries about privacy issues than other technologies, as they can "enter into previously untapped areas in personal households and take on social functions" (Darling, 2017). Given their emotional character and social interactivity, these systems have access to everyday life of users and more sensitive data, such as their emotional and mental states (Lutz, Schöttler & Hoffmann, 2019), at a scale previously unimaginable. When humans develop emotional connections and affective trust in robots, "secrets can be revealed", Lutz, Schöttler & Hoffmann (2019) warn. Trust and attachment to the robot might indeed be used to influence or manipulate the user to spontaneously disclose private or sensitive information (Lee et al., 2011). Interestingly, research has shown that, when disclosing personal information, users are inclined to be more honest and open with AI than with other humans (Glikson & Woolley, 2020).

Related to trust and personal data, two other concerns must be pointed out. First, there is the concern that the data collected about the user might be exploited for manipulation. Research on human-computer interaction has proven that humans are prone to being manipulated by social AI (Darling, 2017). As Scheutz (2012) argues, "it will be only a matter of time before robots are used as sales representatives". For instance, a company might exploit the user's affective trust in the robot to make this latter convince the owner to purchase their goods. Whereas in human relationships, social emotional mechanisms like guilt and empathy might generally prevent the escalation of such scenarios, from the robot's side there is nothing "to stop them from abusing their influence over their owners (Scheutz, 2012).

Secondly, if sensitive data might be divulged, worries regarding digital surveillance automatically follows. Digital surveillance of AEI systems expands into ever-more intimate spaces of users' daily life (Lynch, 2021). Social robots' appearance as genuinely benevolent towards the user may lead people to welcome them in the home and other locations, where for instance a surveillance camera would not be accepted (Sharkey & Sharkey, 2012). Furthermore, Mohammed (2022) expresses the worry that functional characteristics of AEI such as emotion recognition and sentiment analysis can be used for mass surveillance by companies for marketing reasons, and government for, allegedly, political security, without the users' meaningful consent or being aware of such exploitation. Finally, given the highly sensitive data that such systems might collect, the risk of hacking becomes even more alarming. As Lutz, Schöttler and Hoffmann (2019) point out, hacking social robots allows for deeper insights into the user's life than from other devices such as laptops or tablets.

When Trust in Robots Changes Human Relations. Others have focused on long-term consequences of affective trust in social robots based on their appearance. For instance, if it occurs that "robots are generally more believable than humans" (Scheutz, 2012), this might encourage the user to rely more and more on their robots rather than their human fellows, and it might even lead to a general reduction on trust among people (Danaher & Sætra, 2022). Furthermore, Sætra (2021a) analyses the robot's deceptive potential as one of the main causes for overtrusting robots, possibly leading to cultural change and moral revolution. He claims that exploiting trust in HRI have consequences on human-human relationships and might induce a corrosion of trust and cooperation between people in the short and long period. Whenever the user recognises that they have been deceived, they might be inclined to be less trustful in future interactions (Danaher & Sætra. 2022). This could consequently impact how humans relate to each other and, in an evolutionary time frame, the value of trust in human society as we know it now might be eroded (Sætra, 2021b).

To sum up, in the previous section we have explored two opposite perspectives about trust in social robots. In our view, both presented flaws and were susceptible to objections. The first perspective, based on Tallant's argument (2019), required a fundamental change in the design of AEI and social robotic technology, which might nullify the advantages and benefits of such systems for the user. The second, advanced by Coeckelbergh (2012), would implicitly encourage the occurrence of negative effects of granting trust in AEI social robots on the basis of their appearance. We have therefore explored some of these effects and the potential damages brought about to users and society in general. In the next section, by following Sweeney's reasoning (2022), we conclude our argument by presenting our own view.

5.3 Reliability as an Essential Requirement

Our discussion so far has highlighted essential features of social robots with AEI which encourage the user to develop affective trust towards them. Given their anthropomorphic forms, deceptive potential, and ability to elicit emotional responses and affection, people are inclined to believe that the robot possess benevolent and honest behaviours and intentionally act for the sake of the user, despite the robot lacking any genuine intentionality and agency. Merely counting on the appearance of the benevolence and integrity of the robot to grant trust towards these systems might not only negatively affect the user's wellbeing but even endanger the value of trust in the long term. For this reason, we question Coeckelbergh's argument (2012) that an apparent but arguably non-existent agency could be enough to allow robot to be moral objects of trust.

We do not intend to deny the evidence that, *empirically*, the user can develop affective trust attitudes towards AEI social robots. In fact, such attitudes of trust are necessary for the effective functioning of social robots. However, it is crucial to keep in mind that trusting these systems becomes dangerous exactly because we are inclined to accept them as genuinely benevolent entities despite being aware of their deceptive quality. The threshold at which, from the user's point of view, "objects become subjects" (Damiano & Dumouchel, 2018), should arguably not be crossed.

In light of this, to avoid the development of overtrust and the risks associated, robots' synthetic nature should never be disregarded. Considerations of the robot's true capabilities and functionalities – what happens "inside" – and not only what the robot appears to be, have an importance in the assessment of trust towards them. In other words, what should be assessed when placing trust in AEI social robots is their actual reliability to function and perform in accordance with the user's goal. For instance, in cases of errors or malfunctioning of the system, or if it is found out that the owning company sells the collected users' sensitive data to marketing companies, the device is no longer *reliable*, and our spontaneously formed attitudes of affective trust should be necessarily and accordingly readjusted (Sweeney, 2022). Therefore, despite the implementation of AEI into social robotics, the increased robot's capability to deceive and be anthropomorphised, and the consequent importance of the emotional connection which one might developed, users' affective trust should still depend on and be susceptible to positive expectations about the system's reliability.

In conclusion, whereas we cannot deny that the user develops a *feeling* of trust towards the robot, such feeling is not enough to morally justify what we propose calling *trust proper* – a relational conception of trust which necessarily requires authentic capacities of benevolence and integrity. This is distinguished from the "thin" version of trust often used in HRi research, which is arguably very close to the same as simple *reliance*. Relying on the mere appearance of such qualities is not only not enough for trust proper to be established, but it could even expose the user to risks. Importantly, this conclusion does not necessarily necessitate modification of those features which encourage the user to believe the robot capable of benevolence and integrity. Again, a feeling of trust towards these systems could be both necessary and encouraged in certain HRI contexts.

Nonetheless, we claim that people must remain aware of the possibility for the product they are using to become unreliable and recalibrate their affective trust accordingly. Some ethical guidelines might be advanced for the correct development and use of these machines. For instance, informing users of the potential risks involved might be one way to temper an implicit and unwary development of affective trust based on the robot's appearance. Another suggestion comes from Sweeney (2022), who advocates for a need for transparency regarding the actual capabilities of the technology, and for greater responsibility from the manufacturers. As Picard (1997) argues, "In some cases, a machine may need to explain what it can and cannot do", but it will always be essential to help users to set accurate expectations of the technology's actual abilities. Interestingly, also AEI technology might become useful to detect and possibly prevent overtrust behaviours from users (Wagner, Borenstein and Howard, 2018). Whereas such guidelines would be effective remain still to be demonstrated, but the importance of investigating the potential dangers of trusting social robots and finding ways to temper them is nonetheless crucial.

6 Conclusion

We started by asking: What are the conditions for placing affective trust in technology? We explored the issue through the specific case of AEI social robots. Given their significant impact on human emotional and social dimension, we argued that such technologies are the most likely for people to develop attitudes of affective trust. Indeed, the robot's deceptive behaviours induce the user to believe the robot capable of benevolence and integrity. However, we have argued that granting trust based on their appearance involve risks which might endanger the user. We concluded our argument by claiming that it is therefore morally necessary to focus on the actual nature of AEI social robots, as synthetic tools designed for purposes which might differ or even conflict with the ones of the people that interact with it daily. Whereas we cannot deny that people develop a feeling of trust, and such a feeling is functional for the robot to fulfil the purposes it has been created for, we claim that users are nonetheless not morally allowed to grant trust proper towards these systems.

It might be objected that our analysis of the concept of trust is biased and lacks objectivity as affected by the culture we live in. Coeckelbergh (2012), for instance, claims that the identification and application of criteria for trusting, such as integrity and benevolence, are influenced by Western culture and might therefore need to be reformulated according to a different cultural environment. This is an interesting point, which could also provide guidance for further empirical research on this subject. At the same time, we believe that this objection does not undermine our conclusion, as it is based on the consequences that trust in robots might bring about. Even if we agree that no universal definition of trust can be given, then we can at least refer to the implications of trusting the technology to assess the moral permissibility of this.

Finally, as we suggested that social robots equipped with AEI are the most likely candidates for trust to be developed, and we have nonetheless objected such a possibility, it necessarily follows that trust cannot be granted for any kind of technology. To answer our research question, therefore, we conclude that affective trust in technology is not possible, as our tendencies to anthropomorphise and be deceived do and should not guarantee technology to be worthy of trust.

References

Airenti, G.: The cognitive bases of anthropomorphism: from relatedness to empathy. Int. J. Soc. Robot. **7**, 117–127 (2015)

Aroyo, A.M., et al.: Overtrusting robots: Setting a research agenda to mitigate overtrust in automation. Paladyn, J. Behav. Robot. **12**(1), 423–436 (2021)

Beer, J.M., Liles, K.R., Wu, X., Pakala, S.: Affective human-robot interaction. In: Jeon, M. (ed.) Emotion and Affect in Human Factors and Human-Computer Interaction, pp. 359–381. Academic Press, London (2017)

Billings, D.R., Schaefer, K.E., Chen, J.Y., Hancock, P.A.: Human-robot interaction, developing trust in robots. In: Proceedings of the 7th Annual ACM/IEEE International Conference on Human-Robot Interaction, pp. 109–110. ACM, Boston (2012)

Boada, J.P., Maestre, B.R., Genís, C.T.: The ethical issues of social assistive robotics: a critical literature review. Technology in Society 67 (2021)

Bok, S.: Lying: Moral Choices in Public and Private Life. Pantheon, New York, NY (1978)

Boles, T.L., Croson, R.T., Murnighan, J.K.: Deception and retribution in repeated ultimatum bargaining. Organ. Behav. Hum. Decis. Process. **83**(2), 235–259 (2000)

Borenstein, J., Wagner, A.R., Howard, A.: Overtrust in pediatric health-care robots: a preliminary survey of parent perspectives. In: IEEE Robotics & Automation Magazine, vol. 25, pp. 46–54 (2018)

Breazeal, C.: Toward sociable robots. Robot. Auton. Syst. **42**(3), 167–175 (2003)

Breazeal, C.: Designing sociable robots. The MIT Press. Cambridge, MA (2004)

Broadbent, E.: Interactions with robots: the truths we reveal about ourselves. Ann. Rev. Psychol. 8\68, 627–652 (2017)

Campa, R.: The rise of social robots: a review of the recent literature. J. Evol. Technol. **26**(1), 106–113 (2016)

Carpenter, J.: Culture and human-robot interaction in militarized spaces: a war story. Ashgate, New York (2016)

Coeckelbergh, M.: Virtual moral agency, virtual moral responsibility: on the moral significant of the appearance, perception, and performance of artificial agents. AI & Soc. **24**, 181–189 (2009)

Coeckelbergh, M.: Robot rights? Towards a social-relational justification of moral consideration. Ethics Inf. Technol. **12**(3), 209–221 (2010)

Coeckelbergh, M.: Can we trust robots? Ethics Inf. Technol. **14**, 53–60 (2012)

Coeckelbergh, M.: How to descrive and evaluate "deception" phenomena: recasting the metaphysics, ethics, and politics of ICTs in terms of magic and performance and taking a relational and narrative turn. Ethics Inf. Technol. **20**, 71–85 (2018)

Coleman, J.S.: Foundations of social theory. Harvard University Press, Cambridge, MA (1990)

Damasio, A.: Descartes' error: emotion, reason, and the human brain. Avon Books, New York (1994)

Damiano, L., Dumouchel, P.: Anthropomorphism in human-robot co-evolution. Front. Psychol. 9 (2018)

Danaher, J.: Robot betrayal: a guide to the ethics of robotic deception. Ethics Inf. Technol. **22**(2), 117–128 (2020a)

Danaher, J.: Welcoming robots into the moral circle: a defence of ethical behaviourism. Sci. Eng. Ethics **26**(4), 2023–2049 (2020b)

Danaher, J., Sætra, H.S.: Technology and moral change: the transformation of truth and trust. Ethics Inf. Technol. **24**(3), 1–16 (2022)

Darling, K.: Extending legal protection to social robots: the effects of anthropomophism, empathy, and violent behavior toward robotic objects. In: Calo, R., Froomkin, A. M., Kerr, I. (eds.) Robot Law, pp. 213–231. Edward Elgar (2012)

Darling, K.: Who's Johnny? Anthropomorphic framing in human-robot interaction, integration, and policy'. In: Lin, P., Bekey, G., Abney, K., Jenkins, R. (eds.) Robot Ethics 2.0. Oxford University Press (2017)

De Visser, E.J., et al.: Almost human: anthropomorphism increases trust resilience in cognitive agents. J. Exp. Psychol. Appl. **22**(3), 331–349 (2016)

Dumouchel, P., Damiano, L.: Living with robots. Harvard University Press, Cambridge, MA (2017)

Epley, N., Waytz, A., Cacioppo, J.T.: On seeing human: a three-factor theory of anthropomorphism. Psychol. Rev. **114**(4), 864–886 (2007)

Ferrin, D.L., Kim, P.H., Cooper, C.D., Dirks, K.T.: Silence speaks volumes: the effectiveness of reticence in comparison to apology and denial for responding to integrity-and competence-based trust violations. J. Appl. Psychol. **92**(4), 893–908 (2007)

Fong, T., Nourbakhsh, I., Dautenhahn, K.: A survey of socially interactive robots. Robot. Auton. Syst. **42**, 143–166 (2003)

Freedy, A., de Visser, E., Weltman, G., Coeyman, N.: Measurement of trust in human-robot collaboration. In: Proceedings of the 2007 International Conference on Collaborative Technologies and Systems, pp. 106–114. IEEE, Orlando, FL (2007)

Friedman, B., Kahn, P.H., Jr., Howe, D.C.: Structural equation modelling and regression: guidelines for research practice. Commun. AIS **7**(7), 1–78 (2000)

Gaudiello, I., Lefort, S., Zibetti, E.: The ontological and functional status of robots. Comput. Hum. Behav. **50**, 259–273 (2015)

Gino, F., Shea, C.: Deception in negotiations: the role of emotions. Handbook of conflict resolution. Oxford University Press, New York (2012)

Glikson, E., Woolley, A.W.: Human trust in artificial intelligence: review of empirical research. Acad. Manag. Ann. **14**(2), 627–660 (2020)

Goleman, D.: Emotional intelligence. Bantam, New York (1995)

Gompei, T., Umemuro, H.: Factors and development of cognitive and affective trust on social robots. In: Ge, S.S., Cabibihan, J.-J., Salichs, M.A., Broadbent, E., He, H., Wagner, A.R., Castro-González, Á. (eds.) ICSR 2018. LNCS (LNAI), vol. 11357, pp. 45–54. Springer, Cham (2018). https://doi.org/10.1007/978-3-030-05204-1_5

Gunkel, D.J.: Robot Rights. The MIT Press, Cambridge, MA (2018)

Hancock, P. A., Chen, J. Y. C., Schefer, K. E., de Visser, E.: A meta-analysis of factors affectivg trust in human-robot interaction. J. Hum. Fact. Ergon. Soc. 53 (2011)

Hardin, R.: Trust. Polity Press. Cambridge, UK (2006)

Healy, P.: Social robots as partners?. AI & Society (2022)

Heenrik, M., Krose, B., Evers, V., Wielinga, B.: Assessing acceptance of assistive social agent technology by older adults: the Almere model. Int. J. Soc. Robot. **2**, 361–375 (2010)

Heuer, T., Schiering, I., Gerndt, R.: Privacy and socially assistive robots - a meta study. In: IFIP Advances in Information and Communication Technology, pp. 265–281 (2018)

Hoff, K.A., Bashir, M.: Trust in automation: Integrating empirical evidence on factors that influence trust. Hum. Factors **57**(3), 407–434 (2015)

Hung, K., et al.: The benefits of and barriers to using asocial robot PARO in care settings: a scoping review. BMC Geriatrics 19 (2019)

Isaac, A.M.C., Bridewell, W.: White lies on silver tongues: why robots need to deceive (and how). In. Lin, P. Abney, K., Jenkins, R. (eds) Robot Ethics 2.0: From Autonomous Cars to Artificial Intelligence. Oxford University Press, New York, NY (2017)

Kahn, P.H., Friedman, B. Jr., Hagman, J.: 'I care about him as a pal': a conception of robotic pets in online AIBO discussion forums. In: Proceedings of the Extended Abstracts at the Conference on Human Factors in Computing Systems. ACM Press, New York, NY (2002)

Kidd, C.D., Breazeal. C.: Robots at home: understanding long-term human-robot interaction. In: 2008 IEEE/RSJ International Conference on Intelligent Robots and Systems, pp. 3230–3235. Nice, France (2008)

Kim, P.H., Ferrin, D.L., Cooper, C.D., Dirks, K.T.: Removing the shadow of suspicion: the effects of apology versus denial for repairing competence- versus integrity-based trust violations. J. Appl. Psychol. **89**(1), 104–118 (2004). https://doi.org/10.1037/0021-9010.89.1.104

Kim, P.H., Dirks, K.T., Cooper, C.D., Ferrin, D.L.: When more blame is better than less: the implications of internal vs. external attributions for the repair of trust after a competence-vs. integrity-based trust violation. Organ. Behav. Hum. Decis. Processes **99**(1), 49–65 (2006). https://doi.org/10.1016/j.obhdp.2005.07.002

Koyama, T.: Ethical issues for social robots and the trust-based approach. In: IEEE International Workshop on Advanced Robotics and its Social Impacts (ARSO) (2016)

Romportl, J., Zackova, E., Kelemen, J. (eds.): Beyond Artificial Intelligence. TIEI, vol. 9. Springer, Cham (2015). https://doi.org/10.1007/978-3-319-09668-1

Lankton, N.K., McKnight, D.H., Tripp, J.: Technology, humanness, and trust: rethinking trust in technology. J. Assoc. Inf. Syst. 16(10) (2015)

Lee, J.D., See, K.A.: Trust in automation: designing for appropriate reliance. Hum. Fact.: J. Hum. Fact. Ergon. Soc. 46(1), 50–80 (2004)

Lee, M. K., Tang, K. P., Forlizzi, J., Kiesler, S.: Understanding users' perception of privacy in human-robot interaction. In: Proceedings of the 6th International Conference on Human-Robot Interaction, HRI '11. Association for Computing Machinery, pp. 181–182. New York, NY, USA (2011)

Lerner, J.S., Li, Y., Valdesolo, P., Kassam, K.S.: Emotion and decision making. Annu. Rev. Psychol. 66, 799–823 (2015)

Levine, E.E., Schweitzer, M.E.: Are liars ethical? On the tension between benevolence and honesty. J. Exp. Soc. Psychol. 53, 107–117 (2014)

Levine, E.E., Schweitzer, M.E.: Prosocial lies: When deception breeds trust. Organ. Behav. Hum. Decis. Process. 126, 88–106 (2015)

Lewicky, E.J., Bunker, B.B.: Trust in relationships: a model of development and decline. In: Bunker, B. B., Rubin, J. Z. (eds.) Conflict, cooperation, and justice: essays inspired by the work of Morton Deutsch, pp. 133–173. Jossey-Bass/Wiley (1995)

LOVOT. https://lovot.life/en/ (2023)

Lum, H.C.: The role of consumer robots in our everyday lives. In: Pak, R., de Visser, E.J., Rovira, E. (eds.) Living with robots, pp. 141–152. Academic Press, Cambridge, MA (2020)

Lynch, C.R.: Artificial emotional intelligence and the intimate politics of robotic sociality. Space Polity 25(2), 184–201 (2021)

Lutz, C., Schöttler, M., Hoffmann, C.P.: The privacy implications of social robots: scoping review and expert interviews. Mobile Media & Commun. 7(3), 412–434 (2019)

Mann, J.A., MacDonald, B.A., Kuo, I., Li, X., Broadbent, E.: People respond better to robots than computers tablets delivering healthcare instructions. Comput. Hum. Behav. 43, 112–117 (2015)

Matthias, A.: Robot lies in health care: when is deception morally permissible? Kenney Instit. Ethics J. 25(2), 169-162 (2015)

Mayer, R.C., Davis, J.H., Schoorman, F.D.: An integrative model of organizational trust. Acad. Manag. Rev. 20(3), 709–734 (1995)

McAllister, D.J.: Affect-and cognition-based trust as foundations for interpersonal cooperation in organizations. Acad. Manag. J. 38(1), 24–59 (1995)

McKnight, H., Carter, M., Clay, P.: Trust in technology: Development of a set of constructs and measures. In: Digit 2009 Proceedings 10 (2009)

Mohammed, S.M.: Ethics sheet for automatic emotion recognition and sentiment analysis. Comput. Linguistic 48(2), 239–278 (2022)

Mosier, K.L., Dunbar, M., McDonnell, L., Skitka, L.J., Burdick, M., Rosenblatt, B.: Automation bias and errors: are teams better than individuals?. In: Proceedings of the Human Factors and Ergonomics Society Annual Meeting, vol. 42, pp. 201–205 (1998)

Reeves, B., Nass, C.I.: The media equation: how people treat computers, television, and new media like real people and places. Cambridge University Press, New York, NY (1996)

Nickel, P.J., Franssen, M., Kroes, P.: Can we make sense of the notion of trustworthy technology? Knowl. Technol. Policy 23, 429–444 (2010)

Nyholm, S.: Humans and robots: ethics, agency, and anthropomorphism. Rowman and Littlefield (2020)

Picard, R.W.: Affective computing. The MIT Press, Cambridge, MA (1997)

Plaks, J.E., Rodrigues, L.B., Ayad, R.: Identifying psychological features of robots that encourage and discourage trust. Comput. Hum. Behav. 134 (2022)

Prescott, T.J., Robillard, J.M.: Are friends electric? The benefits and risks of human-robot relationships. iScience 24(1) (2020)

Richards, N.M., Smart, W.D.: How should the law think about robots? In: Calo, R., Froomkin, M., Kerr, I. (eds.) Robot Law, pp. 3–24. Edward Elgar, Cheltenham, UK (2016)

Riek, L., Rabinowitch, T., Cjakrabart, B., Robinson, P.: How anthropomorphism affects empathy toward robots. In: Proceedings of the 4th ACM/IEEE International Conference on Human Robot Interaction. Association for Computing Machinery, pp. 245–146. New York, NY, USA (2009)

Robinette, P., Howard, A.M., Wagner, A.R.: Effect of robot performance on human-robot trust in time-critical situations. IEEE Trans. Hum.-Mach. Syst. 47(4), 425–436 (2017)

Rossi, A., Koay, K.L., Dautenhahn, L., and Walters, M. L: How social robots influence people's trust in critical situation. In: 2020 29th IEEE International Conference on Robot and Human Interactive Communication (RO-MAN) (2020)

Rousseau, D.M., Sitkin, S.B., Burt, R.S., Camerer, C.: Not so different after all: a cross-discipline view of trust. Acad. Manag. Rev. 23(3), 393–404 (1998)

Sætra, H.S.: The parasitic nature of social AI: sharing minds with the mindless. Integr. Psychol. Behav. Sci. 54, 308–326 (2020)

Sætra, H.S.: Social robot deception and the culture of trust. Paladyn, J. Behav. Robot. 12(1), 276–286 (2021a)

Sætra, H.S.: Confounding complexity of machine action: a Hobbesian account of machine responsibility. Int. J. Technoethics (IJT) 12(1), 87–100 (2021b)

Sebastian, W., Feiten, L.: Trust in technology: interlocking trust concepts for privacy respecting video surveillance. J. Inf. Commun. Ethics Soc. 19(4), 506–520 (2021)

Severson, R.L., Carlson, S.M.: Behaving as or behaving as if? Children's conceptions of personified robots and the emergence of a new ontological category. Neural Network 23, 1099–1103

Scheutz, M.: The inherent dangers of unidirectional emotional bonds between humans and social robots. In: Lin, P., Abney, K., Bekey, G.A. (eds.) Robo-Ethics: The Ethical and Social Implications of Robotics, pp. 205–221. The MIT Press, Cambridge, MA (2012)

Schoorman, F.D., Mayer, R.C., Davis, J.H.: An integrative model of organizational trust: past, present, and future. Acad. Manag. Rev. 32(2), 344–354 (2007)

Schuller, D., Schuller, B.W.: The age of artificial emotional intelligence. Computer 51(9), 38–46 (2018)

Schweitzer, M.E., Croson, R.: Curtailing deception: the impact of direct questions on lies and omissions. Int. J. Confl. Manag. 10(2), 225–248 (1999)

Schweitzer, M.E., Hershey, J.C., Bradlow, E.T.: Promises and lies: restoring violated trust. Organ. Behav. Hum. Decis. Process. 101(1), 1–19 (2006)

Sharkey, A.J.C.: Should we welcome robot teachers? Ethics Inf. Technol. 18(4), 283–297 (2016). https://doi.org/10.1007/s10676-016-9387-z

Sharkey, A., Sharkey, N.: Granny and the robots: ethical issues in robot care for the elderly. Ethics Inf. Technol. 14, 17–40 (2012)

Sharkey, A., Sharkey, N.: We need to talk about deception in social robotics! Ethics Inf. Technol. 23(3), 309–316 (2020). https://doi.org/10.1007/s10676-020-09573-9

Shim, J., Arkin, R.C.: A taxonomy of robot deception and its benefits in HEI. In: 2013 IEEE International Conference on Systems, Man, and Cybernetics (2013)

Song, Y., Luximon, Y.: Trust in AI agent: a systematic review of facial anthropomorphic trustworthiness for social robot design. Sensors 20(18) (2020)

Sullins, J.P.: Robots, love, and sex: the ethics of building a love machine. IEEE Trans. Affect. Comput. 3(4), 398–409 (2012)

Sung, J.Y., Guo, L., Grinter, R.E., Christensen, H.I.: "My Roomba is rambo": intimate home appliances. In: Krumm, J., Abowd, G.D., Seneviratne, A., Strang, T. (eds.) UbiComp 2007: Ubiquitous Computing. LNCS, vol. 4717, pp. 145–162. Springer, Berlin (2007)

Sweeney, P.: A functional dualism model of social robots. Ethics Inf. Technol. **23**, 465–472 (2021)

Sweeney, P.: Trusting social robots. AI and Ethics (2022). https://doi.org/10.1007/s43681-022-00165-5

Tallant, J.: You can trust the ladder, but you shouldn't. Theoria **85**(2), 102–118 (2019)

Torta, E., et al.: Evaluation of a small socially-assistive humanoid robot in intelligent homes for the care of the elderly. J. Intell. Rob. Syst. **76**(1), 57–71 (2014)

Turkle, S.: A nascent robotics culture: new complicities for companionship. In: AAAI Technical Report Series (2006)

Turkle, S.: In good company? On the threshold of robotic companions. In: Wilks, Y. (ed.) Close engagements with artificial companions: Key social, psychological, ethical and design issues, pp. 3–10. John Benjamins Publishing, Amsterdam, The Netherlands (2010)

Turkle, S.: Alone Together. Basic Books, New York (2011)

Van Maris, A., Zook, N., Caleb-Solly, P., Studley, M., Winfield, A., Dogramadzi, S.: Designing ethical social robots - A longitudinal field study with older adults. Front. Robot. AI **7**(1) (2020)

Wagner, A.R.: The role of trust and relationships in human-robot social interaction. Georgia Institute of Technology (2009)

Wagner, A.R., Borenstein, J., Howard, A.: Overtrust in the robotic age. Commun. ACM **61**(9), 22–24 (2018)

Złotowski, J., Sumioka, H., Nishio, S., Glas, D.F., Bartneck, C., Ishiguro, H.: Appearance of a robot affects the impact of its behaviour on perceived trustworthiness and empathy. Paladyn, J. Behav. Robot. **7**(1) (2016)

Be Me Vest - Exploring the Emotional Effects of Music and Sound-Based Vibrotactile Stimuli

Yulia Sion$^{(\boxtimes)}$ ⓘ, Sunil Sudevan ⓘ, and David Lamas ⓘ

Tallinn University, Tallinn, Estonia
yulia.sion@tlu.ee

Abstract. Music and nature sounds are known for their ability to elicit a wide range of emotional responses; so is physical touch. Nonetheless, tactile feedback seems quite limited in its emotional expressivity. Our goal is to explore whether emotive properties transfer between the aural and the tactile domains. We designed a wearable interface, the "Be Me" vest, which translates sound as vibration on the upper back of a person. Using this interface we then explored whether music compositions and nature sounds can systematically influence a person's affective state when presented via the tactile channel only. For most vibrotactile stimuli, we found a distinct influence on physiological responses. Further, for a subset of the stimuli we also found a distinct influence on self-report evaluations. These findings further our understanding of the role of the tactile modality in the emotional processing of complex sounds and may lead to the development of a rich vibrotactile language.

Keywords: Vibrotactile display · emotion · sound

1 Introduction

Sense of touch is an essential part of our lives, our social interactions, and the way we perceive ourselves and the world around us. Touch elicits comfort and attachment and provides rich information about surroundings [19], showing tremendous potential for perception and communication at the intersection of physical and digital worlds. Yet, despite the fact that tactility has great potential in communicating affective states, vibrotactile feedback is still quite limited in terms of its emotive properties [27]. One of the main reasons for the lack of affective variability of vibrotactile feedback is the complexity of reproducing touch sensations that would resemble natural touch sensations [17]. Allowing haptic designers and researchers to easily prototype a variety of emotive vibrotactile sensations can open the door to a number of novel applications within the tactile affective communication domain.

Accordingly, we posit that projecting music and nature sounds through vibrotactile feedback (creating "tactile compositions") constitutes an important pursuit in the haptics research field. We envision a world in which judiciously-designed "tactile compositions" serve as powerful implicit communicators

© The Author(s), under exclusive license to Springer Nature Switzerland AG 2023
M. Kurosu and A. Hashizume (Eds.): HCII 2023, LNCS 14012, pp. 318–331, 2023.
https://doi.org/10.1007/978-3-031-35599-8_20

of emotions and intentions [19], not unlike real-life touch interactions. We believe that the fact that information based on affect (versus e.g., words or numbers) is more easily and often automatically interpreted by the brain [15] constitutes a strong argument to suggest such "tactile composition" channels will be excellent candidates for implicit interactions; "tactile compositions" will communicate rich emotions, and a variety of states (beyond a commonly communicated by vibration state of alertness) in remote interactions tacitly, or even serve as emotional regulators.

Here **we ask whether emotionally resonant music compositions validated in prior research can be perceived as conveying specific emotion when projected through vibration, and if so, to what extent? Further, we ask whether these "vibrotactile compositions" elicit the same affective response as their sound counterparts.**

We intuit that tactile patterns will result in distinct affective self-reported as well as actual physiological responses and will produce similar emotional effect as the sounds from which they were generated. We find support for this hypothesis in prior research on affective properties of sound and the ability of music to elicit a variety of emotional responses [21], on affective properties of vibration [12,17,23], and how they are shared with sound [13] and on displaying emotive sounds as vibration in the Human-Computer Interaction (HCI) domain [9,12,17]. Only a few HCI works have specifically investigated emotional responses to a set of tactile patterns generated from soundscapes and real-world sounds [9,12,17] with encouraging results. Here we continue this line of research by expanding on the types of stimuli and method.

We conducted a within-subjects exploratory study in a laboratory setting with 18 participants who experienced and rated 6 vibrotactile stimuli through the "Be Me" vest designed for this study. We found distinct influence for most of the vibrotactile stimuli on galvanic skin response (GSR) and significant differences for some stimuli on subjective ratings in terms of valence and arousal. Further, the valence response to the vibrotactile stimuli was similar to its sound counterparts but different in the arousal responses.

The main contributions of this work include:

- Providing further evidence that displaying emotionally resonant sounds as vibrotactile feedback can produce a variety of distinct emotional response.
- Insights about the music properties that may predict the affective response when displayed as vibrotactile stimuli.
- A fully-functional prototype for displaying emotive sounds as tactile feedback on the upper back of a user.

2   Related Work

We ground our work in the prior research on affective properties of vibration and sound, tactile perception as well as on sensory substitution techniques for the deaf.

2.1 Emotive Properties of Music and Vibration

Music and nature sounds have a great potential to communicate a wide range of emotions and influence our affective state. For instance, music evoking calm and relaxing memories can kindle similar emotions [21], reduce stress, and even relieve pain [24,26]. Some natural sounds can create positive emotional feedback, and in other cases, serve as a sleeping aid [11]. Music and nature soundscapes are multisensorial experiences. "Feeling music" is not a new term because music is a sound and sound is essentially a vibration [10]. This explains why we not only hear the music with an ear but also feel it on a skin. For deaf people feeling music is one of the main channels for interpreting and appreciating the affective meaning of music compositions [20].

Vibrotactile stimulation generated from emotionally resonant sounds share many of the fundamental elements that give rise to the emotional expressivity of these sounds. Recent research on cross-modality priming [13] and scalar short-term memory [2] gave us motivation to believe that displaying sound as tactile sensation can be effective. Specifically, the findings strongly suggest that neurophysiological processes, underlying both auditory and tactile information, partially overlap.

Further, prior research on vibrotactile affective perception has established that vibration parameters, such as frequency and amplitude, can map to a specific emotional response. For instance, vibrotactile stimuli at low intensity and low frequency induce a sense of calmness in users, whereas vibrotactile stimuli at low intensity but higher frequency triggers an increased excitement [5,27]. Moreover, recent research on simulating real touch sensations discovered the techniques of producing pleasant sensations similar to a gentle stroke on a hand [14].

2.2 Displaying Sound as Vibration in the HCI

Displaying music or soundscapes as vibrotactile feedback has been predominantly explored in multimodal interactions in virtual reality (VR) and immersive multimedia experiences [5,7,18], social robotics [25], and for sensory substitution [16]. What is not yet fully understood about these devices is whether the affective properties of emotive sounds can be effectively translated to vibrotactile feedback. Below, we discuss studies that directly investigated the effect on an emotional response from perceiving emotionally resonant music and nature sounds as vibration.

Macdonald et al. [17] translated raw emotionally resonant nature sounds as vibration on the palm of a hand. Haynes et al. [12] displayed the processed (using only frequency and melody) music compositions on the forearm. Before experiencing these music compositions tactually, the participants listened to them. Another study by Karam et al. investigated the sensory substitution system that enabled deaf users to perceive the music and appreciate its emotional expressions [16]. The system was designed as a chair with embedded voice coil actuators that were coupled to the back of a person.

Generally, the above-mentioned studies support our hypothesis by demonstrating that affective properties of complex sounds may transfer to a tactile channel. The results also show that the magnitude of emotional response is lower for pleasant sensations and higher for negative sensations when compared to the original sounds. Moreover, tactile sensations evocative of real-world experiences can generate stronger emotional responses. The studies also suggest that parameters such as tempo, frequency, amplitude, and the ability of the stimuli to evoke specific memory or association play crucial roles in generating particular emotional responses.

It is important to note that the previous studies tested either the nature sounds or the processed music sounds and participants were exposed to these sounds aurally before experiencing them tactually. Further investigation of a variety of other stimuli, generated from the emotive sounds not previously experienced by study participants will expand our understanding of how affective properties may transfer between aural and tactile stimuli.

3 Method

The goal of the study was to investigate whether the tactile stimuli generated from the music compositions and nature sounds would produce a distinct emotional response and whether these responses are similar to their sound counterparts. To achieve the goal we conducted a within-subjects experiment in a controlled environment.

3.1 Apparatus

The "Be Me" vest, as shown in Fig. 1, is a sleeveless vest constructed from thin, stretchy material. Six miniature (a 2×3 grid) voice-coil actuators (model: TEAX13C02, Tectonic Elements, UK) were placed between two thin layers of the upper rear of the vest, facing the back of the wearer. The actuators have a relatively wide bandwidth of frequencies ranging from 50 to 2 kHz, with a resonance frequency 560 Hz. An Arduino Nano board controlled a MP3 Module (DF Mini Player), which played MP3 files loaded on an SD card. Each raw sound file on the SD card represented a 20-s music piece. We normalized the peak amplitude of the selected MP3 files to 89 dB using the Mp3Gain software tool. Each MP3 Module was connected to a pair of the voice coil actuators via an amplifier (model MAX98306), resulting in all six actuators outputting each stimulus symmetrically.

As the sounds were directly played by the actuators, only a limited range of frequencies was perceived by the skin. Human vibrotactile sensitivity is highest in the 200–250 Hz range and functional 10 Hz 500 Hz [8]. The stimuli used in this study fit only partially into this range. Although vibrotactile stimuli generated from raw sounds cannot be perceived at the same level of detail and frequency range, it is still possible to assess whether this limited perception can produce emotional responses. The Galvanic Skin Response (GSR) sensor was also controlled by the Arduino Nano; the data was stored on the computer using a custom experiment interface developed in Python script.

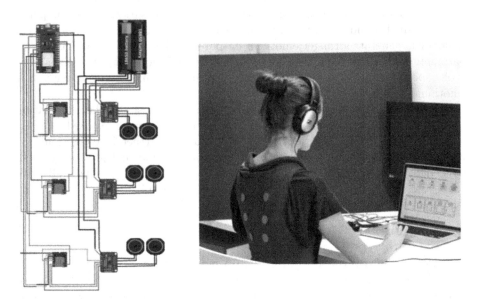

Fig. 1. Right: "Be Me" vest during the experiment. Left: The circuit, enabling the vibrotactile display of the vest.

3.2   Stimuli

Four stimuli were generated using music compositions sourced from the DEAM open source validated sound library [1]. The library provides arousal and valence self-reported ratings (on a Likert scale from 1 to 9) for 1,802 songs. We performed cluster analysis of all songs in the database and selected four stimuli representing an average for each quadrant on the Russell Circumplex Model of Affect. In addition, we chose only instrumental songs to avoid any additional noise from the lyrics. The other two sounds were sourced from prior research on affective responses to nature sounds and were generated from a "heavy human breath" and a "cat purring" sound [17]. We do not have validated arousal and valence ratings for these sounds but prior research shows that people perceive a "cat purring" sound as pleasant and relaxing while a "heavy human breath" sound is considered less pleasant and arousing [17]. Table 1 provides information on the selected songs and the average arousal and valence ratings assigned in the DEAM library.

Stimuli were pilot tested for clarity and some had bass frequencies amplified (0 Hz–100 Hz) using Audacity software. We chose to place the actuators on a person's back because we applied a longer duration (20 s) of stimulation than commonly used, and the lower sensitivity of skin receptors on the back may be beneficial to minimize unpleasant sensations. The rationale behind the longer duration of stimulation is based on prior work that shows longer duration elicits a stronger emotional response to the vibrotactile stimulus [17]. The placement of the actuators along the spine was guided by the body trigger points, utilized in acupuncture and massage therapies. These points are known to be more perceptive to the stimuli [3].

Table 1. The selected songs from which the tactile stimuli were generated. The table specifies the song ID in the library and arousal and valence ratings, sources from DEAM sound library.

Song ID	Arousal Rating	Valence Rating
1	3.3	3.6
2	6.1	6.1
3	3.3	3.7
4	6.2	6.1
"human breath"	-	-
"cat purring"	-	-

3.3   Participants

We recruited 18 (10 males, 8 females) participants with an average age of 34 (range: 24 to 50 years) from a local university. Participants had no tactile impairments and were not exposed daily to excessive vibrations (e.g., special construction equipment or machinery). The participants were not compensated for their participation.

3.4   Procedure

The study included two tasks performed by each participant. During the first task, the participants sat before a computer while wearing noise-canceling headphones and a "Be Me" vest through which they experienced 6 vibrotactile stimuli (independent variables). Each stimulus was randomly presented 6 times. Each time a stimulus lasted for 20 s followed by a 20 s break during which the participants had to report arousal and valence on a 9-point Likert scale (dependent variables), using the Self-Assessment Manikin (SAM) tool [4].

The participants wore one GSR sensor attached to the index and middle fingers of their non-dominant hand. Their GSR measures were collected throughout the duration of the experiment.

There was a 10-min practice session resembling the actual study. The stimuli in the practice session were not used in the actual study. After the practice session, the participants had the opportunity to ask questions to make sure they understood the concepts in the questionnaire and the overall procedure. After the practice session, the task started and finished with a 2-min Resting State period (RS). In the end, the participants completed a demographic survey and questionnaire about their experience. The duration of whole study for the first Task lasted 75 min on average (Fig. 2).

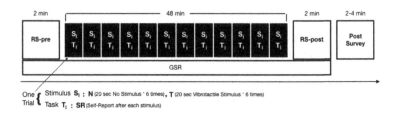

Fig. 2. A schematic representation of experimental procedure for Task 1.

The second task was performed by the same participants several weeks after the first task. Each participant sat before a computer while wearing headphones and listened to the 4 songs from which the vibrotactile stimuli were generated for the first task. We did not include the sounds of "heavy human breath" and "cat purring" as our primary foci of interest were the music compositions and their vibrotactile counterparts. The participants were tasked to rate each sound in terms of valence and arousal using the same scale and questions used in Task 1.

4   Findings

Mapping GSR to Tactile Stimuli: Before performing the analysis, we filtered GSR raw data by removing the high-frequency noise and rapid-transient artifacts and identified event-related skin conductance responses using TobiiPro software algorithm [22]. We then removed any inter-subject variability using the Cousineau approach [6]. The descriptive plot below (Fig. 3) shows the mean and confidence intervals of the normalized GSR values for the six stimuli. The confidence intervals are rather small. The data shows that stimulus 5 resulted in the highest mean values for GSR measures. It is followed sequentially by stimuli 4, 6, 2, 1, and 3. Descriptively we see that the confidence intervals do not overlap so we can infer that the differences are generally significant except for the difference between stimuli 1 and 3.

Mapping Self-report to Tactile Stimuli: The results of the one-way repeated-measures ANOVA showed that vibrotactile stimuli generated from nature sounds and music compositions received significantly different valence (F (5, 85) = 4.1, p = 0.02, and arousal (F (5, 70) = 4.1, p = 0.009) responses. Bonferroni post hoc tests concerning valence measures (Fig. 5) showed that the

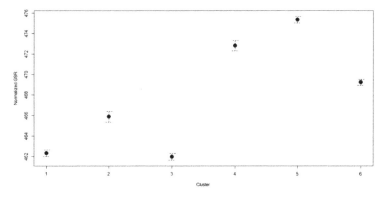

Fig. 3. The mean and confidence intervals of the normalized GSR values for six vibro-tactile stimuli.

stimulus 6 (mean $=$ 4.6, SD $=$ 1.8) is the most distinct stimulus and is signif-icantly different from stimulus 2 (mean $=$ 5.4, SD $=$ 1.4, p $=$ .03), stimulus 3 (mean $=$ 5.9, SD $=$ 1.5, p $=$ .001), and stimulus 4 (mean $=$ 5.9, SD $=$ 1.9, p $=$ .03). Additionally, stimulus 3 is significantly different from stimulus 1 (mean $=$ 4.9, SD $=$ 1.5, p $=$ .02) and 5 (mean $=$ 5.07, SD $=$ 1.9, p $=$ .01). If we look closer at the valence score difference between the four stimuli which were gener-ated from song compositions, we see that only stimuli 1 and 3 are significantly different at p $=$ .02 The Bonferroni post hoc tests concerning arousal measures (Fig. 4) showed that stimulus 4 (mean $=$ 5.5, SD $=$ 1.8) is significantly different from stimuli 1 (mean $=$ 4.3, SD $=$ 1.6, p $=$ .01), 2 (mean$=$ 4.4, SD $=$ 1.3, p $=$ .02), 3 (mean $=$ 4.1, SD $=$ 1.4, p $=$ .001), and 6 (mean $=$ 4.1, SD $=$ 1.1, p $=$ .03). Stimulus 5 (mean $=$ 5.3, SD $=$ 0.9) is significantly different from stimuli 1 (p $=$ .02), 2 (p $=$ .03), 3 (p $=$ .001), and 6 (p $=$ .002). If we compare only the stimuli generated from song compositions we can see that only stimulus 4 is significantly different from all other stimuli generated from songs.

Comparing Affective Responses to Vibrotactile and Sound Stimuli: The 2-dimensional arousal and valence plot (Fig. 6) shows the distribution on a four-quadrant space of the ratings given to songs in relation to the ratings given to vibrotactile stimuli generated from these songs. The statistical analysis shows that only stimulus 4 has a significantly different valence score (p $=$ .001) from its sound counterpart. All other stimuli do not have significantly different valence responses from the songs they were generated from. Conversely, the arousal scores show that stimuli 2 (p $=$ .001), 3 (p $=$ .002), and 4 (p $=$ .04) are significantly different from their sound counterparts. Only stimulus 1 does not significantly differ from the sound it was generated from.

Further, we descriptively compared mean baseline ratings to the sounds sourced from DIAM library to the ratings from tactile and subsequent sound evaluations of the same set of songs we tested in our study (see Fig. 7). We see

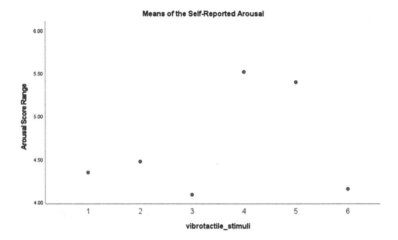

Fig. 4. Means of the Self-Reported measures for Arousal for six vibrotactile stimuli.

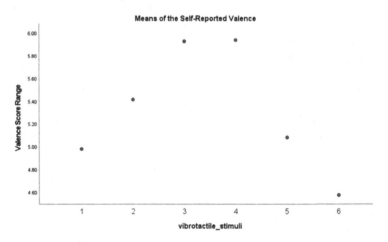

Fig. 5. Means of the Self-Reported measures for Valence for six vibrotactile stimuli.

that the baseline ratings are generally similar to the ratings given to the same sounds by our participants.

Qualitative Feedback: In an open-ended digital survey, after Task 1 was completed, participants were asked which vibrations they found most comfortable and uncomfortable. More than half of the participants mentioned that intensive, fast, constantly-varying in pattern vibrations felt irritating and uncomfortable. Some of these participants mentioned that it was especially uncomfortable when a slow vibration would suddenly become a fast one. Two participants mentioned that weak vibrations with tickling sensations felt uncomfortable, describing them as "there are ants under my skin." The other two participants disliked continuous

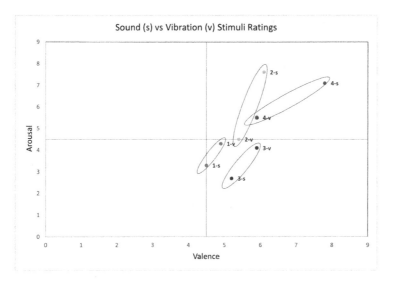

Fig. 6. The valence and arousal responses to the vibrotactile stimuli and their music composition counterparts.

Valence Comparison			
Song ID	Vibration	Sound	Baseline sound
1	4.9*	4.5	3.6
2	5.4	6.1	6.1
3	5.9*	5.2	4.7
4	5.9	7.8	6.1

Arousal Comparison			
Song ID	Vibration	Sound	Baseline sound
1	4.3	3.3	3.3
2	4.4	7.6	6.1
3	4.1	2.7	3.3
4	5.5*	7.1	6.2

Fig. 7. The comparison of means for the valence and arousal responses to the vibrotactile stimuli, their music composition counterparts, and the baseline responses to the same songs sourced from the DIAM library. The values with * are significant at $p < 0.05$

vibration without any peaks and described it as "noise." Eight participants preferred moderate intensity, subtle, and generally slower orderly vibrations. They found it more relaxing. 70 percent of the participants mentioned that orderly patterns with consistent rhythm felt most comfortable.

5   Discussion and Future Work

The findings pointed in the following direction: (1) the vibrotactile stimuli generated from music compositions and other sounds can produce significantly different self-reported and physiological responses; (2) the vibrotactile stimuli produce similar self-reported valence ratings as their music compositions counterparts but differ in terms of arousal. The most distinct stimulus in terms of valence was the sound of human breathing. It was perceived as the least pleasant. It also produced the least arousing tactile sensation. The sound of a cat purr was perceived as more pleasant on average than human breath and significantly more arousing than human breath. These findings are consistent with prior research [9].

In terms of music compositions, stimulus 1 was perceived as the least pleasant and 3 as the most pleasant. Stimulus 1 was generated from a music composition played with a single string instrument with slow Adagio tempo with unpredictable rhythm. Stimulus 3 was generated from a song played with a combination of trumpet and string instruments with slightly faster tempo and distinct rhythm. In terms of arousal, stimulus 4 was the only stimulus which was significantly more arousing than all other stimuli generated from songs. Stimulus 4 was produced from a highly energetic, fast tempo instrumental music composition. We can see that the properties of the music compositions and the affective response to their vibrotactile counterparts are largely consistent with qualitative feedback and prior findings [12,17].

Further, the GSR results are intuitive, especially when looking closely at each stimulus. For instance, stimulus 4 and 5 were rated as highly arousing. Since arousal positively correlates with GSR, it made sense that these stimuli produced the highest response. Conversely, stimulus 3 had the lowest GSR measure similar to the self-reported measure.

By looking at the 2-dimensional arousal and valence plot, we see that the majority of stimuli (both vibrotactile (v) and sound (s)) tend to cluster towards the center and the top right side. This indicates that the stimuli were generally perceived as moderately pleasant and arousing. It also indicates that the response to the stimuli was generally similar to the scores sourced from the DEAM library. By mapping the vibrotactile stimuli together with their sound counterparts we see that, in terms of valence ratings, most of the stimuli are perceived similarly. By contrast, the range of responses for arousal is greater for sound stimuli in comparison to their vibrotactile counterparts. The plot shows that more arousing vibrotactile stimuli are perceived as even more arousing when listened to as a sound, and less arousing vibrotactile stimuli are even less arousing when listened to. The evidence that the sound is perceived more intensely is consistent with prior research. One more reason for this can be the fact that the vibrotactile frequency range is much more limited in comparison to its sound counterpart.

These observations should be tested in future studies with a larger population. We also need to test stimuli that are located on the extreme ends of the Circumplex Model of Affect. Currently, the chosen stimuli were clustered around the middle area of the Circumplex-Model of Effect. Even though we were able to assess the significance of differences between the chosen stimuli, we see it as a limitation of this study.

Further, we plan to use the "vibrotactile compositions" to create meaningful mediated touch support during stressful situations. For instance, during a public speaking situation a friend could approve or encourage a speaker by sending "tactile compositions." If a specific tactile composition can be perceived as a distinct emotion it can carry meaning along the lines of that specific emotion. For instance, rhythmic, moderately intense "tactile composition" can be interpreted as an encouraging message, such as "You are doing great!" We plan to explore this particular scenario and investigate how "tactile compositions" can be interpreted when perceived on the skin during public speaking.

6   Conclusion

The paper investigated whether the vibrotactile stimuli generated from raw music compositions may elicit distinct emotional responses and, most importantly, to what extent or in what way the vibrotactile counterparts draw emotional effects on users from the musical soundtracks. The results demonstrated a significant difference in emotional responses in terms of valence and arousal. Moreover, the results pointed to the common properties of music compositions that may predict the affective response to a vibrotactile counterpart. For instance, low-tempo sounds with weak, unpredictable rhythms are perceived as less arousing and less pleasant tactile sensations. On the other hand, sounds with a moderate tempo with consistent rhythm are perceived as pleasant tactile sensations. Moreover, in terms of arousal, the tactile sensations are perceived with less magnitude than their sound counterparts. We hope these findings can lead to further explorations of the sound-based tactile feedback and inspire novel applications within the affective haptics domain.

References

1. Aljanaki, A., Yang, Y.H., Soleymani, M.: Developing a benchmark for emotional analysis of music. PloS one **12**(3), e0173392–e0173392 (2017). https://doi.org/10.1371/journal.pone.0173392. https://pubmed.ncbi.nlm.nih.gov/28282400
2. Bancroft, T.D.: Scalar short-term memory (2016)
3. Boyles, R., Fowler, R., Ramsey, D., Burrows, E.: Effectiveness of trigger point dry needling for multiple body regions: a systematic review. J. Manual Manipulative Therapy **23**(5), 276–293 (2015). https://doi.org/10.1179/2042618615Y.0000000014. https://doi.org/10.1179/2042618615Y.0000000014, pMID: 26955257
4. Bradley, M.M., Lang, P.J.: Measuring emotion: the self-assessment manikin and the semantic differential. J. Behav. Therapy Exp. Psychiatry **25**(1), 49–59 (1994). https://doi.org/10.1016/0005-7916(94)90063-9. https://www.sciencedirect.com/science/article/pii/0005791694900639
5. Choi, S., Kuchenbecker, K.J.: Vibrotactile display: perception, technology, and applications. Proc. IEEE **101**(9), 2093–2104 (2013). https://doi.org/10.1109/JPROC.2012.2221071
6. Cousineau, D.: Confidence intervals in within-subject designs: a simpler solution to loftus and masson's method (2005)

7. Czech, E., Shibasaki, M., Tsuchiya, K.: Haptic remembrance book series. In: Extended Abstracts of the 2019 CHI Conference on Human Factors in Computing Systems, CHI EA 2019, pp. 1–6. Association for Computing Machinery, New York (2019). https://doi.org/10.1145/3290607.3309685. https://doi.org/10.1145/3290607.3309685

8. Erp, J.V.: Guidelines for the use of vibro-tactile displays in human computer interaction (2002)

9. Erp, J.V., Spapé, M.: Distilling the underlying dimensions of tactile melodies (2003)

10. Gunther, E., O'Modhrain, S.: Cutaneous grooves: composing for the sense of touch. J. New Music Res. **32**(4), 369–381 (2003). https://doi.org/10.1076/jnmr.32.4.369.18856. https://www.tandfonline.com/doi/abs/10.1076/jnmr.32.4.369.18856

11. Handscomb, L.: Use of bedside sound generators by patients with tinnitus-related sleeping difficulty: which sounds are preferred and why? Acta Oto-Laryngologica **126**(sup556), 59–63 (2006). https://doi.org/10.1080/03655230600895275

12. Haynes, A., Lawry, J., Kent, C., Rossiter, J.: Feelmusic: enriching our emotive experience of music through audio-tactile mappings. Multimod. Technol. Inter. **5**(6) (2021). https://doi.org/10.3390/mti5060029. https://www.mdpi.com/2414-4088/5/6/29

13. Huang, J., Sheffield, B., Lin, P., Zeng, F.G.: Electro-tactile stimulation enhances cochlear implant speech recognition in noise. Sci. Rep. **7**(1), 2196 (2017). https://doi.org/10.1038/s41598-017-02429-1

14. Israr, A., Abnousi, F.: Towards pleasant touch: vibrotactile grids for social touch interactions. In: Extended Abstracts of the 2018 CHI Conference on Human Factors in Computing Systems, p. LBW131. ACM (2018)

15. Jang, D., Elfenbein, H.A.: Emotion, perception and expression of. In: Wright, J.D. (ed.) International Encyclopedia of the Social & Behavioral Sciences (Second Edition), 2nd edn., pp. 483–489. Elsevier, Oxford, (2015). https://doi.org/10.1016/B978-0-08-097086-8.25052-6, https://www.sciencedirect.com/science/article/pii/B9780080970868250526

16. Karam, M., Nespoli, G., Russo, F., Fels, D.I.: Modelling perceptual elements of music in a vibrotactile display for deaf users: a field study. In: 2009 Second International Conferences on Advances in Computer-Human Interactions, pp. 249–254 (2009). https://doi.org/10.1109/ACHI.2009.64

17. Macdonald, S.A., Brewster, S., Pollick, F.: Eliciting emotion with vibrotactile stimuli evocative of real-world sensations. In: Proceedings of the 2020 International Conference on Multimodal Interaction, ICMI 2020, pp. 125–133. Association for Computing Machinery, New York (2020). https://doi.org/10.1145/3382507.3418812

18. Mazzoni, A., Bryan-Kinns, N.: Mood Glove: a haptic wearable prototype system to enhance mood music in film. Entertainment Comput. **17**, 9–17 (2016). https://doi.org/10.1016/j.entcom.2016.06.002. http://www.sciencedirect.com/science/article/pii/S1875952116300209

19. Montagu, A.: Touching: The Human Significance of the Skin. Perennial library, HarperCollins (1986). https://books.google.ee/books?id=XU7Z_aqCYggC

20. Nanayakkara, S., Taylor, E., Wyse, L., Ong, S.H.: An enhanced musical experience for the deaf: Design and evaluation of a music display and a haptic chair. In: Proceedings of the SIGCHI Conference on Human Factors in Computing Systems, CHI 2009, pp. 337–346. Association for Computing Machinery, New York (2009). https://doi.org/10.1145/1518701.1518756. https://doi-org.ezproxy.tlu.ee/10.1145/1518701.1518756

21. Ogden, J.J., Lindburg, D.G., Maple, T.L.: The effects of ecologically-relevant sounds on zoo visitors. Curator Museum J. **36**(2), 147–156 (1993). https://doi.org/10.1111/j.2151-6952.1993.tb00787.x. https://onlinelibrary.wiley.com/doi/abs/10.1111/j.2151-6952.1993.tb00787.x

22. Pro, T.: Tobii Pro - GSR Data Filtering and Analysis (2022). https://www.tobiipro.com/learn-and-support/learn/steps-in-an-eye-tracking-study/data/gsr-data-filter-analysis-pro-lab/. Accessed 08-January-2022

23. Tsakiris, M.: My body in the brain: a neurocognitive model of body-ownership. Neuropsychologia **48**(3), 703–712 (2010). https://doi.org/10.1016/j.neuropsychologia.2009.09.034. https://www.sciencedirect.com/science/article/pii/S002839320900390X

24. Tsuchiya, M., et al.: Relaxing intraoperative natural sound blunts haemodynamic change at the emergence from propofol general anaesthesia and increases the acceptability of anaesthesia to the patient. Acta Anaesthesiologica Scandinavica **47**(8), 939–943 (2003). https://doi.org/10.1034/j.1399-6576.2003.00160.x. https://onlinelibrary.wiley.com/doi/abs/10.1034/j.1399-6576.2003.00160.x

25. Wada, K., Shibata, T.: Living with seal robots-its sociopsychological and physiological influences on the elderly at a care house. IEEE Trans. Rob. **23**(5), 972–980 (2007). https://doi.org/10.1109/TRO.2007.906261

26. Welte, J.W., Russell, M.: Influence of socially desirable responding in a study of stress and substance abuse. Alcoholism: Clin. Exp. Res. **17**(4), 758–761 (1993). https://doi.org/10.1111/j.1530-0277.1993.tb00836.x. https://onlinelibrary.wiley.com/doi/abs/10.1111/j.1530-0277.1993.tb00836.x

27. Yoo, Y., Yoo, T., Kong, J., Choi, S.: Emotional responses of tactile icons: effects of amplitude, frequency, duration, and envelope. In: 2015 IEEE World Haptics Conference (WHC), pp. 235–240 (2015). https://doi.org/10.1109/WHC.2015.7177719

How Different Tourist Sites Evoke Different Emotions: Investigation Focusing on the Urban and Rural Sites in Japan

Masashi Sugimoto$^{(\boxtimes)}$ ⓘ, Yasuo Yagi, and Noriko Nagata ⓘ

Kwansei Gakuin University, 1 Gakuen Uegarhara, Sanda 6691337, Hyogo, Japan
{sugimoto.masashi,yagi567,nagata}@kwansei.ac.jp

Abstract. In this research, we examined the affective values realized by two different tourist sites: Sannomiya (Kobe) and Asago. We conducted interviews based on the Evaluation Grid Method with 14 participants. The result of the interviews revealed different affective values according to the site and valence. For Sannomiya, "increasing return motivation" and "enjoyable" were extracted as attractive factors, whereas "unwillingness to walk around," "feeling dangerous," and "uneasiness" were perceived as unattractive aspects. In contrast, for Asago, "relaxing," "feeling of novelty," "feeling of sightseeing," "enjoyable," and "feeling of extraordinariness" were identified as attractive factors, whereas "decreasing return motivation," "decreasing visit motivation," and "feeling of wasting" were determined as unattractive aspects. We also examined the kinds of impressions and tourist resources that influence these affective values. In addition to these qualitative analyses, we conducted a quantitative analysis to verify that these affective factors could distinguish these two sites. These differences in affective values, impressions, and tourist sites enable us to visualize the attractiveness and unattractiveness of each site. The approach used in this research is helpful in investigating different affective values realized in different tourist sites and for describing the characteristics of the sites.

Keywords: Affective Value · Tourist Site · Evaluation Grid Method

1 Introduction

For many countries, sightseeing is one of the most critical industries. Travel and tourism accounted for 10% of the GDP until the outbreak of COVID-19 [1]. Although some changes might be made in the tourism industry after the end of the COVID-19 pandemic [2], sightseeing is still perceived as an effective method for regional vitalization [3].

Although many people enjoy tourism, their motivations for traveling are not necessarily shared. In addition to a general interest in tourism, they have different and specific motivations and evaluate events and items differently depending on the relevance to the motivation for their trip [4]. For example, a suburban area with abundant nature would be an excellent place for those who seek calm and relaxing travel. However, the same area might not satisfy those who want to experience energetic events. To avoid this mismatch,

© The Author(s), under exclusive license to Springer Nature Switzerland AG 2023
M. Kurosu and A. Hashizume (Eds.): HCII 2023, LNCS 14012, pp. 332–343, 2023.
https://doi.org/10.1007/978-3-031-35599-8_21

tourists need to understand the affective values that should be satisfied (e.g., whether they want to be relaxed or energized.). For tourist sites to attract tourists, they need to know what affective values they can impact by using their resources.

Considering the different evaluations of the same events and items, we focused on the affective value generated by the tourist site rather than the items or events of the tourist site itself and attempted to investigate the characteristics of the tourist sites through their affective value. To accomplish this purpose, in this research, we extracted data on how tourist sites evoke different affective values through impression, which is evoked by their tourist resources. We examined two tourist sites (Sannomiya, a central urban area of Kobe city, and Asago, a suburban area full of nature) that would produce different affective values and visualized the affective values they created. In other words, this research focused not on push factors but on pull factors [5]. A pull factor is defined as a factor that emerges due to the attractiveness of a particular tourist site, which distinguishes it from other sites. In contrast, a push factor is defined as a component of the tourists' socio-psychological factors that influences travel decisions and demand.

2 Related Research

2.1 How Tourists Determine Whether to Go and Where to Go

Whether one wants to go on a journey and where he/she goes are matters of decision-making. To examine the process, Mansfeld constructed the conceptual model of tourist destination choice [6] to explain the decision-making process of tourists. In the model, the tourists' decision-making consists of eight steps. In the first step ("travel motivation"), tourists are motivated to travel. In the second step ("information gathering"), they gather information to ascertain the attractive destinations that are within constraint limits and to evaluate the alternative destinations based on "place-utility." In the third step ("establishing alternatives"), the tourists list several alternatives that meet their motivation, constraint limits, and place utility. In the fourth, fifth, and sixth steps ("eliminating destination alternatives," "assessing destination alternatives," and "choosing the best alternative"), tourists select one destination and eliminate the alternatives. In the seventh step ("undertaking the travel"), tourists actually travel to the selected destination. In the eighth step ("choice evaluation"), they evaluate the destination they visited.

In each step of Mansfeld's model, the information about the destination (tourist site) is perceived and processed. Therefore, the aspects perceived as an attribute of the site will determine the tourists' evaluation of the site and whether they will select the site as the destination.

2.2 How Tourists Perceive Tourists Perceive Tourist Sites

Some studies focus on the site's resources that attract tourists to a site. For example, eight factors that relate to the satisfaction of the tourists to Cape Cod, Massachusetts, USA, have been identified: beach opportunities, cost, hospitality, eating and drinking facilities, accommodations, campground facilities, environment, and commercialization

[7]. Since each site has different factors, tourists have various motivations for choosing different sites. For example, tourists who visited Turkey had stronger cultural and physical motivations than those who visited Mallorca [8].

Another study pointed out that the tourist's attributes, not the site's characteristics, affect the tourist's satisfaction. For example, the tourist's preconceived image of the site influences their expectations and loyalty [9]. In addition, the tourist's nationality has an effect on their motivation [8]. These motivations are also known to affect evaluations of tourist resources [10].

3   How Tourist Sites Generate Different Affective Values: An Investigation Using the Evaluation Grid Method for Interviews

3.1   Approach

In this research, we adopt the three-layer hierarchical model of Kansei [11], where the top layer (affective value) is realized by the middle layer (impression), and the middle layer is formed by the bottom layer (physical feature). Physical features are perceived by and used to form impressions, generating value. In the case of tourism, the bottom layer (physical feature) corresponds to concrete tourist resources such as facilities, historic landmarks, and natural environments, the middle layer corresponds to impressions of the site, and the top layer corresponds to the affective value of the site.

3.2   Method

Participants. Fourteen participants participated in the study (seven males and seven females). Thirteen participants were graduate and undergraduate students in architecture courses, and one was a working adult who graduated from an architecture course. Their average age was 21.14 (ranging from 20 to 28). We selected participants who had visited both sites because a previous study pointed out that the visiting experience changes tourists' perception of the site [12]. All participants visited Sannomiya regularly, and the graduate and undergraduate students visited Asago immediately before the interview as a hands-on learning experience for the course.

Materials. For this study, we selected two tourist sites for the theme: Sannomiya and Asago. Both are in the Hyogo prefecture of Japan. Sannomiya is the central urban area of Kobe city with a population of around 1.5 million (Fig. 1). In contrast, Asago is a rural city with a population of around 30 thousand (Fig. 2). These areas were selected for two reasons. First, all of the participants had visited these areas and knew what kind of tourist resources are available and what kind of impressions and values are provided at the sites. Second, the two areas are contrary to each other in characteristics (urban vs. rural) and will provide different values.

Fig. 1. Sites in Sannomiya

Fig. 2. Sites in Asago

Procedure. *Participants' Information.* Participants were asked how many times they have visited Sannomiya and Asago (1: Never, 2: Once, 3: Twice or Thrice, 4: More than four times, 5: I live there or have lived there) and when they had last visited each site (1: A month, 2: Three months, 3: Half a year, 4: A year, 5: More than a year).

Interview. We conducted interviews based on the Evaluation Grid Method [13], which is a semi-structured interview process with a series of open questions. In the Evaluation Grid Method, we premise the interview with a hierarchical information processing mechanism called a construct system, which consists of concrete understanding (bottom layer), sensory understanding (middle layer), and abstract value judgment (top layer). In this system, people first form concrete understandings about an item from perceived information. Afterward, they form sensory understandings based on concrete understandings. Finally, they judge the abstract value using sensory understanding. Through this construct system, people will process outside information, understand their circumstances, and decide on what actions to take.

The Evaluation Grid Method is executed in two steps. In the first step, respondents are asked to compare two items, select the better one, and explain why that item is better than the other one. In the second step, participants were asked to respond to "ladder-up" and "ladder-down" questions. The ladder-up question asks participants about the upper concept of the response with an open question (e.g., "What is the advantage of xxx for you?"). In contrast, the ladder-down question asks participants about the lower concept of the response with an open question (e.g., "What is needed for xxx to be realized?"). By repeating these two questions, the interviewer will develop an evaluation structure of each respondent in a hierarchical network style to visualize how the objective factors conceive the abstract values via sensory understanding. After accumulating the evaluation structures of each respondent, the interviewer will develop an evaluation structure for the whole group of respondents.

The Evaluation Grid Method has three advantages [13]. First, using open questions allows the interviewer to elicit respondents' construct system without relying on the a priori hypothesis. Second, the fixed interview procedure enables the interviewer to collect results while minimizing the bias derived from the interviewer's subjective hypothesis. Third, the results are visualized in a hierarchical network based on the human information processing, which helps the researcher understand the results easily.

In the present research, we modified the procedure in the following ways. First, participants were asked to list attractive aspects of Sannomiya. Second, they were asked to respond to ladder-up questions to extract an abstract value judgment (e.g., "Why is it attractive?") and to ladder-down questions to extract objective understandings of the items (e.g., "What is needed to make the item attractive?"). They responded to all of the attractive/unattractive aspects of Sannomiya/Asago. The order of the four interviews was counterbalanced, and the interviews were about 90 min long in total.

3.3 Results

Participants' Familiarity with Sannomiya and Asago. Figure 3 shows the participants' number of visits to Sannomiya and Asago. All participants have visited Sannomiya more than four times. More than half of the participants have visited Asago once, and the rest have visited it two or more times.

Fig. 3. Participants' experience visiting the sites

Figure 4 shows the participants' last visit to Sannomiya and Asago. Most of them visited both sites within the month before the interview, indicating that their evaluations of the sites are relatively free of recall bias caused by long periods between a visit and an interview.

Fig. 4. Participants' last visit to the sites

Qualitative Difference in Tourist Sites and Valence. The interview data were summarized using the Evaluation Structure Visualization system, which was developed based on [14].

In the data analysis, we first categorized the interview responses with similar meanings. For example, responses such as "I can be relaxed," "I feel relaxed," and "It soothes the mind" are categorized into the "relaxing" category.

The software allows the analyzer to raise or lower the threshold of the results based on Katz's centrality to ensure that more important nodes are enhanced in the graph. In the analysis, we adopted 0.1008 in Katz centrality to make the graph comprehensive and detailed.

Figure 5 shows the attractive aspects of Sannomiya. At the higher level (abstract value judgment), the graph is characterized by words such as "increasing return motivation" and "enjoyable." In the middle level (sensory understanding), the attractive factors are recognized as "enjoy oneself," "easiness to visit," "pleasure of the table," "lively atmosphere," and "convenience." In the lower level (objective and concrete understanding), the participants highlighted "various shops," "many people," "cafe," "store," and "gathered stores."

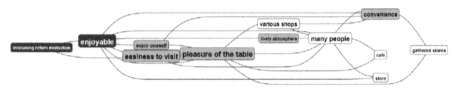

Fig. 5. Evaluation structure of the attractive aspects of Sannomiya (the thick blue nodes indicate affective value, the thin blue nodes indicate impression, and the white nodes indicate tourist resource)

Figure 6 shows the unattractive aspects of Sannomiya. At the higher level, the graph is characterized by words such as "unwillingness to walk around," "feeling dangerous," and "uneasiness." In the middle level, the graph is characterized by words such as "bad atmosphere," "restrictions in walking around," "poor public peace and order," "uncleanness," "need time to travel," "crowdedness," and "pleasure of the table." In the lower level, the graph is characterized by words such as "danger in disaster," "many cars," "touting," "suspicious people," "drunken people," "busy street," "many people," "station and around," and "Center Street."

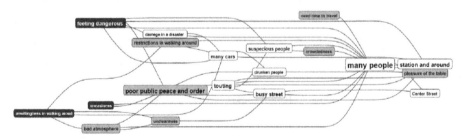

Fig. 6. Evaluation structure of the unattractive aspects of Sannomiya (the thick blue nodes indicate affective value, the thin blue nodes indicate impression, and the white nodes indicate tourist resource)

Figure 7 shows the attractive aspects of Asago. At the higher level, the graph is characterized by words such as "relaxing," "feeling of novelty," "feeling of sightseeing," "enjoyable," and "feeling of extraordinariness." In the middle level, the graph is characterized by words such as "attractive scenery," "distinctive scenery," "quietness," "events that never can be experienced in another place," "pleasures of the table," "being a historical place," "abundant nature," and "beautiful nature." In the lower level, the graph is characterized by words such as "snowfall and snow coverage," "Takeda castle," "station and around," "mountains," "Ikuno area," and "Ikuno silver mine."

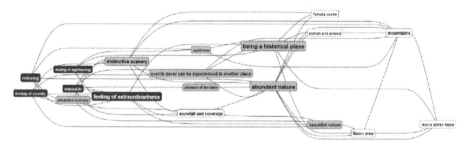

Fig. 7. Evaluation structure of the attractive aspects of Asago (the thick blue nodes indicate affective value, the thin blue nodes indicate impression, and the white nodes indicate tourist resource)

Figure 8 shows the unattractive aspects of Asago. At the higher level, the graph is characterized by words such as "decreasing return motivation," "decreasing visit motivation," and "feeling of wasting." In the middle level, the graph is characterized by words such as "not making use of the tourist attractions," "no pleasures of the table," inconvenience," "difficulty to visit," "no sense of uniqueness," "need time to travel," "limited numbers in options to take." In the lower level, the graph is characterized by words such as "limited numbers in people," "limited numbers in shops," "snowfall and snow coverage," "staying for a short time," "castle town," and "Takeda castle."

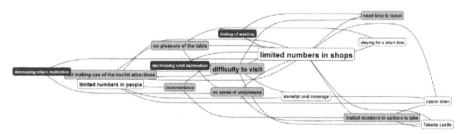

Fig. 8. Evaluation structure of the unattractive aspects of Asago (the thick blue nodes indicate affective value, the thin blue nodes indicate impression, and the white nodes indicate tourist resource)

Quantitative Difference in Tourist Sites and Valence. To determine whether there is a quantitative difference between each site's affective value, we conducted four (site and valence: Sannomiya (attractive)/Sannomiya (unattractive)/Asago (attractive)/Asago (unattractive)) by two (response: referred/did not refer) chi-squared tests on 12 affective values. Figure 9 shows the rate of participants who referred to each affective value in the attractive and unattractive interviews. The chi-squared tests showed significant differences in reference rate ($ps < 0.05$) for almost all affective values, excluding "uneasiness," "unwillingness to walk around," and "decreasing return motivation." Among the nine words that presented significant differences, "enjoyable" was referred to more frequently in the attractive interview on Sannomiya, whereas "feeling dangerous" was referred to more frequently in the unattractive interview. In comparison, "increasing return motivation," "relaxing," "feeling of novelty," "feeling of extraordinariness," and "feeling of sightseeing" were referred to more frequently in the attractive interview on Asago, whereas "decreasing visit motivation" was referred to more frequently in the unattractive interview on Asago. "Feeling of wasting" was not frequently referred to in any condition.

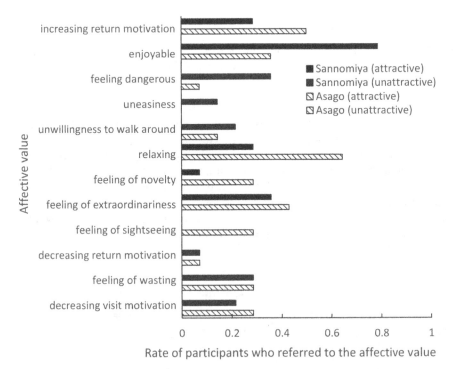

Fig. 9. Rate of participants who referred to each affective value during the interviews.

4 Conclusions

4.1 Summary of the Results

In this research, we conducted interviews on the attractive and unattractive aspects of two tourist sites: Sannomiya and Asago. The results of each interview qualitatively presented different affective values according to the tourist sites and valence. The quantitative analysis revealed the differences between the tourist sites.

From the qualitative analysis of the interview data, Sannomiya was revealed to be an enjoyable site that tourists want to visit more than once ("increasing return motivation"). The attractiveness of Sannomiya was derived from the visitors' impression that it is a lively and accessible city where they can find many places to enjoy themselves and eat delicious foods. These impressions were influenced by the various shops, cafes, and people there.

However, Sannomiya was also revealed to be an uneasy, dangerous place where visitors do not want to walk around. These affective values are a result of the visitors' impression that it is an unclean and crowded place with a bad atmosphere, poor public peace and order, and restrictions on walking around. This impression was derived from many people, who mentioned witnessing touting, suspicious behavior, and drunken people on the busy street near the station.

In contrast, Asago was described as an enjoyable place with a relaxing atmosphere and feeling of novelty, with plenty of sightseeing opportunities and an overall impression of extraordinariness. These affective values were extracted from the visitors' impression that Asago is a quiet and historical place with affective and distinctive scenery and abundant and beautiful nature. These impressions are influenced by artificial (e.g., Takeda castle and Ikuno silver mine) and natural (e.g., snow and mountains) tourist resources.

Unfortunately, Asago was revealed as a tourist site that people don't want to visit. The unattractive aspects of Asago resulted from visitors' belief that they could not feel the uniqueness of the place. This is most likely due to the difficulty to visit and the limited options available, which were derived from the fact that there are few shops there and visitors cannot stay there for a long time.

These feelings of novelty and extraordinariness might reflect people's familiarity with the sites. For most of the participants, Sannomiya was a familiar place that they had frequently visited, whereas Asago was a place that they had only visited once. Because of this difference, the participants might have perceived Asago as a novel and extraordinary place.

The quantitative analysis supported most of the affective differences. The result indicated that Sannomiya is an enjoyable but dangerous place, whereas Asago is a relaxing town with a feeling of novelty and extraordinariness and numerous sightseeing opportunities. One interesting point is that Asago is both attractive ("increasing return motivation") and unattractive ("decreasing visit motivation"), potentially because it is difficult to visit, which prevents Asago from attracting first-time visitors.

The factors of the two tourist sites illustrate their characteristics distinctively. From a valence viewpoint, some factors reflect the attractive aspects of the sites, whereas others reflect the unattractive aspects. From the viewpoint of the site, some factors shed light on the characteristics of Sannomiya, and others describe the characteristics of Asago. This distinctiveness could be useful for grasping the nature of various tourist sites.

4.2 The Novelty and Importance of This Research

This research is novel because we focused not on the tourist resources themselves, but on the affective value created by them. The affective value is realized by the interaction between the site and tourists, which could be a helpful clue for understanding tourism. Considering the increasing interest in co-creating tourist experiences [15], the interactive affective value will play an essential role in future tourism.

Moreover, this research is important because we focused on both the attractive and the unattractive aspects of the sites. Although most sites emphasize their attractive factors exclusively, analyzing the unattractive factors would also be useful. In a previous study, researchers demonstrated the usefulness of examining both sides by investigating both the satisfaction and dissatisfaction of tourists. It revealed that evaluations of the positive attributes and negative attributes lacked concordance [16]. In this research, the opposite of the attractive factors are not the unattractive factors. For example, the attractive affective values of Sannomiya (i.e., "increasing return motivation" and "enjoyable") are not the opposite of the unattractive affective values (i.e., "unwillingness to walk around," "feeling dangerous," and "uneasiness"). In addition, unlike the affective values realized in the Sannomiya and Asago, whose levels of urbanization are opposite, the lack of concordance between attractive and unattractive factors were not opposite. By conducting interviews on the attractive and unattractive aspects of different sites, we were able to reveal the characteristics of the sites more specifically.

This study succeeded in estimating the characteristics of the sites based on affective values, sensory impressions, and tourist resources. By using this method, it is possible to index the affective value of various tourist attractions. In the future, it will also be possible to classify tourist types by examining the degree to which visitors seek out each of the affective values that various tourist sites offer. It will also enable tourist sites to target tourists to whom the region is likely to appeal and allow tourists to select appropriate travel plans.

Acknowledgment. This study is supported by the collaborative special research subsidy of Kwansei Gakuin University.

References

1. Statista homepage. https://www.statista.com/statistics/1099933/travel-and-tourism-share-of-gdp/. Accessed 06 Feb 2023
2. Bhatia, A., Roy, B., Kumar, A.: A review of tourism sustainability in the era of Covid-19. J. Stat. Manag. Syst. **25**(8), 1871–1888 (2022)
3. Japan Tourism Agency homepage. https://www.mlit.go.jp/kankocho/iinkai/after_corona_kankosangyo.html. Accessed 06 Feb 2023
4. Devesa, M., Laguna, M., Palacios, A.: The role of motivation in visitor satisfaction: empirical evidence in rural tourism. Tour. Manage. **31**(4), 547–552 (2010)

5. Uysal, M., Li, X., Sirakaya-Turk, E.: Push-pull dynamics in travel decisions. Handbook of Hospitality Marketing Management, pp. 412–439 1st edn. Routledge, London (2008)
6. Mansfeld, Y.: From motivation to actual travel. Ann. Tour. Res. **19**(3), 399–419 (1992)
7. Pizam, A.: Tourist satisfaction with a destination area. Ann. Tour. Res. **5**(3), 3–14 (1978)
8. Kozak, M.: Comparative analysis of tourist motivations by nationality and destinations. Tour. Manage. **23**(3), 221–232 (2002)
9. del Bosque, I.R., San Martín, H.: Tourist satisfaction a cognitive-affective model. Ann. Tour. Res. **35**(2), 551–573 (2008)
10. Hatano, T., et al.: Measuring attractiveness of tourism resources by focusing on Kansei value structure: possibility of inviting visitors using the Japanese Heritage "Ako Salt". In: 2021 Asia-Pacific Signal and Information Processing Association Annual Summit and Conference (APSIPA ASC), pp. 1–7 (2021)
11. Miyai, S., Katahira, K., Sugimoto, M., Nagata, N., Nikata, K., Kawasaki, K.: Hierarchical structuring of the impressions of 3D shapes targeting for art and non-art university students. In: HCI International 2019 - Posters. HCII 2019. Communications in Computer and Information Science. vol. 1032, pp. 385–393. Springer, Cham (2019). https://doi.org/10.1007/978-3-030-23522-2_50
12. Pearce, P.L.: Perceived changes in holiday destinations. Ann. Tour. Res. **9**(2), 145–164 (1982)
13. Sanui, J.: Visualization of users' requirements: introduction of the evaluation grid method. In: Proceedings of the 3rd Design Decision Support Systems in Architecture Urban Planning Conference, vol. 1, pp. 365–374 (1996)
14. Onoue, Y., Kukimoto, N., Sakamoto, N., Koyamada, K.: E-Grid: a visual analytics system for evaluation structures. J. Visualization **19**(4), 753–768 (2016). https://doi.org/10.1007/s12650-015-0342-6
15. Campos, A.C., Mendes, J., do Valle, P.O., Scott, N.: Co-creation of tourist experiences: a literature review. Curr. Issues in Tourism **21**(4), 369–400 (2018)
16. Alegre, J., Garau, J.: Tourist satisfaction and dissatisfaction. Ann. Tour. Res. **37**(1), 52–73 (2010)

Understanding the User Experience

Research on Usability Evaluation of Online Exhibition Applications

Shih-Chieh Chen[✉] and Yu-Hsuan Lee

National Yunlin University of Science and Technology, Yunlin 640, Taiwan, China
chenshih@yuntech.edu.tw, M11031025@gemail.yuntech.edu.tw

Abstract. The Covid-19 pandemic has caused people to stay at home, and online exhibitions have become a good alternative for people to enjoy arts remotely. To learn more about the user interface and user experience design, this research used three online exhibition applications (apps) (NTMOFA, NPM, A&C) to conducts task analysis, observation, and semi-structured interviews to develop exploratory research. Thirty participants were invited to take part in the experiment, and the time they spent finishing each task was regarded as the objective results; the SUS and NASA-TLX and interview responses were the subjective results. The results showed that the time performance of moving, watching, playing audio, searching and sharing functions of each app was significantly different with NPM and A&C, respectively for VR and AR online exhibitions, usually taking more time. Besides, participants thought that NPM is slightly more user-friendly than the other two apps; however, they preferred the AR online exhibition for its immersion experience. In the interviews, participants also indicated that some elements, such as social interaction and sensory experience, are expected to be added to online exhibition. To sum up, those elements which can create presence of visiting physical exhibitions and can interact with others are critical for the future design of online exhibition apps.

Keywords: Online Exhibition Applications · User Experience · Task Analysis

1 Introduction

1.1 Background and Motivation

Due to the Covid-19 pandemic, online exhibitions have become a similar alternative to real exhibitions for people to view art without leaving their homes (Amorim & Teixeira, 2021). This epidemic has accelerated the digitalization of museums and galleries, rapidly popularizing online exhibitions (Li, Nie, & Ye, 2022). In addition, online museums, with technology innovations, are also breaking down the limitations of time and space, offering further opportunities to change the way of interaction between viewers and exhibitions, and substantially enhancing viewers' autonomy (Choi & Kim, 2021). Therefore, online exhibitions are not just another way of presenting art; understanding viewers' interaction patterns and their feelings about attending online exhibitions is thus necessary.

© The Author(s), under exclusive license to Springer Nature Switzerland AG 2023
M. Kurosu and A. Hashizume (Eds.): HCII 2023, LNCS 14012, pp. 347–362, 2023.
https://doi.org/10.1007/978-3-031-35599-8_22

Online exhibitions upend the display way of traditional museums, shaking the concept of buildings as containers, and switching the center from art works to the audience itself (Li et al., 2022). Moreover, online exhibitions place more emphasis on "interaction" between the audience and the works (Choi & Kim, 2021). Thus, online exhibitions are not just a way of extending the lives of physical exhibitions, their importance is also increasing.

Although some research on online exhibitions has focused on their impact on education (Kraybill, 2015) and sightseeing tourism (Resta, Dicuonzo, Karacan, & Pastore, 2021), little research has placed emphasis on the user interface and user experience of online exhibition applications (apps). Besides, it is also essential for online exhibition apps to satisfy the eight golden rules of interface design (Shneiderman et al., 2016). For this reason, this study, as exploratory research, expected to identify the objective performance and subjective feeling of using different types of online exhibition applications and to explore some design suggestions for the future.

1.2 Purpose

This research mainly considered three types of online exhibition, and discusses the subjective and objective results of uses using online exhibitions, which can be referred to in the future interface designs of online exhibitions. Thus, this study attempted to:

1. understand the user journey map regarding online exhibitions to design the tasks content;
2. realize users' time performance and feelings of using online exhibition applications;
3. learn more about how users interact with online exhibitions; and
4. develop basic design guidelines for online exhibitions.

2   Related Work

2.1   Online Exhibition

Online exhibitions have also been called as "virtual exhibitions, online museums, digital museums", and "e-museums". However, the terms were not clearly defined until Urbaneja (2019) pointed out their ambiguous use in previous research, and redefined an "online exhibition" as a virtual reconstruction of exhibitions and collections with multimedia and interactive resources. As mentioned above, online exhibitions, compared to physical exhibitions, are not object-oriented but user-oriented, and they alter the communication of one-way narrative, emphasizing the experience of "interaction" (Liu, 2006). The new way of showing exhibitions also expend the way of knowledge transfer, and users' participation and autonomy are increased as well (Li et al., 2022). Thus, understanding the difference in interaction in online exhibitions and physical exhibitions is important.

According to the Arts Global Market Report 2020–30: Covid 19 Impact and Recovery (Ken Research, 2020), there is an increasing number of art exhibitions, encouraging more and more artists to engage in producing more art works. With the surge in the number of artists and art works, physical exhibitions are not the only way of presenting the work.

Online exhibitions provide another alternative of presenting art works, spending less time and reducing the costs of establishment (Leong & Chennupati, 2008), while also shedding the high-class and fancy image of arts. On the other hand, online exhibitions evaluate users' autonomy, which coincides with the flexibility, mobility, and accessibility of applications (app) (Ciurea, Zamfiroiu, & Grosu, 2014), so it can be inferred that using applications as the interface of online exhibitions is appropriate. Nevertheless, nowadays, online exhibitions are usually presented through merely pictures and words, which may be less likely to evoke users' interests, or may tire them and fail to attract them to explore the works.

Some studies have discussed such issues as virtual tours in VR online exhibitions (Li et al., 2022) and online exhibitions education (Kraybill, 2015). However, little research has considered how users watch and interact with online exhibitions. Furthermore, online exhibitions are a complicated blend of artistic content, information architecture of platforms, and human-machine interaction mechanisms (Resta et al., 2021).

2.2   Interaction Design and User Experience Interface Design of Interface

Interaction design, originating from human-computer interaction, includes interface design. The interaction design of interfaces is defined as "for digital products with inter-active features, they are designed to be useful and desirable" (Moggridge, 2007). As a result, the interaction design of interfaces not only emphasizes the usability quality, but also focuses on humanity and the emotional value of user experience. It can be divided into two goals: usability and user experience.

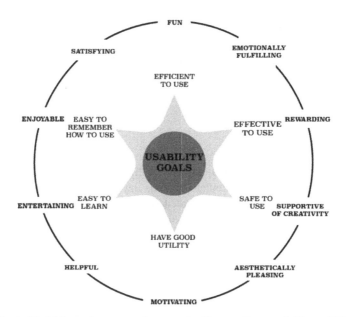

Fig. 1. Usability and user experience goals. (Preece, Rogers, & Sharp, 2007)

Usability goals are concerned with evaluating how useful an interface system is, and include six goals of interaction design. Besides, design should correspond to the six principles established by Norman (1988) in *The psychology of everyday things*: signifiers, feedback, mapping, conceptual models, constraints, and affordances. The interaction design of an interface should also follow Shneiderman's Eight Golden Rules of Interface Design (2016) referred to in *Design the User Interface*, which consider that a good design ought to:

1. strive for consistency
2. enable frequent users to use shortcuts
3. offer informative feedback
4. design dialog to yield closure
5. offer simple error handling
6. permit easy reversal of actions
7. support internal locus of control
8. reduce short-term memory load

As for user experience goals, it relates to users' subjective feelings and emotions, emphasizing all elements regarding user experience, such as environment, media, and so on, and the relationship between users' behaviors and those elements (Schmitt, 1999). To sum up, both usability goals and user experience goals should be simultaneously considered.

According to previous research (Bannon, Benford, Bowers, & Heath, 2005), interaction design can not only promote the interaction of the audience themselves, it can also shorten the gap between arts and the audience, letting the audience to get to know more about the art works. However, little research focuses on the interaction design of the interfaces of online exhibition apps from a user experience perspective. In order to learn more about the interaction patterns and user experience of online exhibition apps, this study was conducted to discover users' objective performance and subjective feelings while using online exhibition apps.

3   Methodology

3.1   Purpose of the Experiment

To understand users' subjective and objective feelings and usability online experience, participants were invited to manipulate the existing online exhibition apps, and their performance and feelings were also recorded. The experiment results were expected to provide some advices on the UI/UX design of online exhibitions and to contribute to future research.

3.2   Experiment Design

We conducted task analysis to investigate users' time performance and usability experience of using online exhibition apps. Before the task analysis, we developed a consumer journey map (Fig. 2) with reference to previous research (Villaespesa & Álvarez, 2020), then used the consumer journey map to develop the task contents.

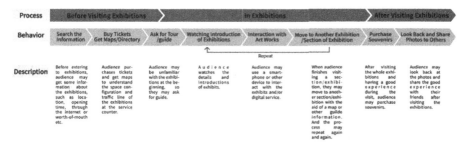

Fig. 2. Consumer Journey Map of Audience Visiting Exhibitions.

The between-subject experiment process of task analysis is shown in Fig. 3. Thirty participants were invited using the purposive sampling method, and eight tasks were conducted (Table 1). The time of performing each task was recorded as the objective results. During the experience, participants' behaviors were also observed and recorded. After finishing the tasks in each app, participants were required to fill out the SUS (Brooke, 1986) and NASA-TLX (Hart & Staveland, 1988) questionnaires as the subjective results to ensure that results recorded their memories while they were still fresh. Besides, the three online exhibition apps of the experiment were ordered by Lantin Square Design (LSD) to avoid the interface of the learning effect. At the end of the experiment, semi-structured interviews were conducted. Participants were requested to answer some questions about their experience of the online exhibition apps.

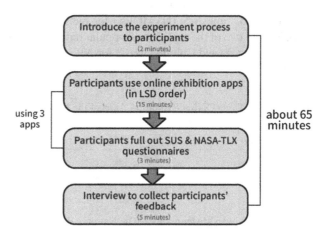

Fig. 3. The Experiment Process.

3.3 Sample

Nowadays, there are mainly three kinds of online exhibitions, namely pictures for simple presentation, VR (Resta et al., 2021) and AR (Kadam, 2021) for exploring a 3D space. To

Table 1. List of Task Analysis.

Number	Tasks	Available App		
		NTMOFA	NPM	A&C
Task 1–1	Find the particular exhibit. (shown on the Powerpoint of the experiment)	●	●	●
Task 1–2	Find the exhibit's name	●	●	●
Task 2	Find the exhibit's introduction	●	●	●
Task 3	Enlarge/zoom on the exhibit	●	●	●
Task 4	Find another particular exhibit inside (shown on the Powerpoint of the experiment)	●	●	●
Task 5	Play the exhibit's audio	●	●	●
Task 6	Use "search" to find another particular exhibit (shown on the Powerpoint of the experiment)	●	●	●
Task 7	Share the exhibition with your friend	–	●	●
Task 8	Switch to another exhibition (shown on the Powerpoint of the experiment)	●	–	●

understand users' usage patterns and preferences for different types of online exhibitions, this study conducted a task analysis (Diaper & Stanton, 2003) experiment using three online exhibitions apps (Table 2) the contents of which was in Traditional Chinese. National Taiwan Museum of Fine Arts (NTMOFA) for pictures and National Palace Museum (NPM) for VR are two of the top 10 most popular online exhibitions in Taiwan (DailyView, 2021); Google Arts and Culture (A&C) for AR is the symbolic AR online exhibition worldwide.

Table 2. The Three Online Exhibition Apps of the Experiment.

	NTMOFA	NPM	A&C
app			
Affiliation	National Taiwan Museum of Fine Arts	The National Palace Museum	Google
Presentation	Pictures	VR	AR

3.4 Participants

Thirty participants (14 male, 16 female), ranging in age from 18 to 26, were selected using the purposive sampling method. All participants had previous experience of watching exhibitions to ensure they were familiar with the task contents.

3.5 Tools

We used the iPhone 12 Pro Max to conduct the experiment. The size is 146.7mm x 71.5mm x 7.4mm with a diagonally 6.68 inches screen and 1284 x 2778 pixels of resolution. The operating system version was iOS 15.6.1.

3.6 Interview

After finishing the task analysis of the three online exhibition apps and the questionnaire for each of them, participants were required to orally answer several questions related to their feelings about using the online exhibition apps, including:

1. Without considering the present interface design of online exhibition apps and merely thinking about their presentation ways of them, which type of presentation (pictures/ VR/ AR) of online exhibition do you prefer?
2. Which online exhibition app do you think is most useful?
3. Regarding these three online exhibition apps (NTMOFA, NPM, A&C), what function(s) is/are poor to you?
4. If online exhibition apps are equipped with some interesting functions, such as VR/AR "Be an Artist" for NTMOFA, painting for A&C, "Art Projector" for A&C, and "Art Transfer" for A&C, will those apps improve your user experience?
5. What kinds of functions/values are you looking forward to being added to online exhibition apps?

   Participants were asked to answer the questions above during the semi-structured interviews, but if they had some other interesting viewpoints to share, that content was also accepted and recorded, and the questions could be extended.

4 Research Results

4.1 Objective Results

We invited participants in the experiment to conduct task analysis. Each time a participants finished each task, the time taken was recorded, as shown in Table 3. The differences and significant findings are discussed below.

Task 1–1. In Task 1-1, it took significantly more time to use NPM and less time to use NTMOFA ($F=20.56, p<0.001$). The reason that participants spent more time on this task may be the difference in moving in each exhibition (app) because most participants were familiar with the "list" form of presentation, compared to "3D digital space." In addition, due to experiencing cyber sickness, some participants needed to spend some time getting

Table 3. Objective Performance of Task Analysis. (second)

	NTMOFA		NPM		A&C			
	M	Sd	M	Sd	M	Sd	F	p
T1–1	3.77	3.69	51.89	46.06	40.77	21.47	20.56	0.00
T1–2	1.23	0.95	6.60	6.56	11.73	14.45	9.48	0.00
T2	3.18	1.99	30.62	34.09	4.32	4.08	18.06	0.00
T3	2.81	1.23	4.16	2.47	4.80	3.19	5.63	0.01
T4	5.31	1.66	42.20	32.64	13.11	11.82	30.48	0.00
T5	7.51	8.28	60.64	39.46	26.45	17.64	35.72	0.00
T6	67.17	29.49	23.63	13.78	69.96	20.52	47.81	0.00
T7	-	-	7.97	6.35	95.32	25.82	-20.04	0.00
T8	6.58	3.42	-	-	12.00	20.29	-1.40	0.17

Table 5. Subjective Performance of Task Analysis. (seconds)

	NTMOFA		NPM		A&C			
	M	Sd	M	Sd	M	Sd	F	p
SUS	31.07	7.62	32.07	6.64	25.37	7.51	6.54	0.00
NASA-TLX	23.87	7.20	25.27	6.91	30.10	6.32	9.03	0.00

used to the manipulation in 3D digital space, and may have felt uncomfortable at the beginning when they entered the exhibition.

Task 1–2. In Task 1-2, A&C took significantly more time for participants to use ($F=9.48$, $p<0.001$) because the names of exhibits do not appear permanently on the interface (Fig. 4). Only when users get closer to the exhibits in the AR 3D exhibition space, does the introduction page of each exhibit pop up. On the other hand, NTMOFA and NPM allow users to directly see the names of each exhibit, whether on the list of art works or the VR 3D exhibition space. Users can firstly read the names of exhibits, and then decide if they would like to see their literal introduction. Nevertheless, some participants thought that it was hard to associate the blue button on NPM with its actual function; besides, many participants thought the resolution of NPM's AR exhibition was too low to see the content clearly. This may be the reason why participants spent more time on using NPM in Task 1-2 than NTMOFA.

Task 2. In Task 2, there was also a significant difference in participants' use of the three online exhibition apps ($F=18.06$, $p<0.001$). The reason participants spent more time using NPM was that the literal introduction of exhibits shown on the VR exhibition was inconsistent with the contents of the blue button, so participants needed to make efforts to find particular information in either of position. Besides, more than half of the participants, by observation, could not precisely tap the blue button at first because they

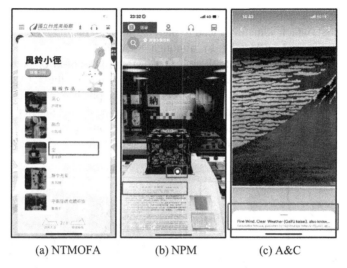

(a) NTMOFA   (b) NPM   (c) A&C

Fig. 4. Manipulation Diagram of Task 1–2.

thought it was too small to tap and it may cause unexpected movement when they were trying to tap it. Thus, compared to NTMOFA with its pictures form and A&C for which the introduction can automatically pop up (Fig. 5), NPM took participants more time to use.

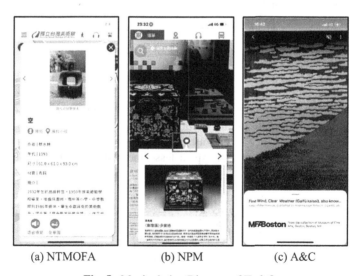

(a) NTMOFA   (b) NPM   (c) A&C

Fig. 5. Manipulation Diagram of Task 2.

Task 3. In Task 3, the time participants spent on using each of the three apps was significantly different, with A&C taking them more time to use. The reason for this result might be that some participants, by observation, were not familiar with the strength of pinching at first, which sometimes lead to piercing through the 3D AR exhibition wall. As for NTMOFA and NPM (Fig. 6), although NTMOFA also has a VR version for watching exhibitions, participants thought the degree of zoom-in of both apps while pinching was so slow that it took effort and time to zoom in on the 3D VR exhibition. Moreover, the exhibits images of both apps could not be pinched, and the resolution of exhibits shown by both VR and picture was too low to see the details clearly. To recap, most participants declared that the present ways of "zooming in" cannot satisfy their needs of seeing more details of the exhibits.

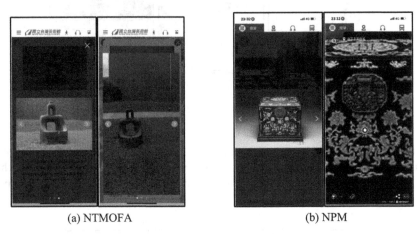

(a) NTMOFA   (b) NPM

Fig. 6. Manipulation Diagram of Task 3.

Task 4. In Task 4, there was a significantly difference in participants using each of the three online exhibition apps ($F=30.48$, $p<0.001$). They spent more time moving to an-other section in an exhibition of NPM than others. There is an interesting finding that participants, in Task 1-1, firstly spent more time moving while using both NPM and A&C; however, they then spent much less time on using A&C than NPM in Task 4. Therefore, we can infer that users spent less time getting used to using AR online exhibition apps than VR online exhibition apps.

Task 5. In Task 5, the time participants took to listen to the audio had a significant difference between each of the three apps ($F=35.72$, $p<0.001$). Because most people thought that the position of the audio of online exhibitions should be near the literal introduction, coinciding with physical exhibitions, it took participants lee time to finish Task 5 in NTMOFA (Fig. 7), as the audio fits the mental map of users. On the other hand, the audio of A&C is organized into each section of the exhibition rather than each exhibit, and the position of the A&C audio does not fit the mental map of users, so it takes more time for participants to use the "audio" function of A&C. Furthermore, many participants suggested that the audio of NTMOFA and A&C should be equipped with an audio track, which ought to be included in future design.

As for NPM, it took the most time for participants to use its audio due to the complicated process of playing audio. If users would like to play NPM audio, they should find the audio numbers of each exhibit in the VR exhibition space, then type the numbers in the "audio" function on the top right of the app (Fig. 7). This process is too difficult for users to be learned the first time, and does not coincide with their mental map. Therefore, we can know by observation that when users use online exhibition apps, they may think of the experience of visiting physical exhibitions and then intuitively behave just like they are watching physical exhibitions. This finding can be considered in future interface design of online exhibitions.

(a) NTMOFA   (b) A&C   (c) NPM

Fig. 7. Manipulation Diagram of Task 5.

Task 6. In Task 6, participants, on average, spent more time finishing because the "search" function of these three online exhibition apps goes against the patterns they are used to. The keyword association tool of NPM is a "drop-up menu" which should be manually tapped to expand (Fig. 8) and does not coincide with the automatically-expanded menus users usually see, causing most participants not to notice the keyword association, and so they typed the whole name of exhibits.

As for NTMOFA and A&C, their "search" functions are not built into the online exhibition but are on the other pages of the apps. The former is built on the list of art works (Fig. 9), and the other is set up on the home page of the app (Fig. 10). Thus, it takes participants more time to find the "search" function because they intuitively think the function related to the exhibition should be on the online exhibition page.

Task 7. There is a significant difference in the time performance of two apps ($t=-20.04$, $p<0.001$), with A&C taking participants much more time to finish the task. Because most

(a) unexpanded keyword association   (b) expanded keyword association

Fig. 8. NPM's Manipulation Diagram of Task 6.

Fig. 9. NTMOFA's Manipulation Diagram of Task 6.

participants gave feedbacks that they would like to share the exhibition only when they had already seen it and found it interesting, they expected that the "share" function should be set up on the exhibition page. Thus, participants spent more time on A&C for which the "share" function is built on the home page of the app (Fig. 11).

Fig. 10. A&C's Manipulation Diagram of Task 6.

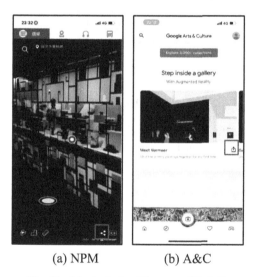

(a) NPM   (b) A&C

Fig. 11. Manipulation Diagram of Task 7.

4.2 Subjective Results

The research requested participants to fill out the SUS and NASA-TLX questionnaires after finishing the tasks contents of each app. They were also asked to answer some questions as the subjective results.

Subjective Performance. Table 4 shows the SUS and NASA-TLX results for each app. From the results, we can find that although NPM's SUS score is significantly higher than that of the other two apps, none of the three apps' SUS score is higher than 68, meaning that none of them is good enough. Therefore, there are still many design features needing to be optimized. Notably, based on the NASA-TLX results, participants thought A&C overall required the most effort to use, so that ought to be the important optimization object.

Interview Results. The interview results were collected and organized as two categories, interface & usage design and interactive design, as summarized in Table 6.

Table 6. Interview Results.

Contents	Feedbacks and Suggestions
Interface & Usage Design	1. Most people like AR online exhibitions, and almost all people think the "pictures" form seems not to be like visiting an exhibit but just like looking for information on the internet 2. They hope to watch exhibits from different angles and be able to enlarge them 3. They hope to add a 2D map in the corner of online exhibition pages to avoid getting lost in the online exhibition 4. They hope the positions of functions, such as search and share, can be set up more intuitively
Interactive Design	5. They hope to have the chance to establish and decorate their own online exhibitions 6. They hope to establish a bulletin board so that users can interact with others 7. Many people think A&C which can interact with body interaction is intuitive and more realistic and immersive 8. Many people think having background music is interesting and can improve the experience of visiting

5   Conclusions

5.1   Discussion

According to research results, there is an interesting finding that although sometimes participants spent more time on A&C, and its SUS and NASA-TLX scores were the worst, without considering the usability design of the sample apps, they still liked AR online exhibitions most because they are the most immersive. They offer users the opportunity to interact with body reaction intuitively so that they can easily engage in visiting the AR online exhibition. Therefore, AR online exhibitions may be a suitable form for online exhibition experience.

However, regarding some frequently-used functions, the usability of A&C and the other two online exhibition apps still need to be optimized. By observation and interview during the experiment, users tend to put their mental map of visiting physical exhibitions on online exhibitions, so the functions that go against the mental map of their usual experience will take users some times and efforts to use. Thus, it would be appropriate to set up some functions according to users' cognitions, for example, "audio" should be built near the introduction and "search" and "share" ought to be set up in the exhibition.

On the other hand, there are some benefits users expect to have in the future, such as social functions and sensory experience. Most participants desired to have some interaction with their friends and other users, including sharing contents with friends, visiting exhibitions with others, and communicating with artists. In addition, participants also wanted some sensory stimulation in the online exhibitions, for example, background music and exhibition decorations, because they believe these elements can improve the experience of visiting. In conclusion, online exhibition users not only pursue the experience similar to that of physical exhibitions, but having social interaction and sensory experience is also important for them and can increase their sense of immersion.

5.2 Limitation and Future Works

This was exploratory research which merely focused on the usability of online exhibitions and aimed to identify the inherent problems. However, beyond usability, users still emphasize features such as social interaction and sensory experience, which means there are still other factors which may affect users' feelings about visiting online exhibitions. Therefore, it is expected that the relationship of how these elements impact the experience of users visiting online exhibitions can be further explored.

References

Amorim, J.P., Teixeira, L.M.L.: Art in the digital during and after Covid: aura and apparatus of online Exhibitions. Rupkatha J. Interdisc. Stud. Hum. **12**(5), 1–8 (2021)

Bannon, L., Benford, S., Bowers, J., Heath, C.: Hybrid design creates innovative museum experiences. Commun. ACM **48**(3), 62–65 (2005)

Brooke, P.P.: Beyond the Steers and Rhodes model of employee attendance. Acad. Manag. Rev. **11**(2), 345–361 (1986)

Choi, B., Kim, J.: Changes and challenges in museum management after the COVID-19 pandemic. J. Open Innov.: Technol., Market, Complexity **7**(2), 148 (2021)

Ciurea, C., Zamfiroiu, A., Grosu, A.: Implementing mobile virtual exhibition to increase cultural heritage visibility. Informatica Economica **18**(2), 24 (2014)

DailyView. Visit art galleries and museums at home! Top 10 "online exhibitions" in Taiwan: bring you to feel the charm of knowledge (2021). https://dailyview.tw/Daily/2021/06/19?page=0

Diaper, D., Stanton, N. (eds.): The Handbook of Task Analysis for Human-Computer Interaction. Mahwah, NJ (2003)

Hart, S.G., Staveland, L.E.: Development of NASA-TLX (Task Load Index): results of empirical and theoretical research. Adv. Psychol. **52**, 139–183 (1988)

Kadam, P.: Virtual Exhibitions-Digitized World in Pre- and Post-Covid. Int. J. Adv. Innov. Res. **8**(3) (2021)

Ken Research: arts global market report 2020–30: Covid-19 impact and recovery (2020). https://www.kenresearch.com/media-and-entertainment/films-and-animation/arts-market-report/342602-94.html

Kraybill, A.: Going the distance: online learning and the museum. J. Museum Educ. **40**(2), 97–101 (2015)

Leong, C.K., Chennupati, K.R.: An overview of online exhibitions. DESIDOC J. Library Inf. Technol. **28**(4), 7–21 (2008)

Li, J., Nie, J.W., Ye, J.: Evaluation of virtual tour in an online museum: exhibition of architecture of the forbidden city. PLoS ONE **17**(1), e0261607 (2022)

Liu, H.Y.: The educational role of virtual art museums. Museol. Q. **20**(1), 55–80 (2006)

Moggridge, B.: Designing Interactions, vol. 17. MIT press, Cambridge, UK (2007)

Norman, D.A.: The Psychology of Everyday Things. Basic books, New York, NY (1988)

Resta, G., Dicuonzo, F., Karacan, E., Pastore, D.: The impact of virtual tours on museum exhibitions after the onset of covid-19 restrictions: Visitor engagement and long-term perspectives. SCIRES-IT-Sci. Res. Inf. Technol. **11**(1), 151–166 (2021)

Schmitt, B.H.: Experiential Marketing: How to Get Your Customer to Sense, Feel, Think, Act and Relate to Your Company and Brands. The FreePress, New York (1999)

Shneiderman, B., Plaisant, C., Cohen, M.S., Jacobs, S., Elmqvist, N., Diakopoulos, N.: Designing the user interface: strategies for effective human-computer interaction. Hoboken, NJ: Pearson (2016)

Urbaneja, M.H.: Online exhibitions and online publications: interrogating the typologies of online resources in art museums. Int. J. Digital Art History **4**, 3–28 (2019)

Villaespesa, E., Álvarez, A.: Visitor journey mapping at the Museo Nacional Thyssen-Bornemisza: Bringing cross-departmental collaboration to build a holistic and integrated visitor experience. Museum Manage. Curatorship **35**(2), 125–142 (2020)

A Study on the Impact of Instagram Influencers Endorsement to Purchase Intention Beauty Brand

Yu-Hsiu Hung and Ying-Kiu Ma[✉]

Department of Industrial Design, National Cheng Kung University, Tainan, Taiwan
p36105019@gs.ncku.edu.tw

Abstract. As social media becomes mainstream in our society, Instagram has become a platform for reaching potential customers. Companies partner with Instagram influencers to promote their products. This study investigates Instagram influencer impact on consumer purchase intention in Instagram-sponsored posts in Taiwan. This research focuses on the difference between Instagram influencers sponsored posts and advertising posts from brand companies. The experiments seek to explore the impact of Instagram influencers on Instagram-sponsored posts by conducting questionnaires. This study provides insights for companies that try to promote their product on Instagram, since Instagram influencer endorsement has a relationship with purchase intention, this information can better strategize their marketing strategy and achieve lean advertising. As lean advertising help companies using the least amount of resource to leaves more impact on the target audience. Result of the research shown influencer endorsements were less impact on purchase intention that advertisement completion, advertisement with more information and without influencer endorsement prove to be more capable of increase purchase intention.

Keywords: Instagram · marketing influencer · purchase intention · lean advertising

1 Introduction

1.1 Research Background

Since social media become mainstream, Instagram are also became part of it, which bring a new opportunity that many companies need to reach out. According to iKala KOL Radar, from their Influencer Marketing Trend Report 2022, Taiwan influencer' posts in Instagram had increased from 90,000 posts in 2019 to 200, 000 posts in 2021, indicating Influencer Marketing is rising. Key Opinion Leader (KOL), also known as the influencer, had become big part of the stoical media, their comment and posts are affect their followers, therefore, their posts can promote product effectively. In the Instagram influencer trend repost from Influenxio, Instagram sponsored posts are mostly beauty brand, more than 18% of them were about beauty product, which is the largest share in the market. And Instagram beauty content influencers are the second large share in the market, which is about 17.6%, those data are shown that a huge opportunity in Instagram influence beauty market. Since beauty product mainly used visual as a attraction to customers, companies using Instagram influencer to promote their product thought image and establish connection with customers will be become a prefer choices [1]. Beauty product ESTÉE LAUDER stated that their customer and beauty product lover are prefer using Instagram, as it have visualization and convenience [2].

1.2 Research Goal

According to the findings of Jarrar, Y., Awobamise, A. O., and Aderibigbe, A. A. (2020), although Instagram influencers are effective in promoting instant sales in marketing, they fail to increase engagement. Engagement helps ensure that consumers interact with brands to obtain information. This can help increase consumers' purchase intention since consumers prefer to keep the advertising information of brand manufacturers to facilitate purchase intention. However, due to a lack of engagement, consumers do not follow the brand companies, and advertisements will no longer appear on consumer pages, resulting in consumers being unable to contact this information [3]. Another study showed influencer marketing has no direct impact on consumers' purchase intention, and influencer marketing is not more effective marketing than regular online advertising strategy [4]. However, the Instagram influencers market continues to grow, indicating that the influencers market has a certain influence on brand companies. Therefore, the purpose of this study is to investigate whether the Instagram influencers market can bring benefits to brand companies so that brand companies can understand if the Instagram influencers market fits their needs and also able to perform lean advertising by not misplace their resource on the promotion.

2 Literature Review

2.1 Purchase Intention

It is a complex process for consumers to make a purchase decision, and purchase intention can affect this process. Morinez et al. (2007) defined purchase intention as a situation in which consumers tend to purchase a specific product under specific conditions, and thus purchase intention is also a decision-making process that can be studied [5]. Purchase intention may change due to the price or the perceived quality and value of the product, so purchase intention can be used as an effective tool to predict the purchase process [6], and purchase intention is also affected by internal or external environmental factors, making consumers think that products produced at low cost, with simple packaging and little-known brands are a high-risk purchase decision, because the quality of these products is not credible [7]. Consumers will make purchase decisions After six stages, they are: awareness, knowledge, interest, preference, persuasion and purchase [8]. Many factors can affect consumers' intentions, and the final decision depends on consumers' intentions. External factors account for a large proportion [9]. The group cohesion of brands affects purchase intentions. Cohesive brands [10]. This information also influences the decisions of other consumers who do not use the brand [11] so other consumers are influenced to use those brands with high cohesion [12].

2.2 Advertise Components

According to Contributor website, there are five advertisement components, the first is an attractive headline, which often appears at the top or in the middle of the advertisement to immediately attract the attention of potential customers. It should be direct and to the point so as not to overwhelm the reader; the second is an effective subtitles, which appears directly below the headline, and it gives you a deeper understanding of what companies are selling while further outlining why customers should care enough to read on; the third is to show the benefits of the product to the consumer, as consumers often buy for the benefits the product provides rather than the product itself or its features; the fourth is imagery and packaging, using pictures of the product or using its The fifth is a call to action, which uses a call to action to get consumers to take action. The call to action usually appears at the end of the advertisement to increase the sense of urgency.

Also a small research was launched focuses on exploring the different components of advertisements. In this research, the definition of an advertisement should be complete with five advertisement components, advertisement with less than five components is defined as an incomplete advertisement. However, the definition of whether an advertisement is complete or not is relatively general and complicated. Therefore, this study collected 50 advertisements posted by brand manufacturers on Instagram to allow consumers to clearly understand their commercial content. By using [13]. The five advertisement components that affect consumers' purchase intentions, we can define whether the classified advertisement is complete or not. According to the collected data, Instagram advertisements now have at least one advertisement component (see Fig. 2), and the distribution is even, and some components will not be too much. The data shows that more than half of the advertisements have five advertisement components (see Fig. 1). However, it is impossible to know from the data whether complete advertisements can increase consumers' intention to purchase. Therefore, this research investigates the relationship between complete advertisements and incomplete advertisements to explore whether the above factors will affect consumers' intentions purchase and help companies to set an lean advertising by more effective components to affect consumers' purchase intention.

2.3 Lean Advertising

Lean advertising means less advertising budget, but at the same time profitable advertising with greater impact. This online video platform provides a perfect way to engage with consumers on a higher level. Today, the cost per impression of advertising in traditional media has been replaced by the cost per viewer engagement of online video advertising. The reason for this is that they give you a lot of tools to measure and track the reaction of your target audience. For example, it is possible to find out how much time viewers spent on a video, how many times it was retweeted (if any), and what links they clicked to visit a website or follow a company on Twitter. In general, an advertising method can be called lean advertising if it costs less while having a greater impact on the target audience [14].

50個instagram廣告具五個廣告元素的比率

Fig. 1. Result on research advertisements completion

元素出現次數 (N=50)

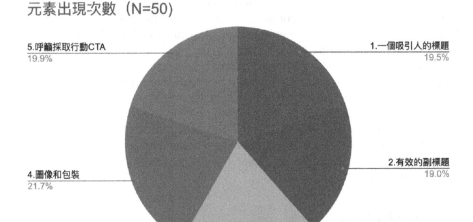

Fig. 2. Result on research advertisements components

3   Research Methodology

3.1   Research Framework and Assumptions

Instagram is no longer just a social media for photos, but a communication platform with multiple functions. The field of online influencer marketing has been defined as "a non-promotional marketing approach in which brands focus their efforts on influencers rather than direct target marketing touchpoints" [15]. According to the survey conducted by

Thomas, M. J., Wirtz, B. W., & Weyerer, J. C. (2019), consumers' trustworthiness of key opinion leaders is particularly affected by external factors, such as website reputation, product/service ratings, and reviewer expertise all show positive effects. Consistency in content posted by influencers reduces followers' perception that they are watching an ad because such consistent posting makes consumers feel natural and spontaneous, thereby reducing consumers' perception of influencers receiving money for sponsorship contents [16].Even if consumers suspect that opinion leaders are not promoting products they themselves use or believe in, posts posted by influencers are considered more trustworthy than traditional advertisements, thereby influencing consumers' purchase intentions [17]. In addition to improving their own credibility, the posts of influencers are also attractive. According to Wilkinson & Light (2011), human images have the ability to grab consumers' attention even in an environment full of distractions. The human figure has always been the factor that prompts the viewer to repeatedly fixate himself or herself in the context of the visual information. This means that a character can capture the attention of consumers in an environment full of distractions [18]. Human face is one of the factors that lead to the fastest recognition by consumers, and a human face with emotional features will quickly attract attention [19]. Celebrity images in advertising appearance has a positive impact on consumers' attention [20]. And using celebrity images when selling products is considered to be one of the effective ways to attract consumers' attention [21].

The above shows that the sales scope of Instagram is not limited to the advertisements released by companies and brands, but has shifted to the influencers. The posts of influencers can influence consumers' purchase intention through credibility and attractiveness. Traditional advertisements cannot produce consistent content due to the need to match the market positioning of the brand. Companies with less affluent brands may not be able to add characters in traditional advertisements, making traditional advertisements less credible and attractive. Based on literature review, this study defines complete and incomplete advertisements components. Influences are more trustworthy and attractive to consumers than traditional advertisements, and can effectively increase consumers' attention, making credibility and attractiveness an important aspect of advertising. Factors that affect consumers' willingness to purchase, so this research assumes that incomplete advertisements lacking advertising elements, with the help of influencers, can achieve the same effects on purchase intention as complete advertisements without advertisement components.

Hypothesis: Incomplete ads achieve the same effect as complete ads when endorsed by influencers.

3.2 Materials and Methods

This research aims to explore the impact of Instagram influencers on sponsored posts compared with advertising posts from brand companies. This research will focus on two variances, purchase intention, and information quality. Purchase intention helps consumers make their purchase decision, which leads to actual profit for the companies. Information quality contains many dimensions, in this study, it includes information that is completeness, easy to understand, and relevant. Brand companies advertising posts contain the same information quality as Instagram influencers, yet Instagram influencers receive more views and attention on Instagram. Therefore, the experiments will be conducted in the form of questionnaires, by comparing Instagram influencers and brand companies with their posts which contain different information quality. The data will be collected from Instagram user with experience in beauty products.

3.3 Research Sample

This research focus on Instagram, according to NapoleonCat website research on Taiwan Instagram users in 2021, there are 25.2% of them aged between 18 to 24, and 35.6% of them aged between 25 to 34, shown that more than half of Instagram users aged between 18 to 34, thus, this research will focus on Instagram users aged between 18 to 34 as our sample group. Although this research focus on beauty product, this research do not limited the gender of users, because according to Chuangshiji's 2019 survey on the use of beauty care and beauty fashion categories, it is found that men are more interested in facial care products, foundation makeup, Fragrance and make-up products have seen significant growth in usage. In order to construct a more homogeneous sample, this study used filtering questions to select users with experience with Instagram and with enough recognition of the influencer in the survey, since the understand of the influencer affect purchase intention.

3.4 Questionnaires

The survey of this research contain to two variances, influencers and advise components, since this research will conduct two-way anova tests, advise components need to be limited, as it contain five components. (A Catchy Headline, An Effective Sub-headline, Selling the Benefits, Images and Packaging and Call-to-action). A small research on incomplete advertisements were launched, to found what components should be remain on the survey. In this research will only remain one components as the variance of the incomplete advise. The result of 100 incomplete advise are shown. (see Fig. 3). The result shown image as the main component, however, Instagram require user to post an image in order to post content, therefore, image is contain in every advertisement. So the research chose the second large component, Call to Action. Consumers of certain age groups are receptive to advertising campaigns that use call-to-action (CTA) buttons only to affect their purchase intent and not yet reach consumers' impulse purchases [22]. Because this research focus on purchase intention, the survey will keep the Call to Action as the components.

Component across 100 advisements

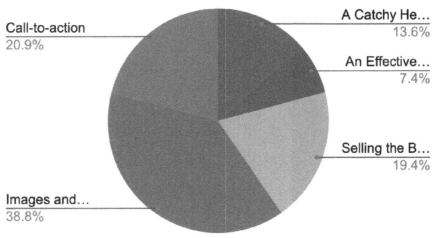

Call-to-action
20.9%

A Catchy He...
13.6%

An Effective...
7.4%

Selling the B...
19.4%

Images and...
38.8%

Fig. 3. Result on research 100 incomplete advertisements

4   Research Result

4.1   Result

The online survey had collected 69 samples with 57 is used for this research. Base on the recognition of the influencers, which in this survey is above 3 scores, were accepted as the data, due the effect of the influencers. In this study, the competition of advertisement and influencer involvement is used as a variable to collect data on whether users will increase their purchase intention and make purchase decisions after exposure to the above four advertising posts. This research questionnaire uses a 5-point Likert scale, and users rate it on a scale from 1 (strongly disagree) to 5 (strongly agree) by answering the following question "Does the above post make or increase your purchase intention?".

Base on the survey data (See Fig. 4), the factors of advertisement with influencer endorsement consider to be more attractive than advertisement without influencer endorsement were consisted with four reasons, easy to access, communication, aesthetic and product description. Easy to access means the post were shown to them, communication means the comment session are crowed, aesthetic means the post is visually attracted to them. There are 40% of users think that the reasons advertisement with influencer endorsement are consider to be more attractive are due product description, 25.7% of them think is because the aesthetic, 20% of them think is the communication and 14.3% of them think is easy to access the post.

你認為網紅推薦的廣告較IG廣告更吸引人的原因是？

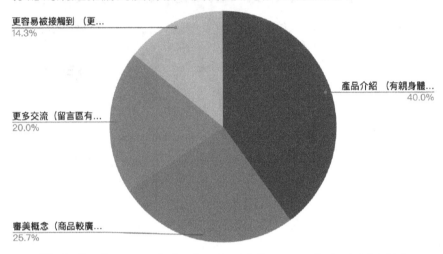

Fig. 4. Result on research attractiveness on influencers endorse advertisement

For the reason that advertisement without influencer endorsement consider to be more attractive than advertisement with influencer endorsement were concentrated brand product, provide sense of security and more detailed information. (See Fig. 5) However, result of the factors are more even, concentrated brand product and more detailed information are the same 32.4%, and provide sense of security are 35.3%.

你認為IG廣告較網紅推薦的廣告更吸引人的原因是？

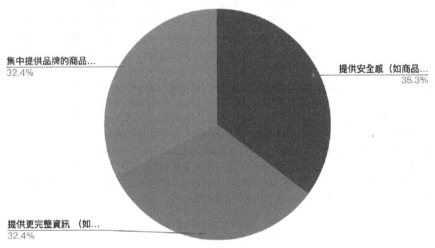

Fig. 5. Result on research attractiveness of advertisements with endorsement

5   Discussion

5.1   Analyze Method

In this research, there are two variances, which is the competition of advertisement and influencer involvement, in order to evaluate the effect of two grouping variables, Two-way ANOVA is used in this research with the tool in R. Two-way ANOVA is used to estimate how the mean of a quantitative variable varies according to the levels of two categorical variables. Two-way ANOVA used when the researcher know how two independent variables combine to affect the dependent variable.

5.2   Analyze Result

This research try to find out if the competition of advertisement and influencer involvement are affect purchase intention, therefore, the null hypothesis of purchase intention is the ads completion and influencer involvement have the same mean. Table 1 shown that ads completion is the most significant factor variable, as the P-value is less than 0.05, These results would lead us to believe that ads completion will impact significantly on the purchase intention. However, the influencer involvement P-value is large than 0.05, showing that influencer involvement does not significantly impact on purchase intention. The interaction between ads completion and influencer involvement are shown significantly impact toward purchase intention, with the P-value of 0.02.

Table 1. Purchase intention.

	Df	Sum Sq	Mean Sq	F value	Pr (>F)
Ads completion	1	17.361	17.361	19.380	0.000112
Influencer involvement	1	0.250	0.250	0.279	0.600956
Interaction	1	1.361	1.361	1.519	0.226693
Residuals	32	28.667	0.896		

Table 2 shown the result of the recommendation toward the users friends and family, since companies also value promotion between user and user. The analysis result also shown ads completion is the most significant factor variable, and influencer involvement were shown less significantly impact toward purchase intention, due to 0.4 P-value. The interaction of two variance are shown significantly impact toward purchase intention.

Table 2. Recommendation

	Df	Sum Sq	Mean Sq	F value	Pr(>F)
Ads completion	1	3.361	3.361	8.491	0.00646
Influencer involvement	1	0.250	0.250	0.632	0.43263
Interaction	1	3.361	3.361	8.491	0.00646
Residuals	32	12.667	0.896		

Combine with the result of the survey, the data shown that users value more on the product information improved by the posts, we can indicate that information of the product increase the purchase intention of consumers. Since anova table shown ads completion provide more significantly impact to the purchase, the hypothesis of incomplete ads achieve the same effect as complete ads when endorsed by influencers are rejected. The ads completion shown an advertisement with more advertisement components, in other way, more information are prove more effectivity increase purchase intention than influencers endorsement. Although many studies shown many factors that influencers endorsement affect purchase intention, endorsement were less powerful compare with advertisement with detail information.

6   Conclusion

6.1   Summary

In this research, Instagram advertisements were studied in order to understand influencers and advertisement components affect toward purchase intention. There are many research on Instagram influencers, some of them mention the factors that affect the purchase intention. However, purchase intention can be affect by many factors, therefore, this research rather the influencers can effective increase purchase intention. As the result, the effectiveness of the influencers endorsement were shown less powerful than advertisements with more advertisement components, or more information. With this information, companies are suggested to blindly using influencer endorsement, even though influencer helps spread the massage, their shown less effect on increase purchase intention. Because the post contents significantly affect purchase intention, companies should choose their strategy more toward their advertisement content. For smaller companies, this would be more easily to achieve lean adverting, smaller companies may not have enough resource for marketing, their advertisements may not have endorsement. Lean should be using less to achieve more, therefore, lean adverting helps reduce the cost by provide a market strategy that do not need to use endorsement from the influencer.

6.2   Research Limitation and Future Research

This research mainly focus on two variable of the advertisements, ads completion and influencer involvement, however, due to the size of the research, there were four other advertisement components were not studied. This research also limited by the influencer ranking, since Instagram contain many influencer, the ranking or follower numbers of influencer were also not included in this study.

The further study of this research can be conduct comparison research on five advertisement to understand their impact individually toward purchase intention, and base different tier of influencer to conduct research in order to understand whether the follower size will affect them on increase purchase.

References

1. Moorhouse, V.: The most popular beauty brands on Instagram-and what they're doing right.StyleCaster, 17 December 2018. https://stylecaster.com/beauty/beauty-brands-instagram/. Accessed 5 May 2022
2. Pathak, S.: Why fashion and Beauty Brands Love Instagram.Digiday, 10 August 2015. Accessed 6 May 2022
3. Jarrar, Y., Awobamise, A.O., Aderibigbe, A.A.: Effectiveness of influencer marketing vs social media sponsored advertising. Utopía y praxis latinoamericana: revista internacional de filosofía iberoamericana y teoría social **12**, 40–54 (2020)
4. Johansen, I.K., Guldvik, C.S.: Influencer marketing and purchase intentions: how does influencer marketing affect purchase intentions? Master's thesis (2017)
5. Shah, H., et al.: The impact of brands on consumer purchase intentions. Asian J. Bus. Manag. **4**(2), 105–110 (2012)
6. Ghosh, A.: Retail Management. Dryden Press, Chicago (1990)
7. Gogoi, B.: Study of antecedents of purchase intention and its effect on brand loyalty of private label brand of apparel. Int. J. Sales Mark. **3**(2), 73–86 (2013)
8. Kotler, P., Armstrong, G.: Principles of Marketing. Pearson Prentice Hall, Upper Saddle River (2010)
9. Keller, K.L.: Building customer-based brand equity: creating brand resonance requires carefully sequenced brand-building efforts. Mark. Manag. **10**(2), 15–19 (2001)
10. Witt, E.B., Bruce, D.G.: Group influence & brand choice congruence. J. Mark. Res. **9**(4), 440–443 (1972)
11. Witt, E.T.: Informal social group influence on consumer brand choice. J. Mark. Res. **6**(4), 443–476 (1969)
12. Moschis, P.G.: Social comparison and informal group influence. J. Mark. Res. **13**(3), 237–244 (1976)
13. Contributor, C.: The 5 parts of an advertising ad. Small Business - Chron.com, 17 November 2020. https://smallbusiness.chron.com/5-parts-advertising-ad-23988.html. Accessed 19 May 2022
14. Yadav, P., Singh, N.:Youtube: Lucrative platform for lean advertising. Chanderprabhu Jain College of Higher Studies & School of Law (2017)
15. Hall, J.: The influencer marketing gold rush is coming: are youprepared?. Forbes (2016). http://www.forbes.com/sites/johnhall/2016/04/17/the-influencer-marketinggold-rush-is-coming-are-you-prepared/#5872a3102964. Accessed 7 Oct 2016
16. Audrezet, A., De Kerviler, G., Moulard, J.G.: Authenticity under threat: when social media influencers need to go beyond self-presentation. J. Bus. Res. **117**, 557–569 (2020). https://doi.org/10.1016/j.jbusres.2
17. Veissi, I.: Influencer marketing on Instagram (2017)
18. Beh, C., Badni, K.: Eye-tracking experiment to test key emerging principles of visual communication of technology, pp. 1–19 (2010)

19. Ohme, R., Matukin, M., Pacula-lesniak, B.: Biometric measures for interactive advertising. J. Interact. Advert. **11**(2), 60–72 (2011)
20. Ryu, Y.S., Suh, T., Dozier, S.: Effects of design elements in magazine advertisements, pp. 262–268 (2009)
21. Li, Y., Lee, Y., Lien, N.-J.: Online social advertising via influential endorsers. Int. J. Electron. Commer. **16**(3), 119–153 (2012). https://doi.org/10.2753/JEC1086-4415160305
22. Handayani, R.C., Purwandari, B., Solichah, I., Prima, P.: The impact of Instagram "call-to-action" buttons on customers' impulse buying. In: Proceedings of the 2nd International Conference on Business and Information Management, pp. 50–56, September 2018

Survey on the Effect of Video Delay in Online Dance with Multiple Participants

Rino Imai[1]([✉]), Ryota Matsui[1,2][iD], Yutaka Yanagisawa[2],
Yoshinari Takegawa[1][iD], and Keiji Hirata[1][iD]

[1] Future University Hakodate, Hakodate, Japan
g2122009@fun.ac.jp
[2] MPLUSPLUS Co., Ltd., Shinagawa, Tokyo, Japan
http://www.mplpl.com/

Abstract. In this survey, we investigated the discomfort of delay between music and movement in online dance performance support. In an online environment, there is a delay due to the communication environment. Due to this delay, when multiple dancers dance simultaneously at a distance, they cannot dance in sync with the music and their movements appear to be out of sync. In previous studies, recommended delay times between audio and video have been investigated. However, the acceptable range of delay when multiple dancers dance has not been verified. Therefore, in this survey, assuming an online dance lesson with multiple dancers, we conducted a questionnaire survey on "discomfort with movement delay," "ease of dancing," and "ease of remembering choreography," using five different dance videos with different interfaces. The results of the survey revealed that grouping the videos according to the size of the delay improved the ease of dancing and the viewability of the videos, and that the number of people on the screen did not affect the ease of dancing or the viewability of the videos. It was also found that people felt uncomfortable if the video was delayed by more than one beat relative to the music.

Keywords: Human Interface · Online Dance · Video Delay

1 Introduction

1.1 A Subsection Sample

In recent years, street dance has been attracting attention since breakdancing was adopted as an Olympic sports. In addition, dance has become compulsory in physical education classes at junior high schools in Japan, and with the spread of SNS and the popularity of K-POP and other cover dances, people from all

Supported by MPLUSPLUS Co., Ltd.

walks of life have many opportunities to come into contact with dance. There are online dance lessons and online live performances, which are environments where people can easily experience and watch dance that have become popular among the general public. These online contents allow dancers to receive instruction from professional dancers in remote locations and watch performances from the comfort of their own homes. The demand for these online contents is increasing due to the impact of the new coronavirus.

When conducting dance lessons in an online environment, there will be delays due to the network environment. Especially when there are multiple students per teacher, the timing of music and movements due to latency becomes a major issue. When multiple students dance together, the start time of the music is different in each student's environment, so the timing of their movements is out of sync with the other students. Therefore, it is impossible to dance together with perfect timing. In addition, in group activities, negative factors such as delayed conversation inhibit cooperation [2].

When learning dance, the learner first observes the movements of the teacher, surrounding dancers, and choreographer, making observations about rhythm and musicality. Therefore, the timing of music and movement is one of the most important elements in learning dance [5].

This study focuses on the impact on dance performance caused by timing differences between music and movement. Studies of speech delays and their impact on collaboration have found that delays of 300 ms or less are rarely a problem. However, delays of 450 to 700 ms have been found to have potentially serious effects on communication. In addition, delays of 700 ms or longer have a dramatic impact on communication and overall task performance [3]. Based on these results, we will examine how much delay and whether there is a difference in ease of dancing with different delay times compared to speech alone.

2   Related Work

One example of motion learning support is a study to support online dance education. The study proposes a system called DanceVis that visualizes the teacher's assessment of student movement and applies vision-based person posture estimation and posture similarity calculation methods to automatically perform individual analysis to accurately identify the strengths and weaknesses of student movement during the practice process. The results of this analysis are accurately recorded as performance details, allowing DanceVis to track individual dynamic changes during online lessons and provide accurate feedback to teachers [4]. Another study conducted a movement analysis to evaluate the movements of multiple individuals using a video dataset called Let'sDance. Let'sDance is a 1000 video dataset consisting of 10 visually overlapping dance categories. To classify categories with many movements, visual information alone is not sufficient, and human movement is an important discriminant. In particular, dance is extremely dynamic due to the diversity of its movements, and video analysis is considered difficult. Therefore, it is possible to support motion learning by performing motion analysis on multiple dancers [1].

As in these studies, several systems have been proposed to provide real-time feedback on movements using motion analysis techniques such as motion capture. However, this study differs from existing studies in that it resolves the gap between movement and music in dance.

3   Survey on Acceptable Video Delay

In this survey, we investigated the effect of video delay on dance video viewing when the following two parameters are varied.

- Number of dance videos (including video delay) to be viewed simultaneously.
- Time of video delay of dance video to be viewed at the same time (same number of pieces).

Three factors were defined as the effects of the video delay on the dance. The three factors are whether the "dancer can dance easily", "whether there is no sense of discomfort from the discrepancy between the music and the movements", and "whether the dancer can feel a sense of unity with the surroundings".

3.1   Method of Survey

Test Subject. The subjects were 10 students who belonged to a dance club at Future University Hakodate. The 10 subjects had been dancing for less than 5 years.

About the Video. The video used in the experiment assumes a real-time dance lesson in which nine students in a remote location dance the same choreography. In an online environment, due to differences in the communication environment, there will be a delay in the video between the teacher and the students, or between students taking the lesson together. Therefore, students taking lessons online will experience a delay between themselves and the students around them. Also, the movements of the students around him appear to be out of sync with the music. Therefore, we have given 9 students, from Student A to Student I, each with a video delay of 0 ms to 800 ms. Regarding the number of seconds of video delay, it is recommended that the delay should not exceed 300 ms in the case of audio [3]. In addition, as a preliminary survey, a questionnaire survey was conducted using several dance videos. The purpose of the preliminary study was to determine whether the ease of viewing and dancing differed depending on the size of the delay. The video footage was created under the same assumptions as in the main experiment. In the preliminary experiment, participants were asked to watch the video footage and select the video footage that most concerned them in terms of the timing of the music and movements. The survey results showed that the largest number of respondents selected a delay of 400 ms. Based on this result, the delay for the nine images was set from 0 ms to 800 ms, with 400 ms as the standard. Figure 1 shows the composition of the images used in the experiment. Table 1 shows a summary of the images used in the experiment.

Timing of songs and movements

| Beat 1 | Beat 2 | Beat 3 | Beat 4 | Beat 5 | Beat 6 | Beat 7 | Beat 8 |

The image the viewer sees (beat 6)

Fig. 1. Overview chart of images used

Table 1. Overview of the video used

	Students who appear	Video Features
Video1	A, B, C, D, E, F, G, H, I	Video showing all participants regardless of the size of the delay
video2	A, B, C	Video showing only three participants with small video delay
Video3	D, E, F	Video showing only three participants with middle video delay
Video4	G, H, I	Video showing only three participants with big video delay
Video5	A, E, I	Three people are selected at random from Video 1 and displayed

The video consists of two different songs and five different interfaces, for a total of 10 videos. The songs are at two different speeds, 80 bpm and 130 bpm, and the delay seconds and interfaces for the five videos are as follows. In video 1, students A to I were randomly given video delays ranging from 0 ms to 800 ms, as shown in Fig. 2-1. In video 2, students A to C are given video delays of 0 ms to 200 ms in alphabetical order, as shown in Fig. 2-2. In Video 3, students D to F were given video delays of 300 ms to 500 ms in alphabetical order, as shown in Fig. 2-3. In Video 4, students G to I were given video delays of 600 ms to 800 ms in alphabetical order, as shown in Fig. 2-4. In Video 5, three students

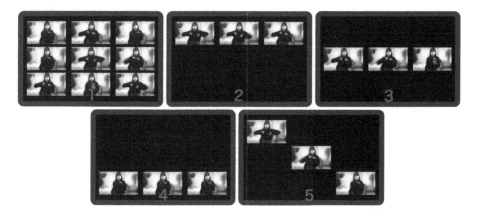

Fig. 2. 5 types of video interfaces used in the survey.

were randomly selected from Video 1, as shown in Fig. 2-5. The video delays are, in alphabetical order, 200 ms, 400 ms, and 700 ms. To survey the effect of the delay of the video on the dance, video 2, video 3, and video 4 were compared. To survey the relationship between the delay of the video and the number of video pieces, video 1 and video 5 were compared.

The investigation was conducted in real time by one subject and one experimenter using zoom, a videoconferencing system. Two surveys were conducted per subject; the second experiment was conducted four days after the first. The experimental procedure was as follows.

1. A 16-s dance choreography was taught to the subject. The teaching period was 3 min and ended when the subject was able to dance the choreography without hesitation. After teaching only the movements without music, the choreography was practiced twice with music.
2. Video 1 to 5 were shared using the screen sharing function of zoom. The subjects were asked to dance the choreography that was first taught to them while watching the videos. When they danced while watching the video, they were told that they could focus on any of the students from Student A to Student I, and that the quality of the choreography was not relevant to the experiment.
3. A survey form was sent to the chats and they were asked to complete the questionnaire. A 5-point Likert scale was used for the survey.

(2) and (3) were performed for each of the five types of videos, for a total of five times. The order of the music and the order of presentation of the five videos were randomized for each subject.

Table 2. Questionnaire Content

	Questions	Answers
Q1	Which video did you watch and dance from	Select from A-I (multiple choice)
Q2	Did you feel the sense of dancing with the people in the video?	1:don't feel–5:feel
Q3	Did you feel that the timing of your movements matched the video?	1:don't feel–5:feel
Q4	Did you feel that it was difficult to time your own movements to the video images?	1:feel–5:don't feel
Q5	Did you find the choreography difficult to dance while watching the video?	1:feel–5:don't feel

4 Results

The contents of the questionnaire are shown in the Table 2.

Figure 5 is a graph of the number of responses per letter of the alphabet for each video for question 1. If the respondents are dancing while watching more than one person, the responses are divided into A and B, D and E, and so on. As shown in Fig. 5, for Video 1, at bpm 80, there were seven responses from Student E, one from Student A and Student E, and two from Student B and Student E, respectively. At bpm 130, there were one student G, one student A, one student D and one student E, five students E, one student A and one student E, and two students E and one student H, respectively. As shown in Fig. 5-(b), for Video 2, at bpm 80, there were one student from Student A, one student from Student C, six students from Student B, and two students from Student A and Student B. At bpm 130, there were three students from Student A, Student B, Student A and Student B, and one student from Student B and Student C, respectively. At bpm130, Student A, Student B, Student A and Student B numbered three, and Student B and Student C numbered one, respectively. As shown in Fig. 5-(c) for Video 3, at bpm 80, there were two responses from Student D, five responses from Student E, and three responses from Student D and Student E, respectively. At bpm130, there were four responses from Student D, one response from Student E, one response from Student F, one response from Student E and Student F, and three responses from Student D and Student E, respectively. As shown in Fig. 5-(d), for Video 4, at bpm 80, there were one student G, six students H, and three students G and H, respectively. At bpm130, there were two responses from Student G, seven responses from Student H, and one response from Student G and Student H. At bpm130, there were two responses from Student G, seven responses from Student H, and one response from Student G and Student H, respectively (Fig. 3).

For questions 2 through 5, we calculated the mean of the responses to the 5-step questionnaire. As shown in Figure ?? and Figure ??, the mean values for Question 2 were 3.7 for Video 1, 3.9 for Video 2, 3.2 for Video 3, 2.2 for Video

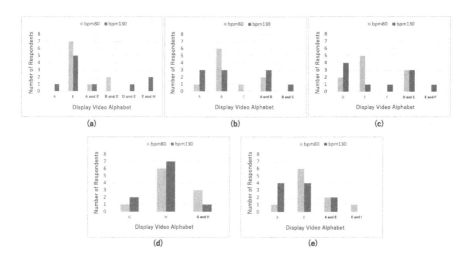

Fig. 3. Q1ans

4, and 3.8 for Video 5 at bpm 80; at bpm 130, 2.7 for Video 1, 3.7 for Video 2, 2.7 for Video 3, 2.3 for Video 4, and 3.1 for Video 5. The results were as follows. In addition, the correlation coefficients were calculated for each of the Videos: Video 1, Video 2 to Video 4, and Video 2 to Video 4. As shown in Fig. 4-Q3 and Fig. 5-Q3, the mean values for Question 3 were 3.0, 3.9, 3.8, 1.8, and 3.2 for Video 1, Video 2, Video 3, Video 4, and Video 5, respectively, at bpm 80. The mean values were 2.7, 3.6, 2.5, 2.3, and 3.4 for Videos 1, 2, 3, 4, and 5, respectively, when bpm was 130. As shown in Fig. 4-Q4 and Fig. 5-Q4, the mean values for Question 4 were 2.8 for Video 1, 3.6 for Video 2, 3.2 for Video 3, 1.6 for Video 4, and 3.3 for Video 5 at bpm 80, respectively. The mean values were 2.1, 3.4, 2.6, 2.2, and 2.7 for Videos 1, 2, 3, 4, and 5, respectively, when bpm was 130. As shown in Fig. 4-Q5 and Fig. 5-Q5, the mean values for Question 5 were 3.0 for Video 1, 4.0 for Video 2, 3.5 for Video 3, 2.2 for Video 4, and 3.4 for Video 5 at bpm 80, respectively. The mean values were 2.6, 3.3, 2.7, 2.4, and 3.2 for video 1, video 2, video 3, video 4, and video 5, respectively, at bpm 130.

Next, a chi-square test was applied to Videos 2, 3, and 4 at bpm 80 and bpm 130, respectively, using Cramer's with a significance level of 0.05 (5 percent). At 80 bpm, Cramer's contingency coefficient was 0.69. The chi-square statistic was 50.70. From the critical value of 15.51 for degree of freedom 8, we obtain the critical value (15.51) < Chi-square statistic (50.70). Therefore, a stronger association was observed for the Cramer's contingency coefficient. At 130 bpm, the Cramer's coefficient was 0.43. The chi-square statistic was 19.10, which is a critical value (15.51) < chi-square statistic (19.10) from the critical value of 15.51 for 8°C of freedom. Thus, the association was confirmed by the Cramer's contingency coefficient.

Similarly, chi-square tests were conducted for Videos 1 and 5 at bpm 80 and bpm 130, respectively, using Clamar's contingency coefficient, with the significance level set at 0.05 (5 percent). When the bpm was 80, the Clamar's correlation coefficient was 0.48. The chi-square statistic was 18.52. From the critical value of 9.49 for degree of freedom 4, we obtain the critical value (9.49) < Chi-square statistic (18.52). Therefore, the association was confirmed by the Cramer's contingency coefficient. In addition, at 130 bpm, the Cramer's coefficient was 0.43. The chi-square statistic was 14.70. From the critical value of 9.49 for degree of freedom 4, the critical value (9.49) < the chi-square statistic (14.70). Thus, the relevance was confirmed by the Cramer's contingency coefficient.

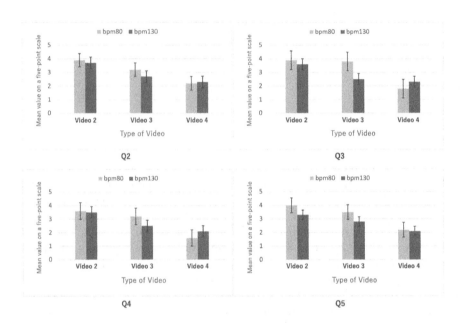

Fig. 4. Q1ans

5   Consideration

First, the results of Question 1 are explained through Video 1 through Video 4. In video 1, student E, who is in the center of the Video and has no delay in the Video, responded the most. In Video 2, Student B, who is in the center of the Video, responded more than Student A, despite having a greater delay than Student A. The same is true in Videos 3 and 4.

These results indicate that when multiple people dance, multiple people tend to focus on the student in the center of the Video.

Next, we focus on the results from video 2 to video 4 for questions 2 to 5. For question 2, the results from video 2 to video 4 show that the values become smaller as the delay increases. Therefore, when the delay becomes large, we cannot feel the sense of unity. For question 3, the results from Video 2 to Video 4 show that the values become smaller as the delay increases. Therefore, the

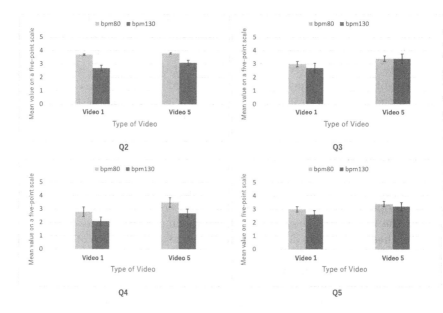

Fig. 5. Q1ans

larger the delay, the greater the sense that one's own movements correspond to those of the Videos. For question 4, the results from video 2 to video 4 show that the value increases as the delay increases. Therefore, it is easier for the user to match the timing of his/her actions to the Video when the Video delay is small. For question 5, the results from video 2 to video 4 show that the value increases as the delay increases. Therefore, it is easier to dance the dance choreography when the video delay is small. The Clamer's contingency coefficient indicates that there is a strong relationship between video 2, video 3, and video 4. Accordingly, as the Video delay increases, the influence of the Video delay on the ease of dancing and viewing the dance choreography increases.

Next, we look at the results for questions 2 through 5, focusing on video 1 and video 5. For questions 2 to 5, the mean value of video 5 was higher than that of video 1. However, there was no significant difference. The relationship coefficients of Clamor's association coefficients also showed no strong relationship. Therefore, it was found that the number of Videos displayed was unlikely to affect the ease of dancing and viewing.

For bpm80, the length of one beat is 750 ms, and for bpm130, the length of one beat is 460 ms. In questions 2 and 3, we focus on the areas where the mean values differ by more than one beat. bpm80 shows a large drop in the mean value in video 4. The range of the video delay given in video 4 is from 600 ms to 800 ms. In the case of bpm130, the mean value drops significantly in Video 3. The range of the video delay given in Video 3 is from 300 ms to 500 ms. Within this range, the length of one beat of bpm130 is 460 ms.

The above results indicate that the influence of the video delay on the ease of dancing and viewing depends on the tempo of the music used in the dance. The results showed that a delay of one beat or more in relation to the bpm of the music affected the sense of unity, ease of dancing, and ease of timing the movements. In this experiment, music at bpm 80 and bpm 130 was used. Therefore, the acceptable range of video delay was from 460 ms to 750 ms. It was also clear that the number of Videos displayed had little effect on the dance.

6   Conclusion

In this survey, we investigated the effect of video delay on online dances in which multiple people participate. When multiple dancers in remote locations dance online at the same time, they cannot dance in time with the music due to the delay, and their movements do not appear to be in sync with each other. To solve these problems, we investigated the acceptable range of delay in dances with both audio and video delay. Using videos of multiple dancers dancing, we conducted an experiment that simulates an online dance lesson for dance beginners. The results of the experiment showed that the acceptable range of the video delay in dancing depends on the tempo of the music used in the dance. In terms of dance learning, it became clear that it was easier to dance and to synchronize the timing when the number of dancers displayed on the screen was reduced. In addition, the larger the delay, the easier it was to dance, the easier it was to feel a sense of unity, and the easier it was to match the timing.

Acknowledgment. This survey was partially supported by JST CREST (JP-MJCR18A3).

References

1. Castro, D., Hickson, S., Sangkloy, P., Mittal, B., Dai, S., andIrfan A. Essa, J.H.: Let's dance: Learning from online dance videos. CoRR abs/1801.07388 (2018)
2. Cornejo, C., Hurtado, E., Cuadros, Z., Torres-Araneda, A., Paredes, J., Olivares, H., Carré, D., Robledo, J.P.: Dynamics of simultaneous and imitative bodily coordination in trust and distrust. Front. Psychol. **9**, 1546 (2018)
3. Gergle, D., Kraut, R.E., Fussell, S.R.: The impact of delayed visual feedback on collaborative performance. In: Proceedings of the SIGCHI Conference on Human Factors in Computing Systems, pp. 1303–1312 (2006)
4. Guo, H., Zou, S., Xu, Y., Yang, H., Wang, J., Zhang, H., Chen, W.: Dancevis: toward better understanding of online cheer and dance training. J. Visualization **25**(1), 159–174 (2022)
5. Rivière, J.P., Alaoui, S.F., Caramiaux, B., Mackay, W.E.: How do dancers learn to dance? a first-person perspective of dance acquisition by expert contemporary dancers. In: Proceedings of the 5th International Conference on Movement and Computing, pp. 1–7 (2018)

Research on the Design of College Students' Offline Social Products Based on AIO Model

Zihao Jia[✉], Hui Jia, and Fanmin Meng

Nanjing University of Science and Technology, Nanjing 210094, China
jiazihao@njust.edu.cn

Abstract. This study aims to investigate, using the AIO model, the characteristic of offline social interactions among university students and to offer recommendations for the development of products that encourage university students to engage in offline activities. Semi-structured interviews with college students were employed in the study. Based on the information provided in the interviews, sensitive factors pertaining to university students' offline social activities were taken from the AIO scale. The lifestyle traits of university students who participated in offline social activities were then determined through qualitative and quantitative assessments of the variables. We created a mental model of the students based on the research findings and spoke about how to design this kind of product. The final section of this essay collects the life form traits of college students' offline social interactions and suggests design thinking for this kind of product in terms of both function and emotion using a mental model.

Keywords: AIO Model · Lifestyle Research · Offline Social Communication

1 Introduction

Maslow's hierarchy of needs hypothesis categorizes human needs into five categories that go from least to most important: physiological requirements, safety needs, belongingness & love needs, esteem needs, and self-actualization needs [1]. Higher-level requirements take precedence when people's basic physiological demands are satisfied. People's needs are always changing. Social requirements are therefore only second in importance to physiological and security demands. Humans are herd creatures, and they place a high value on social interactions. The prevalence of online social connection in 21st-century people's social interactions is distinctive. Online social networking is now a more realistic experience thanks to the development of the model and related technologies. Online socializing differs from offline socializing in that there are fewer non-verbal clues, more anonymity, more opportunity to create new social connections and reinforce existing ones, and greater information dissemination [2].

The fact that university students have grown up in an online world makes them more receptive to online forms of social interaction. However, some people may become unduly reliant on online social interaction as a result of this openness, which can result in psychological problems including social anxiety and loneliness. Louis et al. discovered that loneliness causes people to have emotional disorders and negatively impacts both their physical and mental health as well as their overall wellbeing [3]. We need to gradually transition from online to offline because if we follow the virtual social model without limitations, more and more people would become addicted to the Internet and disregard actual social life. This study examines how to employ online strategies to encourage university students to participate in offline social activities. It does this by analyzing the offline social lifestyles of university students using the AIO model.

2 Lifestyle and AIO Model

Lifestyle refers to the way people live their lives, whether they are individuals or members of typological groups. It includes people's attitudes, consumption habits, social interactions, and opinions and interests in various topics. The concept of lifestyle originated in sociology and has since been widely applied in the field of marketing. William Lazer defines lifestyle as "a systemic concept, a distinctive or characteristic way of life for an entire society or part of it, in a holistic and broadest sense" [4]. Based on this definition we can clearly understand the characteristics of an individual or group lifestyle. Since the early1980s, "lifestyle" has started to appear in Chinese humanities and social science ideas, and Chinese scholars' study on "lifestyle" has mostly taken from Western research findings as well as theoretical frameworks from the former Soviet Union [5]. According to Mo, a person's lifestyle is the way they live their life, which includes social relationships, consumption, and entertainment patterns [6]. From this definition, it is clear that lifestyle refers to a person's or a typological group's way of living, particularly with regard to a person's consumption habits, social interaction styles, and opinions and interests in various topics. Since product design need adhere to the premise of being human-centered and the study of lifestyle is focused on group characteristics, the concept of lifestyle has been introduced into the field of product design since the 1990s and has played a crucial role in product design.

The AIO model is the most widely used method in lifestyle research. It was introduced by William Lazer at the same time as he introduced the concept of lifestyle into the field of marketing. The model focuses on how consumers use their free time, their interests, and their perspectives on various lifestyles [7]. Then it extracts consumer characteristics using a cluster analysis of activities, interests, and opinions [8]. The AIO model has three dimensions: "A" for activities, "I" for interests, "O" for opinions. In 1974, Plummer added demographic variables to the three measures of activity, interest, and opinion to create the full AIO model [9]. Activity refers to a particular visible activity that is known from a behavioral statement but whose cause cannot be measured directly. Interest refers to an individual's sustained attention to something, an object, or a subject that is exciting. Opinion refers to individuals' interpretations, expectations and assessments of external stimuli. Demography refers to the method or study of demographic phenomena in terms of "quantity", which reveals the nature of demographic patterns and phenomena. The modified AIO scale consists of four main dimensions and 36 sub-dimensions, see Table 3. The AIO scale is introduced in this paper in order to study the lifestyles of university students engaging in offline social activities, to comprehend the social traits of university students who struggle with participating in social activities, and to offer recommendations for the design of products that will encourage university students' engagement in offline social activities.

3   Current Status of Products that Promote Offline Social Activities

Social activity refers to the various collective activities held to maintain the interdependent and interconnected social relationships among social groups as a result of the interaction. Currently, popular social networking products in China can be divided into those based on networking, such as WeChat and QQ; those based on information, such as Weibo and Paste; and those based on interest-based social networking, such as Netease Cloud Music and Xiaohongshu. To promote users' active participation in offline social activities, it is necessary to tap into users' interests and recommend activities and people that match their interests. The products involved in this study belong to social products based on interest-based social networking. Interest-based apps share three traits: first, the attributes of the target group are obvious because the product is intended for individuals who share a particular interest; second, the topics are obvious and the information is efficiently delivered; and third, the user-generated content is based on interest topics and users build social relationships by independently producing, sharing, and interacting with content [10].

Zhang et al. studied the interactive effects of online and offline social interaction, pointing out the characteristics of online interactions, such as anonymity and hyperspace, and discussing the relationship between offline and online interactions [11]. Young people frequently project their offline social interactions online and will publish details of their everyday lives on social media platforms as a way to document their lives or develop a sense of identity. Accordingly, attracting users through an online model is the most efficient way to encourage individuals to join in offline social activities based on the relationship between online and offline social networking. First off, gamifying offline actions is a well-liked strategy for facilitating Gamification is the process of incorporating components of games into things that already have certain basic values. This increases user stickiness and gives them an immersive experience that is similar to a game. Xie et al. summarized four gamification features of sports apps through exploration, namely the synergy of multiple motivational elements, the organic integration of internal and external motivations, the replacement of emotions based on sports scenes, and the deep integration of social relationships [12]. The majority of college students enjoy playing video games, therefore this strategy works better with this demographic, which also tends to select and suggest such things to their friends. This gamification concept is also used by the game "Pokémon GO," in which players can only play outside and must move to fulfill missions. Players will get together to acquire Pokémon, and they can trade pets or compete with one another. Pokémon GO "liberates" people from the indoors and gradually shifting from online to offline socializing [13].

In addition, some apps attract users by offering impeccable service and promoting users to participate in offline social activities. This type of approach is commonly found in travel and tourism apps, such as Ctrip and Tuniu Travel. Zhang et al. investigated how to improve the user stickiness and purchase intention of travel apps from the perspective of interactivity, and the study suggested two suggestions always paying attention to users' expectations of interactivity and enhancing the interactive experience of travel apps [14]. Melissa et al. investigated how to promote college travel through smartphone apps, suggesting that such apps should include features such as route planning, information alerts (trip times, weather forecasts), travel logs, and personal achievements [15]. To promote users to travel out of the house, while the travel experience is of primary importance, it is also important as to how the app engages users through online formats, such as impeccable information services and interesting reward mechanisms. What makes university students different from other groups of tourists when it comes to travel is that they are more likely to travel with travel companions they have not previously met [16]. Therefore, travel apps that are based on interest are more likely to attract the attention of university students. For example, the "Film Set" app, a travel service for film fans [17], collects a large number of film locations and tells the story of the film and the location to attract the target group "film In addition to tourism, as the main activity venue for university students, a series of campus activities organized by the university are also the main way for university students to participate in social activities, such as the "Campus Today" app, which serves university students to participate in offline activities by publishing and organizing campus activities, providing information on activities, user registration and sign-in.

A successful app should have a theme that is appealing to users, its functionalities should be user-friendly, and its information should be comprehensive enough to encourage university students to participate in offline social activities. Therefore, it is essential to examine and investigate the social life aspects of college in order to build a product that may offer customers a positive user experience.

4   Analysis of the Life Pattern of Offline Social Activities of College Students

Lifestyle research can help designers to more accurately characterize their target users, and many electronics companies have begun to segment their market categories according to the lifestyles of their users [18]. The lifestyles and attitudes of university student groups are characteristic of the Internet age, with individuality and unlimited possibilities synonymous with them. As the natives of the Internet, their studies, work, life and social activities are all full of the Internet's shadow. These university students are also known as Generation Z. Generation Z refers to people born after 1997, also known as the Internet Generation and the Internet Generation, who are a generation heavily influenced by technology products such as the Internet and smart devices [19]. "The survey of the 2019 Generation Z Consumption Power White Paper" shows that about 80% of Generation Z youth spend 7–9 h a day sleeping, 8 h studying or working, 1.5 h for daily activities such as eating and catching up, and the remaining 6 h are spent on social entertainment, with mobile phone time reaching more than 3 h and offline entertainment only about 1 h. Thus, internet products occupy most of the time of university students' life and entertainment.

When online socializing becomes the mainstream of campus life, problems such as low levels of interpersonal trust, social anxiety, and loneliness arise among university students, and offline activities are important to reduce and prevent the development of mental health problems.

4.1   Lifestyle Sensitivity Variable Construction for College Students

To analyze the characteristics of university students' social lives, semi-structured interviews based on the AIO model were conducted to extract sensitivity variables from the AIO Lifestyle Scale related to the promotion of offline social activities among university students. By understanding the current status of the university student group's participation in activities, their interests, ideological status, and basic personal information, their relevant sensitivity variables within the AIO scale were identified.

Table 1. Interview Outline

Purpose of the question	Question outline
Reduce the interviewee's nervousness. Collect personal information from interviewees	1. Ask interviewees to introduce themselves. (additional demographic information is asked based on interviewees' responses)
Find out what activities the interviewee would like to participate in and has participated in	2. Ask the interviewee what interests they have and what they love about them. Are there any stories?
Learn about the interviewee's current situation	3. What social events have you been attending lately? What are some stories or situations that happened while you were doing these things?
Lead respondents to evaluate recent events and understand their attitudes and opinions about them	4. Any particular concerns or worries? What is the reason?

Semi-structured interviews, one of the methods of interviewing, have certain topics and assumptions in advance, but the actual questions are not fleshed out. An interview outline was first developed. A good interview outline can help the researcher obtain as much valid information as possible and deepen the interviewer's memory of the research questions, to grasp the direction of the interview (Table 1). Four college students who were not good at participating in offline social activities were selected as the interviewees, and the interview format was both online and offline. The whole interviews were recorded, and the interviews were organized and filed as word documents after combining the recordings. The data of the interview results were integrated according to different categories in the three elements of the AIO system, and the sensitivity variables of each interviewee's lifestyle were obtained (Table 2).

Based on the extraction of the sensitivity variables of each of the 4 interviewees in the above table, the 4 were compared to find out the sensitivity variables shared by all 4 and to determine the final variables related to the life patterns of the college student group. The following variables were finally obtained from the AIO life pattern scale: work, social, shopping, leisure, media, self, product, and gain (Table 3, *The sub-dimensions marked in grey underlined are the resulting sensitivity variables*).

Table 2. Data Integration

Interviewee 1 Activities: work, hobbies, social events, shopping Interests: recreation, media Opinions: themselves, education, future Demographics: age, education, income, location
Interviewee 2 Activities: club membership, work, social events, shopping Interests: recreation, media Opinions: themselves, social issues, future Demographics: age, education, income, location, type of residence
Interviewee 3 Activities: work, hobbies, social events, shopping Interests: recreation, media, food Opinions: themselves, product Demographics: age, education, income, location
Interviewee 4 Activities: work, social events, shopping Interests: recreation, media Opinions: themselves, education Demographics: age, education, income, location, family members

Table 3. AIO Lifestyle Scale

Activity	Interest	Opinion	Demographics
Work	Family	**Themselves**	Age
Hobbies	Home	Social issues	Education
Social events	Job	Politics	**Income**
Vacation	Community	Business	Occupation
Entertainment	**Recreation**	Economics	Family size
Club membership	Fashion	Education	Dwelling
Community	Food	**Products**	Geography
Shopping	**Media**	Future	City Size
Sports	Achievements	Culture	Stage in life cycle

4.2 Qualitative Study of College Students' Lifestyle Sensitivity Variables

Based on the results of the first interview, a qualitative study was conducted on the sensitivity variables of college student's lifestyle. A second interview was conducted to discuss and analyze group-related sensitivity variables for the obtained sensitivity variables, to further obtain information about the target users in terms of activities, interests, and opinions, and to qualitatively analyze the interview results.

The outline of the second interview is shown in Table 4. 8 college students who were not good at participating in offline social activities were selected, and the interviews were conducted in both online and offline forms. The whole interview process was recorded, and the interviews were organized and filed as word documents combined with the recordings after the interviews. Six sensitivity variables were analyzed in terms of work, recreation, social events, media, themselves, and product.

Table 4. Interview Outline

Purpose of the question	Question outline
In-depth understanding of the user's state and perception of the product while shopping	1. Have you ever bought anything on a shopping holiday like Double 11? How do you prepare for the shopping festival?
Improve the shape of users' daily life, including study life and entertainment life	2. How do you organize your daily life? How do you organize your study and recreational life?
A more detailed understanding of the user's status in their daily leisure and the media channels they use to access information daily	3. The major video sites are very popular now, do you have any special attention? Besides that, what other leisure projects do you have on weekdays?
Based on the second question, further, determine the user's life trajectory	4. Do you have any hobbies? Is there an activity that stands out to you?
Get the user's focus on the event or others	5. Are there any points of particular interest to you in this activity just mentioned?
Understand the user's attitude and state of life, as well as plans for the future	6. What do you think about your life at the moment? Do you have any expectations for the future?

Work: Studying is the main form of work for the college student group and is an extremely important part of their lives. How to study efficiently is a common goal, and electronic devices are the main tool to improve the efficiency of studying.

Recreation: The interviewees' form of leisure was dominated by activities for better immersion experiences, such as listening to music, watching movies, reading, and physical exercise.

Social events: Interviewees are socially active in a variety of ways, covering both online and offline, and they look for activities in their preferred direction and share them with their friends. For them, communicating their ideas is one of the more important aspects.

Media: The interviewees all use short videos or online videos to watch to learn new information. Since they have a lot of things to do during the day and cannot read or watch relevant content for a long time, using the fragmented time to get information and broaden their knowledge is the most effective way, which is why they choose such media as short videos or online videos.

Themselves: Interviewees give priority to their interests when considering issues. In addition, they all have a clear plan for themselves.

Products: All eight interviewees were more rational in their shopping, shopping mainly for daily consumer goods, school supplies, etc., and paying more attention to the practicality of the products.

The conclusions obtained from the qualitative analysis are shown in Table 5.

Table 5. Qualitative analysis results

Sensitivity variables	Qualitative analysis
Work	It is more of a learning state that takes up a lot of time; offline socializing is mostly for work or study scenarios
Recreation	A form of personal presentation of one's interests
Social events	Often in tandem with leisure, socializing is a way to further enhance the experience after leisure activities
Media	The main way of relaxing and acquiring information for the college student community is to focus more on the efficiency and timeliness of acquiring information
Themselves	The influence of the surroundings and others on self-evaluation in the college student population
Products	A practical, purposeful, and portable tool

4.3 Quantitative Study of Life Pattern Sensitivity Variables of College Students

Based on the construction and qualitative analysis of the sensitivity variables related to the life pattern of college student groups in the first two interviews, a questionnaire survey was conducted to investigate the behavior, environment, and attitude in the life of college student groups by conducting quantitative research on the sensitivity variables of offline social activities of college student groups. Based on the sensitivity variables constructed in the first interview, the questionnaire questions were designed, and based on the information obtained in the second interview, eight in-depth aspects from income, work, social events, shopping, recreation, media, themselves, and product were set, with a total of 21 questions, and finally 40 valid questionnaires were obtained.

Combining the AIO sensitivity variables and the questionnaire results reveals that:

Work: college students generally spend less time studying at work than those who are already in the workforce and have more time to participate in offline social activities in comparison.

Social events: college students have a certain need for socialization, but sometimes lack the "medium" to participate in social activities.

Entertainment: there is plenty of time for recreation, mostly for students at school, and the activities are mostly in the form of various recreational activities on campus.

Recreation: university students have a wide range of leisure forms, including outdoor activities, physical exercise, and shopping, which are highly interactive.

Media: students prefer short videos and graphic readings that are more efficient in acquiring information and knowledge.

Shopping: due to the impact of economic income, players pay more attention to the quality, price, and practicality of products.

Income: university students are financially supported mainly by their parents' allowances, with the vast majority of students having no more than 3,000 yuan at their disposal each month.

Themselves: most students lack plans for the future and are confused, but they do enrich their lives in various ways.

4.4   Mental Model Construction of Offline Social Activities of College Students

A mental model is a "reduced scale model" of the external real world that people use to predict or explain certain events. To understand the mental model of college students when they participate in offline social activities, the mental model of this group was studied. The results of the second interview and questionnaire survey were compiled to build a mental model and propose relevant product features or strategies. Finally, the three mental spaces of "deciding to participate in social activities", "choosing social activities" and "feeling of social activities" were formed (Table 6).

Table 6.   Qualitative analysis results.

5   Thinking About Product Design Based on Promoting Offline Social Activities of College Students

For the target group of this study, i.e. college students who are not good at participating in social activities but are eager to do so, how to provide a suitable "medium" through which the group can participate in offline social activities is the core problem of such product design.

5.1 Design Thinking for the Functional Level

The functionality of the product is the most basic attribute of the product, and the most important thing for users to choose an app is the experience brought by its function. Based on the mental model of offline social activities of college students, the main functions of the product include basic modules such as activity information, interest recommendation, a communication platform, a personal center (including personal information, activity record, activity memo, activity summary), etc. Through these modules, users can meet the needs of "deciding to participate in social activities", "choosing social activities" and "feeling of social activities". "choose social activities", and "the feeling of social activities" needs.

Simplify Functions to Meet Real Needs. Since the purpose of this product is to promote offline activities, the display of interface information is based on the content of the activities, avoiding a purely functional overlay design and focusing on the quality and freshness of the activity information display, such as highlighting the activity keywords and other forms, to attract users to select activities and eventually participate in activities offline.

Fun features to meet the user experience. As college students who are natives of the Internet, fun is a prerequisite for anything they choose to do. Therefore, the interesting nature of product functions is an effective way to enhance user experience. For example, the combination of activity information display interface and real-time communication platform allows users to directly ask for related information or find like minded users.

Weak Communication Format to Highlight the Offline Social Theme. The main function of this product is to provide information services, so the low-cost communication format is sufficient for the basic communication style. The relationship between users is a temporary connection, which is established only to participate in offline activities together. The initial reason for using this product is not to have a social network, but to have accurate access to the content of the event, and the social aspect makes it more efficient.

5.2 Design Thinking for the Emotional Dimension

There is no shortage of socially anxious individuals in the college student population who are extremely sensitive to interpersonal relationships and have difficulty interacting with people face-to-face. Wang Huan et al. found that social anxiety partially mediates the relationship between personality traits and cell phone dependence among college students [20]. Social anxiety causes college students to rely more on their cell phones, while the group of college students who are not good at participating in offline social activities, actually desire deep down to participate in interesting activities.

Gaining Approval to Enhance Emotional Care. Gaining approval to enhance emotional care. College students' reliance on social media is a kind of active satisfaction-seeking behavior because most of them live in a slight stroke deficit reality, and they show a strong desire to express themselves on social media and obtain "stroke" and "identity" through this online interactive behavior [21]. "approval" through such online interaction. By setting up the corresponding reward mechanism and commemorative mechanism to give affirmation and recognition to users' performance in the activities, and sharing the activities and rewards obtained in the communication platform, we can attract more users to participate in the offline activities in the online form.

Interest in Socialization to Enhance Group Relationships. WeChat, QQ, and other apps that live on information exchange belong to pan-social platforms. Due to the needs of study and life, college students often need to deal with a large amount of complicated information on such platforms, and gradually become tired of being pan-social. Therefore, many users shift from pan-social platforms to vertical social platforms, which are divided into different scenarios based on interests or needs, and socialization is carried out in relatively closed communities within each scenario [22], and the strong connection and small circle socialization of vertical networks are more in line with the social preferences of today's college students. With the help of big data, we recommend activities that users may be interested in and strengthen the concept of "interest circle" in the activity push and communication platform so that users can find like-minded partners to participate in activities together.

6   Conclusion

For college students who are full of personalization, offline social forms cannot meet their diverse needs. How to promote college students' active participation in offline social activities under the environment of colorful online social forms is a question worth exploring. Therefore, it is necessary to study the design of such products by analyzing the lifestyle of offline social activities of college students. The article analyzes the typological characteristics of college students in terms of activities, interests, and opinions through the AIO model in the lifestyle analysis, comprehensively and systematically understands the lifestyle characteristics of college students' offline social activities, explores their essential needs, and proposes design considerations for such products at the functional and emotional levels based on the obtained mental model. The use of the AIO scale helps to understand users' needs more clearly, to design products that promote offline social interaction with good user experience.

Please try to avoid rasterized images for line-art diagrams and schemas. Whenever possible, use vector graphics instead (see **Error! Reference source not found.**).

References

1. Maslow, A.H.: A theory of human motivation. Psychol. Rev. **50**(4), 370–396 (1943). https://doi.org/10.1037/h0054346
2. Lieberman, A., Schroeder, J.: Two social lives: how differences between online and offline interaction influence social outcomes. Curr. Opin. Psychol. **31**, 16–21 (2020). https://doi.org/10.1016/j.copsyc.2019.06.022
3. Hawkley, L.C., Cacioppo, J.T.: Loneliness matters: a theoretical and empirical review of consequences and mechanisms. Ann. Behav. Med. **40**(2), 218–227 (2010). https://doi.org/10.1007/s12160-010-9210-8

4. Lazer, W.: Life style concepts and marketing. Toward Sci. Mark. **15**(4), 130–139 (1963)
5. Zhao, P., Lyu, Di.: Lifestyle and its measurements. In: Zhao, P., Lyu, Di. (eds.) Lifestyle Change and Transport in China, pp. 23–58. Springer Nature, Singapore (2022). https://doi.org/10.1007/978-981-19-4399-7_2
6. Mo Lian, F.: Research of product design method based on lifestyle. J. Mach. Des. **60**(07), 127–128 (2013)
7. Akkaya, M.: Understanding the impacts of lifestyle segmentation and perceived value on brand purchase intention: an empirical study in different product categories. Eur. Res. Manag. Bus. Econ. **27**(3), 100155 (2021)
8. Vyncke, P.: Lifestyle segmentation: from attitudes, interests and opinions, to values, aesthetic styles, life visions and media preferences. Eur. J. Commun. **17**(4), 445–463 (2002)
9. Plummer, J.T.: The concept and application of life style segmentation: the combination of two useful concepts provides a unique and important view of the market. J. Mark. **38**(1), 33–37 (1974)
10. Chen, R.: APP design of interest sociality based on social relationships strength. Packag. Eng. **38**(22), 125–130 (2017)
11. Zhang, Y., Du, H., Ding, Q.: Peer interaction for young people: online and offline interaction. Psychol. Res. **9**(01), 53–59 (2016)
12. Xie, Z., Xiong, W.: Research on design characteristics of the internet sports app based on gamification. Design **03**, 134–136 (2017)
13. Xia, W.: Research on the development status and trend of AR handheld games–take the Pokemon Go game as an example. J. Commun. Univ. China (Sci. Technol.) **24**(03), 14–18 (2017)
14. Zhang, C.B., Li, Y.N., Wu, B., Li, D.: Travel app user stickiness and purchase intention: an interactivity perspective. Tourism Tribune **32**(06), 109–118 (2017)
15. Bopp, M., Sims, D., Matthews, S.,Rovinak, L., Poole, E., Colgan, J.: There's an app for that: development of a smartphone app to promote active travel to a college campus. J. Transp. Health **3**(3), 305–314 (2016)
16. Zhu, X.: Backpacker Tourism: Theoretical and Empirical Study Based on China. East China Normal University, Shanghai (2007)
17. Shi, J.: The new experience of film and TV tourism in the internet era: film tourism development of "Film Set" App from the perspective of fan film. Soc. Sci. **02**, 56–64 (2022)
18. Su, J., Zhang, Q., Wu, J.: Evolutionary design of product multi-image styling. Comput. Integr. Manuf. Syst. **20**(11), 2675–2682 (2014)
19. Dimock, M.: Defining generations: where millennials end and Generation Z begins. Pew Research Center **17**(1), 1–7 (2019)
20. Wang, H., Huang, H., Wu, H.M.: Relationship between personality and mobile phone addiction: a mediating role of social anxiety. Chin. J. Clin. Psychol. **22**(03), 447–450 (2014)
21. Liu, Z.: A study of social media dependence and media demand–take the example of college students' reliance on microblogs. Journalism Bimonthly **01**, 119–129 (2013)
22. Luan, C., Jiang, X.: Research on vertical social application design from the perspective of interaction ritual chains theory: a case study of Netease Music. Design **34**(13), 145–147 (2021)

Do People Tend to Select a Delayed Item?

Yuichiro Kinoshita[(✉)], Yuto Sekiguchi, Riho Ueki, Kouta Yokoyama,
and Satoshi Nakamura

Meiji University, Nakano 4-21-1, Nakano-ku, Tokyo, Japan
ev200548@meiji.ac.jp

Abstract. Dark patterns that lead users to unintentionally harmful behaviors are often used in e-commerce and social media, and consumer troubles are frequent. Dark patterns are also seen in choice situations, where some attempt to induce the user's behavior by making specific options prominent. Focusing on user interfaces that seem fair at first glance, but induce users to make a choice, we investigated the effect of delayed display of options for inducing users to make a choice. Specifically, we conducted a crowdsourcing experiment based on the hypothesis that *when only one choice is delayed, the delayed choice is more likely to be selected.* The experimental results showed no tendency for the delayed option to be chosen more often overall. However, we found that the effect of the delayed display of alternatives on choice varied from person to person. Specifically, it was suggested that a delayed display of the option in the upper left corner of the screen with a delay time of 0.1 s for early choosers and a delayed display of the choice in the center of the screen with a delay time of 0.2 s for late choosers might induce their choice behavior.

Keywords: Dark Patterns · Delay · UI · Selection Induction · Pop-out

1 Introduction

It is now possible to collect and disseminate information, make purchases, make reservations, and do many other things on the Web. On the other hand, a problem called dark patterns has emerged [1]. Dark patterns refer to user interface designs that lead users to unintended behaviors. They are often seen, especially in mail-order sites and reservation sites. For example, a message that a product the user is browsing is almost out of stock and a countdown timer that tells the user how much time is left on a sale are among the dark patterns that use scarcity bias to encourage the purchase of a product.

Making certain choices stand out is a type of dark patterns. For such a case, it is easy for users to notice that it induces their choice behavior. However, there are cases in which selection behavior is unconsciously induced by a selection interface that does not appear to be guiding selection at first glance. For example, Yokoyama et al. [2] found that presenting a progress bar that guides the gaze before offering a choice biases the tendency to choose.

Here, we focused on induced visual interference [3], one of the dark patterns. Inspired by the fact that images are displayed with a delay due to network or system problems, we hypothesized that *displaying only one of the multiple choices with a slight delay would induce selection behavior*. To be concrete, we expected that if only one of the six choices were displayed with a slight delay, people would be more likely to choose the one with a delay (Fig. 1). If a delayed display affects selection behavior, it can induce selection behavior by disguising a delayed display as a delay caused by a network or system.

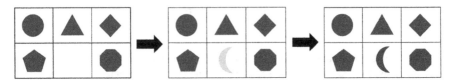

Fig. 1. Interpretation of delayed display of choices.

Therefore, we conducted a large-scale crowdsourcing study of the selection behavior when only one of the six choices was displayed with a delay. The analysis of the results revealed the effect of delayed display on selection behavior.

2   Related Work

Mathur et al. [4] developed an automated web crawler to extract dark patterns from over 11,000 shopping sites. They found 1,818 dark patterns consisting of 15 types and seven categories. They also discovered that dark patterns were more likely to appear on popular websites. Geronimo et al. [5] found that about 95% of 240 popular mobile apps contained at least one dark pattern. Gunawan et al. [6] conducted a comparative study of dark patterns in the mobile app, mobile browser, and web browser versions of 105 popular online services. They found 2,320 dark patterns across all services. They showed that the mobile app version contained slightly more dark patterns than the browser version. Luguri et al. [7] reported that dark patterns effectively induce user behavior and that users have negative feelings toward forceful dark patterns but no emotional repulsion toward mild dark patterns. In other words, dark patterns that appear unguided at first glance are more likely to be accepted by users. Many dark patterns have been discovered and reported, but studies have yet to examine dark patterns related to the timing of choice display. This paper discusses the effect of delayed display of one of the multiple options on choice behavior.

Wilson et al. discussed the relationship between the position of choices and selection behavior [8]. They investigated the selection rate for four stockings arranged horizontally and found that the selection rates were 12%, 17%, 31%, and 40% from the left, indicating the existence of a right-sided bias. On the other hand, Valenzuela et al. [9] found that the choice in the center was more likely to be selected than the choices on either side of the display. We investigate the relationship between the display position of choices and the selection rate.

There is something called 'pop-out' among the human visual characteristics, and research has been conducted on pop-out and choice behavior. Pop-out is an optical property in which a stimulus can be perceived immediately when only one different stimulus is present among multiple stimuli of the same type. Hosoya et al. [10] focused on pop-outs and found that they effectively induced selection in signage-type vending machines when only COLD products were sold but were not so effective when HOT and COLD products were mixed. Maljkovic et al. [11] found that anticipating what will be popped out does not affect attention and that pop-outs must be consciously addressed. A delayed display of only one of the multiple choices could also be considered a variant of pop-outs. We hypothesized that *the delayed choice is more likely to be selected when one of the six choices is delayed*. This paper aims to investigate the effect of delayed display on selection behavior.

3 Methodology

3.1 Experimental Settings

As for the appropriate number of choices, too many would increase the burden of answering. However, if there are only a few options, this might cause experiment participants to select other choices before the delayed choice is displayed. Therefore, the number of choices in this experiment was set to six.

Danziger et al. [12] showed that the more decisions a person makes, the more stressed they feel and the less likely they are to make an accurate decision. Therefore, the number of questions was set to 15 to avoid fatigue caused by decision-making.

The questions asked the experiment participants about their favorite fruits, vegetables, etc. However, such questions could bias the choice toward a particular option depending on its popularity, so we selected options with the same degree of popularity and name recognition as far as possible.

To prevent the experiment participants from becoming accustomed to the delayed display, the delayed display of the choices was only used for five of the 15 questions. Also, we randomized the position of the delayed display and the order of the questions.

Three delay durations of 0.1, 0.2, and 0.3 s were set for the delayed display of the choices. The delay time was randomly selected from the three delay times when the delayed display was used. By comparing the selection behavior at each delay time, we investigated whether the effect of the delayed display on the selection behavior changed depending on the delay time.

3.2 System Overview and Experimental Procedures

The experimental system was created using Vue.js, a JavaScript framework. We first asked the experiment participants to access the experimental system page via a link from a page on Yahoo! Crowdsourcing [13]. When an experiment participant accessed the experiment page, the system generated a unique 16-digit alphanumeric and lower-case ID for each participant and presented a page explaining the experiment. On the page describing the experiment participant was asked to check the checkboxes to confirm the experimental procedure and precautions. The precautions included using Google Chrome, Safari, or Firefox browsers and not pressing the back and reload buttons. In addition, on the page explaining the experiment, participants were asked to select their gender and age from a list before starting the investigation. The experiment could only be started if all the checkboxes were checked, and the page was accessed from a PC.

The sequence of one trial is shown in Fig. 2. When the user moved to the experiment screen, a question and a button were first displayed for each question. Clicking the button below the question displayed six choices. The participant selected one answer to the question from the displayed choices and clicked on it. For each trial, we obtained the user's unique ID, gender, age, current number of trials, selected time, choice content and its display position, delayed display position, delay time, and the date and time when the trial was completed.

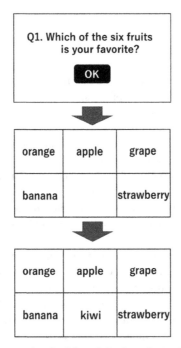

Fig. 2. An example of a delayed display of one of the choices.

After 15 trials of the experiment had been completed, an experiment completion screen was displayed with a common code for the experiment participant to select on Yahoo! Crowdsourcing [13] and a unique ID was generated for each experiment participant. By returning to the crowdsourcing screen, selecting that code and entering the unique ID, the experiment was completed.

4 Results

4.1 Data on Experiment Participants

The experiment was conducted twice using crowdsourcing, with 500 females and 500 males on July 7–8, 2022, and 500 females and 500 males on September 28–29, 2022. Because crowdsourcing experiments can cause some participants to respond inappropriately, we extracted inappropriate participants from the acquired data. In this experiment, problematic participants were removed by referring to the selection position, selected time, and the total number of trials. 89 participants (55 females and 34 males) responded inappropriately in the first experiment, and 101 (56 females and 45 males) responded inappropriately in the second experiment. The data from 1,810 participants (889 females and 921 males), excluding these inappropriate respondents, were included in the analysis.

4.2 Overall Results for Selection Rate of Delayed Choices and Selected Time

Since there were three delay times for the delayed display in this experiment, Table 1 shows the percentage of the delayed display selected for each delay time and the average chosen time when the delayed display was selected and not selected. The chance level of each choice was 16.67% because the number of options in this experiment was six.

Table 1. Selection rate and selected time for delayed display alternatives for the entire body of data.

	Selectivity (%)	Average selected time (s)	
		Selected the delay target	Did not select the delay target
0.1	16.54	4.56	4.60
0.2	17.75	4.53	4.56
0.3	16.47	4.76	4.59
Average	16.92	4.61	4.58

Table 1 shows that for all data with delayed display, the selection rate for the delayed option was 16.92%, which is similar to the chance level. The selection rate of the delayed choice was slightly lower than the chance level when the delay time was 0.1 and 0.3 s. In comparison, the delayed choice was more likely to be selected when the delay time was 0.2 s. Regarding the selected time, when the delayed choice was chosen with a delay of 0.3 s, the selected time was more extended than in the other cases.

4.3 Selected Time in Each Trial

The distribution of the selected time for each trial in the two experiments is shown in Fig. 3. We divided all data obtained in the two experiments into three groups: a group with a selected time of under three seconds (Group Short, N = 7,947), a group with a selected time of over three and under five seconds (Group Middle, N = 10,684), and a group with a selected time of over five seconds (Group Long, N = 8,519) so that the number of data was as equal as possible.

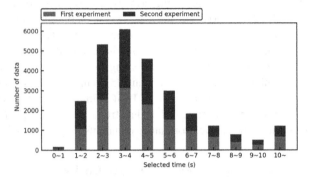

Fig. 3. Distribution of selected time in each trial.

Table 2. The amount of data and average selected time in each group, and selection rate of delayed alternatives displayed.

	Short	Middle	Long
Average selected time (s)	2.20	3.90	7.66
Selectivity (%)	17.10	16.41	17.41

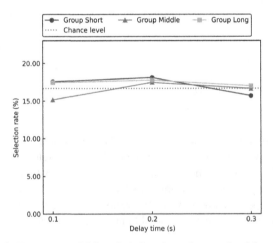

Fig. 4. Percentage of delayed choices in each group by delay time.

Table 2 shows the average selected time and the selection rate of the delayed choices for each of the three data groups. Each group includes both delayed and non-delayed data.

4.4 Percentage of Delayed Choices in Each Group

Table 2 shows that the selection rate of the delayed choice was similar to the chance level for all groups.

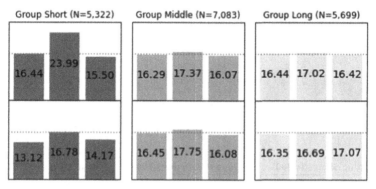

Fig. 5. Selection rate per position without delayed display.

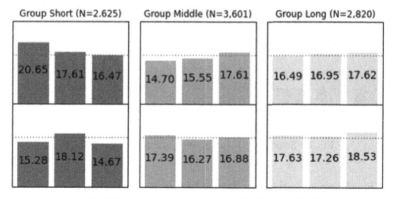

Fig. 6. Selection rate per position with delayed display.

Next, Fig. 4 shows the selection rate of the delayed choice for each group for each delay time. When the delay time was 0.1 s, the delayed choice was slightly more likely to be selected in Group Short and Group Long, while the delayed choice was less likely to be chosen in Group Middle. When the delay time was 0.2 s, the selection rate was slightly above the chance level for all groups. When the delay time was 0.3 s, the selection rate of the delayed choice was slightly below the chance level for Group Short. For Group Long, the selection rate of the delayed choice stayed the same when the delay time was changed.

4.5 Relationship Between Position and Selection Rate in Each Group

As Wilson et al. [8] and Valenzuela et al. [9] pointed out, the selection's tendency depends on the choices' display position. Therefore, we also analyzed the relationship between the position of the options and the selection rate.

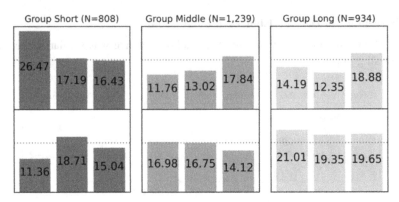

Fig. 7. Selection rate per position at a delay time of 0.1 s.

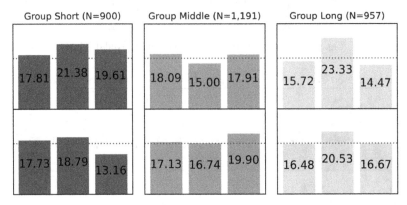

Fig. 8. Selection rate per position at a delay time of 0.2 s.

First, Fig. 5 shows the selection rate (%) for each position when the delayed display was not used. In Fig. 5, the selection rate is shown as a percentage of the total data without the delayed display, where 100 is the complete data without the delayed display for each group. In this experiment, three of the six choices were displayed at the top and bottom of the screen, respectively, and each bar graph corresponds to the position of the real choice. For Group Short, the top of the middle column was the most likely place to be chosen. For Group Middle and Group Long, there was almost no difference in the selection rate due to the difference in location.

Next, Fig. 6 shows the percentage (%) of the delayed display selected for each position. In Fig. 6, the selection rate is shown as a percentage of the total data, with the delayed display at each position in each group. For Group Short, the delayed item was more likely to be chosen when the delayed display was on the top of the left column. For the other groups, there was no significant effect on selection.

Figure 7 shows that when the delay time was 0.1 s, the delayed item was more likely to be selected when the delayed item was displayed at the top of the left column in Group Short. Still, it was less likely to be chosen at the bottom of the left column. In Group

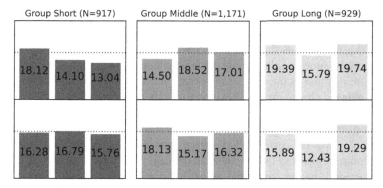

Fig. 9. Selection rate per position at a delay time of 0.3 s.

Middle, the delayed selection was less likely to be selected when the delayed selection is shown at the top of the left column. In Group Long, the delayed item was more likely to be chosen when the delayed item was displayed at the bottom of the left column but less likely to be selected at the top of the middle column.

Figure 8 shows that when the delay time was 0.2 s, the delayed option was more likely to be selected when the delayed display was placed on the top of the middle column in Group Short. For Group Middle, the delayed choice was slightly more likely to be chosen when the delayed display was placed below the right column. Still, the difference between the positions was relatively small. For Group Long, the delayed choice was more likely to be chosen when the delayed choice was displayed in the middle column.

Figure 9 shows that when the delay time was 0.3 s, no position was particularly likely to be selected for the selection rate of the delayed item in Group Short. The same was true for Group Middle. On the other hand, for Group Long, the delayed selection was more likely to be chosen when the delayed selection was displayed at the top of the right column. However, the delayed choice was less likely to be selected when the delayed selection was displayed at the bottom of the middle column.

5 Discussion

The overall selection rate of the delayed choice was 16.92%, which was not different from the chance level, and thus the hypothesis in this study was not supported. The results of the selection rate of the delayed choice in the three groups classified by the selected time showed no tendency to choose the delayed choice in any of the groups. These results suggest that delayed display of alternatives may increase the selection rate of delayed options or, conversely, may decrease it. Specifically, the selection rate increases when the delayed choice is displayed precisely when the user sees the delayed choice. On the other hand, if the choice is not displayed when the user sees the delayed choice, the selection rate is considered low.

Next, the results of the selection rate for each position without the delayed display showed that Group Short was more likely to choose the top of the middle column. This is thought to be because the experiment participants placed a button in the center of the screen that they clicked before moving to the selection page, so they tried to select the item without moving the mouse. On the other hand, the difference in the selection rate between the positions was slight for Group Middle and Group Long. This suggests that people who take time to select compare the contents of the choices regardless of the initial mouse position at the time of the screen transition. The results of the selection rate of the delayed choice for each position for each delay time showed that the delayed choice was more likely to be selected when the top-left choice was delayed by 0.1 s or when the top choice in the middle column was delayed by 0.2 s in Group Short. When the delayed display was not performed, the group was more likely to choose the top of the middle column, suggesting that the delayed display of the top-left option by 0.1 s could induce selection behavior for Group Short. In Group Middle, the delayed choice was slightly more likely to be selected only when the bottom right column was delayed by 0.2 s. When the delay time was 0.3 s, the selection rate of the delayed choice was about the same as the chance level. These results suggest that the delayed display of alternatives is unlikely to affect selection behavior for Group Middle. For Group Long, the delayed choice was more likely to be chosen when the bottom left column was delayed by 0.1 s, and the middle column was delayed by 0.2 s. This difference in the position at which the delayed item was more likely to be selected might be related to eye movement. Since eye movement was not captured in this experiment, we plan to investigate this in future experiments.

6 Conclusion

In this study, based on the idea that some user interfaces seem to be fair but induce selection, we hypothesized that *when only one choice is delayed in a multiple-choice environment, the choice is more likely to be selected*. In addition, we experimented with verifying whether the delayed choice is more likely to be selected when the user selects one answer from among six choices. The experimental results did not support the hypothesis that the delayed choice was more likely to be chosen. This could be due to a significant selection bias toward some options and a lack of removal of inappropriate experiment participants. However, it is also possible that the delayed display of only one of the choices may work as an inducement or a non-inducement and that the effects may have canceled each other out. On the other hand, it was suggested that it might be possible to induce selection by changing the delay time and the position of the delayed display according to the length of the selected time. For example, when the selection time is short, the top-left delay at 0.1 s may induce the user to choose the item, while a bottom left delay of 0.1 s and a middle delay of 0.2 s may induce the user to select the item when the selection time is long.

We plan to reexamine the question and the content of the choices in future experiments. In addition, we plan to conduct a face-to-face investigation using an eye tracker to obtain the eye movements of the participant in order to clarify further the effect of delayed display of choices on selection behavior.

Acknowledgement. This work was partly supported by JSPS KAKENHI Grant Number JP22K12135.

References

1. Brignull, H.: DECEPTIVE DESIGN, https://www.deceptive.design/. Accessed 2022/11/10
2. Yokoyama, K., Nakamura, S., Yamanaka, S.: Do animation direction and position of progress bar affect selections? In: Ardito, C., et al. (eds.) INTERACT 2021. LNCS, vol. 12936, pp. 395–399. Springer, Cham (2021). https://doi.org/10.1007/978-3-030-85607-6_45
3. Gray, M., C., Kou, Y., Battles, B., Hoggatt, J., Toombs, L., A.: The Dark (Patterns) Side of UX Design. In: Proceedings of the 2018 CHI Conference on Human Factors in Computing Systems, no. 534, pp. 1–14 (2018)
4. Mathur, A., Acar, G., Friedman, J.M., Lucherini, E., Mayer, J., Chetty, M., Narayanan, A.: Dark patterns at scale: Findings from a crawl of 11K shopping websites. In: Proceedings of the ACM on Human-Computer Interaction 3, CSCW (2019), pp. 1–32, 2019
5. Geronimo, D.L., Braz, L., Fregnan, E., Palomba, F., Bacchelli, A.: UI Dark Patterns and Where to Find Them: A Study on Mobile Applications and User Perception. In: Proceedings of the 2020 CHI Conference on Human Factors in Computing Systems, pp. 1–14 (2020)
6. Gunawan, J., Pradeep, A., Choffnes, D., Hartzog, W., Wilson C.: A comparative study of dark patterns across mobile and web modalities. In: Proceedings of the ACM on Human-Computer Interaction, vol. 5, pp. 1–29 (2021)
7. Luguri, J., Strahilevitz, L.: Shining a light on dark patterns. Public Law Working Paper, no. 719 (2019)
8. Wilson, T.D., Nisbett, R.E.: The accuracy of verbal reports about the effects of stimuli on evaluation and behavior. Soc. Psychol. **41**(2), 118–131 (1978)
9. Valenzuela, A., Raghubir, P.: Position-based beliefs: the centerstage effect. J. Consum. Psychol. **19**(2), 185–196 (2009)
10. Hosoya, M., Yamaura, H., Nakamura, S., Nakamura, M., Takamatsu, E., Kitaide, Y.: Does the pop-out affect the product selection of signage vending machine? In: 17th IFIP TC.13 International Conference on Human-Computer Interaction (INTERACT 2019), vol. 11747, pp. 24–32 (2019)
11. Maljkovic, V., Nakayama, K.: Priming of pop-out: I. Role of features. Memory Cogn. **22**, 657–672 (1994)
12. Danziger, S., Levev, J., Avnaim-Pesso, L.: Extraneous factors in judicial decisions. Proc. Natl. Acad. Sci. **108**(17), 6889–6892 (2011)
13. Yahoo! Crowdsourcing. https://crowdsourcing.yahoo.co.jp/. Accessed 2022/11/18

Development of Virtual Office System with Awareness-Sharing Function to Facilitate Communication Among Remote Team Members

Kohei Kurosaki, Ryota Sugisawa, and Kinya Fujita[(✉)] [iD]

Tokyo University of Agriculture and Technology, Koganei 184-8588, Japan
kfujita@cc.tuat.ac.jp

Abstract. As the COVID-19 pandemic has forced numerous people to work from home, it has revealed the underlying difficulties of team-based remote work. To address the communication issues, virtual office systems have emerged as a promising new technology. With the objective of motivating workers participation in a virtual office, we developed a prototype virtual office system integrated with an awareness-sharing subsystem that enables the sharing of abstracted statuses among team members without requiring logging in. Results of a preliminary assessment suggests that the developed prototype system may provide presence and sense of activity among team members with minimum reluctance for personal status disclosure.

Keywords: Remote Work · Virtual Office · Awareness

1 Introduction

As the COVID-19 pandemic forced increasing amounts of employees to work from home, information-sharing tools such as video conference, chat, and file-sharing systems have significantly contributed toward the continuous flow of business. Outside the context of the pandemic, remote work offers essential advantages in terms of time efficiency and costs by eliminating the need for commuting. Furthermore, remote work is a promising option to address the social demands associated with child and elderly care. Although tools based on information and communication technology have resolved data-sharing and human communication issues in remote work, several underlying difficulties remain in the context of team members.

Recognized issues in remote work include work-family conflicts [1] and stress [2]. Furthermore, deficiency in communication is one of the most critical issues associated with remote work. As a potential risk in team working, insufficient communication may weaken the network among the members [3], as well as detract the feeling of belonging [4] or instill a sense of isolation [5]. All of these issues may contribute toward the impairment of work efficiency.

One potential cause of insufficient communication encompasses concerns about bothering other members by talking to them. Another conceivable cause is the lack of opportunities for occasional communication.

© The Author(s), under exclusive license to Springer Nature Switzerland AG 2023
M. Kurosu and A. Hashizume (Eds.): HCII 2023, LNCS 14012, pp. 408–419, 2023.
https://doi.org/10.1007/978-3-031-35599-8_27

Accordingly, virtual office systems have been studied with the aim of promoting occasional communication. Sohlenkamp et al. developed a simplified 2D virtual office called DIVA, aiming at providing activity awareness of remote workers and a collaborative environment [6]. Honda et al. developed a 3D virtual office environment called Valentine to realize spatial relationships that parallel those within real office environments [7]. In their system, PC operations and chair motions are remotely shared as potential cues of workers' concentration levels. As a consequence of the COVID-19 pandemic, various virtual office systems have become provided commercially [8–11]. These systems allow workers to share a communication space as needed. However, it appears that most organizations have not yet introduced virtual office systems at the time of this study.

To allow remote workers to unobtrusively communicate with their colleagues, awareness-sharing systems, dedicated to sharing of activity, have been studied. Hubbub is an instant messenger that reflects each user's device operation activity [12]. ActivitySpotter enables the sharing of activity contexts through a semantic analysis of document access [13]. Another line of studies has attempted to estimate and share the interruptibility of remote workers to minimize unintended interruptions. Fogarty et al. [14] developed a system that estimates the remote worker's interruptibility based on the user's PC operation and environmental sound level. Hincapie´-Ramos et al. developed a system that shares the interruptibility and usage of each worker's communication channels [15]. Likewise, we have developed a system that automatically estimates and shares each worker's interruptibility based on their PC operations [16, 17].

Along these two lines of research, this study was conducted to integrate virtual office and awareness-sharing systems, enabling remote workers to transition from individual to collaborative work with less concern regarding bothering their coworkers, thereby facilitating team communication.

2   Virtual Office System with Status Awareness-Sharing Function

In the traditional office setting, workers are mainly engaged in individual tasks, and occasionally engaged in collaborative work such as meetings. In other words, workers transit between individual and collaborative tasks in the process of their work. Furthermore, occasional conversation is necessary to give and receive advice, report minor issues, and confirming unclear points of working processes. To smoothly navigate these occasional conversations, awareness regarding each member's working status, especially interruptibility, is indispensable. This process is illustrated in Fig. 1(a).

In the current remote working environment, tools assisting individual work, such as VPNs to ensure secure remote data access, have already been widely employed. Tools assisting formal collaborative tasks, such as video conference systems, have also gained increasing prevalence. However, these are designed individually, and do not assist in work-status awareness-sharing. Consequently, occasional communication is easily missed, as remote workers have no means to seize the opportunity to talk to their colleagues as shown in Fig. 1(b).

Awareness-sharing system [12–15] may function as potential solutions. However, according to our experience operating an individually developed awareness-sharing system [17] alongside a virtual office system, the simultaneous use of multiple systems inhibits the transitioning from individual work to conversation.

To enable the smooth transition from individual work to occasional conversation, an awareness-sharing among team members and a virtual place for conversation are required. Furthermore, these functions must be integrated seamlessly as shown in Fig. 1(c).

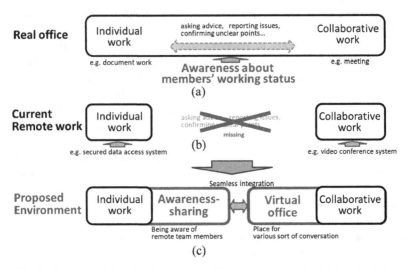

Fig. 1. Concept of virtual office system with remote awareness-sharing function.

A direct solution is the implementation of an awareness-sharing function into a virtual office system. However, the requirement of being logged in to the virtual office just for the purpose of awareness sharing may pose concerns with regards to being disrupted or monitored. These concerns may stress remote workers in situations that necessitate high concentration or privacy consideration. Therefore, the level of shared information must be voluntarily controllable by the workers.

On the other hand, conventional virtual office systems provide no information pertaining to remote coworkers outside of their login sessions. Therefore, a moderate awareness-sharing function must be provided to let workers aware of their colleagues with less concerns relating to self-information disclosure. In other words, both moderate awareness-sharing mode and virtual office mode for conversation are needed. In addition, seamless and intuitive transitions between the two modes are desired.

Figure 2 illustrates the supposed transition of a virtual office system and corresponding working situation of an employee. When the employee turns on their PC, the system automatically starts in awareness-sharing mode, where the worker is anonymized to relieve their stress from being monitored. This mode allows workers to perform their own tasks without being monitored or interrupted, while ambiently and bidirectionally sharing their status with other members. Upon logging in to the virtual office, the employee can view detailed statuses of other team members and communicate with them as needed. This mode allows collaborative work with conversation, as well as individual work. Temporary departures from the virtual office are also permitted.

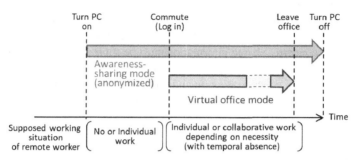

Fig. 2. Supposed transition of virtual office system and corresponding working situation of remote employee.

To realize these two modes, as well as the smooth transition between them, we developed the system illustrated in Fig. 3. This system was designed under the premise that an awareness-sharing subsystem automatically starts when the user turns on their workstation, allowing the user to view an abstract status of the virtual office. It also allows the user to transition to virtual office mode where they can gauge other worker's interruptibility and communicate. Details pertaining to the subsystems are described in the following sections.

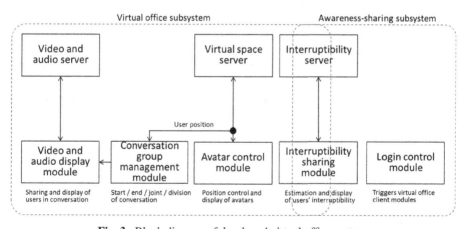

Fig. 3. Block diagram of developed virtual office system.

3 Status Awareness-Sharing Subsystem

3.1 Requirements for Status Awareness-Sharing Subsystem

As discussed previously, to facilitate remote workers login to virtual office, it is beneficial to share detailed information reflecting the coworkers' activity before logging in. However, privacy concerns arise from the perspective of the people being monitored. To address these concerns, shared information must be appropriately abstracted, and the sent (viewed) and received (viewing) information must be balanced.

Furthermore, when concentrating on an individual task, an employee should not be distracted by the system. To ensure practical use, compatibility with existing systems is also desirable.

Summary of requirements:

rq1. Reflection of coworker statuses
rq2. Abstraction of shared information
rq3. Balance between sent (viewed) and received (viewing) information
rq4. Preserving worker concentration
rq5. Compatibility with existing systems

3.2 Implementation of Awareness-Sharing Subsystem

Figure 4 illustrates the designed awareness-sharing window. To satisfy Requirement 1, the statuses of coworkers are categorized into three groups based on estimated interruptibility and displayed as avatar colors: not yet logged in to virtual office but already turned on their PC (gray); already logged in and concentrated in the work (red); and already logged in and available for conversation (green). To display the login status, we use a building metaphor.

Because Requirement 2 demands information abstraction, the avatars are anonymized and the detailed values for estimated interruptibility are hidden to any users who had not yet logged in to the virtual office. Thus, employees must log in to the virtual office and disclose their own status to see other members' statuses. This restriction enables balancing the viewing and being viewed information in accordance with Requirement 3. We provide no means to identify workers who have not yet logged in using the awareness-sharing mode.

To ensure that workers' concentration remains uninterrupted (Requirement 4) with excessive visual stimulation, we avoid the use of animations and set the update interval to one minute.

To facilitate conversation among team members and satisfy Requirement 5, we implemented a function to import and display unread messages from an existing chat system (we used Slack in the present study). The chat system is activated by clicking either of the left two buttons at the bottom of the window.

The commute button at the bottom-right corner of the window allows the user to log in to the virtual office, i.e., the button opens the virtual office window.

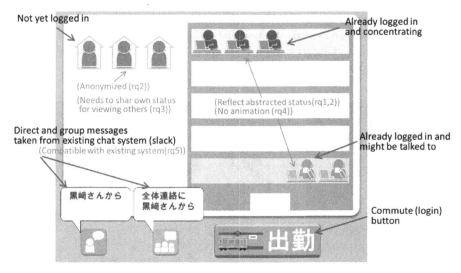

Fig. 4. Displayed window in awareness-sharing mode. (Color figure online)

4 Virtual Office Subsystem

4.1 Requirements for Virtual Office Subsystem

Generally, user interfaces should aim to be simple and intuitive. Furthermore, it is desirable for operations to start or end conversations to mimic occasional conversation in a physical office setting. Although awareness regarding colleagues' working statuses is indispensable for facilitating occasional conversation, we must address privacy concerns, especially among workers who are not currently engaged in conversation.

In addition, even after logging in to the virtual office, workers may desire to concentrate on their own task. For such occasions, the virtual office subsystem must avoid unnecessarily distracting the workers' concentration. From a practical perspective, lower PC performance requirements are desirable.

The following requirements are summarized:

rq6. Intuitive starting/ending of conversations
rq7. Awareness of members' interruptibility
rq8. Privacy protection when not in conversation
rq9. No unnecessary disruptions of workers' concentration
rq10. Lower performance requirements for PC

4.2 Implementation of Virtual Office Subsystem

To reduce the performance requirements (Requirement 10), we adopted a 2D virtual office design, as shown in Fig. 5. Upon logging into the virtual office, workers are displayed as CG avatars when not in conversation mode, thereby alleviating privacy concerns (Requirement 8).

Information regarding other workers' estimated interruptibilities are provided as 4-h transition graphs, displayed on the assigned desks for each worker (Requirement 7). Animations such as walking are minimized to avoid unnecessary disruptions of workers' concentration (Requirement 9).

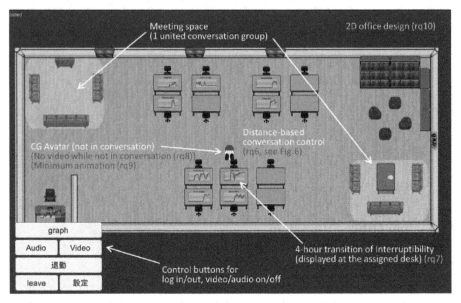

Fig. 5. Displayed window in virtual office mode.

To realize intuitive conversation control, we enables distance-based conversation control (Requirement 6). Although several systems control the sound level proportional to the distance between users, we prioritized ease of hearing and adopted on/off control based on distance.

The detailed algorithm is illustrated in Fig. 6(a). When two users are within threshold distance, a conversation group is automatically formed. Likewise, if two conversation groups are sufficiently close, they are merged in the same manner as our previous system [18]. When a conversation group is formed, video communication is automatically turned on, and the conversation group is displayed as a translucent white circle as shown in Fig. 6(b). Any users outside the conversation group can view the group formation as translucent circles but cannot access the video or audio communication.

The memory usage and network traffic are 170 MB/0.1 Mbps when not in conversation, and 240 MB/2.4 Mbps when in conversation. CPU usage is less than 18% when in conversation on a 5-year old notebook PC with i5-7200U CPU.

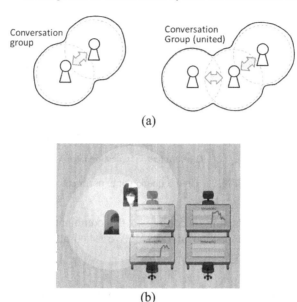

Fig. 6. (a) Algorithm of distance-based conversation control. (b) Example image of conversation group displayed for users in conversation.

5 Preliminary Assessment

5.1 Experiment

We conducted a 30-min preliminary assessment on the impression of remote users using our early-stage prototype. A total of six university and graduate school students belonging to our laboratory, who have known each other for more than five months, took part in the experiment from their homes.

Participants were separated into three teams. Each team was requested to perform one of the three activity sequences shown in Fig. 7, and subsequently evaluate their impressions of the awareness-sharing and virtual office modes.

As shown in Fig. 7, members of Team A were first requested to turn on their PC, so that the awareness-sharing subsystem automatically allowed them to observe other members of their team as gray avatars. Likewise, they could observe Team C members as red or green avatars through the awareness-sharing window. After 10 min of evaluation and questionnaire, they were requested to log in to the virtual office subsystem by clicking the "commute" button. Then, the virtual office windows were opened, allowing them to observe and communicate with other members of their team through avatars. While in this virtual office mode, the awareness-sharing window stayed displayed, allowing Team A members to observe Team B members as gray avatars.

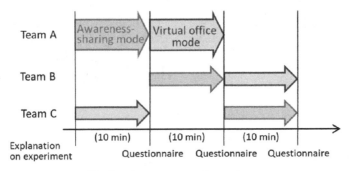

Fig. 7. Time sequence of experiment.

The observable information, according to the combination of own and viewed-member's statuses, is summarized in Table 1. We asked all participants to score the impressions for each of the four cases.

Table 1. Observable information according to own and viewed-member's status.

Members status Own status	Turned PC on (Awareness-sharing mode)	Logged in to virtual office (Virtual office mode)
Turned PC on (Awareness-sharing mode)	Gray avatar at home in awareness-sharing window (reflects turn-on of PC)	Red or green avatar at office in awareness-sharing window (reflects interruptibility)
Logged in to virtual office (Virtual office mode)	No avatar in virtual office (Gray avatar at home in awareness-sharing window)	Avatar in virtual office (can talk to)

Participants subjectively evaluated the following items on a five-point scale:

1. Presence of other members
2. Sense of activity about other members
3. Easiness communicating with other members
4. Sense of togetherness
5. Reluctance against being viewed

Questions 1 and 2 were asked to assess the expected direct effect of the awareness of other members' statuses, whereas Questions 3 and 4 were asked to assess the corresponding indirect effect. Question 5 was asked to assess the negative effect induced by personal information disclosure.

5.2 Results and Discussion

Because the answered scores were widely distributed among the participants for some questions, Fig. 8 shows the raw distributions of the answers. The four bars in each subfigure represent the respective distributions of the four cases listed in Table 1.

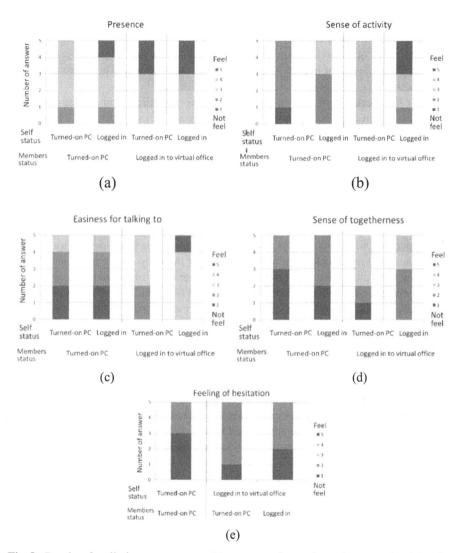

Fig. 8. Results of preliminary assessment; (a) presence of coworkers, (b) sense of activity about coworkers, (c) easiness of talking to coworkers, (d) sense of togetherness, and (e) reluctance against being viewed.

The leftmost bar in Fig. 8(a) suggests that the use of simple gray avatars reflecting the power-on status of colleagues induces moderate presence. The second bar from the left indicates similar results, as the viewable information is the same. On the other hand, the two rightmost bars suggest that the use of avatars to portray interruptibility provides more presence for team members.

As seen in the two leftmost bars of Fig. 8(b), the sense of activity is very weak for avatars not reflecting the remote users' statuses. The second-right bar implies that the interruptibility information provides some sense of activity. However, the strongest sense of activity was perceived by observing avatars move around the virtual office in response to work operations, as indicated by the rightmost bar. Overall, Fig. 8(a) and (b) confirm that the use of avatars to reflect worker status provides presence and some sense of activity.

For the indirect effect of awareness, i.e., ease of communication and sense of togetherness, avatars merely reflecting power-on status were ineffective, as indicated by the two leftmost bars in Fig. 8(c) and (d). Avatars reflecting interruptibility produced somewhat better results as shown by the second-right bars. Avatars in virtual office again scored best; however, the distribution of scores suggests that just seeing avatars does not create a strong sense of belongingness for all individuals.

Figure 8(e) demonstrates that most participants did not claim strong reluctance against being viewed. It appears that an adequate level of abstraction for viewed information contributed to relieving privacy concerns.

As expected, our results suggest that awareness of working status provides a sense of presence and activity among team members without inducing strong reluctance. However, we must be aware that the number of participants was small, and the participants were already in a good relationship. Different types of teams, including those defined by hierarchical relationships or under higher stress, may produce different results. The short duration of the experiment is also a limitation of this study.

6   Conclusion

To address communication deficiencies in the remote working environment, we developed a prototype virtual office system integrated with an awareness-sharing subsystem. Results of a preliminary assessment suggest that the sharing of awareness contributes to presence and a sense of activity among team members with minimum reluctance for personal status disclosure.

To further investigate the effects on conversation facilitation and sense of togetherness, a longer-term assessment with various types of teams is required.

Acknowledgments. This work was partly supported by funds from the Japan Society for the Promotion of Science (KAKENHI).

References

1. Andrade, C., Lousã, E.P.: Telework and work-family conflict during COVID-19 lockdown in Portugal: the influence of job-related factors. Administ. Sci. **11**(3), 103 (2021)
2. Weinert, C., Maier, C., Laumer, S.: Why Are Teleworkers Stressed? An Empirical Analysis of the Causes of Telework-Enabled Stress. Wirtschaftsinformatik Proceedings, vol. 94 (2015)
3. Yang, L., et al.: The effects of remote work on collaboration among information workers. Nat. Hum. Behav. **6**, 43–54 (2022)
4. Mann, S., Holdsworth, L.: The psychological impact of teleworking: stress, emotions and health. N. Technol. Work. Employ. **18**(3), 196–211 (2003)

5. Boell, S.K., Campbell, J., Dubravka, C.K., Cheng, J.E.: Advantages, challenges and contradictions of the transformative nature of telework: a review of the literature. In: Proceedings of the Nineteenth Americas Conference on Information Systems (2013)
6. Sohlenkamp, M., Chwelos, G.: Integrating communication, cooperation, and awareness: the DIVA virtual office environment. In: Proceedings of the 1994 ACM Conference on Computer Supported Cooperative Work, pp. 331–343 (1994)
7. Honda, S., Tomioka, H., Kimura, T., Oosawa, T., Okada, K.I., Matsushita, Y.: A company-office system "Valentine" providing informal communication and personal space based on 3D virtual space and avatars. Inf. Softw. Technol. **41**(6), 383–397 (1999)
8. Gather. https://www.gather.town/. Accessed 24 Dec 2022
9. My Digital Office. https://www.mydigitaloffice.io/. Accessed 24 Dec 2022
10. oVice, https://ovice.in/ja/, last accessed 2022/12/24
11. FAMoffice. https://www.famoffice.jp. Accessed 24 Dec 2022
12. Isaacs, E., Walendowski, A., Ranganthan, D.: Hubbub: a sound-enhanced mobile instant messenger that supports awareness and opportunistic interactions. In: Proceedings of the SIGCHI Conference on Human Factors in Computing Systems, pp. 179–186 (2002)
13. Lim, B.Y., Brdiczka, O., Bellotti, V.: Show me a good time: using content to provide activity awareness to collaborators with activity spotter. In: Proceedings of the 16th ACM International Conference on Supporting Group Work, pp. 263–272 (2010)
14. Fogarty, J., Lai, J., Christensen, J.: Presence versus availability: the design and evaluation of a context-aware communication client. Int. J. Hum. Comput. Stud. **61**(3), 299–317 (2004)
15. Hincapie´-Ramos, J.D., Voida, S., Mark, G.: A design space analysis of availability-sharing systems. In: Proceedings of the 24th Annual ACM Symposium on User Interface Software and Technology, pp. 85–96 (2011)
16. Tanaka, T., Abe, R., Aoki, K., Fujita, K.: Interruptibility estimation based on head motion and PC operation. Int. J. Hum. Comput. Interact. **31**(3), 167–179 (2015)
17. Takashima, K., Yokoyama, H., Fujita, K.: Analysis of observation behavior of shared interruptibility information among distributed offices: case study in a university laboratory. IEICE Trans. Inform. Syst. **E102-D**(9), 1808–1818 (2019)
18. Miyajima, T., Shimoji, T., Fujita, K.: Shared virtual space communication system with pseudo awareness of presence and gaze. Trans. Virtual Real. Soc. Japan **10**(1), 71–80 (2005)

The Influence of Interaction Channel and Difficulty Level of In-Vehicle Information System on Driver's Reading Behavior in Fully Autonomous Vehicle

Tianyi Ma⬤ and Bin Jiang[✉]

Nanjing University of Science and Technology, Nanjing 210094, China
binjiang@njust.edu.cn

Abstract. The autonomous vehicle is developing from a simple means of transportation to an intelligent terminal, and will become the third living space in the future. Previous research on the design of in-vehicle information system mostly focused on non-fully autonomous vehicle. In our research, we focused on the design of in-vehicle information system of fully autonomous vehicle, providing a theoretical reference for the design of the interior space based on driver's reading behavior. The experiment used a mixed design of 2 (interaction channels) × 3 (difficulty levels) to explore the influence of the interaction channel and difficulty level of in-vehicle information system on driver's reading behavior, which took reading accuracy and reading speed as dependent variables to reflect reading performance. The results showed that (1) In terms of interaction channel, auditory manipulation was superior to visual manipulation when the in-vehicle information system was low in difficulty. When in high difficulty, the interaction channel of in-vehicle information system had no significant impact on reading performance. (2) In the aspect of difficulty level, in the design of visual information system, the reading speed of different difficulty levels was significantly different, and the visual information with moderate complexity produced the fastest reading speed. In the design of auditory information system, the reading performance of different difficulties was similar. These results may provide a theoretical basis for the design of in-vehicle information system in fully autonomous vehicle, and improve the acceptance of autonomous vehicle by general population.

Keywords: Fully autonomous vehicle · Reading behavior · In-vehicle information system · Distraction

1 Introduction

The benefits of autonomous vehicle are obvious. It can expand the opportunities for the elderly drivers, the disabled and other socially vulnerable groups to participate in society [1, 2]. At the same time, they can also improve traffic efficiency, reduce emissions, and thus reduce social costs [3]. According to SAE J3016 [4] updated by SAE international in 2021, autonomous driving is divided into six levels, including Level 0 (No Driving

Automation), Level 1 (Driver Assistance), Level 2 (Partial Driving Automation), Level 3 (Conditional Driving Automation), Level 4 (High Driving Automation), and Level 5 (Full Driving Automation).

As we all know, when the driver needs to control the vehicle (L0-L4), the primary task of the driver is to control the vehicle and pay attention to potential road hazards, and the secondary task is to distract the driver from performing in-vehicle secondary tasks [5]. Demands associated with performing in-vehicle secondary tasks, such as manipulating in-vehicle systems while driving, are known to increase workload and cause driver distraction [6], which will lead to a decline in driving performance [7, 8]. However, in Level 5, the autonomous driving function does not require driver to take over the vehicle, and the role of drivers turns into passengers [4].

In September 2022, Roland Berger proposed that with the rapid development of autonomous driving and Internet of Vehicles, autonomous vehicle is changing from a means of transportation to an intelligent terminal, and may become the third living space outside home and office. Bastian Pflying's research [9] also confirmed this change. It mentioned that the driver in a highly or fully autonomous vehicle could be more like a passenger, and highlighted autonomous vehicle as a place of productivity and play.

More and more research aimed to study in-vehicle secondary tasks such as in-vehicle information system [5, 10]. However, most of these studies focused on the situation where drivers still need to drive the car, rather than on the fully autonomous vehicle. It is believed that similar research on fully autonomous vehicle is also extremely urgent, especially at the moment when it is about to be realized [11]. By analogy with the scenario where drivers still need to control the vehicle, we proposed the following three questions.

Q1. In fully autonomous vehicle, how should in-vehicle information system be designed when autonomous vehicle becomes a leisure or productivity space?

Q2. In fully autonomous vehicle, what is the difference between the impact of auditory and visual information on driver's reading behavior?

Q3. In fully autonomous vehicle, how does the difficulty level of information affect driver's reading behavior?

Therefore, the purpose of this study was to explore the impact of the design of auditory and visual in-vehicle information systems on driver's behavior in fully autonomous vehicle. We chose the common behavior "reading" in fully autonomous vehicle as the primary task, and auditory and visual manipulation as the secondary task. We compared reading performance of drivers under different information interaction channels and difficulty levels in order to explore the impact of interaction channels and difficulty levels of in-vehicle information system on driver's reading behavior.

The organization of this study is as follows: Sect. 2 provides literature review, and Sect. 3 introduces our research methods. We explain the data analysis and results in Sect. 4, and discuss the results, limitation, and future work in Sect. 5. We then continue with the conclusions in Sect. 6.

2   Related Research

2.1   In-Vehicle Information System

In-vehicle information system is an information system that conveys the intention and action of vehicle to users and allows machines to interact with users [12]. The design of in-vehicle information system aims to provide the information required by users and improve reliability, acceptability and safety of human machine interaction [13]. However, interaction with in-vehicle information system requires cognitive resources. Regardless of the intention of the system, it will disperse the primary tasks [14, 15]. For example, the use of in-vehicle information system such as navigation and radio can become additional interference sources while driving [16, 17]. All types of in-vehicle information, whether based on hearing, vision or tactile sensing, put forward cognitive demands for users [18].

2.2   Driving Tasks in Fully Autonomous Vehicle

As mentioned in Bubb's research [19], traditional driving tasks can be divided into primary, secondary and tertiary driving tasks. Among them, the primary task covers all tasks directly related to actual driving, that is, longitudinal and lateral control of the car. Secondary task refers to activities that depend on and support primary task. However, the third level driving tasks are not directly related to actual driving. These tasks usually refer to people's entertainment, office and other activities in autonomous vehicle. In a fully autonomous vehicle that can handle all road and environmental conditions, the traditional primary and secondary tasks do not need to be implemented. On the contrary, drivers can devote their attention and time to what we currently call tertiary driving tasks, making them become the major task [9].

In order to avoid calling the same activity (such as turning on the air conditioner) the tertiary tasks during manual driving and "the primary tasks" during fully autonomous driving at the same time, we only studied tasks in fully autonomous vehicle in this study. Therefore, we used "the major task" to describe reading behavior of this study.

2.3   In-Vehicle Information System Design of Auditory and Visual Channels

In the design of in-vehicle information system, auditory information is divided into tone information and speech information. Tone signal transmits information to drivers through special sound while speech information uses language containing content to convey information. During manual driving, auditory information cannot occupy driver's visual resources, so it has greater advantages in information design. However, auditory information also has disadvantages, such as speech information is easily obscured by noise and other messages, and tone information is easily covered by other similar sounds.

With the development of new approaches to interaction, the visual information in the vehicle human-computer interaction interface includes the natural display of the road conditions ahead, the integrated display of mobile devices and vehicles, the auxiliary driving display near the steering wheel, and so on. Due to the large amount of visual information content and the large change of information display position, drivers are more likely to leave the primary visual attention lobe (PVAL).

2.4   Research on Reading Behavior in Fully Autonomous Vehicle

Under the new identity, human behavior has changed greatly. M. Kyriakidis [20] carried out a study on autonomous driving, and the results showed that the number of people who took rest, sleep, reading and other activities increased significantly when driving in a fully autonomous vehicle. In addition, the research of Bastian Pflying [20] investigated the frequency of various activities performed by people as passengers in the car. Among them, reading behavior ranked sixth in all activities, which was a high frequency activity.

Mustafa Yildiz and Ezgi Çetinkaya [21] mentioned that attention significantly affects reading speed and word recognition respectively. Therefore, in our research, we use reading speed and reading accuracy (that is, word recognition in the above research) as indicators to measure reading behavior.

3   Method

3.1   Participants

There were 27 participants in total, of which 1/3 were male (N = 9) and 2/3 were female (N = 18). The inclusion criteria for the selection of participants were to having normal naked or corrected vision and no hearing impairment; willing to drive fully autonomous vehicle. Participants were students aged 18–22, with an average age of 19.9 years (SD = 0.81). Before the experiment, participants needed to understand the whole experiment process, and then signed a written informed consent form.

3.2   Apparatus and Stimulus

The research team conducted the experiment in a quiet indoor environment. Participants were required to be clear about the requirements and the procedures, especially well-trained to perform tasks.

The study used online video. The video simulated the normal driving scene of fully autonomous vehicle, including the lateral control and longitudinal control of the vehicle, and the vehicle obeys the traffic rules.

The HP computer played the video simulating the fully autonomous driving environment. The video was displayed on the screen in front of participants. The size of the screen is 15.6 inches, and the display ratio is 16:9. The iPad (10.5 inches) is used to simulate the visual information interface of the operating system in the autonomous vehicle. It was placed on the left side of the participants. Participants needed to click on the iPad to complete the visual task. The core task of the participants was to read a Chinese novel on a mobile phone (iPhone XR, full screen, 6.1 inches) and simulated the reading behavior of the driver in a fully autonomous vehicle. The other computer was placed in the oblique front of the participant, and the experimenter controlled and played the preset auditory sound to simulate the design of the auditory in-vehicle information system.

3.3 Experimental Design

The research adopts 2 (information interaction channels) × 3 (task difficulties) mixed design. Two types of information interaction channels included auditory tasks and visual tasks. Difficulty level included Level 1 to Level 3. Among them, auditory tasks increased difficulty by increasing the number of target sounds that participants need to distinguish while visual tasks increased difficulty by increasing the number of circles that participants need to click. Interaction channel and task difficulty are independent variables, while reading accuracy and reading speed are dependent variables.

Auditory Tasks. The auditory task is based on the "sound counting" method [22] of the HASTE project, which provides a method to increase the cognitive workload of passengers only from the perspective of hearing, without increasing the visual demand. When the driver was reading the text, the experimenter played a prepared audio of the auditory experimental materials. The audio in the auditory task is fabricated by using ADOBE AUDITION.

Fig. 1. Interface of auditory materials made by Adobe Audition.

The three tracks are audio of three difficulty levels (see Fig. 1). Each level of audio was composed of 15 sound clips, which were divided into target sound and non-target sound, including three target sounds and one non target sound. All target and non-target sounds were the basic scale steps in Natural Major. The sound clip in each audio lasted about 320 ms, with two seconds between each sound clip.

Visual Task. For the visual tasks, a group of images made of circles were displayed on the iPad on the right side of the user, in which one (or more) circles were obviously larger than the others. In the same difficulty level, participants needed to click the big circle on the screen in turn, and the big circle in the point became gray. The "next" button would turn orange only after all the big circles in the interface were clicked. Then the driver clicked the "NEXT" button to jump to the next image at the same level. The response time of each image was as long as 10 s, which meant that even if the passenger did not accurately identify all the big circles within 10 s, the soft-ware would autonomously turn to the next image to prevent the participant from paying too much attention to clicking on the screen and looking for the big circles in the image. The interface in the visual manipulation task was made by Material Design Lite.

Difficulty Level. Auditory task and visual task were composed of three difficulty levels to generate different levels of workload. The auditory task increased the difficulty level by increasing the number of target sounds. Audio in level 1 included non-target sound and one target sound; audio in level 2 included non-target sound and two different target sounds; audio in level 3 included non-target sound and 3 different target sounds. Like auditory tasks, visual tasks also had three difficulty levels. In Level1, only one target circle needed to be pointed out in each image. At Level 2, there were two target circles; Level 3, three target circles (see Fig. 2).

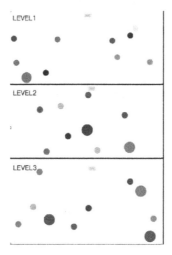

Fig. 2. Visual manipulation interface of three task difficulty levels.

Reading Materials. The reading content was selected from Chinese classic novels, and there were no rare Chinese words. Participants were able to read without barriers. In the experiment with the same interaction channel and task difficulty, all the participants had the same reading materials.

3.4 Experimental Process

At the beginning of the experiment, participants imagined reading a Chinese novel in a fully autonomous vehicle, and the computer in front of them started playing a video of an autonomous driving simulation. At the same time, participants began to read the Chinese novel on their mobile phone and read it out quietly (no loud reading is required). After about a minute, the experimenter played audio from Level 1 auditory task and recorded the starting and ending corresponding time points. After the auditory information was sent out, participants needed to count the number of times the target sound appeared while continuing to read. When the reading material was completely read, the participants informed the experimenter how many times they heard the target sound. Level 1 auditory task was completed. The experimenter replaced the participants' reading materials and increased the difficulty level, then repeated the experiment to complete the auditory tasks at Level 2 and Level 3. In experiments using multiple target sounds, such as Levels 2 and 3, participants were asked to calculate the number of each target sound separately.

When three difficulty levels of the auditory tasks were completed, participants performed the visual task. In visual tasks, participants also needed to imagine reading a Chinese novel in a fully autonomous vehicle. After a minute of reading the novel, participants began to click on the circles in iPad to simulate the click screen operation of the in-vehicle information system. The experimenter recorded the starting and ending corresponding time points of the visual manipulation. After the Level 1 visual task was completed, the experimenter increased difficulty level, and then proceeded with Level 2 visual task and Level 3 visual task in turn. The whole experiment repeated three difficulty levels on two interaction channels. When all three difficulty levels of auditory manipulation and three difficulty levels of visual manipulation were completed, participants were interviewed briefly at the end of the experiment.

During the experiment, if other factors interfered with the experiment and caused participants to regain their attention, the ongoing task would be cancelled and restarted. Each participant's experiment lasted about 10–15 min. The experimenter recorded the whole process and marked the corresponding time points for subsequent data analysis.

3.5 Data Collection

Each participant had 6 recordings because of the mixed design of three difficulty levels and two interaction channels. The experiment collected 162 recordings from 27 participants.

The experimenter replayed the part of the recording of the participants' simultaneous reading and manipulation tasks several times according to the starting and ending corresponding time points recorded in the experiment. Then the experimenter counted the total number of words read, the correct number of words read, and the reading time of the participants in such recording. Among them, the total number of words read referred to the number of words read by participants during the manipulation tasks; The correct number of words read referred to the number of completely correct read words except for the number of words that participants read incorrectly, repeat and skip; Reading time referred to the length of time for participants to simultaneously read and manipulate tasks, in seconds.

All experimental data were recorded in Microsoft Excel, and the reading speed and reading accuracy under the interaction of three difficulty levels and two interaction channels were calculated respectively. Among them, reading speed was calculated by the ratio of the total number of words read to reading time; reading accuracy was calculated by the ratio of the correct number of words read to the total number of words read during the manipulation tasks.

3.6 Data Analysis

All data analysis and data validation were analyzed by SPSS. After calculating reading accuracy and reading speed, the experimenter conducted a Normality Test on them. Because reading accuracy data was abnormal distribution, the research on reading accuracy data adopted non-parametric test. Among them, Mann-Whitney U Test was used to explore the impact of auditory and visual interaction channels on reading accuracy, and Kruskal-Wallis H Test was used to explore reading accuracy at different difficulty levels. According to Normality Test, the reading speed data obtained from all experiments were normal distribution. Therefore, Independent Sample t-test was used to explore the impact of auditory and visual interaction channels on reading speed and one-way ANOVA was used to compare the effects of different difficulty levels on reading speed.

4 Results

4.1 Impact on Reading Accuracy

From the results of Mann-Whitney U Test in Table 1, it could be seen that there was a significant difference between the reading accuracy of drivers in visual manipulation and that in auditory manipulation at level 1, $Z = -2.102$, $p = 0.036$. There was no significant difference between the other two grades.

Table 1. Non-parametric test of the effect of visual and auditory manipulation on reading accuracy.

Difficulty	U	W	Z	Sig
Level 1	243.000	621.000	−2.102	0.036*
Level 2	256.500	634.500	−1.869	0.062
Level 3	265.000	643.000	−1.722	0.085

Note: Grouping variables: 1 = visual, 2 = auditory, * $p < 0.05$

The study used the Kruskal-Wallis H Test to analyze the reading accuracy of different difficulty levels. The results showed that there was no significant difference ($p = 0.722$) in the reading accuracy of auditory manipulation with different difficulty levels. There was no significant difference in the reading accuracy of visual manipulation with different difficulty levels, $p = 0.658$.

When the driver performed visual manipulation tasks, the reading accuracy decreased with the increase of difficulty level (see Fig. 3). The reading accuracy rate of level 1 visual manipulation ($M = 0.921$, $SD = 0.084$) was significantly higher than that of level 2 visual manipulation ($M = 0.893$, $SD = 0.141$) and level 3 visual manipulation ($M = 0.890$, $SD = 0.111$), and the mean difference between level 2 and level 3 visual manipulation tasks was small. The reading accuracy rate of auditory manipulation task increased first and then decreased with the increase of difficulty level. Among them, the reading accuracy rate of level 2 ($M = 0.942$, $SD = 0.069$) was significantly higher than that of level 3 ($M = 0.928$, $SD = 0.085$), while the difference between the reading accuracy rate of level 1($M = 0.941$, $SD = 0.094$) was small.

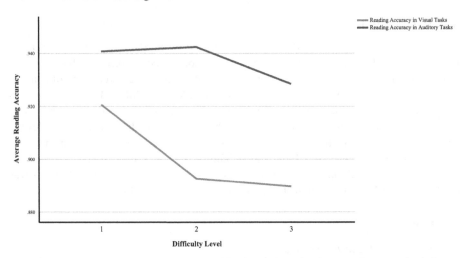

Fig. 3. Changes of reading accuracy with difficulty during visual and auditory manipulation.

4.2 Impact on Reading Speed

It could be seen from the Levene test results that the reading speed data under the three difficulty levels L1 (F = 0.288, p = 0.594), L2 (F = 0.001, p = 0.922), and L3 (F = 2.581, p = 0.114) all met the square difference homogeneity.

From the independent sample t-test results in Table 2, it could be seen that there was a significant difference between the driver's reading speed during visual manipulation and that during auditory manipulation at level 1, and the reading speed during auditory manipulation (M = 3.871, SD = 0.824) was significantly higher than that during visual manipulation (M = 3.103, SD = 0.781), t (52) = −3.516, p < 0.05, d = −0.957. There was no significant difference between the driver's reading speed during visual manipulation and that during auditory manipulation at level 1, t (52) = 0.252, p = 0.802, d = 0.069. Similarly, there was no significant difference at level 3, t (52) = 0.170, p = 0.866, d = 0.046.

Table 2. Independent t-test of auditory and visual manipulation on reading speed.

Difficulty	Auditory task	Visual task	t	df	Sig
Level 1	M = 3.871, SD = 0.824	M = 3.103, SD = 0.781	−3.516	52	0.001*
Level 2	M = 3.653, SD = 0.778	M = 3.707, SD = 0.795	0.252	52	0.802
Level 3	M = 3.415, SD = 0.886	M = 3.452, SD = 0.683	0.170	52	0.866

Note: * p < 0.05

As shown in Table 3, the study used ANOVA to conduct statistical analysis on reading speed of different difficulty levels. The results showed that in the design of auditory information system, there was no significant difference in reading speed under different difficulty levels, F (2) = 2.032, p = 0.138, η2 = 0.050. In the design of visual information system, there are significant differences among different difficulty levels, F (2) = 4.361, p = 0.016, η2 = 0.101. Multiple comparisons showed that the driver's reading speed (M = 3.707, SD = 0.795) during visual manipulation at L2 level was much higher than that at L1 level (M = 3.103, SD = 3.103), and the difference between them was significant (p = 0.004). There was no significant difference between the other groups.

Table 3. Single factor ANOVA of reading speed at different difficulty levels.

Interaction channel	Difficulty level (mean ± standard deviation)			F	P
	Level 1	Level 2	Level 3		
Visual	3.103 ± 0.781	3.707 ± 0.795	3.452 ± 0.683	4.361	0.016[*]
Auditory	3.871 ± 0.824	3.653 ± 0.778	3.415 ± 0.886	2.032	0.138

Note: [*] $p < 0.05$

It could be observed that when the driver performed visual manipulation tasks, the reading speed increased first and then decreased with the increase of difficulty level (see Fig. 4). The reading speed of auditory task decreased linearly with the increase of difficulty level. The results showed that auditory manipulation was significantly superior to visual manipulation in simple manipulation tasks. When the operation steps were difficult, the gap between the two was small.

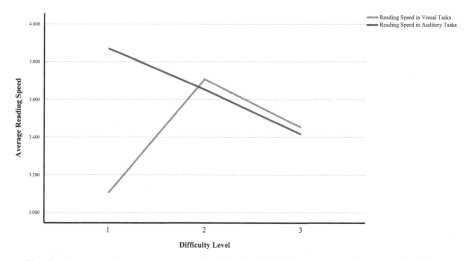

Fig. 4. Changes of reading speed with difficulty during visual and auditory manipulation.

5 Discussion

5.1 Interaction Channel

According to the experimental results, at level 1, compared with visual manipulation, auditory manipulation led to higher reading accuracy and reading speed, thus leading to higher reading performance and the difference was significant. At the same difficulty level, the reading accuracy of auditory manipulation system was higher than that of visual manipulation system. One possible reason is that the visual interface is an important part of the design of in-vehicle information system, and its layout, text and graphics determine the efficiency of users' operation of related functions [23]. As reading is a vision intensive task, according to the Multiple Resource Theory [24], the visual resources required for in vehicle reading behavior overlap with the resources of the in-vehicle control system. In contrast, the in-vehicle information system of the auditory channel still allows the driver to maintain the visual orientation of the reading behavior, and makes the reading performance less affected.

At level 2 and level 3 difficulty levels, there was no significant difference between visual and auditory manipulation on reading accuracy and reading speed. This means that in a fully autonomous vehicle, when the design of the in-vehicle information system is more complex, the selection of interaction channels has little impact on the driver's reading performance. One possible reason is that when there is a serious conflict between the reading behavior and the more complex operation behavior in the car, effective reading will be seriously affected whether it is auditory information or visual information.

Therefore, in the design of the in-vehicle information system of the fully autonomous vehicle, the designer should select the information system design of the auditory channel for the working scenario where the driver reviews the contract and proofreads the manuscript in the vehicle and pays attention to the accuracy of reading. And when the design and operation of in-vehicle information system is relatively simple, the auditory channel should also be given priority to ensure reading performance.

5.2 Difficulty Level

In the design of visual information system, there were significant differences in reading speed under different difficulty levels, and the reading speed reached the peak at level 2. This means that in the design of the information system of fully autonomous vehicle, the design of the visual interface does not fully follow the "less is more", one of the interface evaluation methods proposed by Nielsen [25]. The results showed that too simplified graphics may also lead to lower reading speed, while too complex visual information may also have a negative impact on reading speed. This may be due to reducing the driver's attention to the surrounding environment, which makes the driver lose the ability to focus on key information [26]. The difficulty level of visual manipulation had no significant impact on reading accuracy, but there was a trend that the higher the difficulty, the lower the reading accuracy. This trend needs further research to describe.

In the design of auditory information system, the reading performance under different difficulty levels had similar levels. One possible reason is that the driver was trained in target sound before the experiment, which greatly enhanced the driver's discrimination of auditory information.

5.3 Limitations and Future Work

This study also has some limitations, which can be solved in future research. First of all, this study only took reading behavior in fully autonomous driving as an example to conduct research. In the future, we can further explore the behavior of other users in the car, and broaden the possibility of the future car as the third space. Second, the participants of this experiment were only young people aged 18–22, so different groups can be recruited for in-depth research in the future. Third, the visual and auditory information provided in the experiment was completely accurate, but the real autonomous vehicle may make some errors due to the influence of sensors and complex driving environment. Future research can consider the information reliability factor and measure the driver's trust in it. Fourth, this study only studied the impact of auditory and visual information design on reading behavior. In the future, specific information parameters can be studied to find the auditory and visual information parameters that can bring the best user experience to drivers.

6 Conclusion

Taking the common reading behavior in fully autonomous vehicle as an example, this study compared the effects of auditory and visual information system design on reading behavior in fully autonomous vehicle. The results show that: (1) In terms of interaction channel, auditory manipulation was superior to visual manipulation when the difficulty level of vehicle information system was low. When the difficulty was high, the interaction channel of vehicle information system had no significant impact on reading performance. (2) In terms of difficulty level, in the design of visual information system, the reading speed of different difficulty levels was significantly different, and the visual information with medium complexity could lead to the best reading speed. In the design of auditory information system, the reading performance of different difficulties was similar.

These research results guide significance for the design of in-vehicle information system in fully autonomous vehicle. The research results will provide a theoretical basis for the design of cars as the third living space outside the family and office, and improve the acceptance of autonomous vehicle by the general population.

References

1. Sparrow, R., Howard, M.: When human beings are like drunk robots: driverless vehicles, ethics, and the future of transport. Transp. Res. Part C **80**, 206–215 (2017)
2. Meyer, J., Becker, H., Bsch, P.M., Axhausen, K.W.: Autonomous vehicles: the next jump in accessibilities. Res. Transp. Econ. **62**, 80–91 (2017)
3. Anderson, J.M., Kalra, N., Stanley, K.D., Sorensen, P., Samaras, C., Oluwatola, O.A.: Autonomous Vehicle Technology: A Guide for Policymakers. RAND Corporation, Santa Monica, CA (2014)
4. SAE International: Taxonomy and Definitions for Terms Related to Driving Automation Systems for On-Road Motor Vehicles, Report SAE J3016 (2021)
5. Ma, Y., Hu, B., Chan, C.-Y., Qi, S., Fan, L.: Distractions intervention strategies for in-vehicle secondary tasks: an on-road test assessment of driving task demand based on real-time traffic environment. Transport. Res. Part D Transp. Environ. **63**, 747–754 (2018)

6. Birrell, S.A., Young, M.S.: The impact of smart driving aids on driving performance and driver distraction. Transp. Res. Part F vol. **14**(6), 484–493 (2011)
7. Engström, J., Johansson, E., Östlund, J.: Effects of visual and cognitive load in real and simulated motorway driving. Transport. Res. F: Traffic Psychol. Behav. **8**(2), 97–120 (2005)
8. Tornros, J.E.B., Bolling, A.K.: Mobile phone use - effects of handheld and handsfree phones on driving performance. Accid. Anal. Prev. **37**(5), 902–909 (2005)
9. Pfleging, B., Rang, M., Broy, N.: Investigating user needs for non-driving-related activities during automated driving. In: Proceedings of the 15th International Conference on Mobile and Ubiquitous Multimedia, pp. 91–99. Association for Computing Machinery, New York, USA (2016)
10. Yang, Y., Reimer, B., Mehler, B., Wong, A., McDonald, M.: Exploring differences in the impact of auditory and visual demands on driver behavior. In: Proceedings of the 4th International Conference on Automotive User Interfaces and Interactive Vehicular Applications (AutomotiveUI 2012), pp. 173–177. Association for Computing Machinery, New York, USA (2012)
11. Zhao, X., Yang, J., Tan, H.: The effects of subjective knowledge on the acceptance of fully autonomous vehicles depend on individual levels of trust. In: Rau, P.L.P. (eds.) Cross-Cultural Design. Product and Service Design, Mobility and Automotive Design, Cities, Urban Areas, and Intelligent Environments Design. HCII 2022. LNCS, vol. 13314, pp. 297–308. Springer, Cham (2022). https://doi.org/10.1007/978-3-031-06053-3_21
12. Harvey, C., Stanton, N.A., Pickering, C.A., McDonald, M., Zheng, P.: In-vehicle information systems to meet the needs of drivers. Int. J. Hum. -Comput. Interact. **27**, 505–522 (2011)
13. Kim, M., Heo, J., Lee, J.: In-vehicle information design to enhance the experience of passengers in autonomous public buses. In: Krömker, H. (ed.) HCII 2021. LNCS, vol. 12791, pp. 408–424. Springer, Cham (2021). https://doi.org/10.1007/978-3-030-78358-7_28
14. Hanowski, R.J., Dingus, T.A., Gallagher, J.P., Kieliszewski, C.A., Neale, V.L.: Driver response to in-vehicle warnings. Transport. Hum. Fact. **1**(1), 91–106 (1999)
15. Lee, J.D., et al.: Display alternatives for in-vehicle warning and sign information: message style, location, and modality. Transport. Hum. Fact. **1**, 347–375 (1999)
16. Lee, J.D., Caven, B., Haake, S., Brown, T.L.: Speech-based interaction with in-vehicle computers: the effect of speech-based e-mail on drivers' attention to the roadway. Hum. Fact. **43**(4), 631–640 (2001)
17. Metz, B., Landau, A., Just, M.: Frequency of secondary tasks in driving - results from naturalistic driving data. Saf. Sci. **68**, 195–203 (2014)
18. Jonsson, I.-M., Chen, F.: In-vehicle information system used in complex and low traffic situations: impact on driving performance and attitude. In: Stephanidis, C. (ed.) UAHCI 2007. LNCS, vol. 4555, pp. 421–430. Springer, Heidelberg (2007). https://doi.org/10.1007/978-3-540-73281-5_45
19. Bubb, H.: Das Regelkreisparadigma der Ergonomie. In: Automobilergonomie. A, pp. 27–65. Springer, Wiesbaden (2015). https://doi.org/10.1007/978-3-8348-2297-0_2
20. Kyriakidis, M., Happee, R., de Winter, J.C.F.: Public opinion on automated driving: results of an international questionnaire among 5000 respondents. Transport. Res. Part F Traffic Psychol. Behav. **32**, 127–140 (2015)
21. Mustafa, Y., Ezgi, C.: The relationship between good readers' attention, reading fluency and reading comprehension. Univ. J. Educ. Res. **5**(3), 366–371 (2017)
22. Hamish Jamson, A., Merat, N.: Surrogate in-vehicle information systems and driver behavior: effects of visual and cognitive load in simulated rural driving. Transport. Res. Part F: Traffic Psychol. Behav. **8**(2), 79–96 (2005)
23. Chen, M.-S., Lin, M.-C., Wang, C.C., Chang, A.: Using HCA and TOPSIS approaches in personal digital assistant menu–icon interface design. Int. J. Indust. Ergon. **39**(5), 689–702 (2005)

24. Wickens, C.D., Sandry, D.L., Vidulich, M.: Compatibility and resource competition between modalities of input, central processing, and output. Hum. Fact. J. Hum. Fact. Ergon. Soc. **25**(2), 227–248 (1983)
25. Nielsen, J.: Usability Inspection Methods. Wiley, New York (1994)
26. Gilly, L., Theresa, V., Oya, R., Blazej, K., Phoebe, S.: In-Car GPS navigation: engagement with and disengagement from the environment. In: Proceedings of the SIGCHI Conference on Human Factors in Computing Systems (CHI 2008), pp. 1675–1684 (2008)

Heuristic-Based Evaluation of Transparency Websites of the Municipal Governments Viewed on Web and Mobile Browsers

João Marcelo Alves Macêdo[(✉)] ⓘ, Valdecir Becker ⓘ,
and Felipe Melo Feliciano de Sá ⓘ

Federal University of Paraíba (UFPB), Mamanguape, Paraíba, Brazil
`joao.marcelo@academico.ufpb.br`

Abstract. Public transparency has been a widely debated topic around the world. Research has been conducted, situating the propensity of national and local governments to promote passive and active transparency, as well as the ways in which masses of data, the so-called open data, are made available. When debating this aspect, research has evaluated what is disclosed, but without discussing the means of disclosure, its usability, especially for mobile and design issues that are discussed in the prism of Human Computer Interaction (HCI). In this context, the present study aimed to evaluate, based on heuristics, the electronic sites of public transparency within the local governments of the State of Paraíba in Brazil, assessing responsiveness and accessibility by comparing access via web and mobile browsers. For the current case, we sought to build a study from an experimental strategy, where we worked with accounting students, who will act as experts in the process of creating these transparency spaces aiming at the fulfillment of legal demands. The inductive method was used, with construction in stages, progressing over one academic period and having as a guide the evaluation of mobile device interfaces with the use of a strategy based on heuristics. The results showed that most of the electronic sites have responsiveness, but there are cases that require improvements or even reconstruction. The conclusion is that the lack of this compatibility has hindered the popularization of access, especially by limiting the population that has restrictions on access mechanisms, especially using mobile devices.

Keywords: Government transparency · Heuristic-based evaluation · Transparency websites

1 Introduction

Brazil adopts a codified legal system, thus the debate on public transparency goes back to regulations and legislation's that seek to oblige, at first, the public manager to disclose basic and standardized information and, at second, to provide data and information, which are of public interest, linked to the agencies and their operation. Thus, there are milestones such as Complementary Law 101/2000 [1] and later 131/2009 [2] and, more recently, Law 12.527/2011 [3], known as the Access to Information Law (AIL).

M. Kurosu and A. Hashizume (Eds.): HCII 2023, LNCS 14012, pp. 434–454, 2023.
https://doi.org/10.1007/978-3-031-35599-8_29

However, the debate ought to be deepened and broadened by several factors, namely: what factors impact the understanding of the available information, typology of information, ways and means of access to information, effectiveness of disclosure, among others. Assert that there is a predisposition, in the process of outsourcing of transparency portals, for them to be more fragile and present a greater restriction, even the slowness of maintaining high levels of active transparency and availability of data [4].

Globally, the Public Expenditure and Financial Accountability (PEFA) and the International Budget Partnership (IBP) initiatives have promoted further debate on Public Transparency, influencing the directions and bringing the theme to two distinct perspectives [5]. Respectively, the first is related to the management of government finances, and the second transparency and participation with a focus on the budget process of national and sub-national governments.

PEFA's gaze delves into the quest to identify effective public financial management (PFM) institutions, as these have a critical role to play in supporting the implementation of national development and poverty reduction policies [5]. Thus the PEFA has a pillar of analysis regarding Comprehensiveness and transparency, which is characterized as verifying that budget and fiscal risk oversight is broad and fiscal and budget information is publicly accessible [6]. Verifying that PFM information is comprehensive, consistent, and accessible to users.

Already International Budget Partnership (IBP) has been active on the topic through the Open Budget Survey (OBS) (2021) [7], which self-characterizes itself as the only independent, comparative, fact-based research instrument with internationally received criteria to assess: (i) public access to central government budget information; (ii) formal opportunities for the public to participate in the national budget process; and (ii) the role of budget oversight institutions such as the legislature and the auditor in the budget process.

At the institutional level, the Office of the Comptroller General of the Union (CGU) control body of the Brazilian national government has the Transparent Brazil Scale - 360° Evaluation, is an innovation in the traditional public transparency evaluation methodology adopted by the institution and that seeks to contemplate active and passive transparency, bringing together the two lines of action [8]. According to the CGU in this evaluation, active transparency includes verification of the publication of information related to revenue and expenditure items, bids and contracts, administrative structure, civil servants, monitoring of public works, and others [8]. Thus, the goal is to expand the monitoring of public transparency actions that provide tools for monitoring the actions implemented at the national, sub-national, and local government levels to promote access to information [8].

This demand for inspection can also be the object of National, Sub-national and Local Government Audit Courts, auxiliary bodies of the legislative power with a high degree of specialization that analyze the rendering of accounts, allied to the process of maintaining transparency, which is one of the principles of Brazilian public management. However, if the interference of political decision in the level of transparency of governments is known, in some cases limiting factors are identified, one of them is the integration of systems and the flow of accounting, budgetary or fiscal information, implemented locally, reducing the possibility of parameterization of the portals [4].

However, a pressing concern is what type of device and connection is available to the citizen, especially in a continental-sized country like Brazil. In this sense, the Regional Center for Studies for the Development of the Information Society (Cetic.br) has the mission to produce statistical data and analysis on the impacts of digital technologies on society [9]. In this research Cetic.br presented that the cell phone (smartphone) has been since 2015 the main means of access to the internet for most Brazilians, and when one seeks to isolate the data on exclusive use, there is an increase of 6 percentage points in the exclusive use of the cell phone between 2019 and 2021 [9]. Such data reinforces the need for a deeper analysis of the types of devices, even if the presence of computers in homes remained at 39% [9].

By analyzing the types of internet access devices [10] promoted a study on the responsiveness of electronic sites of public transparency in Paraíba from mobile devices and concluded that there is lack of this compatibility has hindered the popularization of access, especially since it limits the access of the population to public information, resulting in impeding factors of transparency. Along this same path, there are studies relating Human Computer Interaction (HCI) and usability, especially in the approach of Nielsem's Heuristics [10].

Digital technologies have changed the relationship between voters and politicians, especially by expanding channels and increasing interaction. Electronic government (e-government or e-gov) has been boosted, being present in a very important point in the updated that is the mediation of the relationship between citizens and government, fostering debates about the impact of design and usability in the dialogue of the population with public management [11]. Usability addresses the way a system is used, having the impact of user characteristics, especially cognition, ability to act and perceive responses [11].

Given this context, the present study aimed to evaluate transparency systems, based on heuristics, analyzing the responsiveness and accessibility of each local government, comparing each type of access, via web and mobile browsers.

Our view was based on the 223 municipalities that make up the state of Paraíba - Brazil, looking at those institutions where the Brazilian state is closest to the population. It is hoped that with this analysis we will be able to ascertain the situation of public transparency initiatives with the population.

2   Heuristics and Evaluation of Interfaces

There are different methods to evaluate the quality of use of a product. The methods aim to examine usability, accessibility, and user experience, providing guidance to collect and analyze data. The evaluator decides which method best fits the evaluation requirements. HCI evaluation methods can be classified into investigation, user observation and inspection methods [11].

The inspection method strives for prediction of certain user experiences and project possible outcomes from this experience, by identifying design flaws. The observation methods allow the analysis of user data about situations carried out within a system, identifying real problems users face during their experience of use. Finally, the research methods include direct contact with users through interviews, field studies, application of questionnaires, among others, providing the evaluator with access to the user's opinions, expectations, and behavior in relation to the system.

Inspection methods allow the evaluator to examine (or inspect) an HCI solution to anticipate the possible consequences of certain design decisions [11, 12]. By not involving users, this method is designed to identify problems that may arise when using the system. By examining different designs and comparing them, it is possible to find flaws in the design and experiences and can suggest options for product improvements. When inspecting an interface, evaluators put themselves in the shoes of a user with a certain profile, with a certain knowledge and experience in some activities, to identify problems that users may have when interacting with the system, and what ways of support the system offers to help them overcome these problems.

Heuristic evaluation is a usability inspection technique that suggests the evaluator to navigate through the system interface to search potential problems, based on a set of heuristics, such as those proposed by Nielsen [13]. This sort of evaluation is effective for finding different types of usability failures, being a quick and low-cost evaluation alternative when compared to empirical methods [11].

This evaluation technique is useful both in systems development and in evaluating commercial systems, aiming at their evolution. In systems development, heuristic evaluation can be applied at different stages, from prototyping to testing final versions of software before release. In the evaluation of ready-to-use systems, the method aims at redesigning the system, with an increase in improvements in future versions.

The heuristics proposed by Nielsen describe desirable characteristics of the interaction and the interface, composed by 10 items [11, 13]:

1. Visibility and status of the system – through responses to user actions, the system should keep the user informed about what is happening in a reasonable period of time.
2. Conformity of the system with the real world – the system should use a language that is familiar to the user, avoiding technical and specific terms for developers. In addition, real-world conventions must be met, being information appearance in a natural and logical order, as expected by users.
3. User control and freedom – the system should offer an easily identified emergency exit, allowing the user to exit the unwanted state without major problems.
4. Consistency and standards – the system should prevent the user from thinking that different actions or situations mean the same thing. Platform or computing environment conventions should be followed.
5. Recognition rather than recall – the system should minimize the user's memory load by making objects, actions, and options visible. The user should not have to remember information from one part of the dialogue to another. Instructions for use of the system should be visible or easily retrievable whenever appropriate.
6. Flexibility and efficiency of use – the system should enable the optimization of the experience of more experienced users.
7. Aesthetics and minimalist design – the system should avoid the use of irrelevant information on the screen.
8. Error prevention – the system must prevent errors from occurring.
9. Helps users to recognize, diagnose and recover from errors – the system should use simple language to expose the errors that have occurred and suggest a solution.

10. Help and documentation – the system should provide information and instructions easy to search, focused on the user's task, list concrete steps to be carried out, and not be too large.

2.1 Heuristics and Evaluation for Mobile

The Organization for Economic Co-operation and Development [OECD] [15] promoted a study that placed the evolution of government solutions, pointing out that the development of services is linked to the explosion of wireless access points or wi-fi, as well as the expansion of access to smartphones (mobile), expanding the possibility of access to government services. It is known that along the development of electronic government (e-government) initially motivated the advancement of mobile government (m-government), i.e., access to services through applications (app's) and not only through the browser (web browser), which would be a generic application [15].

In this context, Machado Neto and Pimentel [16] evolved the heuristics initially proposed by Nielsen, adapting them to mobile devices, as described in Table 1 and that support the analysis proposed in this paper aimed at measuring public transparency on these devices.

Thus [15] argue that the heuristics proposed by them for mobile devices, extends the performance of the concepts proposed by Nielsen, overcoming cosmetic problems and adapting with new aspects observed from contributions of other authors, as reported in the construction of Table 1.

Table 1. Heuristics for evaluating the usability of mobile device interfaces: second version.

Heuristic Mobile	Description
HM1 - Use of screen space	The interface should be designed so that the items are neither too distant, nor too stuck. Margin spaces may not be large in small screens to improve information visibility. The more related the components are, the closer they should appear on the screen. Interfaces ought to not be overwhelmed with a large number of items
HM2 - Consistency and standards	The application should maintain the components in the same place and look throughout the interaction, to facilitate learning and to stimulate the user's short-term memory. Similar functionalities ought to be performed by similar interactions. The metaphor of each component or feature ought to be unique throughout the application, to avoid misunderstanding

(*continued*)

Table 1. (*continued*)

Heuristic Mobile	Description
HM3 - Visibility and easy access to all information	All information ought to be visible and legible, both in portrait and in landscape. This also applies to media, which should be fully exhibited, unless the user opts to hide them. The elements on the screen ought to be adequately aligned and contrasted
HM4 - Adequacy of the component to its functionality	The user should know exactly which information to input in a component, without any ambiguities or doubts. Metaphors of features ought to be understood without difficulty
HM5 - Adequacy of the message to the functionality and to the user	The application should speak the user's language in a natural and non-invasive manner, so that the user does not feel under pressure. Instructions for performing the functionalities ought to be clear and objective
HM6 - Error prevention and rapid recovery to the last stable state	The system ought to be able to anticipate a situation that leads to an error by the user based on some activity already performed by the user [8]. When an error occurs, the application should quickly warn the user and return to the last stable state of the application. In cases in which a return to the last stable state is difficult, the system should transfer the control to the user, so that he decides what to do or where to go
HM7 - Ease of input	The way the user provides the data can be based on assistive technologies, but the application should always display the input data with readability, so that the user has full control of the situation. The user should be able to provide the required data in a practical way
HM8 - Ease of access to all functionalities	The main features of the application ought to be easily found by the user, preferably in a single interaction. Most-frequently-used functionalities may be performed by using shortcuts or alternative interactions. No functionality should be hard to find in the application interface. All input components should be easily assimilated

(*continued*)

Table 1. (*continued*)

Heuristic Mobile	Description
HM9 - Immediate and observable feedback	Feedback should be easily identified and understood, so that the user is aware of the system status. Local refreshments on the screen ought to be preferred over global ones, because those ones maintain the status of the interaction. The interface should give the user the choice to hide messages that appear repeatedly. Long tasks ought to provide the user a way to do other tasks concurrently to the task being processed. The feedback ought to have good tone and be positive and may not be redundant or obvious
HM10 - Help and documentation	The application should have a help option where common problems and ways to solve them are specified. The issues considered in this option should be easy to find
HM11 - Reduction of the user's memory load	The user should not have to remember information from one screen to another to complete a task. The information of the interface ought to be clear and sufficient for the user to complete the current task

Note. [16]

In this sense, the authors in their results suggest that the heuristics for mobile are more easily adapted to the evaluation of mobile devices and that because they are the largest portal for Internet access they should compose such an evaluation.

3 Public Transparency

In Brazil, public transparency is based on the 1988 Federal Constitution, which is currently in force and is known for encouraging the participation of the population in the formulation of public policies, being commonly called the Citizen Constitution. This role of fostering transparency was initially foreseen in Article 5, subsection XXXIII, through the Principle of Publicity, which guarantees that every citizen can obtain information of his or her interest, except for information whose secrecy is essential to the safety of society and the State [17].

Despite being supported by the Federal Constitution, two other complementary legislations reinforce the legal framework that supports these initiatives, they are Complementary Law 131/2009 [2] (Transparency Law) and Law 12.527/2011 [3] (Access to Information Law - AIL). Respectively the first changed part of the original wording of the Fiscal Responsibility Law (FRL) with regard to transparency of fiscal management, so the new text innovates and determines that detailed information about the budgetary and financial execution of the Union, the States, the Federal District and the Municipalities should be available in real time. The second guarantees that citizens may request information from the public administration, transparency being the rule and secrecy the exception.

Promoted an evaluation of the impact of the Access to Information Law on the behavior of public inspection agents, using for such analysis the conceptual lens of behavior analysis [18]. Thus, it was verified that there was modification in the behavior of professionals of the Court of Auditors of the Municipalities of the State of Goiás in Brazil, because it was shown that after the effectiveness of the law the number of cases was reduced, but the magnitudes of the punishments were higher, both in the form of fines and imputations of debts [18]. Finally, it is concluded that the LAI has impacted the behavior of public inspection agents regarding the imposition of sanctions, not refuting, therefore, the research hypothesis [18].

On the other hand, it is necessary to evaluate if what is made available has Quality, Utility and Sufficiency, in this search, Baldissera et al. [19] evaluated these issues by the perception of members of non profit organization of public transparency. Thus the members of the Social Observatory of Brazil (OSB) have the perception that the quality of information does not meet the objectives of the Access to Information Law and that the information made available by the means of public transparency is not sufficient to exercise social control, although they believe that the tools of public transparency have been useful to strengthen social control.

In the example of Spain, transparency had as a framework for debate after the publication of Law 19 of December 9, 2013, called the Law on Transparency, Access to Public Information and Good Governance, bringing to the center of the debate the concept of transparency [20]. There were some public administrations with a low tradition in providing their accounts, restricting the judgment of society about their actions and activities, but becoming a space for advances and especially a cultural change required by society in general [20]. Thus [20] bring a study on transparency in websites involving 144 Spanish municipalities with a population over 50,000 inhabitants and conclude that there is a great need for improvement in the institutional, organizational and planning areas, as well as in the areas of economic, budgetary and statistical information, of these local governments [20].

4   Transparency Website Infrastructure: Access and Impact

The available infrastructure for public transparency consists of the transparency portal, an electronic site that gathers all the information required by Brazilian legislation and currently known in the literature as passive transparency, but it may also make information available on a voluntary basis, i.e., those that the public manager believes to be important and makes up active transparency. There is also the citizen information system (SIC), which can be local, a physical space, or electronic, by means of an information request form, which is often linked to the transparency portal and is the instrumentation of AIL.

Some governments have invested in the so-called open data, that is, the availability of a conglomerate of raw data that is made available so that the citizen can carry out studies and other means of treating the data in order to increase transparency. We know that there are challenges promoted by the most diverse institutes and even by the government itself aiming at the use of this data. The Hackaton or even hack day, Hackfest or Codefest as these events have become known are a marathon of programming in which hackers gather for hours, days or even weeks in order to explore open data [21]. Thus it becomes interesting to make these masses of data available for such actions and search for logical relationships and products from the available data.

There is a study on transparency initiatives based on open government data conducted by researchers and which are presented the European legislation and initiatives of the Public Sector Information (PSI) Directive in 2003, U.S. President's Obama open data initiative in 2009, the Open Government Partnership in 2011, and the G8 Open Data Charter in 2013 are presented [22]. Another finding of this study are the open government data portals, i.e. data.gov.uk, data.gov, and data.gov.sg, provide means for citizens and stakeholders to obtain government information about the locality or country in question [22]. Authors have identified corruption to be the major problem which triggered open government data initiatives, and one major motivation is transparency. This perspective will avoid governments in publishing for compliance their data only, rather than striving to provide useful data which stakeholders can use, reuse and distribute, and ideally even innovate upon [22].

Given this finding, we know the impact of the construction of the Transparency Portal tool, in Brazil can compromise the provision to citizens of useful information and capable of fostering proper oversight. In Brazil there is a considerable participation of outsourced service providers in this development area. Dias et al. (2020) [4] argue that the transparency portals implemented by outsourcing tend to be more fragile and find it more difficult to maintain the levels of active transparency depending on the integration of systems and the flow of accounting-budgetary information implemented locally, and the level of transparency is a political decision, given the possibility of parameterization of the portals. From this point of view, the existence of own systems and the maintenance of data relative to the various years, so that they can be compared, would be defended.

Another limiting factor stems from the type of device and connection for this access to transparency data. In Brazil the citizen has a very restricted access, provided by not so stable networks and smartphones. A recent study published by the Regional Center for Studies for the Development of the Information Society [9] showed that as of 2015 the cell phone (smartphone) became the main tool for Internet access for Brazilians. Thus, it is verified that one cannot only analyze transparency with the use of computers (desktop or notebook), but reveal the need for a deeper analysis of these devices, their screen sizes and responsiveness.

5 Methodology

The present research used the experimental strategy, from the inductive method, with exploratory outlines and survey strategy for mobile given its representativeness. We made such choices since the participants were motivated at the end of their evaluations to answer a questionnaire, which was used to learn about the extent of transparency and the impact of the vehicles that promote it.

For the execution of the evaluation based on heuristics, we used the 34 (thirty-four) students of accounting sciences from the Federal University of Paraíba who are in the last period of their undergraduate course and who analyzed the performance of experts in the process of creating these transparency spaces aiming at the fulfillment of legal demands. The evaluation of interfaces contemplated the mobile devices with the use of the strategy based on heuristics reached the 223 local governments of the state of Paraíba - Brazil and the web version of a smaller sample, able to understand how the two forms behave.

First, the students had a three-hour class on basic concepts of public transparency, active and passive transparency and their means of consolidation. After this first moment, they accessed the municipal website and made their first observations regarding the web version (desktop) of the transparency portal, answering some initial questions that will be presented throughout this work. The second stage took place with the steps described in Table 2.

Table 2. Stages of the consultation process by mobile device

Stages	Stage Description
1	Connect the cell phone to Wifi, choose a browser, enter the city hall site, take a printout of the home screen in vertical and horizontal mode, check if it was responsive, i.e. if the information molded and or if it is lost, when there is the choice of vertical and horizontal mode.
2	Search the local government website for the tab or new transparency website of the municipality.
3	After accessing the transparency site, print the initial screen in vertical and horizontal mode, check if it reacted, i.e. if the information was shaped and or if it is lost when switching between vertical and horizontal modes.
4	In the transparency site, if you make a query about the municipality's expenses, in this screen, see if it is possible to type or if the information is by choice in predefined options, check this screen in vertical and horizontal position, finally, don't forget to print the screens.

Note: Own elaboration, based on the research script

The data will be treated in the Software GNU PSPP aiming the data tabulation and presentation of the research findings, from the answers provided by the participants. The analysis followed the idea of profiling the respondents, then analyze their interpretations of the transparency sites from the web version, in a reduced perspective and later the survey of all sites by the web version.

6 Data Presentation, Analysis and Discussion

6.1 Respondent's Profile

First, we profiled the respondents by analyzing their age and gender, and found that of the thirty-six (36) survey participants, most are male and have a predominant age range of up to 35 years. Additionally, the study found that all female participants are concentrated in this range up to the age of 35. Such factors denote the participants' attachment to this view of transparency arising from the classes and the nature of the predominant undergraduate degree in accounting sciences (Table 3).

Table 3. Cross-tabulation of participant profiles Age versus Gender

Age	Male	%	Female	%	Total
22 to 25 years old	11	61,11%	7	38,89%	18
26 to 30 years old	5	62,50%	3	37,50%	8
31 to 35 years old	4	66,67%	2	33,33%	6
36 to 42 years old	4	100,00%	0	0,00%	4
Total	24	66,67%	12	33,33%	36

Note: Own elaboration, based on the research results

In this quest to analyze the profile of the interviewees with regard to prior knowledge of transparency, it was found that 96% of them had already accessed the transparency portal. We emphasize that although there was no previous access, this knowledge and the structuring of how this tool works was provided within the experiment (Table 4).

Table 4. Previous access to the transparency portal

Description	Frequency	%
Yes	27	96,0%
No	9	4,0%
Total	36	100,0%

Note: Own elaboration, based on the research results

Aiming to complement this, we questioned how this previous access had been, finding, among the examples: (i) participation in a university extension project on transparency and had found the information; (ii) search for knowledge as a common citizen; (iii) search for information about the university itself; (iv) perception that the sites and transparency in general need improvement and other information; and (v) searches for civil servant salaries.

6.2   Analysis from the Web Profile of Transparency Sites of Local Governments

With regard to the analysis, the respondents were encouraged to get to know the world of transparency, promoting an analysis of the site through the web tool, thus we had a scope of 34 (thirty-four) observations, these being non-exclusive and thus we even obtained the repetition of two cities in the sample, which does not interfere, given that we sought to motivate them and at the same time prepare them for the web evaluation, which promotes a survey on the entire population investigated.

Table 5 shows the respondents' data for the 10 heuristics proposed by Nielson, based on which the transparency websites of Brazilian local governments were analyzed. We have identified that they all present a simple and natural dialog with the user and most of them relate to the user through a language close to the user.

Table 5. Nielsen Heuristics for web evaluating municipal transparency portals

ord	Heuristics	Yes	%	No	%	Not applicable	%
1	Presents simple and natural dialog	34	100	–	–	–	–
2	Speaks in the user's language	33	97,1	1	2,9	–	–
3	Minimizes user memory load	25	73,5	5	14,7	4	11,8
4	It is consistent	29	85,3	3	8,8	2	5,9
5	Provides user feedback	20	58,8	9	26,5	5	14,7
6	It has clear and marked outputs	25	73,5	5	14,7	4	11,8
7	Provides shortcuts	26	76,5	7	20,6	1	2,9
8	Displays constructive and accurate error messages	10	29,4	15	44,1	9	26,5
9	Prevents user errors during navigation	10	29,4	16	47,1	8	23,5
10	They have good support, rescue and documentation	21	61,8	9	26,5	4	11,8

Note: Own elaboration, based on the research results

It can also be seen that for the items such as memory usage, clear and signaled exits and shortcuts, the answers are above 70%, but even so no flaws were pointed out in the systems in general. As for feedback and support, this number drops to around 60%, and for messages and support in case of errors, this positive assessment drops to around 30%. In this sense, it is verified that by accessing the portal on the Web system, it is not seen as a complete system, even knowing the complexity of it, there is room for improvement.

It can be seen in Fig. 1, that the web mode sites have a good consistency, in its initial screen is presented the complete screen, highlighting the Transparency Portal and access to information at the top promoting a good dissemination of these tools.

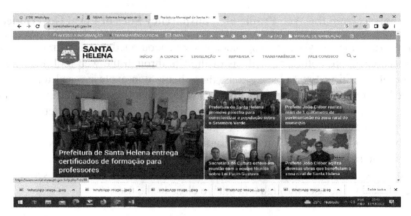

Fig. 1. Home screen of local government site viewed by google chrome® browser in web mode

This transparency denoted by Fig. 2 relates to greater visualization and the completeness of the information that is answered from the screen and promotes public transparency.

Fig. 2. Home screen of transparency local government site viewed by google chrome® browser in web mode

The transparency portal of the state capital, João Pessoa, is presented as one of the most complete and has even been awarded in local rankings of transparency and promotion of the Access to Information Act. So it is verified that it has a good use of the screen, has space for registration of sending periodic information, having a first panel of the expenses with the COVID-19 confrontation, below a set of icons for quick access and at the side the panel with the complete content of it. At the top, it points to the ombudsman, the service body for complaints and the Citizen Information Service (SIC) (Fig. 3).

Fig. 3. Home screen of capital of state site viewed by google chrome® browser in web mode

Continuing the presentation of the evaluations of the transparency portals, we sought to investigate them through mobile devices, since this is the means by which most of the Brazilian population accesses the internet by cell phone (smartphone) (Table 6).

Table 6. Nielsen Heuristics for mobile evaluating municipal transparency portals

order	Heuristics descriptions	Yes	%	No	%	Not applicable	%
1	Presents good use of screen space	172	77,1	47	21,1	4	1,8
2	Have consistency and standards of the interface	178	79,8	39	17,5	6	2,7
3	Visibility and easy access to all existing information	135	60,5	84	37,7	4	1,8
4	Suitability between the component and its functionality	170	76,2	46	20,6	7	3,1
5	Message adaptation to functionality and user	163	73,1	48	21,5	12	5,4
6	Error prevention and quick return to the last stable state	97	43,5	101	45,3	25	11,2
7	Easy data entry	156	70	57	25,6	10	4,5
8	Immediate and easy-to-notice feedback	114	51,1	81	36,3	28	12,6
9	Easy access to functionalities	166	74,4	50	22,4	7	3,1
10	Help and Documentation	147	65,9	59	26,5	17	7,6
11	Minimizing User Memory Load	124	55,6	78	35,0	21	9,4

Note: Own elaboration, based on the research results

Our investigation was based on Machado Neto and Pimentel [16] to evaluate the 223 (two hundred and twenty-three) local governments of the State of Paraíba - Brazil, in it the items were verified from this analysis improvement for mobile. At first we identified that 77.1% present a good use of the screen, that is, they use the space in an adequate way and promote responsiveness, although they still present design problems.

Below we have pasted a figure with four examples of home pages of sites of municipalities in order to present, and in these we found in the first two points that responsiveness generates overlapping of images and information, and in the others they appear. In this study we used the Safari® and Google Chrome® browsers, as can be seen in Fig. 4, we demonstrate that the problems are minimized in HM1.

We also discussed the heuristics in mobile mode, characterized in Table 1 (i) HM2 (ii) HM3 (iii) HM4; and (iv) HM5, which had an adequacy that was higher than 61% going up to 79.8% . This parameter showed that a good portion of the portals had responsiveness capable of compensating for occasional errors and failures.

Fig. 4. Home screenshots of local government sites viewed by Safari® and Google Chrome® browsers.

Thus, within the population analyzed, it was an important finding that they were adequate in their parameters of consistency, visibility and ease of access to the user, adequate functionality and a focus on the user's needs (Fig. 5).

One concern of the evaluators was that the systems do not have a good relation with error prevention, this harms the way the user relates to the system, this way the heuristic that points Error prevention and quick return to the last stable state, so many of the sites are limited to providing navigation manuals, frequently asked questions and help buttons, which refer the user to other modules or to a contact with the site administrator. This, in our view, is quite limited, i.e. error prevention and resuming the last stage needs to be available in order to assist users in achieving their goals when consulting the information on these sites. (see Fig. 6).

Fig. 5. Home screenshots of local government sites viewed by Safari® and Google Chrome® browsers.

Fig. 6. Examples of transparency portal screenshots with help menu, FAQ, and navigation manual

Aiming to present the final part of the evaluation data, we bring the standards of Feedback immediate and easy to be noticed and Minimization of the user's Memory load that point the lowest relation of our research, where it has, that approximately 50% of the sites have. When the question is help and documentation this relation rises to the range of 65.9%, as we have seen the strategy of error prevention and finally the ease of data entry and access to features that are above 70%.

Table 7 presents the data of the cross tabulation between the web and mobile versions of the evaluation on the role of websites and transparency services in relation to accessibility and the promotion of a democratic space for the population. It is noteworthy that "I agree but not strongly" concentrates 41.2% of respondents for the web version and 35.3% for the mobile version, which demonstrates the greater accessibility when the computer is used as a means of access, which by the visualization field promotes this feeling of greater transparency.

While we still evaluate those who oppose the idea that these two systems would promote this transparency, so when we add those who oppose and those who are indifferent, we get to 17.6% of the evaluators. As for those who agree, if we add those who agree more than disagree, agree, agree but not strongly agree, and strongly agree, this number rises to 82.4%, noting that of these 5.9% strongly agree with the existence of this space, this number shows that even with the limitations of responsiveness and design, it has reached a public and promoted public transparency.

Fig. 7. Examples of transparency portal screenshots with help menu, FAQ, and navigation manual

Finally in Fig. 7 we exemplify the adequate space for popular participation with details of the expenses with the confrontation of COVID-19, the vacinometer, control of the vaccines received by the local government, how many were applied to the population and the amount available for application. Then the consultation of an expense is presented and it is exemplified that consultations of previous years are available and it reaches the year 2016. Then we present the summary of public accounts that are available on the transparency portal and finally, the screen with an advanced query and the channels of service of the E-SIC, the Charter of services, where all the services provided to the user are related and finally the ombudsman link for the presentation of criticism, complaints, questions, among others.

Additionally, we present data that points to the conditions under which the test was performed (see Table 8), in terms of operating system in general we had 101 tests performed with IOS, because the devices are Apple iPhone while the other 122 tests were performed with Android System, resulting in this balance between the two types of test. When analyzing the type of browser, it appears that Google Chrome was used in 162 cases, which corresponds to 72.6% of all tests against 23.3 for Safari. In relation to the location of the test the highest concentration was in neighborhoods of the state capital with 31.8%, followed by neighborhoods in medium-sized cities with 27.8%, showing balance in this aspect, capable of impacting the access of the population. Finally we looked at the type of connection, with the majority having Fiber-Optic Internet +5 g/2 g Router with 75.8.

Table 7. Evaluation of the role of websites and transparency services in relation to accessibility and the promotion of a democratic space for the population

Site web version => / Site mobile version	I disagree but not strongly	%	Indifferent	%	More I agree than disagree	%	I agree	%	I agree but not strongly	%	I strongly agree	%	Total	%
I disagree but not strongly	1	2,9	0		0		0		0		0		1	2,9
Disagree	0		1	2,9	0		0		1		0	2,9	2	5,9
Indifferent	0		1	2,9	2	5,9	0		0		0		3	8,8
More I agree than disagree	1	2,9	0		2	5,9	1	2,9	0		0		4	11,8
I agree	0		2	5,9	1	2,9	3	8,8	4	11,8	0		10	29,4
I agree but not strongly	0		2	5,9	0		2	5,9	7	20,6	1	2,9	12	35,3
I strongly agree	0		0		0		0		2	5,9	0		2	5,9
Total	2	5,9	6	17,6	5	17,6	6	14,7	14	41,2	1	2,9	34	100

Note: Own elaboration, based on the research results

Table 8. Additional data on the performance of the tests

Data		Frequency	Valid Percent
Browser type			
1	Google Chrome®	162	72,6%
2	Microsoft Edge®	4	1,8%
3	Opera mini®	5	2,2%
4	Safari®	52	23,3%
Location from where you performed the tests			
1	Inner-city neighborhood (small)	42	18,8%
2	Inner-city neighborhood (average)	62	27,8%
3	Rural Area	11	4,9%
4	Capital City Neighborhood	71	31,8%
5	Center in Inner City	31	13,9%
6	Downtown Capital City	6	2,7%
Connection type from where you performed the tests			
1	Internet way Radio + 5g/2g Router	20	9,0%
2	Internet way Radio + 2g Router only	12	5,4%
3	Fiber-Optic Internet + 5g/2g Router	169	75,8%
4	Fiber-Optic Internet + 2g Router only	22	9,9%

Note: Own elaboration, based on the research results

7   Conclusion

This research aimed to evaluate, based on heuristics, the electronic sites of public transparency within the local governments of the State of Paraíba, measuring responsiveness and accessibility by comparing access via web and mobile browsers. To do so, it used this theoretical support and the experimental construction of the evaluators so that such a result would have a uniform look and could apprehend data in several devices, several operating systems and browsers, capable of representing the citizens who seek such looks.

The results demonstrate an evolution when compared to the results of Jácome Filho & Macêdo [10], especially for covering local governments, the state arms that are closer to the population, meeting the first needs. Hence we find that most of the websites have responsiveness, generating access and enabling public transparency.

This analysis carried out by using a look based on Nielsen's heuristics [13, 14] and by the extended look of Machado Neto & Pimentel [16], identified that there are cases that require improvements or even reconstruction, it is suspected that the adoption of ready-made websites or outsourced systems embedded in the portals of municipalities has generated such problems, which consist of future investigations.

To reduce biases, we tried to distribute the evaluators in a balanced and equitable way, so that there would be no bias in access and thus harm the evaluation. In this way, it was seen that the sample is well representative and managed to present a good evaluation space, being in the places that represent the state of Paraíba - Brazil in all its aspects.

It is concluded with this, that the lack of this compatibility has hindered the popularization of access, especially by limiting the population that has restrictions on access mechanisms, using especially mobile devices. The systems need to be improved so that they can be responsive and adapt to the majority of the mobile devices used.

As limitations, the search for a survey generated a limitation of the view, it is intended to stratify the municipalities by size and other indicators that can better qualify the aspects that lead them to invest in these tools, enabling an adequate space for public transparency and popular participation.

For future research purposes, we see the need to investigate the systems that provide these public transparency modules, analyzing how responsive they are and what the real impact is between the information and its availability, investigating ways to motivate active transparency.

Acknowledgments. This work was funded by the Public Call n. 03 Produtividade em Pesquisa PROPESQ/PRPG/UFPB proposal code PVP13490-2020

References

1. COMPLEMENTARY LAW NO. 101, OF MAY 4, 2000 Establishes norms of public finances focused on responsibility in fiscal management and other provisions. https://www.planalto. gov.br/ccivil_03/leis/lcp/lcp101.htm. Accessed 21 Nov 2022
2. COMPLEMENTARY LAW NO. 131, OF MAY 27TH, 2009. Adds provisions to the Complementary Law no. 101, of May 4, 2000, which establishes public finance norms aimed at fiscal management responsibility and other provisions, in order to determine the availability, in real time, of detailed information about the budgetary and financial execution of the Union, the States, the Federal District, and the Municipalities. https://www.planalto.gov.br/ccivil_ 03/leis/lcp/lcp131.htm. Accessed 21 Nov 2022
3. LAW NO. 12.527, OF NOVEMBER 18, 2011. Regulates the access to information provided for in item XXXIII of art. 5, in item II of § 3 of art. 37 and in § 2 of art. 216 of the Federal Constitution; amends Law No. 8112 of December 11, 1990; revokes Law No. 111 of May 5, 2005, and provisions of Law No. 8159 of January 8, 1991; and makes other provisions. https:// www.planalto.gov.br/ccivil_03/_ato2011-2014/2011/lei/l12527.htm. Accessed 21 Nov 2022
4. da Silva Dias, L.N, de Aquino, A.C.B., da Silva, P.B., dos Albuquerque, F.S.: Outsourcing of fiscal transparency portals by municipalities. J. Account. Organiz. **14**, e164383 (2020). https:// doi.org/10.11606/issn.1982-6486.rco.2020.164383. Accessed 10 Oct 2019 2022/10/19
5. Public Expenditure and Financial Accountability (PEFA). 2011 Public Finance Management - Performance Assessment Framework. https://www.pefa.org/sites/pefa/files/resources/dow nloads/PMF%20Portuguese_HGRFinal.pdf. Accessed 21 Nov 2022
6. Public Expenditure and Financial Accountability (PEFA) 2019 Global Report on Public Financial Management. https://www.pefa.org/sites/pefa/files/resources/downloads/202 0002207PORpor002_Main%20text.pdf. Accessed 21 Nov 2022
7. International Budget Partnership (IBP). Open Budget Survey 2021. https://internationalbu dget.org/open-budget-survey/country-results/2021/brazil. Accessed 21 Nov 2022

8. Controladoria-Geral da União (CGU). Avaliações independentes EBT - Avaliação 360° - 2ª Edição (2021). https://mbt.cgu.gov.br/publico/avaliacao/escala_brasil_transparente/66. Accessed 21 Dec 2022

9. Centro Regional de Estudos para o Desenvolvimento da Sociedade da Informação (Cetic.br). Pesquisa sobre o uso das tecnologias de informação e comunicação nos domicílios brasileiros – TIC Domicílios 2021. https://cetic.br/media/analises/tic_domicilios_2021_col etiva_imprensa.pdf. Accessed 17 Sept 2022

10. de Jácome Filho, E.A., Macêdo, J.M.A.: Analysis of Responsiveness and Usability in Websites Serving Public Transparency in a Mobile Environment: Case Study in the State of Paraíba Through Heuristic Evaluation. In Human-Computer Interaction. User Experience and Behavior: Thematic Area, HCI 2022, Held as Part of the 24th HCI International Conference, HCII 2022, Virtual Event, June 26–July 1, 2022, Proceedings, Part III, pp. 106–127. Springer, Chamhttps://doi.org/10.1007/978-3-031-05412-9_8. Accessed 19 Sept 2022

11. Barbosa, S.D.J., Silva, B.D., Silveira, M.S., Gasparini, I., Darin, T., Barbosa, G.D.J.: Interação humano-computador e experiência do usuario. Auto publicação (2021)

12. Preece, J., Sharp, H., Rogers, Y.: Interaction Design: Beyond Human-Computer Interaction. Wiley (2015)

13. Nielsen, J.: Usability inspection methods. In Conference Companion on Human Factors in Computing Systems, pp. 413–414 (1994)

14. Nielsen, J.: Severity ratings for usability problems. Papers Essays **54**, 1–2 (1995)

15. Organisation for Economic Co-operation and Development: M-government: Mobile Technologies for Responsive Governments and Connected Societies. OECD Publishing, Paris (2011)

16. Machado Neto, O., Pimentel, M.D.G.: Heuristics for the assessment of interfaces of mobile devices. In: Proceedings of the 19th Brazilian Symposium on Multimedia and the Web, pp. 93–96. recuperado de (2013). https://doi.org/10.1145/2526188.2526237

17. BRASIL. Constituição da República Federativa do Brasil de 1988 (1988). http://www.pla nalto.gov.br/ccivil_03/Constituicao/Constituicao.htm. Accessed 29 out. 2022

18. de Machado, L.S., Nalini, L.E.G., Machado, M.R.R.: Freedom of Information Act and Behavior of Auditing Agents. Sociedade, Contabilidade e Gestão, Rio de Janeiro, v. 17, n. 1, jan/abr (2022). https://doi.org/10.21446/scg_ufrj.v0i0.42410. Accessed 21 Nov 2022

19. Baldissera, J.F., Walter, S.A., Fiirst, C., Asta, D.D.: The Perception of Social Observatories on the Quality, Utility and Sufficiency of Public Transparency of Brazilian Municipalities. Sociedade, Contabilidade e Gestão, Rio de Janeiro, v. 14, n. 1, jan./abr (2019). https://doi.org/10.21446/scg_ufrj.v0i0.18404. Accessed 21 Nov 2022

20. Jalón, M.L.D., Heras, E.N., Agudo, L.M.: Cumplimiento de los requisitos de transparencia: un diagnóstico de la situación para los municipios españoles de más de 50.000 habitantes* Innovar, vol. 27, núm. 66, 2017, Octubre-Diciembre, pp. 109–121 Facultad de Ciencias Económicas. Universidad Nacional de Colombia (2017). https://doi.org/10.15446/innovar.v27n66.66806. Accessed 21 Nov 2022

21. Wikipédia, a enciclopédia livre – Hackathon. https://pt.wikipedia.org/wiki/Hackathon. Accessed 21 Jan 2022

22. Attard, J., Orlandi, F., Scerri, S., Auer, S.: A systematic review of open government data initiatives. Govern. Inform. Quar. **32**(4), 399–418 (2015). https://doi.org/10.1016/j.giq.2015.07.006. Accessed 21 Dec 2022

Do Not Shoot the Messenger: Effect of System Critical Feedback on User-Perceived Usability

Georgios Melissourgos[1] and Christos Katsanos[2]([✉])

[1] Multitude SE, Helsinki, Finland
`georgios.melissourgos@multitude.com`
[2] Department of Informatics, Aristotle University of Thessaloniki, Thessaloniki, Greece
`ckatsanos@csd.auth.gr`

Abstract. Measuring perceived usability with questionnaires is a common practice for usability researchers and practitioners. This paper investigates whether there is any user bias towards the perceived usability of a system, when this system administers critical feedback to its users. These systems make decisions that substantially affect their users' lives, such as automated medical diagnosis, bank loan approval etc. In our study, we gathered data from three, almost identical, systems used to apply for a consumer loan and communicate the decision to the applicant. Our dataset involves a total of 332 applicants who completed the UMUX-LITE questionnaire after receiving the system decision (approved, rejected) for their loan. Results showed that participants who had their loans approved (positive system critical feedback) provided significantly higher UMUX-LITE scores compared to participants who had their loans rejected (negative system critical feedback). This finding suggests that one should pay attention when measuring perceived usability of critical feedback administering systems as it tends to be biased from the critical feedback that users received.

Keywords: System Critical Feedback · Perceived Usability · Usability Questionnaire · UMUX-LITE

1 Introduction

1.1 Perceived Usability and Its Measurement

Perceived usability reflects users' subjective assessments of the usability of a system. Hertzum [1] considers perceived usability as one of the six images of usability which "concerns the user's subjective experience of a system based on his or her interaction with it".

Measuring perceived usability with questionnaires is a common practice for usability researchers and practitioners. Examples of such usability questionnaires are the System Usability Scale (SUS) [2], the Post-Study System Usability Questionnaire (PSSUQ) and the Computer System Usability Questionnaire (CSUQ) [3], the Usefulness, Satisfaction, and Ease of use (USE) [4], the Purdue Usability Testing Questionnaire (PUTQ) [5], and the Questionnaire for User Interface Satisfaction (QUIS) [6]. Popular usability questionnaires have been translated into languages other than English. For instance, SUS is available in Greek [7], Slovenian [8], Polish [9], Persian [10], Chinese [11, 12], Danish [13], Arabic [12], French [12], German [12], Hindi [12] and Spanish [12]. As another example, PSSUQ and CSUQ have been translated into Greek [14] and into Turkish [15] and Arabic [16] respectively.

An important trend to perceived usability measurements are short usability questionnaires, which are supported by a growing body of evidence regarding their reliability and validity. The SUS consists of 10 questions and is one of the most used such questionnaires [17] that remains reliable even for a small sample size [18]. Still, there are cases where an even shorter questionnaire is required, such as when the perceived usability measurement is part of a larger questionnaire, or when multiple systems (e.g., versions of a system, competitors' systems) must be evaluated in the same usability study, or when the users' time is in deficit (e.g., studies in the wild). As a result, questionnaires have been developed to measure perceived usability with even less questions than the 10 of SUS. The Usability Metric for User Experience (UMUX) [19] has 4 questions and the UMUX-LITE [20] has only 2 questions.

All questionnaires mentioned so far are administered post study, that is after the participant has finished all the tasks. However, there are also short post-task questionnaires that are completed immediately after finishing a task, such as the After-Scenario Questionnaire (ASQ) [21] with 3 items and the Single Ease Question (SEQ) [22] with 1 item. Even though the latter two questionnaires are very short, they must be completed multiple times in a usability-study session that typically involves multiple tasks. Thus, any time savings from the smaller number of questions might be offset by the additional time required for multiple completions of the same questionnaire.

1.2   The UMUX-LITE Questionnaire

UMUX-LITE [20] is a two-items standardised questionnaire designed to measure perceived usability of a system. It comprises of the following two questions answered on a scale from 1 (strongly disagree) to 7 (strongly agree): "Q1. This system's capabilities meet my requirements" and "Q2. This system is easy to use". These questions are the two positively worded questions of UMUX. A UMUX-LITE score ranges from 0 to 100 and is calculated using Eq. 1, where Q1 and Q2 are the participant's answers in Question 1 and Question 2 respectively [20, 23].

$$UMUX\text{-}LITE = (Q1 + Q2 - 2) * (100/12) \tag{1}$$

In the initial paper that presented UMUX-LITE [20], the scale was found to have high reliability (alpha coefficient from 0.82 to 0.83) and validity (approximately 1% difference with SUS scores). Several other studies have replicated the psychometric properties of UMUX-LITE with alpha coefficients ranging between 0.65 and 0.86 [23–25], which is excellent for a two-items questionnaire, and correlations with the SUS ranging from 0.74 to 0.83 [23, 25]. Given their short form, good psychometric properties, and correspondence to SUS, both UMUX and UMUX-LITE are quickly emerging questionnaires for measuring perceived usability; the paper introducing UMUX-LITE [20] has already

223 citations in Google Scholar as of 07/01/2023, and the initial paper on UMUX [19] has 597 citations in Google Scholar as of 07/01/2023 compared to 144 on 9/12/2017 (as mentioned in [23]).

1.3 Research Motivation

It has been demonstrated that perceived usability questionnaires are affected by user's characteristics. Studies [26, 27] report a significant negative correlation between SUS score and age. By contrast, a more recent study [28] found that SUS scores and age are not significantly associated, while at the same time mentioning that the age distribution of the participants was not varied enough. Additional recent studies have found that SUS, UMUX and UMUX-LITE scores are not affected by age [29]. In addition, numerous studies [17, 27, 28, 30] have consistently shown that there is no effect of respondent's gender on SUS scores. Kortum and Oswald [31] found that SUS scores are affected by gender; females tended to have higher SUS scores, however this result was better explained by their personality traits. They state that SUS is affected by personality traits. Furthermore, previous experience with the evaluated system has been found to significantly increase both the obtained SUS scores [27, 28, 32, 33] and UMUX-LITE scores [25, 29].

However, there is little research on how the system's nature might affect the perceived usability measured. Bangor and colleagues [27] found that the system type (i.e., cell phones, customer equipment such as modems, GUIs, interactive voice response systems, and web pages/applications) significantly affects the obtained SUS scores. One other case of system type that remains rather unexplored is systems used to decide on issues that have a drastic effect on users' life activities, hereafter systems providing critical feedback. Examples of such systems are websites for loan application, automated diagnostic systems (e-health), and online examination systems.

This paper investigates whether there is any user bias towards the perceived usability of a system, when the system in question administers critical feedback. Critical feedback is commonly studied on systems that administer critical feedback for learning purposes to improve students' performance [34]. Our aim is to study the effect of critical feedback on perceived usability, when that is not administered with the objective of learning, rather as a final response. Our hypothesis is that if a system administers positive critical feedback to the user, then its perceived usability will be higher than the perceived usability for a user that received negative critical feedback.

2 Methodology

2.1 Evaluated System

The evaluated system is a web-based system that allows users to apply for a loan and receive a decision (critical feedback) on their application. This system is offered by Ferratum, a business unit within Multitude which is an international provider of digital financial services. Applying for a loan can be quite a complicated process, thus the company is highly interested to measure and improve its usability. The study reported in this paper is only one of the actions that the company takes in order to achieve this.

To apply for a loan, users go through a process of steps filling relevant information and uploading required documents. At the end of the process, the system approves or rejects the loan request based on a proprietary algorithm that calculates a risk score for each applicant. Each operating country is being served in the most commonly spoken languages, most of the time just the native language. Multitude is operating in multiple countries, but this study concerns the system available in three specific countries in Europe (exp1, exp2, exp3); countries are anonymized for privacy reasons as requested by the company. The systems between the countries are almost identical, except being served in different languages, and the existence or absence of some input fields due to local credit regulation.

2.2 Participants

A total of 332 participants from three countries were involved in the study. The participants were actual users of the web-based system who had just applied for a loan and received the systems' decision on their application. They were recruited by a message that asked them to evaluate the usability of the system.

From the 332 participants, 108 had their loan accepted (positive feedback) and 224 had their loan rejected (negative feedback). The participants in exp1 were 74 (positive feedback: 25 vs. negative feedback: 49), in exp2 they were 155 (43 vs. 112), and in exp3 they were 103 (40 vs. 63).

2.3 Instruments

UMUX-LITE was used to measure the perceived usability of the evaluated web-based system. Given that the questionnaire would be addressed to actual customers and administered through the live website, we chose a short questionnaire because it would have a higher likelihood of being answered voluntarily.

The study took place from August to September of 2022 and till that timepoint there were no validated translations of UMUX or UMUX-LITE in the languages used by each country's system. Thus, the English UMUX-LITE was translated by the native speakers responsible for company communications in each of the countries and was provided in the language used on the system serving each country.

2.4 Procedure

The evaluation study took place in the live website of each system for a period of two months. After each loan applicant finished the loan application procedure and received the critical feedback from the system (approved or rejected), they were shown the UMUX-LITE questionnaire that they could optionally complete in their native language. An introductory text informed participants that they participate on a voluntary basis, that their replies to the questionnaire are anonymous and that they would not affect the decision already communicated to them. For each participant, we collected the replies to the UMUX-LITE questionnaire and the system's critical feedback (positive or negative).

3 Results

We collected three datasets of UMUX-LITE scores, one per system used in each country of our participants.

An initial analysis was conducted to investigate whether a cross-country aggregated dataset of UMUX-LITE scores could be compiled. The assumption of normality was violated for all three countries; exp1: $W(74) = 0.892$, $p < 0.001$, exp2: $W(155) = 0.894$, $p < 0.001$, and exp3: $W(103) = 0.869$, $p < 0.001$ respectively. Thus, Kruskal-Wallis one-way ANOVA, a non-parametric test, was applied. Results found no significant differences among the UMUX-LITE scores for the systems used in the three countries; $H(2) = 0.854$, $p = 0.652$. Hence, a cross-country dataset can be compiled.

In the following, we report analyses both for the cross-country aggregated dataset and for each system (experiment) separately for completeness purposes. Table 1 presents descriptive statistics of the UMUX-LITE scores for each study dataset segmented by type of system critical feedback.

Table 1. Descriptive statistics of the UMUX-LITE scores for each study dataset segmented by type of system critical feedback.

Dataset	Critical feedback	Mean	Median	SD	95% C.I
Exp1	Negative	45.75	50.00	33.68	(36.07, 55.42)
Exp1	Positive	85.67	91.67	18.25	(78.14, 93.20)
Exp2	Negative	47.02	50.00	35.51	(40.37, 53.67)
Exp2	Positive	75.97	83.33	27.53	(67.50, 84.44)
Exp3	Negative	38.76	33.33	36.02	(26.69, 47.83)
Exp3	Positive	79.58	87.50	25.53	(71.42, 87.75)
Aggregated	Negative	44.42	50.00	35.29	(39.77, 49.07)
Aggregated	Positive	79.55	91.67	24.97	(74.79, 84.32)

3.1 Questionnaire Reliability Analysis

Reliability analysis on the cross-country dataset showed that the UMUX-LITE scale had high reliability; $\alpha = 0.828$, $N = 332$ respondents. Cronbach's alpha coefficients for all three experiments were also above the 0.70 threshold for adequate internal consistency [35]; exp1: $\alpha = 0.829$, $N = 74$, exp2: $\alpha = 0.774$, $N = 155$, and exp3: $\alpha = 0.904$, $N = 103$ respectively. These results align with previous research [23–25] on the good reliability of the UMUX-LITE scale.

3.2 Effect of System Critical Feedback on Perceived Usability

A two-tailed Mann-Whitney test found that the UMUX-LITE scores provided by participants who had received positive critical feedback by the system (M = 79.55, SD

= 24.97) were significantly higher compared to the ones provided by participants who had received negative critical feedback by the system (M = 44.42, SD = 35.29); z = 8.301, p < 0.001, r = 0.460. A non-parametric test was used because the assumption of normality was violated for both the negative and positive feedback groups; W(224) = 0.898, p < 0.001 and W(108) = 0.809, p < 0.001 respectively.

Figure 1 presents the mean UMUX-LITE scores per experiment segmented by critical feedback received by the participants. In all three cases, the assumption of normality was violated for at least one level of the independent variable, thus non-parametric tests were used; Shapiro-Wilk tests, p < 0.001. Two-tailed Mann-Whitney tests found a significant effect of system critical feedback on loan applicants' UMUX-LITE scores; exp1: z = 4.629, p < 0.001, r = 0.538, exp2: z = 4.524, p < 0.001, r = 0.363, and exp3: z = 5.323, p < 0.001, r = 0.524, respectively. Analytically for each experiment, the mean UMUX-LITE score of the participants who received positive critical feedback (i.e., had their loans approved) was rather high; exp1: M = 85.67, SD = 18.25, exp2: M = 75.97, SD = 27.53, and exp3: M = 79.58, SD = 25.53. By contrast, the participants in the negative feedback condition gave significantly lower UMUX-LITE scores; exp1: M = 45.75, SD = 33.68, exp2: M = 47.02, SD = 35.51, and exp3: M = 38.76, SD = 36.02.

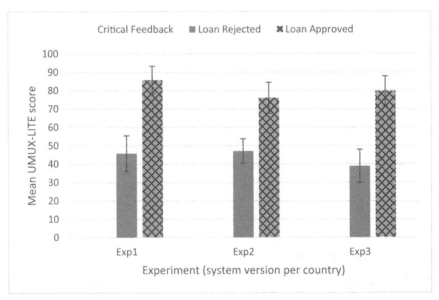

Fig. 1. The mean UMUX-LITE scores per experiment segmented by critical feedback received by the participants. Error bars represent the 95% confidence interval.

In sum, we consistently found that the participants who received negative critical feedback rated the perceived usability significantly lower than the participants who received positive critical feedback. In all the analyses, a medium to large effect size was observed [36], which demonstrates the magnitude of bias introduced to the participants' perceived usability ratings due to the critical feedback they had received.

3.3 System Critical Feedback and UMUX-LITE Questions

Our study participants interacted with the evaluated system to apply for a loan. Strictly speaking, this is the user task they had to perform. However, participants' overall goal was to get a loan. The latter goal was either met or not met based on the system decision which either approved (positive feedback) or rejected (negative feedback) their loan application.

UMUX-LITE is constructing a single usability score from the replies to two questions: "Q1. This system's capabilities meet my requirements" and "Q2. This system is easy to use". Although UMUX-LITE is a unidimensional measure of perceived usability, users who received negative critical feedback could interpret the first question as that the system didn't have enough capabilities to meet their requirements, that is getting a loan. At the same time, ease-of-use which is measured directly by the second item shouldn't be affected by the system's critical feedback. Thus, the observed differences in UMUX-LITE scores could be affected by lower scores in the first question only, which in turn might raise concerns for using this scale in our study and for systems providing critical feedback in general.

We conducted hypothesis testing on the cross-country aggregated dataset to investigate whether the type of system critical feedback (positive, negative) had a significant effect on the ratings of each UMUX-LITE question. The assumption of normality was violated for at least one level of the independent variable for both UMUX-LITE questions, thus non-parametric tests were used; Shapiro-Wilk tests, $p < 0.001$. Two-tailed Mann-Whitney tests found a significant effect of system critical feedback on participants ratings for both UMUX-LITE questions; Q1: $z = 8.073$, $p < 0.001$, $r = 0.443$, and Q2: $z = 6.756$, $p < 0.001$, $r = 0.371$ respectively. Study participants who had their loans rejected provided significantly lower ratings for both questions (Q1: $M = 3.33$, $SD = 2.33$, Q2: $M = 4.00$, $SD = 2.37$) compared to users who had their loans approved (Q1: $M = 5.67$, $SD = 1.78$, Q2: 5.88, $SD = 1.40$).

The same pattern was observed after analysing each of the three datasets separately (see Fig. 2 and Fig. 3). Again, the assumption of normality was violated in all cases and thus non-parametric tests were used; Shapiro-Wilk tests, $p < 0.001$. Two-tailed Mann-Whitney tests found a significant effect of system critical feedback on loan applicants' ratings for UMUX-LITE Q1; exp1: $z = 4.663$, $p < 0.001$, $r = 0.542$, exp2: $z = 4.532$, $p < 0.001$, $r = 0.364$, and exp3: $z = 4.798$, $p < 0.001$, $r = 0.473$, respectively. Participants' ratings for UMUX-LITE Q2 were also significantly affected by the system critical feedback; exp1: $z = 3.680$, $p < 0.001$, $r = 0.428$, exp2: $z = 3.337$, $p < 0.001$, $r = 0.268$, and exp3: $z = 5.185$, $p < 0.001$, $r = 0.511$, respectively.

In sum, we consistently found that participants' ratings in both UMUX-LITE questions were significantly lower for participants in the negative feedback condition compared to ones in the positive feedback condition.

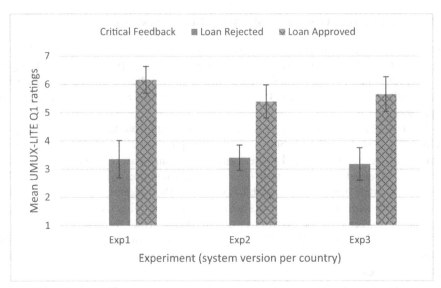

Fig. 2. The mean ratings for UMUX-LITE Q1 ("This system's capabilities meet my requirements") per experiment segmented by critical feedback received by the participants. Error bars represent the 95% confidence interval.

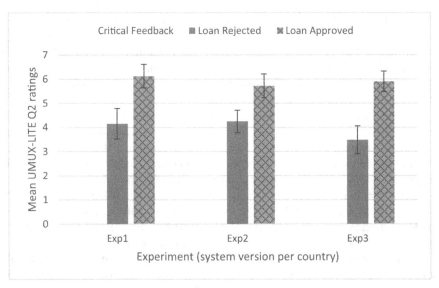

Fig. 3. The mean ratings for UMUX-LITE Q2 ("This system is easy to use") per experiment segmented by critical feedback received by the participants. Error bars represent the 95% confidence interval.

4 Discussion

4.1 Why is Perceived Usability Affected by System Critical Feedback?

Subjective over Objective Effort. We can define "objective effort" as the observed user effort, measured by objective, deterministic metrics like time-to-complete-task, number-of-errors, etc. By contrast, "subjective effort" is the mental effort required to complete the task as perceived by the user. Subjective effort doesn't always correlate with objective effort. For example, it has been found that uncertain choices are significantly more subjectively effortful than random [37].

A possible explanation of the observed difference in perceived usability ratings might be that users tend to assess usability compared to final outcome. In our study, the objective effort required to get to the end of the loan application process was the same regardless of the critical feedback received. However, the subjective effort of the users might be different due to the final outcome (i.e., loan application approved or rejected). For users who received positive feedback, the subjective effort could be characterized as low, given that they received a loan for their effort. For users who received negative feedback, the subjective effort could be characterized as high since they didn't receive a loan regardless of their effort. That differentiation in perceived effort could have driven the differentiation of the perceived usability scores we observed in our study results.

In Sect. 3.3, we presented an analysis focusing on each separate UMUX-LITE question, which might be viewed as a first attempt to explore this differentiation in perceived usability scores. However, this perspective assumes that the first question of UMUX-LITE reliably captures only the subjective effort, whereas the second question measures only the objective effort, both of which are assumptions that we cannot support by referring to the literature or our own data analysis.

Complementary Explanations. Based on the data presented in Table 1, one can observe that the variance of scores tends to be higher for users who received negative critical feedback compared to the ones who received positive critical feedback.

That could be an indication that users who received positive critical feedback evaluated the system from a rather utilitarian point of view (i.e., "I needed to do these actions to receive the loan, and for that reason I evaluate the usability as x"), thus relying more on the system functionality for their perceived usability rating, which might also explain the lower variance of the values. By contrast, users who received negative critical feedback might have relied more on their expectation of the minimum objective effort to receive negative feedback and/or their ratings might have been hedonically driven by their disappointment for having their loan rejected, thus making their evaluations more varied.

In any case, sentiment could play a particularly important role in usability ratings of systems providing critical feedback. Users who get positive critical feedback might tend to have more positive view of the system; users who get negative critical feedback might tend to have more negative view of the system.

4.2   Issues to Consider When Measuring Perceived Usability of Systems Providing Critical Feedback

When to Collect Perceived Usability Ratings?   One might argue that perceived usability of systems providing critical feedback should be measured before users receive any type of feedback (positive or negative). This would certainly nullify the effect of system critical feedback on users' perceived usability ratings. However, this excludes from the evaluation the UI part that communicates the decision to the user and any task(s) that might rely on the user knowing the system feedback (e.g., issue the loan online after the loan application has been approved).

In addition, measuring perceived usability before users receive any critical feedback might be particularly challenging to achieve in some cases due to practical constraints (e.g., unmoderated remote user testing and the questionnaire can be made available only through a separate URL/screen after interacting with the evaluated system). At the same time, measuring perceived usability pre-admission of the critical feedback is adding unnecessary delay towards achieving the user's goal (e.g., get the loan). The user is asked to answer a usability questionnaire before getting the outcome, which potentially increases the risk of skipping the questionnaire completion or answering the questions without paying the required attention to do so.

Should We Split Perceived Usability Ratings by Feedback Type?   It could be argued that splitting participants' ratings by feedback type (positive, negative) would provide a cleaner measure of perceived usability. However, this might not always be practical (e.g., too few users in one of the feedback types), and we would still be missing a single score that reflects the overall perceived usability of the system. To this end, the perceived usability scores per feedback type group could be first calculated and then they could be combined in a (weighted) average. Finding what weights to use, if any, could be the objective of future research.

5   Conclusion and Future Work

Questionnaires, such as SUS, UMUX and UMUX-LITE, are typically used to measure perceived usability in HCI practice. Previous research has explored how ratings in usability questionnaires are affected by user characteristics, such as gender, age, personality traits and previous experience with the evaluated system. However, there has been little investigation into how the nature of the system may impact the assessed perceived usability.

This paper explores whether there is any user bias towards the perceived usability of a system, when the system in question administers critical feedback, not administered with the objective of learning, rather as a final response. To this end, we gathered perceived usability data from three, almost identical, web-based systems used to apply for a consumer loan and communicate the decision to the applicant. The dataset involves a total of 332 applicants, 108 with approved loans and 224 with rejected loans, who had also answered the UMUX-LITE after receiving the system decision for their loan. Results showed a significant effect of system critical feedback on loan applicants' UMUX-LITE scores. Participants who received positive system feedback provided significantly and largely higher UMUX-LITE scores compared to participants who received negative system feedback.

One possible limitation of the presented research is that it adopts a between-subjects research design: one group of participants received the positive system feedback and another one received the negative system feedback. This means that individual user characteristics might have affected the findings. Future research could employ a one-group pretest-posttest research design by asking from the same group of participants to provide perceived usability ratings both before and after being exposed to the system critical feedback.

Additional research with systems providing critical feedback in other domains is also needed to confirm that our findings are generalizable. In case this study's results are reproducible in other domains, it is worth investigating how to systematically analyse perceived usability ratings for such systems in order to calculate the overall "real" perceived usability. Furthermore, we know from our previous research that user-reported emotional ratings (e.g., valence-arousal ratings) are also affected by user characteristics [38, 39]. Our future work also involves investigating the effect of system critical feedback on user-reported emotional ratings.

For the time being, we advise usability researchers and professionals to pay attention when measuring critical feedback administering systems as users' perceived usability tends to be significantly biased from the critical feedback they received. We encourage anyone who is evaluating such systems to segment the perceived usability data by feedback type to further investigate the possible bias.

Acknowledgments. We thank Multitude for allowing us to use the collected usability data for our research purposes in this paper. We also thank the anonymous participants that volunteered to assess the perceived usability of the evaluated system and thus made this research possible.

References

1. Hertzum, M.: Images of usability. Int. J. Hum.-Comput. Interact. **26**, 567–600 (2010). https://doi.org/10.1080/10447311003781300
2. Brooke, J.: SUS: a "quick and dirty" usability scale. In: Jordan, P.W., Thomas, B., Weerdmeester, B.A., McClelland, A.L. (eds.) Usability Evaluation in Industry. Taylor and Francis, London (1996)
3. Lewis, J.R.: IBM computer usability satisfaction questionnaires: psychometric evaluation and instructions for use. Int. J. Hum.-Comput. Interact. **7**, 57–78 (1995). https://doi.org/10.1080/10447319509526110
4. Lund, A.M.: Measuring usability with the USE questionnaire. Usabil. Interface **8**, 3–6 (2001)
5. Lin, H.X., Choong, Y.-Y., Salvendy, G.: A proposed index of usability: a method for comparing the relative usability of different software systems. Behav. Inf. Technol. **16**, 267–277 (1997). https://doi.org/10.1080/014492997119833
6. Chin, J.P., Diehl, V.A., Norman, K.L.: Development of an instrument measuring user satisfaction of the human-computer interface. In: Proceedings of the SIGCHI Conference on Human Factors in Computing Systems, pp. 213–218. ACM, New York (1988). https://doi.org/10.1145/57167.57203

7. Katsanos, C., Tselios, N., Xenos, M.: Perceived usability evaluation of learning management systems: a first step towards standardization of the system usability scale in Greek.
In: Proceedings of the16th Panhellenic Conference on Informatics (PCI 2012), pp. 302–307
(2012)

8. Blažica, B., Lewis, J.R.: A Slovene translation of the system usability scale: the SUS-SI.
Int. J. Hum.-Comput. Interact. **31**, 112–117 (2015). https://doi.org/10.1080/10447318.2014.
986634

9. Borkowska, A., Jach, K.: Pre-testing of Polish translation of system usability scale (SUS). In:
Borzemski, L., Grzech, A., Świątek, J., Wilimowska, Z. (eds.) Information Systems Architec-
ture and Technology: Proceedings of 37th International Conference on Information Systems
Architecture and Technology—ISAT 2016—Part I. AISC, vol. 521, pp. 143–153. Springer,
Cham (2017). https://doi.org/10.1007/978-3-319-46583-8_12

10. Taheri, F.,Kavusi, A., Faghihnia Torshozi, Y., Farshad, A.A., Saremi, M.: Assessment of
validity and reliability of Persian version of system usability scale (SUS) for traffic signs.
Iran Occup. Health **14**, 12–22 (2017)

11. Wang, Y., Lei, T., Liu, X.: Chinese system usability scale: translation, revision, psychological
measurement. Int. J. Hum.-Comput. Interact. **36**, 953–963 (2020). https://doi.org/10.1080/
10447318.2019.1700644

12. Gao, M., Kortum, P., Oswald, F.L.: Multi-language toolkit for the system usability scale. Int. J.
Hum.-Comput. Interact. **36**, 1883–1901 (2020). https://doi.org/10.1080/10447318.2020.180
1173

13. Hvidt, J.C.S., Christensen, L.F., Sibbersen, C., Helweg-Jørgensen, S., Hansen, J.P., Lichten-
stein, M.B.: Translation and validation of the system usability scale in a Danish mental health
setting using digital technologies in treatment interventions. Int. J. Hum.-Comput. Interact.
36, 709–716 (2020). https://doi.org/10.1080/10447318.2019.1680922

14. Katsanos, C., Tselios, N., Liapis, A.: PSSUQ-GR: a first step towards standardization of the
post-study system usability questionnaire in Greek. In: CHI Greece 2021: 1st International
Conference of the ACM Greek SIGCHI Chapter, pp. Article23:1–Article23:6. ACM, New
York (2021)

15. Erdinç, O., Lewis, J.R.: Psychometric evaluation of the T-CSUQ: the Turkish version of the
computer system usability questionnaire. Int. J. Hum.-Comput. Interact. **29**, 319–326 (2013).
https://doi.org/10.1080/10447318.2012.711702

16. Al-Hassan, A.A., AlGhannam, B., Naser, M.B., Alabdulrazzaq, H.: An Arabic translation
of the computer system usability questionnaire (CSUQ) with psychometric evaluation using
Kuwait university portal. Int. J. Hum.–Comput. Interact, pp. 1–8 (2021). https://doi.org/10.
1080/10447318.2021.1926117

17. Lewis, J.R.: The system usability scale: past, present, and future. Int. J. Hum.-Comput.
Interact. **34**, 577–590 (2018). https://doi.org/10.1080/10447318.2018.1455307

18. Tullis, T., Stetson, J.: A comparison of questionnaires for assessing website usability. In:
usability professionals association (UPA). In: 2004 Conference, pp. 7–11 (2004)

19. Finstad, K.: The usability metric for user experience. Interact. Comput. **22**, 323–327 (2010).
https://doi.org/10.1016/j.intcom.2010.04.004

20. Lewis, J.R., Utesch, B.S., Maher, D.E.: UMUX-LITE: when there's no time for the SUS. In:
Proceedings of the SIGCHI Conference on Human Factors in Computing Systems, pp. 2099–
2102 (2013)

21. Lewis, J.R.: Psychometric evaluation of an after-scenario questionnaire for computer usability
studies: the ASQ. SIGCHI Bull. **23**, 78–81 (1991). https://doi.org/10.1145/122672.122692

22. Sauro, J., Dumas, J.S.: Comparison of three one-question, post-task usability questionnaires.
In: Proceedings of the SIGCHI Conference on Human Factors in Computing Systems, pp.
pp. 1599–1608. ACM, New York (2009). https://doi.org/10.1145/1518701.1518946

23. Lewis, J.R.: Measuring perceived usability: the CSUQ, SUS, and UMUX. Int. J. Hum.-Comput. Interact. **34**, 1148–1156 (2018). https://doi.org/10.1080/10447318.2017.1418805
24. Borsci, S., Buckle, P., Walne, S.: Is the LITE version of the usability metric for user experience (UMUX-LITE) a reliable tool to support rapid assessment of new healthcare technology? Appl. Ergon. **84**, 103007 (2020). https://doi.org/10.1016/j.apergo.2019.103007
25. Lewis, J.R., Utesch, B.S., Maher, D.E.: Investigating the correspondence between UMUX-LITE and SUS scores. In: Marcus, A. (ed.) DUXU 2015. LNCS, vol. 9186, pp. 204–211. Springer, Cham (2015). https://doi.org/10.1007/978-3-319-20886-2_20
26. Granic, A., Cukusic, M.: Usability testing and expert inspections complemented by educational evaluation: a case study of an e-Learning platform. Educ. Technol. Soc. **14**, 107–123 (2011)
27. Bangor, A., Kortum, P., Miller, J.: An empirical evaluation of the system usability scale. Int. J. Hum.-Comput. Interact. **24**, 574–594 (2008). https://doi.org/10.1080/10447310802205776
28. Orfanou, K., Tselios, N., Katsanos, C.: Perceived usability evaluation of learning management systems: empirical evaluation of the system usability scale. Int. Rev. Res. Open Distrib. Learn. **16**, 227–246 (2015)
29. Berkman, M.I., Karahoca, D.: Re-assessing the usability metric for user experience (UMUX) scale. J. Usabil. Stud. **11**, 89–109 (2016)
30. Kortum, P., Bangor, A.: Usability ratings for everyday products measured with the system usability scale. Int. J. Hum.-Comput. Interact. **29**, 67–76 (2013). https://doi.org/10.1080/10447318.2012.681221
31. Kortum, P., Oswald, F.L.: The impact of personality on the subjective assessment of usability. Int. J. Hum.-Comput. Interact. **34**, 177–186 (2018). https://doi.org/10.1080/10447318.2017.1336317
32. Sauro, J.: Does prior experience affect perceptions of usability?. https://measuringu.com/prior-exposure. Accessed 30 Jan 2023
33. McLellan, S., Muddimer, A., Peres, S.C.: The effect of experience on system usability scale ratings. J. Usabil. Stud. **7**, 56–67 (2012)
34. Cutumisu, M., Schwartz, D.L.: The impact of critical feedback choice on students' revision, performance, learning, and memory. Comput. Hum. Behav. **78**, 351–367 (2018)
35. Nunnally, J., Bernstein, I.: Psychometric Theory. McGraw-Hill Humanities/Social Sciences/Languages (1994)
36. Cohen, J.: A power primer. Psychol. Bull. **112**, 155–159 (1992)
37. Robinson, M.M., Morsella, E.: The subjective effort of everyday mental tasks: attending, assessing, and choosing. Motiv. Emot. **38**(6), 832–843 (2014). https://doi.org/10.1007/s11031-014-9441-2
38. Liapis, A., Katsanos, C., Xenos, M., Orphanoudakis, T.: Effect of personality traits on UX evaluation metrics: a study on usability issues, valence-arousal and skin conductance. In: Extended Abstracts of the 2019 CHI Conference on Human Factors in Computing Systems, pp. LBW2721:1–LBW2721:6. ACM, New York (2019). https://doi.org/10.1145/3290607.3312995
39. Liapis, A., Katsanos, C., Sotiropoulos, D., Xenos, M., Karousos, N.: Stress recognition in human-computer interaction using physiological and self-reported data: a study of gender differences. In: Proceedings of the 19th Panhellenic Conference on Informatics, pp. 323–328. ACM, New York (2015). https://doi.org/10.1145/2801948.2801964

Research on the Influence of Automotive Instrumentation HMI Design on Driving Behavior

Fanmin Meng[✉], Zhixin Wu, and Zihao Jia

Nanjing University of Science and Technology, Nanjing 210094, China
mengfanmin@njust.edu.cn

Abstract. Instrument HMI is an interface directly related to driving behavior, and the interaction experience between humans and instrument HMI directly affects the safety and comfort of driving activities. Nowadays, there are various types of automotive instrumentation HMI designs with complex interface elements and numerous display data. Different design styles of HMI information display priorities will inevitably have an impact on the interaction experience of actual driving activities. This study aims to investigate the interface design factors affecting driving behavior in automotive instrumentation HMI, and design experiments based on these factors to explore the most suitable interface design guidelines for driver cognition. In this paper, a comparison experiment with controlled variables was used to randomly ask questions to the driver during the driving simulation, and the time required for the driver to answer the questions reflected the degree of influence of different HMI designs on driving behaviors. This is a quantitative analysis to investigate the impact of HMI on driving behavior. The final conclusions are provided for the two main components of HMI, namely, resident display information and temporary display information.

Keywords: Human-computer interaction · HMI design · Driving behavior

1 Introduction

1.1 Automotive Instrumentation HMI Concept

HMI (Human Machine Interface), also translated as "human-machine interface", is an important medium for information exchange and interaction between the vehicle system and the driver. Compared with the general car interior design, HMI is more focused on the experience and feeling of human interaction with the car interface. Automotive instrumentation HMI plays an important role in different aspects such as safety, reliability, user communication and technology. The instrumentation HMI is also used to operate switches in the vehicle, such as the instrument panel, audio and video devices, which are distributed within the vehicle and communicate with each other, and the instrumentation HMI is a key way to achieve communication (Praveen Padagannavar 2016). With the deepening penetration of information technology, digitalization, and networking into the automotive industry, the rapid development of smartphone technology, mobile computing, and GSM mobile communications that support connected vehicles has contributed to the rapid development of in-vehicle information systems (IVIS) (Birrell et al. 2014). Intelligent human-computer interaction systems have become standard in new vehicles. The automotive instrumentation HMI is the component that a person touches most frequently as far as the eye can see when driving a car. The development of automotive instrumentation has experienced up to now, evolving from the traditional mechanical pointer type to the current full LCD screen type. The space of instrument design has made a qualitative leap. Instrument HMI is the key element in the whole automotive HMI system and plays a vital role in driving activities. Instrument HMI establishes the bridge between the driver and the car, and the interaction between human and car related to driving activities mainly occurs through the instrument HMI. Especially in today's booming autonomous driving technology, HMI has a more important significance as it covers all the interfaces inside the vehicle and enables passengers to interact with the DAS (Driving Automation System). As the level of automation increases, the scope of the automated system expands and the role of the passenger changes. Therefore, the HMI must transparently communicate the system status of the automation to the passenger to ensure that the driver can clearly and intuitively perceive the automation mode and switch between automation modes safely, efficiently and comfortably. (Bengler, et al. 2020).

1.2   The Impact of Automotive HMI on Driving Behavior

Driving Distractions. Distraction is the shifting of attention from the driving task to a concurrent activity; distraction may or may not be related to driving, and events, objects, or people inside or outside the vehicle may cause driving distraction (Chapon et al. 2006). The HMI is the second most important point of gaze during driving activities after the road area ahead and is a major contributor to visual distraction. A National Highway Traffic Safety Administration (NHTSA) naturalistic driving study of 100 vehicles showed that 78% of crashes involved some degree of driver inattention and that more than 22% of crashes and near-crashes were caused by driver distraction from secondary tasks (Cauffman et al. 2022). Distractions are important for automotive HMI design research, and many interface design factors can reduce the impact of distractions, such as text, graphics, and color of the HMI interface. 17.5 mm (Kim et al. 2014).

Cognitive Load. Cognitive load refers to the mental load caused by the demands of complex tasks (Chalmers 2003). As the operation of machine interfaces has become more complex, the stress of human-HMI interaction has shifted from physical stress to cognitive workload (Naveen Kumar and Jyoti Kumar 2016). In-vehicle information systems have the potential to greatly enhance mobility and comfort (e.g., navigation aids and traffic information systems, media players, web browsers, etc.), but at the same time increase the risk of excessive and dangerous neglect of vehicle control tasks (Amditis et al. 2010). According to currently available research, some existing HMIs in autonomous vehicles do not provide accurate feedback to the driver, and according to previous research, no matter which design of instrumentation HMI is used, there is more or less mode confusion (inability to accurately feedback the current autonomous driving mode to the driver) in real driving situations (Noé Monsaingeon et al. 2021) In real-life situations, mode confusion can cause drivers to misjudge the current autopilot status of the car, which can lead to wrong driving decisions and eventually cause serious traffic accidents.

Research Significance. Despite the important influence of automotive instrumentation HMI on driving behavior, there is still a lack of clear understanding of the impact of CV (connected vehicle) HMIs on driver recognition and response. A well-designed HMI has the potential to provide active decision support to the driver, thus reducing the likelihood of traffic accidents (Gaweesh and Yang 2019). Therefore, it is important to study the design of HMI interface in order to improve the cognitive efficiency and reduce the cognitive load of the driver for HMI, which in turn increases the speed of the driver in capturing the required information from HMI and effectively reduces the time the driver takes his eyes off the front and improves driving safety.

In addition, Driver Behavior Analysis (DBA) has the potential to improve driver performance, road and traffic safety, fuel management, and the design of efficient intelligent transportation systems. One of the key entry points for driving behavior analysis (Azadani and Boukerche 2021).

1.3   Automotive Instrumentation HMI Element Analysis

Classification of instrumentation HMI

Fig. 1. HMI Classification: Vehicle-centric HMI (left); Driver-centric HMI (right)

Based on Noé Monsaingeon et al.'s interface analysis and research on instrumentation HMI, the interface can be mainly divided into two categories according to the priority of the information displayed: driving-centric HMI, vehicle-centric HMI (Fig. 1).

Vehicle-Centered HMI. Evolved from the classic instrument manipulation interface, the interface design focuses on displaying driving data related to the vehicle itself such as speed and RPM, retaining the classic dashboard design and making it more intuitive to grasp speed changes.

Driver-Centered HMI. Focusing more on comfortable driving experience, the speed dashboard is removed, and the form data is expressed by numbers, and the HMI will focus on displaying the current vehicle driving status in 3D simulation, which mostly appears in self-driving cars.

Analysis of the Functional Composition of the Instrument HMI. Through extensive analysis of existing instrumentation HMI, it is found that the functions of instrumentation HMI mainly focus on: 1. Docking the car and the driver, reporting the current driving status of the car to the driver (speed, RPM); 2. Displaying the car itself and internal data information (fuel level, air conditioning); 3. Displaying real-time navigation and mileage statistics; 4. Displaying alert messages (safety alerts, automatic driving); 5. Part HMI will display the information received by the driver's cell phone (phone call, SMS), etc. through wireless connection (Table 1).

Table 1. Instrument HMI function composition

Instrument HMI functional composition
1. Indicator light is displayed along the top to provide status information
2. When you actively navigate to a destination, the navigation indicator displays the real-time location and distance from the destination
3. Body state 3D effect display, such as door opening. Headlights, etc
4. Gear state display, the current selected gear: parking gear, reverse gear, neutral gear or forward gear
5. Range and energy recovery state display
6. Driving speed
7. Energy usage state display, including energy consumption, speed, power and other related display
8. Total mileage and subtotal mileage display
9. Real-time time, date and temperature display

Analysis of the Interface Information Composition of the Instrument HMI

Table 2. Instrument HMI information composition

Permanent display information	Temporary display Information
Speed of car	Alarm warning light
Speed of rotation (Fuel oil vehicle)	Lane departure
Water temperature	Vehicle distance warning
time	Autopilot mode
temperature	
Oil volume	

Instrument HMI interface information components according to the display time and display logic can be divided into: resident display information and temporary display time information. The permanent display information mainly includes speed, speed (oil and natural car), water temperature, fuel, time, temperature; temporary display information: alarm indicator, basic vehicle information, menu, active safety information (lane departure, distance ahead, left and right incoming traffic, etc.); temporary display information is also divided into: active information and passive information. Active information: can be understood as a reminder of the alarm information requires the driver to take the initiative to operate, prompt the interface to disappear; passive information: no driver to operate, it automatically disappears after a few seconds (can be set) (Table 2).

1.4 Research Objectives

Instrument HMI design is closely related to driving activities and some studies have shown that HMI interface design can be effective in reducing distractions in driving behavior and thus improving safety, for example, Reimer et al. emphasize that the font design in the automotive user interface affects task completion time and visual demands while driving. (Reimer et al. 2014). However, the sources of interface design interference with driving behavior are complex. The purpose of this paper is to investigate the main factors affecting driver cognitive efficiency in a fixed basic HMI interface design, starting from the visual aspect of the instrument HMI, identifying variables, designing experiments, comparing the efficiency of driver-HMI interaction under different variables, and exploring the degree of influence of different HMI designs on the efficiency of driver information acquisition, and finally determining To determine a relatively suitable HMI interface design standard for driving activities.

2 Experimental Design

2.1 Variable Determination

According to the basic components of automotive instrumentation HMI, the best design forms of resident display information and temporary display information are to be studied separately. In the following, the most representative influence factor will be searched for according to its information reality characteristics and realistic content respectively, combined with the realistic driving environment, and the design scale that is most suitable for the driver to obtain information under the influence of this independent variable will be studied.

Permanent Display Information. The speed display is the most basic and important display information of the instrument HMI. Currently, there are two main types of speed display designs: the classic instrument-based speed display form of vehicle-centered HMI, and the sub-centered digital speed display form of driving-centered HMI. Therefore, in this experiment, the research variable for the resident display information is: speed display form (Fig. 2).

Fig. 2. Different forms of speed display

Temporary Display of Information. The study of temporary display information is intended to take automatic driving tips, speeding tips and other driving event tips as an example. The current display graphics and text forms for temporary display information tend to be homogeneous, so this study intends to start with the temporary display information display position and study the efficiency of drivers to capture information in different display positions (Fig. 3).

Fig. 3. Different temporary message display positions

Variable Summarization. In summary, this experiment consists of two parts. In the first phase of the experiment, the effect of the speed display format on the efficiency of the driver in capturing speed information will be investigated; in the second phase of the experiment, the effect of the driver on the efficiency of capturing temporary display information for different position displays will be investigated (Fig. 4).

2.2 Experimental Ideas

The research objectives of this paper are to investigate the effects of different speed display types on the efficiency of speed information acquisition, and the effects of different display positions of cue information on the efficiency of cue information acquisition. Take speed information as an example, the driver's efficiency of capturing speed information in the instrument can be measured by time. In summary, the driver's efficiency in capturing speed in the HMI can be shown by the response time required to answer speed questions when driving simulations are performed with the HMI (Fig. 5).

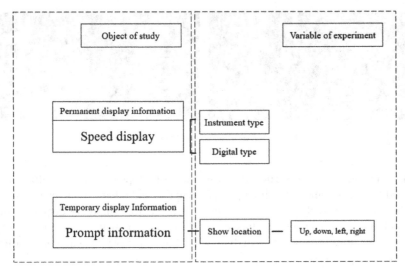

Fig. 4. Experimental subjects and variable settings are summarized

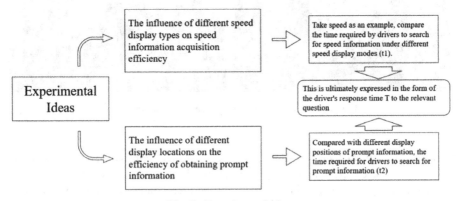

Fig. 5. Experimental ideas

2.3 Experimental Environment

The study proposes to use a combination of screens, simulating a real driving environment, to reflect the efficiency of the driver's interaction with the HMI by measuring the response time (time spent searching for information from the interface) when the driver answers questions; Screen B is a highly simulated driving game (Figs. 6 and 7).

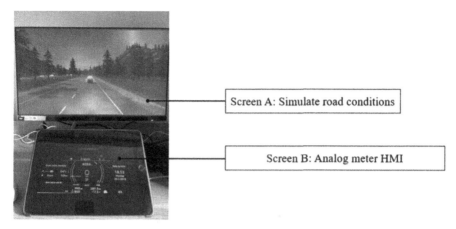

Fig. 6. Experimental environment

Fig. 7. Driving simulation game

2.4 Experimental Procedure

First of all, 8–10 subjects were recruited, requiring a uniform gender and roughly the same age. At the beginning of the experiment, the rules of the test were first unified, and in the test, the subjects manipulated the simulated driving game vehicle, requiring: minimizing collisions and collecting as many gold coins as possible; the test will be conducted one by one. First subjects will have six minutes to familiarize themselves with the simulation driving game, then the first phase of the experiment begins, the staff will ask the driver questions about speed at a random moment, requiring the driver to quickly scan the HMI and answer questions while taking into account the driving, each speed display form the HMI will ask questions twice; after the questions are finished informing the subjects to enter the second test phase and start the temporary display information test, this When the instrument HMI will appear special information on a random position, the device will ring when the information appears, requiring the subject to quickly check and report the information content after hearing the ringing prompt, a total of four positions, each position to ask questions twice; after the end of the questions to inform the subject of the end of the test, how to interview their driving feelings and evaluation; the whole process of the experiment video (Fig. 8).

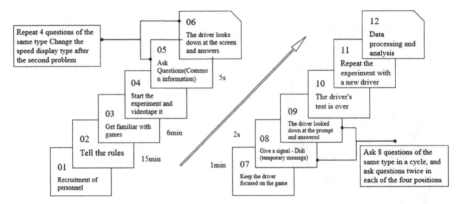

Fig. 8. Experimental steps

2.5   Data Extraction

The efficiency of the driver in capturing information in this HMI can be shown by the response time required to answer relevant questions when driving simulations are performed with this HMI. Therefore, in this experiment, it is necessary to extract the thinking time of the driver in answering questions, and the data is extracted by using the recording extraction method, where the test video is imported into Premiere and the subject's thinking time is extracted by the waveform of the audio track (Fig. 9).

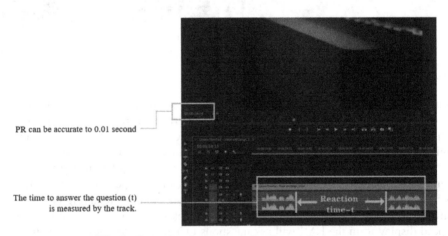

Fig. 9. Extracting time information through Premiere

2.6   Data Processing Methods

The specific data processing method should be based on the actual situation of the data. After the data are collected and imported into SPSS software, we will first verify the significance of the effect of the experimental variables on the experimental results to prove the research significance of this experiment, and then analyze the data visualization of the two groups of data separately and draw experimental conclusions.

We will first analyze the data for normality, and then choose the next test method according to the results of the normality analysis. If the data conform to normal distribution, we will first use ANOVA or T-test to prove the correlation, and then transform the data into box plots to more intuitively compare the information capture efficiency of drivers under different variables; if the data are non-normally distributed, we will first use Mann-Whitney If the data were not normally distributed, the correlation was first proved by Mann-Whitney test or Kolmogorov-Smirnov test, and then the data were also transformed into box plots for comparative analysis. By observing the morphology of the box line plot and the data, we can visually reflect the central location and scattering range of the continuous quantitative data distribution, so as to grasp the overall characteristics of the data set and draw experimental conclusions.

3   Participants

Fig. 10. Experimental records

A total of 8 subjects (all male) were recruited for this experiment, they held a driver's license for 2 years on average, they had no visual or auditory impairment, they were all master students from Nanjing University of Science and Technology, they were familiar with and mastered the rules of the experiment, the average test duration was 26 min, and the whole experiment was videotaped (Fig. 10).

4 Data Analysis and Processing

4.1 Data Logging

A total of eight subjects were recruited and each subject participated in the research test for both the resident display information and the temporary display information, where one variable and two variable factors were present in the research test experiment for the resident display information, and each variable factor was tested twice in the experiment, yielding a total of four data; in the research test experiment for the temporary display information, one variable and four variable factors, with two tests for each variable factor in the experiment, yielding a total of eight data. Therefore, for each subject, there were two tests for each single factor, yielding a total of 12 data, and at the end of the experiment time data were intercepted from the video one by one and entered into SPSS data analysis software (Fig. 11).

Fig. 11. Data logging

4.2 Permanent Display Information Data Processing and Analysis

Data Normality Analysis. In order to verify whether the test data are correlated with the test variables, the data were first analyzed for normality, and the data were tested to be significant less than 0.01 and P < 0.05, so the data were non-normally distributed, and parametric tests could not be used for the processing of resident display information (Fig. 12).

正态性检验

		柯尔莫戈洛夫-斯米诺夫[a]			夏皮洛-威尔克		
	组别3	统计	自由度	显著性	统计	自由度	显著性
时间	车辆为中心的HMI	.338	16	<.001	.733	16	<.001
	驾驶为中心的HMI	.406	16	<.001	.641	16	<.001

a. 里利氏显著性修正

Fig. 12. Data normality analysis

Correlation Test of Data Variables. Using the Mann-Whitney test, significance < 0.01 and P < 0.05 was found, so the distribution of the data for the two groups of variables was not correlated, indirectly proving the correlation between the variable factors and the data results (Fig. 13).

假设检验摘要

	原假设	检验	显著性[a,b]	决策
1	在组别3的类别中，时间的分布相同。	独立样本曼-惠特尼 U 检验	<.001[c]	拒绝原假设。

a. 显著性水平为 .050。

b. 显示了渐进显著性。

c. 对于此检验，显示了精确显著性。

Fig. 13. Mann-Whitney test

Box Line Chart Analysis. Box line plots were generated after data entry using SPSS, and the box line plots were used to visually analyze the differences in speed data capture speed for different speed display formats (Fig. 14).

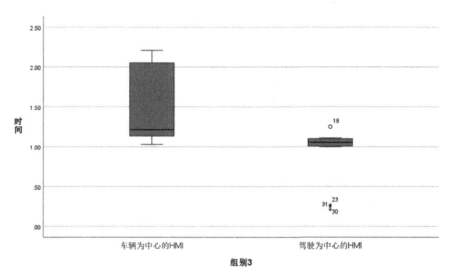

Fig. 14. Box line chart analysis

The graphical observations revealed that.

(1) The vehicle-centered HMI data fluctuated the most. Participants spent different amounts of time performing meter readings, resulting in high data fluctuations, presumably due to differences in driving experience, with participants with longer driving experience reading meters faster than those with less or no driving experience.
(2) Driver-centered HMI data were the most stable and generally lower. (b) A sub-centric data-based speed display captures speed information faster than a traditional gauge-based speed display.

4.3   Temporary Display Information Data Processing and Analysis

Data Normality Analysis. In order to verify whether the test data are correlated with the test variables, the data were first analyzed for normality, and after testing, the data significance were all less than 0.01 and $P < 0.05$, so the data were non-normally distributed, and parametric tests could not be used for the processing of temporary display information (Fig. 15).

正态性检验

| | 组别2 | 柯尔莫戈洛夫-斯米诺夫[a] | | | 夏皮洛-威尔克 | | |
		统计	自由度	显著性	统计	自由度	显著性
时长2	下	.372	16	<.001	.663	16	<.001
	左	.316	16	<.001	.707	16	<.001
	上	.377	16	<.001	.620	16	<.001
	右	.413	16	<.001	.535	16	<.001

a. 里利氏显著性修正

Fig. 15. Data normality analysis

Correlation Test of Data Variables. The Kolmogorov-Smirnov test was used and the significance was found to be 0.306, $p < 0.05$, so the distribution of the data for the two groups of variables was not correlated, indirectly proving the correlation between the variable factors and the data results (Fig. 16).

➡ 非参数检验

假设检验摘要

	原假设	检验	显著性[a,b]	决策
1	在 组别2 的类别中，时长2 的分布相同。	独立样本克鲁斯卡尔-沃利斯检验	.306	保留原假设。

a. 显著性水平为 .050。

b. 显示了渐进显著性。

Fig. 16. Kolmogorov-Smirnov test

Box Line Chart Analysis. A box plot was generated after data entry using SPSS, and the box plot was used to visually analyze the comparative relationship between different temporary display information display positions on the speed of information capture by the subjects (Fig. 17).

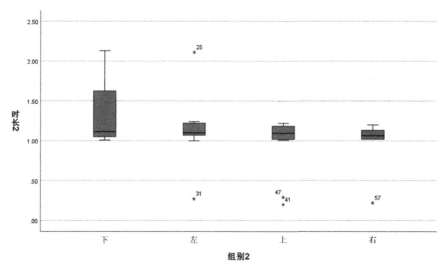

Fig. 17. Box line chart analysis

The Graphical Observation Shows that

1. The data fluctuates the most when the temporary information display position is "down". Since "down" was the first test, some testers were not yet familiar with the interface, resulting in large fluctuations in data.
2. The most abnormal values were found when the temporary information was displayed in the "down" position. Due to the limitations of the interface design of this experiment, the prompt information displayed in the "upper" position was not visually obvious, resulting in a more even capture time for most people, but some participants could be acutely aware of it, thus causing three outliers.
3. The data were most stable and efficient when the temporary message was displayed at the "right" position. When the temporary information was displayed on the "right", the speed capture time was generally concentrated and stable, and the median was lower than that of other groups.

4.4 Test Conclusion

(1) The driver-centered digital speed display HMI allows for more efficient data capture with respect to frequently displayed information.
(2) For temporary information, when the display position is "right", information can be captured more efficiently.

4.5 Interview Analysis

After each experiment, a brief interview was conducted with the subjects to collect their feelings and experiences about the whole experimental process, and it was found that five subjects indicated that although the digital speed format with a driving-centered sub-center display could provide more direct and clear access to speed information, the traditional instrument-based speed display could provide a more intuitive grasp of speed changes. This is in addition to the experimental hypothesis that the proposed combination of instrumentation and digital design will allow drivers to quickly and accurately access speed information while intuitively grasping speed changes.

5   Results and Discussion

5.1   Experimental Conclusions

The purpose of this study is to investigate the influence of HMI on drivers' driving behavior. "After analyzing the experimental data, we can basically conclude that, compared with the classic instrument-based HMI, the driver-centered digital HMI can capture the speed information faster and more accurately". In terms of temporary display information, when the display position is "right", the driver can capture the temporary display information faster.

5.2   Design Optimization

The experimental findings are translated into a design to form an HMI design standard that best suits driving behavior. In this design, the speed display is digital, but the classic speed meter is retained so that the driver can intuitively grasp the speed change trend; the temporary display information position is set on the right side, which allows the driver to capture the prompt information from the HMI faster (Fig. 18).

Fig. 18. Design optimization

5.3   Discussion and Outlook

Discussion. In terms of experimental findings, there is a discrepancy with previous studies. Noé Monsaingeon et al. had explored the difference between the effects of driver-centered HMI and vehicle-centered HMI on driving behavior, and eventually found that the conventional instrument HMI could allow drivers to capture speed information faster than the driver-centered digital speed display HMI, which is the opposite of the findings in this study. The analysis may be due to the difference in details of the experimental material HMI, as the instrument HMI design used in this study does not contain a pointer, and drivers with some driving experience may have a higher sensitivity to pointer speed gauges.

During the experiment, we noticed that the response time of the subjects was generally very short, which made the data interception and differential comparison difficult. Therefore, we tried to increase the cognitive load for the subjects as much as possible in the actual experiment, such as asking the participants to prohibit collisions and collect as many gold coins as possible. For example, we asked participants to prohibit collisions and collect as many gold coins as possible. We also asked questions at the moment when participants were making a turn, passing through a narrow road or collecting gold coins, so as to enlarge the subtle differences, but the actual effect was still not obvious.

Outlook. In the short term, the design of automotive HMIs is limited by technological developments and the range of functions that the technology can achieve. (François et al. 2017) Therefore, we need to improve the existing HMI under the existing conditions, in addition to studying the impact of interface element arrangement on interaction efficiency, we also need to study the excessive cognitive load and distraction caused by the HMI to the driver, for example, Strayer et al. compared the cognitive load caused by the traditional in-vehicle HMI and the new intelligent in-vehicle operating systems (For example, Strayer et al. compared the cognitive load on the driver caused by traditional in-vehicle HMI and new intelligent in-vehicle operating systems (Carplay, Carlife, Hicar, etc.) and their impact on the efficiency of interaction while driving, and found that the latter could interact with the driver more quickly and effectively with less cognitive load (Birrell et al. 2014). The new intelligent in-vehicle operating system is an in-vehicle system developed based on users' high familiarity and awareness of smartphone systems, with low learning costs and clear and easy-to-understand information presentation, and will flourish in the coming decades.

In the long term, the Volkswagen Group's 2025 Strategy, released in March 2017, articulates four major directions for future automotive technology development: lightweighting, new energy, sharing, and smart network connectivity (Welch 2019). Sharing and intelligent network connectivity have put forward new requirements for the design of automotive HMI. There will no longer be a division of work for people in the car, and all people will be in the role of passengers, and the HMI will no longer be just for the driver alone, but equally for every passenger. What kind of new interaction methods will be brought? What kind of HMI design will bring higher interaction efficiency? This will be the topic that scholars will face in the future. The development of technology is bound to bring creative innovation to automotive HMI design, but no matter what stage of technology development, people will always have to deal with machines, and we look forward to more in-depth and up-to-date research on automotive HMI in the future.

References

Ahmed, M.M., Gaweesh, S., Yang, G.: A Preliminary investigation into the impact of connected vehicle human-machine interface on driving behavior. IFAC-PapersOnLine **51**(34), 227–229 (2019)

Amditis, A., et al.: Towards the automotive HMI of the future: overview of the AIDE-integrated project results. IEEE Trans. Intell. Transp. Syst. **11**(3), 567–578 (2010)

Azadani, M.N., Boukerche, A.: Driving behavior analysis guidelines for intelligent transportation systems. IEEE Trans. Intell. Transp. Syst. (2021)

Bengler, K., Rettenmaier, M., Fritz, N., Feierle, A.: From HMI to HMIs: towards an HMI framework for automated driving. Information **11**(2), 61 (2020)

Birrell, S.A., Fowkes, M., Jennings, P.A.: Effect of using an in-vehicle smart driving aid on real-world driver performance. IEEE Trans. Intell. Transp. Syst. **15**(4), 1801–1810 (2014)

Cauffman, S.J., Lau, M., Deng, Y., Cunningham, C., Kaber, D.B., Feng, J.: Research and design considerations for presentation of non-safety related information via in-vehicle displays during automated driving. Appl. Sci. **12**(20), 10538 (2022)

Chalmers, P.A.: The role of cognitive theory in human–computer interface. Comput. Hum. Behav. **19**(5), 593–607 (2003)

Chapon, A., Gabaude, C., Fort, A.: Défauts d'attention et conduite automobile: état de l'art et nouvelles orientations pour la recherche dans les transports (No. 52). INRETS (2006)

François, M., Osiurak, F., Fort, A., Crave, P., Navarro, J.: Automotive HMI design and participatory user involvement: review and perspectives. Ergonomics **60**(4), 541–552 (2017)

Kim, H., Kwon, S., Heo, J., Lee, H., Chung, M.K.: The effect of touch-key size on the usability of in-vehicle information systems and driving safety during simulated driving. Appl. Ergon. **45**(3), 379–388 (2014)

Kumar, N., Kumar, J.: Measurement of efficiency of auditory vs visual communication in HMI: a cognitive load approach. In: 2016 International Conference on Advances in Human Machine Interaction (HMI), pp. 1–8. IEEE, March 2016

Ma, J., Gong, Z., Tan, J., Zhang, Q., Zuo, Y.: Assessing the driving distraction effect of vehicle HMI displays using data mining techniques. Transport. Res. F: Traffic Psychol. Behav. **69**, 235–250 (2020)

Monsaingeon, N., Caroux, L., Mouginé, A., Langlois, S., Lemercier, C.: Impact of interface design on drivers' behavior in partially automated cars: an on-road study. Transport. Res. F: Traffic Psychol. Behav. **81**, 508–521 (2021)

Padagannavar, P.: Automotive product design and development of car dashboard using quality function deployment. Int. J. Ind. Eng. Res. Dev. (IJIERD) **7**(1), 10–23 (2016)

Reimer, B., et al.: Assessing the impact of typeface design in a text-rich automotive user interface. Ergonomics **57**(11), 1643–1658 (2014)

Welch, J.: The Volkswagen recovery: leaving scandal in the dust. J. Bus. Strateg. (2019)

Does the Average Color Influence Selection?

Yuto Sekiguchi[(✉)], Riho Ueki, Kouta Yokoyama, and Satoshi Nakamura

Meiji University, Nakano 4-21-1, Nakano-ku, Tokyo, Japan
yuutosekiguchi@gmail.com

Abstract. The Goldilocks effect is the tendency to select the middle choice when three choices that can be expressed in three levels, such as size and price, are presented. We investigate the possibility that the Goldilocks effect can also be applied to color and that it unintentionally distorts the choice. Specifically, we hypothesized that when presented with three choices consisting of two different colors and their average color (the average of the two colors), people would choose the average color, and we conducted a crowdsourcing experiment. The experiment results showed that people did not tend to choose the average color option. However, analysis by gender showed that females tended to select the average color option while males did not. In addition, when the average colors were similar to one of the two colors in the three options, both males and females tended to select the less similar different color option.

Keywords: Color · Selection Behavior · Goldilocks Effect

1 Introduction

People make many choices in everyday life, such as when purchasing products, making hotel reservations, voting in popularity contests and elections, eating food, and selecting what to wear. The choice of a single product's choice is influenced by various factors, for example, price, quantity, package design, color, display location, and the absence of pop-outs.

Many studies have been conducted in cognitive science and developmental psychology on selection behavior. One of the psychological effects of choice is the Goldilocks effect, in which people tend to choose the middle option when given three choices in a stepwise manner. For example, when French fries are sold in three different sizes (S, M, and L), the middle-sized serving is more likely to be chosen.

Priluck et al. [1] suggested that the color factor may influence product selection and that sellers should consider the color of the product and package in their marketing strategies. Kobayashi et al. [2] also showed that color variation influences purchase intention, enjoyment, anxiety, and satisfaction at the time of selection. As shown in the above studies, it is clear that a product's color has some influence on selection behavior. It is common for a certain product to have color variations, but if the choice is guided by the color of other products, not the product itself, the choice may be distorted. If this

M. Kurosu and A. Hashizume (Eds.): HCII 2023, LNCS 14012, pp. 485–496, 2023.
https://doi.org/10.1007/978-3-031-35599-8_32

applies to choice behavior other than product selection, such as elections and popularity contests, it would be a significant problem.

We expected that the Goldilocks effect might also apply to color. Specifically, we hypothesized that, given a choice of three colors, if one of the three was a color with values intermediate between those of the other two choices in terms of hue, saturation, lightness, or RGB value (hereafter referred to as an "averaged color"), people would be more likely to choose it. If the Goldilocks effect also appears with color, then it is likely that the selection would be distorted by the type of colors in the selection target group.

In this paper, we investigate the influence of the color factor on choice behavior by using crowdsourcing to examine the choice behavior on a large scale when two and three choices are presented. In addition, we compare the averaged color choice rate between the two- and three-choice scenarios and clarify whether the Goldilocks effect is also manifested in color.

2   Related Work

Regarding package design, Terry et al. [3] found that the product name's font strongly influences product evaluation. However, as well as font and design, color is also considered an essential factor in package design.

In an investigation of the influence of color on things, Priluck et al. [1] showed that a product's color is a significant factor in marketing strategies, and the color factor is thought to have some influence on choice behavior. Fergus [4] studied food color and consumer consumption behavior and found a correlation between beverage consumption and color. However, only a few studies on product colors, such as these, have focused on multiple product colors. We investigate the influence of color factors on choice behavior by conducting a survey focusing on the color of multiple products.

Yokoyama et al. [5] investigated the influence of the design of the progress bar displayed during the waiting time on the web screen on the participant's subsequent selection behavior. They found that a right-to-left animation and a progress bar on the upper side tended to maintain fairness in selection behavior. Focusing on a visual characteristic called pop-out, Hosoya et al. [6] implemented a digital signage-type vending machine and investigated how pop-outs affect participants. They found that participants were likelier to select products that had been popped out.

These studies suggest that various factors are involved in choice behavior, and that product package design significantly impacts the impression of a product and is an essential factor in choice behavior. In addition, studies on the Goldilocks effect and color have yet to be conducted. This study aims to clarify the influence of color on choice behavior when a person is given three choices.

3   Experiments

3.1   Outline of the Experiment

In this experiment, we investigate the influence of color on choice behavior based on the hypothesis that when a product is presented in two colors and an average color simultaneously in a three-choice scenario, the average color product is more likely to be chosen. To investigate the influence of color on choice behavior, we created an experimental system (Fig. 1 and Fig. 2) in which images of the same product, with only the color, changed, are presented in two or three choices, and conducted a large-scale experiment using *Yahoo! crowdsourcing* [7].

Fig. 1. An example of the screen during the presentation of two choices in the experiment.

Fig. 2. An example of the screen during the presentation of three choices in the experiment.

3.2 Experimental Design

We designed experiments using various colors and products to show the relationship between color and selection behavior.

Specifically, we selected 10 product categories such as clothing, food and drink, electrical appliances, and household goods frequently selected in everyday life. Then, we prepared one product image in each product category and created two product images in each category from the original image by changing the saturation and brightness. Table 1 shows the product images in each category. In each category, there are three product images.

Table 1. Examples of selection targets in each product category.

	hue+0 x	hue+30 average	hue+60 y			brightness+70 x	brightness+0 average	brightness-70 y
Desktop PC					**Mask**			
	hue+0 x	hue+20 average	hue+40 y			hue+0 x	hue-15 average	hue-30 y
Car					**Men's Hoodies**			
	chroma+0 x	chroma-50 average	chroma-100 y			(R,G,B)= (223,228,232) x	(R,G,B)= (159,190,216) average	(R,G,B)= (95,152,200) y
Pants					**Shirt**			
	hue+0 x	hue+25 average	hue+50 y			hue+0 x	hue+40 average	hue+80 y
Ice cream					**Women's Hoodies**			
	hue+35 x	hue+0 average	hue-35 y			hue+0 x	hue-30 average	hue-60 y
Drink					**Cups**			

We studied the difference in the selection rate of the average color product in two choices and in three choices to test our hypothesis. In the experiment, our system selected five product categories randomly for the three-choice task, and the other five for the two-choice task. Since three combinations of two choices can be created from three types of color images, the number of questions is 5 three choices and 15 two choices, for a total of 20 questions.

We implemented the experimental system using Vue.js, a JavaScript framework.

3.3 Experimental Procedure

A participant first accessed the experiment system page through *Yahoo! crowdsourcing* in this experiment. The first page of the experiment system explained the experiment. At that time, a unique 16-digit alphanumeric and lower-case ID was generated for each participant. The survey procedure and precautions were confirmed on the page explaining the experiment, and the participants were asked to check a check box. The instructions included the following: enlarge the window size, experiment on a PC, do not press the reload button, and use a browser other than Internet Explorer. In addition, the explanation page also asked participants to select their gender and age. The experiment could only be started if all the checkboxes were checked. Note that the experimental system allowed access only from PCs, and the browsers were limited to Google Chrome, Mozilla Firefox, and Apple Safari.

When the participant moved to the experimental screen, he/she was given three seconds to compare the products for each question. Afterward, the participant clicked on the button displayed and selected a product. This was one trial. The purpose of presenting the button on each trial was to reset the mouse cursor position by having the participant click the button, thereby eliminating the influence of the mouse cursor position at the start of the trial as much as possible. The choices on the experimental screen consist of three two-choice questions and one three-choice question, repeated five times for a total of 20 trials. For each trial, we recorded the selected image, the selected image's position, the selection time, the number of clicks, the window width, window height, and so on.

After 20 trials of the experiment were completed, the participant was taken to a questionnaire screen. On the questionnaire screen, there were two columns: one for selecting their favorite color and the other for writing about what was problematic in the experiment and whether or not there were any errors.

In a crowdsourcing experiment, participants might give inauthentic responses. To reduce such responses, we blocked 1,312 inappropriate participants from past experiments in advance. In addition, we extracted the data from participants who gave inauthentic or inappropriate responses from the acquired body of data. In this experiment, we extracted inauthentic responses and inappropriate participants by referring to the selection time, window size, and the number of clicks.

4 Results

In this experiment, we recruited 1,000 participants (500 females and 500 males). In total, 102 participants (42 females and 60 males) gave inauthentic or inappropriate responses. Therefore, we analyzed the data of 898 participants (458 females and 440 males), excluding the 102 inappropriate participants.

4.1 Results and Analysis of the Overall Selection Rate

First, in the free description section of the questionnaire conducted in this experiment, there was a group of options in which there were multiple opinions that the colors of the products were similar or indistinguishable. Therefore, we will refer to the set of colors that were not easily distinguishable as similar colors, and to one color that is different from the two similar colors as dissimilar colors. In addition, the four choices (ice cream, drink, women's hoodies, and cup) that include similar and dissimilar colors are denoted as "Choice Group Pop-out," and the other six choices that are distinguishable are denoted as "Choice Group Normal."

Table 2 shows the selection percentage of each item in the "Choice Group Normal." In Table 2, the blue text indicates a decrease in the percentage of the three choices, and the red text indicates an increase. The results show that the percentage of average color choices increased for pants and men's hoodies while it decreased for the other items. The average color selection rate for "Choice Group Normal" was 38.93% when two choices were presented, and 36.01% when three choices were presented, indicating that average color products were not more likely to be selected when three choices were presented. Table 3 shows the selection rate of each item in the "Choice Group Pop-out." In Table 3, the choice with an orange background is dissimilar, and the other two are similar colors. In Table 3, the selection rate of the average color choice was lower for all items when three choices were presented than when two choices were presented. However, the selection rate of the dissimilar color choice increased significantly in the three-choice presentation compared to the two-choice presentation.

Table 2. Selection rate of each item in "Choice Group Normal."

Category		x	average	y
Desktop PC	two choices	29.33	42.67	28.00
	three choices	38.89	39.58	21.53
Car	two choices	21.19	39.28	39.53
	three choices	18.57	35.00	46.63
Pants	two choices	44.69	37.28	18.02
	three choices	37.31	40.30	22.39
Mask	two choices	44.19	39.14	16.67
	three choices	46.72	36.50	16.79
Men's Hoodies	two choices	37.83	41.13	21.04
	three choices	32.03	41.41	26.56
Shirt	two choices	44.36	34.07	21.57
	three choices	47.37	23.31	29.32
Average	two choices	36.93	38.93	24.14
	three choices	36.82	36.01	27.17

Table 3. Selection rate of each item in "Choice Group Pop-out."

Category		x	average	y
Ice cream	two choices	17.20	37.90	44.89
	three choices	17.93	29.66	52.41
Drink	two choices	29.85	32.03	38.13
	three choices	39.66	21.55	38.79
Women's Hoodies	two choices	43.66	38.03	18.31
	three choices	61.42	19.69	18.90
Cups	two choices	43.75	31.77	24.48
	three choices	56.03	20.57	23.40
Average	two choices	33.62	34.93	31.45
	three choices	43.76	22.87	33.38

4.2 Results and Analysis of Selection Rates by Gender

Abramov et al. [9] showed that there might be differences in the way males and females see and perceive color. Therefore, we analyzed the results for each gender, assuming that each gender sees and perceives colors differently.

Table 4 shows the results of the selection rates for each item in the "Choice Group Normal" for females. Comparing the average color selection rates for the two-choice group and the three-choice group, the average color selection rates for the three-choice group were higher than those for the two-choice group for five of the six items, except the shirt. The mean average color choice rate for the two-choice group was 39.52%, while the mean average color choice rate for the three-choice group was 42.92%, indicating that females were more likely to select an average color item when presented with three choices than when presented with two choices. The $\chi 2$ test on the total number of choices for all items in "Choice Group Normal" with a significance level of 5% confirmed a significant difference in the number of choices in terms of whether or not respondents chose average colors ($\chi 2(1) = 4.06, p = .044$).

Table 5 shows the results of the selection rate for each item in the "Choice Group Pop-out" for females. The results for "Choice Group Pop-out" were similar to those shown in Table 3, with the average color choices having a lower selection rate when presented with three choices than when presented with two. Table 5 shows that the selection rate for the three choices was much higher than that for the two choices for the dissimilar-colored choice with an orange background. The $\chi 2$ test on the total number of selections for all items in "Choice Group Pop-out" with a significance level of 5% confirmed a significant difference in the number of selections for the dissimilar color ($\chi 2(1) = 35.65, p < .001$).

Table 4. Selection rate of each item in "Choice Group Normal" for females.

Category		x	average	y
Desktop PC	two choices	32.18	42.96	24.86
	three choices	37.17	46.02	16.81
Car	two choices	28.71	38.91	32.38
	three choices	23.94	45.07	30.99
Pants	two choices	43.14	37.25	19.61
	three choices	40.08	40.51	19.41
Mask	two choices	42.94	42.80	14.27
	three choices	40.93	48.84	10.23
Men's Hoodies	two choices	37.31	40.47	22.22
	three choices	35.35	42.79	21.86
Shirt	two choices	44.60	34.70	20.70
	three choices	43.93	34.31	21.76
Average	two choices	38.15	39.52	22.34
	three choices	36.90	42.92	20.18

Table 6 shows the results of the selection rate of each item for males in "Choice Group Normal." Unlike females, males showed a lower average color selection rate when presented with three choices than when presented with two choices. In addition, males' average color selection rates were lower when they were presented with three

Table 5. Selection rate of each item in "Choice Group Pop-out" for females.

Category		x	average	y
Ice cream	two choices	16.42	36.52	47.07
	three choices	21.62	22.01	56.37
Drink	two choices	36.10	31.30	32.61
	three choices	47.60	23.58	28.82
Women's Hoodies	two choices	37.76	38.59	23.65
	three choices	52.53	23.50	23.96
Cups	two choices	44.95	34.40	20.64
	three choices	52.92	27.92	19.17
Average	two choices	33.81	35.20	30.99
	three choices	43.67	24.25	32.08

Table 6. Selection rate of each item in "Choice Group Normal" for all males and males.

Category		x	average	y
Desktop PC	two choices	26.18	40.98	32.85
	three choices	32.34	38.72	28.94
Car	two choices	16.90	37.98	45.12
	three choices	15.11	34.67	50.22
Pants	two choices	43.08	36.44	20.48
	three choices	43.14	30.88	25.98
Mask	two choices	39.29	36.23	24.48
	three choices	41.20	31.76	27.04
Men's Hoodies	two choices	34.22	38.64	27.14
	three choices	35.98	37.85	26.17
Shirt	two choices	39.62	33.81	26.57
	three choices	47.81	19.30	32.89
Average	two choices	33.22	37.35	29.44
	three choices	35.93	32.20	31.71

choices than when they were presented with two choices for all six items, indicating that males were less likely to select average colors when presented with three choices than when presented with two choices. Similar to the results for females, the $\chi 2$ test confirmed a significant difference in the number of choices for the choice of average colors ($\chi 2(1) = 11.22$, $p < .001$).

Table 7 shows the results of the selection rates for each item in "Choice Group Pop-out" for males. As in Tables 3 and 5, the selection rate of the average color choice was lower in the three-choice group than in the two-choice group. In addition, the selection rate of the dissimilar color choice was much higher when the three choices were presented than when the two choices were presented. Similar to the results for females, the $\chi 2$ test showed that there was a significant difference in the number of choices for the dissimilar color among males ($\chi 2(1) = 65.47$, p $<$ .001).

Table 7. Selection rate of each item in "Choice Group Pop-out" for all males and males.

Category		x	average	y
Ice cream	two choices	23.15	37.96	38.89
	three choices	20.98	30.80	48.21
Drink	two choices	33.33	28.99	37.68
	three choices	44.29	20.48	35.24
Women's Hoodies	two choices	54.06	35.51	10.43
	three choices	76.19	14.29	9.52
Cups	two choices	38.71	33.33	27.95
	three choices	60.37	12.90	26.73
Average	two choices	37.31	33.95	28.74
	three choices	50.46	19.62	29.93

These results support the hypothesis when limited to females. In addition, it was found that both males and females tended to select the non-similar color choice when there was a non-similar color choice among the similar color choices. When focusing on the selection rate of dissimilar colors, the selection rate of females was 41.47% when presented with two choices and 52.36% when presented with three choices, and the selection of males, when presented with two choices, was 41.25% and 57.27% when presented with three choices., the rate of increase was slightly higher in males than in females.

4.3   Results and Analysis for Selection Position

Figure 4 shows the average selection rate by gender for each position when the three choices were presented. Figure 4 shows that females tended to select the middle choice. Males tended to select the choice in the middle and on the right, similar to the results of Wilson et al. [7].

We also analyzed the average choice rate of average color according to the position of the average color when the three choices were presented (see Fig. 5). This figure shows that females tended to select the most average color choice when the color choice was presented in the middle. On the other hand, males tended to select the average color choice when the average color choice was presented on the right.

Comparing Figs. 4 and 5, we can see that females tended to select the average color choice more than the non-average color choice in all positions. Males tended not to select the average color choice when it was presented on the left or in the middle but were more likely to select it when it was presented on the right.

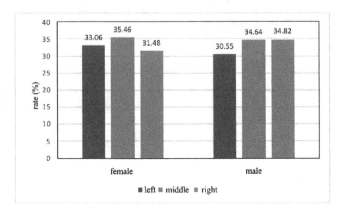

Fig. 4. Average selection rate by gender for each position in the three choices.

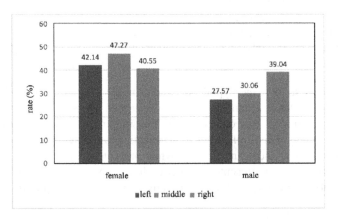

Fig. 5. Average color selection rate per average color presentation position.

5 Discussion

This experiment showed that the results for the average color choice rate for both genders as a whole were different from our hypothesis. However, we found that the dissimilar color tended to be selected more often in "Choice Group Pop-out," in which the average color was similar to one of the two colors in the three choices. This result may be similar to the induction of choice by pop-outs, as revealed by Hosoya et al. [6]. We believe that the presence of dissimilar-colored products among similar-colored products influences selection behavior and distorts fairness in the same way as pop-outs. The effect of dissimilar colors on selection behavior was smaller for females than for males. This result suggests that females can discriminate finer color differences better than males.

The results for both genders as a whole contradicted the hypothesis, but when only females, they tended to choose average colors. The results also showed that males tended to avoid the average colors. These results suggest that the presence of average color distorts the fairness of the selection behavior. The difference between females and males may be that males and females see or perceive colors differently, as found by Abramov et al. [9].

This experiment showed that when presented with three choices, females were more likely to select the choice in the center, while males were more likely to select the choice on the right. This suggests that females are more likely to be influenced by center bias, while males are more likely to be influenced by right-side bias. In addition, females were more likely to select the average color, regardless of where it was displayed, whereas males were more likely to select the average color only when it was placed on the right side. These results suggest that placing the average color on the right side can induce males to select the average color choice and significantly reduces the gender difference in choices that include average colors.

6 Conclusion

In this study, we conducted two-choice and three-choice experiments to test the hypothesis that when two colors and their average color product are presented simultaneously in a three-choice scenario, the average color product tends to be selected more often. Specifically, we experimented using *Yahoo! Crowdsourcing*, by presenting two colors and their average colors together, and presenting products in two of those three colors were presented together.

The analysis of this experiment showed that within "Choice Group Normal," there was a significant difference in females' average color choice rate when presented with two choices and when presented with three choices, and that females tended to choose average colors when presented with three choices, which was in line with the hypothesis. On the other hand, there was a significant difference in the rate with which males chose average colors when presented with two choices and when presented with three choices. However, males tended to avoid choosing average colors when presented with three choices, which differed from the hypothesized result. We hypothesized that this difference between females and males was due to the differences in the way they see, feel, and perceive colors depending on their gender. We plan to verify this point by conducting further experiments.

In the case of "Choice Group Pop-out," where the average color was similar to one of the two other colors among the three choices, both males and females tended to choose the dissimilar color. However, this result differed from the hypothesis that they would be more likely to choose the average color. This result may be similar to the induction of choice by pop-out, as shown by Hosoya et al. [6]. The analysis of the selection position revealed that placing the average color choice on the right side decreases the difference in the selection rate between male and female participants.

In this experiment, we showed that the presence of average color affects the choice behavior in a three-choice task. However, the effects of average color on choice behavior differed between males and females. In the future, we plan to conduct a detailed investigation of the reasons for the differences in the effects and to study the construction of a system to maintain the fairness of choice behavior based on the results obtained in this experiment.

Acknowledgment. This work was partly supported by JSPS KAKENHI Grant Number JP22K12135.

References

1. Priluck Grossman, R., Wisenblit, J.Z.: What we know about consumers' color choices. J. Market. Pract. Appl. Market. Sci. vol. **5**(3), no. 11, 78–88 (1999)
2. Kobayashi, H., Yoshitake, M., Tsuchiya. H., Tanaka, Y., Vinai, N., Shinichi, K.: Effect of Color Variation on Consumer Satisfaction with Choice: The Case of Fashion- and Style-oriented Products. International Association of Societies of Design Research 2011 Proceedings (4 pages on conference CD−ROM) (2011)
3. Terry, L.C., Jeffrey, J.: All dressed up with something to say: effects of typeface semantic associations on brand perceptions and consumer memory. J. Consum. Psychol. **12**(2), 93–106 (2008)
4. Fergus, M.C.: Color as a factor in food choice. Critical Reviews in Food Science and Nutrition, pp. 83–101 (2009)
5. Yokoyama, K., Nakamura, S., Yamanaka, S.: Do animation direction and position of progress bar affect selections? In: Ardito, C., et al. (eds.) INTERACT 2021. LNCS, vol. 12936, pp. 395–399. Springer, Cham (2021). https://doi.org/10.1007/978-3-030-85607-6_45
6. Hosoya, S., Yamaura, H., Nakamura, S., Nakamura, M., Takamatsu, E., Kitaide, Y.: Does the pop-out affect the product selection of signage vending machine?. In: 17th IFIP TC.13 International Conference on Human-Computer Interaction (INTERACT 2019), vol. 11747, p. 24–32 (2019)
7. Yahoo! Crowdsourcing. https://crowdsourcing.yahoo.co.jp/
8. Wilson, T.D., Nisbett, R.E.: The accuracy of verbal reports about the effects of stimuli on evaluation and behavior. Soc. Psychol. **41**(2), 118–131 (1978)
9. Abramov, I., Gordon, J., Feldman, O., Chavarga, A.: Sex and vision II: color appearance of monochromatic lights. Biol Sex Differ **3**(21), 21–35 (2012)

Does the Type of Font Face Induce the Selection?

Riho Ueki[✉], Kouta Yokoyama, and Satoshi Nakamura

Meiji University, Nakano 4-21-1, Nakano-ku, Tokyo, Japan
riho1itigo@gmail.com

Abstract. When people buy products, they are influenced by various factors. For example, it has been reported that both fonts and pop-outs affect product selection. Here, we focused on the Goldilocks effect whereby people tend to choose the middle option in three-tier choices. We applied this effect to the font-face of the options' name and conducted an experiment on crowdsourcing based on the hypothesis that when three different fonts are presented on the impression axis, the font with the middle impression is more likely to be chosen. The results showed that a fusion font in the middle of the impression axis was not selected. However, in the selection of ramen flavor, we found that people were influenced by the font face. On the other hand, it was found that people tend to select the choice in the center on a PC and the choice on the right on a smartphone.

Keywords: Font · Choice · Choice behavior · Goldilocks effect · Crowdsourcing

1 Introduction

When making a choice, people are influenced by a variety of factors. For example, even when purchasing drinks from vending machines, the choice depends on taste preference, temperature, price, and mood at the time. Recent studies have shown that the impression of a product's package can be a factor that influences consumers' product preferences and purchasing behavior [1]. We are conscious of the problem of not only guiding the choice but also making a choice fair by clarifying what influences the choice of a certain object among multiple alternatives.

Childers et al. [2] studied the relationship between product name fonts and consumer behavior. As a result, they revealed that the font affects consumers' evaluation of products. There are various elements of package design, such as shape, color, and material. Among them, Zhang et al. [3] revealed that the logo design of a product even affects the taste of the product as perceived by the purchaser.

As described above, it is clear that the letter shape of the product name has some influence on selection behavior. However, if the font (the type of font face) itself influences selection, regardless of the impression of the product, the font may promote selection bias. In other words, if the influence of fonts on selection behavior can be clarified, it would be possible to induce selection or eliminate selection bias, regardless of what the product is.

In the field of psychology, there have been many studies on choice. The Goldilocks effect has been applied to choice induction in behavioral economics and marketing. The Goldilocks effect is an effect that people tend to choose the middle option when there are three choices. For example, when French fries are available in three sizes (S/M/L), most people choose the middle size (M). Here, Saito et al. [4] have proposed the Fontender system, which can generate a new font by fusing two fonts (see Fig. 1) and found that the impression value of the fused font is between the impression values of the two fonts before fusion. Based on this research, we expected that this Goldilocks effect could be applied to the relationship between fonts and choice behavior. Specifically, we predicted that when three choices are presented simultaneously in three different fonts on the impression axis, people will choose the one that gives the middle impression

In this study, referring to the Goldilocks effect, we hypothesized that "if three choices are presented simultaneously as three different fonts: two fonts on a particular impression axis and a fusion font in the middle of the impression axis, the option with the fusion font, which is the middle impression, is more likely to be chosen. This study aims to verify this hypothesis through an experiment using crowdsourcing, and to investigate the influence of the impression of each font on choice. In addition, we will clarify what influences the choice by analyzing various factors in the experiment.

Fig. 1. An example of the fusion of the Square Style font and the Hannotate font

2   Related Work

Thomas et al. [5] conducted an experiment to evaluate the design of a fictitious brand of bottled beverages. Specifically, they asked participants to evaluate a total of four different designs, combining two types of bottle shapes and two types of logo typefaces. The results revealed overall positive effects of meaning congruence on perceptions of brand credibility and price expectations.

For font impressions, Kimura et al. [6] investigated the impression of Japanese kana fonts in printed documents. In this study, they selected six Japanese kana typefaces and physically measured the width of the vertical and horizontal sides and the area ratio of the black area. A psychological experiment was also conducted on the typefaces. Subjects responded to a sample of the typefaces with 40 different adjectives. These measurements and this psychological experiment revealed that the newer typefaces with constant letter spacing created a good impression. In comparison, the older typefaces with long vertical or horizontal spacing created an unfavorable impression. Saito et al. [4] asked subjects to rate their impressions of 18 existing fonts using 35 adjective pairs. In addition, they proposed Fontender, which allowed users to generate a font with the impression they want to create by inputting the impression words. From the above studies, we think that people have impressions of fonts and that the fonts themselves may influence their choices.

Simonson et al. [7] experimented with demonstrating the Goldilocks effect by preparing descriptions of low-quality and low-priced, medium-quality and medium-priced, and high-quality and high-priced cameras, and conducted a questionnaire survey for participants to ask which cameras they would be willing to purchase. The results showed that 60% of the participants chose medium-quality and medium-priced cameras. Many people consider low-priced cameras to be of inferior quality to high-priced cameras, and high-quality cameras to be too expensive and difficult to afford. This effect, in which a medium-quality and medium-priced product are more likely to be chosen as a compromise between low-priced and high-quality, is called the compromise effect. Simonson et al. concluded that the results of this survey show a compromise effect. There have been many other studies on the Goldilocks effect, most of them in behavioral economics. In behavioral economics, the causes of the Goldilocks effect are generally considered to be the compromise effect, the context effect, the anchoring effect, and loss aversion. In this paper, we examine the likelihood of choosing a font with an intermediate impression in terms of font impression, based on the idea that the middle option is more likely to be chosen among the three options.

There have been various other studies on choice behavior. Hosoya et al. [8] focused on the visual effect of pop-outs and investigated the influence of pop-outs in vending machines. Specifically, they implemented a digital signage-type vending machine. They analyzed how users are affected by pop-outs when purchasing drinks and found that users are more likely to select products with pop-outs. These pop-outs can be combined with the current method. Yokoyama et al. [9] investigated the effects of visual feedback on choice induction. Specifically, they conducted experiments that the effects of the display position of the progress bar and the orientation of the animation on the subsequent selection made. The experiments revealed that the presentation of a progress bar that animated from left to right tended to bias the selection. It was also suggested that presenting a right-to-left animated progress bar on the upper side of the screen might make the selection fairer.

3 Experiments

3.1 Experiment Summary

The purpose of this experiment is to test the hypothesis that "if three choices are presented simultaneously as three different fonts, namely two fonts on a particular impression axis and a fusion font in the middle of the impression axis, the choice with the fusion font, which is the middle impression, is more likely to be chosen. To test this hypothesis, we designed a task in which participants had to select an object from three choices with two conditions. One condition was the mixed condition, presenting multiple choices in three different fonts (Fig. 2). The other was the unified condition which presented multiple options in the same font (Fig. 3). The primary purpose of the unified condition experiment was to confirm the preference of the alternatives.

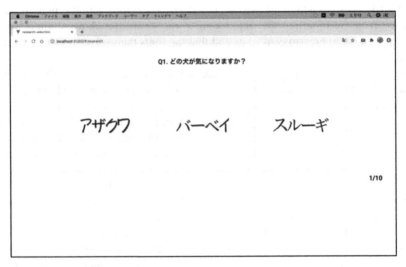

Fig. 2. Screenshot of the experimental page for the mixed condition experiment

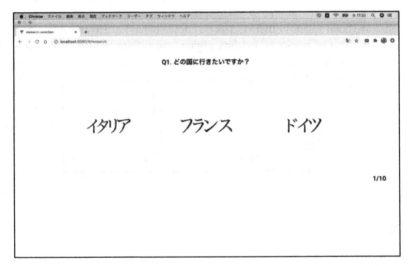

Fig. 3. Screenshot of the experimental page for the unified condition experiment

In addition, we prepared four types of fonts and their fused fonts using Saito et al.'s method [4]. We also used *Yahoo! Crowdsourcing* to conduct a large-scale investigation on choice.

3.2   Task Design

In the experiment, three choice questions were presented, and the participants were asked to answer one of them, assuming an actual choice situation. Here, Danziger et al. [10] clarified that the more decisions a person makes, the more stressed the person feels and the less likely they are to make accurate decisions. Therefore, in this experiment, we set the number of questions to 10 to avoid decision fatigue.

As for the theme of the questions, common questions, for example about favorite ramen flavor or favorite dog breed, are expected to be less influenced by the font because the preferences are clear. Therefore, it is desirable to present questions that are not common to measure the effect of choice induction. However, if only difficult questions are asked, the participants will be forced to make a choice concerning something they do not know about, and there is a risk that they will not respond seriously to the task. Thus, we prepared five questions in which the choices were immediately obvious to everyone (hereafter to as "easy questions") and five questions in which the choices were real but not well known (hereafter to as "difficult questions"). Note that the names of the aliens in the difficult questions are fictitious.

To eliminate the influence of the Japanese letters themselves as much as possible, only two types of notation (Hiragana or Katakana characters) were used, and the questions were unified into one of them. The number of questions in each notation was limited to five. The questions and options are as shown in Table 1.

Table 1. Prepared categories and options

Easy

Category	Option		
Ramen	Miso	Soy sauce	Pork bone broth
Dog	Chihuahua	Poodle	Bulldog
Sushi	Tuna	Mackerel	Sea bream
Flower	Cosmos	Cherry blossoms	Pansy
Country	Italy	France	Germany

Difficult

Category	Option		
Dog	Azawak	Sloughi	Barbet
Flower	Umbrella leaf	Hydnora	Cistus albidus
Country	Niue	Belize	Suriname
Alien	Ubeohta	Kagachanm	Rokipikin
Sweets	Crumpets	Papanache	Palatschinken

3.3   Font Selection

What is important for the font used in the selection task is that the fusion font generated by the two fonts has an intermediate impression. Here, Saito et al. [4] analyzed the factor structure of impressions when evaluating existing fonts. As a result, they extracted four factors: softness, attractiveness, cheerfulness, and activity. Based on these four factors, we selected fonts with strong and weak impressions so that the fusion fonts will have an intermediate impression. Also, considering the ease of application, fonts were selected from existing relatively commonly used fonts. In addition, to ensure that the fusion of fonts did not reduce visibility, fonts with a consistent thickness were selected.

The fonts selected were "Hiragino Mincho", "Kako Gothic", "Kako Kaisho", and "Hannotate" (Hiragino Mincho will be referred to as Mincho, Kako Gothic as Gothic, and Kako Kaisho as Kaisho). Mincho and Hannotate differed significantly in cheerfulness and softness, while Gothic and Kaisho differed significantly in activity. We created two combinations of each of the four fonts and fused the two fonts. For font fusion, we used Fontender [4]. Figure 4 shows an example of a string actually generated. Table 2 shows the question and font combinations used in the mixed condition and unified condition experiments.

Fig. 4. Example of generated strings

3.4   Innovations in Conducting Experiments in Crowdsourcing

In crowdsourcing experiments, the experiment supervisor cannot monitor the participants. Therefore, it is possible that participants may give inauthentic answers or perform inappropriate operations [11]. The proper analysis could not be carried out without excluding such userious responses and inappropriate experimenters.

Therefore, we were supposed to pay rewards to those who participated in this selection task. However, we first added a warning that we could not pay the reward if the

Table 2. Combination of questions and fonts used

Easy		Difficult	
Category	**Font Style**	**Category**	**Font Style**
Ramen	Mincho	Dog	Mincho
	Gothic		Hannotate
	Min×Got		Min×Han
Dog	Mincho	Flower	Kaisho
	Kaisho		Hannotate
	Min×Kai		Kai×Han
Sushi	Gothic	Country	Mincho
	Kaisho		Kaisho
	Got×Kai		Min×Kai
Flower	Gothic	Alien	Mincho
	Hannotate		Hannotate
	Got×Han		Min×Han
Country	Mincho	Sweets	Gothic
	Gothic		Kaisho
	Min×Got		Got×Kai

answers were clearly inauthentic. Our laboratory has conducted more than 15,000 questionnaires and experiments using Yahoo! Crowdsourcing. From the results of these experiments, we registered 840 participants in a block list before this experiment. In this experiment, we recruited participants from the crowdsourcing service and conducted the experiment in our Web system.

To check for inappropriate answers, we measured the selection time for each question. If the responses suggesting that the participant had not read the question exceeded a certain number we excluded that participant. In this experiment, respondents who answered more than three out of ten questions in less than 1000 ms were considered as inappropriate respondents.

3.5   System Overview

Our system first presented the procedure and precautions for the experiment (Fig. 5). The 'Start Experiment' button on the first page could only be pressed if all the checkboxes next to these procedures and precautions had been ticked. This was done to ensure that the precautions were read carefully and to prevent access congestion.

When accessing the experiment system, a unique 16-digit alphanumeric and lower-case ID was generated for each user. On the experimental screen, the question was displayed at the top, and three options were displayed side by side in the center, as shown in Figs. 2 and 3. The choices' display locations were shuffled in the mixed condition and unified condition experiments. For each question, the user's unique ID, gender, age, selected image, selected image location, selection time, and device information were recorded.

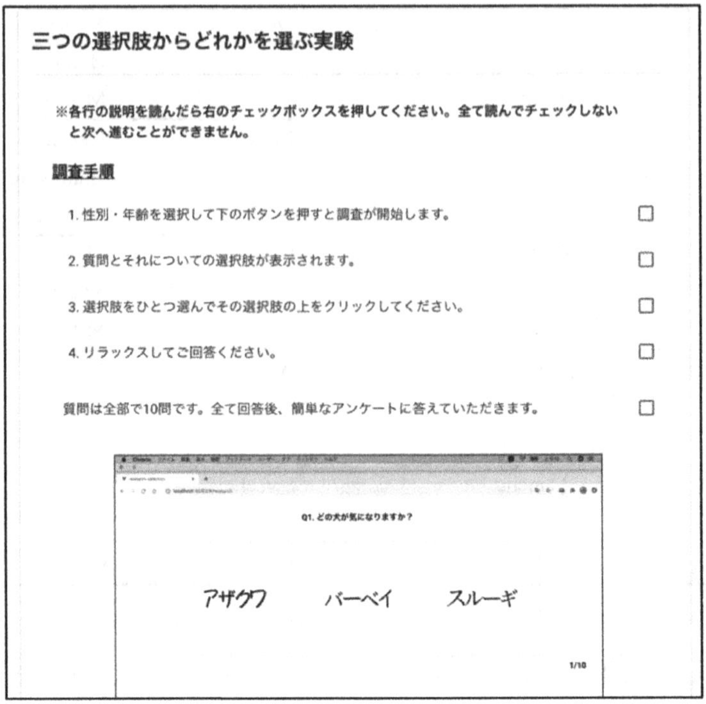

Fig. 5. Screenshot of the explanatory page

After the user finished answering the ten questions, a questionnaire was displayed at the end. Here, the user was asked if they had understood all the options and if there had been any problems in the experiment. After the questionnaire, the user's unique ID and a code common to all experiments were displayed.

We implemented the experimental system using Vue.js. In order to see the possibility of unconscious choice induction, we set the experiment title as "An experiment to choose one of three options," and did not mention the differences in fonts.

3.6 Experimental Procedure

Participants accessed the experimental page by clicking on the button presented in the Yahoo! Crowdsourcing task. On the first screen, they ticked the checkboxes next to the instructions and precautions, selected their gender and age, and then pressed the start button. When they did so, the selection task started, and they had to answer ten questions with three choices.

After answering the ten questions, participants were asked to complete a questionnaire to ensure that there were no glitches in the system and that they were eligible for the analysis. The questionnaire content was whether all options were displayed (mandatory), multiple answers for unknown options, and free-text answers such as impressions (optional). After the questionnaire, the user's unique ID and the common code were displayed so they could enter them into the screen on Yahoo! Crowdsourcing.

This experiment was conducted on PCs, smartphones, and tablets, and the system automatically recorded what devices they used.

4 Experimental Results

4.1 Basic Experimental Data

In the experiment, 500 males and 500 females were asked to respond to the mixed condition experiment. The unified condition was conducted twice, and 750 males and 750 females were asked to respond in the second round.

From 1000 answers collected in the mixed condition experiment, the data of those who did not follow our instructions or whose response time was less than 1000 ms three or more times were eliminated, yielding results for 946 respondents (465 males, 477 females, and four no-gender respondents). From 1500 answers collected in the second round of the unified condition experiment, the results for 1404 respondents (689 males, 709 females, and six no-gender respondents) were obtained by excluding those who were not serious.

The gender ratio of PCs and mobile devices in the mixed condition experiment is shown in Fig. 6, with males having the same usage rate for PC and mobile device usage rate, while females had a higher usage rate for mobile usage rate (e.g., smartphones). This was also the case in the unified condition experiment.

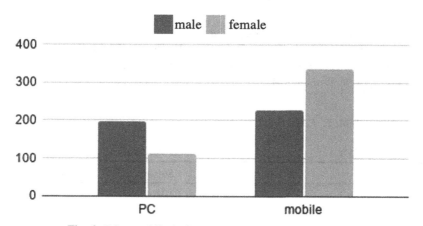

Fig. 6. PC to mobile device gender ratio in mixed conditions

4.2   Results and Analysis of Selection Guidance by Fonts

First, we test the hypothesis that when three different fonts are presented on a certain impression axis, the font with the middle impression is more likely to be chosen from the results of a mixed condition experiment.

The expected value of the fusion font being selected in the mixed condition experiment is 33.3%. If the expected value is higher than this value, it could be said that the fusion font is more likely to be selected, and if it is lower than this value, it could be said that the fusion font is less likely to be selected. The results were summarized: the actual selection rate was 32.7% (male 32.3%, female 33.1%, PC 32.3%, mobile device 33.0%). Therefore, the results did not differ significantly from the expected values, and this hypothesis was not supported.

Fig. 7. Example of Ramen broth in Mincho and Gothic fonts

Next, when the effect of selection guidance by font was examined for each category, differences were found only for the Ramen broth category. The results for the ramen broth in the unified condition experiment are shown in Table 3, and those in the mixed condition experiment in Table 4.

Table 3. Ramen broth selection rate under the unified condition

Font Style	Option		
	Miso	Soy sauce	Pork bone broth
Mincho	27.4%	26.6%	46.0%
Mincho×Gothic	35.8%	26.3%	38.0%
Gothic	45.9%	23.4%	30.6%
Average	36.4%	25.4%	38.2%

Table 4. Ramen broth selection rate under mixed-condition

Font Style	Option		
	Miso	Soy sauce	Pork bone broth
Mincho	28.4%	34.9%	36.7%
Mincho×Gothic	27.7%	33.2%	39.0%
Gothic	32.1%	34.4%	33.4%
Average	29.4%	34.2%	36.4%

Table 3 shows that the selection rate of 'Soy sauce' was low in the unified condition experiment and that 'Pork bone broth' was selected with high probability when all the fonts were presented in the Mincho font. In contrast, 'Miso' was selected with a high probability when all the fonts were presented in the Gothic font. Furthermore, when all the fonts were presented in the Mincho and Gothic fonts, 'Miso' and 'Pork bone broth' were selected with equal probability. This result supports what Saito et al. [4] found, that the fused font produces impression values that are intermediate between the two pre-fusion fonts. Figure 7 shows an example of ramen broth in Mincho and Gothic fonts.

Next, in the mixed condition experiment (Table 4), unlike in the unified condition experiment, the selection rate of 'Soy sauce' was higher. There was no difference between 'Soy sauce' or 'Pork bone broth' using the Mincho font, 'Soy sauce' or 'Pork bone broth' using a fusion of the Mincho and Gothic fonts, and selections when using the Gothic font for any kind of broth.

4.3 Results and Analysis by Position and Device

The three choices are arranged in three rows on the left and right. The number of choices by display position in the mixed condition is shown in Fig. 8, and the number of choices by display position in the unified condition is shown in Fig. 9. The results show that in the mixed condition, the number of selections for the left option was not much different for either males or females compared to the middle and right display for both males and females. On the other hand, in the unified condition, the left option was less often and the right option was selected more often.

Table 5 shows which of the left, middle and right options was selected the most for PC and mobile device in the unified and mixed conditions, respectively. The results show that the center or the right side is more likely to be selected overall, while the left side is less likely to be selected, and that the center is more likely to be s elected when using a PC and the right side when using a mobile device. This suggest that the display position influences selection.

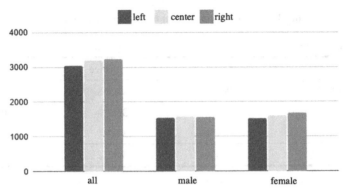

Fig. 8. Number of selections by position by gender in mixed conditions

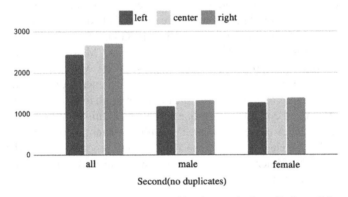

Fig. 9. Number of selections by position by gender in unified conditions

Table 5. Selection rate by display position per device

Device	Selected Position		
	Left	Center	Right
PC (unified)	29.9%	35.6%	34.5%
Mobile (unified)	31.8%	33.4%	34.8%
PC (mixed)	32.2%	34.8%	33.0%
Mobile (mixed)	32.3%	33.1%	34.6%
Average	31.6%	34.2%	34.2%

5 Discussion

The results for the mixed condition show that, contrary to our hypothesis, fused fonts are not more likely to be selected. The Goldilocks effect is mainly numerical. We speculate that this is due to the fact that the impression of the font was different from that of the numerical middle.

On the other hand, a tendency for selection according the position of the three choices was revealed, with a high tendency to select the center position for PCs and the right position for mobile devices. Smartphones and tablet devices may be used as mobile devices other than PCs, and many users of Yahoo! Crowdsourcing are smartphone users. If the participants were smartphone users, it is possible that right-handed users answered with one hand and were more likely to select the right side of the questionnaire, which is closer to the thumb. However, we do not have data on the percentage of users who used smartphones among the mobile device users, whether they were right-handed or not, and whether they answered with one hand or not, so we cannot be sure of the exact results.

To eliminate the difference in the number of selections depending on the display position, it was found that the best way was to present the choices on a PC under mixed conditions, where the choices are presented in three types of fonts. However, the differences by display position for each item were large, and it is possible that aliens and flowers of the minor question categories and ramen and flowers of the major question categories caused these differences. By finding the characteristics of the items with large bias, it is expected to be possible to reduce the bias caused by the display position.

The Fontender system [4] proposed by Saito et al. was used to create the image of the choices, but due to system limitations, the edges of the text were uneven, and there was some variation in the text size. Some respondents in the questionnaire expressed concern about this issue, suggesting that the distorted character shapes may have influenced the selection process. We plan to resolve this issue in the future.

6 Conclusion

In this study, we designed a three-choice task to test the hypothesis that the font with the middle impression is more likely to be chosen when three different fonts are presented on an impression axis. We conducted two large-scale crowdsourcing experiments: a mixed condition experiment in which participants were presented with a choice between two fonts, and a unified condition experiment in which participants were presented with a choice in the same font and their fusion font.

Analysis of the mixed condition revealed that the fusion fonts were not easily selected, and the hypothesis was not supported. This may have been because the impression of the font was not expressed as a numerical value or quantity to begin with, or because of the specification of the genre of the question, or the large bias in the preferences. The results of the unified condition revealed that preferences also appeared in the minor questions. In particular, in the ramen category of the major question, respondents had an image of the choices. In addition, the analysis of display position by device revealed that the middle position for PCs and the right position for mobile devices were more likely to be selected, suggesting the possibility of eliminating selection bias by display position by taking account of this feature.

In this paper, we used only four fonts that are commonly used, and the use of other existing fonts or fonts with complex shapes, such as design fonts, was not assumed. Therefore, we consider increasing the number of font types and using English fonts as well as Japanese fonts when we conduct further experiments.

Acknowledgment. This work was partly supported by JSPS KAKENHI Grant Number JP22K12135.

References

1. Henderson, P.W., Cote, J.A., Leong, S.M., Schmitt, B.: Building strong brands in Asia: selecting the visual components of image to maximize brand strength. Int. J. Res. Mark. **20**(4), 297–313 (2003)
2. Childers, T.L., Jass, J.: All dressed up with something to say: effects of typeface semantic associations on brand perceptions and consumer memory. J. Consum. Psychol. **12**(2), 93–106 (2008)
3. Zhang, A., Paul, H.: Design aesthetics: principles of pleasure in design. Psychol. Sci. **48**(2), 157–172 (2006)
4. Saito, J., Nakamura, S.: Fontender: interactive japanese text design with dynamic font fusion method for comics. In: Kompatsiaris, I., Huet, B., Mezaris, V., Gurrin, C., Cheng, W.-H., Vrochidis, S. (eds.) MMM 2019. LNCS, vol. 11296, pp. 554–559. Springer, Cham (2019). https://doi.org/10.1007/978-3-030-05716-9_45
5. van Rompay, T.J.L., Pruyn, A.: When visual product features speak the same language: effects of shape-typeface congruence on brand perception and price expectations*: shape-typeface congruence. J. Prod. Innov. Manage. **28**(4), 599–610 (2011). https://doi.org/10.1111/j.1540-5885.2011.00828.x
6. Kimura, S., Taguti, T.: Impression of japanese kana typefaces in typeset texts. Inform. Process. Soc. Japan **38**(11), 2209–2216 (1997)
7. Simonson, I., Tversky, A.: Choice in context: tradeoff contrast and extremeness aversion. J. Mark. Res. **29**(3), 281–295 (1992)
8. Hosoya, M., Yamaura, H., Nakamura, S., Nakamura, M., Takamatsu, E., Kitaide, Y.: Does the pop-out make an effect in the product selection of signage vending machine? In: Lamas, D., Loizides, F., Nacke, L., Petrie, H., Winckler, M., Zaphiris, P. (eds.) INTERACT 2019. LNCS, vol. 11747, pp. 24–32. Springer, Cham (2019). https://doi.org/10.1007/978-3-030-29384-0_2
9. Yokoyama, K., Nakamura, S., Yamanaka, S.: Do animation direction and position of progress bar affect selections? In: Ardito, C., et al. (eds.) INTERACT 2021. LNCS, vol. 12936, pp. 395–399. Springer, Cham (2021). https://doi.org/10.1007/978-3-030-85607-6_45
10. Danziger, S., Levev, J., Avnaim-Pesso, L.: Extraneous factors in judicial decisions. Proc. Natl. Acad. Sci. **108**(17), 6889–6892 (2011)
11. Maniaci, M.R., Rogge, R.D.: Caring about carelessness: Participant inattention and its effects on research. J. Res. Pers. **48**, 61–83 (2014)

Integrating the Kano Model and IPA to Measure Service Quality of Pet Grooming

Kai-Chieh Yen and Yu-Hsiu Hung[(⊠)]

Department of Industrial Design, National Cheng Kung University, Tainan, Taiwan
P36101081@gs.ncku.edu.tw

Abstract. In recent years, there are huge business opportunities for pet grooming services, but the market competition has become increasingly fierce. In order to stand out in this competitive environment, operators need to identify customer needs (i.e., what customers care about). Therefore, the purpose of this study is to investigate the design of pet grooming services with customer satisfaction and to conduct a study with case studies of pet groomers. By introducing KANO Model and IPA to analyze customer needs and design customer satisfaction pet grooming services. The contributions are (1) to fill the research gap of pet owners' expectations and satisfaction of the quality of services received by their pets. (2) Help pet grooming operators to classify and set strategic priorities for service quality for practical application.

Keywords: Service quality · IPA-Kano model · Pet grooming

1 Introduction

1.1 Background

The recent revolution in the status of pets has changed the way we view pet care. First, the social significance of pets to humans has gradually changed from being human property to a psychological support function [1, 2], and owners are willing to spend more on pet-related goods and services to satisfy their love for their pets, creating a huge consumer market. According to the Census and Statistics Department, Ministry of Finance, the sales of pet care services industry (e.g., grooming, medical) increased nearly five times from 2008 to 2018 [3], in which the Taiwan Institute of Economic Research According to the Research Center for Biotechnology Industry, the top three percentages of daily spending on pets in 2020 are food, medical care, and grooming, and owners spend an average of $2,254 per pet per year on grooming [4]. In summary, there is a huge business opportunity for pet grooming services, and not only is the number of pets growing, but owners are also willing to invest money in pet grooming.

M. Kurosu and A. Hashizume (Eds.): HCII 2023, LNCS 14012, pp. 511–527, 2023.
https://doi.org/10.1007/978-3-031-35599-8_34

1.2 Research Motivation

According to the Census and Statistics Department in 2019, the number of pet care service businesses has grown significantly from 269 in 2008 to 1,516 in 2018, which means that customers have more options to find stores that meet their needs for consumption [3]. In order to stand out in this competitive environment, operators need to identify customer needs (i.e., what customers care about).

In recent years, many papers in the service industry have used the SERVQUAL questionnaire, an extension of the PZB model proposed by Parasuraman et al. [5], to investigate the quality of service. To enhance customer satisfaction and meet the service quality demanded by customers. There are two main research directions: understanding the classification of service quality [6], or the assessment of expectations (importance) and satisfaction [7].

However, there are gaps in the above studies: First, in terms of service quality classification, Martilla and Jame suggest that operators can apply importance-performance analysis (IPA) to identify critical improvement attributes and assess the adequacy of certain quality attributes [8]; or apply the Kano model to analyze the types of service quality attributes based on customer satisfaction and dissatisfaction with how their personal requirements are met [9]. However, the Kano model usually classifies service quality and ignores the impact of quality on the increase or decrease of user satisfaction; IPA only analyzes customer expectations and satisfaction for operators to prioritize improvement of service quality by identifying those that perform well and those that need improvement [10]. In summary, the use of a single analysis to study customer expectations of pet grooming service quality is limited in that it is not possible to classify and prioritize pet grooming service quality at the same time. Second, Carman pointed out that when applying SERVQUAL to evaluate service quality, it is better to revise the questionnaire content with the specific needs of the service industry [11]; otherwise, the discussion of service quality items will be incomplete. The difference between the pet grooming service industry and the general service industry is that owners care about the quality of service their pets receive, and Belk mentioned that the problems of animal companions affect consumer behavior [12] (e.g., owners purchase superior goods or services for their pets [13]. However, the quality of services received by pets has not been measured by SERVQUAL.

In summary, the remaining problems in the pet grooming field are: (1) the quality of services received by pets has not been discussed in the SERVQUAL questionnaire (2) there is no research that combines the use of Kano and IPA to classify and prioritize the quality of pet grooming services.

1.3 Research Purpose

This study aims to examine (1) pet owners' expectations and satisfaction with the quality of services received by their pets through a case study of pet grooming operators. (2) How the combined application of IPA-Kano model can help pet grooming operators to classify service quality and set strategic priorities.

1.4   Research Contribution

The practical contributions of this study are (1) to fill the research gap of pet owners' expectations and satisfaction of the service quality received by their pets (2) to help pet grooming operators to classify and set strategic priorities for service quality for practical application.

2   Introduction

2.1   Service quality and SERVQUAL

Service quality will affect the company's marketing performance and consumer satisfaction [14]. And Chen Junting's research pointed out that what customers care most about pet grooming shops is service quality [15], and good service quality is the most decisive factor for a company to gain a competitive advantage in the market [16]. To sum up, this study intends to explore the service quality of pet grooming.

First of all, service quality is subjective. Grönroos defined service quality as the result of consumers' evaluation of the service process [17]. Parasuraman, Zeithaml, and Berry further summarized the reasons why service quality is difficult to control into several main characteristics such as intangibility, indivisibility, heterogeneity, and perishability, and established a PZB service quality model [5]. Parasuraman, Zeithaml & Berry further developed the Service Quality Evaluation Scale (SERVQUAL) based on the PZB model [18]. The study confirmed the operational definition of "Service Quality = Customer Perception (Satisfaction) - Customer Expectation (Importance)". The five facets of SERVQUAL are defined as follows:

1. Tangibility: Refers to the appearance of venues, physical equipment and service personnel.
2. Reliability: The ability to provide the promised service reliably and correctly.
3. Responsiveness: The willingness of service personnel to assist customers and provide immediate service.
4. Assurance: The service personnel's professional knowledge, courtesy and ability to generate trust and trust from customers.
5. Empathy: The Company cares about customers and provides exclusive services.

To sum up, the method of measuring service quality in this study adopts Parasuraman's view on service quality in the PZB model, that is, service quality is based on customer expectations (importance) (ES) and customer It is measured by the gap between the service satisfaction (PS) actually felt, and the questionnaire items to measure the service quality are based on the updated SERVQUAL service product quality table proposed by Parasuraman et al. [19], and according to the suggestion of Carman's suggestion that the contents of the "SERVQUAL" questionnaire were revised and adjusted according to the specific needs of the service industry [11]. Therefore, this study added questions about the owners' expectations and satisfaction with the quality of pet grooming services received by their pets.

2.2 Importance-Performance Analysis (IPA)

The importance-performance analysis (IPA) proposed by Martilla and James [8] is a technique that compares the importance (the extent to which customers expect the service) with the performance level (the satisfaction of consumers after receiving the service) [20]. The importance score is used as the X-axis, and the satisfaction score is used as the Y-axis. This two-dimensional matrix is divided into four quadrants. According to the scores of service quality in importance and satisfaction, the coordinates of the service quality are marked in specific quadrants. According to the quadrant where the service quality coordinates are located, the operator can know the customer's requirements and the customer's current evaluation of the service quality, which can be used as a reference for the operator to propose strategies and set priorities in the future [21, 22].

Referring to the method of Hollenhorst et al. [23], this study divides the four quadrants by using the average value of importance and satisfaction as the separation point, as shown in Fig. 3.2. In addition, the meanings represented by the four quadrants are as follows:

(1) The first quadrant: Keep up good work. Consumers expect high importance and satisfaction with this service quality, so operators should maintain service quality in this quadrant to maintain competitiveness with peers.
(2) The second quadrant: Concentrate here. It means that consumers have high expectations for this service quality but low satisfaction, and the industry cannot meet consumers' expectations. This is the main disadvantage of the industry. Therefore, the industry should be listed as a key item for immediate priority improvement to improve service quality.
(3) The third quadrant: Low priority. Indicates that the importance of consumers' expectations and satisfaction with this service quality is low, because consumers pay little attention to the service quality in this area, which means that customers do not have a strong demand for services in this area, so low satisfaction will not be a obvious disadvantages, low priority for improvement.
(4) The fourth quadrant: Possible overkill. It means that consumers have low expectations for this service quality but high satisfaction, which means that the industry has invested too much unnecessary resources to meet consumers' weak needs. The industry should save resources and invest in this area, and allocate resources to areas that need more improvement.

2.3 Kano Model

The Kano two-dimensional quality model proposed by Kano is a way to classify and describe the quality of a product or service [9]. x-axis represents the degree of possession of a service quality element, and y-axis is customer satisfaction, using the relative relationship between the horizontal axis and the vertical axis, the service quality is divided into the above five quality elements, as shown in Fig. 1; in addition, the meanings represented by the five quality elements are as follows.

1. Attractive quality (AQ): When this element is sufficient, people will feel satisfied, and when it is not sufficient, it is also acceptable and will not cause dissatisfaction.

2. One dimension quality (ODQ): When this quality element is present, it will make customers feel satisfied and increase satisfaction; if not, it will cause customer dissatisfaction and decrease satisfaction; that is, there is a linear relationship between consumer satisfaction and quality elements.
3. Must-be quality (MBQ): This quality element is taken for granted when it is sufficient and does not increase satisfaction, but when it is insufficient, it will cause dissatisfaction with the quality. Therefore, this quality element is the basic index of the product or service. 4.
4. Indifferent quality (IQ): When quality attributes or elements, whether they are present or not, do not cause customer satisfaction or dissatisfaction. That is, there is no impact on consumer satisfaction of the product.
5. Reverse quality (RQ): When this quality element is sufficient, the dissatisfaction level will be increased; when the claim is not sufficient to be satisfied. Service providers should try to avoid this.

In the questionnaire design part, in order to conform to the concept of the two-dimensional model, a two-way questionnaire with positive and negative questions is used to ask consumers' feelings and satisfaction levels when they have or do not have the service quality elements as the research basis. This study adopts the terminology and classification method of Matzler and Hinterhuber [24], in order to conform to the concept of two-dimensional model, a two-way questionnaire with positive and negative question sets was used to ask consumers about their feelings and satisfaction when the service quality elements were present or not present respectively. The five levels of user perceptions, namely, "like", "take for granted", "no matter", "barely accept", and "don't like", were used as the questionnaire questions, and the service quality elements were categorized with reference to Table 1.

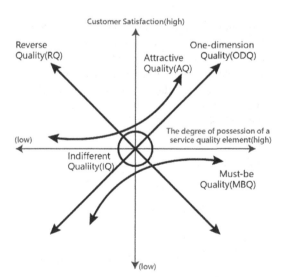

Fig. 1. KANO two-dimensional matrix diagram

Table 1. KANO quality elements categorization table

Characteristics		Their feelings when the service quality were not present				
		don't like	barely accept	no matter	take for granted	Like
Their feelings when the service quality were present	don't like	IVQ	RQ	RQ	RQ	RQ
	barely accept	MBQ	IQ	IQ	IQ	RQ
	no matter	MBQ	IQ	IQ	IQ	RQ
	take for granted	MBQ	IQ	IQ	IQ	RQ
	like	ODQ	AQ	AQ	AQ	IVQ

3   Research Methods

3.1   Research Framework

In this study, the method of measuring service quality in this study adopts Parasuraman's view on service quality in the PZB model, and the questionnaire items to measure the service quality are based on the updated SERVQUAL service product quality table proposed by Parasuraman et al., which is divided into: Tangibility, Reliability, Responsiveness, Assurance and Empathy five dimensions [5], according to this as a dimension to measure the service quality perceived by pet grooming customers to study the views of pet grooming service customers [19].

According to the IPA proposed by Martilla and James, this study combines the importance and satisfaction with comparative analysis [8]; in addition, according to the Kano two-dimensional quality model, the consumer's perception of service quality is analyzed, and further classified into five categories: There are five quality elements: attractive quality, must-be quality, one-dimensional quality, reverse quality and indifferent quality [9]. Finally, according to related research [25, 26], Kano Model and IPA are combined to discuss the method of service quality that needs to be improved first.

The research framework is shown in Fig. 2.

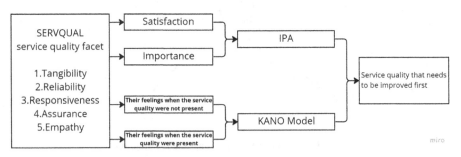

Fig. 2. Research framework

3.2 Research Case Introduction

The object of this study is pet grooming shop A in Tainan City. Since its establishment in 2020, pet grooming shop A has provided services including a full set of grooming (bathing + trimming), accommodation, grooming, etc. Statistics of the service items in 2021–2022 Sales volume, the full set of grooming (bathing + trimming) is the service item with the highest sales volume in pet grooming store A. Compared with other service items provided by the pet grooming store, the full set of grooming (bathing + trimming) services accounted for 90% of the average annual overall turnover %, which is the most popular sales service item of the store.

The capital of Pet Grooming Shop A is NT 240,000, and the number of employees is 4 (including 1 operator, 1 full-time employee and 2 part-time employees). In principle, it is closed on last Thursday, and the operator and 1 full-time employee during the rest of the working hours will always be on duty in the store. There are more customers on Tuesdays, Saturdays, and Sundays, so 1–2 part-time employees would assist in these days. The business hours are from 9:00 am to 7:00 pm. According to the store's statistics, in 2022, the majority of customers who come to the store are female dog owners aged 21 to 40, accounting for 41% of the store's visits, and the average number of daily visitors is about 10–20.

Figure 3 shows the plane layout of pet grooming shop A. The gray block represents the contact point for customers to go to the pet grooming shop. Customers make an appointment to check out and pick up their pets at the counter at the door of the store. In addition, the pet cage and the waiting area for uncaged pets are the waiting areas for customers' pets. The load capacity is 10 in total.

The service area of the pet grooming industry is divided into two major areas, including the backstage work area, the pet waiting area (including the pet cage and uncaged waiting area), and the counter. A full set of grooming (bathing + trimming) work items include two baths, oil silk care, hair blowing, pre-shearing work (shaving soles, belly, anus, inner ear hair), and body hair trimming. For pets with limited mobility, bath and massage services will be added before two baths, and infrared phototherapy services will be added after trimming the whole body hair.

When a customer brings a pet to the counter, the staff will move the pet to the "pet cage" or "uncaged waiting area", and then move the next pet after the work of the previous pet in the working area is completed, and so on. After the full grooming service, the pet will be moved to the pet cage or uncaged waiting area until the owner comes to pick it up.

3.3 Research Objects and Questionnaire Distribution Process

This study adopts a paper-based questionnaire survey. The research objects are customers who come to pet grooming shop A to consume pet grooming services. Simple Random Sampling is used to distribute and fill in the questionnaire after the customer has experienced the entire service process. Each person is limited to fill in once. The data collection time is Weekdays and holidays are covered from January to February 2023.

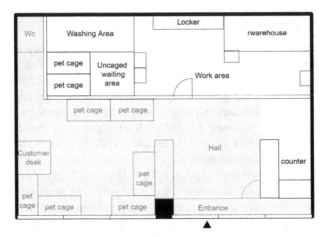

Fig. 3. Layout plan of pet grooming shop A

4   Analysis and Results

4.1   Background Narrative Statistical Analysis

A total of 71 paper-based questionnaires were distributed in this study, 42 questionnaires were returned, 41 valid questionnaires, and the response rate of questionnaires was 59%. Table 2 presents the sample's demographics.

Table 2. Background narrative statistical

Characteristics	Items	Frequency	Percentage
Identity	pet owner	37	90%
	Not pet owner	4	10%
Gender	Male	3	7%
	Female	38	93%
Age	<10	0	0%
	11–20	0	0%
	21–30	9	22%
	31–40	9	22%
	41–60	15	37%
	> 60	8	20%
Current Residence	Tainan City	41	100%
	Other Cities	0	0%
Is it the first time to come to our store to consume pet grooming services?	Yes	6	15%
	No	35	85%
The type of pets that consume pet grooming services	Dog	41	100%
	Cat	0	0%

4.2   Reliability Analysis

This study refers to Cuieford who considered Cronbach's α value as a measure of the consistency of internal variables [27]. Four Question aspects of Cronbach's alpha(Kano positive, Kano negative, Satisfaction and Importance) for all dimensions—tangibility, reliability, responsiveness, assurance, empathy—value more than 0.7. This indicates that the constructs for these scales have high reliability [28, 29].

4.3   Kano Model Results for Respondents

This study employed the Matzler and Hinterhuber's two-dimensional classification method [24] to classify 41 valid questionnaires using the majority principle listed by the respondents under the six quality types: attractive quality, must-by quality, one-dimension quality, indifferent quality and reverse quality, invalid quality.

Table 3 shows the 26 quality factors in this study. Specifically, 13 quality factors were classified under attractive quality, 12 quality factors were classified under one dimension quality, 1 quality factors were classified under indifferent quality.

Table 3. Categorization of quality factors listed by respondents (%).

No	Quality Factors	AQ	ODQ	MBQ	IQ	RQ	IVQ	Categorization
Tan1	Pet grooming shop has modern equipment	41	2	5	**51**	0	0	**IQ**
Tan2	The physical facility (environment) of the pet grooming shop is visually appealing	**56**	22	5	17	0	0	**AQ**
Tan3	The environment of the grooming shop (such as a work area or waiting area) is comfortable for your pet	24	**51**	17	7	0	0	**ODQ**
Tan4	Employees in pet grooming shop look tidy	**34**	29	17	20	0	0	**AQ**
Tan5	In pet grooming shops, service-related materials (such as literature or notices) are visually appealing	**56**	0	5	39	0	0	**AQ**
Rel1	When a pet grooming shop promises to do something at a certain time, it does so	34	**37**	5	24	0	0	**ODQ**
Rel2	When you have a problem, the pet grooming shop shows a sincere interest in solving it	29	**56**	12	2	0	0	**ODQ**
Rel3	Pet grooming shop provides the service right at the first time	29	**59**	12	0	0	0	**ODQ**
Rel4	Pet grooming shop provides its services at the time it promises to do so	39	**49**	7	5	0	0	**ODQ**

(continued)

Table 3. (*continued*)

No	Quality Factors	AQ	ODQ	MBQ	IQ	RQ	IVQ	Categorization
Rel5	Pet grooming shop insists on error-free records	24	**56**	20	0	0	0	**ODQ**
Res1	Employees of pet grooming shop tell you exactly when services will be	**41**	39	15	5	0	0	**AQ**
Res2	Employees of pet grooming shop give you prompt service	**57**	37	5	5	0	0	**AQ**
Res3	Employees of pet grooming shop are always willing to help you	**46**	44	5	5	0	0	**AQ**
Res4	Employees of pet grooming shop are never too busy to respond to your requests	**49**	32	19	5	0	0	**AQ**
Res5	The average time you wait for pet grooming services is not long	**41**	29	10	20	0	0	**AQ**
Ass1	The behavior of employees of pet grooming shop instills confidence in customers	39	**51**	10	0	0	0	**ODQ**
Ass2	You feel safe in your transactions with pet grooming shop	15	**76**	10	0	0	0	**ODQ**
Ass3	'Your pet' feels safe when receiving services at pet grooming shop	12	**68**	20	0	0	0	**ODQ**
Ass4	Employees of pet grooming shop are consistently courteous with you	37	**51**	5	7	0	0	**ODQ**
Ass5	Employees of pet grooming shop have the knowledge to answer your questions	41	**46**	12	0	0	0	**ODQ**
Emp1	Pet grooming shop gives you individual attention	**61**	32	5	2	0	0	**AQ**
Emp2	Pet grooming shop has operating hours convenient to all its customers	**71**	22	2	5	0	0	**AQ**
Emp3	Pet grooming shop has employees who give you personal attention	**59**	24	2	15	0	0	**AQ**
Emp4	Pet grooming shop has employees who give 'your pet' personal attention	**39**	37	10	15	0	0	**AQ**
Emp5	Pet grooming shop has your best interests at heart	**41**	34	5	20	0	0	**AQ**
Emp6	Employees of pet grooming shop understand your specific needs	37	**49**	5	10	0	0	**ODQ**

Notes: AQ, attractive quality; MBQ, must-by quality; ODQ, one-dimension quality; IQ, indifferent quality; RQ, reverse quality; IVQ, invalid quality. The bold stands for the majority

The results show that overall, customers have different classification results for quality factors in pet grooming services, but one dimension quality (ODQ) and attractive quality (AQ) account for the vast majority. In addition, the service classification results in the Reliability and Assurance facets are both one dimension quality (ODQ) (e.g. Rel1-Rel5 and Ass1-Ass5 in Table 3), while the service classification results in the Responsiveness facet are all attractive quality (AQ) (e.g. Res1-Res5 in Table 3).

4.4 Importance-Performance Analysis (IPA) Results

Customers evaluate overall quality based on what quality factors they deem important. Importance-Performance Analysis is divided into four quadrants according to Hollenhorst, Olson & Fortney's suggestion, and the average value of importance and satisfaction is used as the dividing point of the quadrant: excellent, needs improvement, superior and careless [23].

Table 4 summarizes IPA's results for pet grooming services. These scores are rated by survey respondents. Among these 26 projects.

The highest average importance is 'Ass3: Your pet' feels safe when receiving services at pet grooming shop (4.9 out of 5.0), Rel3: Pet grooming shop provides the service right at the first time (4.8), Rel4: Pet grooming shop provides its services at the time it promises to do so (4.7) and Ass2: You feel safe in your transactions with pet grooming shop. On the contrary, Tan1: Pet grooming shop has modern equipment (3.7), Tan5: In pet grooming shops, service-related materials (such as literature or notices) are visually appealing (3.7) and Emp3: Pet grooming shop has employees who give you personal attention (4.0) has the lowest average importance.

The highest average satisfaction is Ass4: Employees of pet grooming shop are consistently courteous with you (score 4.8 out of 5.0) and Ass5: Employees of pet grooming shop have the knowledge to answer your questions (4.8). On the contrary, Tan5: In pet grooming shops, service-related materials (such as literature or notices) are visually appealing (4.1) and Tan1: Pet grooming shop has modern equipment (4.1) have the lowest average satisfaction.

In addition, we found that the service items in the Tangibility and Empathy dimensions are generally classified into the third and fourth quadrants, which means that the priority of improvement is low, while all the service items in the Assurance dimension are classified into the first quadrant, which means that they need to continue to maintain.

According to Fig. 4, we can understand the distribution of service items in each quadrant of pet grooming services. Not all service quality attributes are considered equally important, and most of the service items are classified into the first and third quadrants. Part of the improvement priority is less urgent, and the use of resources will not be excessively wasted. Therefore, priority should be given to improving the service items representing the second quadrant, and checking whether the resources occupied by the service items in the fourth quadrant are necessary.

Table 4. Summary of IPA result (%).

No	Quality Factors	Imp	Sat	Quadrants
		Mean + sd	Mean + sd	
Tan1	Pet grooming shop has modern equipment	3.7 ± 0.6	4.1 ± 0.7	3
Tan2	The physical facility (environment) of the pet grooming shop is visually appealing	4 ± 0.6	4.4 ± 0.7	3
Tan3	The environment of the grooming shop (such as a work area or waiting area) is comfortable for your pet	4.5 ± 0.5	4.5 ± 0.6	2
Tan4	Employees in pet grooming shop look tidy	4 ± 0.5	4.4 ± 0.7	3
Tan5	In pet grooming shops, service-related materials (such as literature or notices) are visually appealing	3.7 ± 0.5	4.1 ± 0.7	3
Rel1	When a pet grooming shop promises to do something at a certain time, it does so	4.5 ± 0.5	4.5 ± 0.6	2
Rel2	When you have a problem, the pet grooming shop shows a sincere interest in solving it	4.6 ± 0.6	4.7 ± 0.4	1
Rel3	Pet grooming shop provides the service right at the first time	4.8 ± 0.4	4.7 ± 0.4	1
Rel4	Pet grooming shop provides its services at the time it promises to do so	4.7 ± 0.5	4.7 ± 0.5	1
Rel5	Pet grooming shop insists on error-free records	4.6 ± 0.5	4.5 ± 0.5	2
Res1	Employees of pet grooming shop tell you exactly when services will be	4.4 ± 0.6	4.6 ± 0.6	1
Res2	Employees of pet grooming shop give you prompt service	4.3 ± 0.7	4.7 ± 0.5	4
Res3	Employees of pet grooming shop are always willing to help you	4.4 ± 0.7	4.7 ± 0.6	1
Res4	Employees of pet grooming shop are never too busy to respond to your requests	4.2 ± 0.7	4.5 ± 0.8	3
Res5	The average time you wait for pet grooming services is not long	3.9 ± 0.8	4.3 ± 0.7	3
Ass1	The behavior of employees of pet grooming shop instills confidence in customers	4.6 ± 0.5	4.6 ± 0.6	1
Ass2	You feel safe in your transactions with pet grooming shop	4.7 ± 0.5	4.7 ± 0.6	1
Ass3	'Your pet' feels safe when receiving services at pet grooming shop	4.9 ± 0.4	4.7 ± 0.6	1
Ass4	Employees of pet grooming shop are consistently courteous with you	4.4 ± 0.7	4.8 ± 0.4	1
Ass5	Employees of pet grooming shop have the knowledge to answer your questions	4.5 ± 0.5	4.8 ± 0.4	1

(*continued*)

Table 4. (*continued*)

No	Quality Factors	Imp	Sat	Quadrants
		Mean + sd	Mean + sd	
Emp1	Pet grooming shop gives you individual attention	4.2 ± 0.8	4.5 ± 0.7	3
Emp2	Pet grooming shop has operating hours convenient to all its customers	4 ± 0.8	4.6 ± 0.5	4
Emp3	Pet grooming shop has employees who give you personal attention	3.9 ± 0.7	4.4 ± 0.7	3
Emp4	Pet grooming shop has employees who give 'your pet' personal attention	4.3 ± 0.7	4.5 ± 0.6	4
Emp5	Pet grooming shop has your best interests at heart	4.1 ± 0.6	4.5 ± 0.6	4
Emp6	Employees of pet grooming shop understand your specific needs	4.5 ± 0.6	4.5 ± 0.5	2

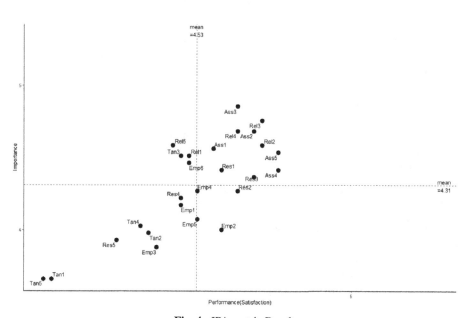

Fig. 4. IPA metric Result

4.5   Combining KANO Model and IPA Results Discussion

Table 5 combines the opinions of KANO and IPA to prevent the quality attributes of each item from being ignored when only using IPA, or only using Kano Model to ignore the actual perceived satisfaction after receiving the service, and we can clearly give priority to improvement Therefore, the service quality improvement priority and discussion order of pet grooming shop A in the case is as follows:

Starting from the second quadrant "concrete here", since there are no MBQ items in this study, ODQ will start to improve, including four items as follows:

1. Tan3: The environment of the grooming shop (such as a work area or wait-ing area) is comfortable for your pet
2. Rel1: When a pet grooming shop promises to do something at a certain time, it does so
3. Rel5: Pet grooming shop insists on error-free records
4. Emp6: Employees of pet grooming shop understand your specific needs.

It is worth noting that Tan3 shows that customers care about whether the environment in which their pets are waiting or receiving grooming work is comfortable, which is different from the situation in the general service industry, so practitioners should focus on meeting the comfort of pets when planning space Planning, rather than designing with a space environment that attracts customers' vision; moreover, Rel1 is related to the reliability of service time, so improving time control and completing services on time is a very high priority for pet grooming stores; in addition, Rel5 representatives The store needs to reduce the error rate of the service process as much as possible, and the standardization of the process is one of the directions that can be carried out; finally, Emp6 means that the store needs to improve in empathizing with the specific needs of customers, because each pet has individual differences, There are some diseases or additional needs in personality. However, the pet grooming shop is busy with work, and sometimes it is difficult for the current industry to spare enough time to communicate with customers to meet their needs. It is recommended to further understand this type of needs through follow-up interviews, etc. developing strategies for improvement.

There are 10 items in the first quadrant "Keep up good work", including 2 AQ items and 8 ODQ items. The AQ items are as follows:

1. Res1: Employees of pet grooming shop tell you exactly when services will be
2. Res3: Employees of pet grooming shop are always willing to help you.

According to Res1 and Res3, we can find that customers expect to get a response when the service is performed and when they request help from the store. However, these two service items are not required for every service, similar to the "intimate" behavior of the store, when the pet grooming store continuously and fully provides Res1 and Res3 services, it will be attractive and satisfying to customers. The ODQ items are as follows:

3. Rel2: When you have a problem, the pet grooming shop shows a sincere in-interest in solving it
4. Rel3: Pet grooming shop provides the service right at the first time
5. Rel4: Employees of pet grooming shop are never too busy to respond to your requests.
6. Ass1: The behavior of employees of pet grooming shop instills confidence in customers.
7. Ass2: You feel safe in your transactions with pet grooming shop.
8. Ass3: 'Your pet' feels safe when receiving services at pet grooming shop
9. Ass4: Employees of pet grooming shop are consistently courteous with you
10. Ass5: Employees of pet grooming shop have the knowledge to answer your questions

We can find that most of the items in this quadrant are related to reliability and guarantee. When pet grooming stores provide these services continuously and fully, customers will be satisfied, otherwise it will lead to dissatisfaction. Therefore, it is necessary to maintain the service quality of this part at all times. Above a certain level.

There are 8 items in the third quadrant "Low priority", including 1 IQ and 7 AQ items. The IQ items are:

1. Tan1: Pet grooming shop has modern equipment.
    And the AQ items are as follows:
2. Tan2: The physical facility (environment) of the pet grooming shop is visu-ally appealing.
3. Tan4: Employees in pet grooming shop look tidy.
4. Tan5: In pet grooming shops, service-related materials (such as literature or notices) are visually appealing.
5. Res4: Employees of pet grooming shop are never too busy to respond to your requests.
6. Res5: The average time you wait for pet grooming services is not long.
7. Emp1: Pet grooming shop gives you individual attention.
8. Emp3: Pet grooming shop has employees who give you personal attention.

Customers pay little attention to the service items here, especially Tan1, which is a low-ranking improvement item.

Finally, there are 4 items in the fourth quadrant "possible overkill" as follows:

1. Res2: Employees of pet grooming shop give you prompt service
2. Emp2: Pet grooming shop has operating hours convenient to all its customers.
3. Emp4: Pet grooming shop has employees who give 'your pet' personal attention.
4. Emp5: Pet grooming shop has your best interests at heart.

There is no need to invest too much resources here. Instead, the resources used in these services should be transferred to other quality items that customers really need.

Table 5. Combination of IPA and Kano Model results.

Improve priority	IPA Quadrant	Kano Categorization	Service
1	Two	MBQ	/
2	(concrete here)	ODQ	Tan3, Rel1, Rel5, Emp6
3		AQ	/
4	One	AQ	Res1, Res3
5	(keep up good work)	ODQ	Rel2, Rel3, Rel4, Ass1, Ass2, Ass3, Ass4, Ass5
6		MBQ	/
7	Three	MBQ	/
8	(low priority)	ODQ	/
9		AQ	Tan1, Tan2, Tan4, Tan5, Res4, Res5, Emp1, Emp3
10	Four	ODQ	/
11	(possible overkill)	MBQ	/
12		AQ	Res2, Emp2, Emp4, Emp5

5 Conclusion

This study aims to examine improvement priorities in pet grooming services by using IPA and Kano Model. The results indicated that the following four service qualities should be improved as a priority:

1. Tan3: The environment of the grooming shop (such as a work area or waiting area) is comfortable for your pet
2. Rel1: When a pet grooming shop promises to do something at a certain time, it does so
3. Rel5: Pet grooming shop insists on error-free records
4. Emp6: Employees of pet grooming shop understand your specific needs.

On the other hand, there is no need to invest too much resources in the following four service qualities. Instead, the resources used in these services should be transferred to other quality items that customers really need:

1. Res2: Employees of pet grooming shop give you prompt service
2. Emp2: Pet grooming shop has operating hours convenient to all its customers.
3. Emp4: Pet grooming shop has employees who give 'your pet' personal attention.
4. Emp5: Pet grooming shop has your best interests at heart.

By applying the IPA combined with the Kano Model approach, this study provides pet grooming practitioners with a useful implementation framework to help owners develop pet grooming service improvement prioritization strategies. In addition, the findings shed light on the environment in which pets wait for or receive grooming jobs Quality, reliability of time control, error rate of service process, and specific needs of customers need to be improved. These items are related to the service process provided by the background. Therefore, it is suggested that future researchers can according on the findings of customer need form the front stage in this study, further import back stage improvement related research.

References

1. Carmack, B.J.: Companion animals: social support for orthopedic clients. Nurs. Clin. North Am. 33(4), 701–711 (1998)
2. Veevers, J.E.: The social meanings of pets: Alternative roles for companion animals. Marriage Fam. Rev. 8(3–4), 11–30 (1985)
3. Statistics Office of the Ministry of Finance. Number of profit-making enterprises and sales statistics (2019). Retrieved from https://www.mof.gov.tw/htmlList/100
4. Taiwan Economic Research Institute Biotechnology Industry Research Center (2020) - Survey on the consumption structure and breeding attitude of pet owners in my country
5. Parasuraman, A., Zeithaml, V.A., Berry, L.L.: A conceptual model of service quality and its implications for future research. J. Mark. 49(4), 41–50 (1985)
6. Chiang, T.Y., Perng, Y.H.: A new model to improve service quality in the property management industry. Int. J. Strateg. Prop. Manag. 22(5), 436–446 (2018)
7. Tamanna, T.: Consumer perceptions and expectations of service quality: assessment through SERVQUAL dimensions. J. Econ. Bus 3(2) (2020)

8. Martilla, J.A., James, J.C.: Importance-performance analysis. J. Mark. **41**(1), 77–79 (1977)
9. Kano, N.: Attractive quality and must-be quality. Hinshitsu (Quality J. Japn. Soc. Qual. Control) **14**, 39–48 (1984)
10. Wong, M.S., Philip, G., Fearon, C.: Evaluating E-government in Ma-laysia: An importance-performance grid analysis (IPA) of citizens and service providers. Int. J. Electron. Bus. **7**(2), 105–129 (2009)
11. Carman, J.M.: Consumer perceptions of service quality: an assessment of T. J. Retail. **66**(1), 33 (1990)
12. Belk, R.W.: Possessions and the extended self. J. Consum. Res. **15**(2), 139–168 (1988)
13. Johnson, T.P., Garrity, T.F., Stallones, L.: Psychometric evaluation of the Lexington attachment to pets scale (LAPS). Anthrozoös **5**(3), 160–175 (1992)
14. Mahamad, O., Ramayah, T.: Service quality, customer satisfaction and loyalty: a test of mediation. Int. Bus. Res. **3**(4), 72 (2010)
15. Chen, J.: A study on the important factors affecting the behavior intention of pet grooming customers—a case study of dog owners in greater Taipei area. Master thesis (2010)
16. Chang, T.Z., Chen, S.J.: Market orientation, service quality and business profitability: a conceptual model and empirical evidence. Journal of services marketing (1998)
17. Grönroos, C.: A service quality model and its marketing implications. Eur. J. Mark. **18**(4), 36–44 (1984)
18. Parasuraman, A., Zeithaml, V.A., Berry, L.: SERVQUAL: a multiple-item scale for measuring consumer perceptions of service quality **64**(1), 12–40 (1988)
19. Parasuraman, A., Berry, L., Zeithaml, V.: Refinement and reassess-ment of the SERVQUAL scale. J. Retail. **67**(4), 114 (2002)
20. Sampson, S.E., Showalter, M.J.: The performance-importance re-sponse function: Observations and implications. Serv. Ind. J. **19**(3), 1–25 (1999)
21. Emmanuel, J.C., Ronald, M., Jean, P.: Segmentation of bank commercial markets. Int. J. Bank Mark. **7**(6) (1989)
22. Chapman, R.G.: Brand performance comparatives. Journal of Product & Brand Management (1993)
23. Hollenhorst, S.J., Olson, D., Fortney, R.: Use of importance-performance analysis to evaluate state park cabins: the case of the West Virginia state park system. J. Park. Recreat. Adm. **10**(1), 1–11 (1992)
24. Matzler, K., Hinterhuber, H.H.: How to make product development projects more successful by integrating Kano's model of customer satisfaction into quality function deployment. Technovation **18**(1), 25–38 (1998)
25. Pan, W.: Combining Kano Model and IPA to Examine the Service Quality Attributes of National Highway Passenger Transport - Taking Guoguang Passenger Transport as an Example, Master Thesis of the Institute of Marketing and Circulation Management, National Changhua Normal University(2008)
26. Kuo, Y.F., Chen, J.Y., Deng, W.J.: IPA–Kano model: a new tool for categorising and diagnosing service quality attributes. Total Qual. Manag. Bus. Excell. **23**(7–8), 731–748 (2012)
27. Cuieford, J.P.: Fundamental Statistics in Psychology and Education, 4th (Ed), NY McGraw Hill. Day, RL (1977). Toward a Process (1965)
28. Kerlinger, F., Lee, H.: Foundations of behavioral research: Harcourt College Publishers (2000)
29. Cortina, J.M.: What is coefficient alpha? An examination of theory and applications. J. Appl. Psychol. **78**(1), 98 (1993)

Author Index

© The Editor(s) (if applicable) and The Author(s), under exclusive license
to Springer Nature Switzerland AG 2023
M. Kurosu and A. Hashizume (Eds.): HCII 2023, LNCS 14012, pp. 529–530, 2023.
https://doi.org/10.1007/978-3-031-35599-8